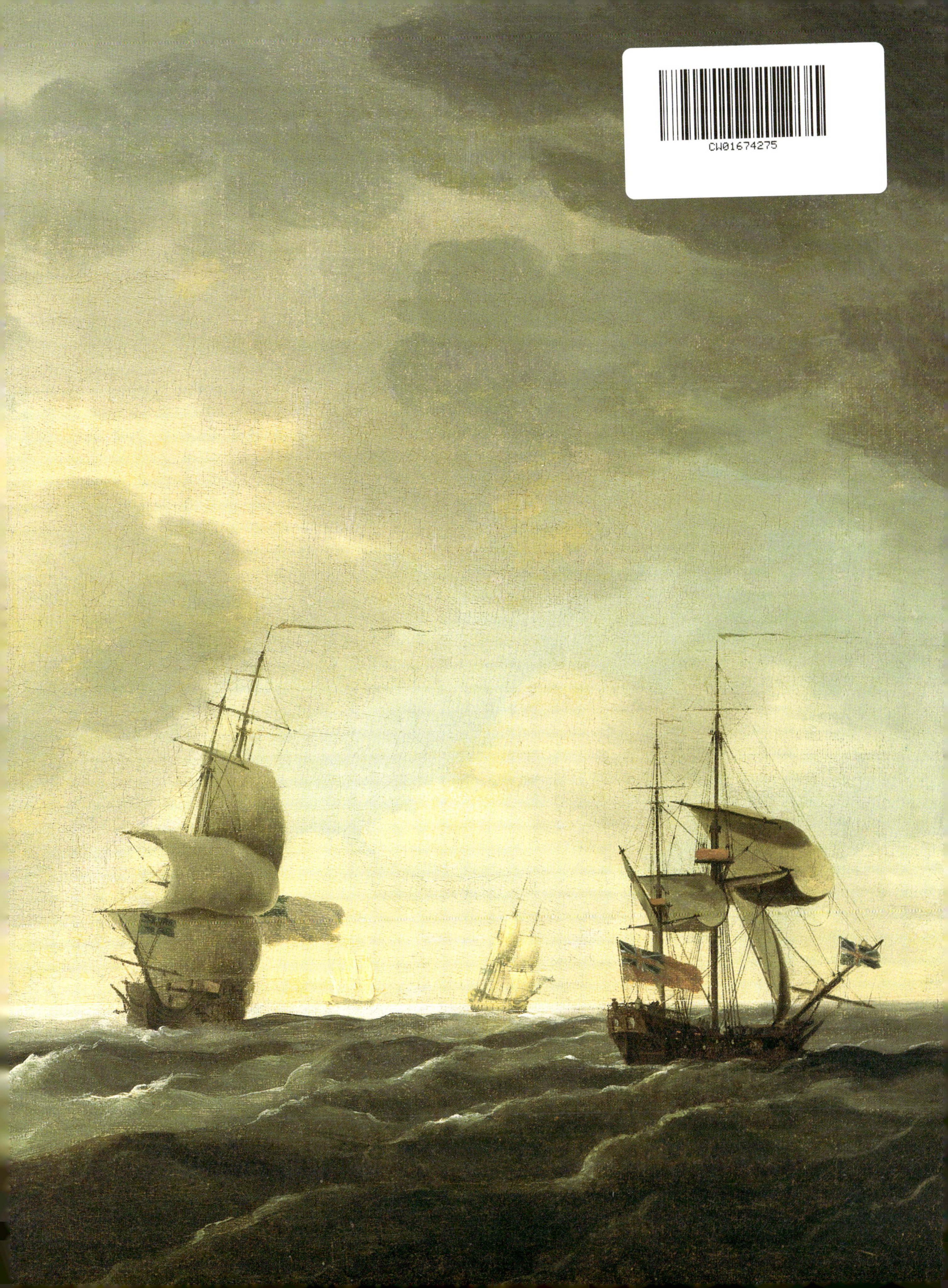

CHARLES BROOKING

1723-1759

and the 18th Century British Marine Painters

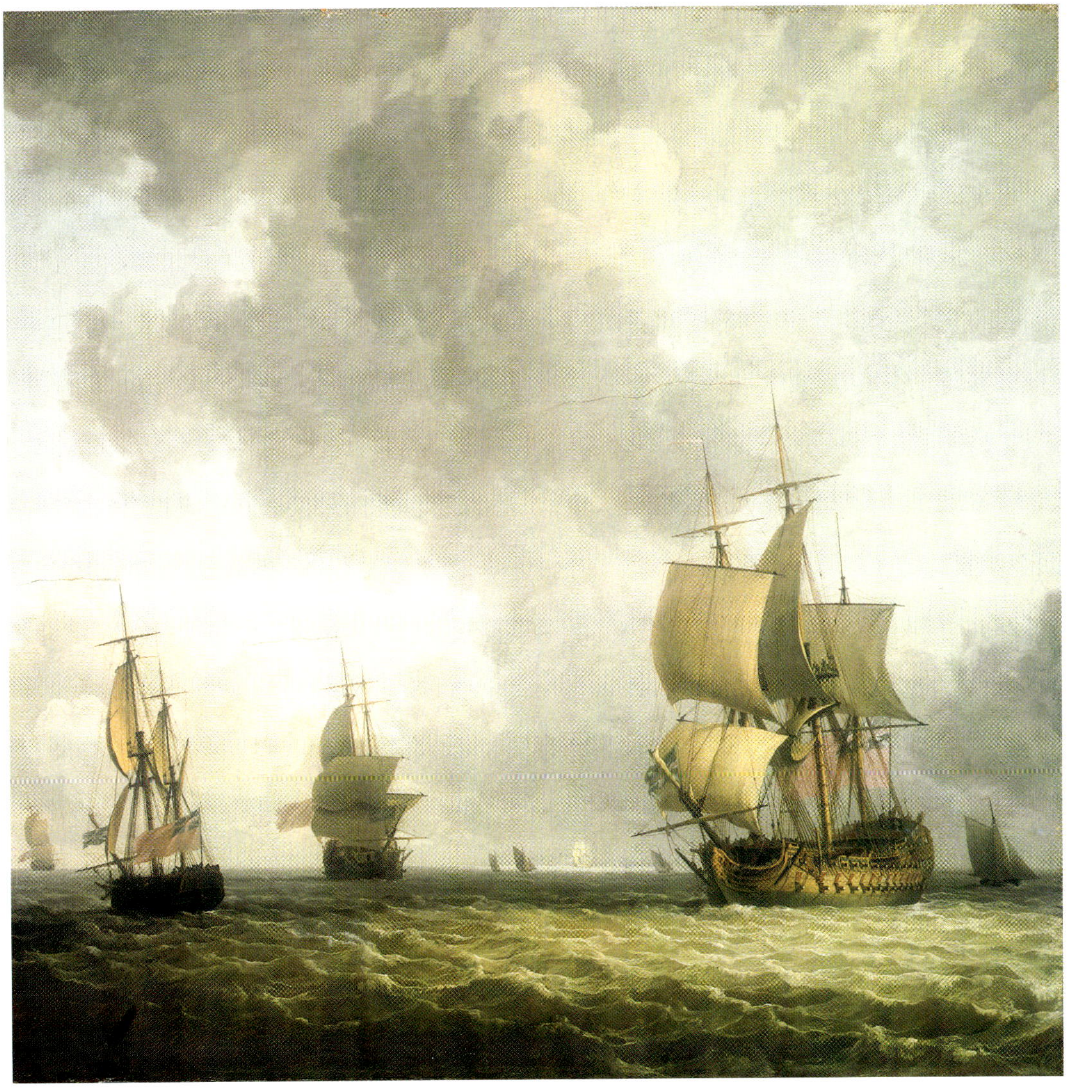

244

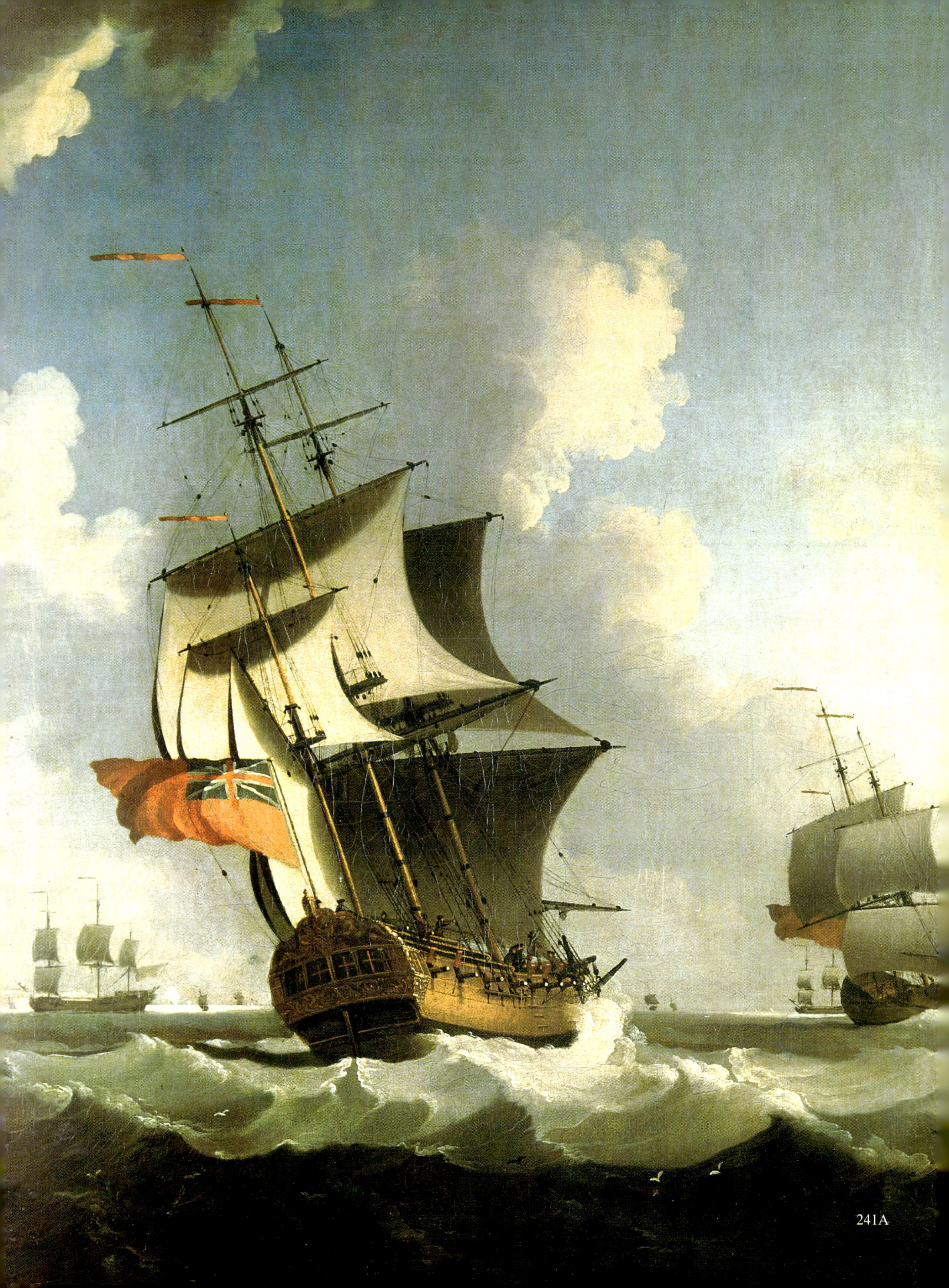

241A

CHARLES BROOKING

1723-1759

and the 18th Century British Marine Painters

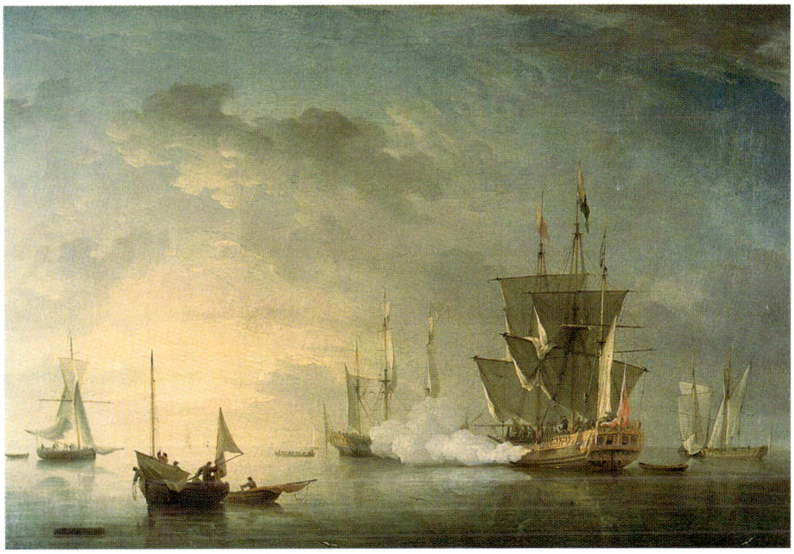

1B

David Joel

ANTIQUE COLLECTORS' CLUB

For Jenifer, my wife, and my daughters Jane, Suzy and Emma who for long have supported my endeavours

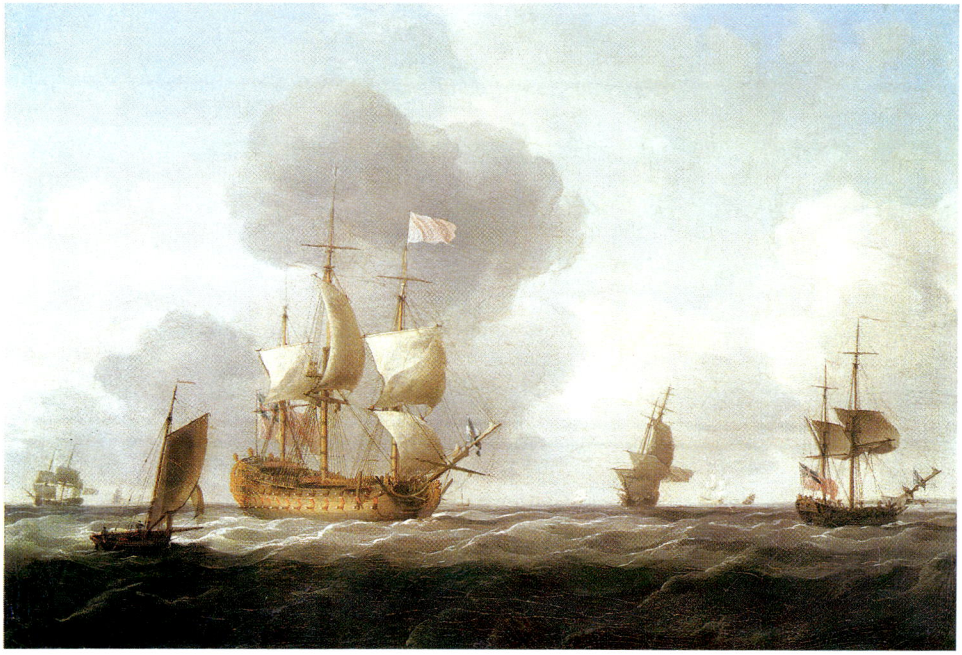

231G

ISBN 1 85149 277 1

British Library Cataloguing-in-Publication Data
A Catalogue record for this book is available from The British Library

Printed in England by the
Antique Collectors' Club Ltd.,
5 Church Street, Woodbridge, Suffolk IP12 1DS

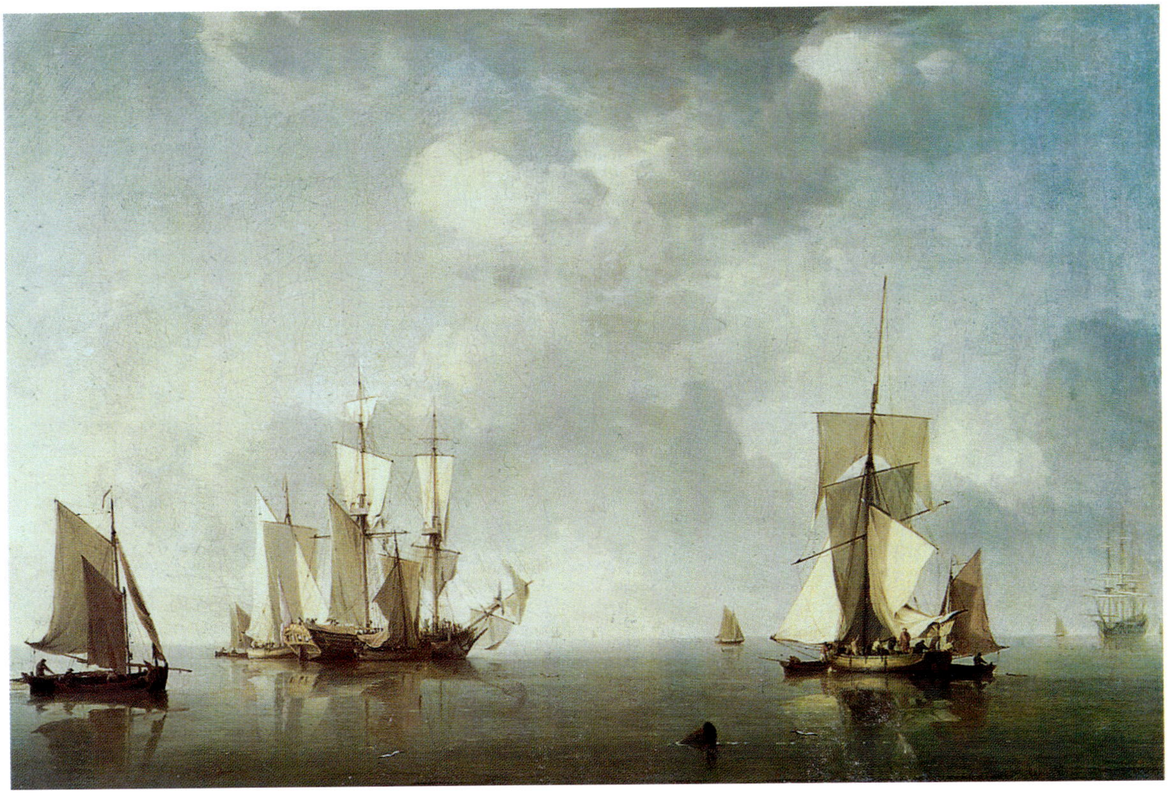

3A

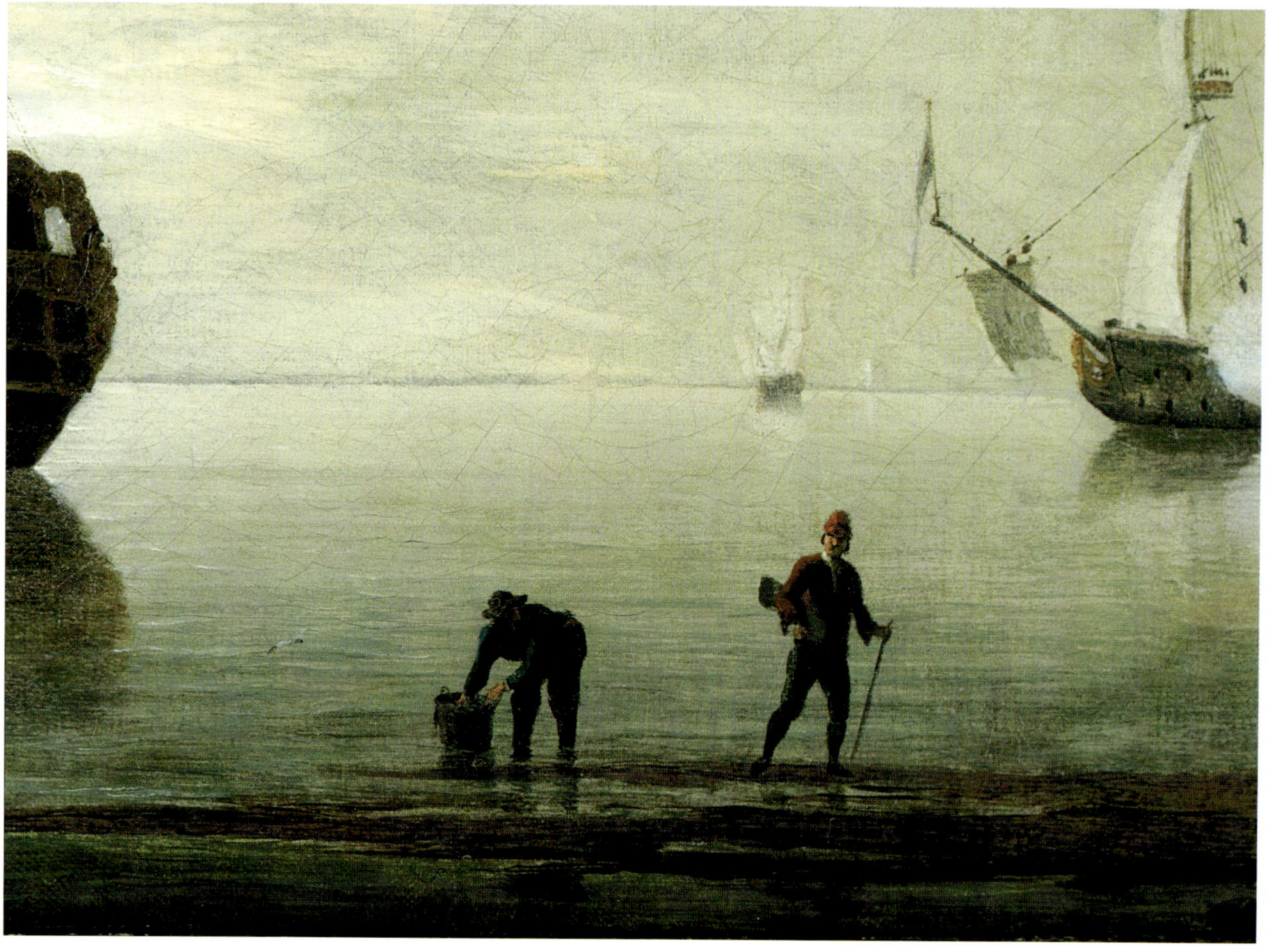

Detail from 27, *A flagship firing a gun and another two-decker getting under way at dawn*. The artist comes ashore. Oil on canvas 20¾ x 27¾. Signed C Brooking on jetty lower right.

Charles Brooking's only self portrait. He is carrying a large landscape sketch book under his right arm as he sets off for a day's sketching on the Isle of Sheppey in the Thames estuary.

Charles Brooking's signature

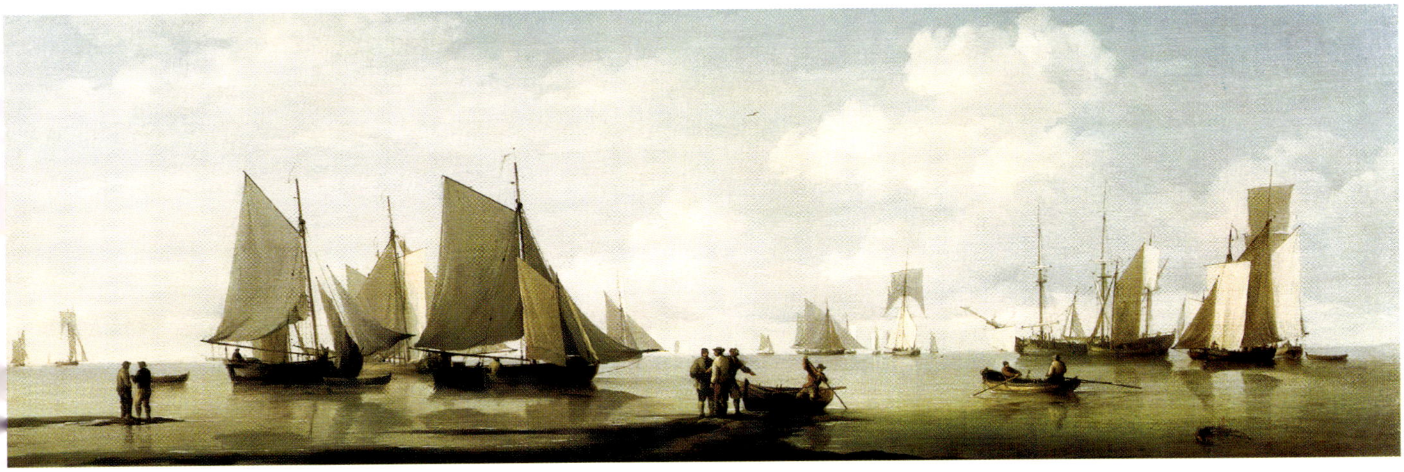

17 *Fishing Smacks becalmed near a shore*. Oil on canvas, 10¾ x 33. Tate Gallery, London

Contents

***Note. As in Brooking's day, all measurements are given in inches. The reference numbers beneath Charles Brooking's illustrations refer to the Catalogue, Chapter 7.**

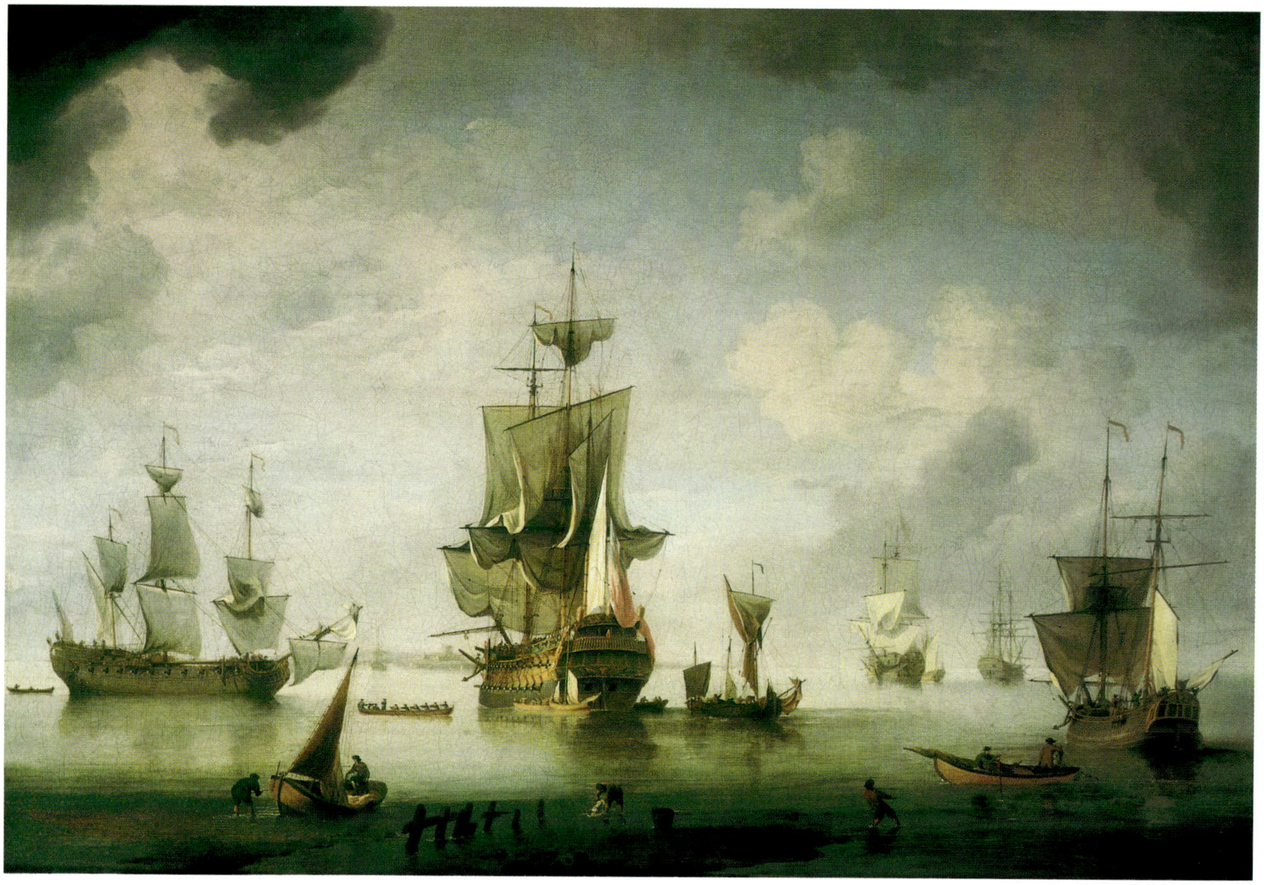
8A
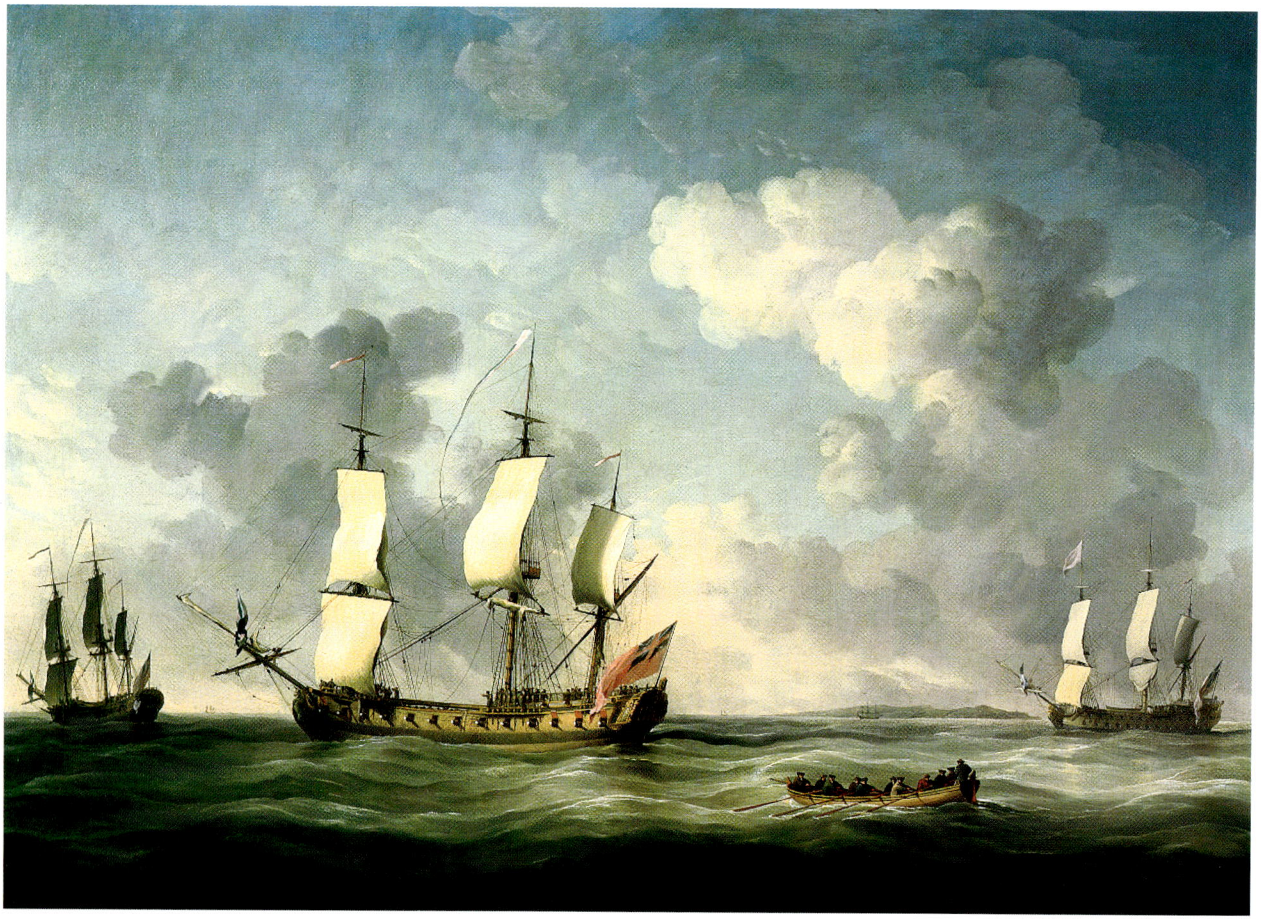
26A

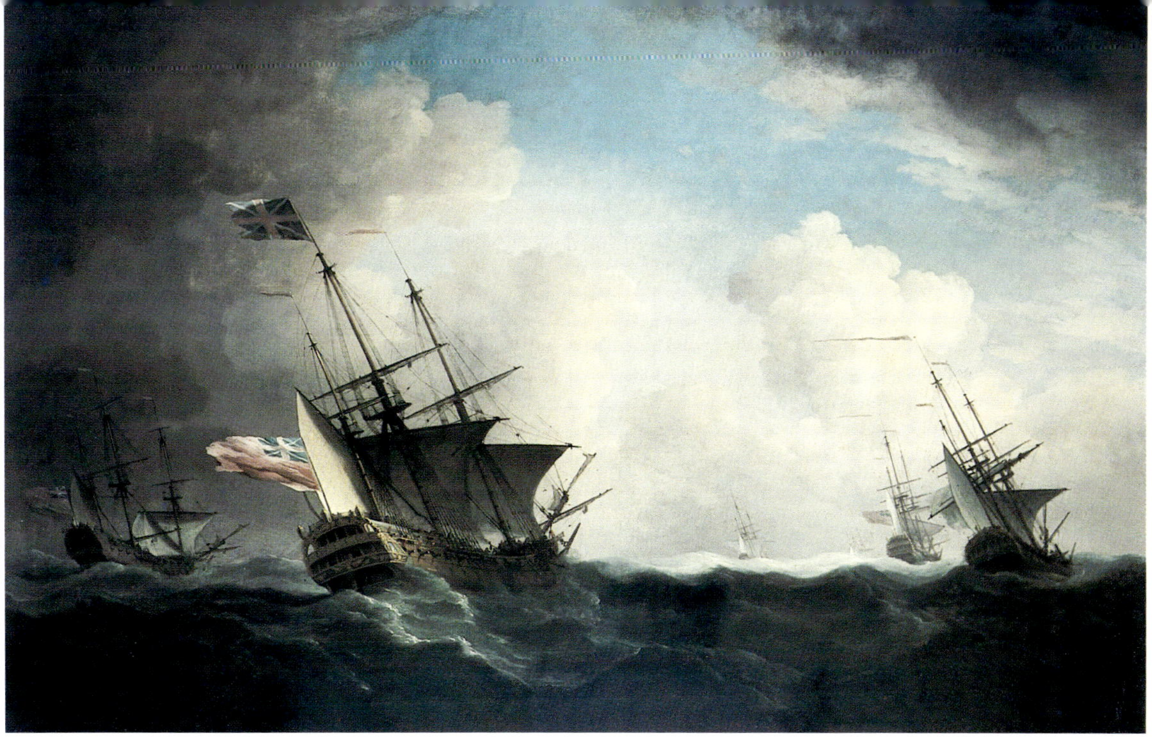

201A

Acknowledgements

A. E. Edwards Esq. deserves special mention, for having the imagination and foresight to sponsor this publication. Without his support, this book would not be in print. His contribution has now made it possible for academics, artists, historians, and collectors and anyone with a passion and respect for the sea, and its fascinating history, to gain an overview of the remarkable work of Charles Brooking: his life, work and times.

I owe a considerable debt to my two early tutors, Michael Robinson, ex-Keeper of Paintings at the National Maritime Museum, and his late deputy E. H. H. Archibald, who encouraged me to study eighteenth century maritime art and to start cataloguing Charles Brooking's work. Michael Robinson's masterwork, *The Paintings of the William van de Veldes*, has been an invaluable aid, and I have quoted, with his permission, from some of the relevant descriptions. However, I based my Charles Brooking catalogue section from the beginning in 1959 on wind strengths, and left open additional catalogue numbers for his paintings, drawings and prints so that pictures discovered in the future may be incorporated and referenced in any later publications.

Sadly Teddy Archibald died on 27 May 1998 whilst this book was with the publisher. He had been the Curator of Paintings and served the Museum from 1952 to 1984. He was responsible for the acquisition of over 60 per cent of the 4,000 oil paintings, which is an enormous purchase, though most of it was done for low prices. No one is ever likely to equal this record in any major museum. With his unrivalled knowledge of both marine paintings and portraiture, and of British Naval history, he produced the great reference work *Dictionary of Sea Painters*, now in its third revision. After retirement, he continued to advise the art trade and his collector friends. He also encouraged this book on Brooking and allowed me to quote from his books and other writings extensively.

Colin Sorensen gave me access to all his research work prepared for the exhibition on the artist held first at the Aldeburgh Festival, June 1966 which was moved to Bristol the following month. Sorensen located many new paintings, drawings and almost all of Brooking's prints and has also most generously made available his entire collection of photographic prints and transparencies of the first hundred or so paintings recorded by the end of the 1960s.

The following auction houses, galleries, and individuals have also greatly assisted in this project:

Antony Griffiths, Department of Prints and Drawings, British Museum; David Moore Gwyn and Lucy Hodson, Sotheby's; John Stainton, Margie Christian, Sue Leach, Jane

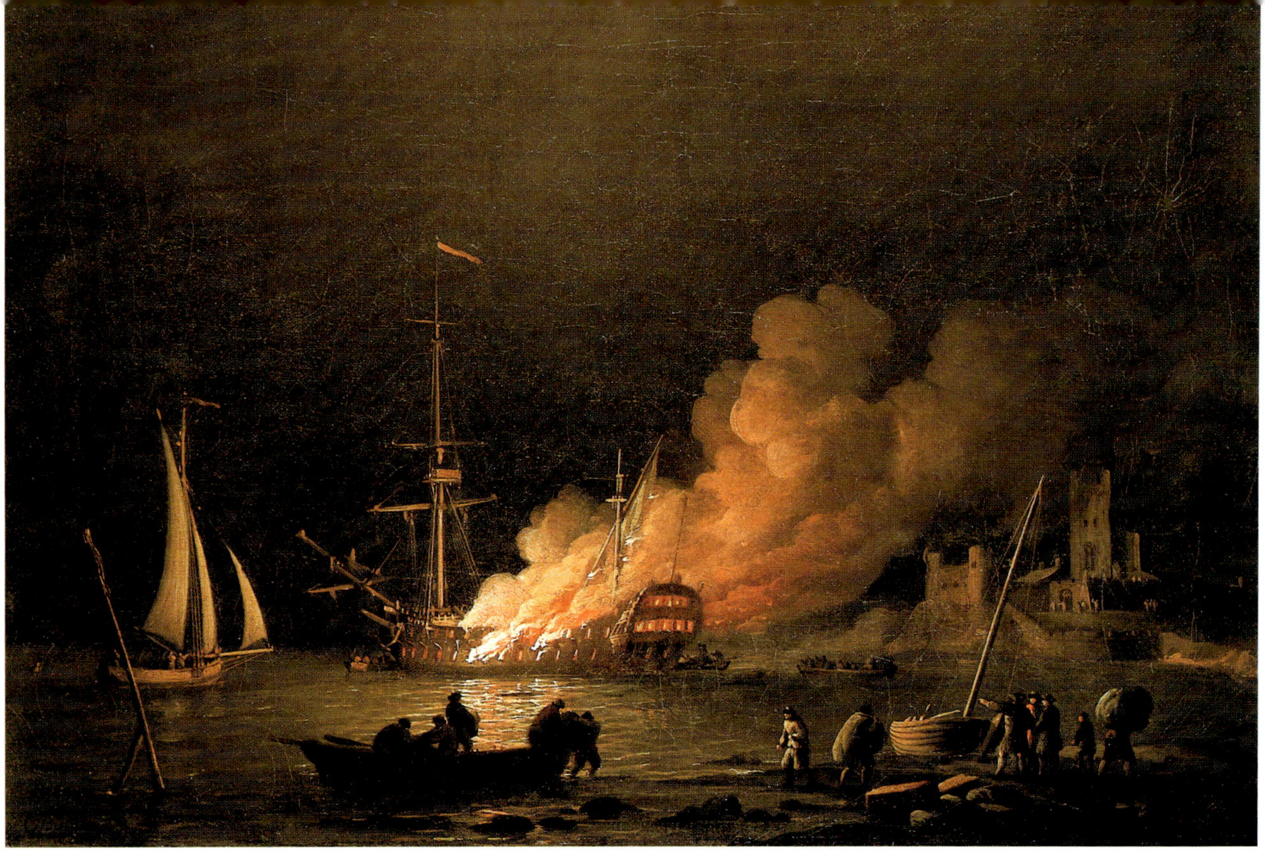

153A *A two-decked ship on fire at night close to shore*. Oil on canvas, 12½ x 17½.
Yale Center for British Art, Paul Mellon Collection

Turner, and Jeremy Rex-Parkes, Christie's; John Dabney and Sophie Money, Phillips; Alastair Laird, Charles O'Brien and James Glennie, Bonhams; Agnew's; Richard Green, Richard Green Galleries; Lane Fine Art; Leggatt Bros; David Messum; N. R. Omell Gallery; Parker Gallery; Oliver Swann, Tyron and Swann Gallery; Royal Exchange Art Gallery; Spinks; Simon Carter Gallery; Oscar and Peter Johnson; Rupert-Preston Ltd and the Witt Library. I am also most grateful to Douglas Smith (Paul Mellon Foundation), the late Dr Peyto Slatter for photographic services, Philip Stevens, and to all the owners of paintings and drawings for giving me access to the sources, many of them wishing to remain anonymous. I must thank the librarian staff of the Royal Academy of Arts; the Witt Library of the Courtauld Institute; the Painter Stainers Company; Rhian Harris, archivist at the Thomas Coram Foundation; Ralph Hyde of the Guildhall Library; Jane Maxwell, Assistant Librarian of Manuscripts at Trinity College, Dublin and Dr Noel Kissane of the National Library of Ireland for answering so many questions. Charles Harrison Wallace gave much appreciated assistance providing details of Peter Monamy and his grandson, Monamy Swaine. I wish also to thank my secretary, Mrs Katrina Legg, for typing the early manuscripts. From the Brooking Society I wish to thank Bob Brooking, Barry Brooking, Don Steel, Thorsten Sjolin, and their genealogist Helen Allen; and Sylvia Guthrig of the Devon Family History Society for details from *Devon Extracts 1665-1850*. The Yale Center for British Art, New Haven, USA awarded James Taylor a month long Fellowship in March 1998 to study their extensive Brooking collection. The fruits of the Fellowship are evident in Chapters 1 and 5. Thanks to Timothy Goodhue, Registrar of the Yale Center for British Art.

I am also indebted to Diana Steel, my editor Diana McMillan and the team at the Antique Collectors' Club for bringing this project to fruition, and current staff of the National Maritime Museum, especially Roger Quarm and Lindsey MacFarlane of the Picture Library, and Chris Gray, Colin Starkey, David Taylor and Tina Chambers in Photographic Services. Photographic prints and oleographs after Brooking's pictures are available for purchase by contacting the Photographic Services Department of the National Maritime Museum, Romney Road, Greenwich, London, SE10 9NF Telephone: 0181-858 4422. To Blandford Press Ltd. and E.H.H. Archibald for permission to quote from his book *The Wooden Fighting Ship in the Royal Navy 897-1860*, which was illustrated by Ray Woodward.

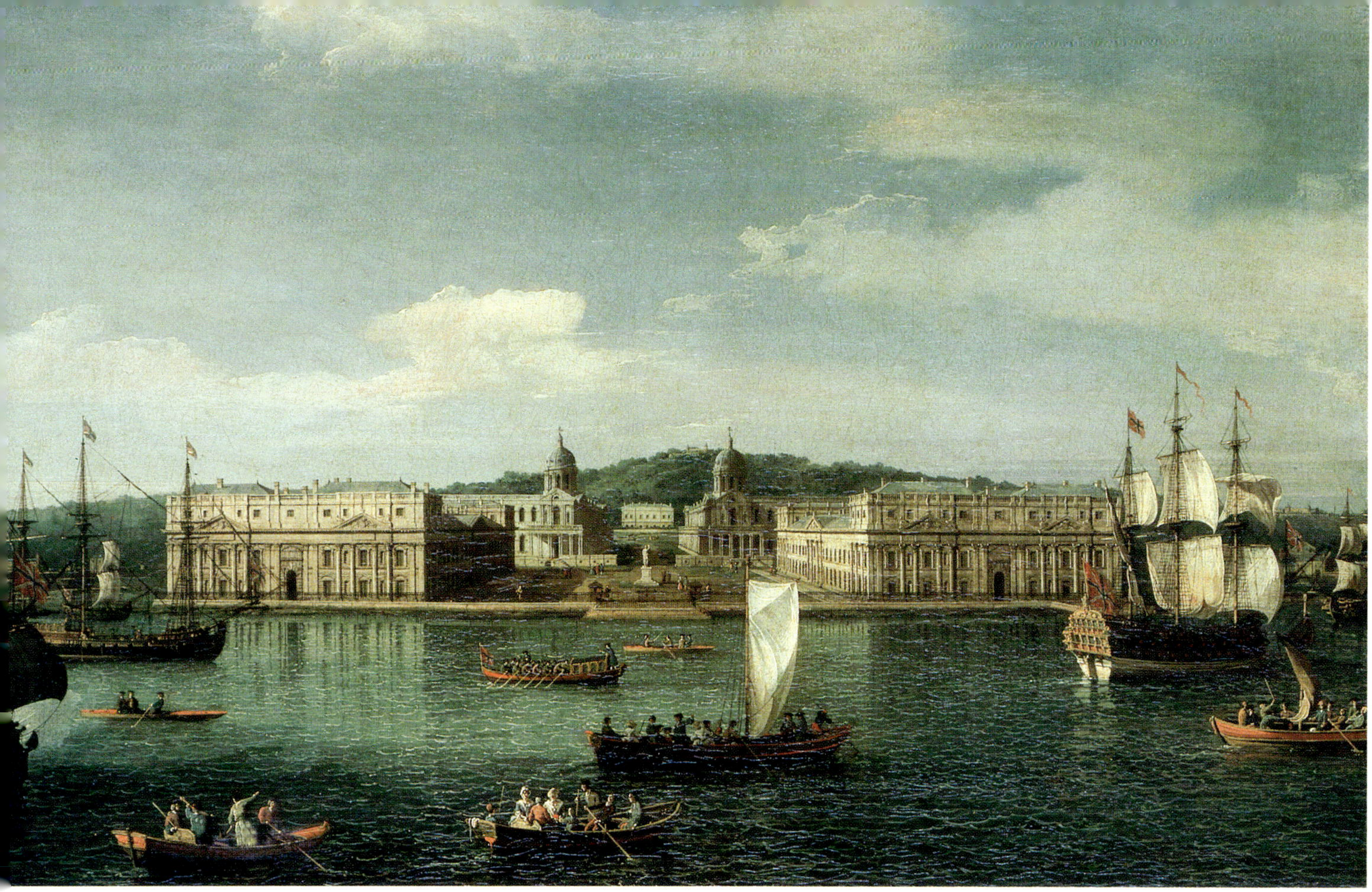

Foreword

Canaletto (1697-1768). *A View of Greenwich from the River*, c.1750. Private Collection

Commander David Joel RN has done more than anyone to promote the work of Charles Brooking (1723-1759). His career in the Royal Navy has spanned forty-three years and has taken him worldwide. He has commanded six of Her Majesty's ships and was second-in-command of a further eight, including the assault ship *Fearless*. He was based in the West Indies as Royal Naval Liaison Officer and Defence Adviser Caribbean from 1975-78 and later was to be the only Commander recalled for service in the Falkland War, where his special knowledge was required.

David Joel's secondments to the Royal Naval College [RNC] at Greenwich, regarded by naval officers as the Royal Navy's university (founded in 1694, and originally called Greenwich Hospital: a home for old and disabled sailors), provided him with the ideal opportunity to study the extensive picture collection of the National Maritime Museum, located in buildings literally across the road.

The National Maritime Museum's picture collection comprises 4,000 oil paintings and more than 60,000 watercolours, drawings and prints, ranging from the sixteenth century to the present day. Many of the Museum's oil paintings originally hung in the Painted Hall of Greenwich Hospital where they formed an impressive gallery of maritime art, the first of its kind in the world, celebrating Britain's naval achievements.

The Greenwich Hospital collection of pictures includes not only dramatic naval

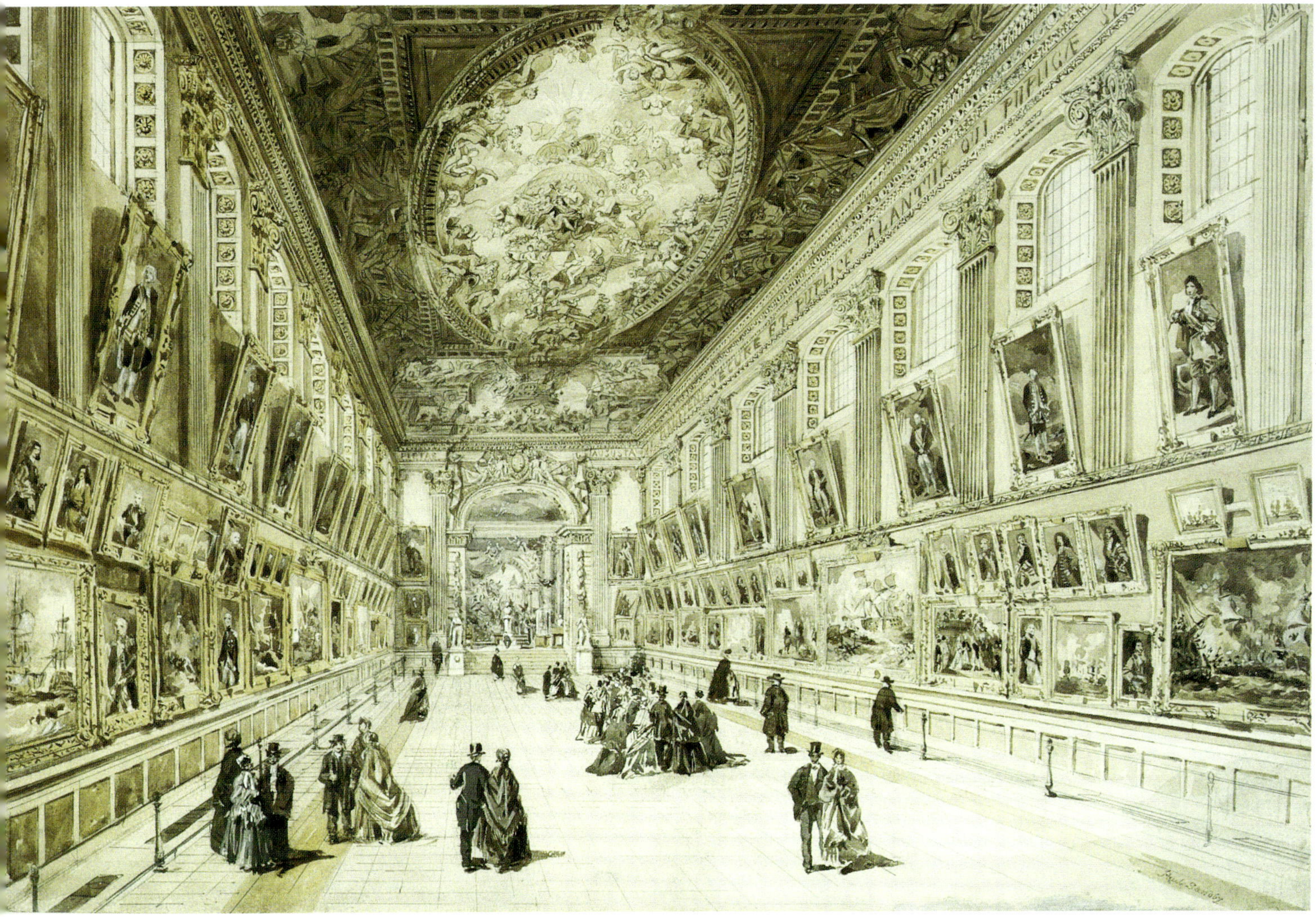

L.V. Michael. *The Painted Hall with the Admiralty Collection of paintings on display*, circa 1850. Wash, brown and grey heightened with white, 13½ x 21½. From the *Illustrated London News* Collection, given by Sir Bruce Ingram. National Maritime Museum, London

The Greenwich Hospital Collection is shown here decorating the walls of the Painted Hall for Victorian visitors to see. This was the Admiralty Collection and it formed the basis for the Maritime Museum's initial collection. Today, at the Millennium, almost all of this collection and most of the great national collection of marine paintings is in storage by the Blackwall Tunnel. It cannot be seen by the public, which is most unfortunate. Once the National Maritime Museum has completed its rebuilding it is hoped that the greatest collection of marine art in the world will again be on view.

actions, but also portraits of the admirals and captains who fought in the battles, portraits of their ships, as well as allegorical works and genre subjects. Paintings were specially commissioned, donated and bequeathed to hang in the Hospital. Victorian visitors would pay to enter the Painted Hall and marvel at the collection. In fact, many Victorian artists painted scenes showing the interior of the Painted Hall itself, views of splendid baroque buildings, and depictions of everyday life of the Greenwich Pensioners. Perhaps the best known views of the Greenwich Hospital in oils were painted by Canaletto from the north bank of the Thames. They were painted around 1750, when the complex of buildings had been completed.

On David's first visit to the NMM in 1948 he studied, albeit briefly, the maritime paintings on display, as all young naval officers were encouraged to do. During later visits he decided to study them more seriously, and made use of the National Maritime

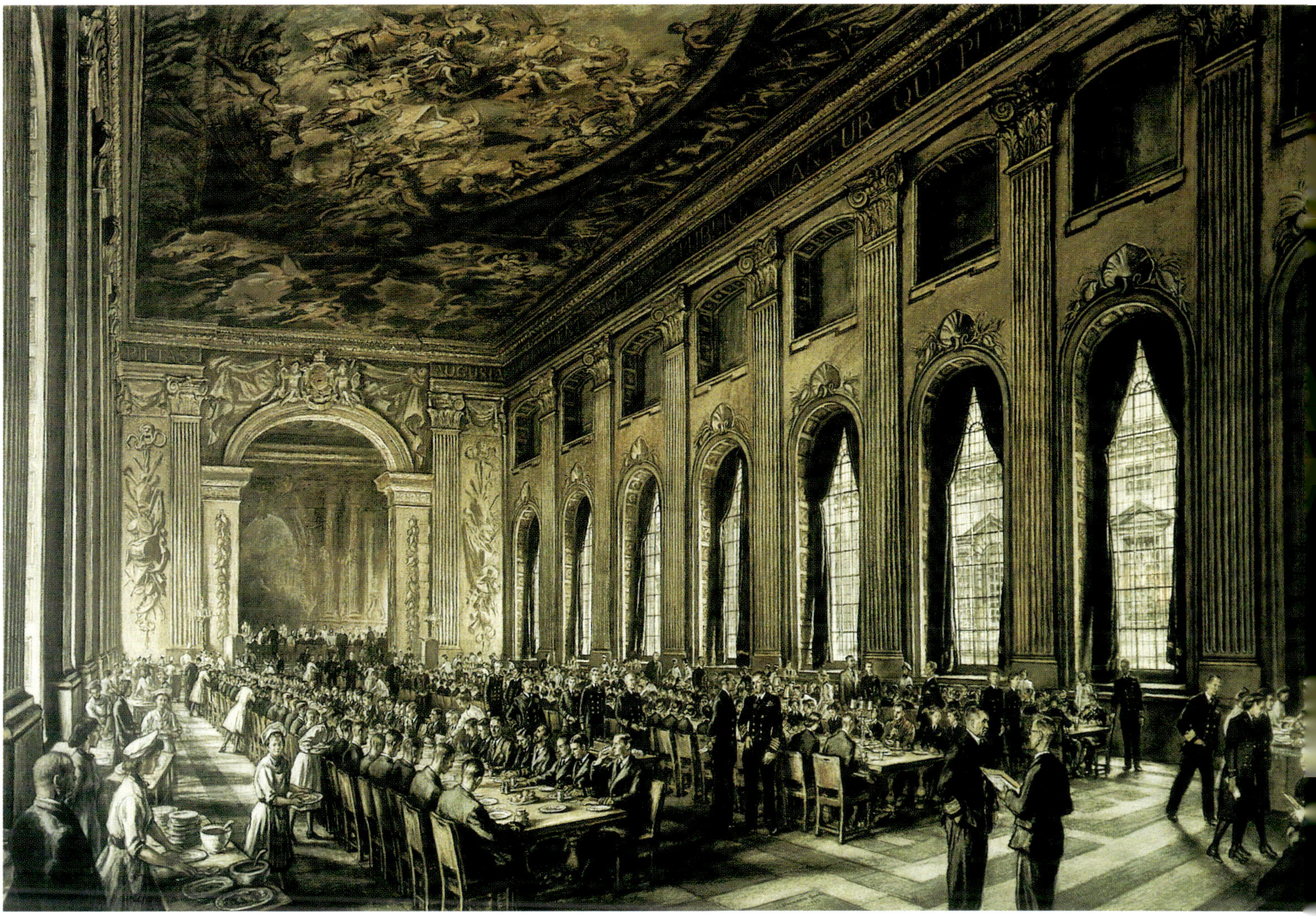
Sir Muirhead Bone (1876-1953). *Luncheon in the Painted Hall*, 1942. Watercolour heightened with white, 20 x 30. National Maritime Museum, London

Museum's superlative Print Room, sadly demolished in 1991. Joel's fascination for Brooking and eighteenth century marine painting was heightened further when in 1958, whilst browsing in the 'Lanes' of Brighton, then famous for its many fine antique shops, he discovered a small oil painting by Brooking. It was the start of a lifelong interest in maritime art and the beginning of what is now a significant private collection of eighteenth century marine paintings.

This publication will be of interest to all collectors of maritime art, and especially to those with an enthusiasm for the marine artists of the eighteenth century.

James Taylor, Curator of Paintings/Corporate Development
National Maritime Museum, Greenwich

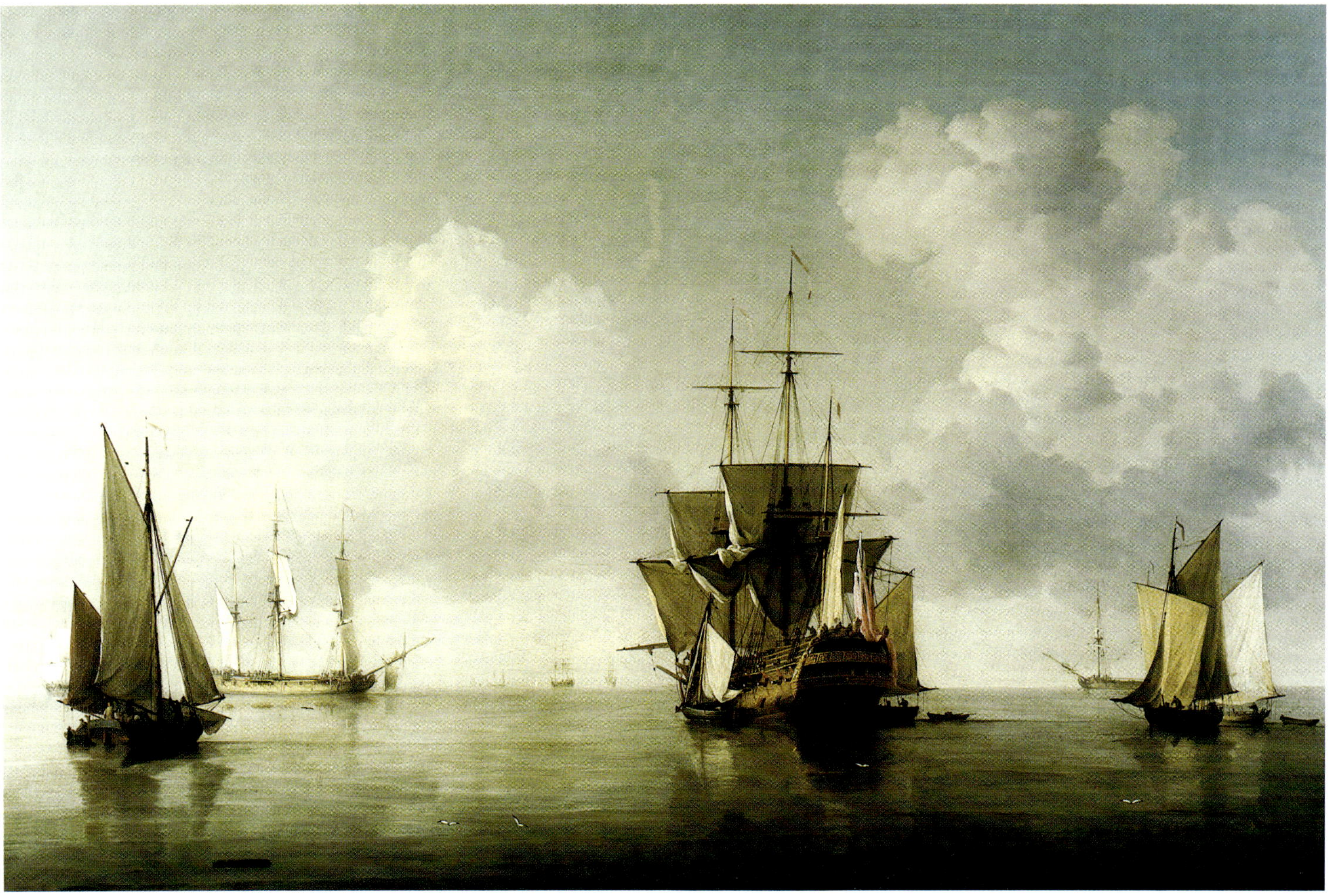

41 *An East Indiaman becalmed with fishing boats.* Oil on canvas, 20 x 30. Signed C Brooking on plank lower left. See detail on facing page.

Introduction

Few English artists of great talent have been as neglected as Charles Brooking, now generally acknowledged by maritime historians as the most accomplished of all eighteenth century British marine painters. Perhaps his premature death at the age of thirty-six in 1759 in part explains this neglect. He would have submitted work, and been a favourite to win a premium (or prize), from one of the marine painting competitions organised by the Society of Arts (now the Royal Society of Arts), held between 1764-68. If he had been active in 1768, the year of the foundation of the Royal Academy of Arts, in London, Brooking would have almost certainly been elected as a founder member. As it happened this honour was bestowed on Dominic Serres, traditionally believed to be Brooking's pupil.

Concerning Brooking, the late Basil Taylor of the Paul Mellon Foundation for British Art suggested that only Richard Wilson and Thomas Gainsborough could be regarded as his superiors in the treatment of nature before 1760, also that Brooking was as significant in changing the scope of his specialisation as was the celebrated sporting artist George Stubbs in his particular sphere.

This book lists all of Brooking's known paintings, drawings and prints, and illustrates over 200 of them. It shows the influences on Brooking, and the impact of his artistic legacy on his followers. The artist's working method and the relationship between his

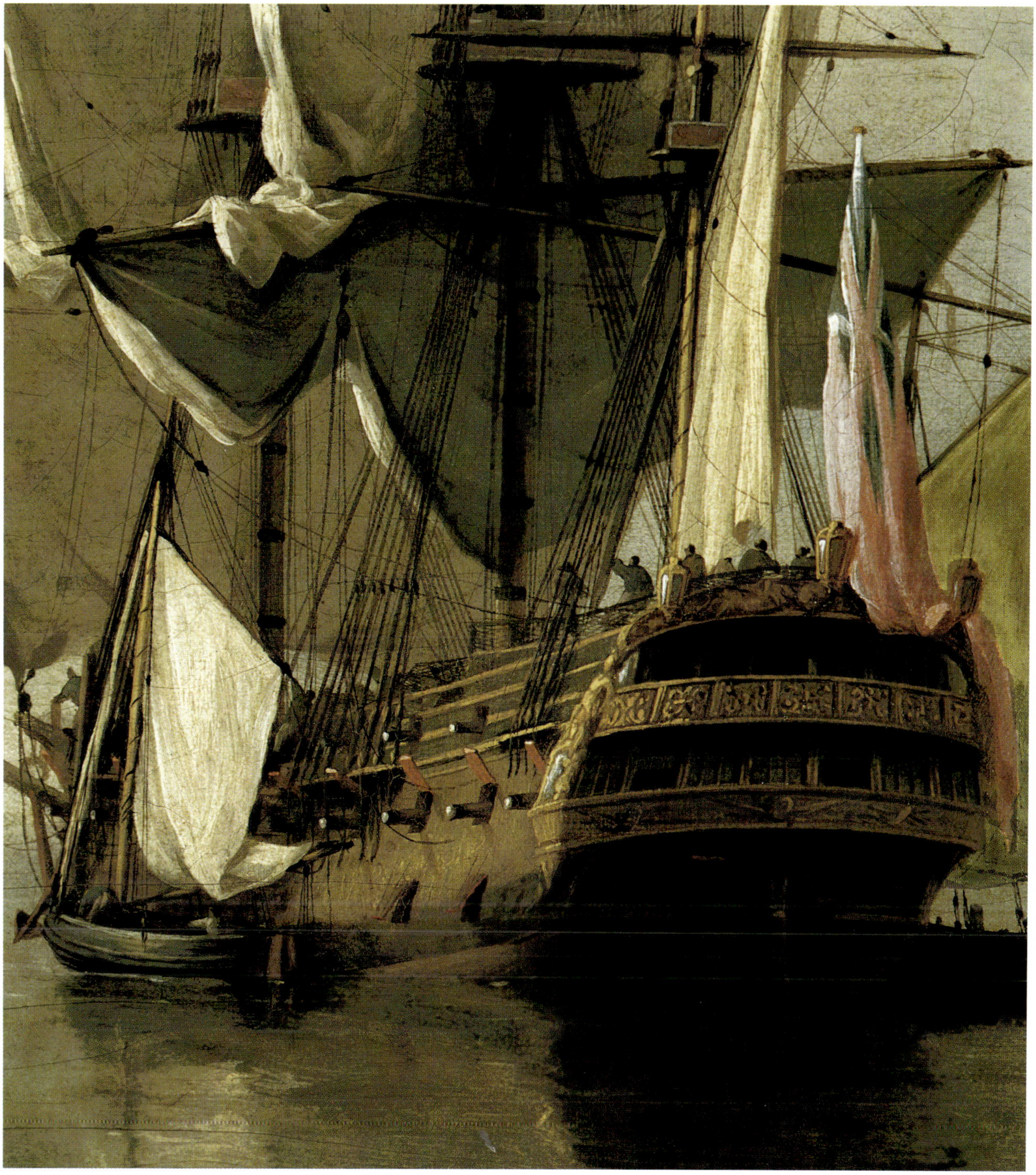

preparatory sketches and drawings to his finished work is discussed. Also his preference for re-working and updating the compositions of the Willem van de Veldes, and other artists of the seventeenth century. It will be revealed that in many instances Brooking actually enhanced, and improved, upon their original designs.

Brooking's position amongst marine painters will be established at last, and will enable custodians of his paintings to take an overall view of his *oeuvre*, to appreciate his sense of light and atmosphere which fifty years later, in the art of John Crome and John Constable, became two of the most expressive and influential characteristics of the English School.

Chapter 1

Charles Brooking and the Dutch School of Marine Painting

by David Joel and James Taylor

The birth of marine painting took place in Holland during the latter part of the sixteenth century. The Haarlem-born artist, Hendrik Cornelisz Vroom (1566-1640), is now widely recognised as its founding father. The reason for the development of the genre in Holland remains open to question. Certainly the dependence of the country on the sea and the extensive inland canals and waterways offered no shortage of subject matter. By the second quarter of the seventeenth century the trading successes of the Dutch East India Company (founded in 1602) had greatly enhanced the economy of Holland, and increased trade was reflected in a lively art market.

Vroom's prominence cannot be underestimated, as it is now believed that he was largely responsible for creating the demand for ship painting significantly before the establishment of the Dutch Republic as a major maritime power. By the middle of the seventeenth century many Dutch trading companies, as well the merchants themselves, were eager to commission artists to paint portraits of the vessels that had contributed to their good fortune. Other popular maritime subjects included portraits of private vessels and yachts, general shipping scenes, coastal and harbour views, and naval actions.

Vroom helped to popularise many of the subject categories of maritime art, notably naval battles, marine views of everyday life with small sailing craft, and lively harbour scenes such as *Ships Trading in the East*. He had originally followed his father's profession as a painter of pots and ceramics before turning to marine painting. In addition to painting he also designed tapestries, of which his most famous work was the series of ten designs depicting the major incidents of the *Spanish Armada*, commissioned by Lord Howard of Effingham, to commemorate the English success under his overall command. In 1650 they hung in the House of Lords until they were destroyed by fire in 1834.

Carel van Mander, Vroom's friend, fellow painter and biographer, published a lively account of the artist's life in *Het Schilder-Boeck* (Haarlem, 1604). Mander was a loyal friend and wrote of Vroom's work: '...not only does [he] understand the construction of the ships, their ropes and rigging, the direction of the winds, the sails and other relevant matters, but he also excels in all other aspects, such as backgrounds, landscapes, waves, towns, small figures, fish and the subjects which enliven and enhance his ships.'

From Mander's account of Vroom's life it is known that he was fond of playing practical jokes, and that he received some tuition from the Flemish artist Paul Bril (1554-1625). Vroom had firsthand experience of the sea and even survived being shipwrecked. He painted storms and shipwrecks, and excelled at beach and fishing scenes, and

1/1
Hendrik Cornelisz Vroom (1566-1640). *Ships trading in the East*, detail. Oil on canvas, 38½ x 59½, signed and dated 1614.
National Maritime Museum, London

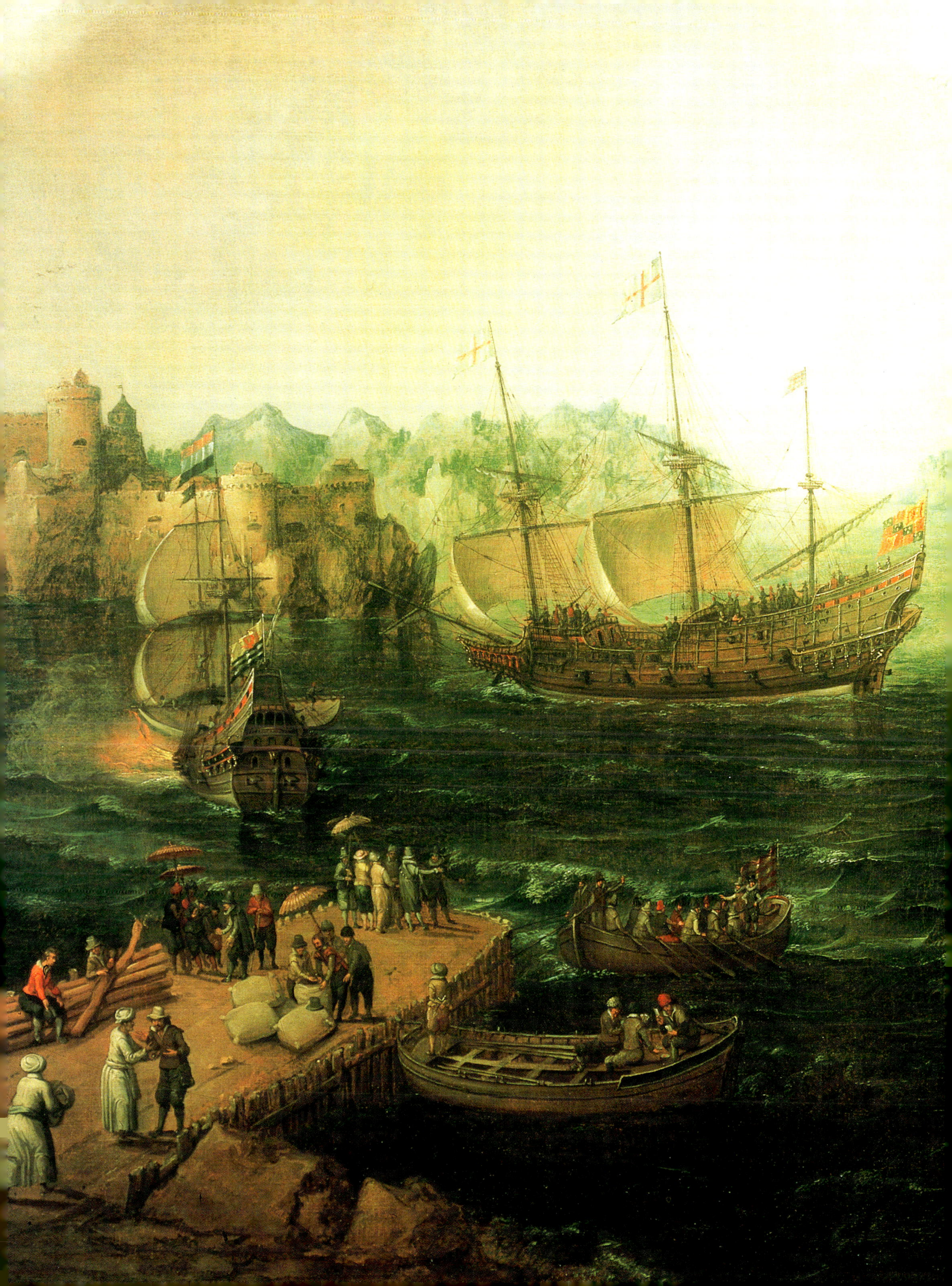

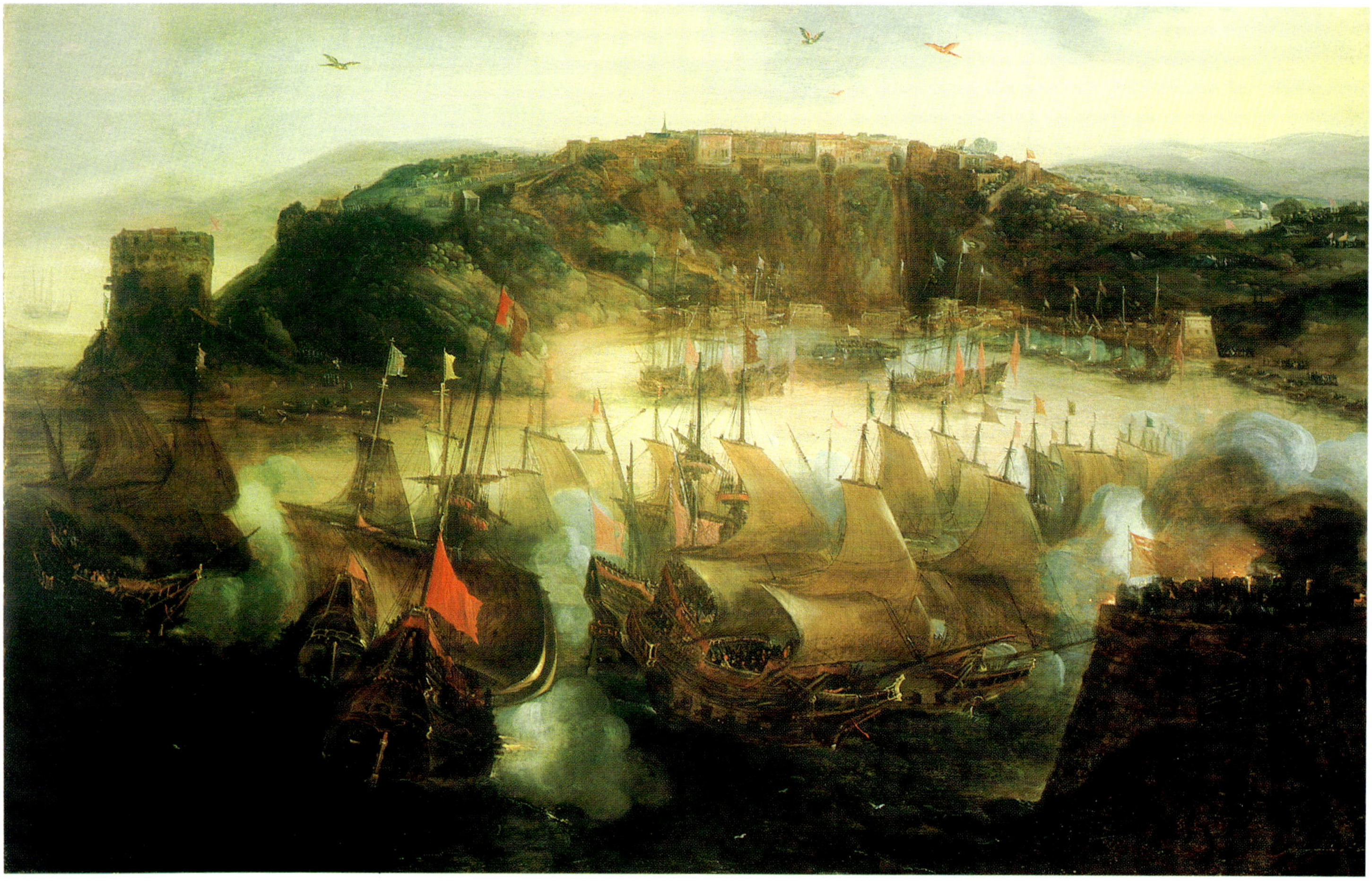

1/2
Andries van Eertvelt (1590-1652). *Attack on San Salvador, 9 May 1624*. Oil on panel, 26½ x 42.
National Maritime Museum, London

especially at scenes of royal arrivals and departures.

Andries van Eertvelt (1590-1652), one of Vroom's pupils, copied his master's work, although his ships are less accurately handled. He would often group them too closely together, and would distort the size and scale of the ships themselves with the effect of coincidentally heightening the visual drama of his compositions. Eertvelt's *Attack on San Salvador, 9 May, 1624* is a good example. Many of Eertvelt's pictures, and those of his master, were inspired by cartography; adopting a high viewpoint to show the scene from above, rather like a map or plan. This artistic device may well have been less naturalistic but at least it helped the viewer to make visual sense of the ships as they appeared at sea. Some of these early views also included a key, identifying ships. It was an ideal format to convey the visual appearance of a complex naval battle, or a series of encounters at sea such as the *Spanish Armada* that took place over several days and in different locations.

Vroom, and Eertvelt were less interested in naturalistic effects. Their dark, green seas were invariably punctuated with brilliant highlights of colour. Eertvelt preferred a cool, metallic palette. It was left to Jan Porcellis (c.1584-1632), also a pupil of Vroom, or 'Old Vroom' as he was popularly known in England, and later followers, notably the Rotterdam born artist Simon de Vlieger (c.1600-1653), and the Willem van de Veldes, a father and son, generally referred to as the Elder (1611-1693) and the Younger (1633-1707), to develop representational techniques and a palette of colours that reflected local subjects and climate with greater fidelity. De Vlieger's *The Beach at Scheveningen* is a remarkable early coastal view, painted in 1633, and without question a maritime masterpiece.

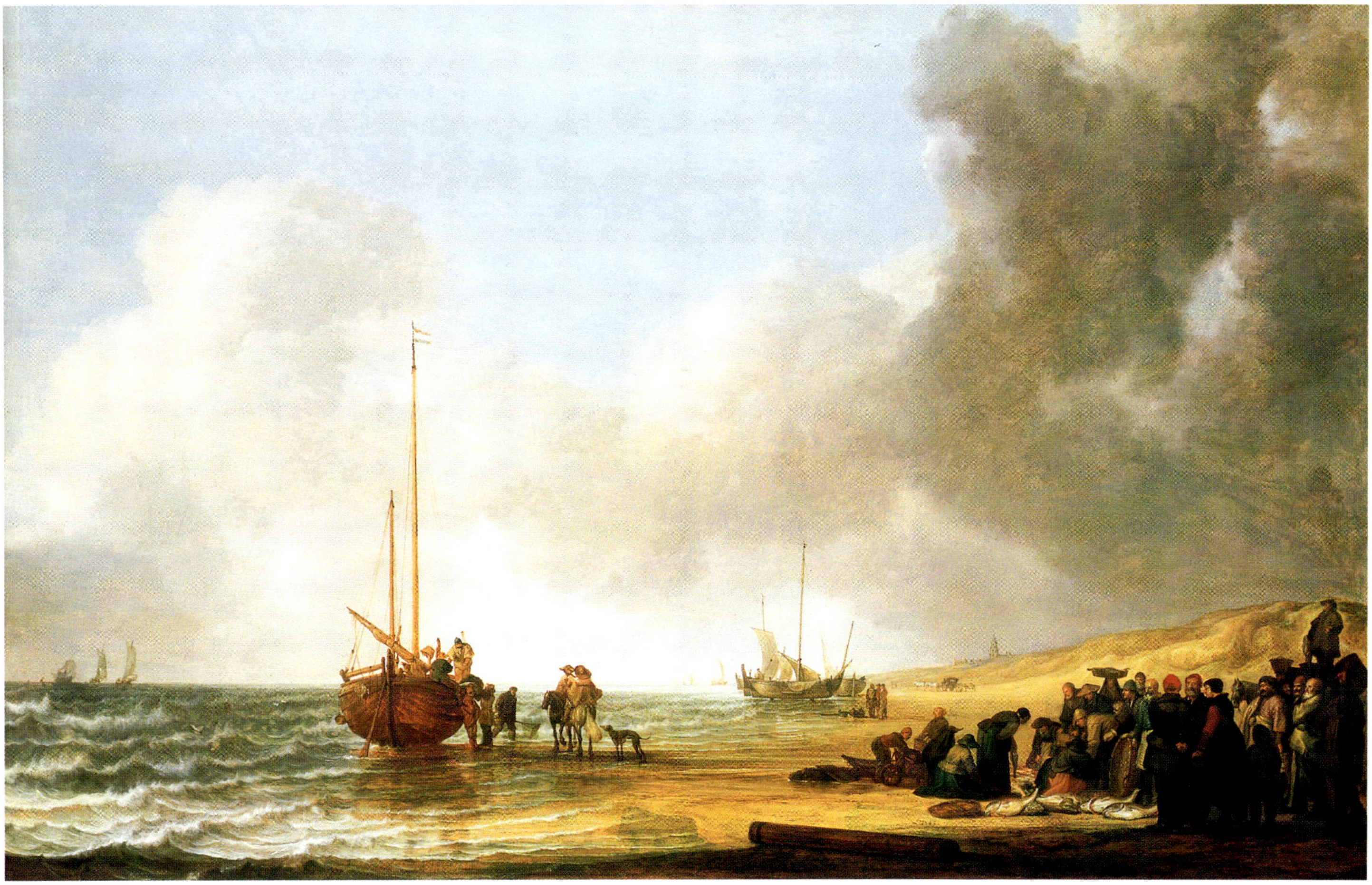

1/3
Simon de Vlieger (c.1600-1707). *The Beach at Scheveningen*. Oil on panel, 27 x 42. Signed and dated 1633.
National Maritime Museum, London

De Vlieger was the most gifted student of Jan Porcellis. Although de Vlieger was an extremely accomplished painter, frustratingly little is known of his life. In fact the scant knowledge that we do possess is typical of our general comprehension of many marine artists of the seventeenth and eighteenth centuries. We know through studying de Vlieger's work that he preferred coastal views, and scenes of everyday maritime life, and generally avoided naval actions and historical subjects. It is traditionally believed that he was a pupil of van de Velde the Elder, and in turn de Vlieger taught the eldest son, van de Velde the Younger, to paint in oils. De Vlieger is credited with several other celebrated pupils, including Jan van de Capelle (1624-1679), Hendrik Dubbels (c.1620-1676) and Lieve Pietersz Verschuir (1630-1686), all of whom were to influence the work of Brooking.

Dubbels' celebrated pupil, Ludolf Bakhuizen (1631-1708), was an extremely successful artist in his own right, and although German by birth, rightly belongs to the Dutch School. He was influential on Willem van de Velde the Younger and Charles Brooking. Verschuir was a native of Rotterdam. It is known that Brooking copied his work.

Brooking studied de Vlieger's work closely. He made two copies (see 101A-B) of de Vlieger's beach scene, now in the Wallraf-Richartz Museum in Cologne, Germany. Van de Velde the Younger also copied de Vlieger's composition. It is likely that Brooking had ready access not just to the engravings after de Vlieger's work, but to the oil paintings themselves. This would account for the fact that of all the artists of the Dutch School, Brooking's colour range of warm ochres, greys and greens, has the closest affinity to de Vlieger's palette.

De Vlieger and the Willem van de Veldes, among others, introduced a lower, more

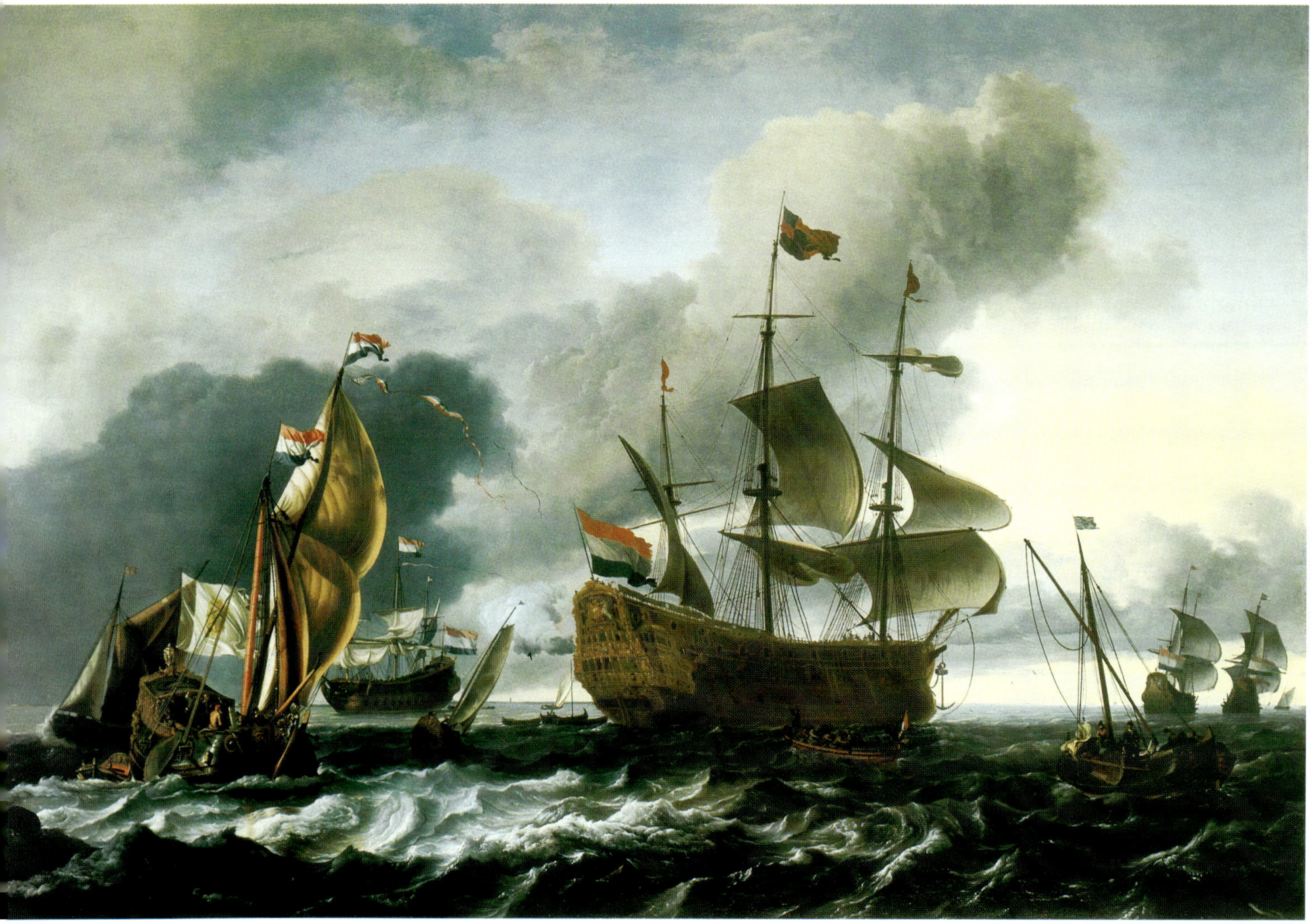

1/4
Ludolf Bakhuizen (1631-1708). *Dutch attack on the Medway – HMS* Royal Charles *carried into Dutch waters, 1667.* Oil on canvas, 48 x 78. Signed. National Maritime Museum, London

realistic viewpoint, although they continued to use the high horizon viewpoint when necessary. They adopted perspective to good advantage and popularised the 'visual step', a dark, narrow, horizontal band in the immediate foreground of their compositions, usually stretching across the sea. This artistic device helps to lead the viewer into their pictures, and breaks up an expanse of sea, creating a more convincing sense of spatial recession. It was a popular device with eighteenth century European marine artists, including Brooking, who would vary the depth and arrangement of the 'visual step' to achieve particular visual effects. It fell from favour during the early years of the Victorian era.

The influence of the Dutch artists who specialised in riverscapes, estuary views, and coastal scenes, often with fishing craft and figures strolling on the shore, on the early English marine painters, has often been overlooked, or underestimated. Porcellis, Jan van Goyen (1596-1666) and their followers were responsible for introducing a greater realism into marine painting. The local weather conditions, and the fleeting changes of nature themselves were often the main preoccupation of these artists. These natural features would invariably be their primary subjects. Van Goyen's marines were usually small-scale works, highly atmospheric, and sometimes almost monochromatic in appearance. He used a careful balance of ochres, greens, and silvery-greys, imbuing his works with a delicacy of great beauty that has yet to be surpassed. Brooking shared van Goyen's

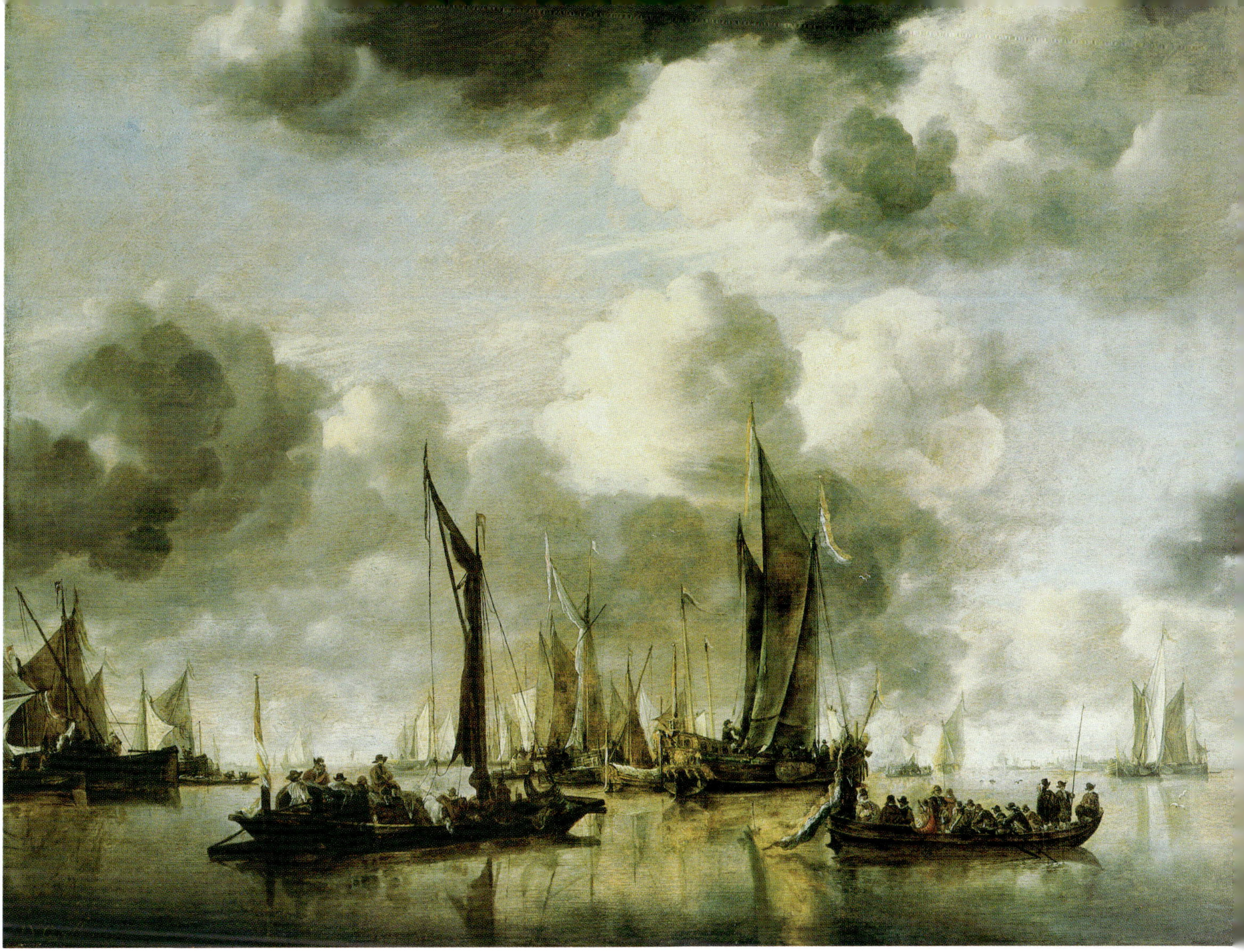

1/5
Jan van de Capelle (1624-1679). *A Dutch Yacht firing a salute as a barge pulls away, and many small vessels at anchor.* Oil on oak panel, 33⅛ x 45, signed and dated 1650. National Gallery, London

interest in portraying naturalistic effects, and to a lesser degree the Dutch artist's penchant for extreme contrasts of light and shade. Brooking was certainly familiar with van Goyen's work, and made a copy of the Dutch artist's *Blankenburg Castle off the Coast of Flanders* (see catalogue No. 104).

Van Goyen's contemporaries, Solomon van Ruisdael (1600-1670), probably better known for his landscapes, and his cousin Jacob Isaakszoon van Ruisdael (1628/9-1682), also excelled at inshore seascapes and focused on naturalistic effects conveyed via a muted palette. Albert Cuyp (1620-1691) and Jan van de Capelle are two of the best known painters instrumental in the transition from a subdued palette of van Goyen and his circle to warmer, brighter colours, and compositions suffused with light. These artists are noted for their scenes of everyday maritime life, often observed at close-quarters, and arranged into visually arresting compositions. In particular they are acclaimed for their carefully observed reflections of ships, small craft and figures, that imbue their work with a sense of heightened realism, and tranquillity of astonishing beauty.

Something of that essence of tranquillity and calm is evident in Brooking's work. One of the most readily identifiable features of his painting is the extraordinary sense of stillness. It can found in almost all his work. This characteristic was aptly summed up by Basil Taylor in his introduction to the Paul Mellon Foundation for British Art's exhibition catalogue in 1966. '[Brooking's] compositions often present a most precarious equipoise, as if a film, arrested at the point of a well designed frame, is about to dissolve into the fluidity of motion.' There is a wonderful lyrical quality to many of his paintings.

The Willem van de Veldes are now acknowledged as two of the most gifted, successful, and influential of all marine painters. Their artistic legacy remains a significant influence on many marine artists working today. Brooking openly acknowledged his debt to them by studying, copying, adapting and updating their compositions. Their popularity lies in their ability to create harmonious compositions, containing accurate depictions of all manner of ships, brought to life by skilful handling of naturalistic effects. They often featured seamen actually working the ships, or seashore strollers. Flags flutter convincingly, the wind really does appear to be acting on the sails, and the vessels portrayed actually sit correctly in the water. Marine painting offers numerous challenges to an artist.

Van de Velde the Elder was born in Leiden, South Holland, the son of a shipmaster. He went to sea at an early age and later served aboard transport vessels trading with Norway. Little is known about his formal artist's training but he clearly inherited his father's love

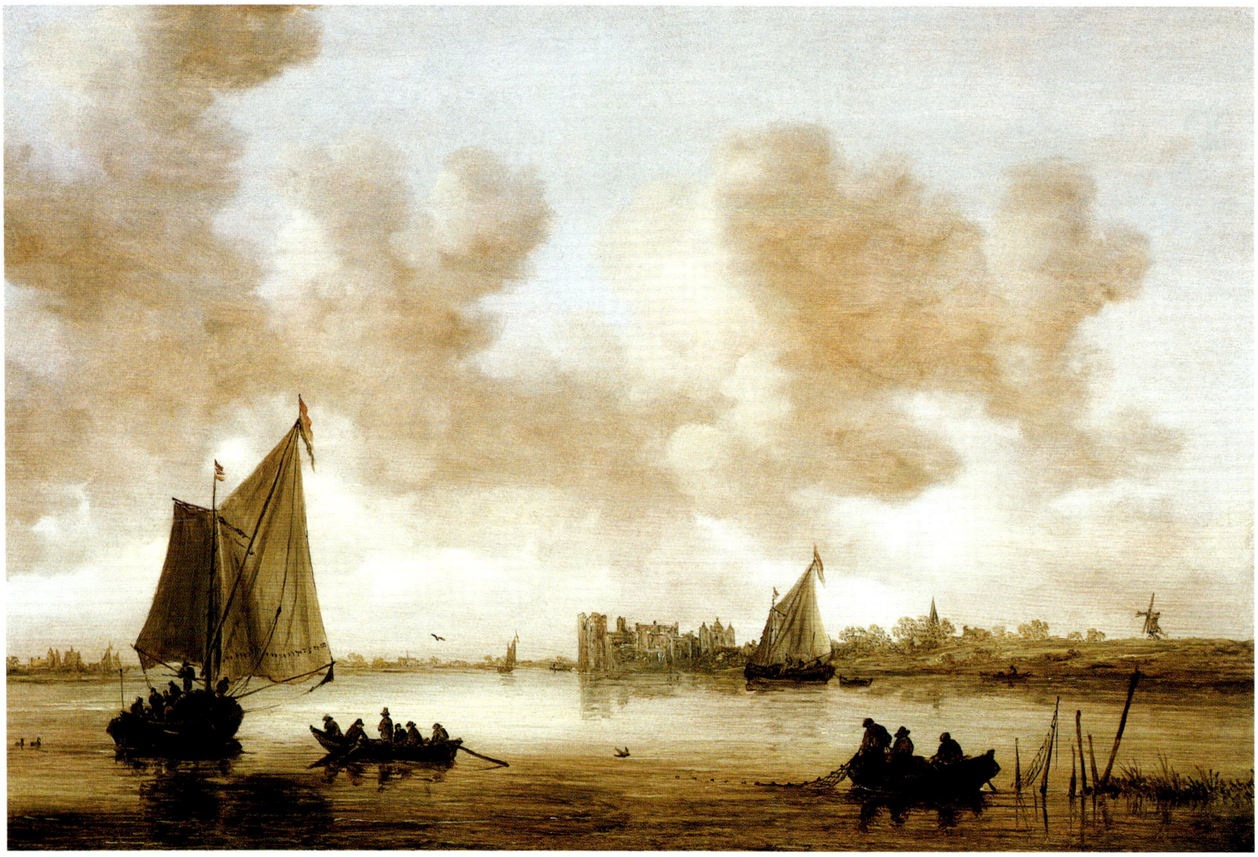

1/6
Jan van Goyen (1596-1666). *A river landscape with a boat in the foreground*. Oil, 15¾ x 23¾, signed with monogram and dated 1641. Richard Green Gallery

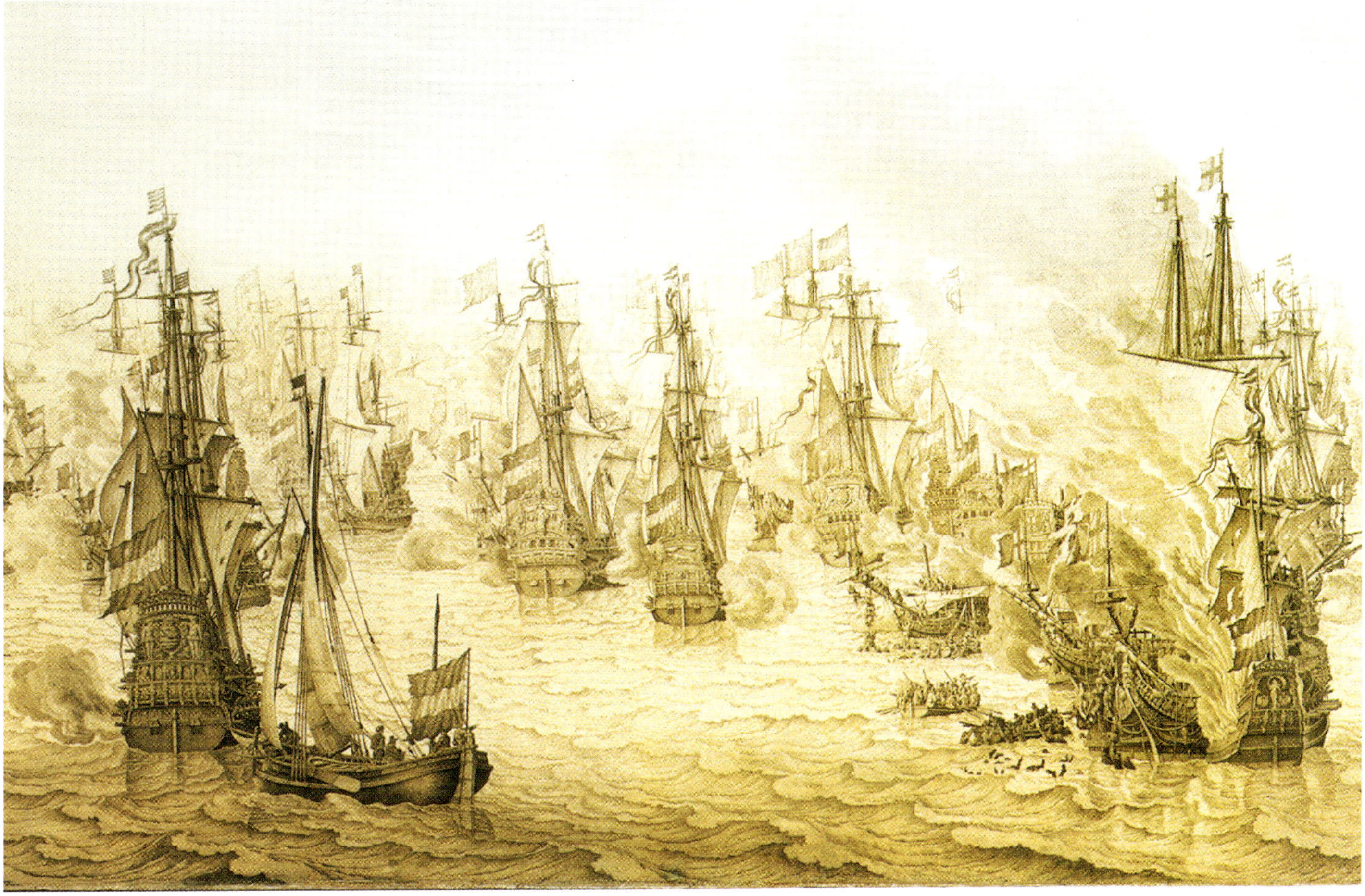

1/7
Willem van de Velde the Elder (1611-1693). *The Battle of Scheveningen, 10 August 1653.* Grisaille on panel, 44⅜ x 61⅜.
National Maritime Museum, London

of ships and the sea. His eldest son, Willem, was also his most promising pupil. They worked individually and sometimes in partnership, van de Velde the Elder providing sketches and drawings which his son would work up into finished oil paintings.

The Elder developed new recording skills in Holland derived largely from his precarious experiences escorting the Dutch fleet at sea. To assist him in his work, his naval patrons provided him with a galliot but gave him specific instructions to keep his distance. He sketched key subjects and made detailed notes of the ships' positions and the sequence of events. Thus probably for the first time, it was possible to achieve greater accuracy and to offer a more authentic representation of naval action.

After the outbreak of the First Anglo-Dutch War in 1652, van de Velde the Elder was operating as an official war artist. One drawing bears the revealing inscription: *View of the fleet, ready to sail, before the harbour, when I put to sea in the galliot with letters for Admiral Tromp on Friday afternoon at 2 o'clock, 8 August 1653.* Two days later he was also present at the Battle of Scheveningen, 10 August 1653, and in one notable painting, showed himself sitting on the galliot's deck with sketchbook firmly balanced on his knee while all around him the battle raged.

Van de Velde the Elder used boats as a floating studio. He also made use of ship models to improve his draughtsmanship. Writing in 1706, the translator of Roger de Pile's *Art of Painting* mentions that van de Velde the Elder 'for his better information in this way of Painting had a Model of the Mast and Tackle of the Ship always before him'. Similar models were also used by van de Velde the Younger to ensure nautical accuracy. The Younger also made many drawings. An inscription on one of his studies shows the fastidious nature of his working method. It reads: 'To be noted: a ship or small vessel in pitching nearly always throws up spray, as shown here.' A series of ten sketch plans reveals that van de Velde the Younger was almost certainly designing a yacht for himself. These sheer plans and several hundred other sketches and drawings by the van de Veldes, many of them annotated, can be seen in the collection of the National Maritime Museum, Greenwich.

The van de Veldes were active during the so-called 'Golden Age' of Dutch painting: the era of Rembrandt, Hals and Vermeer. Admirals, captains, state officials, city guilds and the States General itself, the collective assembly of the seven provinces forming the Dutch Republic, all of whom were proud of their own successes, commissioned artists to commemorate their achievements on canvas. Some had their portraits painted showing them wearing their finest clothes. Some preferred to have themselves painted with their families in domestic or social settings. Others commissioned exquisite still lifes depicting luxury goods, such as gold and silver plates and goblets, or opulent displays of flowers and food.

A familiar feature of Dutch painting from this period is its accurate detail, perhaps reflecting patrons' concerns with all things material. Fine silks (brought back from the trading expeditions to India and China), lace, intricate interior decorations, and rotten, decaying apples are all rendered with such skilful precision that they seem almost real.

Although van de Velde the Elder occasionally painted in oils, the bulk of his work comprises drawings and sketches. He was one of the earliest practitioners of pen-painting, or *penschilderij*, sometimes called grisaille. Quill pens were used to create sharp lines on panels or canvas which were sometimes heightened with grey wash. Using this

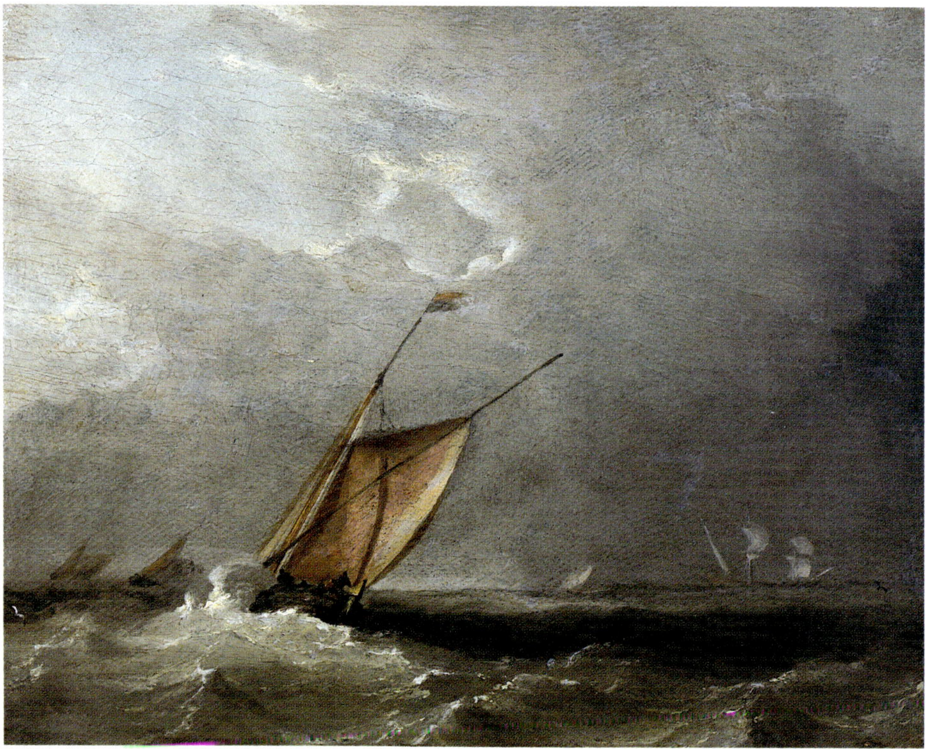

1/8
Willem van de Velde the Younger (1633-1707). *A kaag close-hauled in a strong breeze and a heavy sea.* Oil on canvas, 7¾ x 10¼.
Private Collection

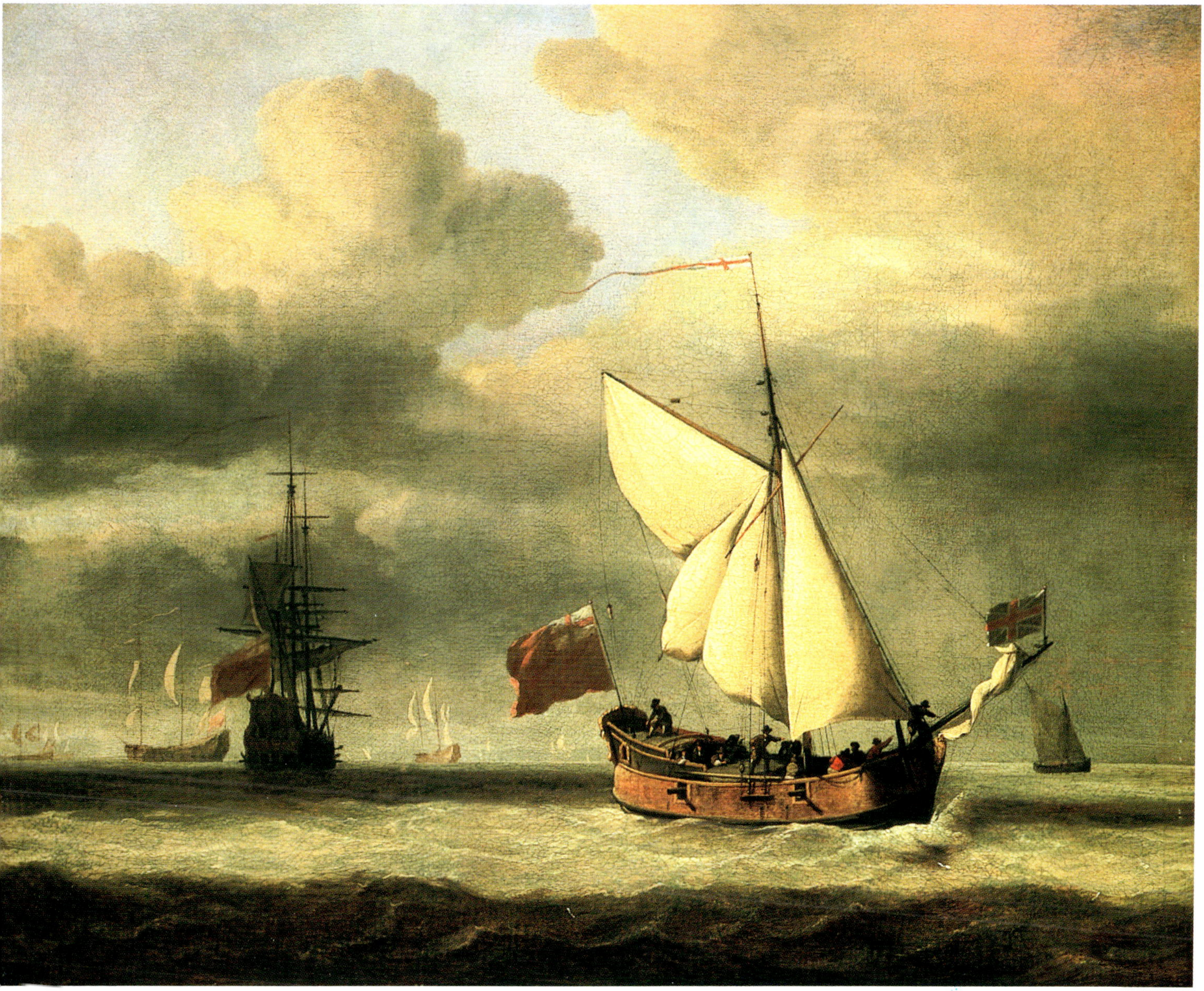

1/9
Willem van de Velde the Younger (1633-1707). *The Royal Escape*. Oil on canvas, signed, 24 x 29.
National Maritime Museum, London

technique artists could create far more detailed works than they could with oils, and pen-painting became the nautical equivalent of the highly detailed still lifes. Although they took considerably longer to complete than oil paintings, pen-painted works, which in many ways resembled engravings, were much admired by naval officers, mariners, merchants and states officials who demanded above all accuracy and exacting detail.

In 1672 Charles II issued a declaration encouraging Dutch citizens to settle in England. The van de Veldes were among those who responded, no doubt spurred on by the fact that France had recently invaded the Netherlands and commissions had dried up. One further factor was also instrumental in encouraging van de Velde the Elder to move to England, his wife had discovered her husband's infidelity and that his illicit liaison had resulted in illegitimate children. The threat of legal action no doubt settled the matter, and in 1671, or in the following year, he moved to England. His son followed suit.

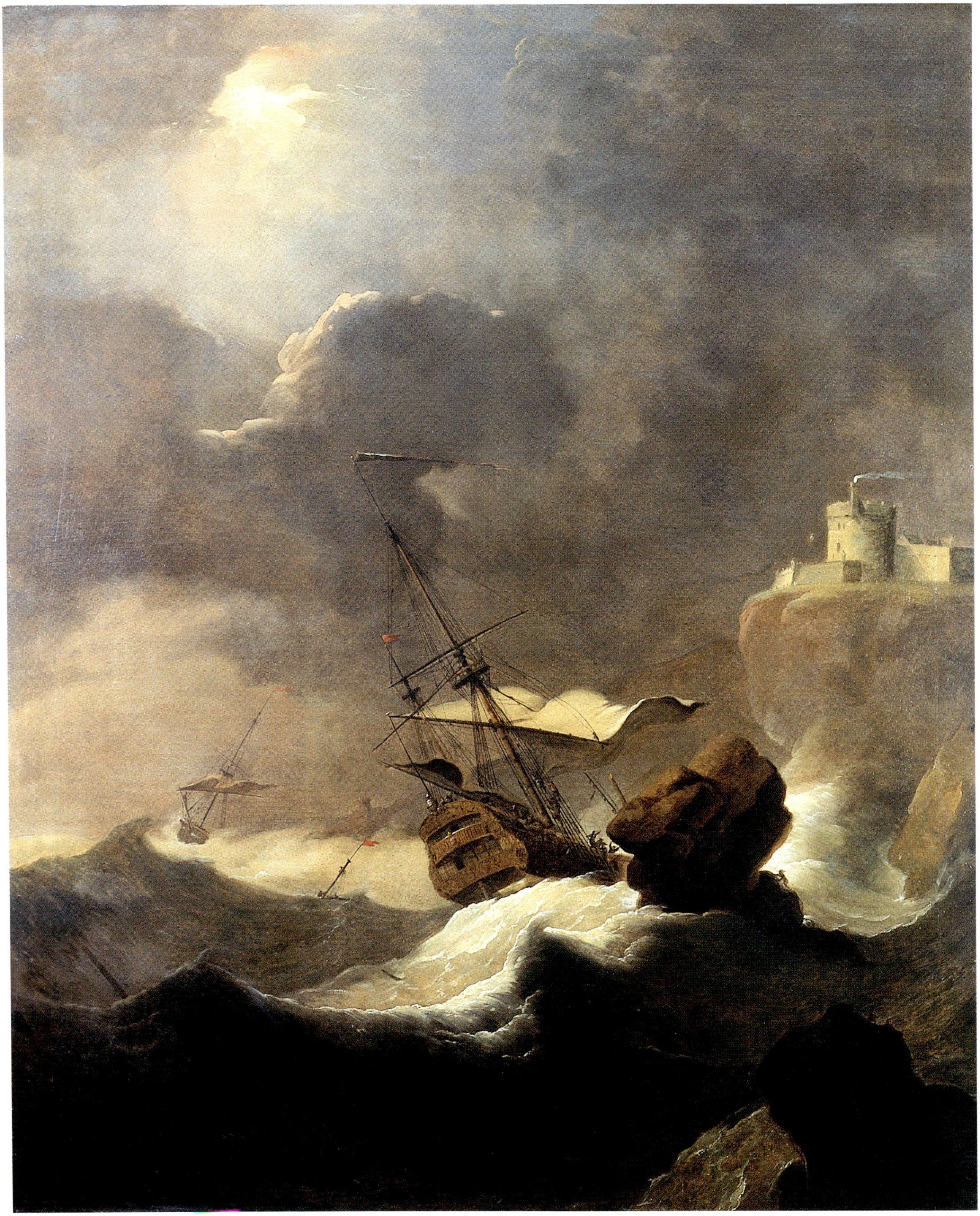

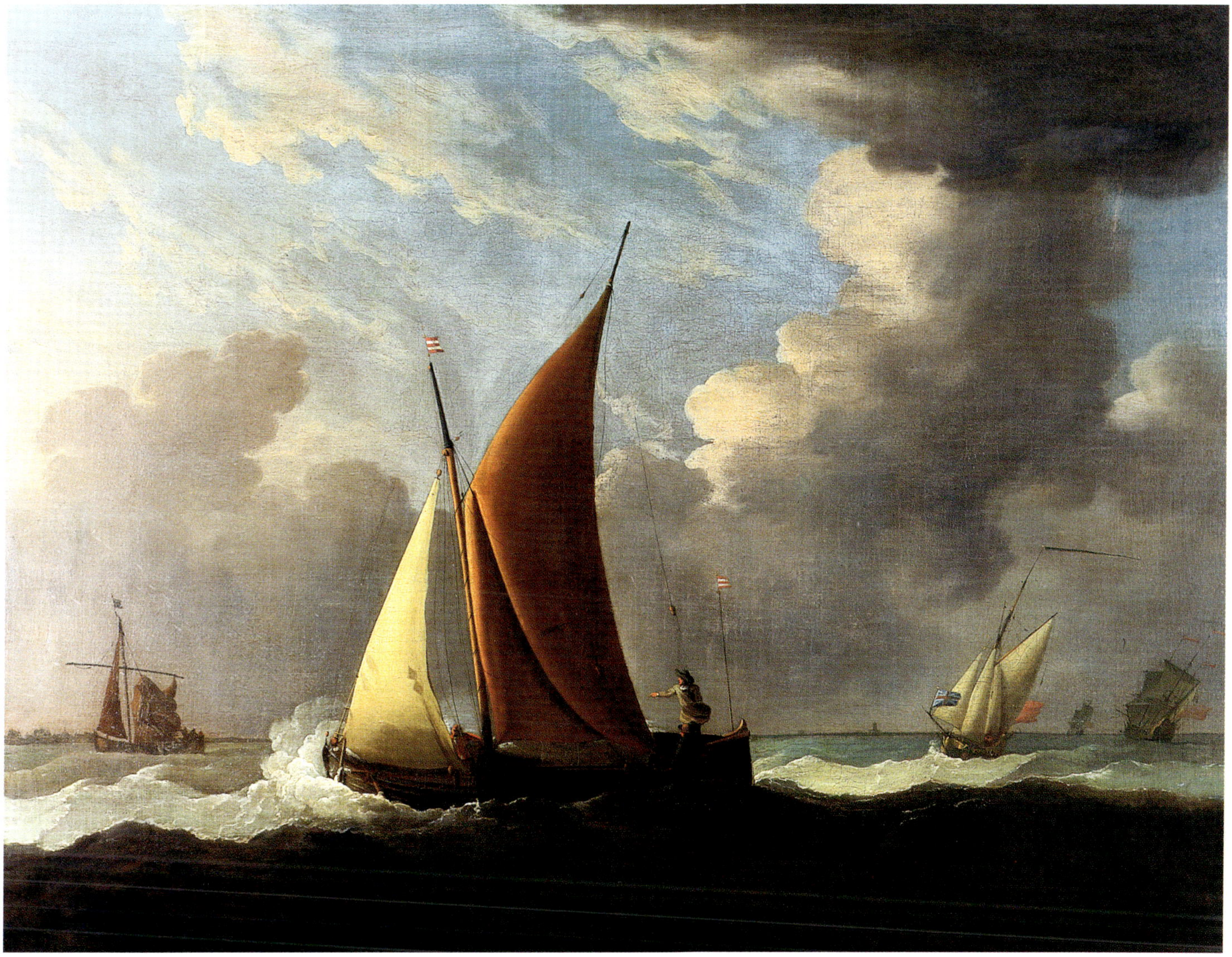

1/11
Peter Monamy (1681-1749). *A smallschip in a stiff breeze with an English Royal Yacht and two English Frigates.* Oil on canvas, signed, 29 x 39½. Collection Miss Emma Joel

1/10 (Left)
Peter Monamy (1681-1749). *Storm and Shipwreck off a rocky coast with a fortress above.* Oil on canvas, 65 x 54. Signed P Monamy pinx. Collection M. D. Joel

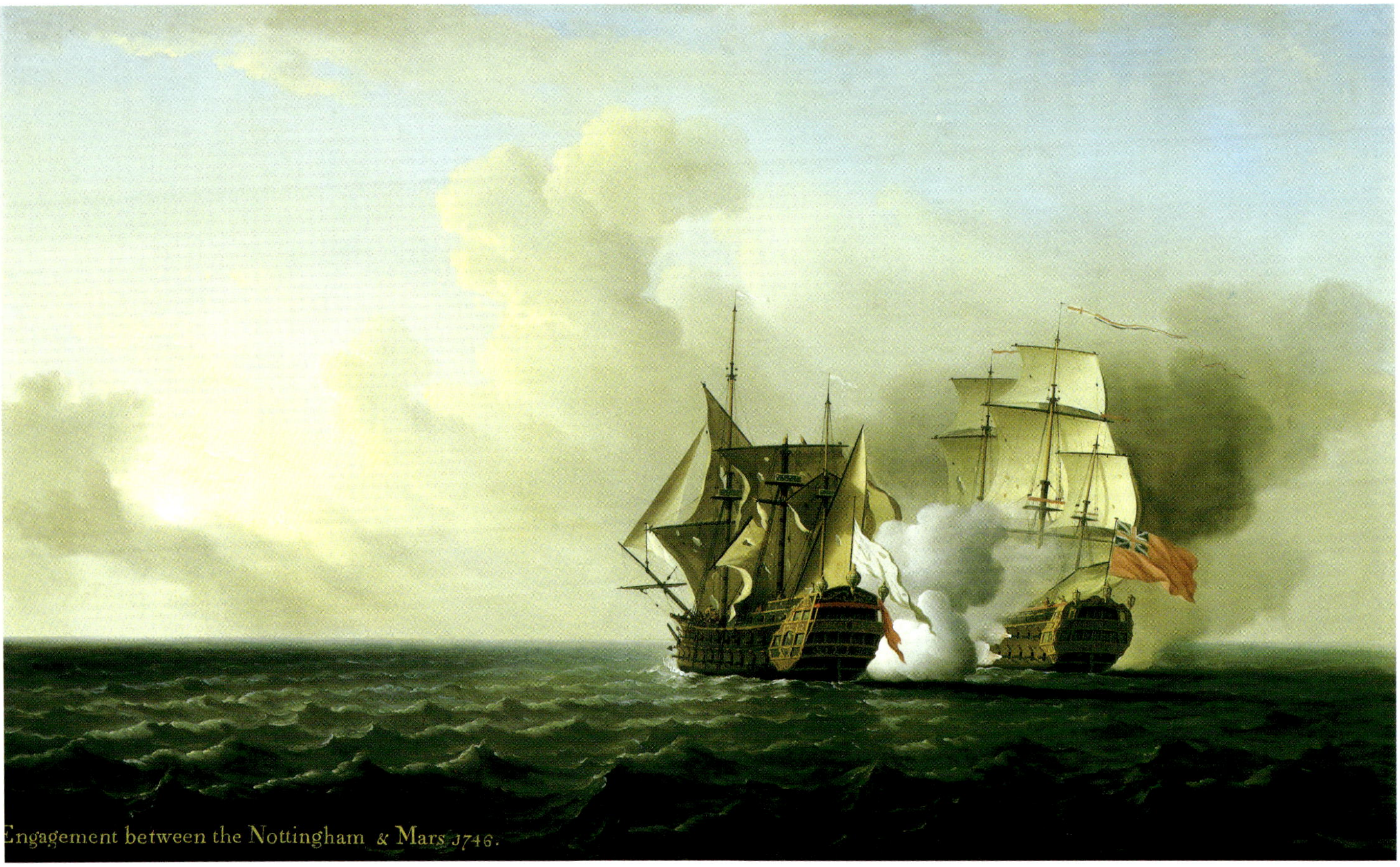

1/12
Samuel Scott (c.1702-1772). *Engagement between the* Nottingham *and* Mars *11 October 1746*. Oil on canvas, 24 x 39½. Richard Green Gallery

King Charles II offered the van de Veldes studio space in the Queen's House, in Greenwich, now part of the National Maritime Museum. They worked in the ground floor rooms painting royal reviews, state occasions, naval actions, and less official subjects including seashore scenes with fisherfolk and bathers, yacht and barge designs, even drawings designed to aid up-and-coming artists with the rudiments of marine painting. In addition to painting, they also made tapestry designs of subjects from the protracted Anglo-Dutch Wars. The King was eager to retain their services and the division of their labours was drawn up in royal records. The Treasurer of the Navy was instructed to pay 'the salary of One hundred pounds per annum unto William Vandeveld the elder for taking and making the Draughts of Sea Fights, and the like Salary of One Hundred pounds per annum unto William Vandevelde the younger for putting the said Draughts into Colours for Our particular use.'

The van de Veldes were not constrained to paint for the British Royal Family, or the British Navy. Their skills were widely appreciated by collectors and connoisseurs in England, and Europe. As the market for art improved in Holland they once again started to receive commissions from Dutch naval officers and merchants. Patrons were eager for marine subjects to decorate their town houses and country residences. In England, Ham

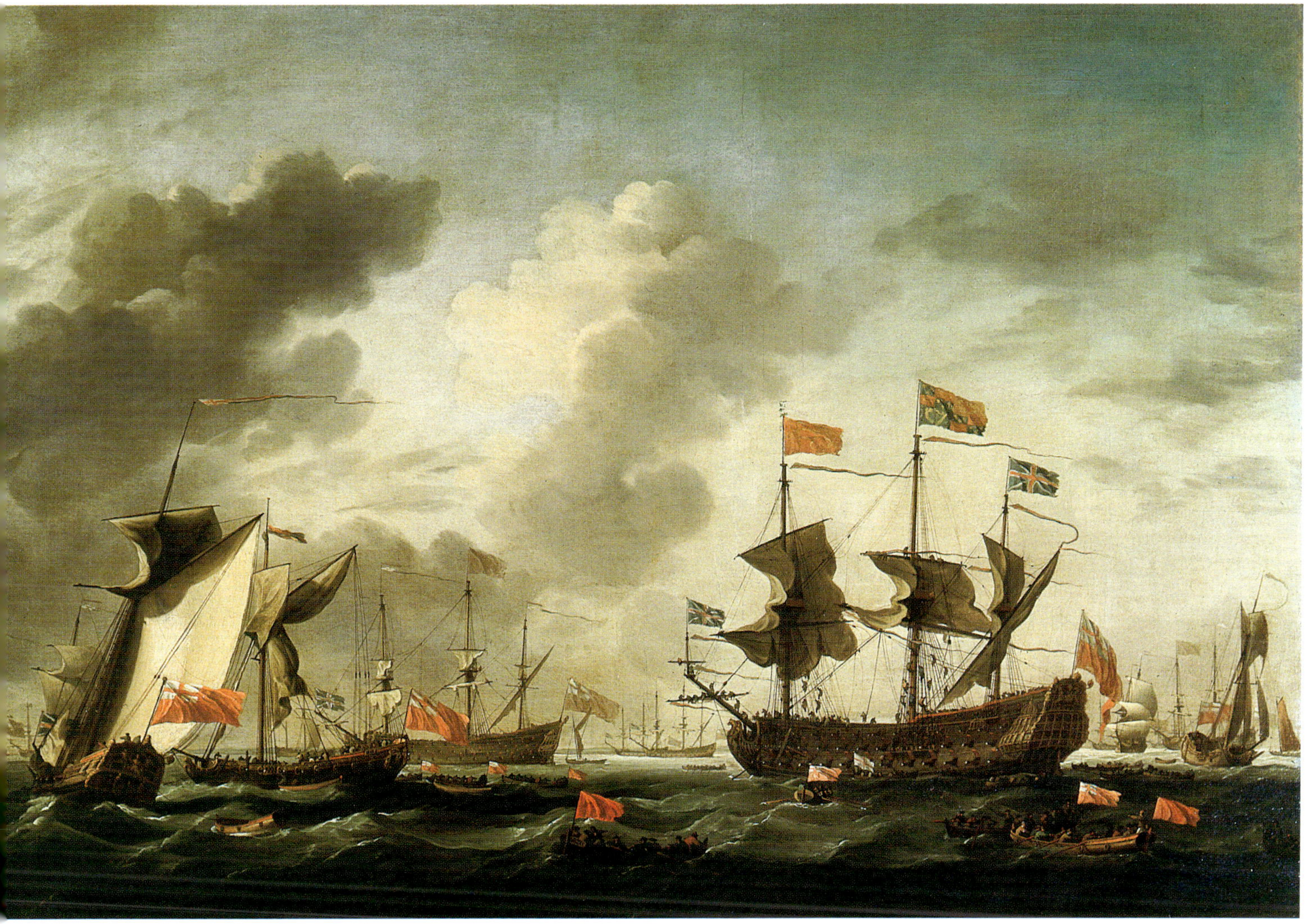

1/13
Charles Brooking (450A) *The Royal Visit to the Fleet in the Thames Estuary, 10 September 1673.*
Oil on canvas, 25¼ x 38. Unsigned. Collection Sir Nicholas Bacon

House, in Surrey, still possesses the four original oils painted by van de Velde the Younger for the Duke and Duchess of Lauderdale in 1673. They were originally commissioned for the Duke's Bedchamber to hang either side of his bed, and over the doorways. A visit to Ham House is a journey back into the seventeenth century. It is now the property of the National Trust in England, and open to the public.

By the mid-1670s Greenwich became a centre for marine painting. The demand for the van de Veldes' work ensured greater numbers of studio assistants, among them van de Velde the Younger's son, Cornelis van de Velde (active 1675-1729). Cornelis' son-in-law Johann van der Hagen (1675-c.1745) is also closely associated with the studio, and some sources have claimed him to be Brooking's master. This busy studio explains the presence of a large body of work loosely attributed to the van de Veldes, and much of it of variable quality. The van de Veldes themselves were instrumental in encouraging English artists to take up marine painting, and because of the lack of local role models English artists studied, copied, adapted, and collected the Dutch artists' sketches, drawings and oil paintings. The van de Veldes provided the benchmark to which many marine artists aspired.

Peter Monamy (1681-1749) and Samuel Scott (c.1702-1772), the first two English

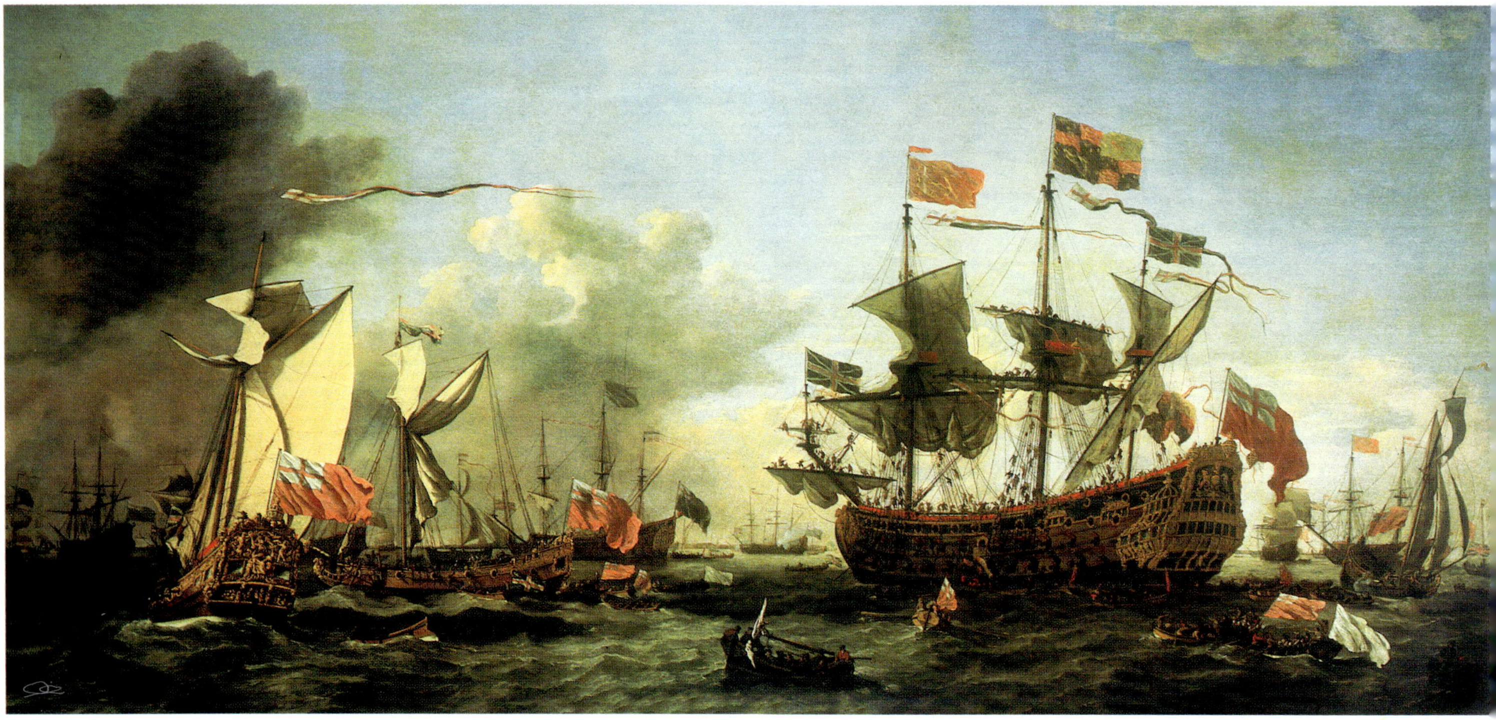

1/14
Willem van de Velde the Younger (1633-1707). *The Royal Visit to the Fleet in the Thames Estuary, 10 September 1673*. Oil on canvas, 65 x 128, signed and dated 1696.
National Maritime Museum, London

marine painters of note, even used the van de Veldes' name to promote their own work. By associating themselves closely with these Dutch artists they hoped that they too would become popular and successful. Monamy described himself as: 'Second only to van de Velde'. Scott was promoted by many influential figures in the eighteenth century, including the writer and art collector, Horace Walpole, an avid admirer of Scott's work. He described the artist as: '...one whose works will charm in every age. If he was but second to Vandeveld in sea pieces, he excelled him in variety, and often introduced buildings in his pictures with consummate skill.'

Monamy and Scott copied and updated the compositions of the van de Veldes, and other Dutch artists of the seventeenth century. If original work by the van de Veldes was not readily available they would turn to engravings after their work for inspiration. Brooking did the same and as E. H. H. Archibald has pointed out, the copies he made of Willem van de Velde the Younger's *Royal Visit to the Fleet in the Thames Estuary, 10 September 1673,* commissioned by Charles II (previously believed to portray a royal event of 6 June 1672) show that he did them from the mezzotint engraving (see Chapter 5, page 67) and never saw the original. He did not understand that the boat in the foreground was French and should have had white flags where he has put in red ones.

Charles Brooking also made several versions of van de Velde the Younger's *English ships at sea beating to windward in a gale* in which he substituted the seventeenth century ships for those of his own time. One of these is in the National Maritime Museum, Greenwich. Other copies or 'modernized' versions of van de Velde's compositions, or themes, by Brooking can be seen in the series of paintings of the *Evening Gun* (see 1A-G) which are closely related to Willem van de Velde the Younger's painting *A small English ship with yachts and other vessels near the shore*, now hanging in the Schilderijenzaal Prins Willem V, The Hague. This painting was originally in the collection of Charles Jennens in London, where Brooking would have been able to study it at first hand.

Brooking was inspired by, and made versions of, several other van de Velde compositions. His series of paintings (see 102A-B) of the *Beach scenes with Men O'War*

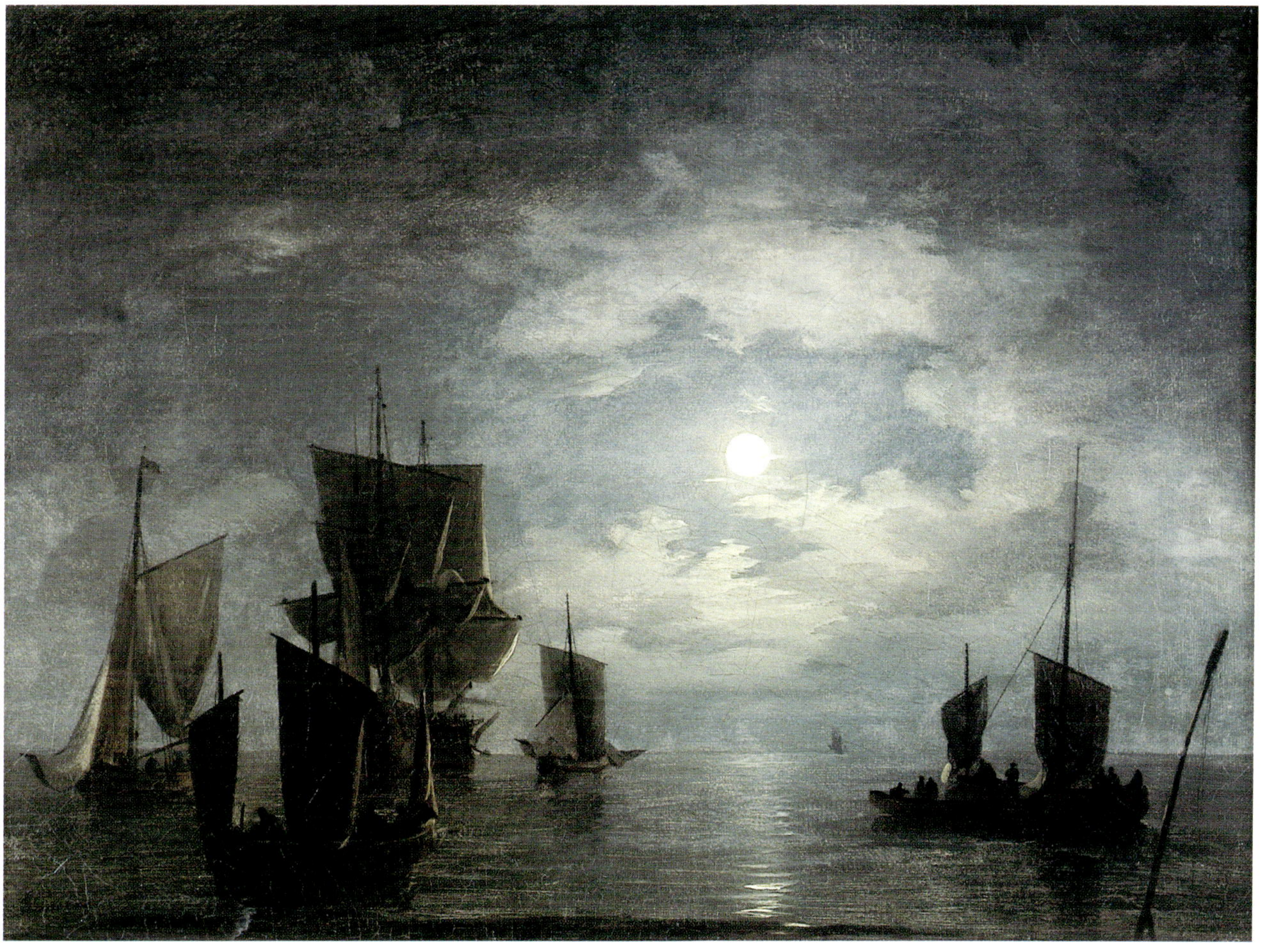

1/15
5A *A frigate becalmed by moonlight with cutters and luggers.* Oil on canvas 11 x 15. Signed C Brooking lower left. Mrs S. J. Herrtage

in the distance derive from the van de Velde the Younger picture now in the Institute Netherlandais, Paris. Also Brooking's *Ships near a coast of sand dunes* (see 105) based on Willem van de Velde the Younger's composition, part of the Assheton Bennett collection No. 72, in the Manchester City Art Gallery.

The selection of one of Brooking's oil paintings: *An English merchant brig and coastal craft becalmed by moonlight'* (catalogue ref. 5B), for the dust jacket of E. H. H. Archibald's classic work *Dictionary of Sea Painters* (1st Edition, 1980), certainly helped to raise interest in the artist. In the entry on Charles Brooking, Archibald also made a bold claim that: '...no painter of the second generation of British marine artists contributed so much to the emergence of a national style as did Brooking, and no painter, then or after, did it better.' *Charles Brooking and the 18th Century British Marine Painters* will attempt to substantiate that claim, and explain as well as illustrate the nature of Brooking's contribution to maritime art.

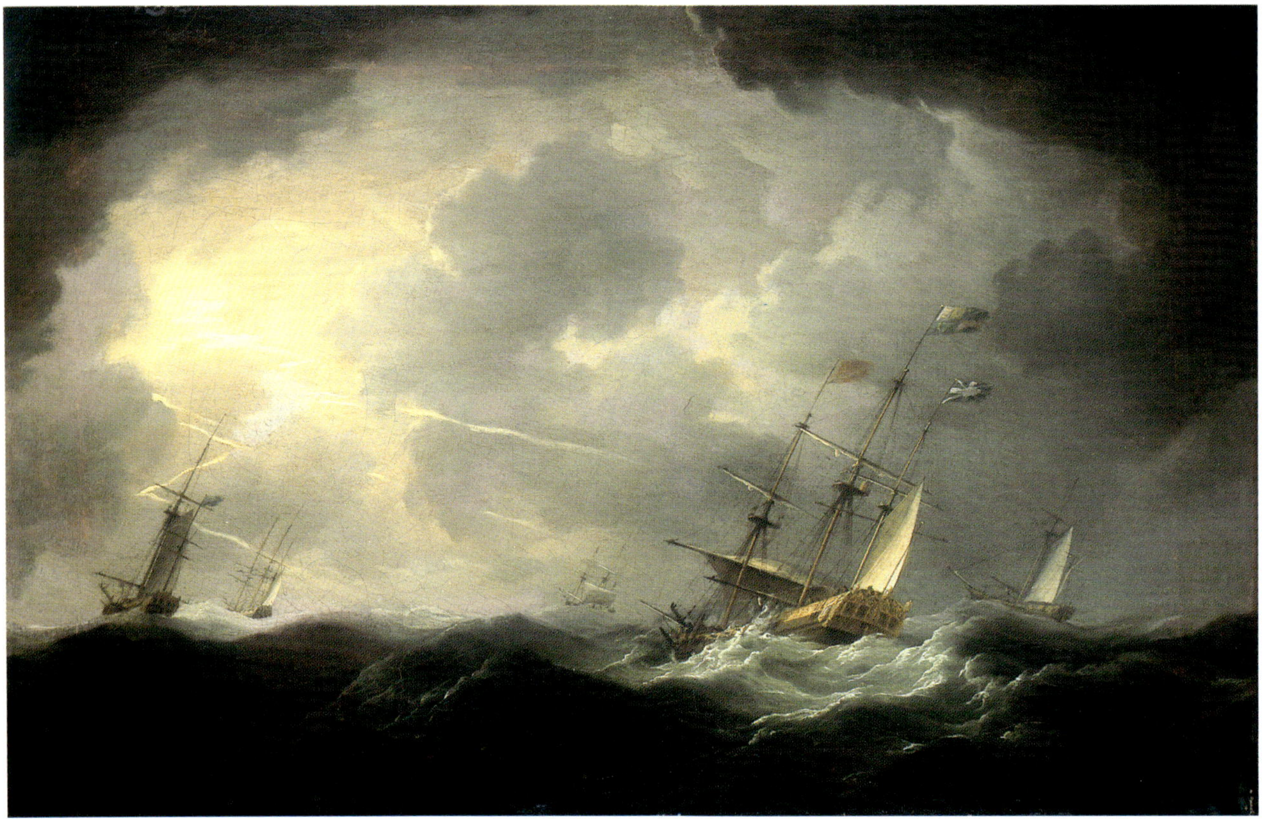

Chapter 2

Biography of Charles Brooking and his Family

2/1
202 *A Royal Yacht in a gale*.
Oil on canvas 14½ x 23½.
Signed C Brooking lower left on spar.
National Maritime Museum, London

2/2
Map of the city and suburbs of Dublin. Drawn from an actual survey. Made by Charles Brooking [senior]. Printed and sold by John Bowles. Print & Mapseller at Mercers Hall in Cheapside 1728, 23½ x 56¼.
Cat. No. 10015 National Library of Ireland British Museum. Map Room Edition 1728 – c.7.a.28

According to the Brooking Society, founded in 1982, Brooking is a rare English name and even today they number but a few. It is now known that the Brooking family hailed from the West Country. During the seventeenth and eighteenth centuries Brookings were located in Damerel, East Stonehouse, Newton Ferrers, Plymouth, and Wembury. Unfortunately the original registers of East Stonehouse were destroyed in the bombing of Plymouth during the Second World War. However, it is now believed that the father of Charles Brooking the marine painter, also called Charles, was baptised there in about 1677 and that he married Catherine Coward at East Stonehouse on 25 September 1701. She died and was buried at King Charles Church, Plymouth on 12 October 1703. Charles senior worked in Plymouth Dockyard where he became a ship's painter. He was later made a Freeman of the City of Plymouth on 2 October 1711.

Charles Brooking senior married again to Jane Hardy. Their daughter Elizabeth was baptised at King Charles Church on 28 October 1714, and their son Charles, the marine painter, is believed to have been born in 1723, but to date no actual record has been found. His mother died in the following year and is buried at Stoke Damerel.

In 1715 the Parish Church overseers accounts for the village of Linkinhorn, located sixteen miles north-west of Plymouth, include a series of entries for labour and charges by Mr Brooking, 'the painter from Plymouth'. They reveal that he was paid £5 for 'drawing the Commands, Lords Prayer and Creed with two figures representing Moses

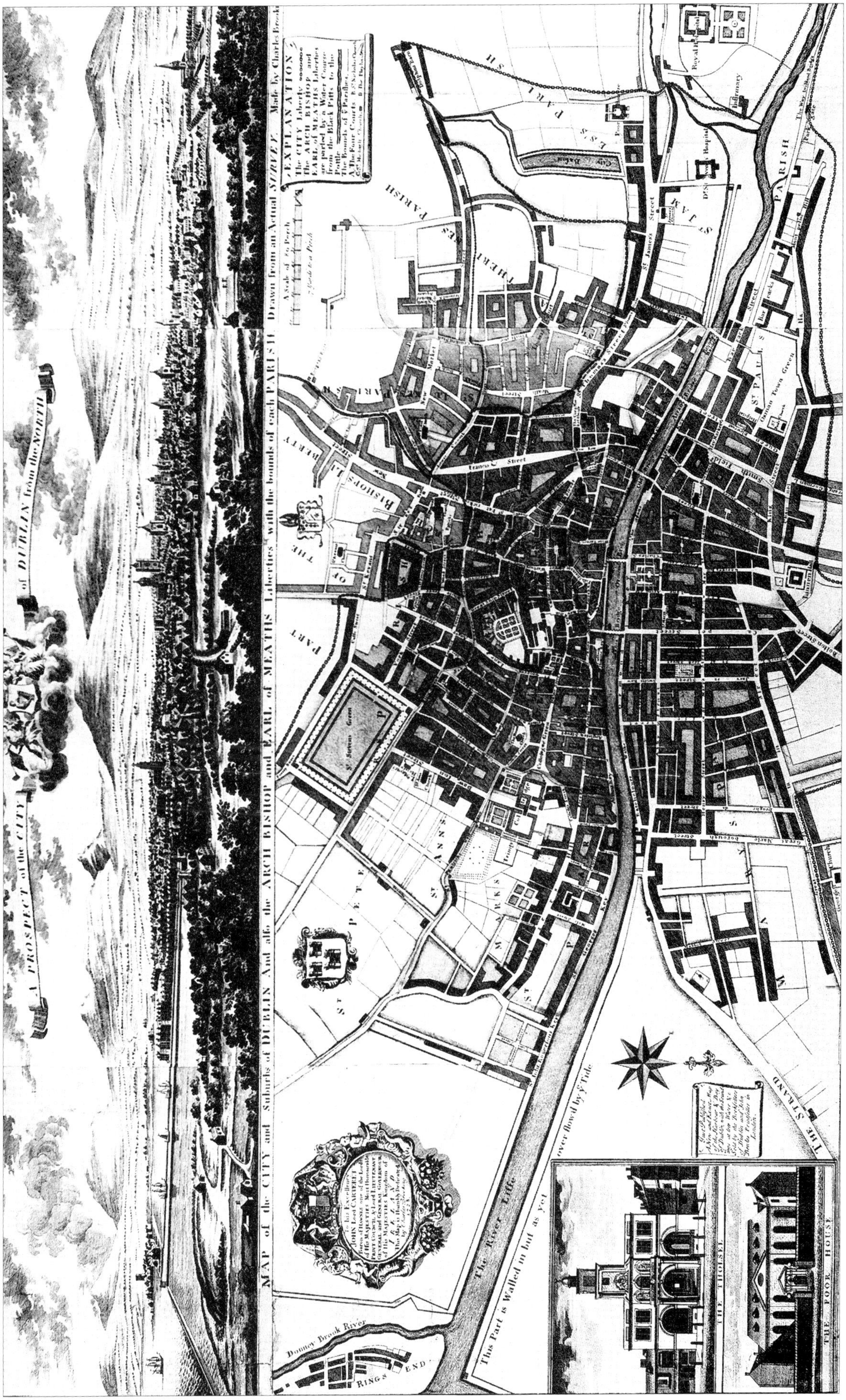
A PROSPECT of the CITY of DUBLIN from the NORTH
MAP of the CITY and Suburbs of DUBLIN And also the ARCH BISHOP and EARL of MEATHS Liberties with the bounds of each PARISH Drawn from an Actual SURVEY Made by Charles Brooking
THE THOLSEL
THE POOR HOUSE
This Part is Walled in but as yet over flowd by ye Tide
The River Liffe
THE STRAND
Donney Brook River
RINGS END

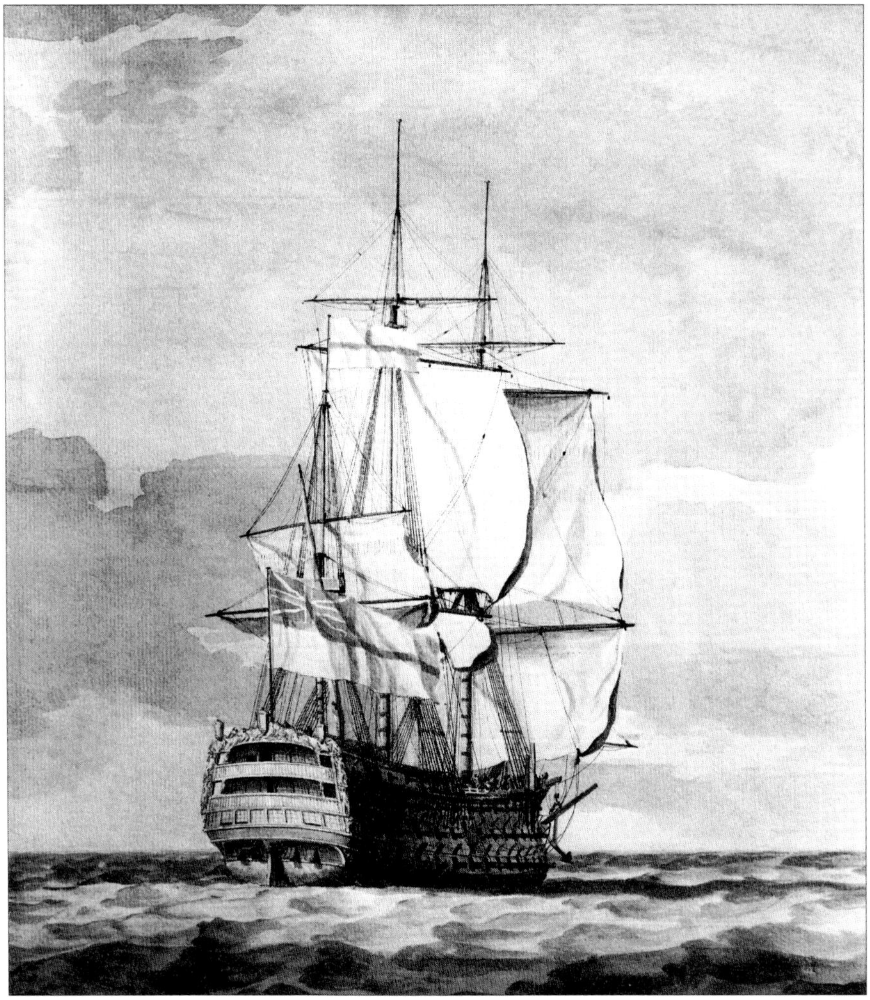

2/3
720 *A three-decked man of war from the starboard quarter*. Pen, ink and grey wash 12⅜ x 11½.
Victoria & Albert Museum, London

and Aaron'. He spent five days at the church and also painted the font, parson's pew and desk, the clerk's seat, 'ye pulpit ye rails and canopy and railes about Comund table, brandishing ye pannels of ye sd work because it was more than the bargaine.' That additional cost to the church was £2.2s.4d. The Parish Church's accounts reveal Brooking senior to be a journeyman artist-cum-painter and decorator.

Three years after completing the work for the Linkinhorn Parish Church Brooking senior was declared bankrupt. He was either a bad businessman, or a poor painter/decorator or possibly a bit of both. The bankruptcy proceedings went on for an agonising four years, starting in the Plymouth Court, and moving on to the Guildhall in London. From extracts discovered in the *London Gazette* by the South Devon Family Historical Society, we learn that Charles Brooking senior had had a substantial estate in Plymouth. It included a '...dwelling house called the Mill Tenement and a Curtilage and Garden, with the Oil Mill and another Mill for Colours, and also a Field thereto adjoining containing about 9 Acres with a Rope-Walk and Cellar thereon being all in Plymouth.' In addition to painting and decorating, Brooking senior manufactured paints for commercial use. His house, land, and mills were sold at the Guildhall. There is no record of Brooking senior in a debtors' prison, and so it would appear that by 1722 he had paid off his creditors. Rather than return to Plymouth he travelled to Ireland and settled temporarily in Dublin.

A Map of the city and suburbs of Dublin was drawn by Charles Brooking senior and published in 1728. It was the first commercial map of Dublin, but was more than just a map for it included a panoramic drawing of the city taken from the North, looking southwards with the mountains of Wicklow beyond. The accurate street map is illustrated below the drawing. Around the periphery of the map the surveyor included twenty

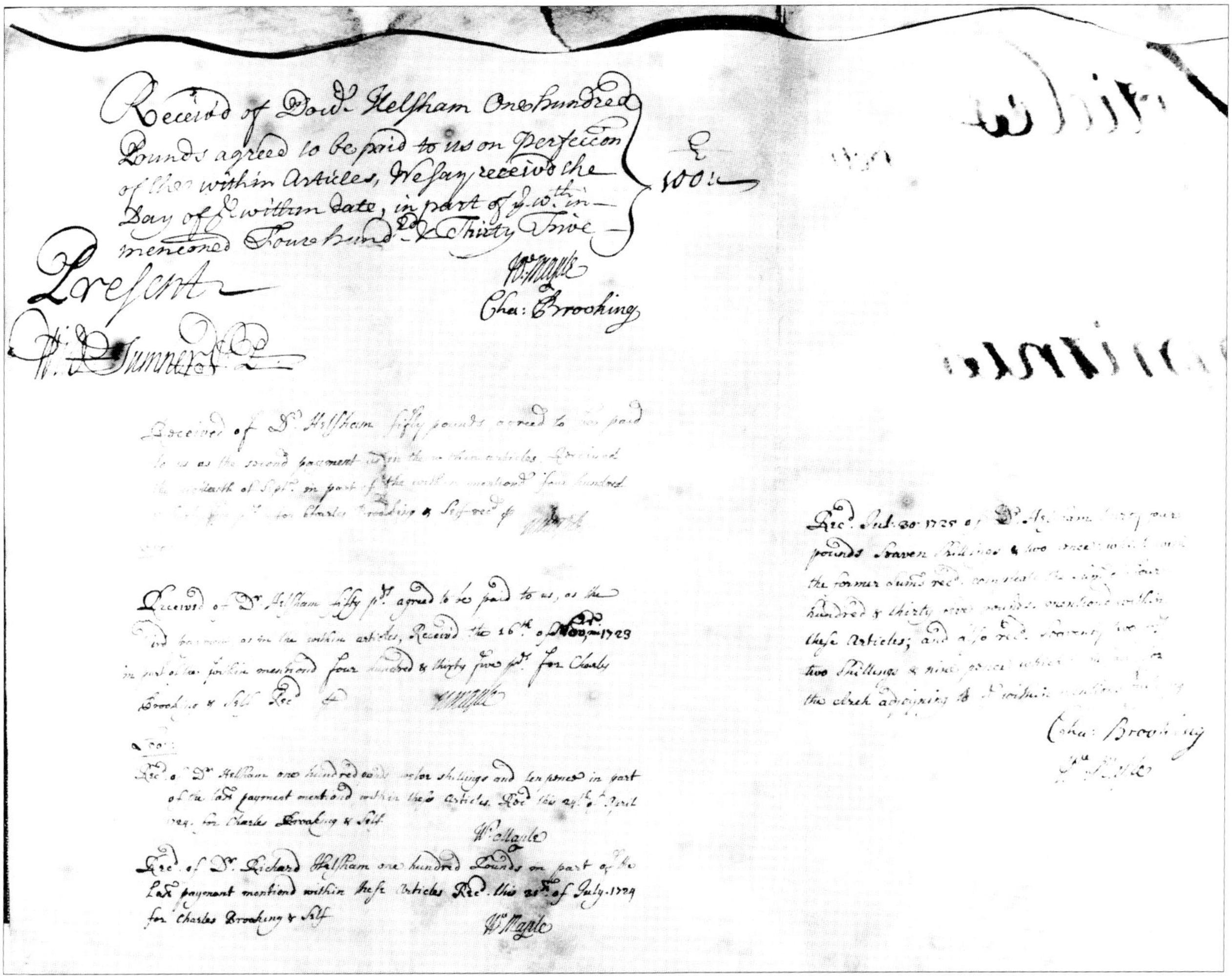
Received of Docr. Helsham One hundred Pounds agreed to be paid to us on Perfection of the within Articles, We say received the Day of ye within date, in part of ye within mentioned Four hundd & Thirty Five

£ 100:

Present

Wm Maple

Cha: Brooking

Recd. of Dr. Richard Helsham one hundred Pounds in part of the last payment mentiond within these Articles Recd. this 25th of July 1729 for Charles Brooking & Self

Wm Maple

2/3
Trinity College Dublin, signatures in Account Book for the year 1725.
Trinity College Archives

drawings of the principal buildings and the coats of arms of the City's Livery Companies. The main drawing represents an excellent eighteenth century prospect of Dublin which together with the map is the first well drawn record of the Irish capital. It was printed and sold by John Bowles, Print and Mapseller at the Mercer's Hall in Cheapside, London from 1728 until it was superseded by John Rocque's map of 1756, some twenty-eight years later after much development of the outskirts of the city. The Brooking map was priced initially at one crown (five shillings).

According to John H. Andrews, who was a professor of geography at Trinity College, Dublin, a Charles Brooking received several payments for carpentry and building work at the college in 1724 and 1725. Brooking senior was coming to the end of his residency in Ireland and the next we hear of him is in connection with his work as a decorator at Greenwich Hospital, where he worked from 1729 to 1736. Amongst other items painted by Charles were the marbling of the columns in Sir James Thornhill's Painted Hall, and the lettering in the Queen Anne's block – both can be seen today. On 24 December 1729 Brooking senior was taken to task by the officials of Greenwich Hospital for poor workmanship. The records state: 'The painter was called in (to the General Court) and questioned about not doing his work well and Admonished to perform better, which he promised to do.'

On 27 November 1732 Brooking senior took as apprentices 'Banches Mathew Vickers of Woolwich Dockyard for 5 years from ye 25 March last £10.0.0., Master Charles Brooking [his son who became the marine painter] for £5.0.0.'

Brooking senior died on 22 May 1738 in Greenwich and Administration was given to his daughter Elizabeth in August that year. He was described in the Administration as 'late of Plymouth Yard but in the Parish of East Greenwich, in the county of Kent,

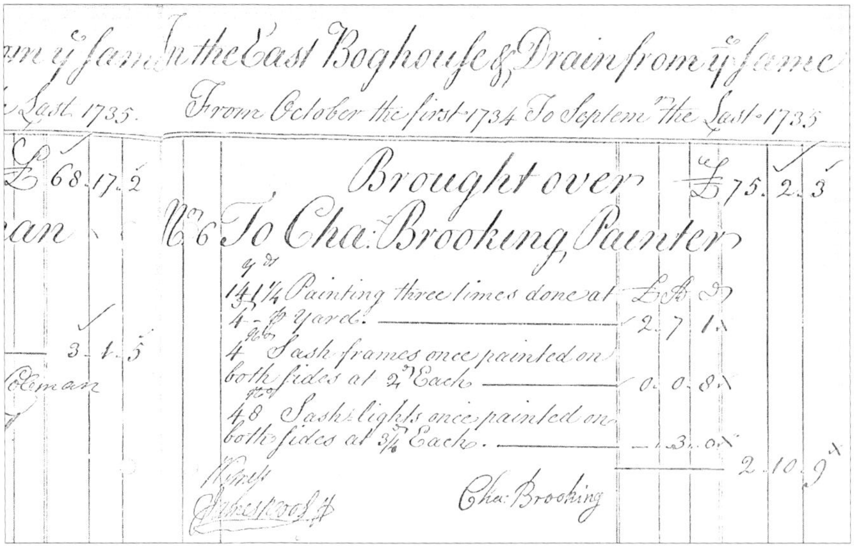

...m ye same In the East Boghouse & Drain from ye same
... Last 1735. From October the first 1734 To Septem.r the Last 1735
£ 68.17.2 Brought over £75.2.3
No 6 To Cha: Brooking Painter
yds 141¼ Painting three times done at 4d p yard — £ s d 2.7.1
4 Sash frames once painted on both sides at 2d Each — 0.0.8
48 Sash lights once painted on both sides at ¾ Each — 0.3.0
2.10.9
Cha: Brooking

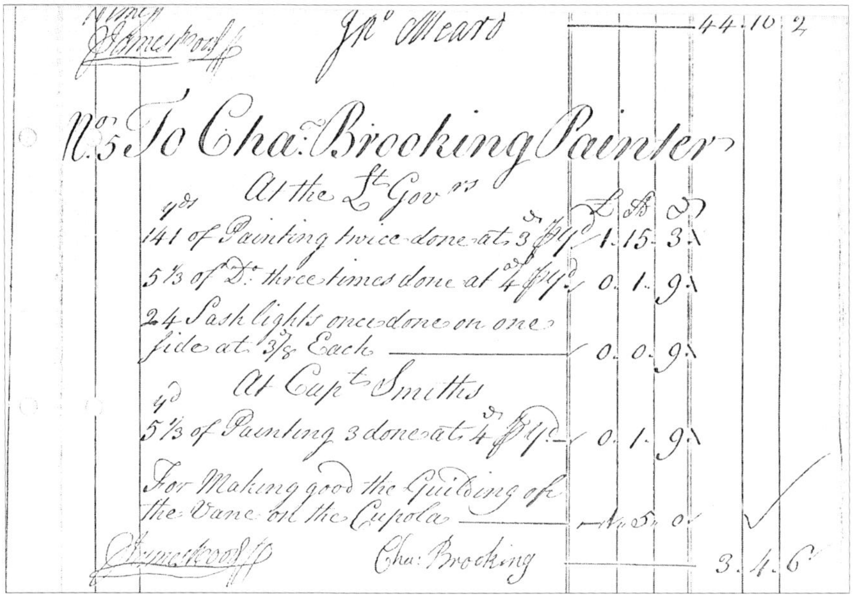

Jno Meard 44.10.2
No 5 To Cha: Brooking Painter
At the Lt Govrs
yds 141 of Painting twice done at 3d p yd — £ s d 1.15.3
5⅓ of Do three times done at 4d p yd 0.1.9
24 Sash lights once done on one side at ⅜ Each — 0.0.9
At Capt Smiths
5⅓ of Painting 3 done at 4d p yd — 0.1.9
For Making good the Guilding of the Vane on the Cupola — 1.5.0
Cha: Brooking 3.4.6

2/4
Greenwich Hospital accounts, signed by Charles Brooking senior.
Royal Hospital at Greenwich, Book of Works April to Sept. 1735. ADM/721.

widower'. Elizabeth by this time was married to Robert McGill, a shipwright. She was twenty-four and her brother Charles fifteen years of age.

What literary sources tell us about Charles Brooking the marine artist

One of the major challenges in reassessing Charles Brooking the marine painter is the paucity of primary literary material, and the general absence of contemporary, or later, printed references to his life and work, in eighteenth century newspapers, magazines and books. *The Universal Magazine of Knowledge And Pleasure*, established in July 1748, and published monthly by John Hinton, in London, occasionally mentioned living marine artists. In the November 1748 issue, in a short piece written by 'Pictor' entitled the *Art of Painting*, only two English marine artists were listed – Monamy and Scott. They were named as '...esteemed eminent masters...'

A likely explanation for the lack of recognition received by Brooking during his own lifetime, and for that matter for some time afterwards, is offered in *The works of the late Edward Dayes including professional sketches of Modern Artists,* published in London, and printed by T. Maiden, Sherbourne Lane, Lombard Street in 1805. It is in fact the first book to mention Brooking, albeit briefly. Dayes came straight to the point:

'I cannot learn anything of the history of this artist than he lived for the most part dependant on the picture dealers, who kept him in a wretched state of obscurity;

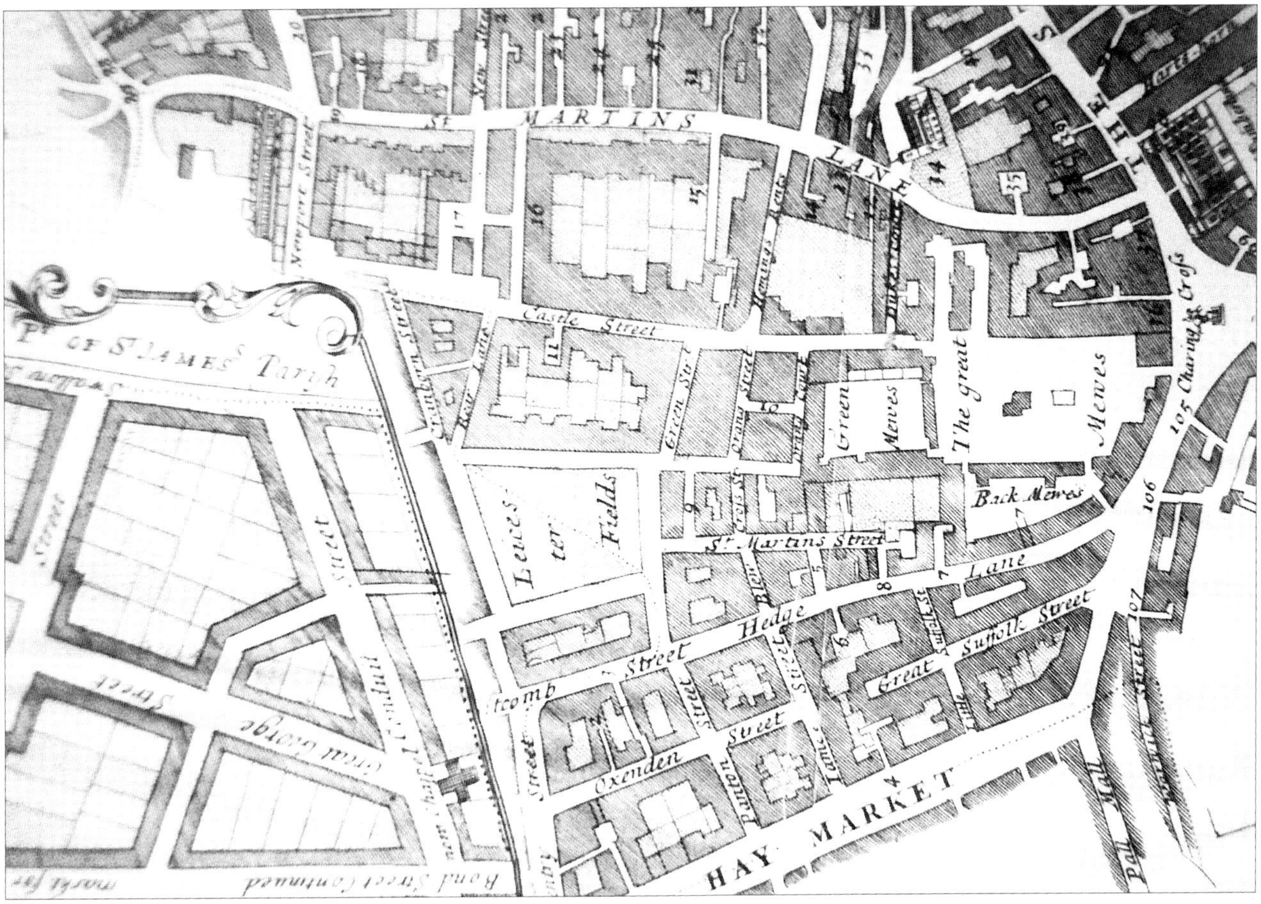

2/5
Map showing Castle Street, London, 1754.
Guildhall Library
Ref. V2 B6 P67

from which he emerged a short time before his death. His works possess considerable merit, he had an extensive knowledge of naval tactics, his colouring is bright and clear, his water pellucid and transparent with a firm broad, spirited touch. Had he lived he could have been one of the finest marine painters that ever appeared in the world of arts. He died prematurely, through injudicious medical advice given to remove a perpetual headache.'

This is a fine critique and succinctly sums up Brooking as an artist. Michael Robinson, the leading scholar of the van de Veldes has said, perhaps surprisingly, that in his opinion the English artist excelled these Dutch artists too, in many of his works.

Horace Walpole's *Anecdotes of Painting*, originally published in a series of four volumes between 1765 and 1771, is arguably the major reference source on the lives of painters and engravers working in London at that time. These volumes include biographies on several marine painters including: the Willem van de Veldes, Isaac Sailmaker (c.1633-1721), Robert Woodcock (1692-1728), Monamy and Scott, but they are sadly silent on Brooking. Walpole had based his work on the note books and manuscripts of the antiquarian George Vertue, and even a firsthand investigation of these original sources has so far drawn a blank on details of Brooking's life and work.

From Edward Edwards (1738-1806), a 'Teacher of Perspective' at the Royal Academy Schools in London, although now regarded as an indifferent artist of various subjects, but fortunately an informative writer, we learn a great deal more about eighteenth century marine painting and Brooking in particular. Edwards' *Anecdotes of Painters*, published in 1808, was designed as a continuation of Horace Walpole's work, obtained from firsthand information from Dominic Serres, who apparently knew Brooking well. Edwards tells us that Brooking:

'Had been in some department in the dock-yard at Deptford, but practised as a ship painter, in which he certainly excelled all his countrymen; nor has any since Vandevelde equalled his productions in that department of painting: but his merits were scarcely known before his death prevented him from acquiring the honour and profit which, by his abilities he had just right to expect. He died of a

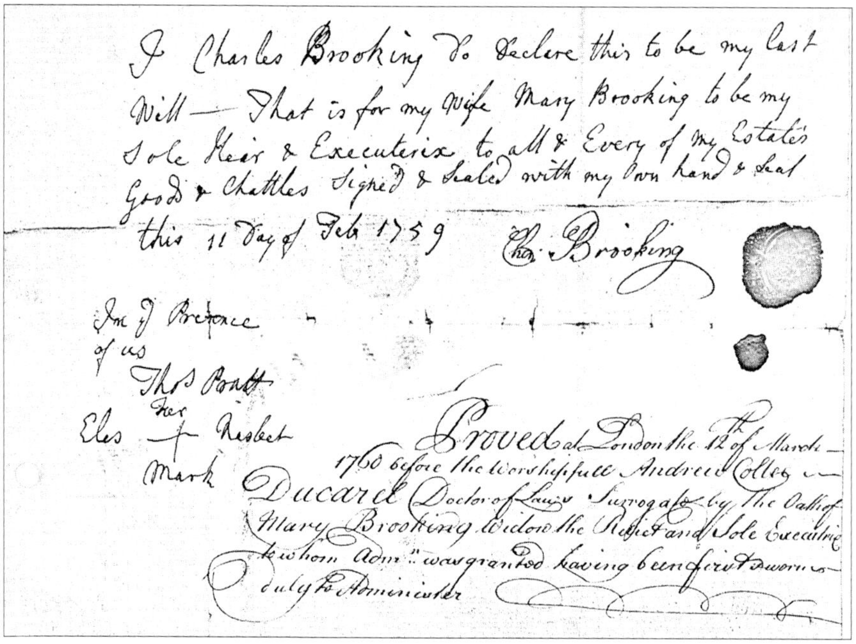
I Charles Brooking Do Declare this to be my last Will — That is for my Wife Mary Brooking to be my Sole Heir & Executerix to all & Every of my Estates Goods & Chattles Signed & Sealed with my Own hand & Seal this 11 Day of Feb 1759 Chas Brooking

In ye Presence of us
Thos Pontt
Eles her mark Nesbet

Proved at London the 12th of March 1760 before the Worshipfull Andrew Coltee Ducarel Doctor of Laws Surrogate by the Oath of Mary Brooking Widow the Relict and Sole Executrix to whom Admn was granted having been first sworn duly to Administer

2/6
Charles Brooking's Will, dated 11 Feb. 1759 and proved 12 March 1760.
PRO Chancery Lane
8.7.65 Q/B 431.
6W/1760.

consumption at his lodging in Castle-Street, Leicester Square, in the Spring of the year 1759, under forty years of age. The following anecdote is given upon the authority of the late Mr. D. Serres, to whom he was well known.

Many of the artists of that time worked for the shops, and Brooking like the rest, painted much for a person who lived in Castle-Street, Leicester-Square, not far from the Mews, who coloured prints, and dealt in pictures, which he exposed at his shop window.

A gentleman, who sometimes passed the shop, being struck with the merits of some sea pieces, which were by the hand of this artist, desired to know his name; but his inquiries were not answered agreeably to his wishes; he was only told, that if he pleased they could procure any that he might require from the same painter.

Brooking was accustomed to write his name upon his pictures, which mark was as constantly obliterated by the shopkeeper, before he placed them in his window; it however happened that the artist carried home a piece, on which his name was inscribed, whilst the master was not at home; and the wife, who received it, placed it in the window, without effacing the signature. Luckily, the gentleman passed by before this picture was removed, and discovered the name of the painter whose works he so justly admired.

He immediately advertised for the artist to meet him at a certain wholesale linen draper's in the city. To this invitation Brooking at first paid no regard, but seeing it repeated with assurances of benefit to the person to whom it was addressed, he prudently attended, and had an interview with the gentleman, who from that time became his friend and patron. Unfortunately the artist did not live long enough to gratify the wishes of his benefactor, or to receive any great benefit from his patronage.'

The anecdotes are intriguing and for the first time we learn that Brooking had been in some department of the dockyard at Deptford, that he lodged in Castle Street, Leicester Square, that his dealer was in the same street and lastly that he died of consumption – presumably tuberculosis.

Before the introduction of commercial art exhibitions in London during the 1760s the main retail outlets for artists were the 'shops'. Professional picture dealers were rare at this time, and the 'shops' were retailers who sold a wider range of items, and frequently adorned their windows with 'furnishing' pictures to attract the attention of prospective customers.

Edwards' revelation of Brooking's suffering at the hands of an unscrupulous dealer was not an isolated case. Dayes tells us of the trials and tribulations of Canaletto, who was the victim of a fraudulent campaign by dealers to deny the Italian artist the benefits of the English art market. Such was the reputation of Canaletto that the dealers commissioned English artists

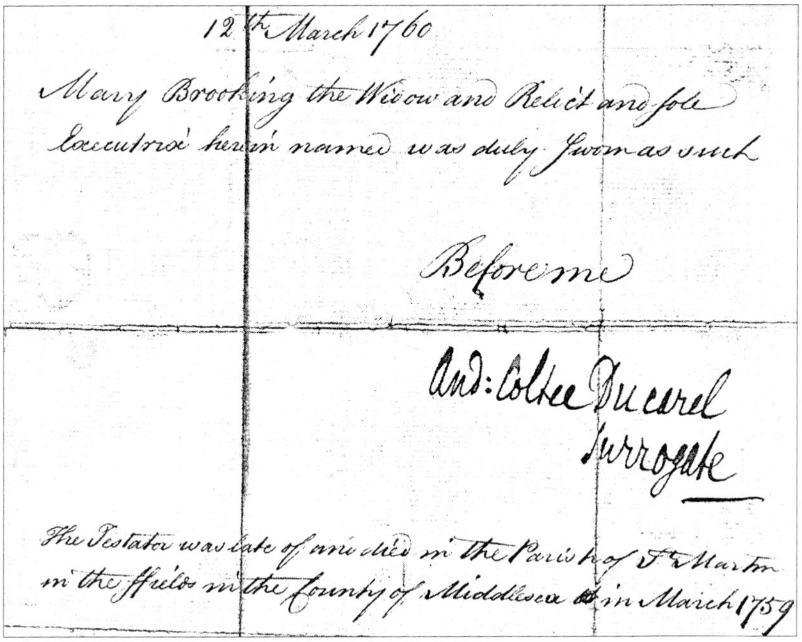
12th March 1760
Mary Brooking the Widow and Relict and sole Executrix herein named was duly sworn as such

Before me

And: Coltee Ducarel
Surrogate

The Testator was late of and died in the Parish of St Martin in the ffields in the County of Middlesex in March 1759

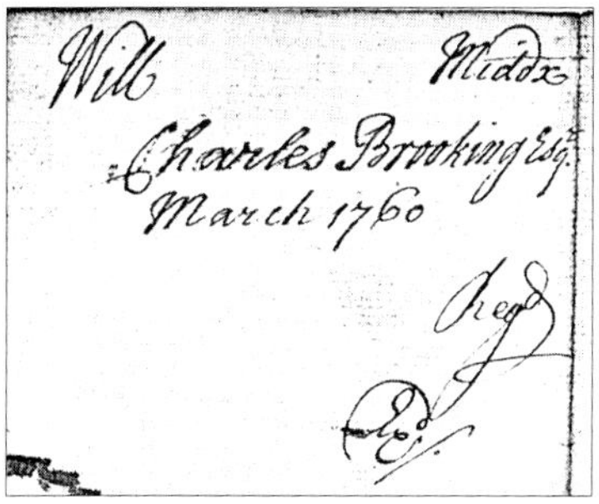
Will Middx
Charles Brooking Esq
March 1760

to make copies of his work, which they sold as 'original' works. When he arrived in England the dealers claimed Canaletto as an artistic imposter and his pictures as fakes. Dayes claimed that: 'By this scheme they hoped to drive him from the country and thereby to prevent him from detecting the copies they had had made from his works, which were in great repute. Certainly the dealers disreputable actions damaged his reputation for a time.'

The only other revealing detail on Brooking's life is to be found in Joseph Farington's *Diary, 1793-1821*. Farington was a landscape and topographical artist but his reputation today rests on his illuminating diary. He records a meeting with the animal painter Sawrey Gilpin (1733-1807), who had been apprenticed to Samuel Scott, the marine painter, between 1749-56, and stayed on as his assistant in Covent Garden until 1758, afterwards specialising in horse subjects. Farington's brief note states: 'Gilpin once saw Brooking. He was a man of sickly appearance – he had been much at sea – Scott greatly admired his works'. Farington's *Diary* includes one other comment of note that: 'William Wells of East India Dock Office told Farington he would give me one of his pictures by Brooking.' William Wells belonged to the celebrated shipbuilding family who built many ships for the East India Company, and the Navy at their Deptford yard. It is not known if Farington ever received the Brooking painting as a present.

Farington's statement that Brooking '...had been much at sea' has been followed up relentlessly, but to no avail. There were other Brookings who had had successful careers in the Navy during this period, one even became an Admiral, but there is no trace of Charles Brooking himself listed as an officer, or a mate, and no record of him serving on the lower deck. His topographical views of Dover, Harwich, Sheerness, Portsmouth and Jersey are very accurate from seaward, and certainly suggest that he had firsthand experience of the sea. Brooking could also have acquired this knowledge as a pilot in the employ of Trinity House, although he is not included in any official record, nor he is shown in the exemption lists from the press gang as a fisherman over the significant parts of his lifetime. There is no trace of him in the East India Company records, nor those of any other shipping concern.

Brooking's Will, located in the Public Records Office, London, is short and simple. It reads as follows:

> *'I Charles Brooking do declare this to be my last will – that is for my wife Mary Brooking to be my Sole Heir and Executrix to all & Every of my Estate's Goods & Chattles Signed & Sealed with my Own hand & Seal this 11 day of Feb 1759.*
>
> *Charles Brooking*
>
> *In the presence of us*
> *Thos Pratt   Eles Nesbet + Her Mark.'*

Thomas Pratt could have been the Brandy Merchant who lived near Castle Street at Broadcourt, Leicester Square. Elizabeth Nesbet was perhaps a relation of the linen draper in Castle Street.

The Will was proved on 12 March 1760 and Administration was granted to Mary Brooking, the Widow and Relict. A note also states that 'the Testator was late of and died in the Parish of St. Martins in the Fields in the County of Middlesex in March 1759'. There is no inventory to the Will.

The last we know of the artist himself is that he died in March 1759, before his thirty-sixth birthday. He left his widow Mary, and children, Charles, aged two, William aged just over six months, and a daughter Mary who was considerably older, although her exact age is not known.

The entry in the Burial Register states that Brooking was buried at St Martins in the Fields on 25 March 1759. The cemetery for that church was where Trafalgar Square and the National Portrait Gallery now stand. The tombstones were moved away many years ago to Camden Town cemetery, and now there is no record, though because of his family's poverty after his death, his grave is unlikely to have been marked.

The fact that Brooking died in poverty is tragic, more so, when the artist and his family should have benefited from the estate of his wealthy uncle, John Hardy of the parish of St Botolph without Aldgate. Hardy had died in 1758, and his Will proved on 13 October of the same year indicates that his nephew was left £200 in 3½% Bank Annuities and a subscription, plus a share in the balance of the estate to be divided between the two nephews and two nieces. He also, in a codicil, bequeathed five guineas quarterly to him, his silver watch, his bureau and a share of all his books.

Brooking received the £200 of 3½% Bank Annuities and the first twenty guineas but then died, leaving his estate to his wife Mary. The executor, Thomas Thornley, then became infirm and seemed incapable of winding up the Hardy estate. By this time Mary Brooking had remarried; her second husband's surname was Waddon, but she was fully entitled to Charles' residue of the estate.

Mary and others brought a libel case in the Ecclesiastical Court of Arches, which is fully recorded at Lambeth Palace. It appears to have taken until 30 June 1762 for this to be settled correctly, by which time Mary Waddon (Brooking) had received £21 and her proctor Nathaniel Bishop £5.5s.0d. Later on Mary and her daughter were to receive financial assistance from the Society of Artists.

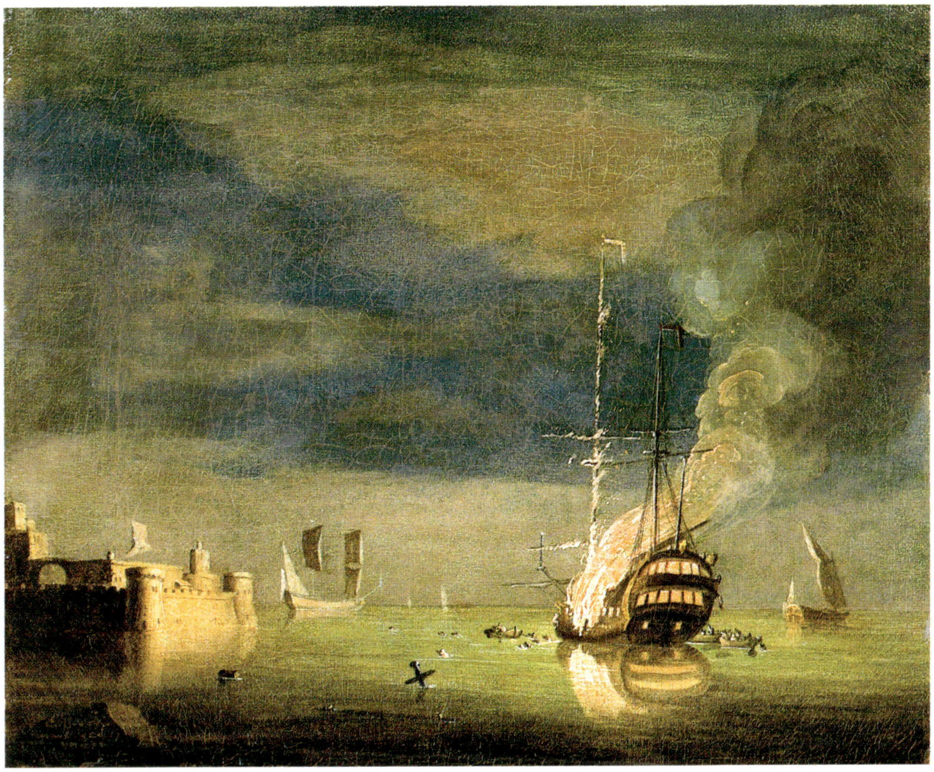

3/1
151 *A two-decker on fire at night off a fort*. Oil on canvas, 10 x 12½. Signed C Brooking pinxit aged 17 years.
Yale Center for British Art, Paul Mellon Collection

Chapter 3

Charles Brooking: Marine Painter

Charles Brooking's early years were spent in East Greenwich, within close proximity to the River Thames, the busiest river in England, and the neighbouring dockyards of Deptford and Woolwich. He was apprenticed to his father, a painter and decorator, who no doubt encouraged him to take up marine painting.

The scarcity of dated Brooking paintings and engravings, and the fact that Brooking's life was tragically cut short, make it nearly impossible to establish a precise chronology of his work. The first of his paintings we know of is *A two-decker on fire at night off a fort* (151). The painting is signed and inscribed 'C. Brooking pinxit aged 17 years'. There is no reason to dispute the inscription, and so it is likely that Brooking's first oil painting dates from 1740. This picture is almost certainly one of a pair to *A bomb ketch becalmed by moonlight near a fort* (152). They are ambitious marine paintings for a teenage artist, competent in terms of overall design although a little crude in execution and attention to nautical detail.

Brooking almost certainly had access to marine paintings by other artists. Although the celebrated Greenwich Hospital collection of paintings and other artefacts was in its infancy, there would have been pictures from the collections of resident naval officers on display in their own quarters. These collections would have included naval actions, ship portraits and general shipping scenes by, among others, the van de Veldes, Peter Monamy and Samuel Scott. Brooking may also have had the opportunity to see maritime paintings in the various shipyards, and in homes of ship owners.

The subject of a ship on fire was a popular one. Several versions by the van de Veldes, Scott and notably Peter Monamy are known. Monamy, by this time aged fifty-nine, was well established as an artist. Monamy's family originated in the Channel Islands, although he was born in London. He had a similar training to Brooking, and was

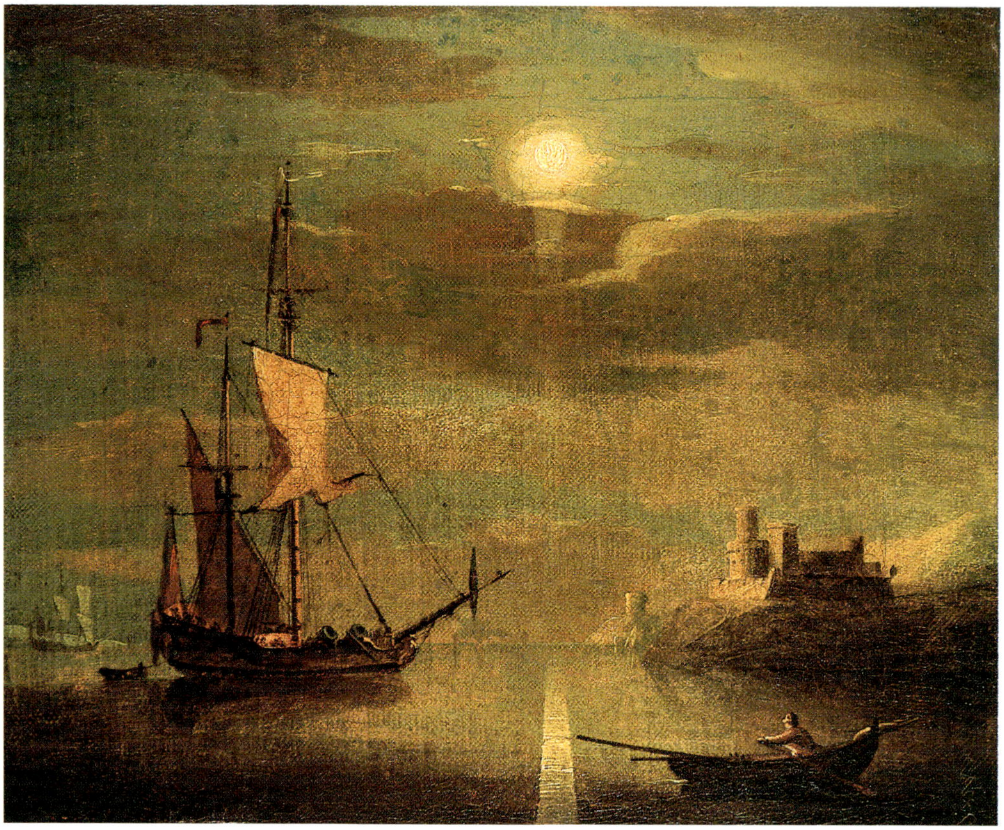

3/2
152 *A bomb ketch becalmed by moonlight near a fort*. Oil on canvas, 10 x 12. Signed C Brooking.

apprenticed to William Clarke, of the Painter-Stainers' Company who, according to Horace Walpole, was a sign and house painter living on London Bridge. Monamy is known to have decorated the carriage of the unfortunate Admiral Byng with ships and naval trophies, and 'painted a portrait of Admiral Vernon's ship for a famous public-house'. He received commissions from both naval and merchant patrons. It has been suggested that Monamy may have given Brooking some tuition in his early years, although there is no firm evidence to substantiate this claim. Certainly Brooking was familiar with Monamy's work, either the original oils, or engravings after them.

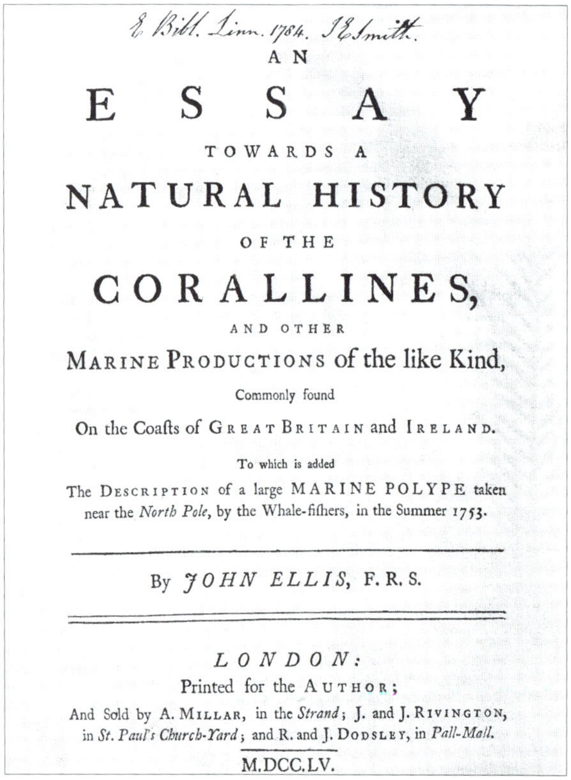

E Bibl. Linn. 1784. J E Smith.

AN
ESSAY
TOWARDS A
NATURAL HISTORY
OF THE
CORALLINES,
AND OTHER
MARINE PRODUCTIONS of the like Kind,
Commonly found
On the Coafts of GREAT BRITAIN and IRELAND.
To which is added
The DESCRIPTION of a large MARINE POLYPE taken near the *North Pole*, by the Whale-fifhers, in the Summer 1753.

By *JOHN ELLIS*, F. R. S.

LONDON:
Printed for the AUTHOR;
And Sold by A. MILLAR, in the *Strand*; J. and J. RIVINGTON, in *St. Paul's Church-Yard*; and R. and J. DODSLEY, in *Pall-Mall*.
M.DCC.LV.

3/3
Cover plate for *Natural History of the Corallines*, by John Ellis FRS, published in 1755.

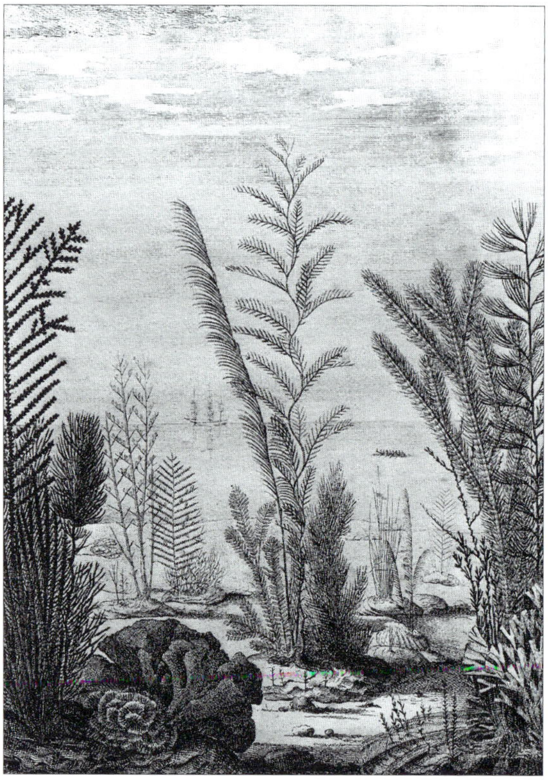

3/4
622 *Corallines at low tide*, 9 x 6, frontispiece for *Natural History of the Corallines* by John Ellis FRS. Illustrated by Charles Brooking and published in 1755. It was drawn in 1752, showing corallines in the Isle of Sheppey. But note the ships and their boats on the sea beyond.

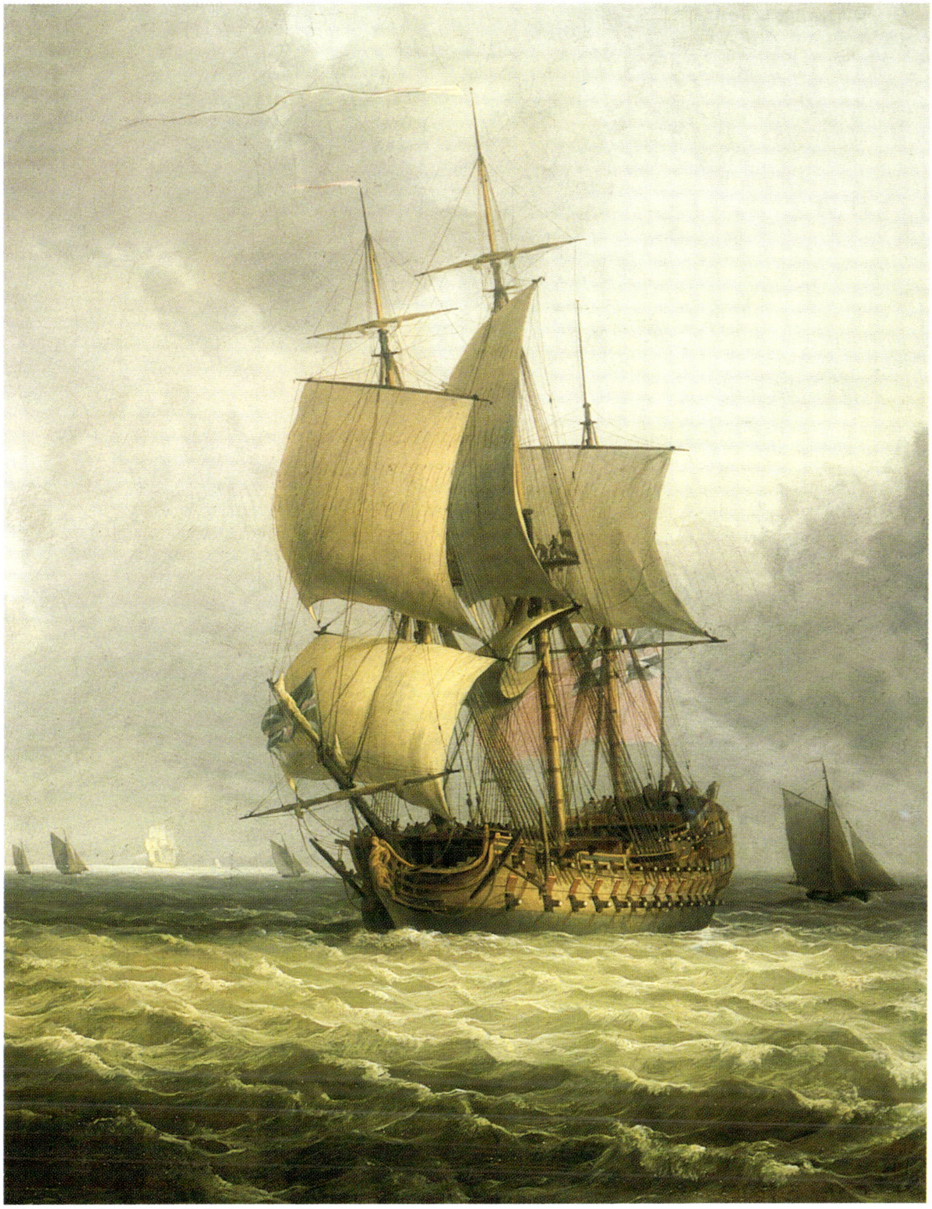

3/5
244 *Ships in a light breeze*, detail. Oil on canvas 27 x 27. Signed C Brooking on spar left foreground.
Caird Collection, National Maritime Museum, London

That Brooking was familiar with a significant collection of van de Velde's work is now, thanks to the research of Michael Robinson, no longer a matter of supposition. By 1761 we are reliably informed in R. and J. Dodsley's *London and its Environs described* (Vol.5, pp.78-90), that Jennens had amassed seventeen van de Veldes and that they were displayed in his London townhouse in Great Ormond Street. Jennens, or Selymann the Magnificent, as he was sometimes whimsically called, had commissioned his country residence Gopsall Hall, in Leicestershire. The collection later passed into the Penn family, and moved to Penn House in Buckinghamshire, when in 1933 some of the paintings were sold by Christie's on behalf of Lord Howe. Brooking visited and made copies of Charles Jennens' collection.

According to Robinson, 'The only marine painter who could paint as softly and as accurately [as Willem van de Velde the Younger] is Charles Brooking, who must have learned to paint by copying van de Velde, but he was only painting as well as this towards the end of his life; so far as is known, he always modernised the types of vessel he shows.' (Ref. Robinson: Vol. I p.519.) However this final observation is not wholly correct as paintings by Brooking, after van de Velde's work, have subsequently come to light where he has not altered or modernised the ships.

Natural History of the Corallines

The first major dated commission undertaken by Brooking was a series of designs for John Ellis' *Natural History of the Corallines,* published in 1755. In the month of August 1752,

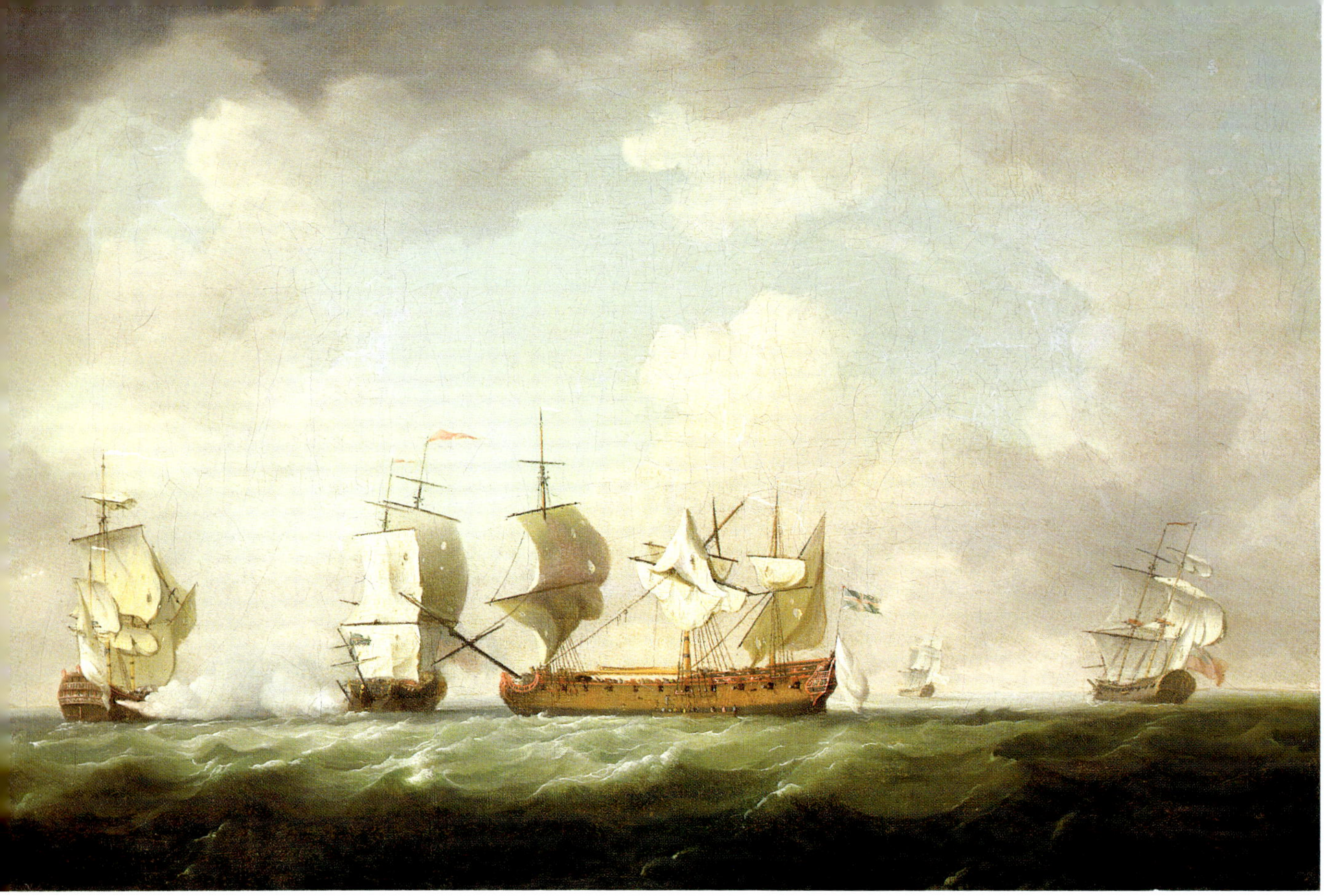

3/6
351 *The taking of the* Marquese d'Antin *and the* Louis Erasme *by the* Prince Frederick *and* Duke *Privateers, 10 July 1745.* Oil on canvas, 13 x 19⅛.
Yale Center for British Art, Paul Mellon Collection

Brooking accompanied John Ellis on a scientific expedition to the Isle of Sheppey at the entrance to the Thames estuary on the north coast of the county of Kent. John Ellis was a Fellow of the Royal Society, a distinguished naturalist, and a friend and correspondent of Linnaeus. Ellis asked Brooking to undertake the preparation of a series of botanical studies to illustrate his work on Corallines. They explored the foreshore of Sheppey 'by the help of a very Commodius Microscope of Mr Cuff's, the optician in Fleet Street' to study the branching forms of Corallines, plant-like creatures which attach themselves to the shells of oysters, mussels and similar molluscs, and which, wrote Ellis, had hitherto been considered by Naturalists as Marine Vegetables. In the introduction to the publication *Natural History of the Corallines,* Ellis described Brooking as '...a celebrated painter of sea-pieces...'.

For additional illustrations to Ellis' book he employed Georg Dionysius Ehret (1710-1770), the famous botanical draughtsman and painter, with whom he visited Brighthelmstone (Brighton) in June 1754. It seems unlikely that Ellis was dissatisfied with Brooking's work, for those plates which can be identified as having been made from his drawings compare favourably in terms of accuracy and subtlety of effects, and accurate draughtsmanship, with those of Ehret, and it is an engraving after Brooking's design which was used as the frontispiece of the book (see 622).

Brooking's frontispiece, entitled: *Groups of different Corallines drawing on shells, supposed to make this Appearance on the Retreat of the Sea at a Very Lowe Ebb Tide,* was engraved by A. Walker. All the corallines are erect, as they would be if the tide was in, and it is a very apt way of illustrating them. However, Brooking has gone one step further and has drawn clouds in the sky, and placed a horizon centrally in the picture. Upon it are two full-rigged ships and between the corallines on the right, an eight-oared gig is rowing out to the nearer vessel. These additional maritime features had obviously been approved by Ellis.

The Royal Family Privateers

In 1753 John Boydell published the first of a series of engravings relating to the adventures of the 'Royal Family' Privateers, so called because each vessel bore the name of a member of the Royal Family. Under the overall command of Commodore James Talbot on 10 July 1745, the *Prince Frederick* and the *Duke* engaged and captured two

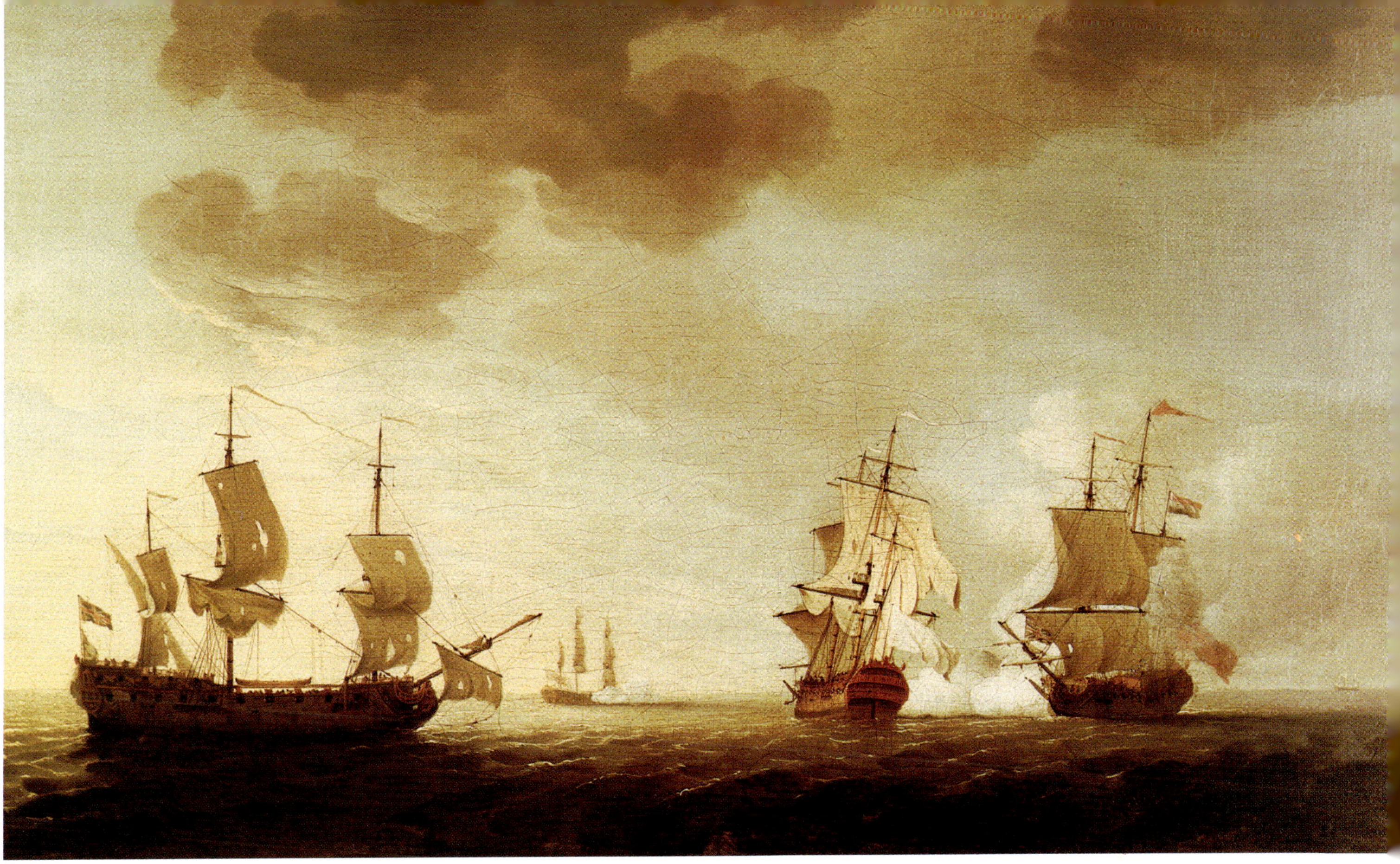

Frenchmen, the *Marquese d'Antin* and the *Louis Erasme* which were found to be carrying over one million pounds in bullion. Boydell knew that there would be a popular demand for prints of the patriotic exploits of the 'Royal Family' Privateers.

Simon Francois Ravenet engraved the first, entitled *The taking of the Marquese de Antin and Louis Erasme two rich prizes from the South Seas by the Prince Frederick and Duke Privateers with a view of the third ship which escaped, 10th July, 1745 Lat 43° 50' Off the coast of Portugal* (see 608A).

The preliminary drawing for Ravenet's engraving (see 707A, below) once belonged to President J. F. Kennedy and hung in the White House, Washington, DC from 1961 to

3/8
357. *Capture of the* Marquese d'Antin *and the* Louis Erasme, *10 July 1745.* Oil on canvas, 14½ x 24.

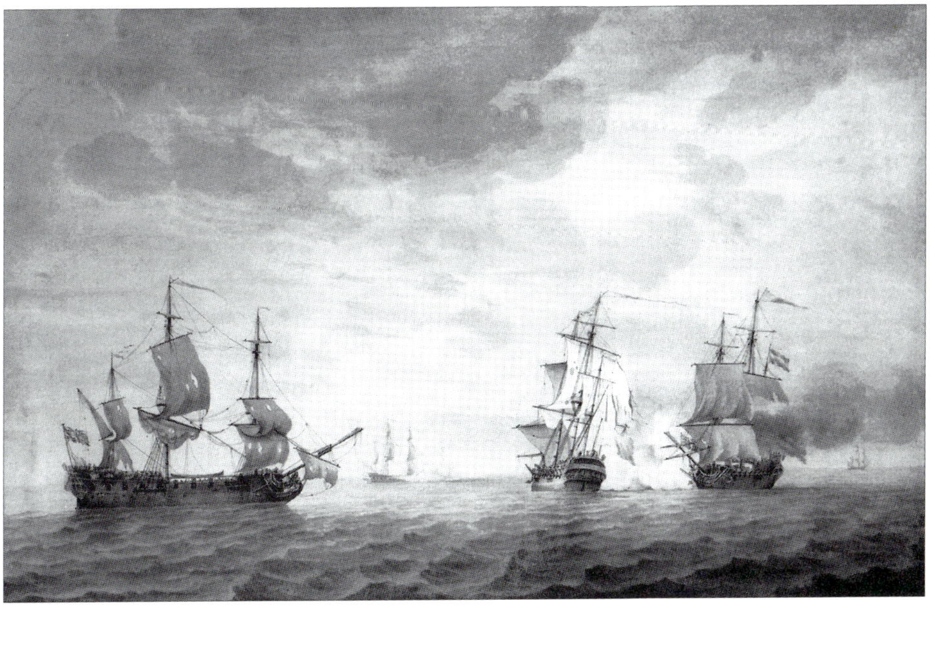

3/9
707A *The taking of the* Marquese d'Antin *and the* Louis Erasme *by the* Prince Frederick *and* Duke *Privateers, 10 July 1745.* Wash drawing on cream paper. Laid down on backing board, 11½ x 17¾. Not signed.

Bequeathed by President John F. Kennedy to the National Maritime Museum in memory of his brother, Lieutenant Joseph P. Kennedy Jnr., USNR.

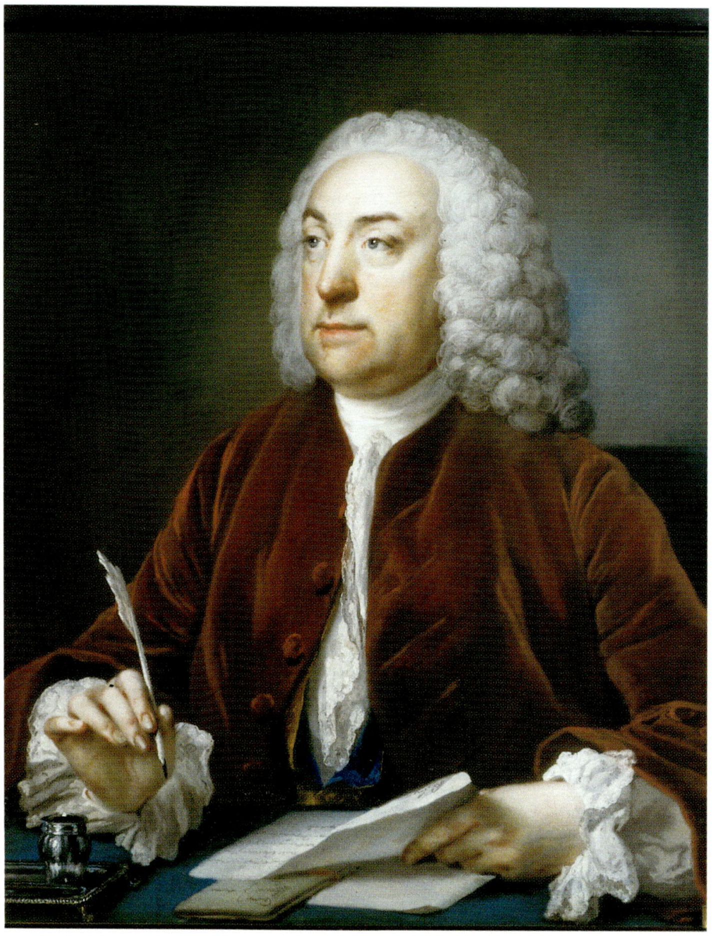

3/11
Francis Cotes (1726-1770).
Portrait of Taylor White, Treasurer of the Foundling Hospital, 1758, pastel.
Coram Foundation, London/Bridgeman Art Library London/New York

1964. The related oil painting of this subject has survived and is a highly accomplished work. There is another oil painting of this action (351), and that subject was also engraved by Peter Mazell, engraver in Windmill Street, Tottenham Court Road, London, and published on 28 August, 1766 (see engraving 621). This painting at that time was owned by Mr Panton Betew. Betew was a collector and dealer who owned a second painting by Brooking (15A), which was also engraved (engraving 611), by R. B. Godfrey and published by T. Bradford in Fleet Street. The engraving is not dated.

The Foundling Hospital Commission

In 1754 Brooking received his most prestigious commission from Taylor White to paint a seascape for the Foundling Hospital – *A Vice-Admiral of the Red and his Squadron at Sea*. It was to be Brooking's largest oil painting, measuring 68¾ x 121ins, and one of his most popular successes (see page 48). It is curious that to date no engravings after the subject have come to light, if indeed they were undertaken. But Brooking painted many replicas, and versions, of the Foundling Hospital painting in various formats and sizes (see 231A-J).

In 1739 Captain Thomas Coram, a retired sea captain, shipbuilder and philanthropist, secured a royal charter for a Foundling Hospital in London 'for the maintenance and education of exposed and deserted children'. The Hospital, the world's first incorporated charity, actively encouraged artists, including the marine painters Monamy and Scott. William Hogarth, a founder Governor of the Hospital, conceived the idea of adorning the walls of the Court Room and other rooms with paintings and sculpture and was made responsible for organising a committee to 'consider what further Ornaments may be added to this hospital without any expence to the charity'. It was hoped that paintings of marine subjects might inspire the foundling boys to seek a career at sea. In exchange for their donations the artists benefited from the exhibition of their work, making the Foundling Hospital the first non-paying public exhibition forum for the arts in England. In addition, contributors were appointed Governors and Guardians of the Hospital.

John Brownlow's *Memoranda or Chronicles of the Foundling Hospital*, London, 1847,

3/10 (Opposite)
William Hogarth (1697-1764).
Portrait of Captain Coram, 1740. Oil on canvas, 94 x 58. Signed W. Hogarth Pinx[t] 1740.
Coram Foundation, London/Bridgeman Art Library London/New York

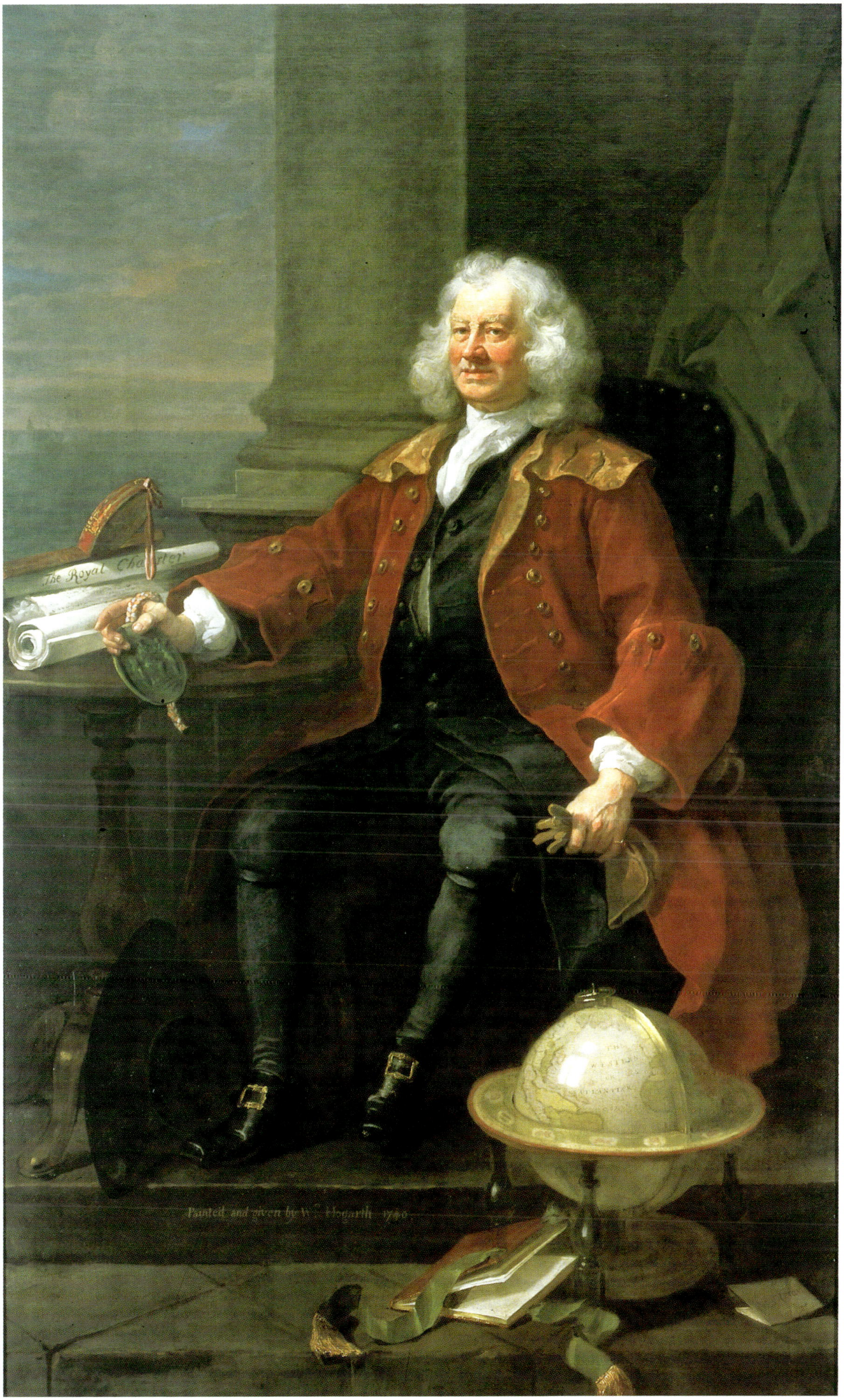
The Royal Charter
Painted and given by Wm Hogarth 1740

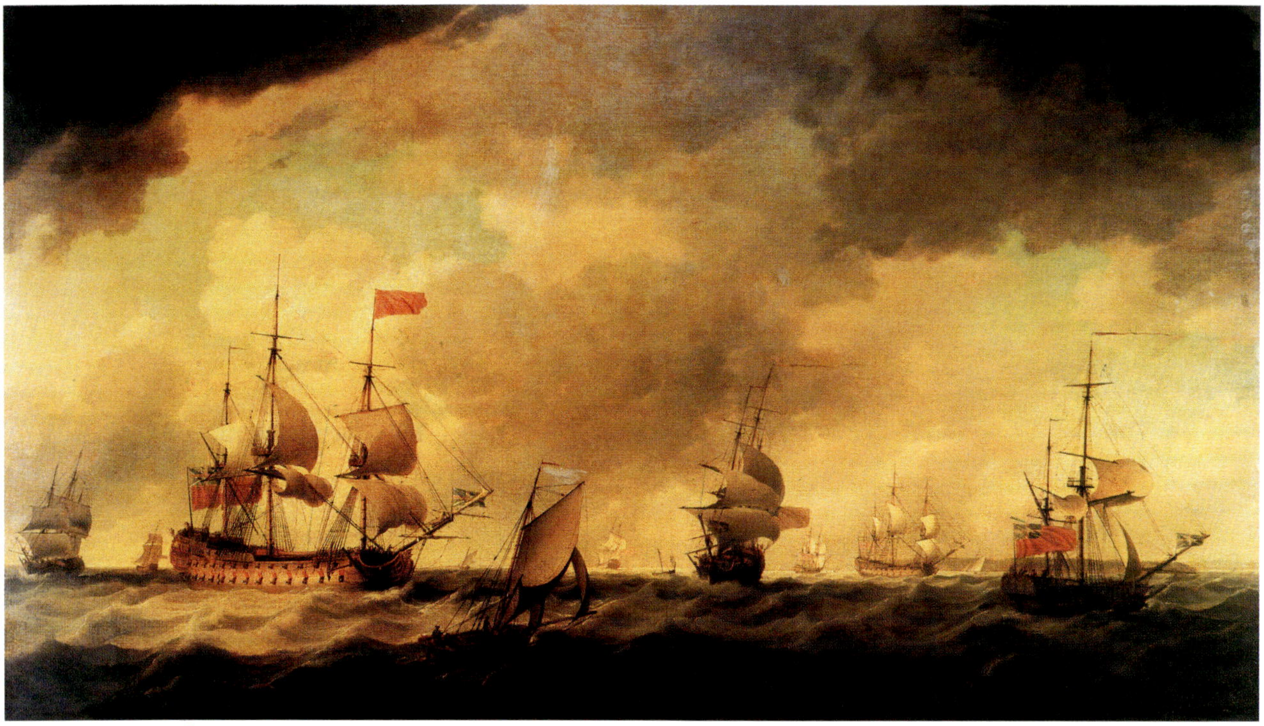

3/12
231A *A flagship, wearing the flag of a Vice Admiral of the Red, before the wind off the English coast, with a cutter, a ketch-rigged sloop and other shipping*. Oil on canvas, 68¾ x 121. Signed C Brooking Pinx lower left. This huge painting is in need of cleaning and restoration.
Foundling Hospital Collection (presented by the painter in 1754)

identifies Taylor White, the Treasurer of the Hospital, as the gentleman recorded in Edwards' *Anecdotes of Painting* who advertised to meet Brooking after seeing a signed painting in the window of the 'shop' in Castle Street, Leicester Square. It is more likely that this meeting actually happened in 1753, or even earlier.

Taylor White was a barrister with a large practice on the Northern circuit. He was Treasurer

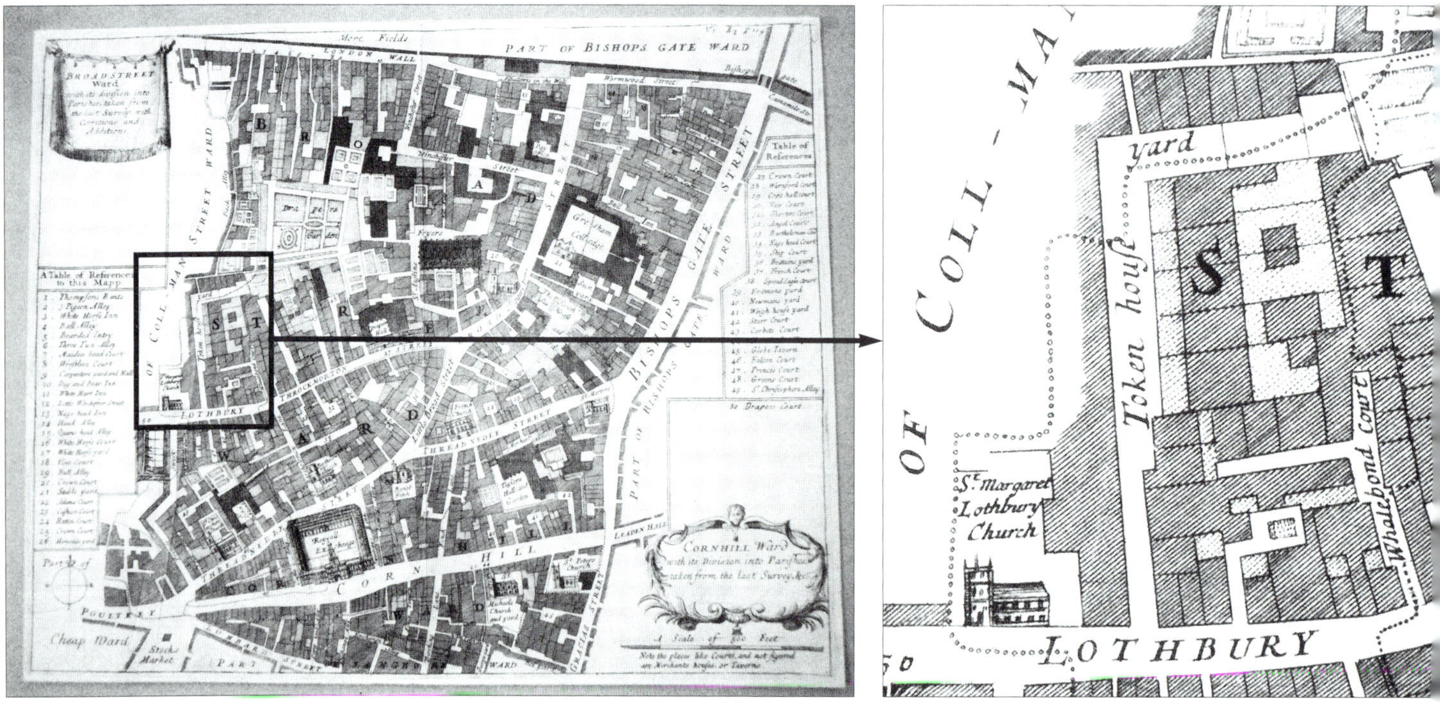

3/13
Cornhill Ward and *Broad Street Ward* showing the city around Cornhill and the Royal Exchange, Lothbury and Token House Yard, where Charles Brooking lived, and St Margaret's Church, Lothbury.
Guildhall Library, London.
V1 B2 P139 Photo: Author

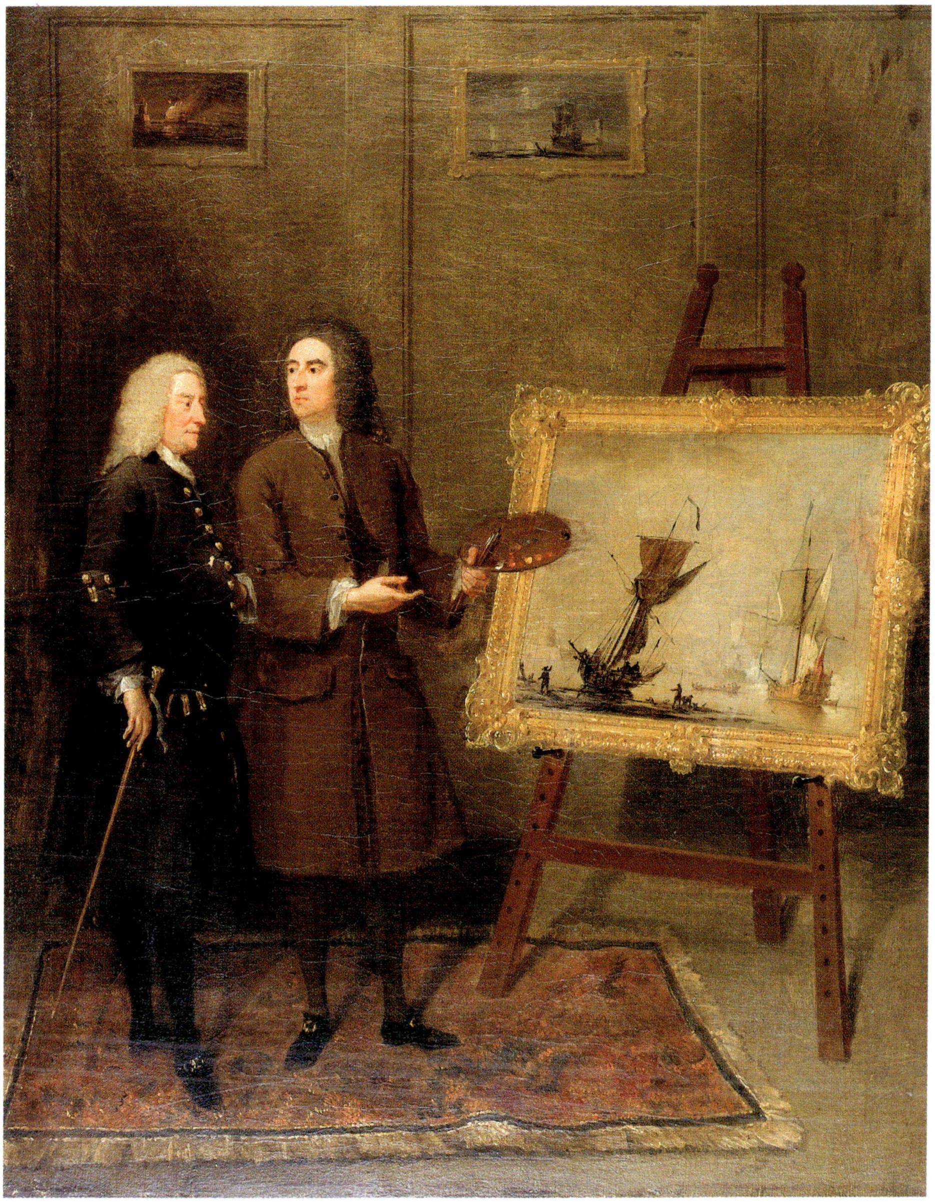

3/14
Peter Monamy (1681-1749) and William Hogarth (1697-1764). *Monamy the Painter exhibiting a Sea-Piece to Mr Thomas Walker, his Patron.* Oil on canvas, 24 x 19.
Private Collection

of Lincoln's Inn 1764, Judge of North Wales, afterwards Judge of Chester County Palatinate, Deputy Recorder of Nottinghamshire and steward of East Retford. He was keenly interested in the arts, an avid collector himself, and a member of the Society of Arts (now the Royal Society of Arts). White was also concerned about the welfare of foundlings and was Treasurer of the Foundling Hospital from 1745-1772. He assisted Hogarth in the search for leading contemporary artists, sculptors and craftsmen, many of them from the St. Martin's Lane Academy. Those artists who became Governors before Brooking include Francis Cotes, Thomas Gainsborough, Francis Hayman, Joseph Highmore, Thomas Hudson, John Pine, Allan Ramsay, Sir Joshua Reynolds, and Richard Wilson. The public flocked to the Hospital to see the foundlings and the paintings, sculptures and furnishings. It was a great success.

Taylor White persuaded Brooking to paint and present a painting as a companion picture to one completed earlier by Peter Monamy (see page 50). This Monamy painting was in the Hospital until around 1909 when it was removed, perhaps for cleaning. The painting has recently been re-discovered in a private collection in London. The subject depicts *An English Fleet in the Downs* and although traditionally acknowledged as a companion picture to the Brooking, it is in fact of a slightly smaller size, at 70 x 106½ ins. Clearly Brooking had been advised to make his painting larger than the Monamy.

Brownlow also identifies the 'shop' as being in Fleet Market, and not in Castle Street, the address mentioned by Edwards, and further states that Brooking resided in a garret

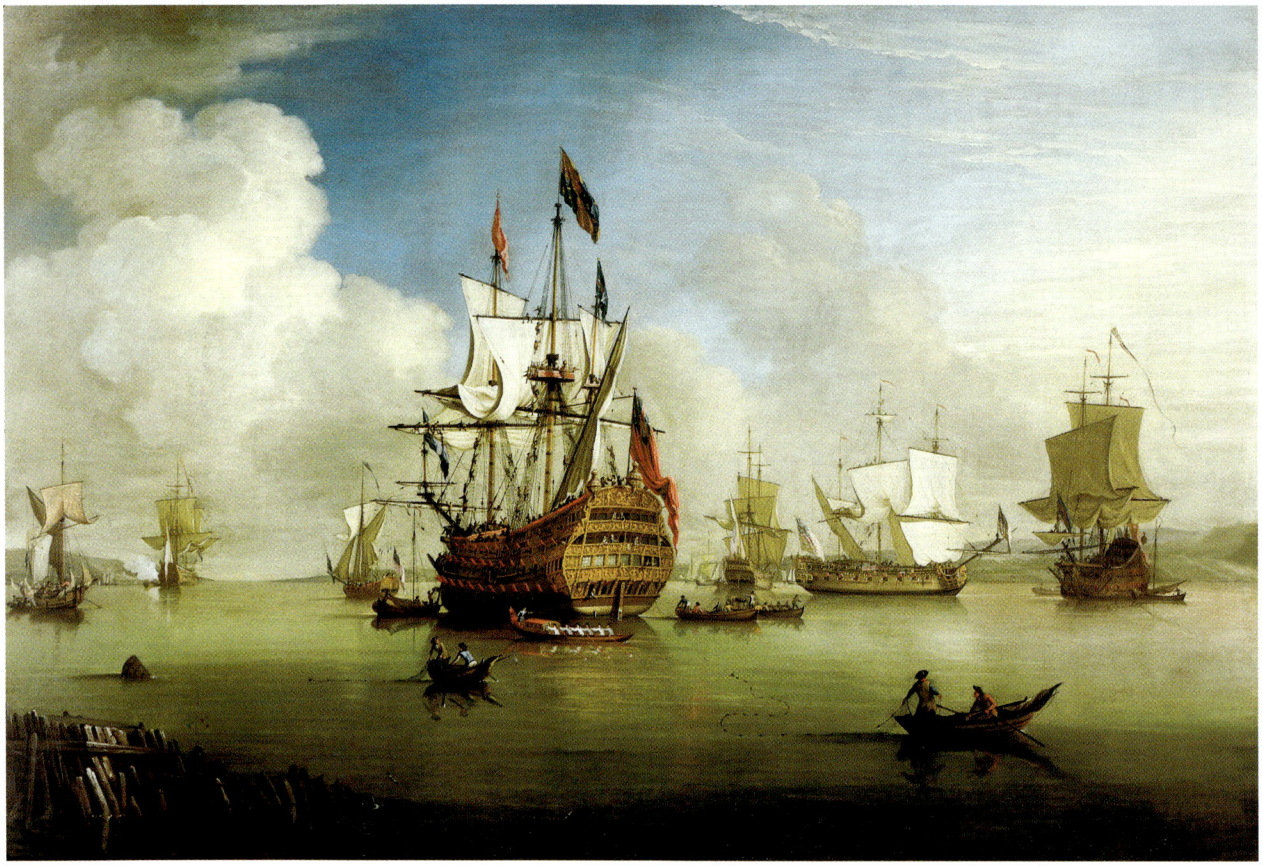

3/15
Peter Monamy (1681-1749). *An English Fleet in the Downs.* Oil on canvas, 70 x 106½. Signed P. Monamy pinx. Believed to be the Monamy missing since 1909 from the Foundling Hospital. Brooking painted No 231A to accompany this painting but made his 15 inches wider. Private Collection, London

belonging to the shopkeeper. He goes on to report that Taylor White proposed to Brooking that he should paint a sea-piece for presentation to the Hospital and that this was carried out in a room there, Brooking's garret 'not affording sufficient space'.

The garret occupied by Brooking may not have been in the Fleet Market (which, incidentally, consisted of single-storey structures), as a first reading of the story would seem to imply, but in Token House Yard, Lothbury, the address given for Brooking when his name was entered in the Register of Governors of the Foundling Hospital on the occasion of his election in June 1754. In 1720, Strype, a celebrated writer on the history of London, described Token House Yard as 'a large place with well built houses, fit for good inhabitants' – but the upper floors may well have been broken up into tenements by the 1740s. That Brooking lived in Lothbury for some years seems clear from the fact that his first son, Charles, was baptised in the parish church of St. Margaret's on 6 February 1751.

An explanation of the confusion as to the site of the shop in which Taylor White is reported to have noticed Brooking's pictures may be explained by the fact that Brooking did move to the Castle Street district in the last year of his life (his second son, William, was baptised at the nearby church of St Martin's in the Fields on 1 October 1758), and Edwards, quoting Dominic Serres, reports that that Brooking died at lodgings in Castle Street.

Brownlow states that the Foundling Hospital picture was completed in eighteen days. If this is correct, it seems certain that Brooking must have made elaborate preparations for it to be painted *in situ*, using and enlarging a composition which he had already produced. We know that it was a popular picture as there are eight recorded versions extant today, although all of them are much smaller. No drawings relating to the original have to date been traced. Hogarth himself no doubt had intimate knowledge of the painting, as it is known that he designed the picture frame. The two artists would have been acquainted, although no record of their conversations is known.

A note in the *Catalogue of the Burlington Fine Arts Club Exhibition* in 1929, derived

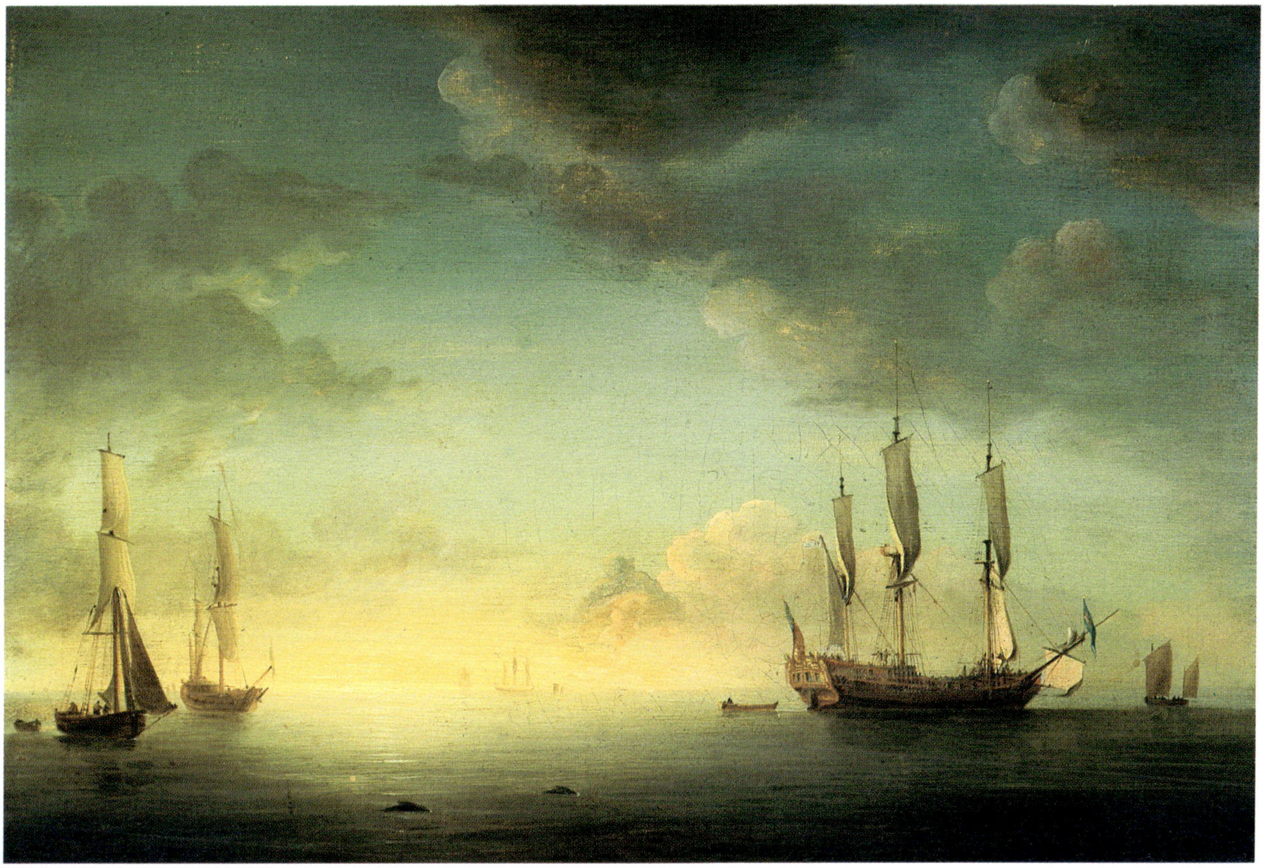

3/16
2E *Sunset. A ship-rigged Royal Yacht and other shipping in calm waters*. Oil on canvas, 11⅛ x 16.
Private Collection

from 'the records of the Foundling Hospital' (the exact source has not been identified), states that the picture was commissioned in February 1754. It was certainly completed and on exhibition at the Foundling Hospital by June of that year. On Wednesday 26 June that year Brooking was elected a Governor and Guardian of the Hospital, having presented 'a very valuable sea piece in painting'.

It is clear that Taylor White admired Brooking's work, for the sale of the former's pictures after his death by the auctioneers Christie's in December 1774 lists three examples by the painter. One of these, described as *A capital sea-piece with a view of Dover*, was sold for the then remarkable sum of £43.1s.0d. Such a considerable sum of money would suggest that it was a large commissioned work, and not one of the speculative works to be displayed in a shop window.

The four years between the completion of the Foundling Hospital picture and Brooking's death should, it might be supposed, have been a period of increased activity, wider patronage, greater financial security and the recognition of his fellow artists. Alas, there was no fairy-tale ending to Brooking's career. By 1754 he was probably already suffering from the illness that prevented him from following up the success of his Foundling Hospital commission, although he was well enough to attend the 'Dilettanti and Virtuosi' Dinner, held at the Foundling Hospital on 5 November 1757.

Family Poverty

After Brooking's demise, his widow and children struggled to make ends meet. They received the sum of ten guineas allocated from the profits of the 1761 exhibition of the 'Society of Artists of Great Britain'. Gainsborough, Hogarth, Hudson, Scott, Wilson and Zoffany, and many other artists exhibited at this Society and part of the monies raised through the sale of catalogues was put aside as a relief fund to assist artists and their families. Mrs Brooking received a further sum of five guineas on 31 January 1766. The Brooking family was not alone in receiving assistance from the Society of Artists, the

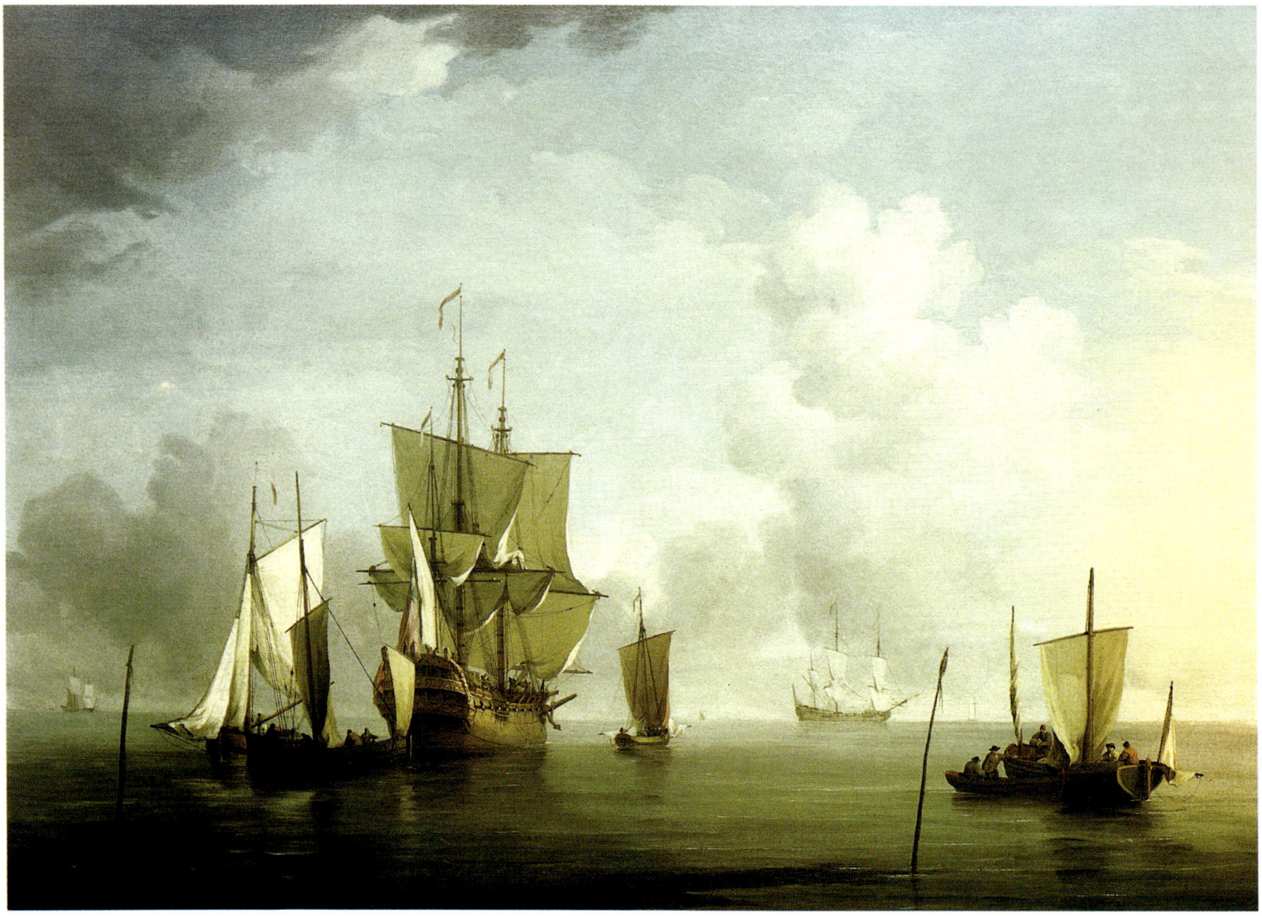

3/17
4A. *East Indiaman becalmed with Cutters and Luggers*. Oil on canvas, 22¾ x 32. Signed C Brooking. Private Collection

sum of five guineas was also given to Mrs Monamy and Mrs van der Hagen.

Charles Brooking's widow, Mary Waddon, died on 30 May 1769. We know this from a letter written by Sarah Waddon, addressed to the Royal Incorporated Society (the new name at that time for the Society of Artists of Great Britain) at the Turk's Head in Gerard Street, Soho, now in the Society of Artists' records at the Royal Academy. A family friend of the Brookings revealed that the mother's death 'hath left the Children in the utmost Distress. The eldest [Charles] who is now about Thirteen Years of Age is an Errand Boy and the Youngest [William] about eleven is in St. Luke's Workhouse'. Sarah Waddon, who named her own profession as that of a peruke (wig) maker received £2.4s.9d in aid for Brooking's sons.

In October 1769 a letter from Mary Brooking was sent to the marine artist Richard Paton (1717-1791) in the Old Jewry, near Cheapside to seek his advice on how to help her brother achieve his wish to go to sea. This is the first time we have heard of this Mary Brooking. A Mary Brooking is recorded as being baptised at the Foundling Hospital on 12 April 1752. If she was adopted by the Brookings, by this time she would have been at least seventeen years of age.

Paton's reply is not known. It would have been surprising if she had not also written to Dominic Serres for advice, as it is now generally believed that Serres was a pupil of Brooking. As a founder marine painter of the Royal Academy of Arts, London, in 1768, who was later appointed official marine artist to King George III, perhaps Mary Brooking felt that by 1769 Serres had become too important and was therefore embarrassed, or reluctant, to approach him for financial help for her family.

On 5 December 1769, Mary Brooking wrote another letter, this time addressed to The Society of Arts via Mr James Payne Esq, Salisbury Street, Strand in which she states that 'she is much troubled with convulsion fits this last 11 years'. Later on it seems that

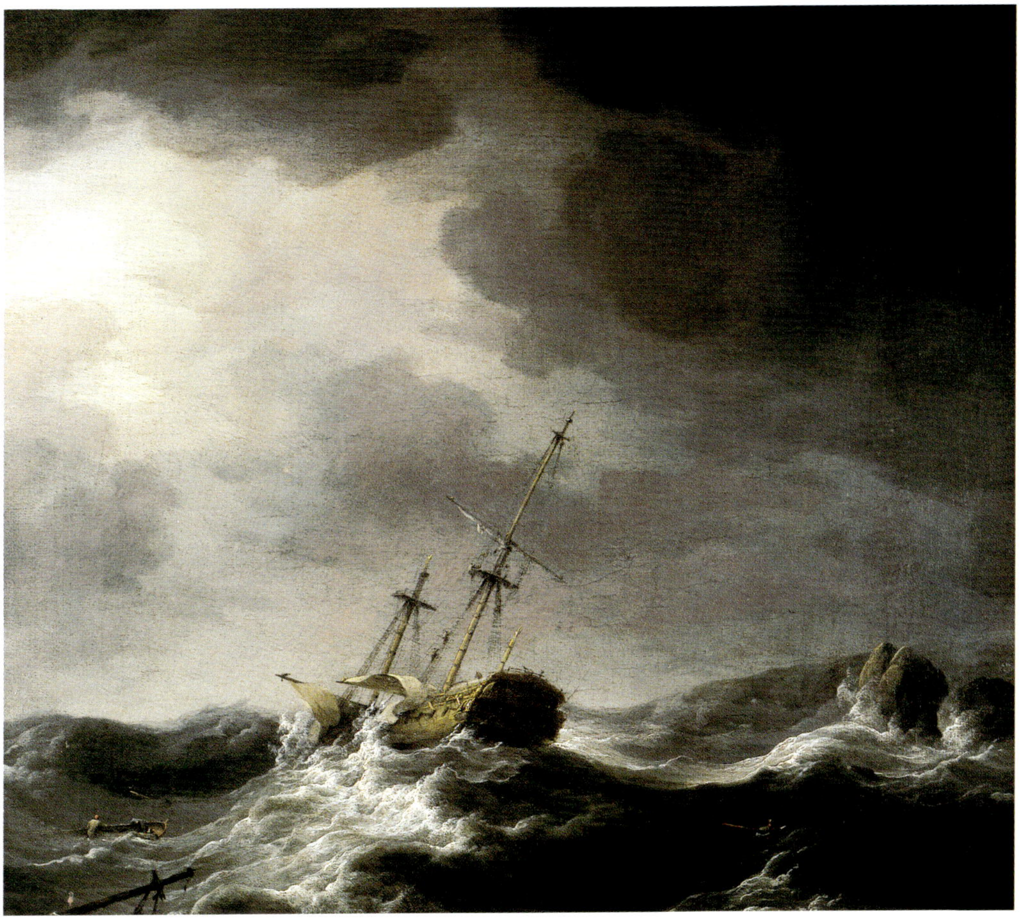

3/18
401A *A dismasted ship driving ashore in a gale*. Oil on canvas, 12 x 13¾. Signed C Brooking on broken mast, lower left foreground. Author's Collection

brother Charles has run off to sea and she thanks them for their trouble on his behalf. From 1768 to 1773 Mary received a pension then of 10/6d per month from the Society, who also assisted Mrs Monamy and Mrs van der Hagen.

So there is little doubt that, like so many other artists, Charles Brooking was unable to provide for his family. Life today is comparatively easy. London was pretty foul in the eighteenth century, though Brooking lived in the West End, which was healthier than either the East End or Greenwich, due to the prevailing south-westerly wind, which made Tower Hamlets most objectionable before sewers were constructed. Disease and illness were prevalent and life was expected to be short.

For copies of letters, see Appendix H.

Charles Brooking's artistic legacy

Although Brooking failed to provide adequately for his family, he left behind him a lasting artistic legacy. Whereas Peter Monamy and Samuel Scott closely followed the artistic models established by the Willem van de Veldes, Brooking to some extent broke away from their conventions.

In Roger Quarm's essay 'The Art of Marine Drawing', written for the exhibition catalogue *Masters of the Sea* (Phaidon Press, Oxford, 1987), Brooking's artistic achievement is succinctly summed up: 'In Brooking…there is a freshness, a reappraisal of subject, and to a large extent a freeing from the Van de Velde stereotype. His drawings as well as his paintings reveal extraordinary observation of sea and weather as well as shipping, conveying a strong sense of the first hand and the locale. Even his pictures of naval engagements have an originality of composition, sometimes with unusually atmospheric effects. None of his immediate followers, even Dominic Serres and Richard Paton, despite their greater prominence, gave their subjects the same degree of lyricism as Brooking.'

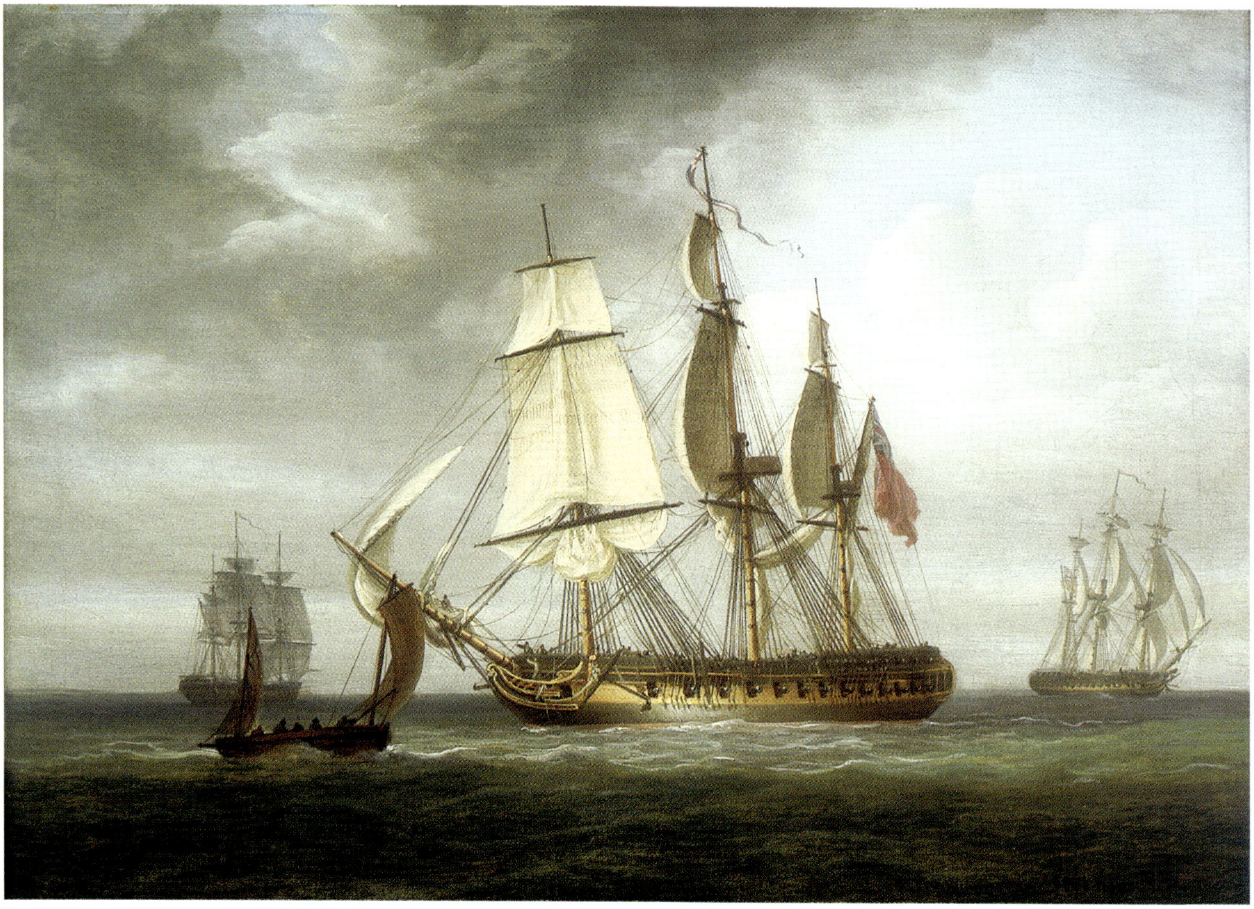

3/19
Nicholas Pocock (1740-1821) *HMS Triton and other vessels*. Oil on canvas, 15½ x 22, signed and dated 1797.
National Maritime Museum, London

Brooking's artistic influence can be discerned in the positioning of ships, and atmospheric effects, compared with the compositions of the watercolours and oils of several prominent followers, notably Dominic Serres (1722-1793), Nicholas Pocock (1740-1821) and William Anderson (1757-1837). Unlike these artists, Brooking was generally not interested in naming ships, or producing ship portraits. In fact, apart from his notable series of oils on the 'Royal Family' Privateers, in which individual ships are named, it is extremely rare to be able to identify specific ships, or other vessels, in his work. He moved away from the documentary tradition of marine painting popularised by the Willem van de Veldes, and slavishly imitated by mediocre followers to such an extent that the influential Victorian art critic John Ruskin described their work as under the influence of 'the Dutch infection'.

Brooking was the first British marine artist of note to treat ships and the sea as works of art. His predominant interest was in conveying the varied moods and beautiful atmospheric effects of marine subjects. The heightened stillness of his most accomplished work is a trademark of the artist. It is a characteristic usually associated with photography and film, not widely available until more than a century after his death. He was ahead of his time and should be rightly credited for elevating British marine painting to new heights. Around 1800, P. J. de Loutherbourg and J. M. W. Turner broke away from the documentary tradition of marine painting, and practised a more personal and expressive form of painting, sacrificing nautical accuracy and detail in favour of experiments in artistic expression and emotive effects.

Charles Brooking never lost his eye for nautical detail, but his preference for atmospheric and naturalistic maritime effects at a time when buyers of marine paintings, notably ships' masters, captains and admirals, demanded above all heightened nautical detail, and recognisable ships, preferably their own, had a liberating effect on later artists, and no doubt contributed to his lack of commercial success. Fortunately Brooking carried on regardless, and has left behind him some of the most beautiful of all marine paintings.

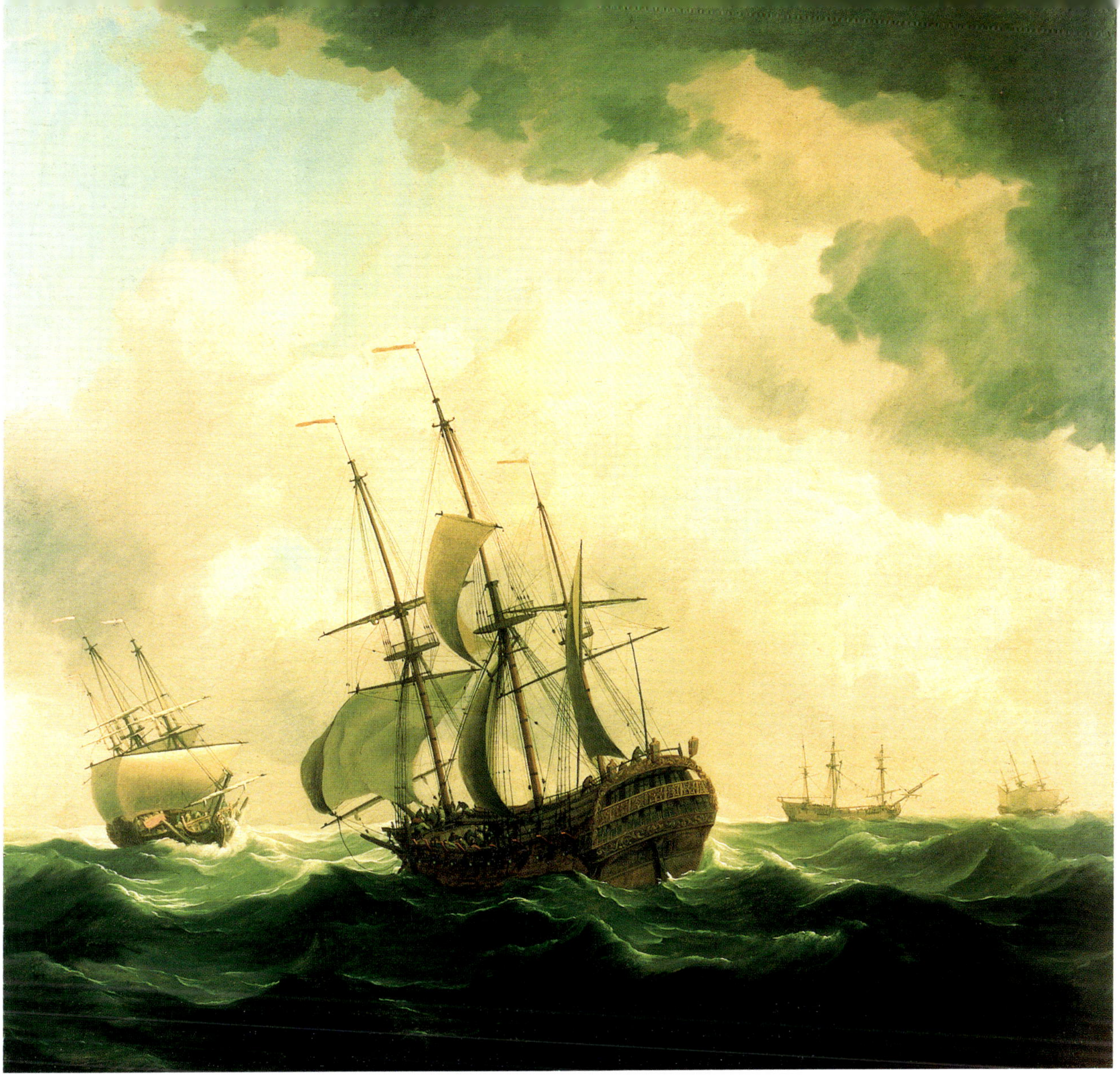

Chapter 4

Examination of Brooking's artistic technique

Charles Brooking almost always painted his pictures on canvas. Of the 228 pictures recorded, all but eight are on canvas and of those eight, five are on oak wooden panels (39B, 234D, 239, 247B and 278), whilst two small paintings (23 and 247A) are on copper. *Two Merchant ships with a smack* (262) is painted in oils on paper and laid down on canvas. This is unusual, for many of his Dutch predecessors preferred panel and of his contemporaries Francis Swaine, in particular, favoured copper for many of his smaller pictures.

The cheaper canvas was made from hemp strands and the more expensive from flax, which in its strongest form was called linen. If indeed Brooking was brought up in a seafaring family, or in the Royal dockyards, then he would have been surrounded with

4/1
248 *Indiamen in a fresh breeze*. Oil on canvas, 45½ x 48. Signed C Brooking on a barrel, left foreground.
National Maritime Museum, London

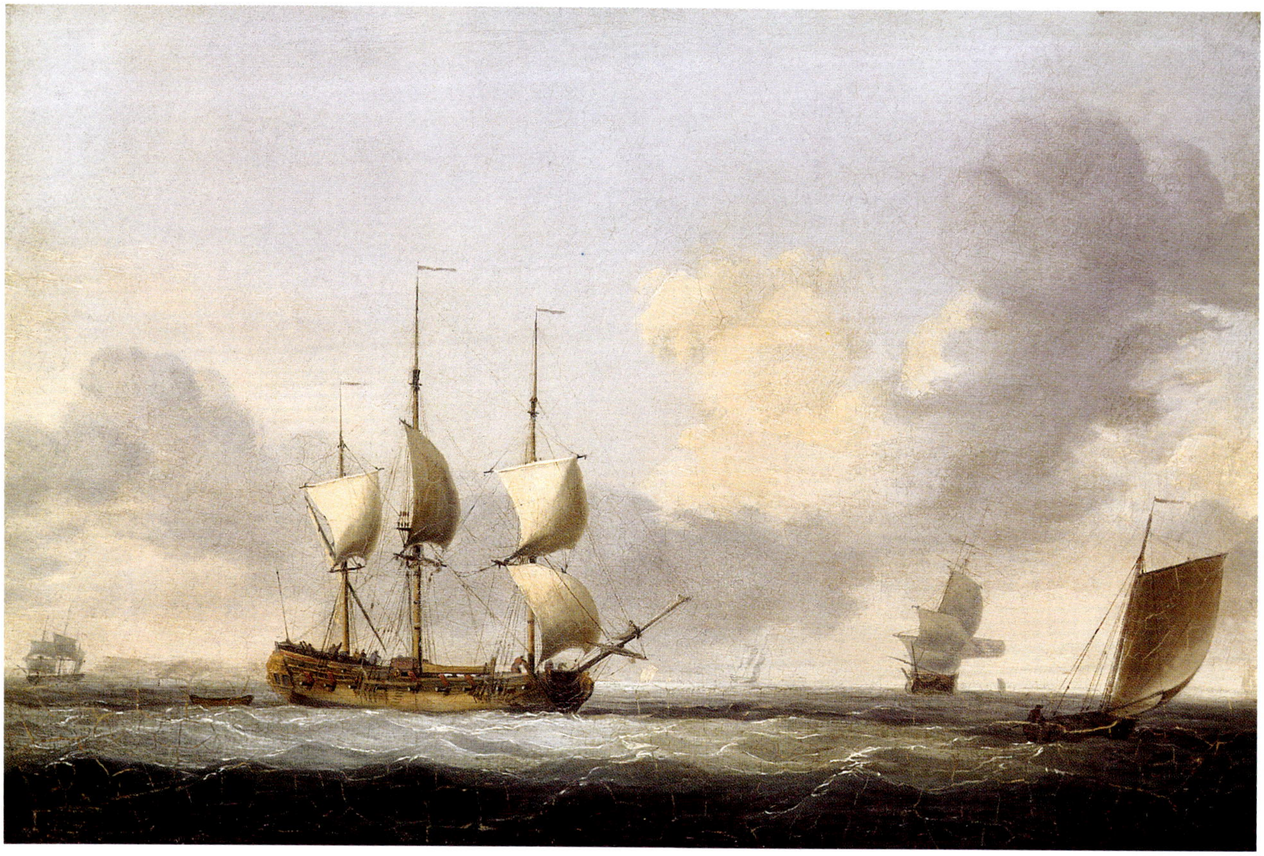

4/2
262 *Two merchant ships with a smack to the right*. Oil on paper laid down on canvas, 10⅛ x 15¼.
Collection of Mr and Mrs Welch

canvas. Great quantities were used for making sails and in the Navy it was supplied in two foot wide strips in up to six different thicknesses. All of this, at the time, would have been hand-woven and very strongly made, but uneven, compared to today's machine-made cloth. This is an important point to note in eighteenth century canvases. Surely when Brooking first started to paint on canvas it would have been on scraps from the sail lofts. Later on, he would have been able to afford his own, making up his stretchers and mounting the canvas on them. For the Foundling Hospital commission (231A), his largest painting, the stretchers would have been made up individually, however the majority of his paintings would fit within a two foot strip.

Clearly, he must have been careful in the preparation of the canvas for it to have remained in such good condition for so long, for many of his paintings were painted a quarter of a millennium ago. A number of these pictures have not been relined, so the preparation must have been good and sound.

First, he would have sized the canvas with an animal glue size to protect the fibres of the canvas and this would have been brushed into the gaps between weft and warp, or the weave of the material. This strengthens and protects the canvas, which when dry can be given the necessary priming coat of gesso, composed of white lead paste and perhaps a little chalk. He would have done this at least twice, rubbing down between coats with a light pumice stone. Once he had made a sound and very flat surface, he probably waited a few weeks before using the canvas. It was extremely important for him to achieve a totally flat surface so that he could draw in the design, and later on the masts and rigging. It is difficult to do this on uneven canvas. Similarly, he would not build up a heavy impasto anywhere in his paintings, and we find them generally uniformly even.

Now and again there is some impasto (paint that stands in relief from the canvas, or panel), perhaps on the edge of a cloud, and the accurate observer can see that the painter has smoothed it down with his finger. Impasto is also of course used to highlight the

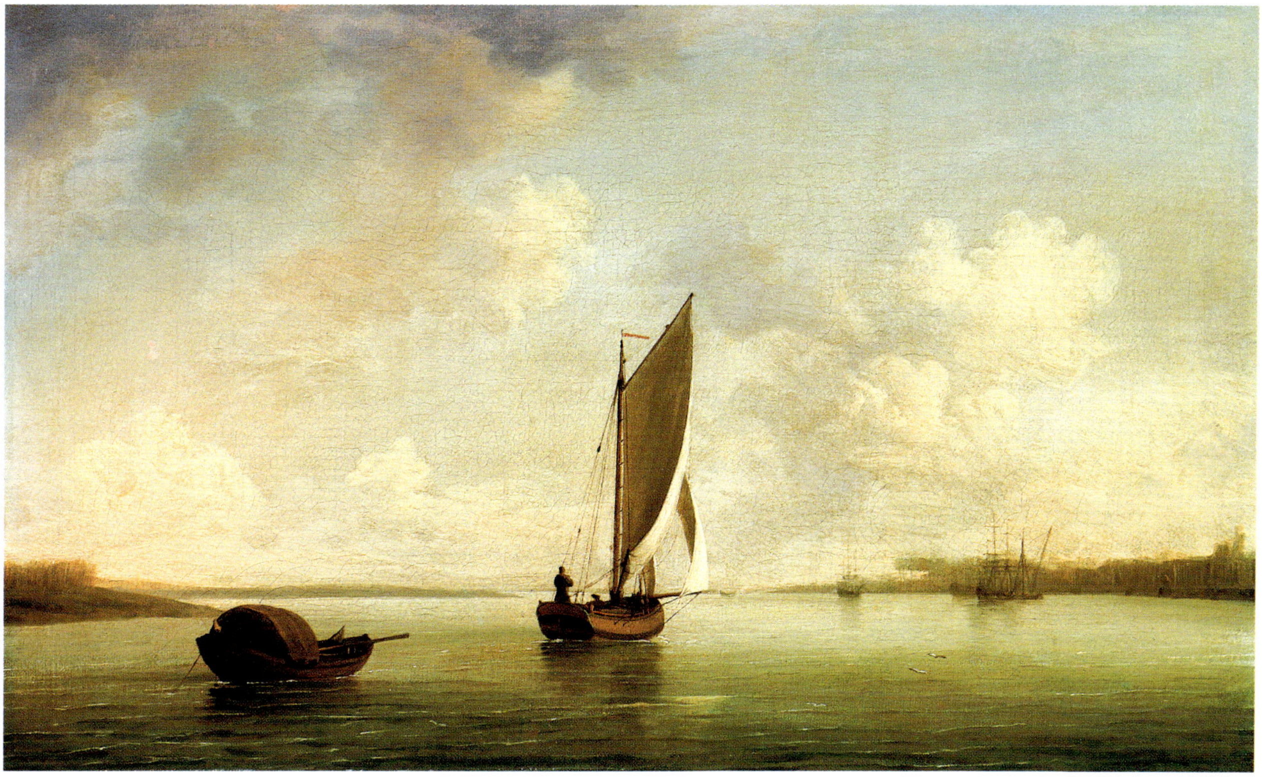

4/3
30 *A smack under sail in a light breeze going down river.* Oil on canvas, 14½ x 24½. Signed C Brooking. Brooking sketching at the tiller. Collection of Mr and Mrs Paul Mellon

peaks of breaking waves, and also to show sea spray. Brooking did not normally use impasto to highlight the rigging of his ships, or other vessels.

Brooking's next step was to draw in the ships. He did this very accurately, using the same outline of various ships over and over again. Similarly, when there is a pair of paintings which both look and measure the same he was able to make one so accurate a copy of the other, that today we can only tell the difference by the craquelure in the paint, which has evolved over the last two and a half centuries.

There are standard drawings, which were used in reverse for the engravings by Boydell and others, and in some cases the marks of the engraver are still to be found on the back of the drawings. This may explain the repetition of many successful compositions. However, there must have been many more standard drawings than those in existence today.

It is possible that Brooking made sketches in pencil or ink and wash whenever he could, either in his boat at sea (No. 30) or when on shore (27 and 622), as on the Isle of Sheppey. The sketches were then worked up for his oil paintings and retained for further use. There is no sign of any sketch book having survived for the moment, but one can always hope that somewhere, hidden away in some library in a stately home, one or more of them may come to light. However, fire and damp and neglect in the past are destroyers of such very valuable documents.

Like every other painter of his day, Brooking would have ground up and made his own colour mixtures. It is now known that his father manufactured paints for commercial use. The colour mixtures would have been kept in glass

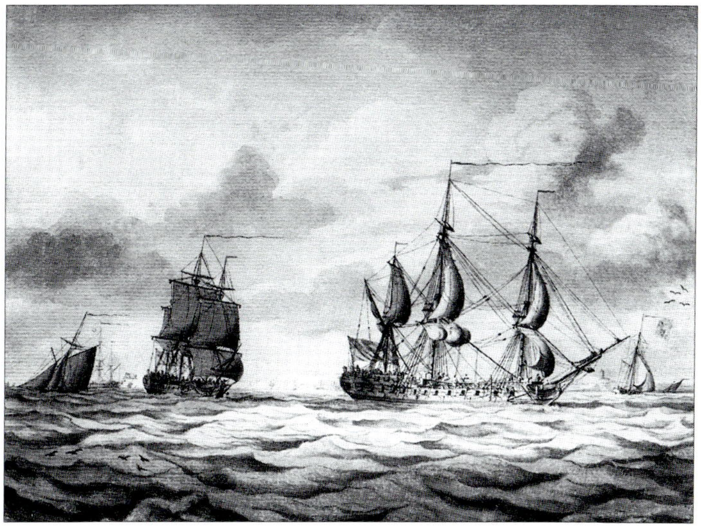

4/4
701 *Two frigates before the wind.* Pen, ink and grey wash, 7⅞ x 10⅛. Signed C Brooking on the plank left foreground.
Collection of Mr and Mrs Paul Mellon

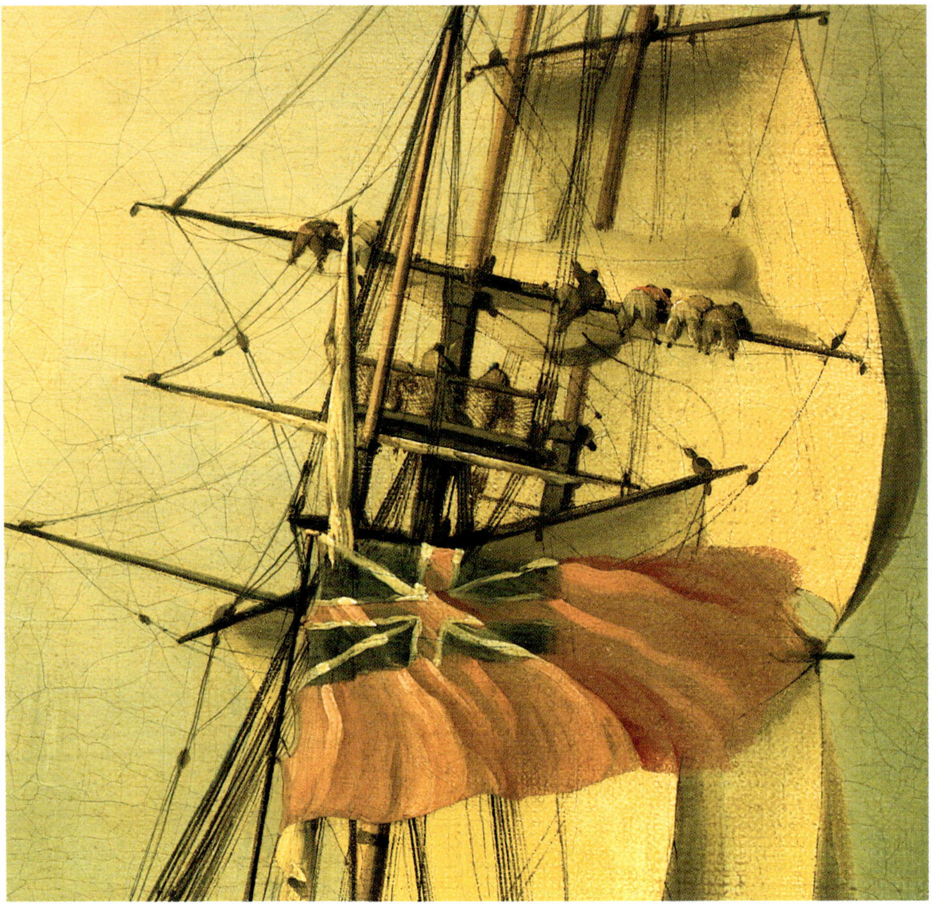

4/5
250 *A bomb ketch, a two-decker and other shipping in a stormy sea*, detail. Oil on canvas, 26½ x 35. There are eight seamen aloft furling the main topsail.
National Maritime Museum, London

jars (the powder) and the mixtures ready for use in bladders. Almost all his painting must have been carried out indoors. Perhaps he had a studio, more likely he did not, and worked within the hours of daylight, so restrictive in winter, particularly in a city, unless he could paint on a top or garret floor with a skylight window.

His palette, we are told by Edward Dayes, writing in 1805, produced pictures where 'his colouring is bright and clear, his water pellucid and transparent with a firm broad spirited touch'. Marine painting in the eighteenth century generally had a muted palette; there are no primary colours at sea and very little green. Bright colours are only really apparent in sunsets, sunrises, ships on fire at night and of course in flags. Today's marine paintings are lighter and brighter with a greater variety of colouring, but rarely achieve the subtlety of effects achieved in the eighteenth century.

Many of the colours that we take for granted today were not available until quite recently. For instance, the main blue which Brooking would have used was from ground-up lapis lazuli. There were no chromes of cadmiums or ultramarine substances. He would have used mainly the earth colours, lapis lazuli and possibly prussian blue (available from 1724), rose madder or indian red or vermillion, naples yellow, yellow ochre, lead white and lamp black (carbon). That this is quite enough to paint masterpieces is clearly demonstrated by our earlier masters. A simple palette is easier to maintain balance and control and is a lot less expensive to purchase. As a matter of interest, lead paint tubes from which paint can be squeezed were not available until about 1860, so it was not an easy task to carry these bladders of paint around.

For his media, Brooking would have used turpentine or linseed oil or poppy seed oil, and as is clearly evident he used these extensively for his glazes, which are so important in his work. Where paintings have been damaged or over cleaned, this will almost certainly extend to the top glazing, which regrettably will have altered the balance of the painting, losing certain effects. Often the rigging and fine details are removed and later restoration incorrectly applied. Neither glazes nor rigging can be put back exactly as in the original. This feature is common to so many restorations in marine paintings.

Damage to the 'in depth glazing' is more of a problem in eighteenth and nineteenth

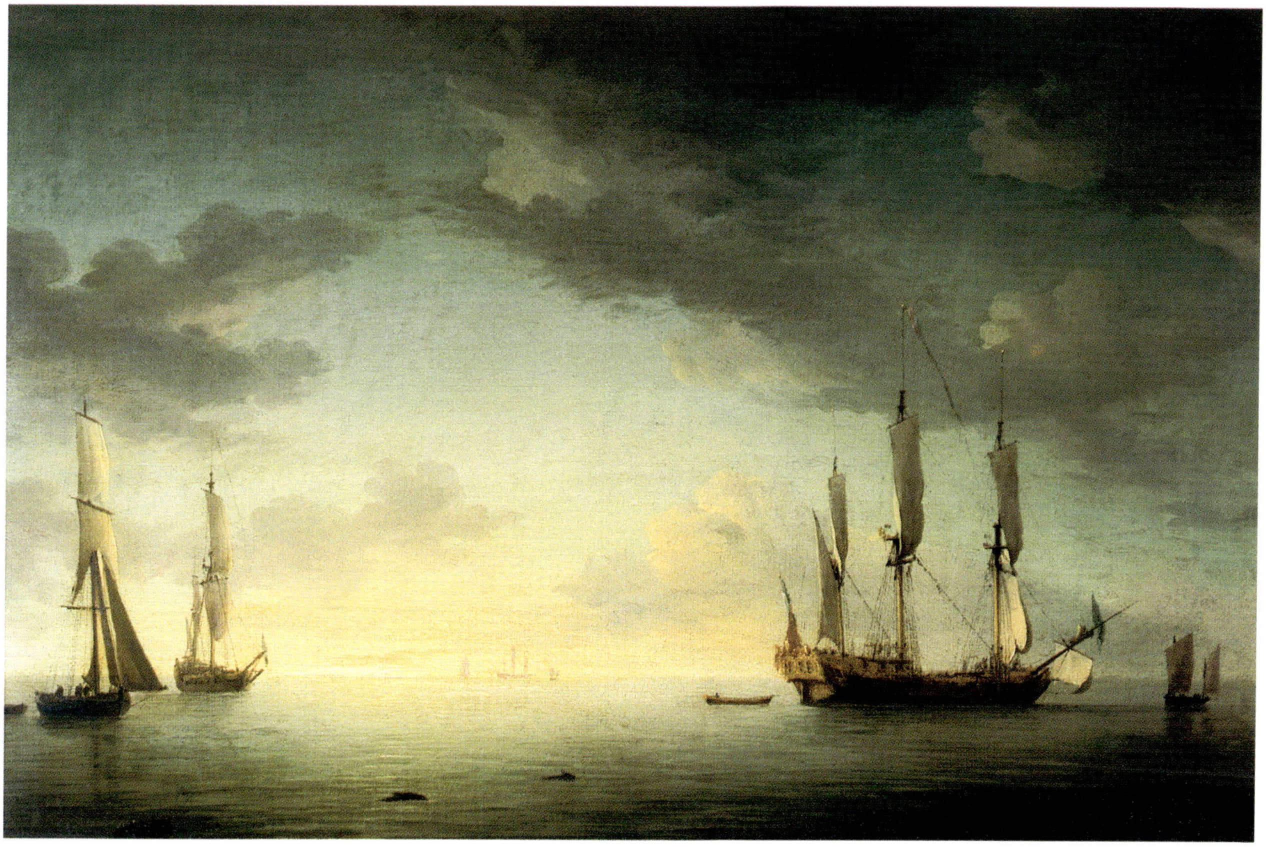

4/6
2D *Sunset. A ship-rigged Royal Yacht in a light air with another yacht and a cutter.*
Oil on canvas, 9½ x 14¾.
Signed C. Brooking.
Private Collection

century marine paintings than to those of the twentieth century. In very many nineteenth century paintings there has been relatively little damage through the years and if some restoration is necessary, the present day restorer has a much greater awareness of the techniques required to restore and conserve them, without causing damage. In particular, there is a problem with ancient varnishes from the eighteenth century which discolour and bind with the paint and glazes below. Modern varnishes, by contrast, are mostly resin-based and easy to remove without damaging what lies beneath. It is a horrid thought, but many old paintings were cleaned with fine pumice stone with consequent loss of paint and detail. There are many chemical processes available today which are relatively safe by contrast. Good restorers have to have a thorough knowledge of the chemistry of the compounds they use nowadays. In general they are most careful of the pictures in their trust. Pumice is never used today for cleaning paintings.

Clouds and Seas by Brooking (details)

In this book, many paintings are reproduced in colour. One has only to look at them to see how much interest Brooking took in the portrayal of the skies and the sea. The division in each painting is generally about three-quarters sky and one quarter sea, though this is obviously altered as required. It would seem that van de Velde the Younger was used to a higher horizon line of say two-thirds sky and one-third sea.

Thus it was necessary for Brooking to study the sky in detail for his atmospheric compositions. It is probable that he recorded his skies with as much care as John Constable (1776-1837). Constable's cloud studies were painted in the 1820s, some seventy years after Brooking had died, and are in oil on thick paper. It is understood that Constable made these studies using a rapidly evaporating type of petroleum mixture as a medium, which would not have been available in Brooking's day, but facilitated Constable's rapid sketches in the open air.

Four paintings have been chosen to show how Brooking painted skies and to show their structure over 240 years ago, long before others had approached such observations. The following paintings have been selected to show fine weather (2D and 276), bad weather (203D) and a complete frontal system (358). Today we understand these systems, for they

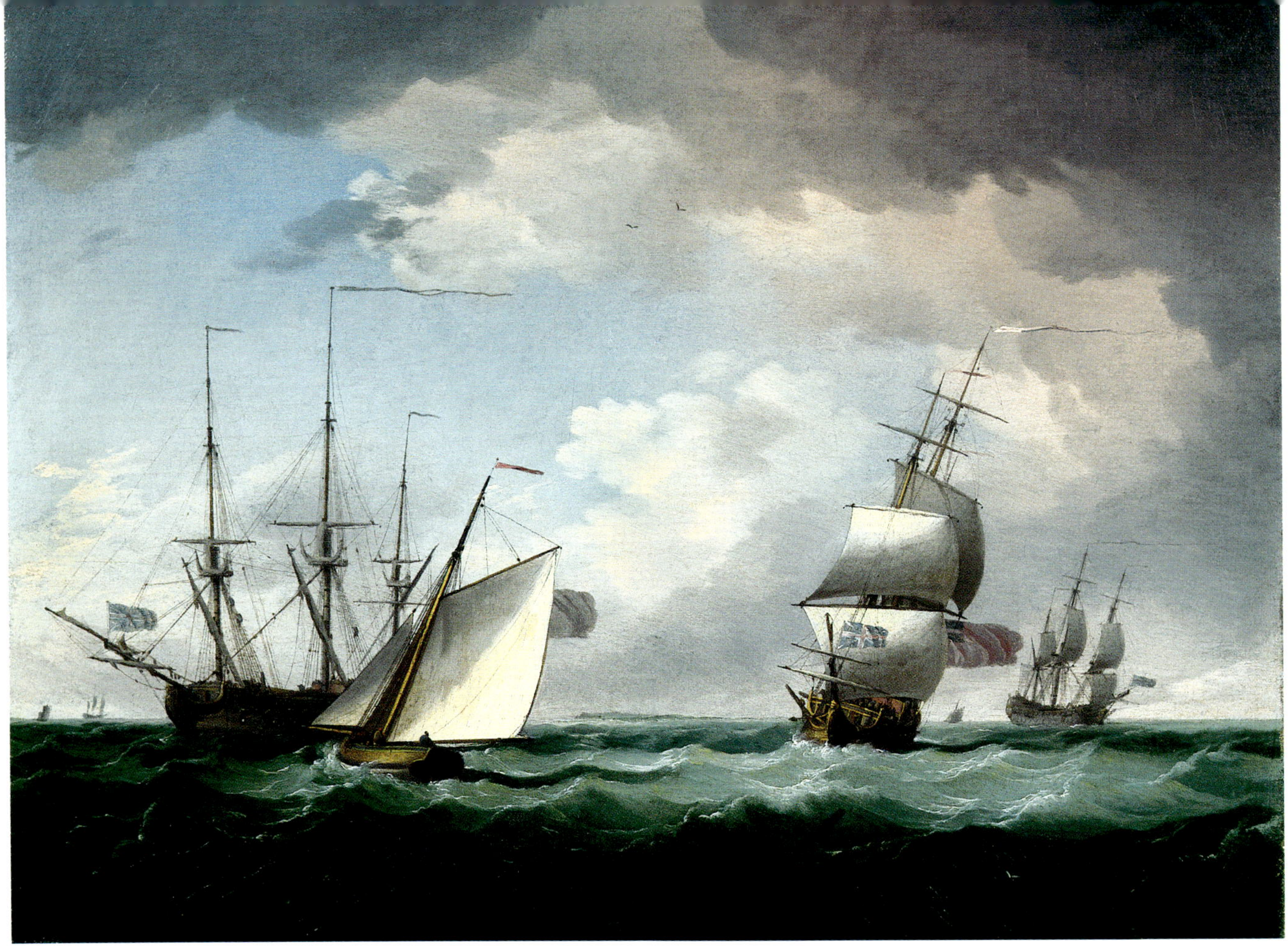

4/7
276 *A frigate, a cutter close-hauled and two ships of the line, one at anchor, in a breeze*. Oil on canvas, 17½ x 23½. Signed. Private Collection

are constantly shown to us on television forecasts.

In the eighteenth century one had to make one's own weather forecasts and predictions, and there is no doubt that Brooking was among the first to understand how this could be done, and to show exactly what they looked like – he must have been a good observer to do this. He must also have been able to memorise the cloud systems, for his paintings would have been done indoors.

Painting 2D shows a royal yacht and other shipping towards sunset in a calm. There is a bit of cumulo-nimbus which has formed during the day and some stratus toward the horizon, whilst in the calm waters which reflect the clouds and the evening light two porpoises are lazily cruising in the foreground. This painting had always remained in the Barrington family. It was probably bought by the 2nd Viscount (1717-1793) who was Secretary of State for War several times between 1755-75, and also during the American War of Independence. In 1960 it was given by Patrick William, 11th Viscount Barrington, to his kinsman Vice Admiral B. C. B. Brooke CB, CBE, DL, together with three other paintings, also by Brooking. He gave these paintings to Admiral Brooke because he was the only sailor in the family. The Barrington family home was at Becket, Shrivenham.

Painting 276 shows us bright summer day with a stiff breeze. The clouds are white cumulus towering up into the distance, whilst a rain squall seems imminent overhead. The man with the red hat in the cutter in the foreground seems to be sketching: perhaps it is Brooking himself, for he portrays himself like this in two other paintings. There is a lovely short sea running to the right across the painting,which had belonged to a Miss Honey in 1920. It was sent to Christie's on 8 March 1920 and remained unsold at 30 guineas!

In painting 203D the storm, having done its damage, is passing away to the right of the painting, leaving the ships in a very rough sea, but in sunshine. The weather is improving as the bad weather system moves to the right and out of the painting. This is one of a set

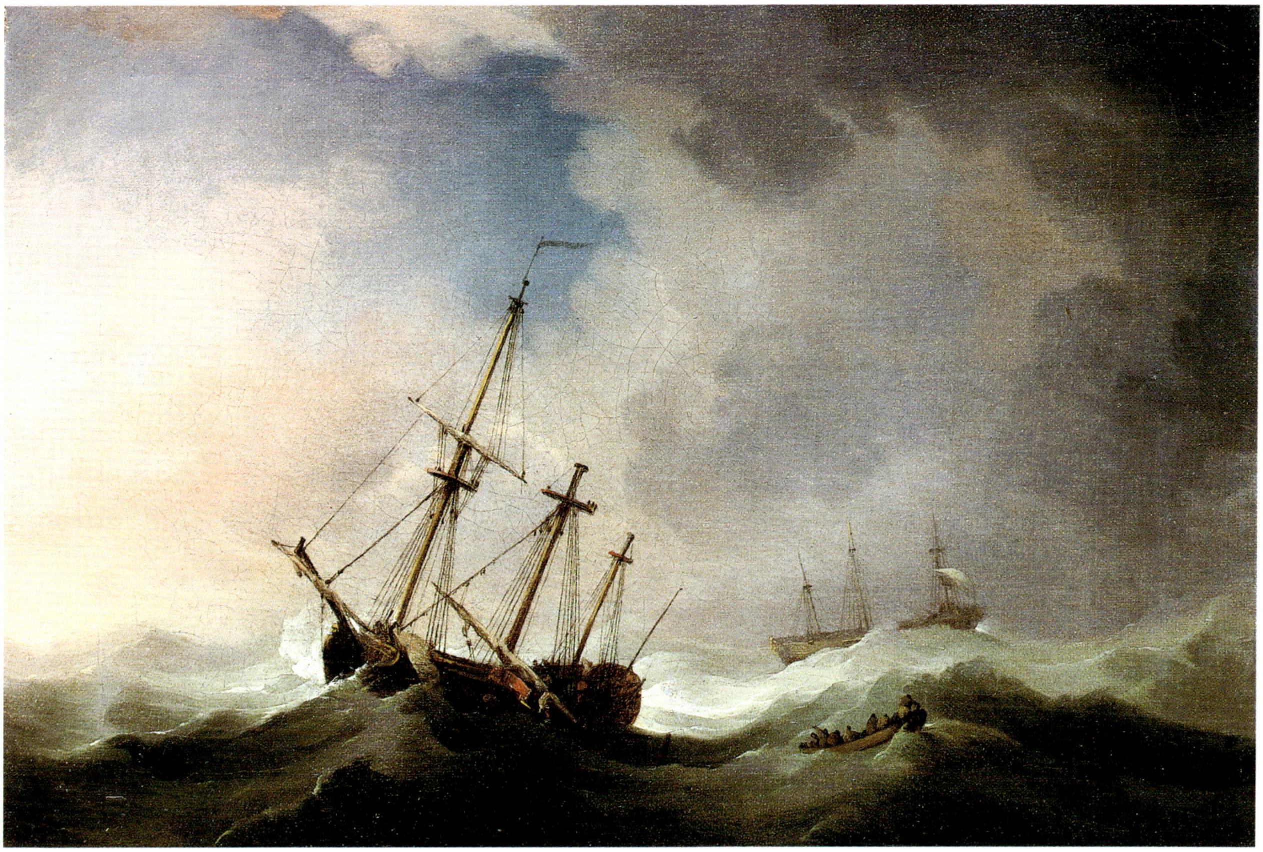

4/8
203D *A flagship in a gale shortening sail.* Oil on canvas, 10½ x 14½. From a set of six Brooking paintings (see 15B). Signed lower right C Brooking. Private Collection

of six Brookings which belonged to a solicitor, Mr Robert Taylor of Lincoln's Inn, since about 1850, and were given to his nephew in 1915. The set was broken up and sold finally by Sotheby's in 1985.

Painting 358 is an astounding and magnificent painting, quite unique in Brooking's oeuvre. It is the largest of his paintings after that in the Foundling Hospital, and so far as we know is the only painting with an aerial perspective of a sea battle. It was sold by Lord Howe to Spink's on 7 December 1933. This must have been the 5th Earl Howe, Francis Richard Henry Penn Curzon, PC, CBE, Commodore in the Naval Reserve and a racing driver who sold this painting, perhaps to finance his racing cars. Colin Sorensen suggested in the Mellon exhibition of 1966 that this painting was made soon after the action on 10 April 1746 in which, in the Privateer *Alexander*, Captain Phillips, on sighting the *Solebay*, earlier captured from the British, was bold and daring enough to attack and recapture her off Isle de Ré, just off the French base of La Rochelle. By his very sudden and vigorous attack under the nose of the French fleet, Phillips was able to recapture the *Solebay*. For this exploit he received a gold medal from King George II and a gratuity of 500 guineas.

The painting is very large, measuring 44 x 95ins. The sky shows a great Atlantic front going through from right to left and a good sea running straight across from the Bay of Biscay. It also shows a French fleet at anchor and six ships in La Rochelle. What a superb cutting out operation to carry out, in a force six gale with a beam wind. What fine seamanship and such a prize to recapture, needing great enterprise and valour from every man on board the *Alexander.*

The various phases of the engagement are portrayed and each is given a letter; the key to this is given in a panel in the centre foreground which the painter has signed 'Chas Brooking Pinx' but was alas not dated. If it was painted in the year following, that is 1747, then Brooking was aged twenty-six years.

Westby Percival-Prescott, who was the principal paintings' conservator at the National

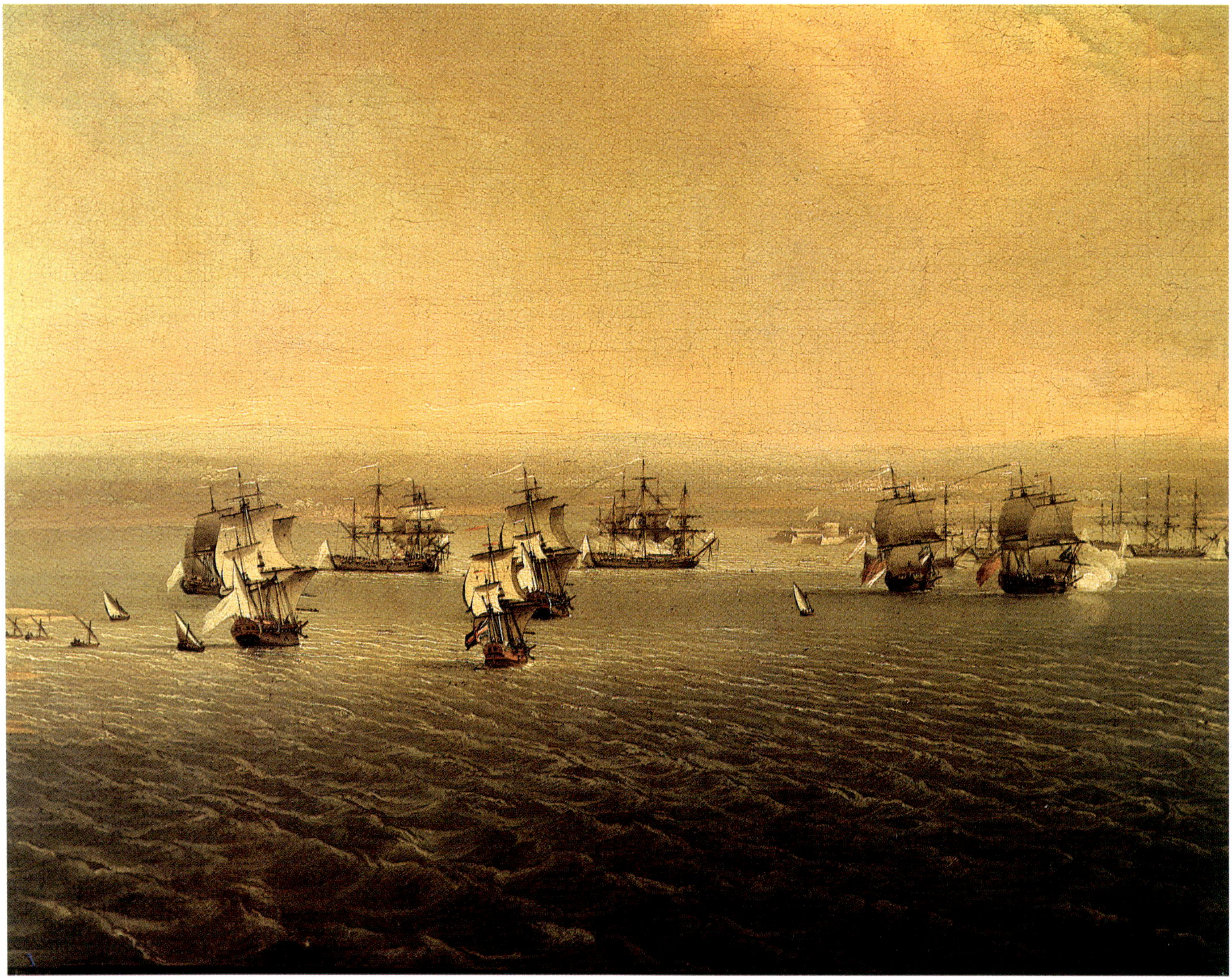

4/9
358 *The* Alexander *in action with the* Solebay *off the island of Ré* – La Rochelle – *10 April 1746*, detail (of centre section). Oil on canvas, 44 x 95. Signed Chas Brooking Pinx centre foreground below the description of the action. Private Collection

Maritime Museum and had restored many of the Brookings there, wrote about this painting in the *Burlington Magazine* (August 1966). His observations are most appropriate. With permission, the quote follows:

'Departing from the earlier conventions of large sea battle pictures, with their high horizons and overlapping patterning of ships, he invites the spectator to view the engagement as though from an immense distance and with the eye level raised several hundred feet. Brooking gave himself entirely new problems of composition and perspective by making the sea and the sky the major part of the picture; the incidents of the engagement occupy only a fraction, about a thirty-sixth part of his painting. The principles of Dutch marine painting and the baroque diagonal arrangements of the Van de Velde the Younger were abandoned, with their linear thrusts and counter-thrusts, and he introduced a new way of representing space in terms of movement in depth within the picture, movement in which the viewer must participate. This form required new techniques to suggest the illusion of space and give aerial perspective, and it demanded devices which would draw the spectator's attention from one area of the picture to another. Brooking achieves this in a series of shallow diagonal movements, which sweep from side to side,

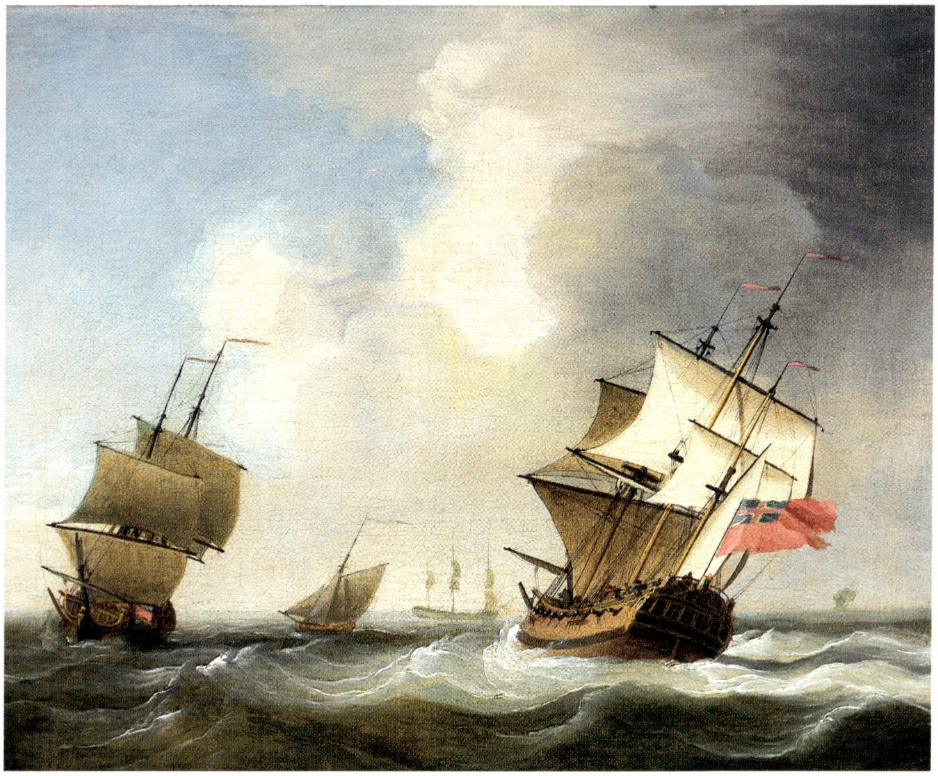

4/10
241B *Merchant ships passing in the Channel.* Oil on canvas, 13¾ x 17⅞. Traces of signature lower right. Collection of Miles Joel

> *leading the eye eventually towards the horizon, resolving into distance and into the sky which acts as a stabilising counterpoise to these motions. These innovations, which were Brooking's solutions to the problems presented by this particular subject, were returned to repeatedly throughout his career.'*

In the magnificent exhibition organised by Westby Percival-Prescott and David Cordingly in 1982 at the Queens House, Greenwich called 'The Art of the Van de Veldes', the former was to write the following:

> *'The popularity of the work of the Van de Veldes inevitably brought with it the wave of derivative painting. The use of assistants in his studio only increased this tendency. Some of his followers rose to become masters in their own right, establishing even more firmly the importance of the principles they had learnt. Yet only one of these painters followed with any success the interest in naturalism which could be observed in some of Van de Velde's later works.*
>
> *It fell to Charles Brooking (1723-59) to form this link and in his quest for greater reality to continue the search for truth which the Van de Veldes had pursued throughout the whole of their careers.'*

Meanwhile, the late Edward Archibald wrote in his *Dictionary of Sea Painters* in 1980 regarding Brooking that 'No painter of the second generation of British marine artists contributed so much to the emergence of a national style as did Brooking, and no painter, then or after, did it better.'

So the leading authorities on British marine painting, including the comments of the late Basil Taylor (page 14, Introduction) and Michael Robinson (page 43, Chapter 3) are already in the text. Thus the author feels it unnecessary to push his subject further and expects the illustrations in this book to complete the case for Brooking's pre-eminent reputation in marine painting, pre-eminent despite his all too short life. Colin Sorensen is, I know, in agreement too, and it is his work that underpins much of this book.

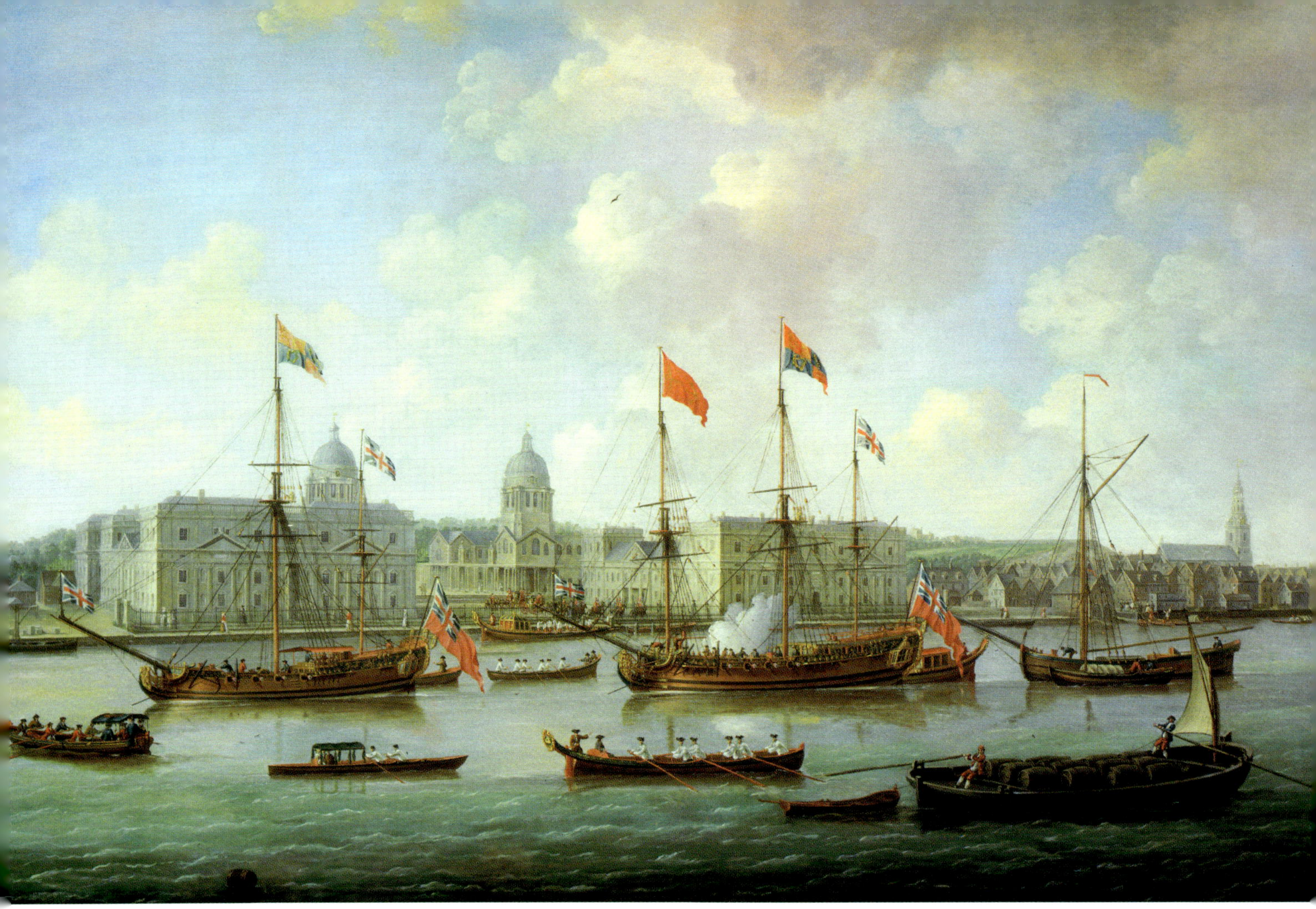

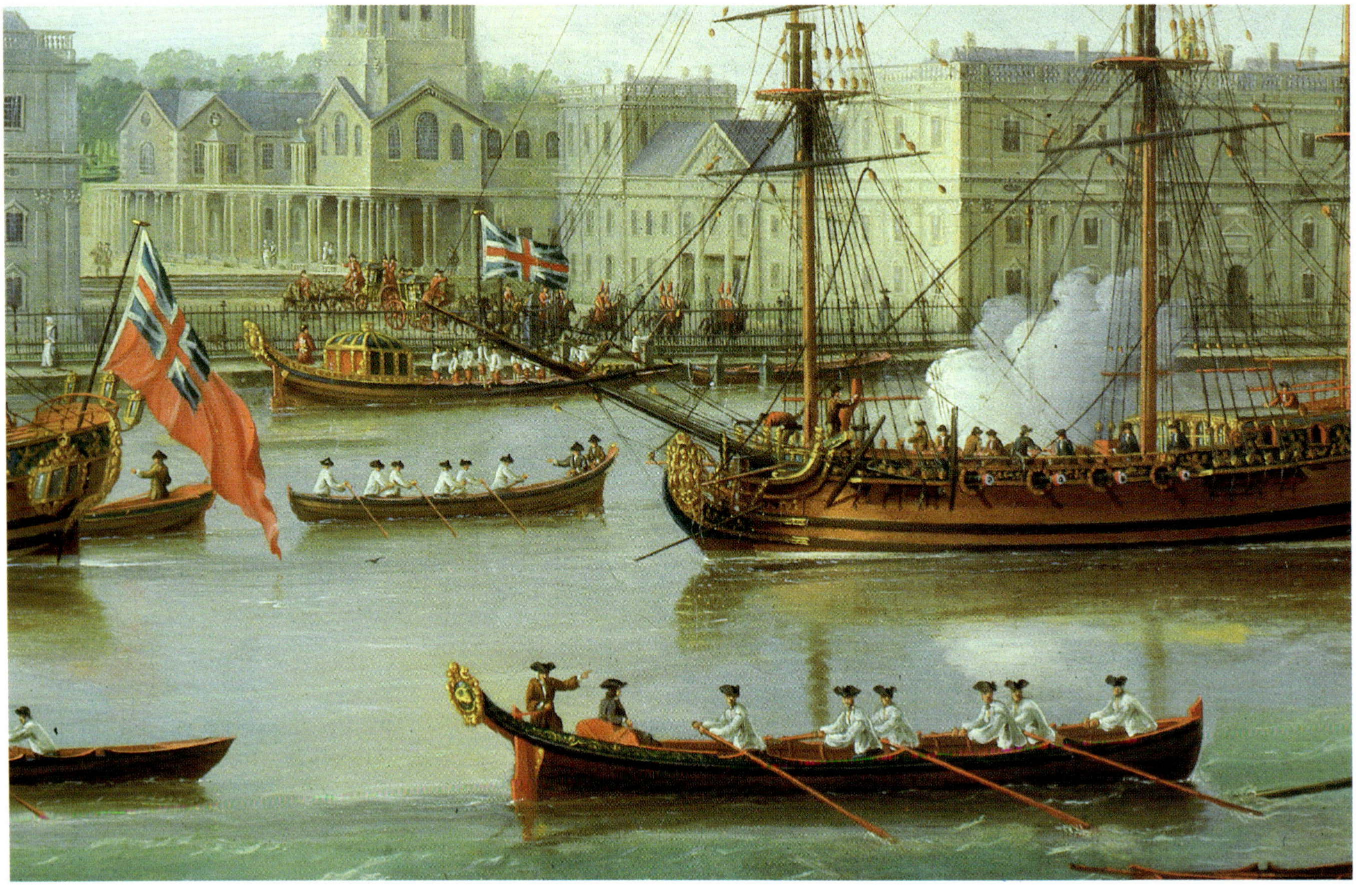

Chapter 5

18th Century Maritime Painters, Printmakers and Publishers

by James Taylor

Curator of Paintings/Corporate Development, National Maritime Museum

Throughout the eighteenth century London was the major centre for printmaking and publishing in Britain. During the early years of the century, the Overton and Bowles families were leading publishers, and arch rivals. Maritime prints made up only a small proportion of their stock. Print publishers had a preference for engraving the artists' subjects of the seventeenth century, such as Rembrandt, David Teniers and Claude Lorraine, as well as Simon de Vlieger, Jan van Goyen, Albert Cuyp, and Ludolf Bakhuizen, and above all the Willem van de Veldes. The van de Veldes remained by far the most popular marine painters in print well into the 1760s.

Although there was a predilection for artists of the seventeenth century, a small number of eighteenth century British marine painters were featured in print publisher's catalogues. Monamy and Scott were especially popular during the first half of the century. Brooking, the Cleveley family, Dodd, Paton, Serres and Swaine were among the most popular names in print from the 1750s to the early years of the nineteenth century. Their prints were promoted by Overton, Bowles, Sayer, and the Boydells, the principal publishers and retailers of the period.

Maritime prints were purchased by officers and officials of the British Admiralty and Navy, also Livery companies, merchants, shipbuilders, owners, captains, masters, and senior crewmen. From the 1760s there was also a growing demand for prints from an increasingly prosperous 'mercantile class' driven by patriotic interest in Britain's victories and trading achievements at sea, as well as a general interest in seafaring.

John Overton issued his first catalogue in 1667. The family business prospered into the following century under his son Henry Overton the elder. Henry's catalogue of 1717 offered engravings of various subjects and sizes, as well as maps and decorative prints, including: 'nine several sorts of landskips and sea-pieces, designed for sashes for windows'. Presumably these prints were a type of transparency allowing light to shine through the specially prepared 'cut away' areas of the design.

During the first half of the eighteenth century, marine paintings were usually described as 'Sea Pieces', and were often promoted by print publishers for use as 'interior decoration'. In Robert Sayer's *New and Enlarged Catalogue* of 1766 he describes prints that are: 'Proper to collect in the Cabinets of the Curious and also make Furniture elegant and genteel when framed and glazed, or may be fitted up in a cheaper Manner, to ornament Rooms, Staircases etc...' Prints were also recommended to adorn 'chimneypieces', possibly to decorate the centrepiece of a fireplace surround, but more usually to hang over fireplaces. Certainly oil paintings were commissioned for this purpose. One of Dominic Serres' Royal Academy exhibits in 1790 was described as 'Lord Rodney carrying the Ville de Paris and other prizes into Port Royal, Jamaica; a frieze for a chimney-piece.'

5/1 (facing page)
John Cleveley the Elder. (1712-1777). *The Royal Palace, The King arriving at Greenwich.* Oil on canvas, 35 x 50, signed, 1752. Richard Green Collection

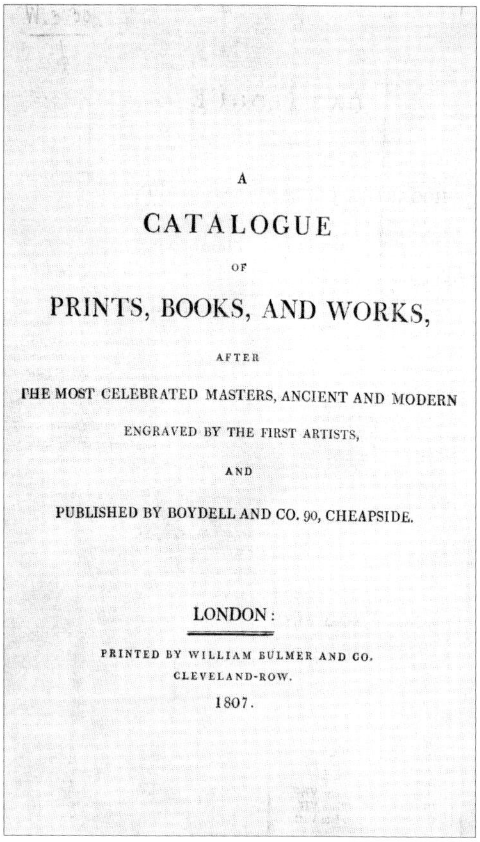

A

CATALOGUE

OF

PRINTS, BOOKS, AND WORKS,

AFTER

THE MOST CELEBRATED MASTERS, ANCIENT AND MODERN

ENGRAVED BY THE FIRST ARTISTS,

AND

PUBLISHED BY BOYDELL AND CO. 90, CHEAPSIDE.

LONDON:

PRINTED BY WILLIAM BULMER AND CO.
CLEVELAND-ROW.

1807.

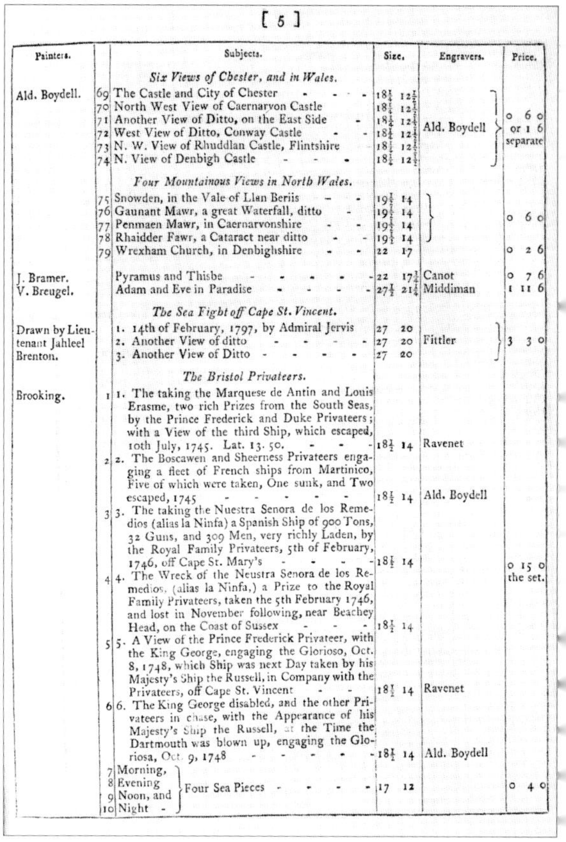

[5]

Painters.		Subjects.	Size.	Engravers.	Price.
		Six Views of Chester, and in Wales.			
Ald. Boydell.	69	The Castle and City of Chester - - - -	18¼ 12½		
	70	North West View of Caernarvon Castle	18¼ 12½		
	71	Another View of Ditto, on the East Side -	18¼ 12½	Ald. Boydell	o 6 o or 1 6 separate
	72	West View of Ditto, Conway Castle - -	18¼ 12½		
	73	N. W. View of Rhuddlan Castle, Flintshire	18¼ 12½		
	74	N. View of Denbigh Castle - - -	18¼ 12½		
		Four Mountainous Views in North Wales.			
	75	Snowden, in the Vale of Llan Beriis - -	19½ 14		
	76	Gaunant Mawr, a great Waterfall, ditto -	19½ 14		o 6 o
	77	Penmaen Mawr, in Caernarvonshire - -	19½ 14		
	78	Rhaidder Fawr, a Cataract near ditto - -	19½ 14		
	79	Wrexham Church, in Denbighshire - -	22 17		o 2 6
J. Bramer.		Pyramus and Thisbe - - - - -	22 17¼	Canot	o 7 6
V. Breugel.		Adam and Eve in Paradise - - - -	27½ 21¼	Middiman	1 11 6
		The Sea Fight off Cape St. Vincent.			
Drawn by Lieutenant Jahleel Brenton.		1. 14th of February, 1797, by Admiral Jervis	27 20		
		2. Another View of ditto - - - -	27 20	Fittler	3 3 o
		3. Another View of Ditto - - - - -	27 20		
		The Bristol Privateers.			
Brooking.	1	1. The taking the Marquese de Antin and Louis Erasme, two rich Prizes from the South Seas, by the Prince Frederick and Duke Privateers; with a View of the third Ship, which escaped, 10th July, 1745. Lat. 13. 50. - - -	18½ 14	Ravenet	
	2	2. The Boscawen and Sheerness Privateers engaging a fleet of French ships from Martinico, Five of which were taken, One sunk, and Two escaped, 1745 - - - - - -	18½ 14	Ald. Boydell	
	3	3. The taking the Nuestra Senora de los Remedios (alias la Ninfa) a Spanish Ship of 900 Tons, 32 Guns, and 309 Men, very richly Laden, by the Royal Family Privateers, 5th of February, 1746, off Cape St. Mary's - - - -	18½ 14		o 15 o the set.
	4	4. The Wreck of the Neustra Senora de los Remedios, (alias la Ninfa,) a Prize to the Royal Family Privateers, taken the 5th February 1746, and lost in November following, near Beachey Head, on the Coast of Sussex - - -	18½ 14		
	5	5. A View of the Prince Frederick Privateer, with the King George, engaging the Glorioso, Oct. 8, 1748, which Ship was next Day taken by his Majesty's Ship the Russell, in Company with the Privateers, off Cape St. Vincent - -	18½ 14	Ravenet	
	6	6. The King George disabled, and the other Privateers in chase, with the Appearance of his Majesty's Ship the Russell, at the Time the Dartmouth was blown up, engaging the Gloriosa, Oct. 9, 1748 - - - - -	18½ 14	Ald. Boydell	
	7 8 9 10	Morning, Evening Noon, and Night - } Four Sea Pieces - - - -	17 12		o 4 o

5/1A and 5/1B
Boydell and Co. Catalogue cover, 1807 and page 5, which lists engravings by Brooking.
British Museum, London

Maritime prints were also promoted as subjects for viewing through a perspective glass, known too as a diagonal mirror, or optical pillar machine. The perspective glass is traditionally believed to be a French invention that '...exaggerated correct linear perspective'. This novel way of viewing prints was quickly adopted by English printsellers in the 1740s and remained popular into the following century. Bowles and Carver's *New and Enlarged Catalogue* of 1795 offered 'Perspective views of Shipping...' among other subjects, 'specially designed for viewing with surprising beauty and effect, in the Diagonal Mirror.' In fact it was not necessary to engrave prints specifically for the perspective glass, but the claim 'specially designed' worked well as a means of sales promotion. The Bowles & Carver 'views' were priced at 1s each plain, and 2s coloured. The mirror itself was also offered for sale 'neatly fitted up in mahogany, with Looking-Glass, &c...' for one guinea. Among the many marine prints sold in association with the perspective glass were those by Peter Monamy and the Cleveley family of artists.

In 1734 Henry Overton issued *A Catalogue of maps, prints, copy-books &c...* which revealed that at that time he was in partnership with John Hoole. After his death in 1751 his nephew, also called Henry Overton, took over the business, although it was short-lived. John's brother Philip also had a shop in Fleet Street. Far from being rivals, they collaborated on the production of prints and catalogues.

The Bowles family of print-publishers and sellers also worked closely together. The earliest known Bowles catalogue was issued by Thomas senior in 1720. Thomas Bowles' shop was in St Paul's Churchyard. His son, Thomas junior, also worked in the business. By 1734 Thomas senior's younger brother John had moved his shop from Mercer's Hall in Cheapside to the Black Horse in Cornhill. From the previous address John Bowles had published Charles Brooking Senior's *Map of the city and suburbs of Dublin* (see Chapter 2, page 33) in 1728. John's son, Carrington Bowles (1724-1792), joined the business as a partner in 1753. In turn his son Henry Carrington Bowles (1763-1830) carried on the family firm and from 1793 he traded as Bowles and Carver.

In the *Daily Advertiser* of 24 March, 1743 Henry Overton offered a selected number of

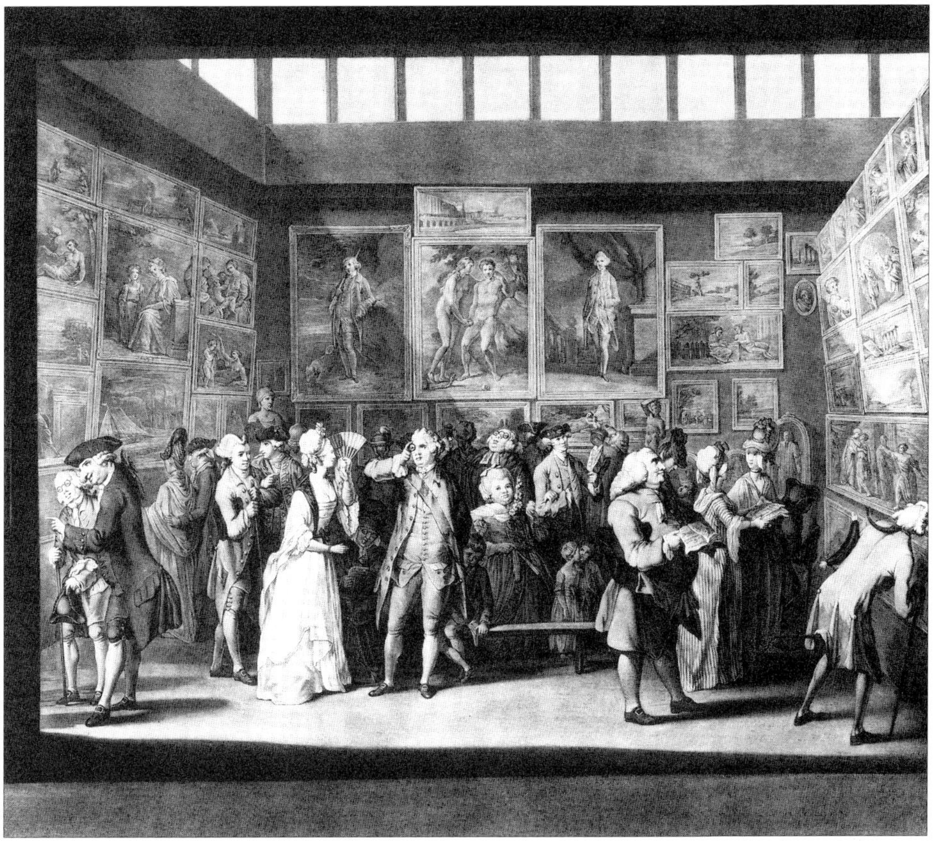

5/2
Robert Sayer. *Print Saleroom*, mezzotint, published 15 May 1772. Private Collection

four sheet prints of the man-o'war *Britannia* after Willem van de Velde the Younger. The print was originally published in 1692. Overton promoted the print as a 'very proper Ornament for the Cabbin of a Ship'. There is no doubt that naval officers and their merchant equivalent would have adorned the bulkheads and cabins of ships, yachts and other vessels with such prints. Apart from nautical decoration they would also have provided distraction from the monotony and danger of long sea voyages.

Van de Velde prints also feature in Thomas Major's *A catalogue of prints engraved from the finest paintings...* published in 1754. This 'catalogue' was in fact a broadsheet.

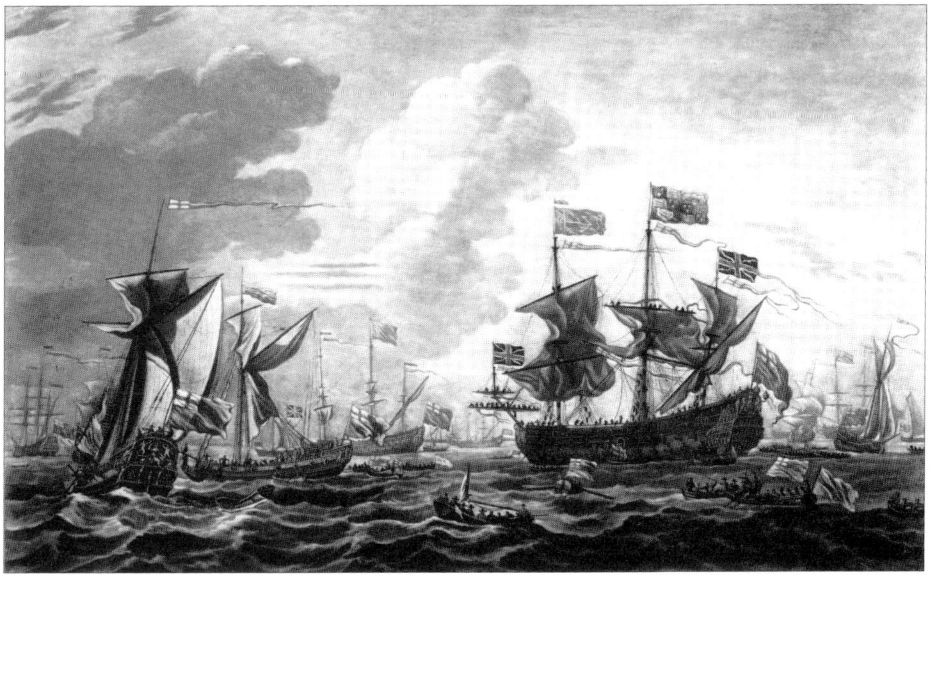

5/3
Willem van de Velde the Younger, *Review of the Fleet, 10 September 1673*. Mezzotint engraving.
National Maritime Museum, London

Engravings were printed on 'grand eagle paper; to be had either in sheets or bound fit for Gentlemen's libraries'. Many of the engravings were after pictures in the collection of Frederick, Prince of Wales, to whom he had been appointed as official engraver. He was later engraver to George II and George III. The titles of the van de Velde's engravings were in French: *Le Calme* and *Vent Frais* were both offered at 2s each. *A Sea Piece* by Cuyp was listed for 1s 6d and *A Sea Port* by Claude Lorraine for 2s 6d.

The engraving *Vent Frais* was published according to an Act of Parliament on 18 February 1751. Other descriptive information on the print itself reveals it was: 'Grave d'après Le Tableau original de Vandervelde de 21 ½ pouces de large sur 16 pouces de haut A Londres chez Major Graveur de S.A.R. Le Prince de Galles a la Tete d'or dans West Street'. At this time it was common for prints to have titles and descriptions in both English and French, indicating the popularity of these prints in the respective countries. The original oil painting described by M. S. Robinson as *A Kaag and a Weyschuit running before a strong breeze* (see M. S. Robinson *Van de Veldes* Vol II pp.837-844) is now in a private collection. It has been identified as having once belonged to the collection of Charles Jennens. It is therefore likely that Brooking would have been familiar with this picture, as copies made by him of other van de Veldes from the same collection are known.

Vent Frais was engraved by Pierre-Charles Canot (1712-1777), a leading printmaker of his day. Born near Paris, he settled in England in 1740. In 1770 he was elected an Associate of the Royal Academy of Arts in London. Canot engraved a series of ten maritime scenes after Peter Monamy. An eleventh print to the series after Monamy is thought by Charles Harrison Wallace to have been published as an afterthought. Canot also engraved the work of Canaletto, the Cleveley family, Paton, Scott, and Serres, among others. In addition to marines he also engraved topographical views, and sporting subjects.

Thomas Major (1720-1799) studied in Paris under the French draughtsman and printmaker Hubert Gravelot (1699-1773), Charles-Nicholas Cochin, the elder (1688-1754) and Jacques-Philippe Le Bas (1707-1783). Upon returning to London in 1748 he set up a studio at the Golden Head in Chandos Street, at the lower end of St. Martin's Lane. Although based in London, he maintained close links with Paris and was one of the major distributors of French prints in England. In 1762 he exhibited five pictures at the Free Society, including *A ship-wreck*. Five years later Major was elected an Associate of the Royal Academy. He exhibited one engraving at the Royal Academy in 1776.

During the second half of the eighteenth century, maritime prints gained in popularity, and many more were published. The growing market for prints was largely stimulated by the demand for images of British naval conquests at sea. Prints commemorating Admiral Vernon's capture of Porto Bello, off Panama, during the War of Jenkins' Ear 1739-40 were particularly popular; also incidents during Commodore (later Lord) Anson's remarkable circumnavigation in the *Centurion* of 1740-44, the exploits of the 'Royal Family' Privateers, and the notable actions of the Seven Years War, 1756-63. Printmakers and publishers also satisfied the demand for other subjects, including views of London from the Thames, and depictions of the principal settlements of the English East India Company, responsible for introducing silks, spices, tea, and new wealth into Britain.

The leading London-based print publishers of the second half of the eighteenth century were Robert Sayer (1725-1793) and John Boydell (1719-1804). In 1745 Sayer took over the stock of the print dealer Philip Overton, and set up shop at what was later numbered 53 Fleet Street. He was a sole trader until he formed a partnership with John Bennett as Sayer and Bennett from 1774 to 1786, and later traded as Sayer & Co. from 1791 until his death. The company was then sold to Laurie & Whittle who published their first catalogue in 1795. Sadly, the earliest surviving Sayer catalogue is for the year 1766. The catalogues of 1763 (the first issued), and 1768 have not been traced.

Sayer's *New and Enlarged Catalogue...* of 1766 reveals that in addition to single and sets of 'Scarce and Valuable' prints, maps, 'Drawing and Copy-Books' could be acquired by 'Gentlemen for Furniture, Merchants for Exportation, and Shopkeepers to Sell Again...on the most Reasonable Terms...' The index from Sayer and Bennett's Catalogue for 1775 shows that the customer was spoilt for choice, although maritime prints formed only a small part of their extensive stock. There were: 'Theatrical Prints', 'Portraits', 'History', 'Droll', 'Royal Personages', 'Beauties', 'Miscellaneous and Humorous Subjects', 'Naked Figures', 'Sporting Pieces, Horses, Scripture Pieces, Topograpical views', as well as 'Miniature Designs for Watch-Cases', 'Writing Books', 'Books of Flowers', 'Architecture,' and 'Maps and Sea Charts'. Maritime prints in this catalogue could be found under various headings, including: 'Sea Pieces, Landscapes, Cattle, Moral, and other subjects' and 'Sets of small Prints – Views, Landscapes, Horses, Hunting, Hawking, Shipping, History Pieces, & c.'

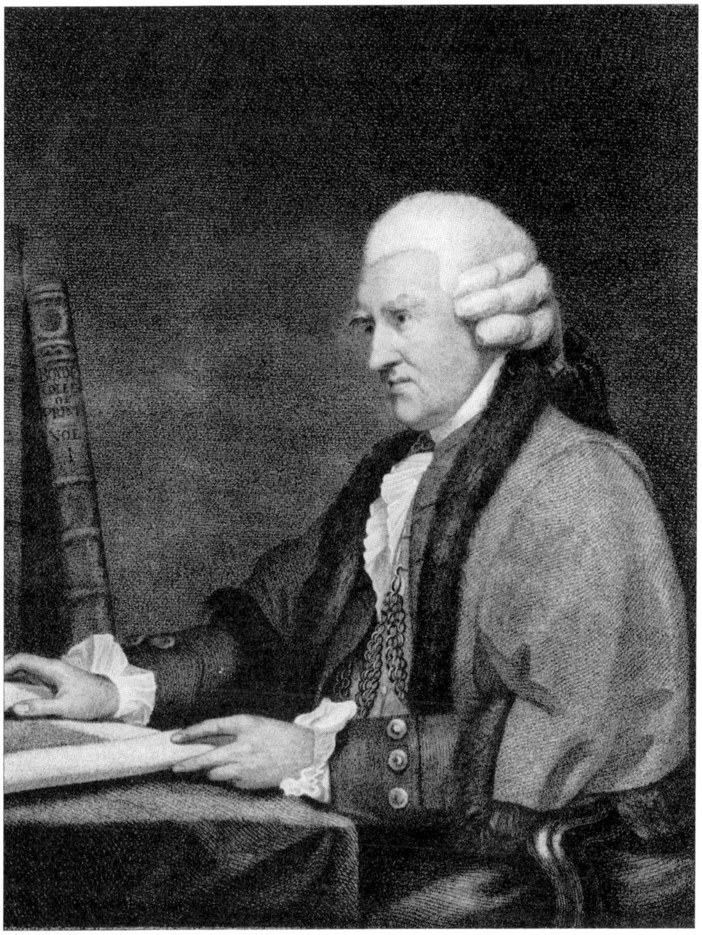

5/4
Portrait of John Boydell.
Engraving. Private Collection

According to the British print specialist Antony Griffiths, John Boydell '...almost singlehandedly created a market for fine engravings in England and made English prints an eagerly collected commodity throughout Europe.' Boydell was a competent and occasionally excellent printmaker, an inspired publisher and for the best part of his career an astute businessman. The grandson of a parson in Shropshire and son of a land surveyor, he studied at the St. Martin's Lane Academy. He was later apprenticed to the London etcher and line engraver William Henry Toms (active from 1735-55) who produced naval and military subjects, a small number of portraits, and architectural and topographical views.

In 1751 Boydell set up shop, initially at the Unicorn in Cheapside. Although he engraved and published his own landscapes, at this time the main source of income derived from selling imported foreign prints. However, in the early 1760s Boydell took the initiative to publish prints himself: '...from the most Capital Paintings in England'. His printselling business earned him a considerable fortune, although an ambitious plan to commission leading artists and engravers to illustrate scenes and characters from Shakespeare's plays for his Shakespeare Gallery in Pall Mall was a financial failure. He became Sheriff of the City of London in 1785, and Lord Mayor of London in 1790.

The first known Boydell catalogue dates from 1764, although it is likely that there were earlier publications as yet untraced. In Boydell's 1767 publication entitled *A catalogue of prints, ...from the most capital paintings in England, ...to which are added, a catalogue of the copper-plates belonging to...John Boydell* he takes the opportunity to thank the 'Nobility and Gentry, who have generously granted him the use of their Pictures, and otherwise encouraged him to proceed in this undertaking.' Boydell also acknowledged the assistance of the members of the '...Academy of Painting and Sculpture, in St. Martin's Lane, ...and the generous contribution of the Society of Arts, Manufactures and Commerce, for the Encouragement of the Science of Painting, have been the means of

63.

SEA PIECES, *after* VANDEVELD *and* BROOKING.

64. Morning.
65. Evening.
66. Noon.
67. Night.
68. Greenland Fishery.
69. A Small Breeze.
70. A Calm.
71. A Brisk Gale.
72. Sun Setting.
73. Privateers engaging French Ships.
74. Wreck of La Ninfa
75. Privateers in Chase.
76. A Calm.
77. A View of the Port of Marseilles.
78. A View of the New Port, or the Arsenal of Toulon.
79. A Large View of Elizabeth Castle, in the Island of Jersey.

5/5
Page from Boydell's 1790 catalogue listing van de Velde and Brooking engravings.
British Museum, London

bringing the art of design to a degree of perfection not before known in this nation.'

'The Society of Arts, Manufactures...', now called the Royal Society of Arts, is located off the Strand, London. In 1773 the Society of Arts awarded Boydell a Gold Medal 'for encouraging the Art of Engraving'. Although Boydell certainly did help to promote English engraving, many of his best-sellers were engravings after Dutch, Flemish, French, German, and Italian masters. He commissioned Canot to engrave *A Brisk Gale* and *A Moderate Gale*, after Willem van de Velde and Ludolf Bakhuizen respectively. They were from the collections of Sir Lawrence Dundas, Bart and the Earl of Bute, and sold for 5s each (see Appendix B, page 184, under Highcliffe Castle sale by Mr Christie). These prints were featured in Boydell's 1767 catalogue. They were still listed in catalogues during the early years of the nineteenth century. Although not painted as companion pictures, Boydell promoted them as such, and with great success. They were also included in the first of his remarkable nine volume folio format series entitled *A Collection of Prints engraved after the most capital paintings in England*, published between 1769-92, accompanied by the predominant religious, landscape, portrait and genre subjects after Holbein, Rembrandt, Rubens, Van Dyck, Murillo, Lorraine, and Cuyp, among many others. The price asked for a Rembrandt engraving was 7s 6d, and for Cuyp 5s.

In Volume I of the folio series Boydell included extensive descriptive captions on the various engravings. Of *A Brisk Gale* (see page 71) he observed: 'It is impossible to give a minute description of pictures of this kind. Vanderveldes's excellency being so universally known, and this picture so great a masterpiece in its kind, it is sufficient to say, that whoever views it, whether he considers the bright, delicate, and beautiful colouring of the sky, the transparency and natural agitation of the sea, or the artful position, variety of grouping, and truth of the vessels, must support himself either standing upon the beach of the sea, or else viewing the real objects from a deck, or cabin-window. Every part of the picture is an undoubted proof that Vandervelde was one of the greatest painters that ever lived.'

Boydell was equally effusive of Bakhuizen's *A Moderate Gale*, claiming he was 'The painter who approached nearest to Vandervelde'. He went on to describe the picture in greater detail: '...The drawing of this picture is perfect, the waves are touched with the utmost spirit and truth, and the masses of light and shadow are particularly well understood. His colouring was generally grey and rather cold, but there is a fine glowing warmth throughout this picture.' Boydell was obviously describing the original oil paintings by Bakhuizen and van de Velde. Canot's engravings after these subjects were largely sold uncoloured, although coloured examples are known, usually of a later date.

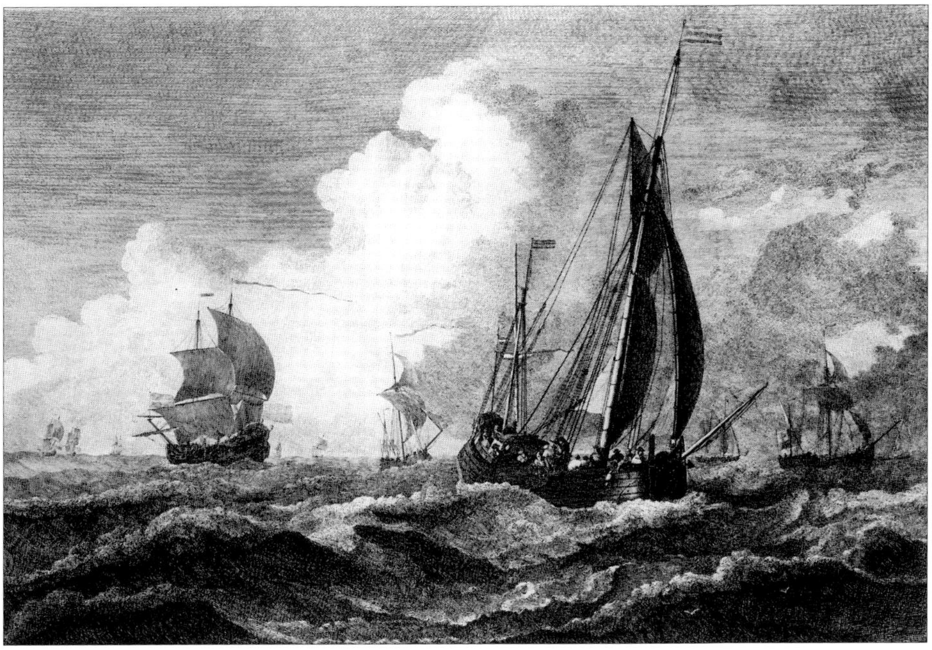

5/6
Engraving by Boydell. *A Brisk Gale* by Willem van de Velde the Younger. Private Collection

Fifteen of Boydell's catalogues have been traced. The first was issued in 1764 and the last published in 1812. Boydell was a sole trader until he invited his nephew Josiah to become a partner in 1786. Josiah was born in Flintshire, North Wales. His study of art was encouraged by his uncle, and Josiah became a competent artist, and mezzotint engraver of various subjects. After his uncle's death he became an Alderman of the City of London.

Peter Monamy (1681-1749), the elder statesman of British marine painting, enjoyed popularity with prints issued individually, as well as sets of prints, published in the first half of the eighteenth century. In around 1740 he was commissioned to paint a series of four large-scale marines for Vauxhall Pleasure Gardens, a leading London attraction in the eighteenth century. Under the ownership of Jonathan Tyers, Vauxhall offered paying visitors a range of outdoor and indoor attractions, including elegant formal gardens, visually exciting architecture, music, decorative arts, and a choice of 'supper boxes' in which to dine, decorated by leading contemporary artists of the day.

Monamy's original oils for Vauxhall have not been traced but their subjects are known through extant engravings by Paul Fourdrinier (active 1740s-50s) and Remy Parr (1723-c.1750). Parr engraved 'The taking of Porto Bello by Vice Admiral Vernon', published by Thomas and John Bowles and Son in 1743 (see page 72). Bowles and Carver's 1795 catalogue featured engravings described as: 'Five Sea-Pieces in Vauxhall Gardens, after Monamy: Sweet William's farewell to Black-eyed Susan, a Sea engagement, between the English and Algerines, the taking of Portobello by Vice-Admiral Vernon, the taking of the Princessa, a Spanish man of war.' The first four subjects were painted by Monamy for his commission for Vauxhall Gardens in the 1740s. 'The taking of the Princessa, a Spanish man of war' was painted at a later date. A small-scale version of the oil painting described as *The Taking of the St. Joseph, a Spanish Carracca Ship*, is now in the National Maritime Museum, Greenwich. The popularity of the Vauxhall series probably encouraged Monamy to paint smaller scale versions, and perhaps a replica set.

'Original Sea Pieces and Shipping, by P. Monamy, representing many of the capital ships of his Majesty's Royal Navy in various situations' were featured in Sayer and Bennett's *Enlarged Catalogue of New and Valuable Prints...* of 1775. There were twelve prints priced at 12s for the set. A customer could purchase individual prints, but would be charged a higher price. The set included *A Calm*, *A fresh gale*, *Morning, or Sun Rising*, *Evening, or Sun Setting*, *Moon-light*, *Night, and a ship on fire*, *A strong gale or a squall*, *Shipwreck*, *Chace*, *Commodore Anson in the Centurion...*, *The Nottingham, Capt.*

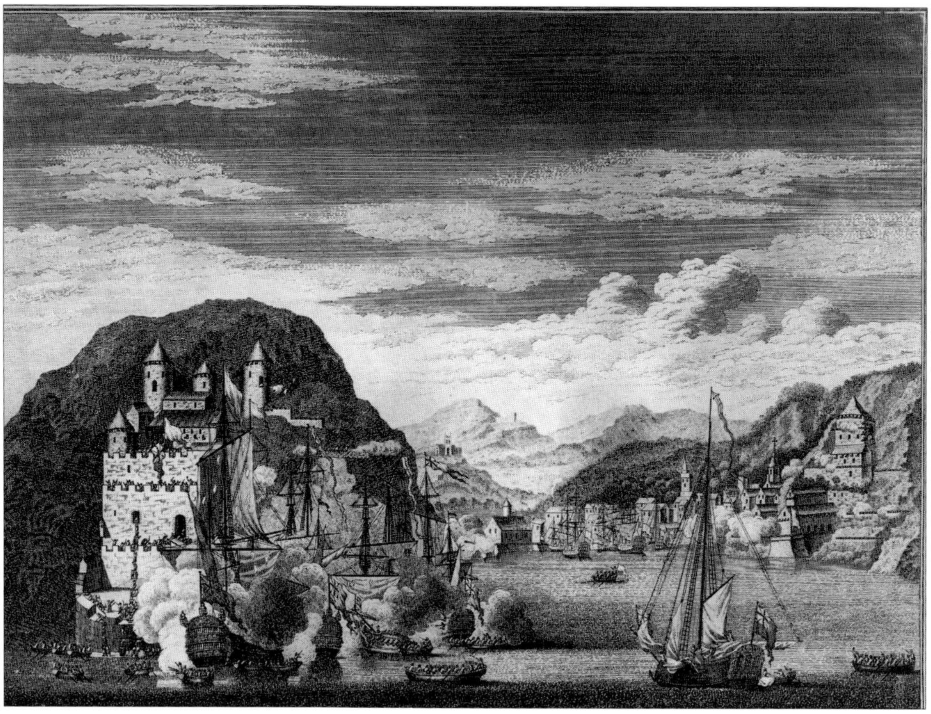

5/7
Engraving by Parr, after Peter Monamy. *The taking of Porto Bello, 22 November 1739.*
Private Collection

Saumarez, taking the Mars, and *A general engagement between two squadrons*. The dimensions of the prints were listed as '...12 inches deep, and 16 inches wide...' There was an additional note reminding collectors that '...They may be had neatly coloured after the original paintings', although no price is mentioned.

This set of Monamy engravings had in fact originally been published by John Bowles between 1745-46. Bowles included English and French titles on the prints and sometimes acknowledged the owner of the original oil painting. For example, *Morning, or Sun Rising* was from the collection of Baptiste-May, and the engravings entitled *Moon Light* and *A Strong Gale or Squall* were after oil paintings from the collection of Alexander Stuart.

Sayer and Bennett also offered *Shipping from Monamy*, under a section called 'Drawing Books'. These 'Books' were designed to assist aspiring artists as well as for general interest. The 'Books' were described as '...New and Curious Drawing Books, Six Leaves in each' and were sold at sixpence each. Demand for Monamy's prints waned towards the end of the century. Although Boydell showed little interest in promoting his work, during the 1790s his prints were promoted by Bowles and Carver. Their *New and Enlarged Catalogue* of 1795 included the 'Twelve Sea-Pieces'. They were the same prints sold earlier by Sayer and Bennett.

Francis Swaine (c.1720-1783) would almost certainly have received some painting lessons from Monamy. In fact Harrison Wallace has established that Swaine was Monamy's son-in-law. Swaine married Mary Monamy at Allhallows, London in 1749. The son was called Monamy Swaine (c.1750-1770s). Of the meagre information we have on Monamy Swaine we know that he was baptised at St. Dunstan's, Stepney on 27 February 1754. In 1735 Francis Swaine is recorded working as a messenger for a department of His Majesty's Navy. By the 1740s he was probably established as an artist. Swaine was popular and prolific, and although his pictures are of uneven quality, he was capable of inspired work. It is known that he copied and adapted Brooking's pictures and occasionally their work has been confused. Swaine worked mainly for 'the shops' and according to Edwards he was prepared to try his hand at various commissions, including painting the 'face of a wind-dial, with sea and ships'.

Engravings after Francis Swaine's pictures '...of memorable Sea Engagements with

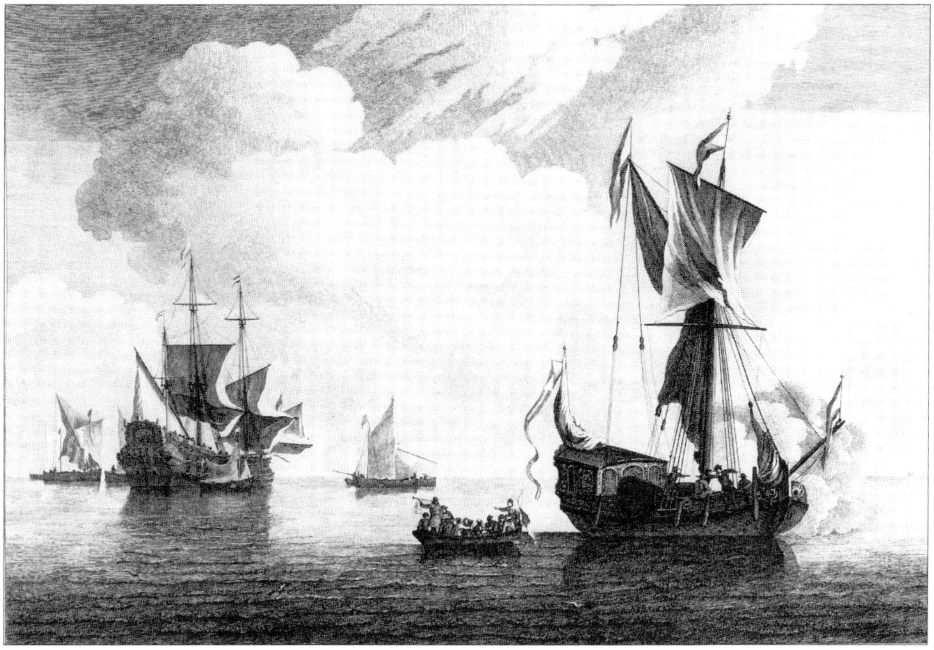

5/8
Engraving by Boydell. *A Calm* by Willem van de Velde the Younger (see illustration 5/5, page 70).
Private Collection

the French in the last War…' and two prints depicting incidents from the invasion of Quebec in 1759 engraved by P. C. Canot, were included in Sayer and Bennett's 1775 catalogue. The last named prints were priced at 4s for the pair. These prints were also featured in the Bowles and Carver's catalogue issued in1795.

In 1758 the March edition of *The Critical Review, or, Annals of Literature* (Ref: Vol 5, pp.265-66) announced that 'Mr. Scot [Samuel Scott] has lately favoured the public with two very agreeable views of the bridges of London and Westminster…' The anonymous art critic goes on to claim that 'the ingenious artist, to whom we are obliged for these prints is the only ship painter of any note or eminence now living; and, in the opinion of the judicious, no way inferior to the celebrated names of Vandervelde and Monamy…' A bold claim and notable for the absence of any reference to Brooking.

The writer is believed to be the editor of *The Critical Review*, Tobias George Smollett (1721-1771), who continued to offer some encouragement to Scott by way of open criticism of the British admirals: 'We heartily wish, that some of our admirals would, if it was only for the sake of encouraging the liberal arts, give this gentleman an opportunity of shewing his skill in the representation of, what we have almost forgot, a victory at sea.'

Scott certainly painted naval actions, notably the capture of the *Covadonga* by Anson's *Centurion*, 20 June 1743, Lord Anson's victory off Cape Finisterre, 3 May 1747, and French fireships attacking the English fleet off Quebec, 28 June 1759. Examples of these actions are in the National Maritime Museum, Greenwich. Although it is true that, once under the influence of Canaletto, he largely gave up sea battles in favour of painting views of wharfs, bridges, and notable landmarks along the River Thames, albeit in a more matter-of-fact style, Scott, like Canaletto and Vernet, would often animate his views with people going about their daily business.

Engravings by Canaletto (or Canaletti, as Sayer and Boydell and others called him), were in constant demand, especially his Venetian views. Boydell & Co. offered a set of twelve views engraved by Henry Fletcher (fl.1720s-60s) in their 1790 catalogue for 12s. Vernet also sold well and Boydell & Co. offered four of his engravings in their 1807 catalogue ranging in price from 2s for *A Shipwreck* in an oval format engraved by John Pye (1746-c.1790s) to Lerpiniere's engraving of *A Calm* at 10s 6d.

Scott's views of the bridges of London and Westminster were two of the best-selling prints after his work and they overshadow the prints engraved after his naval actions. The

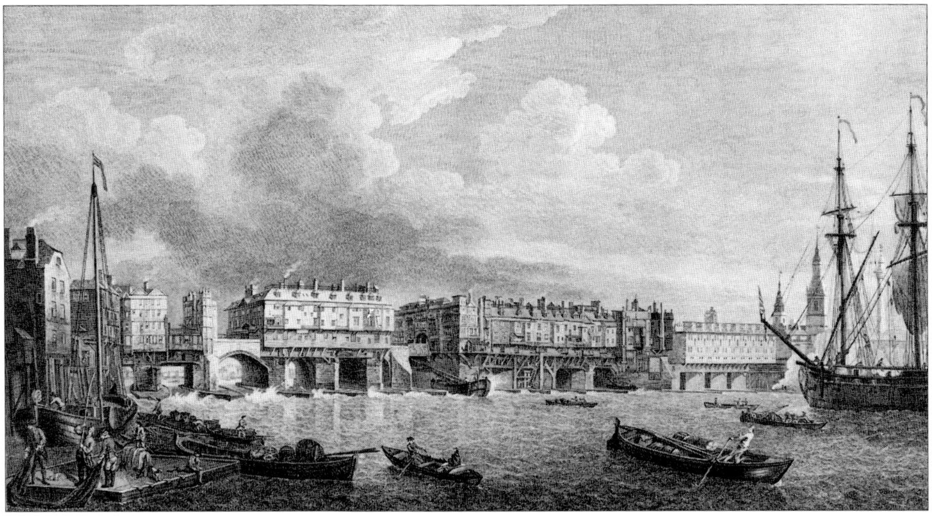

5/9
Samuel Scott's *A View of London Bridge before the late Alteration as in 1757*, published 25 February 1758, engraved by P. C. Canot.
Private Collection

views of bridges were promoted in several of the leading printsellers' catalogues throughout the eighteenth century. In Robert Sayer's 1766 catalogue Scott's views are described as: 'Two agreeable Views from capital Pictures, painted by Mr. Samuel Scott, and engraved in a masterly manner by P. C. Canot 1. London Bridge before the Alterations, as in the Year 1760 2. Westminster Bridge, with the adjacent buildings, as in the Year 1760. Each print is 21 and Half inches wide by 13, Price 5s the pair.' Scott exhibited a 'View of London Bridge as in the Year 1757' at the Society of Artists in 1761. The National Maritime Museum has an example of Canot's engraving entitled *A view of London Bridge before the late Alteration as in the Year 1757*.

John Boydell promoted Scott's views of the London bridges in his *A Catalogue of A Collection of Prints Now Engraving by Subscription from the most capital paintings in England...*, published on 24 June, 1767. The catalogue also included prints that were completed. Boydell's sales description of Scott's prints was prosaic in comparison to Sayer's entry. The prints were offered for 2s 6d each. Bowles and Carver offered the engravings in their *New and Enlarged Catalogue* of 1795 for 5s the pair, or 'Neatly coloured 12s'. They must have been popular as they were also listed in the 1807 Boydell & Co. catalogue as '...Prints, Books, and Works after the Most Celebrated Masters, Ancient and Modern' although the price of the prints remained the same as that stated in the 1767 catalogue.

In 1730 Scott was sub-contracted to the landscape painter George Lambert (1700-1765) to supply the shipping in a series of six paintings of the English East India Company's settlements for the Company's headquarters at East India House, in Leadenhall Street, London. The set of pictures comprising: Bombay, Fort William, Calcutta, Fort St George, Madras, Tellicherry and Cape of Good Hope and St Helena, was certainly completed by 1732. It is known that Lambert received £94 10s 0d for his greater contribution.

The East India settlement pictures attracted great interest and two sets of engravings are known. An inferior series of mezzotint prints were engraved by Elisha Kirkall, and published by John Bowles in 1734. Kirkall (c.1682-1742) is perhaps best known for his popular series of green-tinged mezzotint *Sea Pieces*, after Willem van de Velde the Younger, circa 1720, one of which, according to J. M. W. Turner, was his inspiration to be a painter. Brooking was almost certainly familiar with Kirkall's engravings and is likely to have had a small collection for nautical reference (see paintings 450A and B). In 1736 Kirkall's set of East India Settlement engravings was on sale for 15s. A second set, of superior quality, was engraved by Gerard Vandergucht (c.1698-1777) and published on 19 April, 1736. Both sets of prints were offered in the Bowles and Carver catalogue of 1795. Kirkall's series was printed in green.

Vandergucht was a gifted engraver and a printseller, stationer and picture restorer. His trade card of 1758, now in the British Museum, reveals that by that date he had moved his premises from Hanover Square to Grosvenor Square, also that he sold 'all sorts of

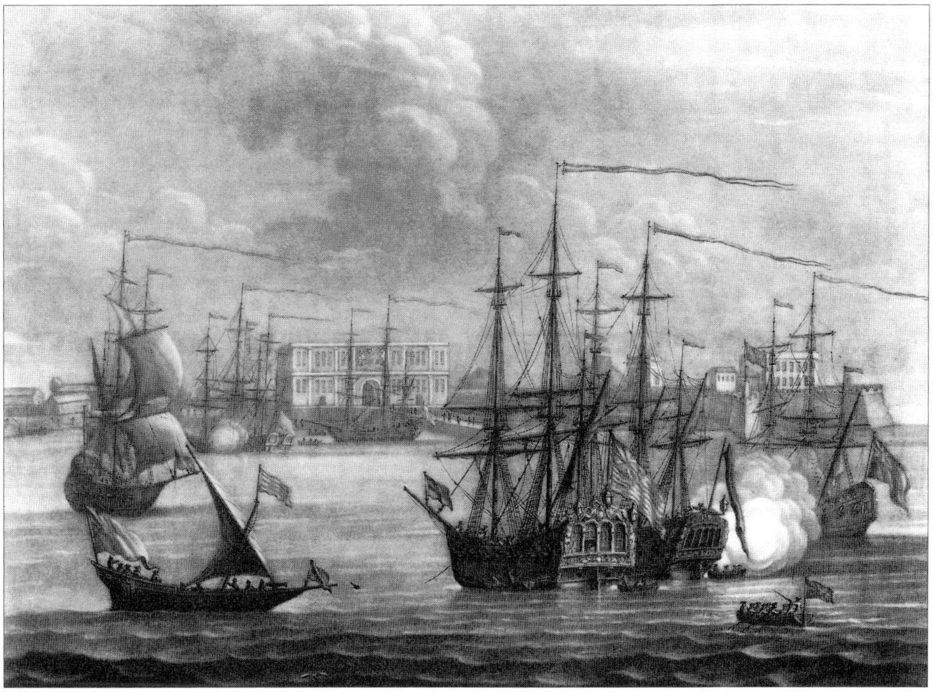

5/10
Samuel Scott and George Lambert, *Bombay Harbour,* engraved by Kirkall.
National Maritime Museum, London

Italian, Dutch, French & Flemish Prints and Drawings; both of the Ancient and Modern Masters…'

In January 1736 Vandergucht's set first appeared in *The London Daily Post and General Advertiser* inviting subscribers to make a down payment of one and a half guineas. In 1766 Robert Sayer's *New and Enlarged Catalogue* offered the Vandergucht set for £1 1s and claimed that the original paintings had been drawn on the spot. However, as Brian Allen has pointed out, it is unlikely that either Lambert or Scott visited the settlements and judging by the generalised background detail it would appear that the Company had not been particularly helpful in supplying visual reference material. That said, they are the earliest depictions in oils of these settlements and important examples of Anglo-Indian topography.

Brooking would have been familiar with the popular East India Settlement pictures, either the original oils themselves, or more likely the engravings.

Scott and Lambert also collaborated on a series of five views of Mount Edgcumbe engraved by James Mason and published in 1755. Mason (1710-c.1780) engraved several plates for Boydell, and collaborated with Canot, and François Vivares (1709-1780). The Mount Edgcumbe views were listed in Sayer and Bennett's *Enlarged Catalogue of New*

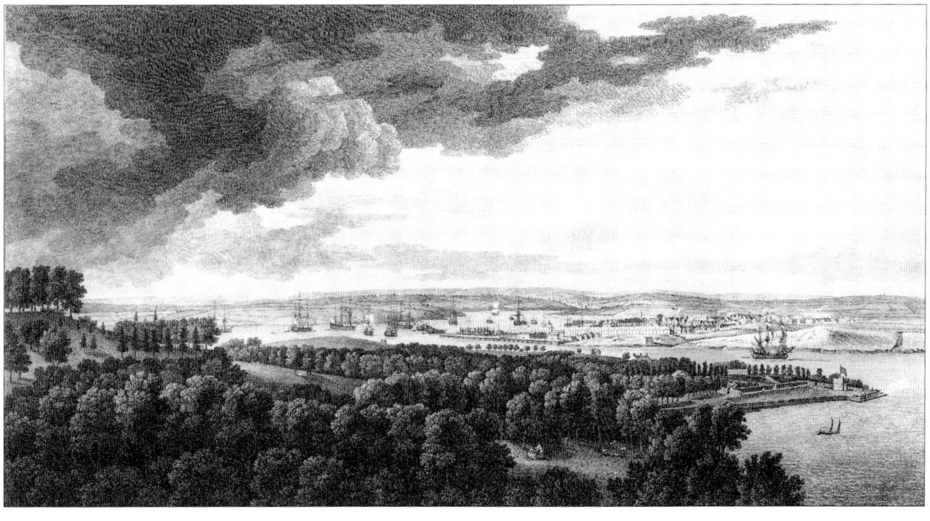

5/11
Samuel Scott and George Lambert, *Plymouth Dockyard from Mount Edgcumbe*, 1755.
National Maritime Museum, London

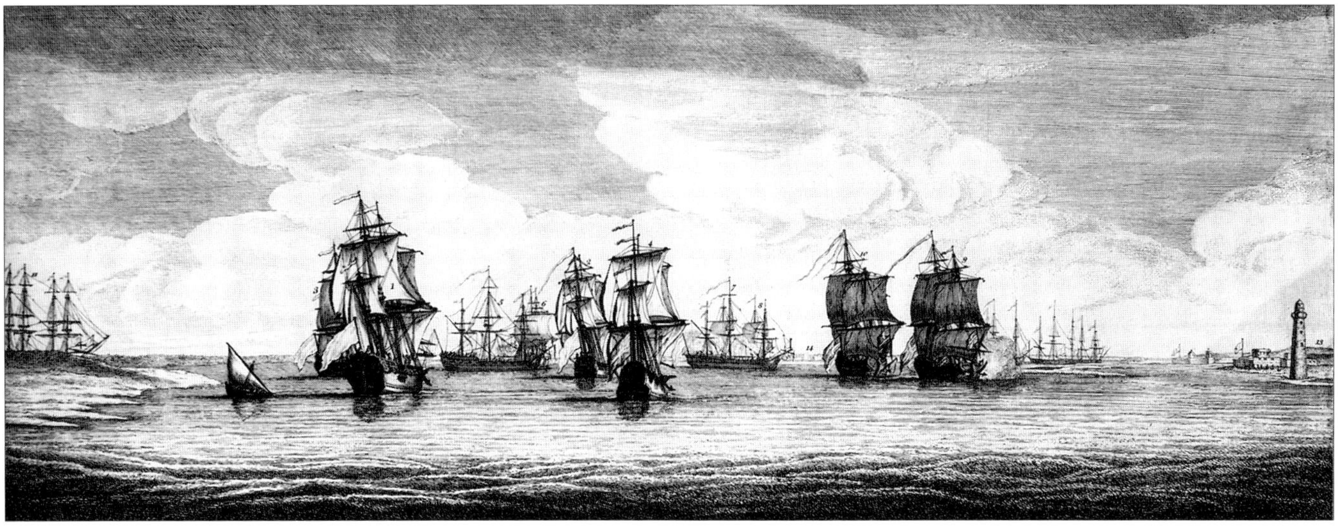

5/12
617 *An exact Representation of the taking of the Solebay Man of War by Captn Phillips of the* Alexander *Privateer of 20 Guns &140 Men belonging to Bristol.*

and Valuable Prints of 1775, as 'Five Views composed of Land and Sea, being Prospects of Plymouth and of Mount Edgcumbe, engraved by Canot and Mason. Price 15s the set', or 'Finely coloured, £1 10s.' John and Josiah Boydell's 1787 catalogue listed the prints at the lower price of 15s for the set. Bowles and Carver's 1795 catalogue also featured the prints at 15s plain, and 'finely coloured' for £1 11s 6d.

Maritime engravings after Brooking's work were among the most sought after of the eighteenth century. Judging from the number of entries in printsellers' catalogues, the artist was arguably the most popular English marine painter in print during the second half of the eighteenth century. The earliest recorded engraving after Brooking portrayed *An exact Representation of the taking the Solebay Man of War by Captn Phillips...* It was published by Thomas Bakewell (fl.1729-48) on 25 February 1753. Although Bakewell is less well known than Bowles, Sayer or Boydell, his business was successful and lasted until the third quarter of the century. Brooking's name is not actually acknowledged on the print, although it relates closely to his oil painting (see 358).

By 1729, Bakewell had taken over the business of Thomas Taylor, who sold foreign prints and maps, as well as glass pictures, oil paintings and frames from the Golden Lion in Fleet Street between 1710-26. In 1745 Bakewell re-located to Birchin Lane in Cornhill and after his death the business was continued by his widow, Elizabeth. She was joined by Henry Parker (1726-1809) who became a partner, and subsequently ran the business until the 1770s.

John Boydell's catalogue of 1767 was almost certainly the first to feature Brooking prints. They were listed as 'Six Sea Pieces, representing the most remarkable action of the Royal Family Privateers in the Years 1745 to 1748. Painted by Mr Brooking and engraved by Messrs Ravenet and Boydell, 14 by 19 in length. Price 6s'. Paris-born Simon François Ravenet (1706-1774) was a pupil of J. P. LeBas and was encouraged to settle in England by William Hogarth to engrave plates for his celebrated series of paintings entitled *Marriage-a-la-Mode*. In addition to marines, Ravenet also engraved and etched genre, landscape, and sporting subjects, as well as portraits and caricatures. Ravenet was made an Associate of the Royal Academy where he exhibited. He also exhibited at the Society of Artists and the Free Society.

The prints after Brooking's *Royal Family Privateers...* were originally published by Boydell in 1753 to be sold as a set, or individually (see catalogue illustrations 601, 608A, 609, 613, 616, and 620). Ravenet engraved two of the plates: *The taking of the Marquese de Antin & Louis Erasme...*, and *A View of the Prince Frederick privateer with the King George engaging the Gloriosa...* Eight preparatory and associated drawings for the set have been traced (see 707A-D, 710, 714, 721 and 722). There are also seven oil paintings extant that relate to the engraved series (see 351, 353, 355, 356, 357, 359 and 402A). If

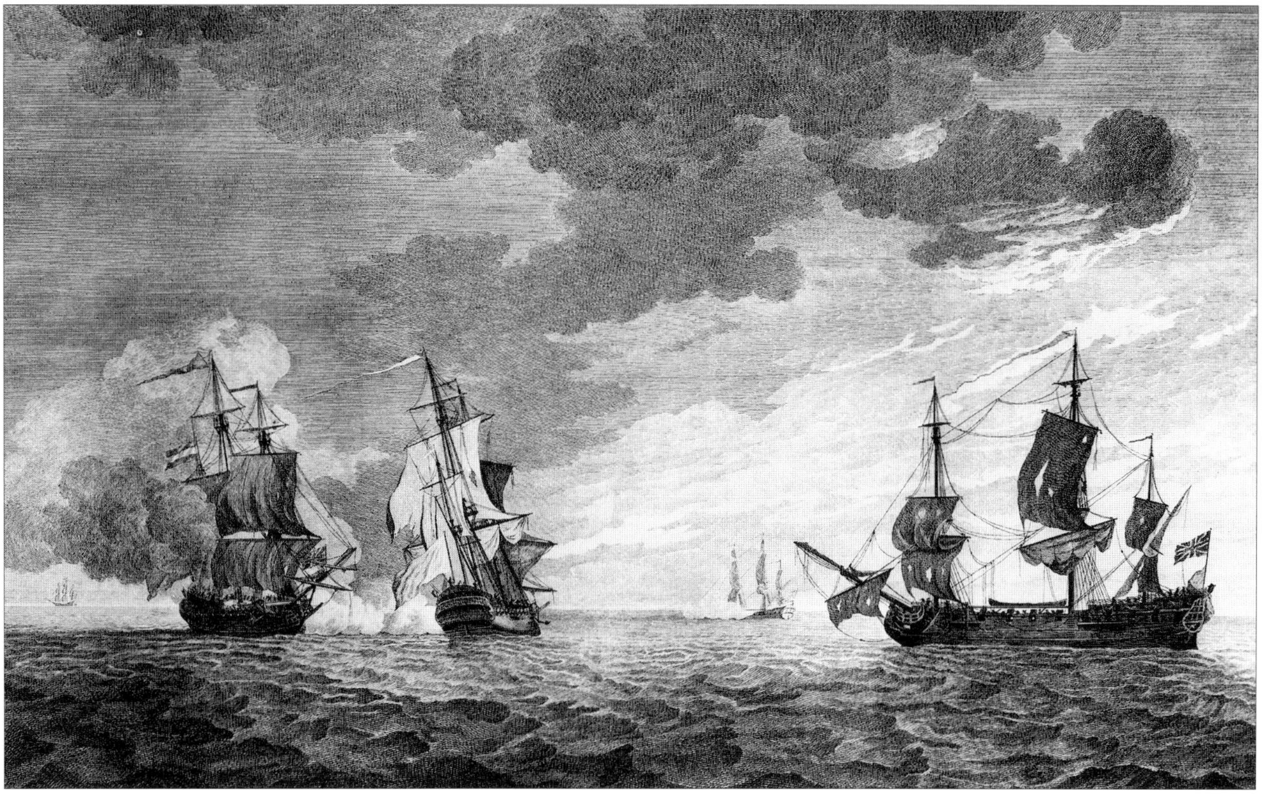

5/13
608B *Taking of the* Marquese de Antin *and* Louis Erasme *by the* Prince Frederick *and* Duke, *Privateers.*

Boydell had published catalogues in the 1750s then it is likely that the Brooking set would have been included.

The *Royal Family Privateers...* series was featured in the Boydell catalogue of 1787 priced at 10s 6d, and in the 1803 John and Josiah Boydell catalogue the set was offered for 15s. The series was also published by Laurie and Whittle in 1818. There is scant biographical information on James Whittle (active 1770s-1820s) and Robert Laurie, or Lawrie (c.1775-c.1838), who was a prominent London mezzotint engraver of various subjects. In 1776 Laurie was awarded a premium from the Society of Arts for inventing a method of printing mezzotints in colours.

Sixteen 'Sea Pieces, after Vandeveld and Brooking' were listed in John Boydell's 1790 catalogue *A Collection of Views in England and Wales... To which are added some miscellaneous subjects after various masters...* The prints were drawn and engraved by Boydell and priced at 'Five Guineas, in sheets; bound in calf, six guineas' (see illustration 5/5, page 70). The engravings after Willem van de Velde the Younger have been identified as *A Calm* and *A Brisk Gale*. There were also prints after Van der Neer, Vernet and Canaletto.

The itemised list of Brooking prints in Boydell's 1790 catalogue included: *Greenland Fishery*, *Privateers engaging French ships* and *A large view of Elizabeth Castle, in the Island of Jersey*. Two other subjects, *A View of the Port of Marseilles*, and *A view of the New Port, or the Arsenal of Toulon* appear from Boydell's promotional index to be by Brooking. However, an examination of the prints themselves reveals that they were in fact after the French artist Claude-Joseph Vernet. Vernet's ambitious series of French port views was commissioned by Louis XV of France. Boydell published engravings of Marseilles, the first painting to be completed, and Toulon in 1762. The paintings and engravings are full of maritime detail of the period. Vernet's work had little bearing on Brooking but it was influential on other English marine artists, notably Dominic Serres, and the Cleveley family of artists.

A remarkable series of views of English dockyards described as 'Six Prints of His Majesty's Dock-yards, elegantly Engraved, by Mr Canot, from the correct surveys made

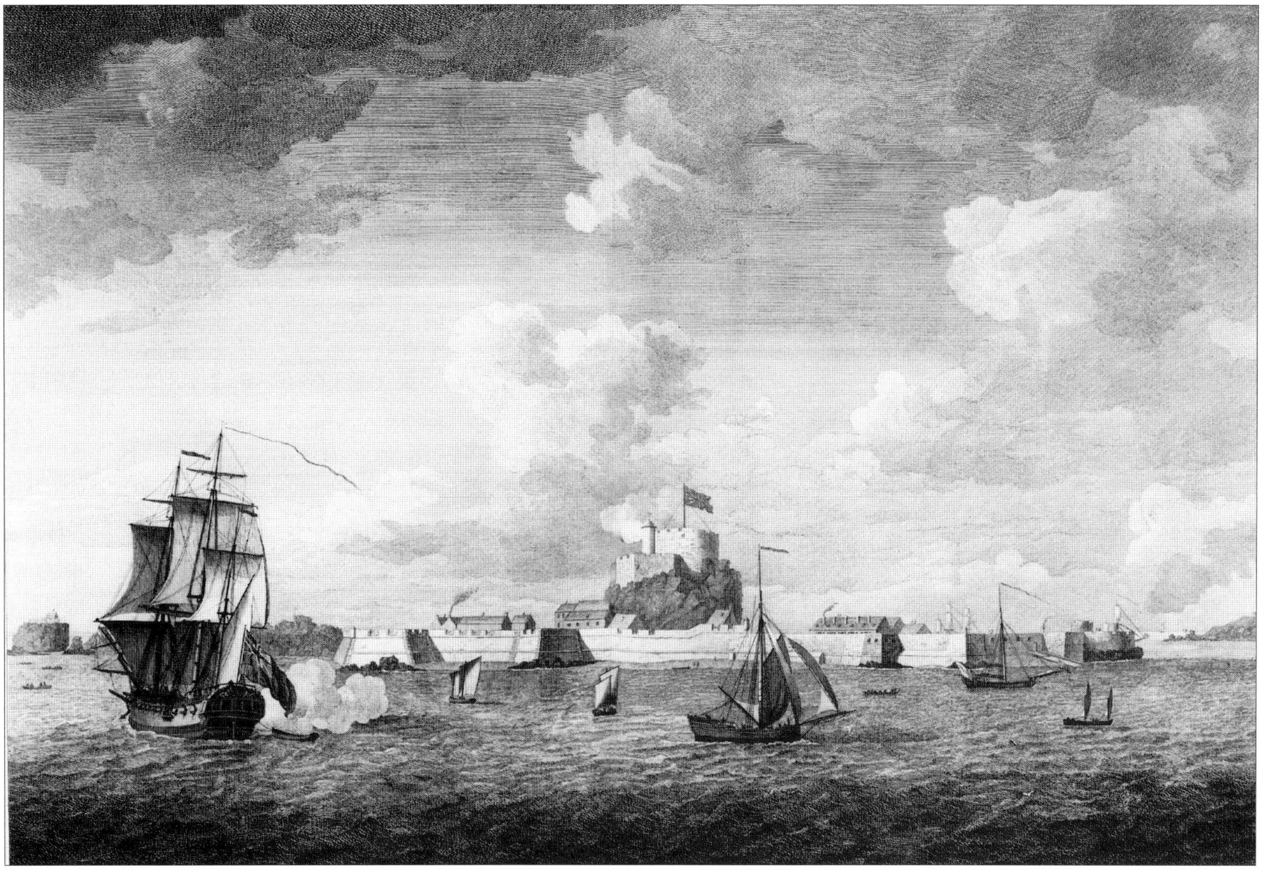

5/14
615B *East Prospect of Elizabeth Castle in Jersey*, 20⅞ x 28½. Published by John Boydell.

by Mr Milton' was in preparation at around the same time as Vernet's series. Milton's dockyard views were published separately: Woolwich (18 June, 1753), Deptford (30 July, 1753), Portsmouth (29 April, 1754), Chatham (2 September, 1755) and Sheerness (14 April, 1755) and Plymouth (2 February, 1756). The prints were issued as a set priced at 12s.

In Boydell's 1767 catalogue the set of engravings was carefully described. 'The Plates measure 26½ inches by 19½, and are divided into two parts. In the uppermost is given an exact view of the yard and town, with the shipping lying before it; and the division at the bottom contains a correct plan of the yard, with reference to each particular. Each print is decorated with an elegant border, in which it shows the method of building a Man of War, from its being first put upon the stocks, to the launching: Also the different proportions of a ship under sail, and correct views of the principal Men of War taken from the French in the late war.'

John Cleveley the Elder (c.1712-1777) was sub-contracted to provide the vignettes of ship building scenes, ship launches, naval actions and other marine subjects. Some of the original watercolour designs are in the National Maritime Museum, Greenwich. Generally referred to as John Cleveley the Elder, he was the senior member of a remarkable artistic family. His twin sons John Junior (1747-1786) and Robert (1747-1809) were also marine artists. A third son, James, was a carpenter on Captain James Cook's third voyage of discovery and he brought back sketches which John Junior translated into aquatints.

The Elder Cleveley was born in Southwark, London, and had been apprenticed to Thomas Miller, a joiner. Cleveley was probably a self-taught artist. It is believed that his twin sons received some tuition from the watercolourist and aquatinter Paul Sandby (1731-1809). The Cleveleys painted dockyard scenes, ship launches, ship portraits, harbour views, royal occasions and sea battles. They exhibited at the Royal Academy and

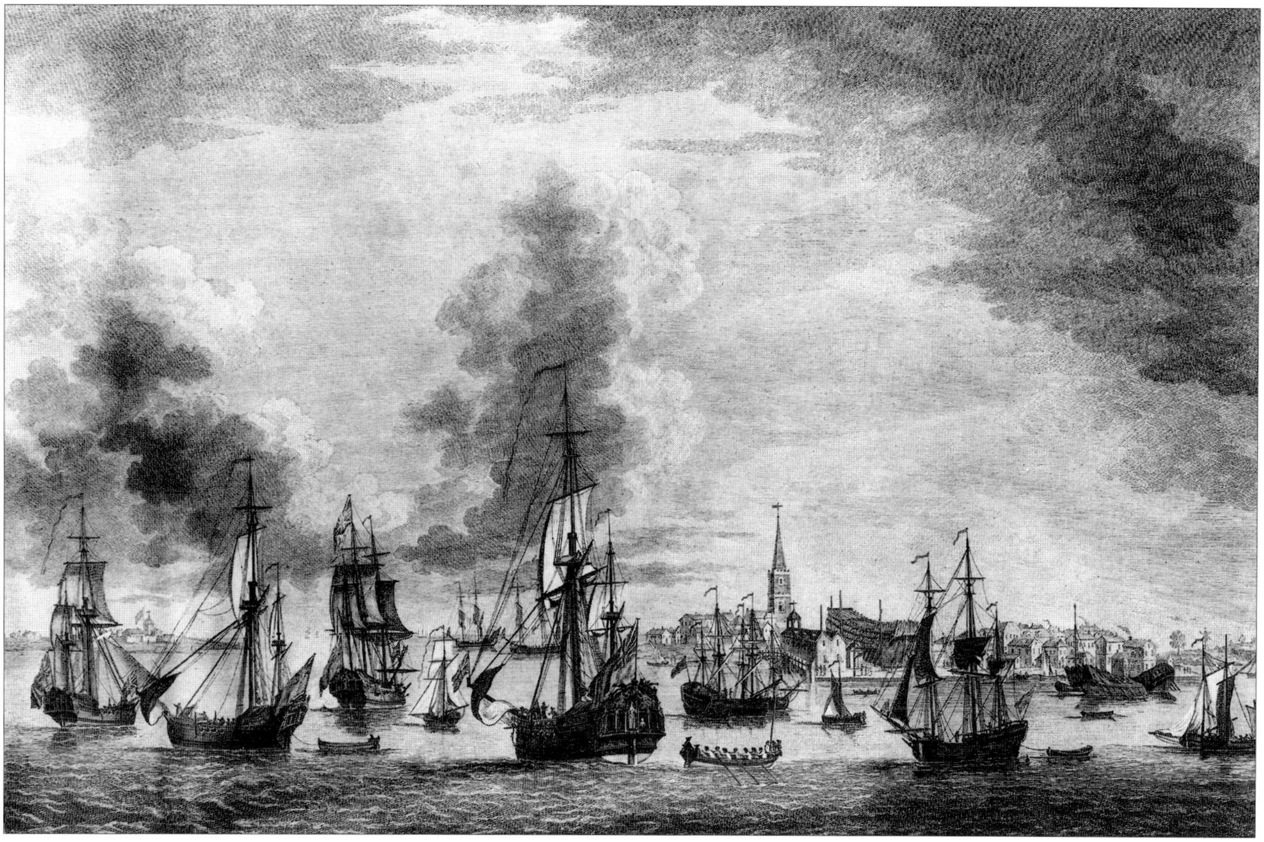

5/15
Thomas Allen, *Harwich*, engraved by P.C. Canot. National Maritime Museum, London

the Free Society.

Farington recorded that 'Robert Cleveley, the ship painter when young was bred a Caulker but not liking the business quitted it. Admiral Vandeput has been his great friend. He was clerk to the Admiral when Captn. of a Yacht & on other service...' The diarist also reveals that Robert was teased while he worked as a caulker for his habit of '...working in Gloves'. After his discharge in 1777 Robert was determined to be a painter. He was appointed 'Marine Draughtsman' to the Duke of Clarence, and was the only family member to enjoy royal patronage. His depiction of *The Rowing match at Richmond on his Royal Highness the Duke of Clarence's birthday* was exhibited at the Royal Academy in 1793.

John Cleveley Junior exhibited six drawings at the Free Society in London between 1767-80, including *A man of war going out of port*. His work in oils is rare. John Junior was selected as draughtsman for a Royal Society expedition to Iceland in 1772, and after his return he exhibited two views at the Royal Academy in 1773. In the following year he exhibited two 'tinted drawings' of the *Racehorse*, and *Carcass* in the ice at Spitsbergen during another Royal Society expedition led by Captain Phipps in an attempt to reach the North Pole. The expedition had departed on 3 June 1773. According to the polar specialist Ann Savours, Cleveley Junior was not in fact on the expedition but produced the 'tinted drawings' from sketches made on the spot by Midshipman Philippe D'Auvergne, later the last Duc de Bouillon.

Edward Edwards tells us that Cleveley Senior '...was brought up in some department in the dock-yard, at Deptford'. Edwards reveals a similar biographical detail about Brooking stating that he 'had been bred in some department in the dock-yard at Deptford, but practised as a ship painter...' It is likely that they would have been acquainted.

The Cleveley family of artists was not alone in becoming associated with a particular dockyard. Thomas Allen (active 1730s-70s) was described as 'painter to His Majesty's yard at Woolwich'. Allen exhibited fourteen marine subjects at the Free Society from 1767 to

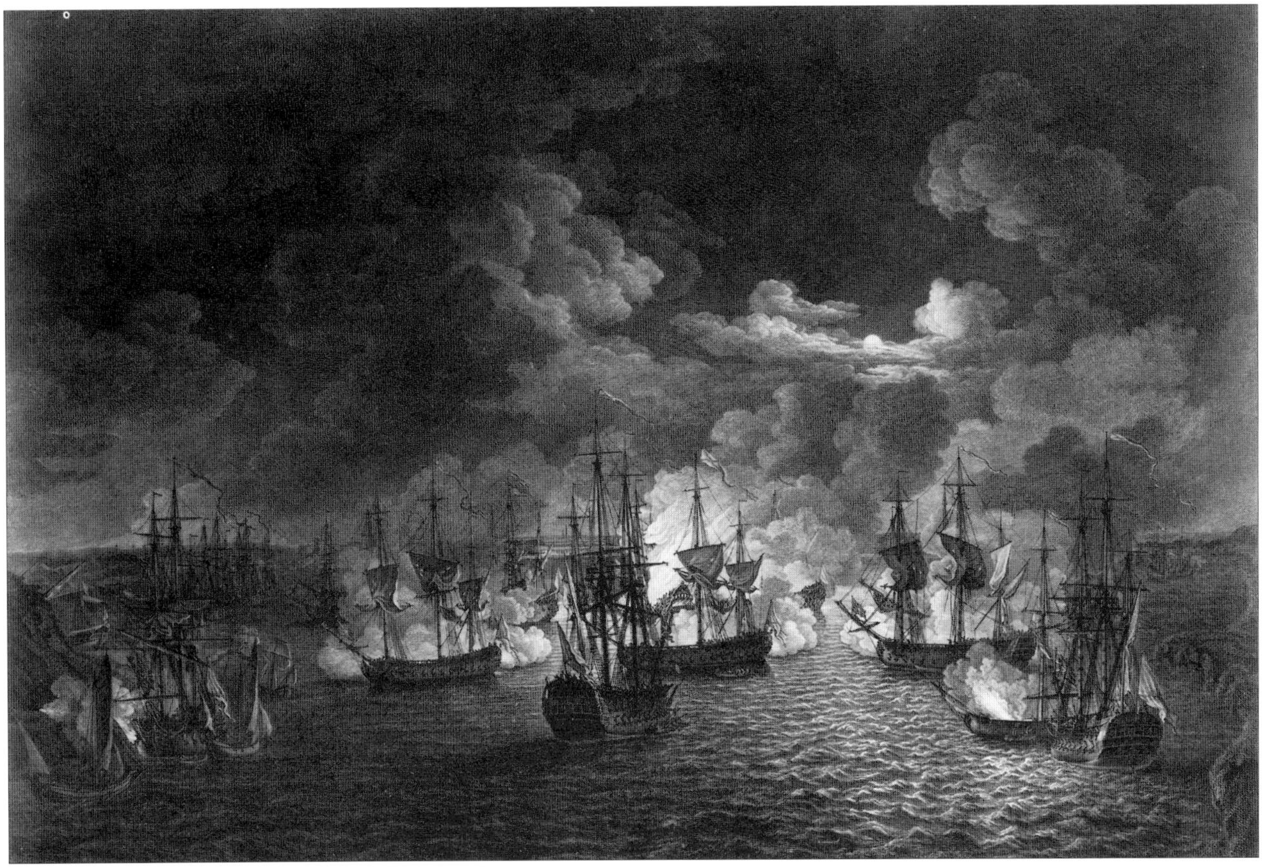

5/16
Richard Paton. *Russian fleet attacking the Turkish fleet, 6/7 July 1770.* Engraved by P. C. Canot.
National Maritime Museum, London

1772. His series of three oil paintings depicting the despatch of the English Royal Yachts to collect Princess Charlotte, the return voyage, and her arrival in 1761 were engraved by P. C. Canot. The set of three prints was listed in Bowles and Carver's 1795 catalogue priced at 15s for the set. The catalogue description also revealed that 'in order to make the designs, [Allen] performed the voyage outward and home, in the Mary yacht'.

Thomas Mitchell (1735-1790), like Cleveley Senior, also had first hand experience of the ships he painted. He was a shipwright to the Admiralty. In 1774 he exhibited his first oil painting at the Royal Academy entitled *His Majesty's Yacht* Augusta, from an address 'Of his Majesty's Yard at Deptford'. For a time he was 'Builders' Assistant' at the royal dockyard of Chatham. He exhibited sea-battles, royal yachts and general shipping scenes at the Free Society and the Royal Academy.

Although Mitchell had been barred from submitting any further pictures to the Society of Arts because of his disreputable conduct in removing an oil painting he had submitted for one of the marine painting competitions without prior permission, he decided nonetheless to submit an engraving to the Society of Arts maritime printmaking competition established in January 1769. It was decided that a premium, or prize, of 20 Guineas would be awarded 'For the best engraving of a Sea Piece (after a picture of which there is no print) not less than sixteen inches by twelve'. The claimants were instructed to produce the pictures together with the plates on or before the third Tuesday in March 1770. On 20 April 1770 it was revealed that Thomas Mitchell had won the prize, but as he had been barred from entering, the competition was cancelled. By March 1771 the Society of Arts decided to abandon the printmaking competitions. It is not known who else entered the competitions. Mitchell's submission has not been traced. His son, Thomas Mitchell, Junior, also exhibited at the Free Society in 1780 and was described as an engraver. Engravings after the Mitchells' pictures are rare.

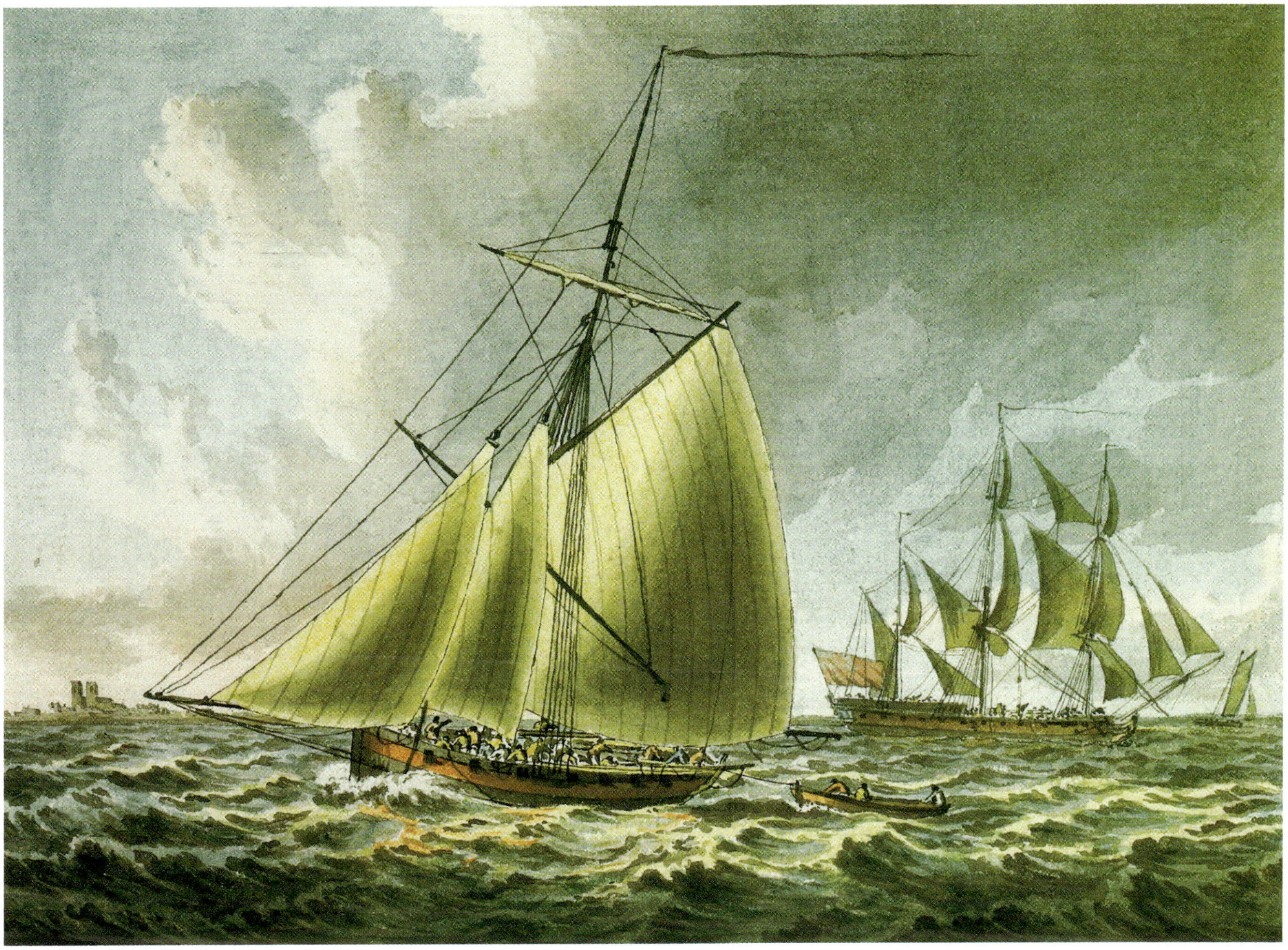

5/17
John Cleveley the Younger. *The Relentless*, pen and watercolour. Private Collection

The vague information supplied in eighteenth century sales catalogues and exhibition records has made it difficult to determine which John Cleveley painted a particular picture. The Elder and Junior painted and drew similar subjects, although Junior is better known for his watercolours and drawings, in which he exhibits considerably greater skill. His oil paintings lack the sophistication of his father's work. None the less they are full of nautical detail and charm. A small number of prints after the Cleveley family was featured in eighteenth century catalogues, and so presumably they sold fairly well.

In Bowles and Carver's 1795 catalogue it is likely that the 'John Cleveley' who supplied the drawings for the engravers to produce 'Small Drawing-Books' in which some plates were 'outlined only' ready to be coloured in, 'Books of Prints, or Demy-Sets', and landscape 'Views in Kent and Surrey' was actually John Junior. In the same print catalogue 'Six beautiful views of ships of different Rates in the Royal Navy of Great Britain drawn by John Cleveley...' were priced at '3s plain, or 5s colourd' and 'Six Striking Views of His Majesty's Dock Yards' specially designed for the perspective glass. Each print measured 17 by 11ins. John Junior's oil painting of Deptford and one of the handcoloured engravings after this subject are now in the Kreigstein collection, USA. In the 1770s the price asked for the coloured engraving was 2s.

The earliest recorded royal commission to paint a series of views of English ports, which often showed the dockyards, dates from the mid-1670s. King Charles II engaged the Dutch artist Hendrik Danckaerts (c.1625-1679) to paint the principal English ports of England and Wales, as well as the royal palaces for the Palace of Whitehall. Among those completed were views of Greenwich including Inigo Jones' Queen's House completed around 1638, and the ports of Portsmouth and Plymouth. All were painted in the traditional bird's-eye view format.

Richard Paton (1717-1791) and Robert Dodd (1748-1815) also painted dockyard views. Dodd completed a series of six views and engraved them as a set. Paton received permission from King George III to paint the Royal Dockyards but this ambitious project was not completed. Paton's decision to scale down the commission may well have irked the King, and perhaps for this reason he failed to gain an official royal appointment.

At the Royal Academy in 1776 Paton exhibited *A view of his Majesty's dockyard at Deptford and the royal Hospital at Greenwich, with the procession of the Trinity Masters...* The painting may have been finished in the previous year, or earlier, as the celebrated engraver William Woollett exhibited his engraving *A View of the royal Dockyard at Deptford; from a Picture of Mr. Payton* at the Society of Artists exhibition in 1775. Paton also described the painting as 'being part of a set of views of the royal dock yards'. This was an advertisement of what was intended to follow. Two years later he exhibited a *View of his Majesty's dockyard at Chatham.*

Richard Paton has been overshadowed by Dominic Serres, although Paton deserves greater attention. According to the recollections of the architect James Gandon: 'When a boy he is said to have attracted the notice of Admiral Sir Richard Knowles, who took him to sea in his squadron (I presume as his clerk, Paton having been well educated, and being an excellent accountant).' Edwards tells a different story, stating that '...he was born in so low a sphere of life, that Sir Charles Knowles took him out to sea, having found him a poor boy on Tower-hill.'

Paton held the appointment of Accountant-General in the Excise Office, and according to Edwards rose early so that he could paint for several hours before starting his official work. Apparently his 'appearance and manners were prepossessing, although to strangers he was reserved. His official duties and his close application to the arts, left him little time for mixing in society'. Like Brooking, he devoted himself to his work and this in part explains the lack of biographical details on their lives. Paton was encouraged by John Boydell, who presented several of his paintings to the Guildhall in London. Paton presented his series of pictures portraying the Destruction of the Turkish Fleet in the Bay of Chesme to the Empress of Russia who, Gandon informs us, 'in return sent him one thousand pounds, with a gold medal containing her portrait.' She had them engraved and gave the artist a further sum of six hundred pounds. Paton's work was engraved by Canot, James Fittler (1758-1835), Lerpiniere, Mason and Woollett. Fittler was an acclaimed line engraver of maritime subjects. He studied at the Royal Academy Schools and became an Associate of that Academy. He was appointed marine engraver to George III.

On 30 March 1792 the London auctioneer Mr Christie sold Paton's art collection at his Great Room in Pall Mall. This impressive collection reveals something of the artist's personal taste and working method. One picture by Brooking was itemised and described simply as *A Sea piece*. The sale also included pictures by Rembrandt, Brueghel, Rubens, Teniers and Ruisdael, and many of his own pictures, copper plates and prints, including his dock-yard views. Several of Paton's pictures are listed as 'from' or 'after Vanderveldt', and he shared the Dutch artist's interest in ship models to ensure nautical accuracy. The last lot of the sale was described as: 'A very accurate and complete model of a frigate, in a large mahogany case, glazed'.

It is doubtful that Robert Dodd amassed such an extensive art collection to rival Paton, although he was a prolific artist and printmaker. His six views of 'Dock-Yards', including Deptford, Blackwall, Woolwich, Chatham, Portsmouth and Plymouth, were published in stages. The first two were published 25 March, 1789, the next pair on 29 October, 1789, and the following prints separately on 1 September, and 1 November respectively. John and Josiah Boydell issued them as a set in their 1794 catalogue.

Robert Dodd has often been confused with Ralph Dodd (c.1756-1817), an engineer and artist, who is presumed to be his younger brother. Both exhibited at the Society of Artists

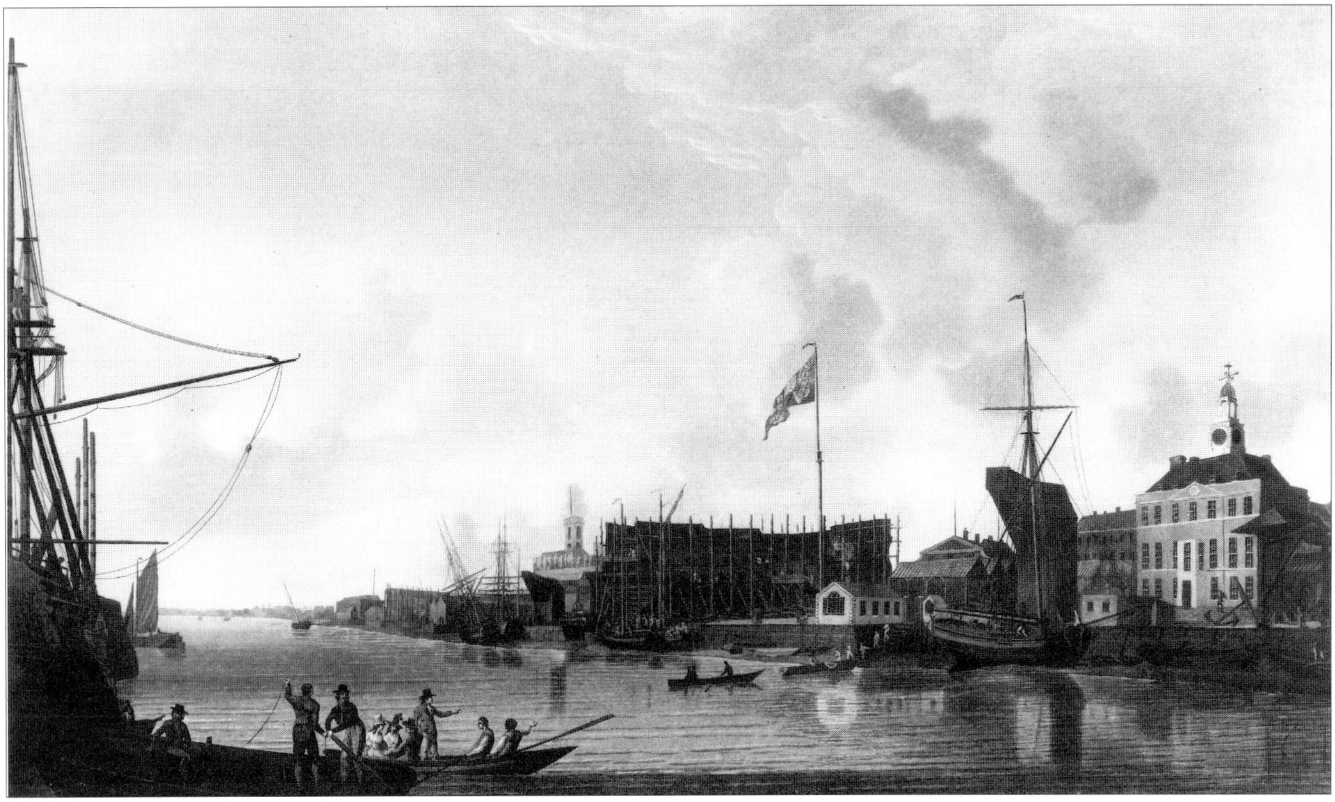

5/18
Robert Dodd. *Royal Dockyard at Woolwich*. Engraving, published by Boydell.
National Maritime Museum, London

and Royal Academy. It is now generally agreed that Robert was the principal artist, and he painted and aquatinted many incidents of the War of American Independence and the French Revolutionary Wars. Like Paton, he has been neglected by art and maritime historians. His work is often full of incident and of considerable charm, although his draughtsmanship is of variable quality.

There is little biographical information on the Dodd family and despite G. W. Younger's explorative articles on the Dodds in the *Connoisseur* in 1925 (Ref: 1925, Feb. pp.73-80, October, pp.87-94), in which he asked readers to furnish more information on the Dodd family, little has been forthcoming. It is believed that Ralph had firsthand experience of the sea, probably in the Navy. Robert Dodd painted a variety of subjects, although he is probably best known for his naval actions. Ralph Dodd, or more likely Robert Dodd, also exhibited the following subjects at the Royal Academy: *A small portrait of a gentleman; in oil colours* and *A Cat, and Rook, and Grey Cod*.

In 1784 the writer of the Royal Academy *Notes* [being a continuation of Sir Joshua Reynold's Pictures], commenting on Robert Dodd's exhibits of that year, spoke in glowing terms of this '...very promising Marine Painter'. Of one of Dodd's sea battles the anonymous witty writer observes: 'L'Amazone after an hour and a quarter's engagement, striking to his Majesty's frigate, Santa Monica, commanded by Captain Salter. The hulls, masts and rigging of the ships are delineated with architectural proportion, the hulls are bright and clear, equal to Backhuysen. The water possesses great transparency, and the distant sky good keeping. The rigging and sails of both ships appear shot to pieces. The damage seems mutual and if the enemy found the English Captain a SALTER, he proved himself a PEPPERER in return!' Although better known for his naval actions, Dodd's depiction of *The Royal Hospital, Greenwich from the Isle of Dogs*, painted in 1792, is now in the National Maritime Museum, Greenwich. Dodd also made a large engraving after his own design.

In general Dodd's prints, and those after Paton, did not enjoy the same popularity as Brooking's. John and Josiah Boydell's *An alphabetical catalogue of plates...* of 1803

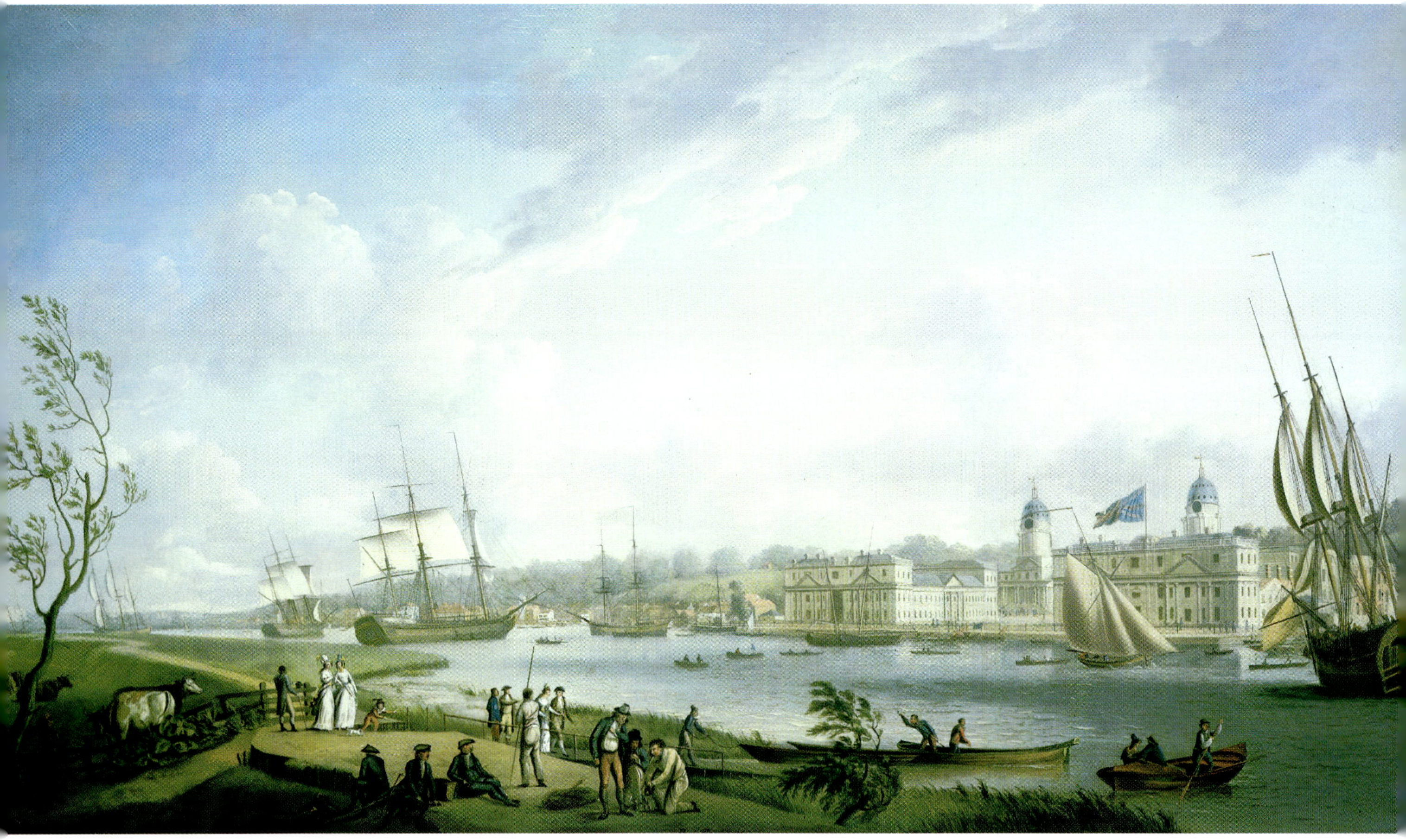

5/19
Robert Dodd. *Greenwich from the Isle of Dogs*. Oil on canvas, 33 x 56½, dated 1792.
National Maritime Museum, London

reveals that the engravings after Brooking were still selling well almost fifty years after his death. Fifteen engravings after Brooking are listed. Fourteen are itemised in the main section of the catalogue, with an additional item, *View of Elizabeth Castle*, engraved by Le Comte and priced at 1s, included in the section 'The Following PRINTS have been unavoidably omitted in their respective Places in the Catalogue'.

Brooking had almost certainly based his oil painting of Elizabeth Castle on the drawing made by James D'Auvergne (see painting 265 and engravings 615, 615A and 615B). In John and Josiah's catalogue of 1803 D'Auvergne was listed as a 'painter'. According to Philip Stevens, a specialist on Channel Island artists, Major-General James D'Auvergne (1726-1799) was the uncle of Philippe D'Auvergne, Duc de Bouillon (1754-1816), who produced an image of the South prospect of Mount Orgueil, Jersey, as well as a sketch of Prince's Town, Jersey. John Boydell also engraved the subject with a different title: *East View of Elizabeth Castle in Jersey*. This engraving is listed as measuring 28 by 20 ins and priced at 5s. A 'copy' of this subject measuring 19½ and 10½ inches was also available for 1s. Although it is tempting to suggest that the less expensive 'copy' was the engraving after Brooking, the dimensions of the prints do not correspond. John and Josiah Boydell's catalogue of 1803 reveals the Brooking print to measure 16 by 11 inches. So it is almost certain that three engraved versions of Elizabeth Castle of differing sizes were issued. Laurie and Whittle reissued the Boydell catalogue print of 1803 on 24 June, 1818 (see 615A).

Although there are several French engravers named Le Comte, or Lecomte, none appear likely candidates. Benezit lists the Paris-born engraver and amateur artist, Marguerite Le Comte (c.1719-c.1786) and although she was active during this period the association is speculative.

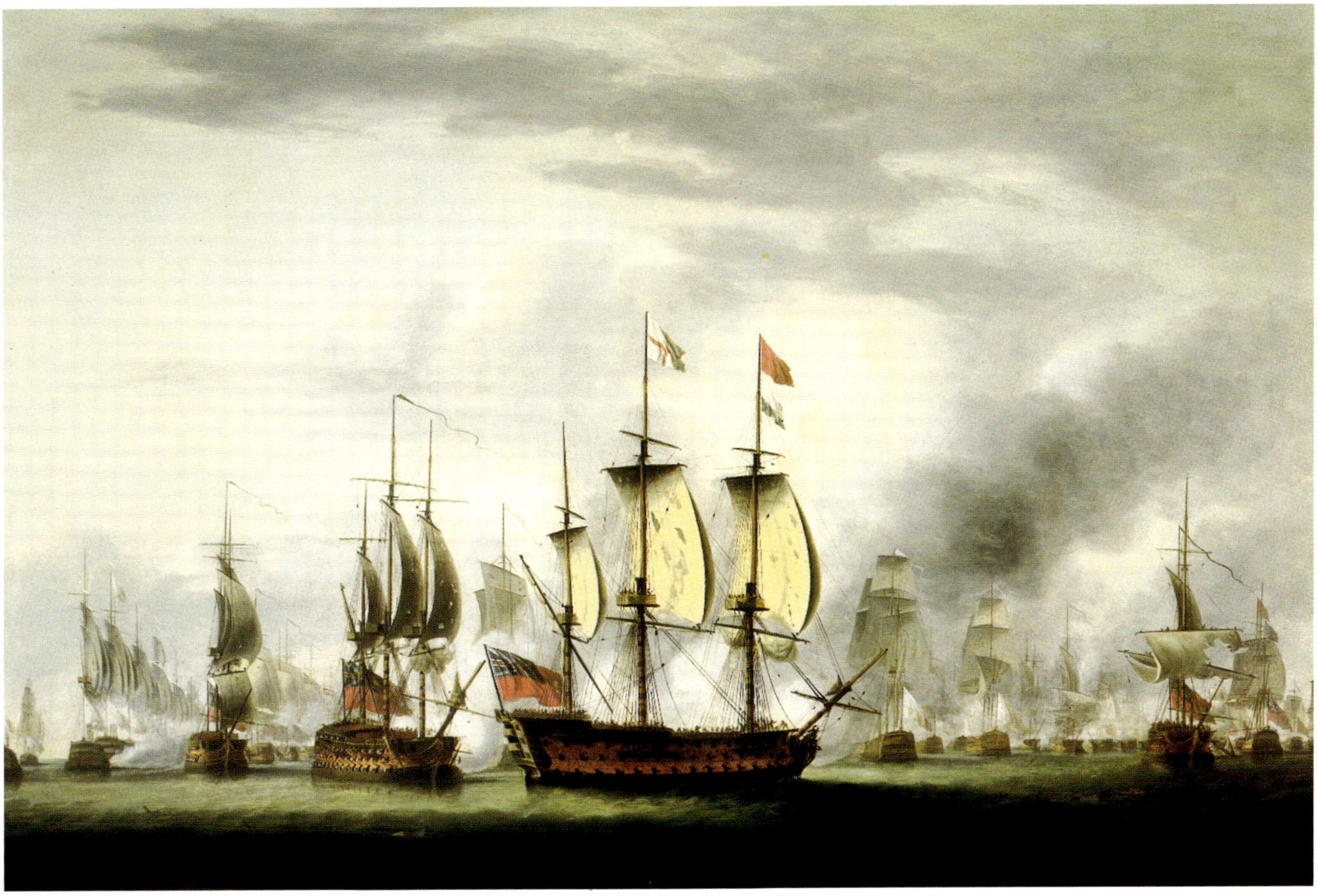

5/20
Robert Dodd. *Battle of the Saints*. Oil on canvas, 32½ x 49½, not signed. The picture shows Sir George Rodney's flagship, the *Formidable*, centre foreground, 98 guns. Richard Green Gallery

John and Josiah Boydell's 1803 catalogue also featured the following numbers of prints after some of the principal marine painters of the period: one after de Vlieger, two after Scott, three after Van Goyen, four after Vernet, nine after Dodd, ten after the van de Veldes, eleven after Paton, twelve after Canaletto, fifteen after Serres, and the same number after Brooking. Van de Velde engravings were still commanding good prices with the cheapest available at 1s 6d. A Brooking could be purchased for 1s and was therefore more readily affordable. In part this would explain the popularity of the Brooking prints.

It is well known that Brooking copied, adapted and updated, or 'modernized', the compositions of the van de Veldes, and other marine painters of the seventeenth century. For example *Hazy Weather* (see engraving 610A) is openly described as being 'After an Original Picture of Vanderveldt'. The inscription on *Sun Setting* (see engraving 607) reveals that it was 'Engraved from picture of Vandeveldes modernized'. Both prints were published by Boydell, who would have been well aware of the consequences of artistic piracy, although it was an excellent sales ploy to associate Brooking with one of the most acclaimed names of marine painting. A Brooking print inspired, or copied, from a van de Velde was considerably cheaper to purchase than a Canot engraving after one of these Dutch artists.

Brooking's oil painting of the *Whalers in the Ice* (see 22A) ranks highly among his most accomplished work. It was also a popular subject. Three engravings after Brooking's composition are known, the first engraved and published by John Boydell in 1754 (605A). Robert Sayer also published a version engraved by Wilson. The publication date is not known but is probably of a later date. It is certainly of inferior quality. The engraver Wilson may be James Wilson (active 1740s-80s). His engraving of the *Greenland Whale Fishery* was after a picture by Sieuwert van der Meulen (c.1698-1730),

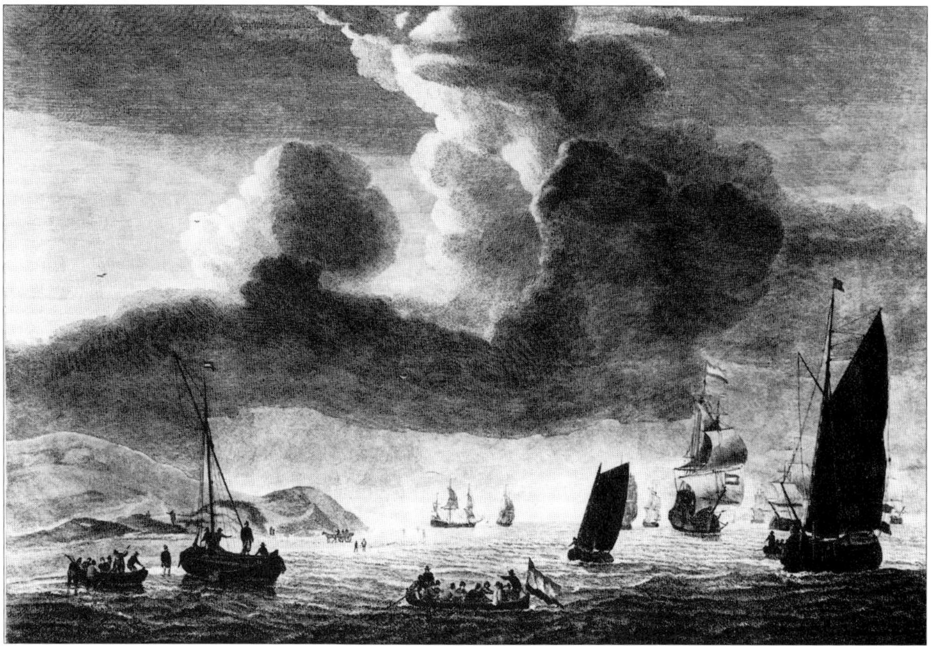

5/20
610A Charles Brooking. *Hazy Weather*. Engraved and published by Boydell.

a Dutch painter, draughtsman and etcher. Van der Meulen and other Dutch artists and printmakers, notably Adriaen van Salm (c.1660-1720), his son Roelof van Salm (1688-1765), Adolf van der Laan (c.1684-c.1755) and Adam Silo (1674-1766) popularised images of whaling and herring fishing in northern waters, and it would have been their compositions, either the original oils, or engravings, that Brooking would have turned to for inspiration. A third print, a coloured reverse copy of Sayer's engraving, is recorded in the Francis B. Lothrop Collection of the Peabody Museum, in Salem, Massachusetts.

Scenes of whaling and fishing in northern waters were also painted and engraved by Robert Dodd. Dodd exhibited a *View of the Whale Fishery in Greenland* at the Royal Academy in 1782. A print after the painting was published by John and Josiah Boydell on 1 January, 1789, and listed in their 1794 catalogue. Dodd's engraving of *The North-West of Davis's Straits Whale Fishery*, originally published by Boydell on 1 May, 1789, was also included.

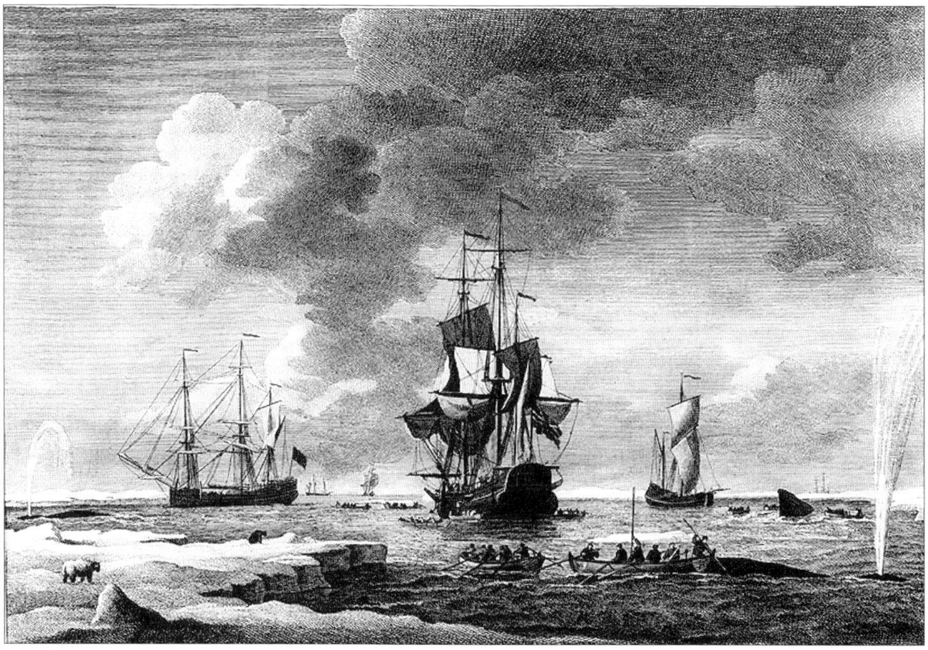

5/21
605A Charles Brooking. *Greenland Fishery*. Engraved and published by Boydell, 1754.

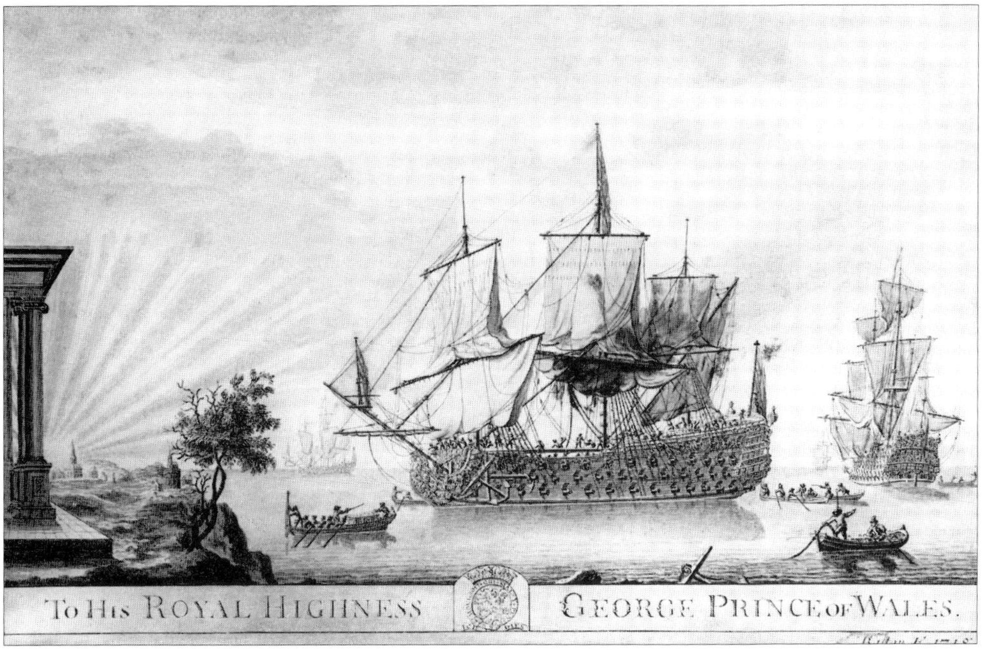

5/22
Thomas Baston. *HM Ship* Britannia, *a 1st Rate.* Engraving and etching, published *c.*1730.
National Maritime Museum, London

Thomas Baston (active 1700-c.1725) drew scenes of fishing and whaling that were published by Bowles and Carver's *New and Enlarged Catalogue* of 1795. This catalogue included: 'Ten Views of the Royal Navy and Fishery of Great Britain' and included *The fishery of Great Britain, viz herring, cod, and Whale Fishery* and *Greenland, or Whale Fishery*. Priced at 1s plain or 2s coloured. Earlier Thomas Bowles had published 'Twenty two Prints of several of the CAPITAL SHIPS of His Maj.ties ROYAL NAVY with Variety of other SEA PIECES after the drawings of T. Baston' circa 1725. Elizabeth Ingalls, the cataloguer of the Francis B. Lothrop Collection of whaling prints, believes that the early date of circa 1721 ascribed to Baston's prints is unlikely, as the first English whaleship under the South Sea Company and Sir John Eyles did not arrive in Greenland waters until 1725.

Examples of Baston's preparatory designs for this series, including *A First-rate Man-of-war in a Calm at Sun Rising*, dated 1718, are in the National Maritime Museum, Greenwich. Little is known of Baston, whose style has an affinity with that of Peter Monamy and Isaac Sailmaker. Baston's designs were engraved by Elisha Kirkall and by

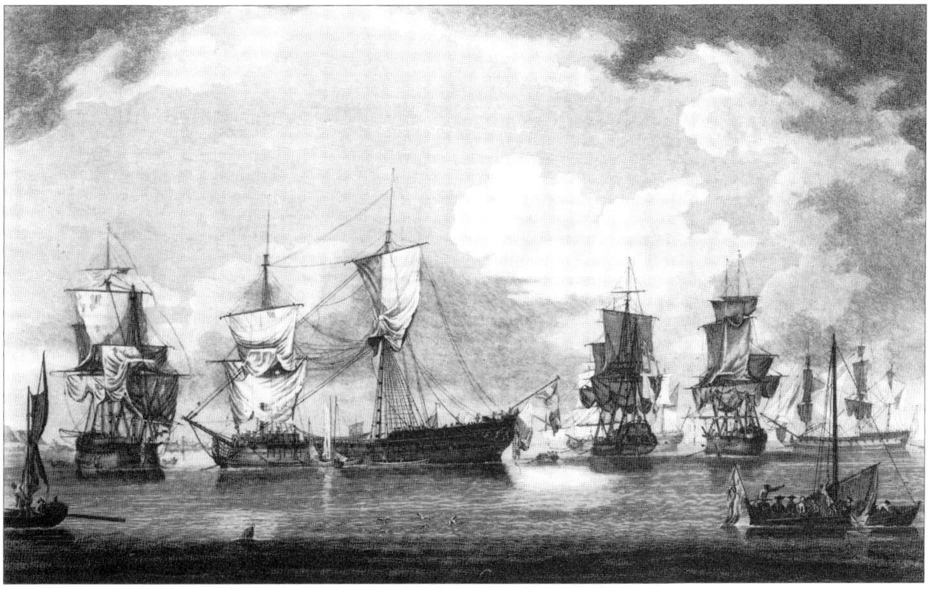

5/23
Richard Wright. *Ramsay Bay, the Isle of Man, 28 February 1760.* Engraving, published 30 May 1762.
National Maritime Museum, London

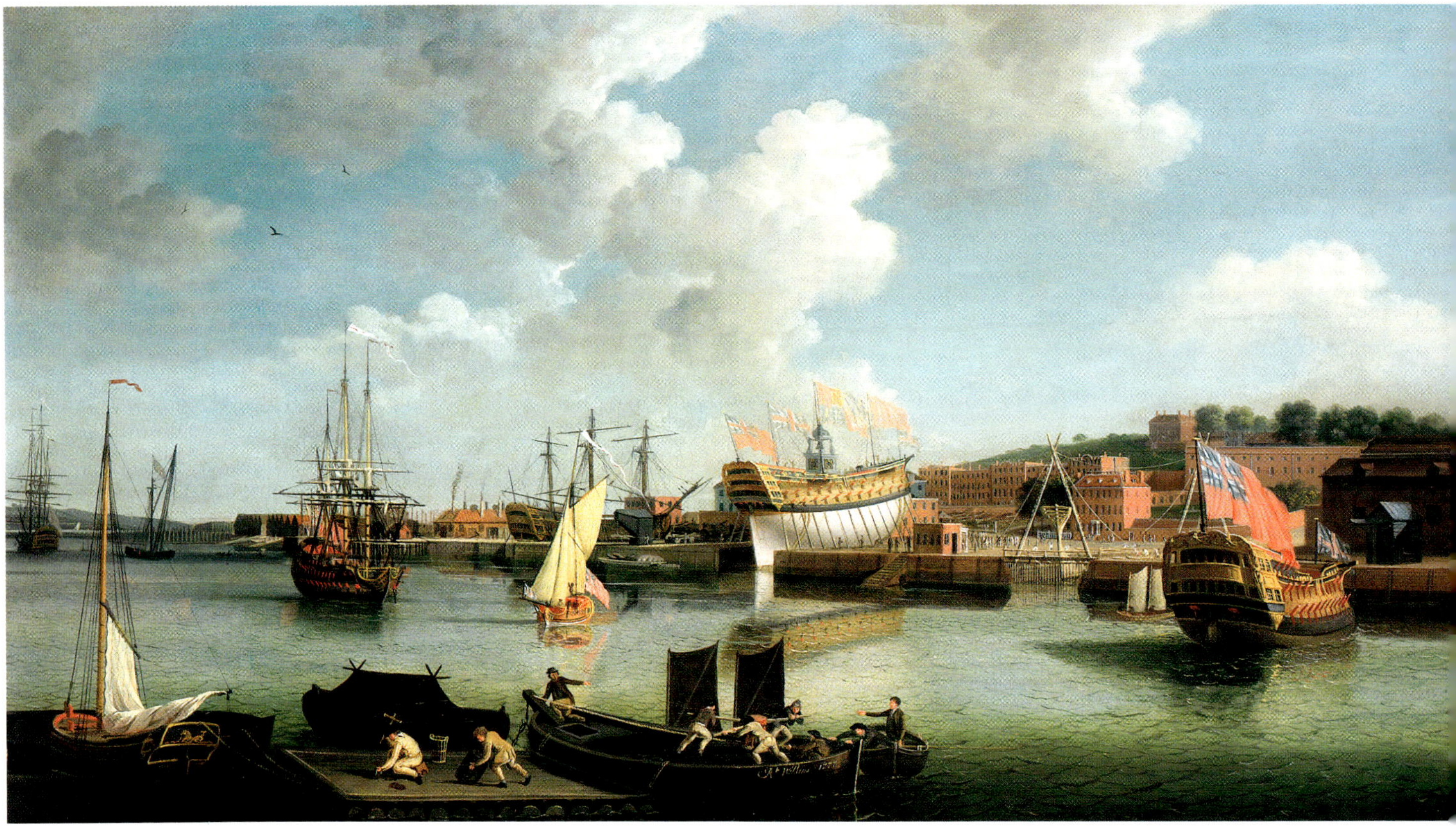

5/24
Robert Wilkins. *Woolwich dockyard,* oil on canvas, 29¼ x 54, signed and dated 1777.
Richard Green Gallery

James Cole (active 1708-46), a printmaker and seller who kept a shop at the Crown in Great Kirby Street, Hatton Garden.

The most popular marine subject associated with fishing was painted by Richard Wright (1735-1775). *A Sea Piece, with a Squall of Rain*, or *The Fishery*, as it is generally known after the title of William Woollett's engraving, was awarded the first premium, or prize, for the marine painting competition organised by the Society of Arts in 1764. The prize-winning painting was exhibited at the Free Society in the same year. Woollett's engraving was published in 1768 and exhibited at the Society of Artists in that year. It was one of the most popular of all maritime prints and was featured in many printsellers' catalogues. In the Boydell catalogue of 1803 it was priced at 10s 6d. William Woollett (1735-1785) was one of the most accomplished printmakers of his generation. In 1775 he was appointed honorary engraver to King George III. Woollett was a member of the Society of Arts, and also received an award from the Society for a drawing of a nude, which survives in the Society's archives. He worked for John Boydell, among others. Woollett received a premium from the Society of Arts for his contribution in raising the standard of British printmaking.

According to Edward Edwards, a contemporary writer and artist, Wright 'paid a compliment to the Society, by introducing an allusion to their encouragement of the scheme for supplying the metropolis with fish by means of a land-carriage'. This bizarre composition, inspired by the stormy coastal scenes of Vernet, exists in several painted and engraved versions. It has not been possible to identify the original, although it is known that the Society of Arts had advertised for 'the best original Sea Piece on a canvas 5 feet 6ins in length and 3 feet and a half in height'. Whether the submitted painting actually corresponded to these dimensions is open to question.

Wright was born in Liverpool. He befriended the celebrated animal painter George Stubbs, and for a time they shared a studio in London. Wright was a self-taught artist of little original talent, although possessed of a talent for selecting popular and prize-winning subjects, usually copied, or adapted, from other artists. In addition to his success in 1764, he also received the first premium for his *Sea-Pieces* submitted to the Society of Arts' painting competitions in 1766, and in 1768. Wright also painted naval actions. His engravings were often expensive at 5s each, or 10s for a pair.

Wright's flair for self-promotion was unrivalled among English marine artists. One of a pair of prints dedicated to the Worshipful Corporation and Merchants of Liverpool portrays 'a view of both squadrons lying in Ramsay Bay in the Isle of Man after the defeat of the daring Mons Thurot who was killed in the action the 28th of Feb 1760.' An inscription on the companion print was clearly intended to promote sales as it stated that the engravings could 'be had at Mills Coffee House opposite the Admiralty, and Grigsby's Coffee house side of the Royal Exchange, and at Mr Millers Printshop in Maiden Lane'. The prints were engraved by John Goldar (1729-1795) and John Miller (active 1740s-80s). Wright had based his paintings on pictures 'drawn from the Real ships by...Capt. Elliott'.

In 1768 the Society of Arts' competitions to encourage English marine painting abruptly ended. There had been a public media outcry in the London newspapers alleging that the Society's marine and landscape competitions had been rigged. Blame was passed to one of the Society's active Members, Jared Leigh, an amateur marine artist, who according to Mortimer's *Director* (1763) was 'by profession, an Attorney'. After an official enquiry in which Wright himself was asked to submit evidence, it was revealed that Leigh was the culprit, and that he had colluded with the marine artists Thomas Mitchell and Robert Wilkins (active 1760s-1770s). Leigh resigned before he was expelled and the last two named were barred from entering any further competitions.

The Society of Arts awarded premiums to John Cleveley the Elder (third prize 1765), Thomas Mitchell (second prize 1766), Francis Swaine (second prize in 1764) and Robert Wilkins (third prize 1766). By the 1760s Dominic Serres was already established as a marine painter and so he probably did not enter the competitions. If Richard Paton and Francis Holman (1729-1784) submitted pictures, there are no records of them winning a prize. Holman was a notable marine artist of merchant ship portraits, ship launches and occasional naval actions, although prints after his work are extremely rare. Unfortunately a list of those who entered has not been traced, if indeed one had been compiled.

Dominic Serres was a popular artist in print and one of the most successful marine painters of the eighteenth century. He was born near Auch in Gascony and attended the English Benedictine school at Douai. It is believed that his uncle was the Archbishop of Rheims. In order to avoid his family's wishes for him to pursue a religious career, he ran away firstly to Spain and later to the West Indies. After some time in Havana (other sources state that Serres visited Havana in 1752) he enlisted on a Spanish ship and was captured by the English in 1748, or 1749 and brought to England where he was interned at Marshalsea prison. After his release Walpole's *Anecdodes of Painting* reveal that he '...settled in a shop upon London-Bridge; whence he removed to Piccadilly, nearly opposite the Black Bear inn, where in a small shop, he exposed his pictures at the window for sale, which were mostly sea views, and sometimes landscapes'. From this situation he developed his reputation, and enjoyed patronage from, among others, 'gentlemen of rank in the naval department'. In 1768 he was the only marine painter to be appointed as a founder member of the Royal Academy.

By 1772 the King acknowledged his achievements by appointing him as an honorary marine painter. Not surprisingly, among the various subjects Serres painted were portraits of royal yachts, and naval reviews and state occasions. He also painted landscapes. In addition to being a painter he was also a skilled printmaker, and etched and published a series of six prints illustrating naval officers' and seamen's dress in November 1777.

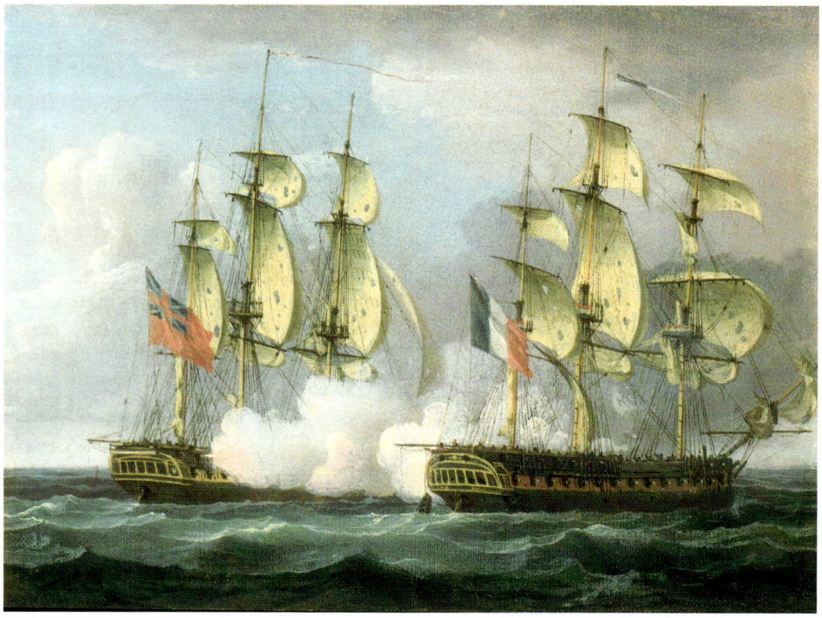

5/26
Thomas Whitcombe. *The capture of the 42-gun French frigate* L'Immortalité by Fisgard, *24 October 1798.* 7½ x 10½ engraved by James Jenkins. Richard Green Gallery

William Sandby's *The History of The Royal Academy of Arts* (Longman, Green, Longman, Roberts, & Green, London, 1862) considered Serres to be '...the best artist in that style of the time...[who]...acquired considerable renown as a painter of sea-pieces and landscapes. The gallant Lord Hawke and other naval commanders patronised him to paint their nautical exploits; and one of his most important pictures was a view of Lord Howe's engagement with the French and Spanish fleets off Gibraltar in 1782'.

A commentator in the *London Courant* of 6 May 1780 observed that Serres' exhibits of naval engagements at the Royal Academy, 'are very capital paintings; the events represented are rendered highly interesting; the shipping very highly finished and the sea expressed that accuracy of colouring which distinguishes the works of Brooken [Brooking] and Monamy'.

In addition to the tuition Serres is traditionally believed to have received from Brooking, it is likely that he was assisted by his friend Paul Sandby who was his neighbour in St. George's Row in Hyde Park. It is known that both artists had extensive collections of drawings and other pictures by the van de Veldes. Sandby's art collection was sold by the auctioneer Mr James Christie (later known as Christie's) in a three-day sale that commenced on 2 May, 1811. The sale included: '..nearly 200 original Drawings of shipping by W. V. de Velde'. These were variously described as: 'single ships and hulls', 'large hulls of ships', 'fleets at sea', 'pen-drawings', and 'three long drawings of fleets at sea'. Two of Serres' exhibits at the Royal Academy in 1786 are described as 'Sea piece, in the style of Vanderveld, by the particular desire of a gentleman'.

The Boydell family actively promoted prints after Serres' work. In their catalogue of 1787 'Seven Views of Belleisle and of the City of Sanzon' were listed as engraved by Canot and Mason. They measured 14ins by 21ins long, at 'Price £1 1s'. In this series Serres had collaborated with the marine artist and publisher Richard Short, of whom no biographical details are known. The set depicting the capture of Bellisle, April 7 to June 7, 1761, was republished on April 15, 1777 with Boydell's name as publisher. The plates were engraved by Benoist, Canot, Elliott and Mason. A reduced set of six oil paintings closely related to the engravings after Dominic Serres, dated 1762, is in an American private collection.

Boydell's 1787 catalogue also included 'Six Views of Halifax, in Nova Scotia' engraved by Mason. These prints measured 14ins by 21ins long and cost £1 1s. The above-mentioned were among the most popular of Serres' prints offered in the printsellers' catalogues, although many more engravings after his work are known. His celebrated series of oil paintings depicting the Capture of Havana, 11 June - 16 August 1762, is arguably his greatest artistic achievement. The series of pictures can be seen at the National Maritime Museum, Greenwich. They were painted in the 1760s and 1770s

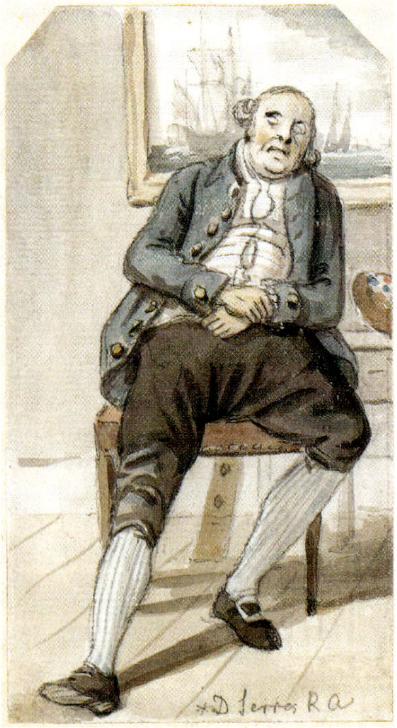

5/25
Paul Sandby. *Portrait of Dominic Serres asleep in a chair*, signed, watercolour.
Courtesy Sotheby's

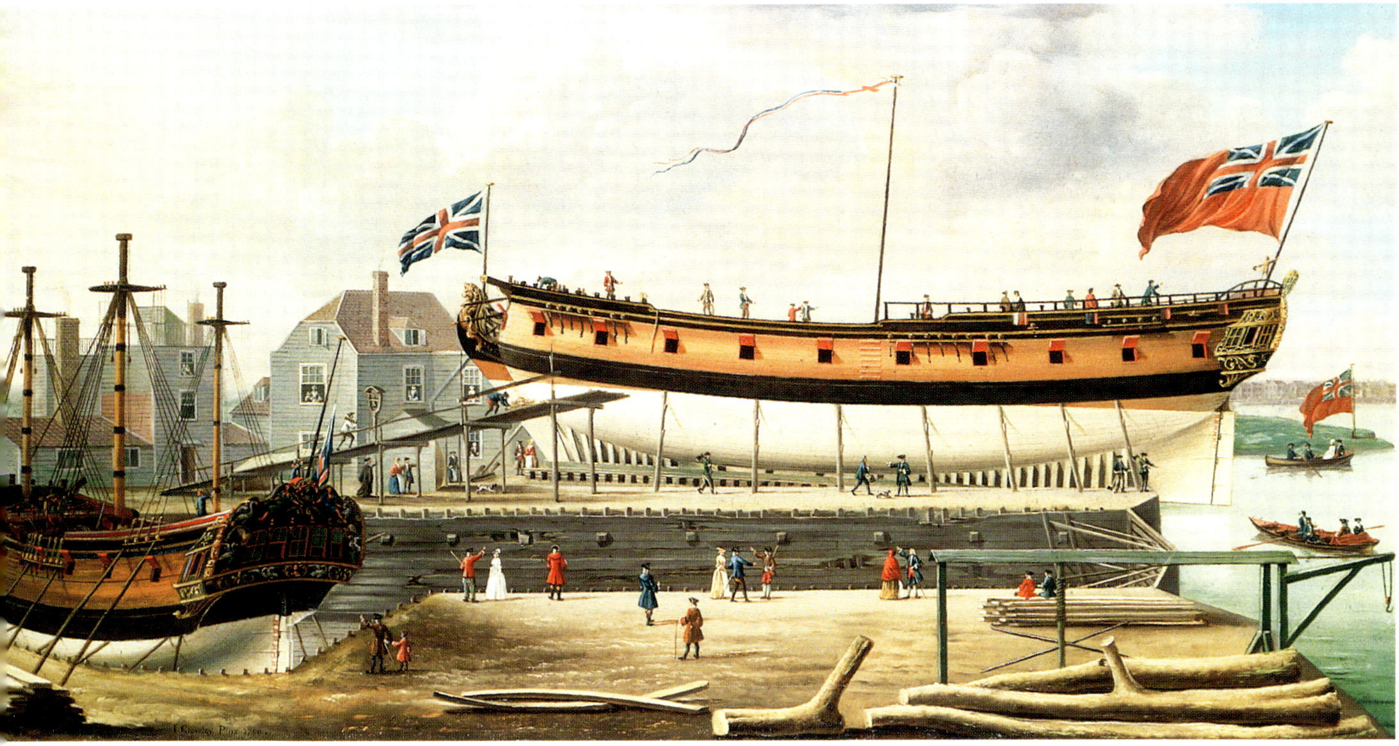

probably to the commission of Commodore Augustus Keppel who led the Red Squadron during the action. Serres' paintings were based on a set of engravings produced in the 1760s. An advertisement in the London newspaper *The Gazetteer and New Daily Advertiser*, Friday 12 April 1765 informs readers that: '12 Historical Views conquest & Taking of Havannah. Taken by an officer on the spot. Nos. 9 and 10 will be completed by the latter end of this month. He will close the said subscriptions. Whole will be completed in July.' The officer was Lieutenant Durnsford who collaborated with Serres on this speculative commission. Durnsford published the engravings.

5/27
John Cleveley the Elder. *A sixth rate on the stocks.* Oil on canvas, 26½ x 51, signed and dated 1758.
Caird Collection
National Maritime Museum, London

Print publishers would use the subscription method to defray part of their initial production costs. Publishers would advertise in newspapers for prospective customers to make a down payment in exchange for a guaranteed discount on the prints purchased. A series of prints would usually take several months to complete. Sometimes an ambitious publication plan would take years to come to fruition.

Serres did not live long enough to record the incidents of the Napoleonic Wars. The principal naval actions of that era were recorded by Nicholas Pocock (1740-1821), Robert Dodd (1748-1815), Thomas Luny (1759-1837) and Thomas Whitcombe (*c.*1752-1824), among others. During the later years of Serres' career he witnessed the introduction of aquatints, popularised by Paul Sandby in England from the 1770s, enabling a greater range of subtle atmospheric effects. The 'watery grain' appearance of the new printmaking process was ideally suited for maritime subjects, and especially the rendering of sea.

Serres and his son, John Thomas Serres (1795-1825), who was also a marine artist, used the process to good effect in their collaborative publication called *Liber Nauticus, and Instructor in the Art of Marine Drawing*, published by Edward Orme in two parts in 1805 and 1806. During the early years of the nineteenth century the rise in demand for hand-coloured aquatints corresponded with a falling interest in the black-and-white line engravings and etchings of the artists of the previous century. Even engravings and etchings that were carefully hand-coloured lacked the sophistication of aquatints.

Aquatints dominated printmaking processes until the adoption of colour lithography in the 1830s. Many of the popular English marine artists of the eighteenth century who had made their reputations with black-and-white engraving fell into obscurity. Only after the Second World War, with the publication of Oliver Warner's *British Marine Paintings* (1948), has there been a renewed and sustained general interest in their work.

Chapter 6

Brooking's Contemporaries in the 18th Century

E.H.H. Archibald compiled details of these marine artists in his *Dictionary of Sea Painters* and with permission I have selected all those painters of the eighteenth century who were either painting at the same time as Charles Brooking or who were painting later on in the century. Many of the latter copied or were influenced by his work. In many instances the information given has been revised.

ANDERSON, William **1757–1837**

Little is known of his early life except that he was born in Scotland and became a shipwright. He also learned to be a very finished painter, and when he was about thirty made his way south to London and set up as a marine painter. His style is firmly based on the Dutch seveteenth century school and, though he lived well into the nineteenth century, he never made any concessions to the Romantic movement.

Although he did some large canvases he is best known for his small, sometimes rather vapid calms, which sold well and still do. He first exhibited at the Royal Academy in 1787, and at the British Institution in 1810.

He was a friend of Julius Caeser Ibbotson, who is believed to have collaborated with him on some paintings. He had a son, William Guido Anderson, who joined the Royal Navy and was mortally wounded as a midshipman in the *Bellona*, at the Battle of Copenhagen in 1801.

ATKINS, Samuel **fl. 1787–1808**

A watercolourist who specialised in charming little shipping scenes. He first exhibited, from a variety of London addresses, at the Royal Academy in 1787 and then every year (except 1790) until 1796. He then went on a voyage to the East Indies. By 1804 he had returned and exhibited a Chinese subject at the Royal Academy. He last exhibited in 1808 from an address in The Strand. It may be he died at this time.

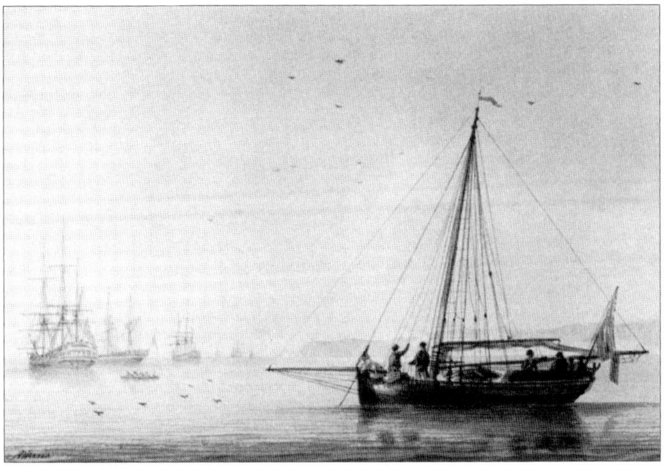

6/2
Samuel Atkins (fl.1787-1808). *A Fishing Boat at anchor with Men O' War beyond*. Watercolour on paper, 6¼ x 4¼.
Winster Collection, Royal Naval College, Greenwich

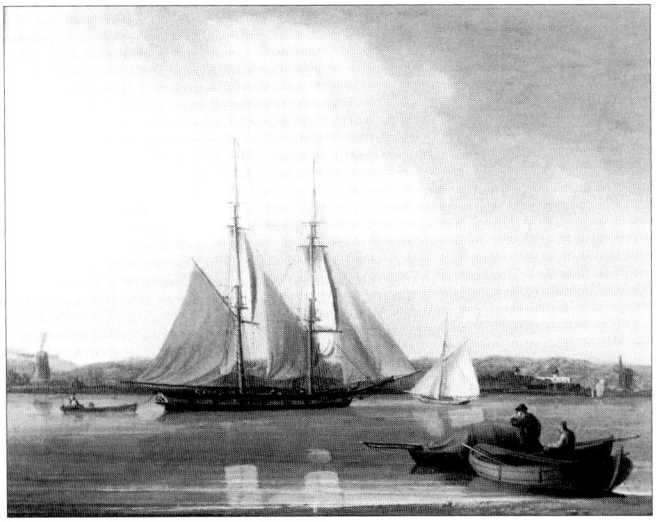

6/1
William Anderson (1757-1837). *A Brig and Fishing Boats in a calm.* Oil on board, 8½ x 6½. Winster Collection, Royal Naval College, Greenwich

BAKHUIZEN, Ludolf **1631–1708**

Although Bakhuizen belongs to the Dutch school, he was German and first worked as a calligrapher in his native town of Emden, where he was born on 18 December. While still a young man, an interest in drawing and painting prompted him to emigrate to Amsterdam, where he at first followed his trade.

The early 1650s was the period when Willem van de Velde the Elder was perfecting his grisaille drawing technique in Amsterdam; these drawings appear to have inspired young Bakhuizen and he may well have taken tuition from van de Velde. Bakhuizen's grisailles are closely textured with tiny strokes of the reed pen in sepia ink.

He learnt to paint in oils in the studio of Allaert van Everdingen, a landscape painter who did some marines, and more importantly in the studio of Hendrik Dubbels. Even in oils Bakhuizen, used to working in black and white, seems to have approached colour with caution. In his early works he

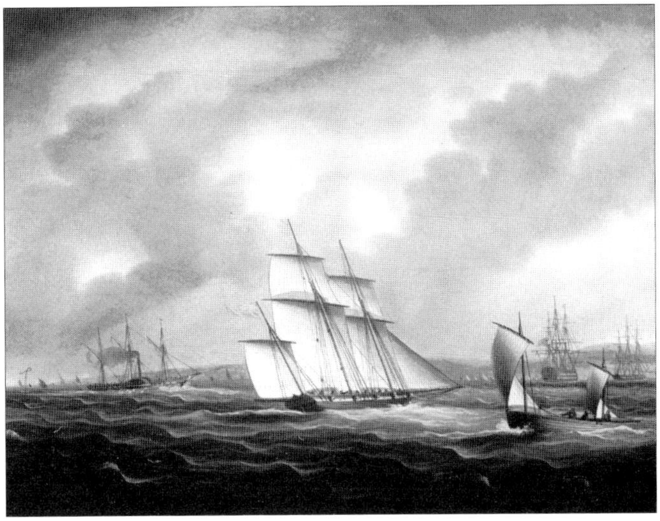

6/3
Thomas Buttersworth (1768-1842). *Shipping in an Estuary.* Oil on canvas, 15½ x 11½. Winster Collection, Royal Naval College, Greenwich

was unique in the adoption of a black palette, relieved with grey-brown and flushes of pink on the landscape area of the pictures, which are generally wreck scenes. By the middle 1660s he had perfected a technique of luminous glazes with blue-grey seas, majestic skies and very dramatic light-and-shade compositions. This was his best period. Later his palette warmed and the dramatic effects became less sharp. At Greenwich there are two large monochrome views of a Dutch factory port in the East Indies, but they are not like the early black pictures and must have been a special commission later on.

Bakhuizen was a contemporary of the younger Willem van de Velde, and shared with him an accurate understanding of the ships he painted. He was deservedly successful in his lifetime and this must have influenced van de Velde to adopt some of his style, to the point where some van de Veldes of about 1670 have been mistaken for Bakhuizens.

Bakhuizen must be placed in the first rank of marine painters; besides his oils he left drawings and engravings. He was also a convivial, generous man, who left money for a great wake to be held for him by his many friends after his death in Amsterdam on 17 November.

See Chapter 1, page 20.

BASTON, Thomas **fl. early18th century**

Artist working in the first quarter of the eighteenth century. In the reign of George I, Thomas Bowles published an important set of prints, 'Twenty two PRINTS of several of the CAPITAL SHIPS OF HIS Maj^{ties} ROYAL NAVY with Variety of other SEA PIECES after the drawings of T. Baston'. The compiler knows of no oil paintings.

See Chapter 5, page 87.

BUTTERSWORTH, Thomas **1768–1842**

Born on the Isle of Wight on 5 May, one of three sons of a butcher in West Cowes. A seaman-painter, who enlisted aboard His Majesty's Receiving Ship *Enterprise*, moored off the Tower, on 17 August 1795. On 19 August he joined the *Caroline*, a new frigate fitting out for sea at Deptford and was rated an able seaman at the age of twenty-seven. The following November he was appointed a master-at-arms, and in 1800 a midshipman. That same year he was invalided at Minorca and sent home. Nothing more is known of his naval service but the National Maritime Museum, Greenwich, has a number of large watercolours of the Battle of St. Vincent, 1797, and of the subsequent inshore blockading squadron off Cadiz, done in such a way as to make the compiler believe he witnessed the events. There are Mediterranean subjects dated 1797, 1799, and 1800, which must also have been worked there.

He was never a very good painter but the best examples of his work are reasonably well crafted and, understandably, he well understood the ships he painted. He was a prolific painter, and dealers have priced his works high, since they know many more will come on to the market.

Until recently it was supposed that he died about 1827 but a painting by him of Queen Victoria's visit to Edinburgh in 1842, and other evidence, seems to establish that he died in London in November 1842.

CLEVELEY, John, the Elder **c.1712–1777**

Born in Southwark, London; his father was a joiner and young Cleveley was apprenticed to another, Thomas Miller, in 1726. He later worked in the Royal Dockyard at Deptford, where he settled, dying there 21 May. Where then, and from whom did he learn his considerable skills as a painter? One explanation could be that following the scandal of the cost of the carved decorations on the *Royal Sovereign* of 1701, the Admiralty decreed in 1704 that only the head and stern galleries of ships could have carved decorations, while the rest of the decorations must be in paint. Thus many woodcarvers were paid off in the Royal dockyards and decorative painters taken on to paint the trophies of arms, classical figures, chariots, and so on, which adorned the sides of most ships from head to stern at the level of the upper-deck gunwales and above. John Cleveley could have learnt to paint from one or some of these dockyard painters and by his own genius refined his work to easel painting.

A weakness of Cleveley's output was a tendency to repeat a successful composition, with the result that a number of almost identical paintings of East Indiamen merely have different names on their sterns.

He had three sons: James became a ship's carpenter and was the *Resolution*'s carpenter on Cook's third voyage. He never was an artist in the formal sense but apparently did bring back from that voyage some competent sketches, from which his brother John made finished drawings which were then engraved. John and his twin brother Robert, born in 1747, were presumably younger than James.

See Chapter 5, page 91.

CLEVELEY, John, the Younger **1747–1786**

One of the twins born to John Cleveley, the Elder at Deptford on Christmas Day; the other was Robert. He followed his father into the Royal Dockyard at Deptford, where he trained as a shipwright. At the same time he shared his father's interest in painting, became his pupil and also took lessons from Paul Sandby at Woolwich. The fact that his father was an established painter evidently helped this side of his career, for having

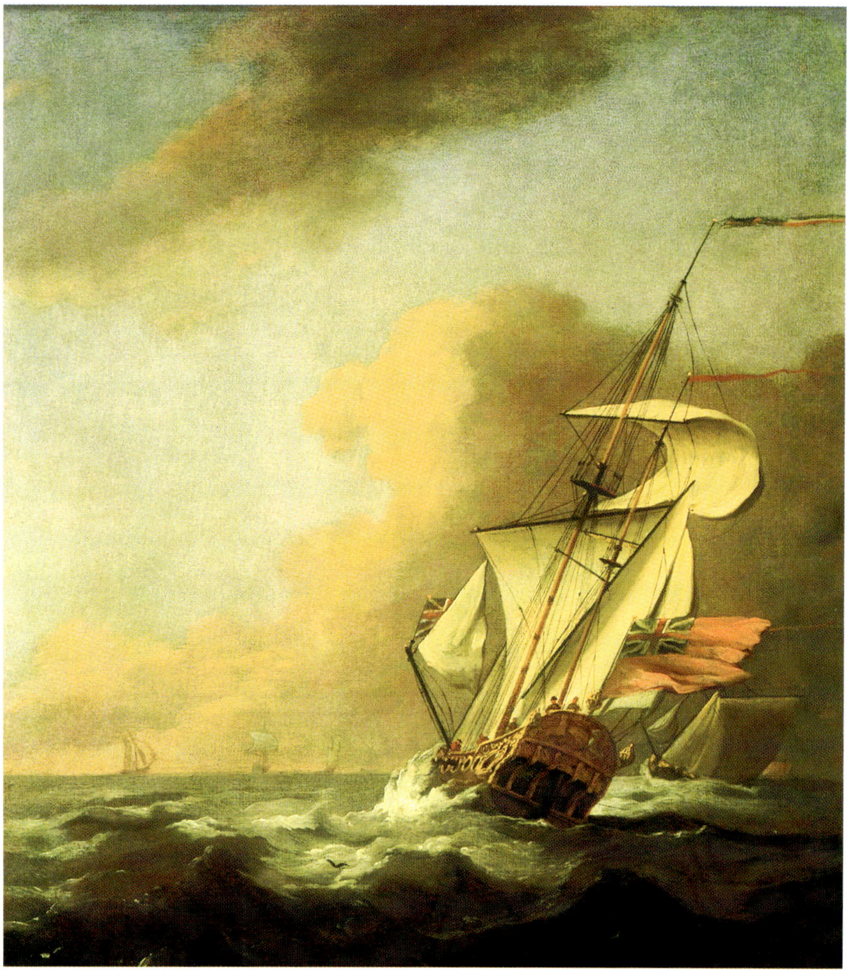

6/4
Johann van der Hagen (b.1675-*c.*1745). *A Ketch rigged Royal Yacht in a breeze.* Oil on canvas, 18 x 16, signed. National Maritime Museum, London

6/5
William Hodges (1744-1797). *HMS* Resolution *and* Adventure *with fishing craft in Matavi Bay, circa 1773.* Oil on canvas, 53½ x 76.
Admiralty House Collection, National Maritime Museum, London

exhibited two drawings at the Society of Artists exhibition as early as 1767 and three at the Royal Academy in 1770, he was chosen as draughtsman for a Royal Society expedition to Iceland in 1772. On his return he exhibited two Icelandic views at the Royal Academy in 1773.

His style is close to his father's but in signed works he used a 'J' as the initial whereas his father used an 'I'.

See Chapter 5, page 81.

CLEVELEY, Robert **1747–1809**
Twin brother of John jnr., he also went into the Royal Dockyard at Deptford, a place in which his father John snr. had influence, and became a caulker. Not surprisingly he did not care for it and was apparently a fastidious lad, for he is said to have been the butt of his workmates for working in gloves. In 1770 he volunteered into the Royal Navy as a clerk and served as Captain William Locker's clerk in the *Thames* until 1773. Then Captain George Vandeput took over command and Robert subsequently followed him to the *Asia*, thus serving in her on the North American and West Indies stations until discharged on her return in 1777.

His ambition was to be a painter and as his brother John was the pupil of his father and Paul Sandby, then it is fair to assume that Robert was too. Whereas his brother John went in for voyages of discovery, Robert took up battles, since this was a profitable line during the American War of Independence. The profit lay in getting commissions for paintings that were to be engraved, for these engravings of British victories were bestsellers with the public. This was also an area where important patronage could be sought and Robert, who had first exhibited at the Royal Academy in 1780, showed two paintings in 1790 on the subject of the Duke of Clarence's public engagements; he was appointed Draughtsman to His Royal Highness the following year. This connection must have been instrumental in his appointment as Marine Painter to the Prince Regent.

His work is not very like that of his father and brother, being more atmospheric and in tune with the later trends of the eighteenth century. He died in Dover 28 September 1809.

DODD, Robert **1748–1815**
One of the principal recorders of the naval aspects of the American War of Independence and the French Revolutionary Wars. He not only painted the actions but also engraved and published over a hundred of them, mostly in aquatint.

He first exhibited at the Society of Artists in 1780, the same year as his younger brother, Ralph. Both painted battle pieces in a very similar manner and in Graves' dictionary of contributors to the Royal Academy exhibitions, all the works by Dodd, starting in 1782, are lumped together as by Ralph Dodd. This must be a mistake.

Robert Dodd's major work was the very large painting (76 x

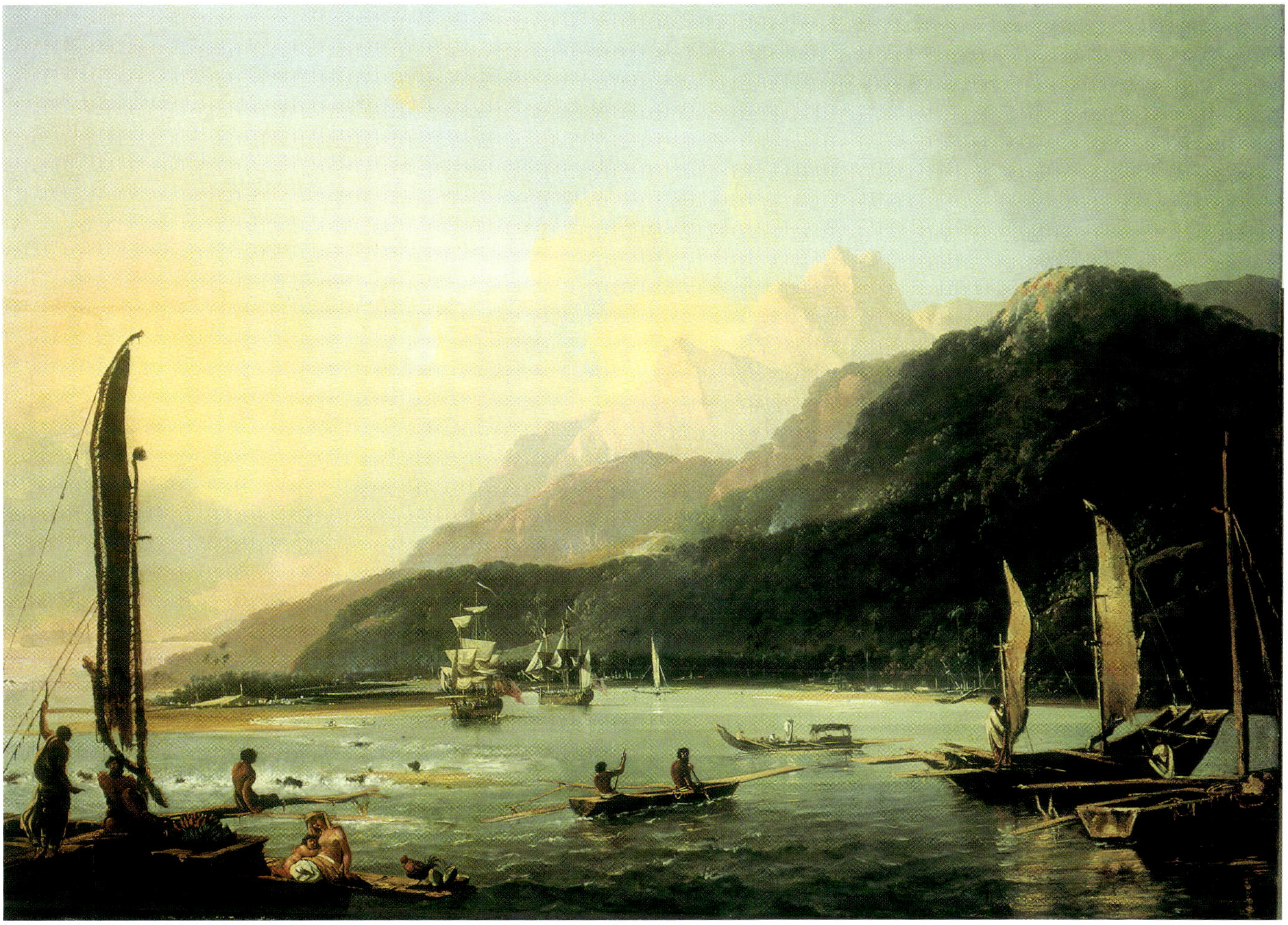

134 ins.) of the end of Lord Howe's victory on 1 June 1794, showing the rescue of the crew of the sinking *Vengeur du Peuple*. This he painted in 1795, to hang in the dining room of his local inn, the Half Way House in the Commercial Road. Because of its size it was painted *in situ*. It is now in Greenwich.

Although he could occasionally turn out a nicely finished work, his pictures on the whole are rather dull. He last exhibited at the Royal Academy in 1809. He died in London in February 1815.

See Chapter 5, pages 83 and 84.

ELLIOTT, Lieutenant William, R.N. fl. 1770–1791

The confusion as to which of the William Elliotts in the Royal Navy was the painter has never been satisfactorily resolved. The favourite has been the man who, having been previously in the merchant service, was master's mate of the *Roebuck* for four years, before passing for lieutenant on 11 May 1782. He went on to be promoted to commander in 1790 and captain in 1810 and died in 1838.

If this identification is correct then it is odd that he should have ceased to exhibit in 1791 and that his latest known picture is of the *Victory* off Bastia in 1794. A painting of George III reviewing the fleet at Spithead in 1789, signed Lieutenant W. Elliott, was exhibited at the Free Society in 1790; he exhibited there again in 1791. Previous to this he had exhibited at the Royal Academy every year from 1784 to 1789.

He went in for large canvases and painted battle pieces of reasonable quality.

GORE, Charles 1729–1807

Born in Horkstow, Lincolnshire, 5 December. His family was well off so he drew and painted in watercolours, not for a living but as recreation. Although he never exhibited, he was extremely industrious and skilled. He greatly admired the Willem van de Veldes and did numerous drawings of seventeenth century subjects in their manner, some based on their drawings. He was working in Southampton in the middle of the century but in 1773, in an effort to recoup his wife's health, they went to Italy by sea and travelled there, in Corsica and on the Riviera. During this tour he made valuable drawings of the ancient ruins they visited.

He returned to England in 1781 and became a member of the Dilettante Society. After visiting Florence again he settled for the rest of his life at the court of the Duke of Weimar. He died in Weimar 22 January.

HAGEN, Johann van der (Jan van Hagen) b.1675–c.1745

Born in The Hague, he is said to have come to London about the end of the seventeenth century. However, this artist, and his relation Willem van der Hagen, are to be approached with caution. In recent times eminent scholars have added their labours to others in attempting a positive identification of both men and have largely failed. What we do know is that certain extant paintings in the style of Willem van de Velde the Younger are signed 'J.v.Hagen' and that it was his daughter, Bernarda, who married van de Velde's son, Cornelis.

Strickland's *Dictionary of Irish Artists* claims that he moved from London to Dublin at the end of his life. His death occurred before 1745 for he is mentioned as the 'late' in a note of that date. His work is so modelled on van de Velde's that one wonders if he was not working in the latter's studio.

See page 94.

HAGEN, Willem van der **fl. c.1736**

A view of Waterford, Ireland, dated 1736, and the strange allegorical signed painting of William III landing at Carrickfergus have brought up the question of which van der Hagen went to Ireland. The answer may be both. For if Johann van der Hagen went to Dublin, why not his family? There is no evidence to support the theory that Willem was Johann's son, except that he was apparently in Ireland in 1736. He was given to painting large panoramic port scenes; including Gibraltar, Portsmouth and Falmouth.

Charles Brooking senior was in Dublin 1724/25 working at Trinity College. In 1728 his map of Dublin was published. Could this be the point at which the van der Hagens and the Brookings first met?

HODGES, William, R.A. **1744–1797**

London born, he was the son of a blacksmith in Drury Lane. He went to William Shipley's School and afterwards, in 1757 or 1758, was apprenticed to the painter Richard Wilson for five years or more. Before photography it was the practice to take artists on major scientific expeditions to record what was found. Hodges was offered such a post on James Cook's second voyage in 1772, the aim of which was to establish or debunk once and for all, the presence of a great inhabited southern continent (what we now know as Antarctica). The expedition returned in 1775, bringing with it a vast number of Hodges' drawings and small oils on panel. Some of these he used as a basis for large canvases which he exhibited at the Royal Academy in 1776.

They were of great artistic interest and originality of style, neither romantic nor academic, but sometimes bordering on the impressionist in his bold handling of the paint; perhaps it was this that the public was not quite ready for, since he did not get the patronage he needed. He did, however, win enough patronage from Warren Hastings to take him to India in 1780, where he stayed for four years and returned having made a fortune. He resumed exhibiting at the Royal Academy and was elected R.A. in 1787.

None the less, success again eluded him. Nearly all his exhibits until 1789 are of scenes from his travels to the East, which might have been unfashionable had not Thomas Daniel painted Eastern scenes exclusively and successfully for years; so it seems that his style was again the trouble. In 1794 he admitted defeat and retired to the West Country. Here he was involved in a banking venture which failed and he committed suicide.

See page 95.

HOLMAN, Francis **1729–1784**

In spite of being one of the major marine painters of the eighteenth century, little is known about this artist. He first exhibited at the Free Society in 1767 from an address in Bell Dock, Wapping. Except for 1769, he continued to exhibit with the Free Society until 1772. He then switched to the Royal Academy in 1774, where he exhibited marines every year until 1784 from addresses in Shadwell.

He was an industrious artist, whose views of shipyards, sea actions, ship portraits and general shipping scenes are still plentiful. His one famous pupil was Thomas Luny, whose early work is like his master's but who went on to greater things.

See page 97.

LEEMANS, Thomas **fl. c.1720**

Surviving paintings signed 'T. Leemans' show him to have been a follower of Willem van de Velde, the Younger, in the generation of Peter Monamy. Known examples date to around 1720; though inferior to Monamy they have a finished, glossy quality. One distinctive feature is his tendency to exaggerate the sparring of his ships, particularly the length of the yards.

See page 98.

LOUTHERBOURG, Philippe-Jacques de, R.A. **1740–1812**

Born in Strasbourg 31 October. He studied first under his father, a miniaturist, then in Paris under Carl Vanloo, the genre and portrait painter, and last under the battle and marine painter, Francesco Casanova. He was already an established painter in France, painter to the King, a member of the French Royal Academy and of the Academy of Marseilles, when in 1771 he came to London. The man instrumental in causing de Loutherbourg to settle in London was the actor David Garrick, who, after some trial work, engaged him in 1773 as scenic director at Drury Lane Theatre with the enormous salary of £500 per year. He continued in this position for ten years, and in 1781 first exhibited his Eidophusikon or mechanical theatre, in which one of the most successful displays was of a painted

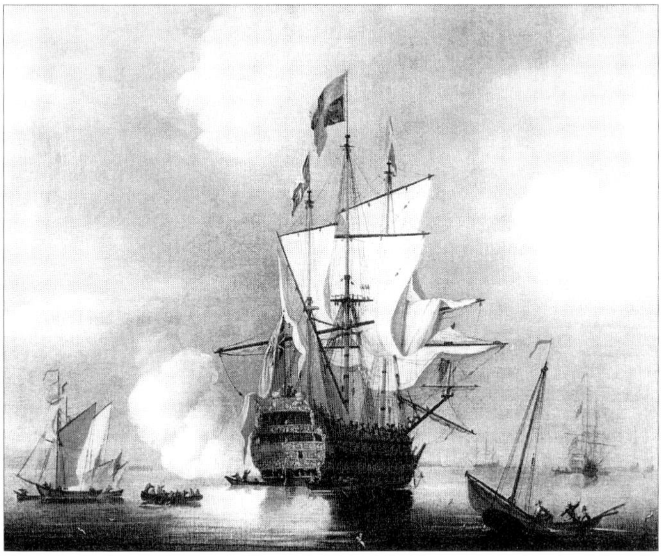

6/6
Thomas Leemans. *Morning Gun*. Oil on canvas, 30¼ x 35½. Bonhams

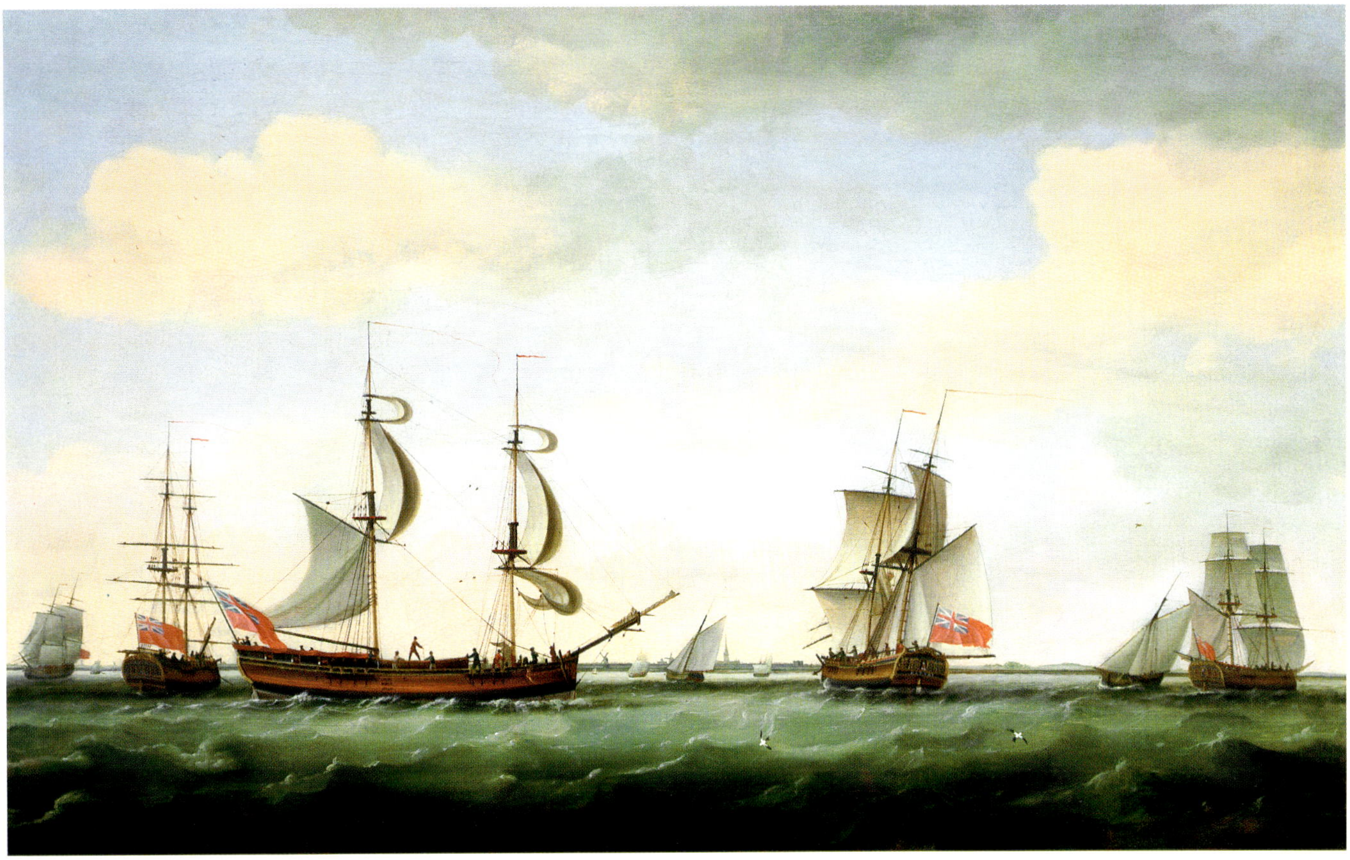

6/7
Francis Holman (1729-1784). *The Brigs of War* Nancy *and* Bettey. Oil on canvas, 26 x 42, signed and dated 1782.
Richard Green Gallery

and mechanical shipwreck.

In this, in his theatre work and his general art, de Loutherbourg was preoccupied with the recreation of dramatic, naturalistic light effects. He was a leader of the Romantic movement and had a considerable influence on the direction marine painting was to take in the early nineteenth century. He particularly influenced the young J. M. W. Turner, who had a high regard for his work. He died in Chiswick on 11 March.

LUNY, Thomas **1759–1837**

For many years Luny was believed to have been born in London, in fact he was from the West Country. When he first exhibited at the Society of Artists in 1777 his address was given as 'At Mr. Holman's, Johnson Str. St. George's'. This means that Luny was Francis Holman's pupil and assistant at that time, and he may well have continued with Holman until he moved to Ratcliffe Highway, Stepney, in 1781–82.

His early work is very close to Holman's except that Luny used a slightly lighter, warmer palette. He ceased to exhibit at the Society of Artists after 1778 and only ever exhibited one picture at the Free Society, in 1783, concentrating instead on the Royal Academy exhibitions every year from 1780 to 1793. He showed nothing after 1793 until 1802, when he exhibited *Battle of the Nile*, and then nothing until the year of his death, when he exhibited three pictures.

He had ceased to paint by 1837 but the decision to exhibit would have been connected with the simultaneous exhibition of 130 of his pictures in Old Bond Street. The fact that the R.A. exhibits cease in 1793, the year of the outbreak of the long French Revolutionary Wars, indicates that he probably joined up. Why he should have done so we do not know but he is supposed to have been a purser in the Royal Navy, and to have served under Captain George Tobin, R.N. That officer retired to Teignmouth after paying off in 1814 and was certainly a close friend of Luny's there.

Luny's own retirement from the Navy, due to rheumatoid arthritis, is usually given as 1810, but by his own account seems to have been earlier. He kept an inventory of the pictures he painted with the title, the purchaser's name and the price. The first entries are in February 1807 and include views of London Bridge and of Blackfriars Bridge; however, two views of Teignmouth are among the entries for June, so it seems he arrived there in the summer of 1807. He remained there to paint for the rest of his life.

His disability was severe, confining him to a wheelchair and affecting his hands, so that he had to hold the brush between both hands, or strapped to his wrist. Even so, his output was prodigious, over 2,200 pictures between February 1807 and the last crabbed entry in his journal in December 1835. In some months there are twenty-five or twenty-six entries, which means that, assuming he did not work on Sundays, he was turning out a picture every working day. Add to this his output from the late

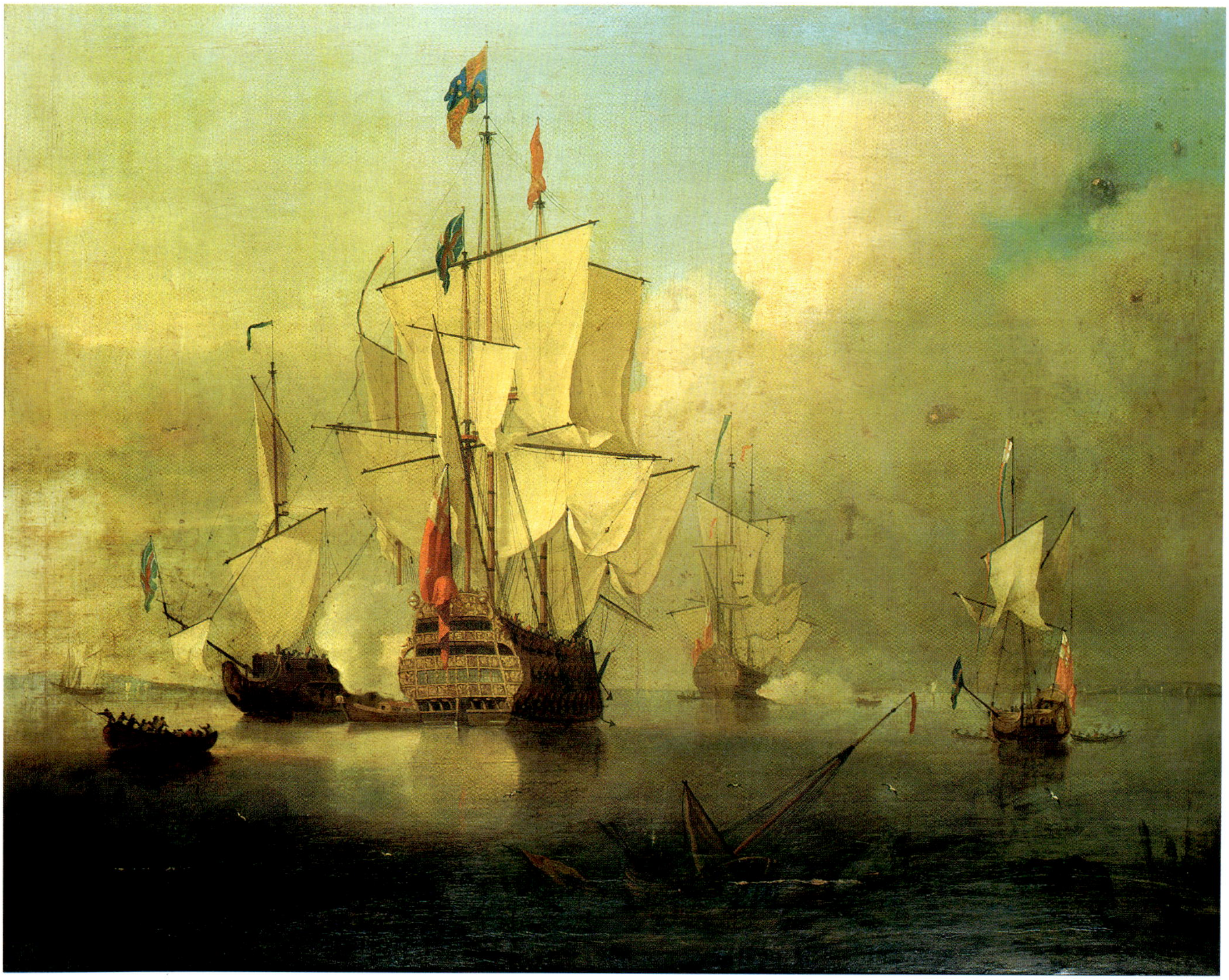

6/8
Thomas Leemans (*fl. c.*1720). *Calm – A first rate bearing the Royal Arms of 1707*. Oil on canvas, 41 x 53½.

1770s until 1793 and his total life's work must have been close to 3,000 pictures. It is no wonder that the sale-rooms are full of them.

Most of Luny's paintings sold for less than £5, a proportion for around £10, and some occasionally for £25. He left £14,000 when he died in Teignmouth on 29 September.

See page 99.

MAN, L. D. (or L. de) **fl. 1707–1725**
This artist was painting in England but was probably not British, as his style is Dutch, though not in the Dutch tradition as manifested in England. It is carefully finished and rather static. Cockett states that he flourished in England from 1707-25 and that he had found many examples of his work, of which eight were clearly signed 'L. d. Man'.

MELLISH, Thomas **fl. 1761–1778**
Artist who exhibited a pair of sea pieces at the Society of Artists in 1761 and a moonlight scene in 1763. In 1766 he exhibited a moonlight view with shipping and a view of Dover with shipping, from an address in Hoxton Square in London. The latest dated pictures known are of 1778.

His quality varies but at his best he has been mistaken for Samuel Scott, and some years ago some of his paintings hung in an exhibition devoted to Scott. Indeed, one of them had for many years been attributed to Charles Brooking.

MITCHELL, Thomas **1735–1790**
Like John Cleveley, the Elder, whom he must have known well, Mitchell combined the professions of marine painter and shipwright to the Admiralty throughout his career, and went far further in the latter service. In 1771 he was Builders' Assistant at His Majesty's Dockyard, Chatham, then filled the same position at Deptford; lastly he became Assistant Surveyor of the Navy. He did a supplement to the survey of harbours in 1774.

If he surpassed Cleveley in his naval career, he did not approach him as a painter. Although there was nothing amateur

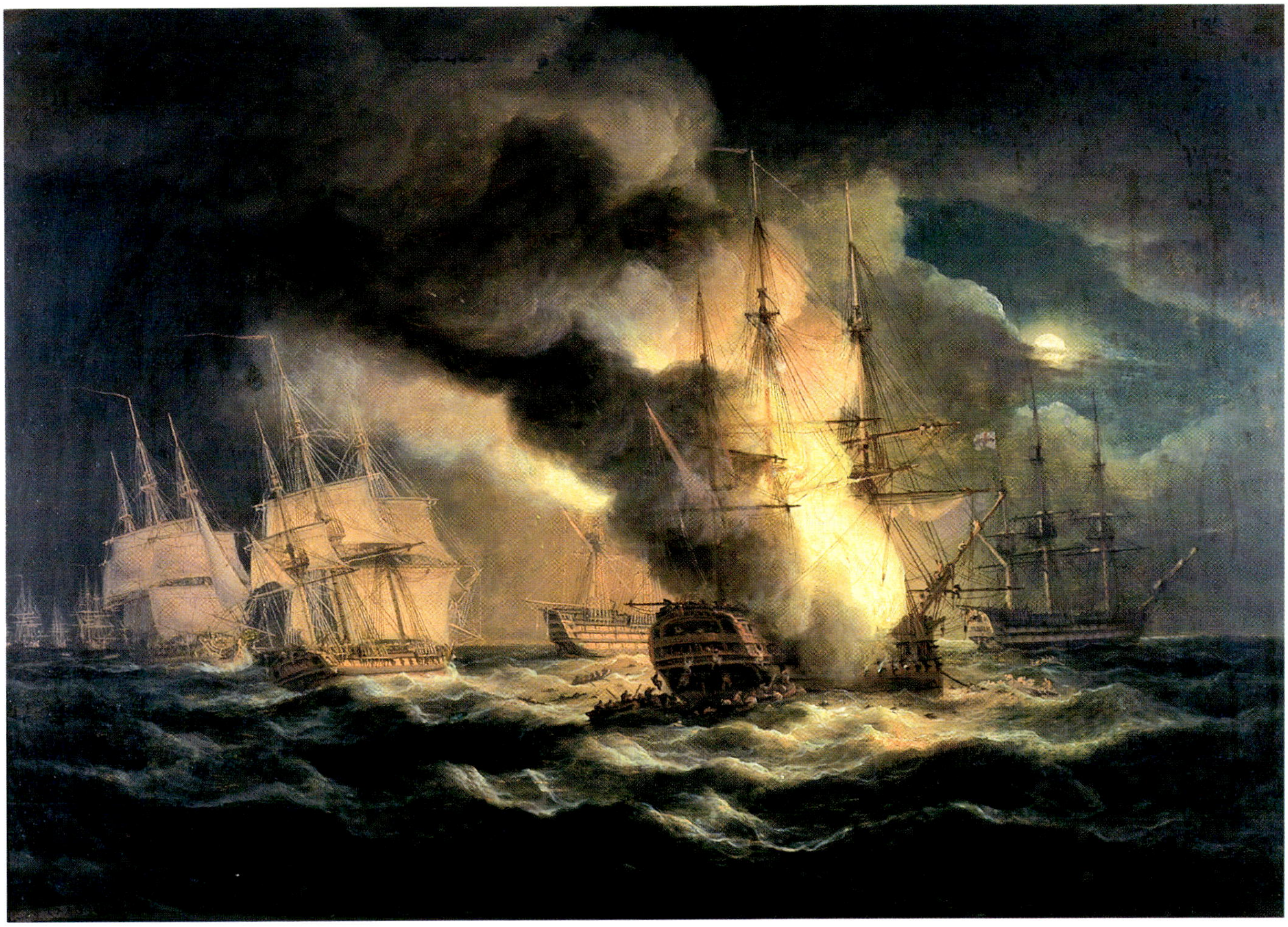

6/9
Thomas Luny (1759-1837). *Loss of the* Ajax *14 Feb. 1807.* She was in Admiral Duckworth's fleet off the Dardanelles. Oil on canvas, 24 x 34, signed T. Luny 1833. Private Collection

about his approach his style was dull and strongly influenced by Richard Paton. He liked to undertake large battle pieces and exhibited at the Free Society between 1763 and 1780, and at the Royal Academy between 1774 and 1789.

MONAMY, Peter 1681–1749
Peter Monamy was born in London, the youngest son of a Guernseyman, to a family known in the Channel Islands since 1540 AD. He was baptised at St. Botolph's without Aldgate, 12th January 1681. In 1696 he was apprenticed to William Clarke, a former Master of the Painter-Stainers Company. Clarke was a well-established tradesman, based on Old London Bridge and nearby Thames Street, serving London merchants in the decoration of their houses, and as a painter of the ornate trade signboards advertising City businesses. Peter was freed of his apprenticeship in 1704, on the same day as Thornhill, who later decorated the Painted Hall at Greenwich Naval College.

George Vertue, a well-known engraver, wrote two accounts (1726 and 1749) of Monamy. He notes that Monamy "took to the study and inclination of painting of ships or sea-pieces from the variety of those views he had continually before his eyes where he lived when 'prentice." Vertue records his "constant practice... his industry and understanding in the forms and buildings of shipping with all the tackles, ropes and sails... his neatness and clean pencilling of sky and water... his many excursions to the coasts and seaports of England to improve himself from nature" and that he was "by many much esteemed, especially seafaring people, officers and others, merchants, etc."

For some of his early years Monamy lived in Red Lion Street, off the Minories, near the Tower of London, before moving to Westminster (about 1720), where he is recorded as living in St. Margaret's Lane, Fish Yard and Old Palace Yard, between the House of Commons and Westminster Abbey.

Monamy's early works are painted in a manner reminiscent of his native English contemporaries. Until the mid-1730s he also absorbed a variety of North European, Dutch and French influences. Vertue mentions "other famous masters of paintings in this manner, van de Veldes etc." The van de Velde studio was carried on after the Younger's death in 1707, by his son Cornelis (c.1675-1729) and Cornelis' father-in-law Johann van der Hagen (1675-c.1745). It declined until Cornelis left for Holland in about 1720. For ten years after 1720 Monamy may

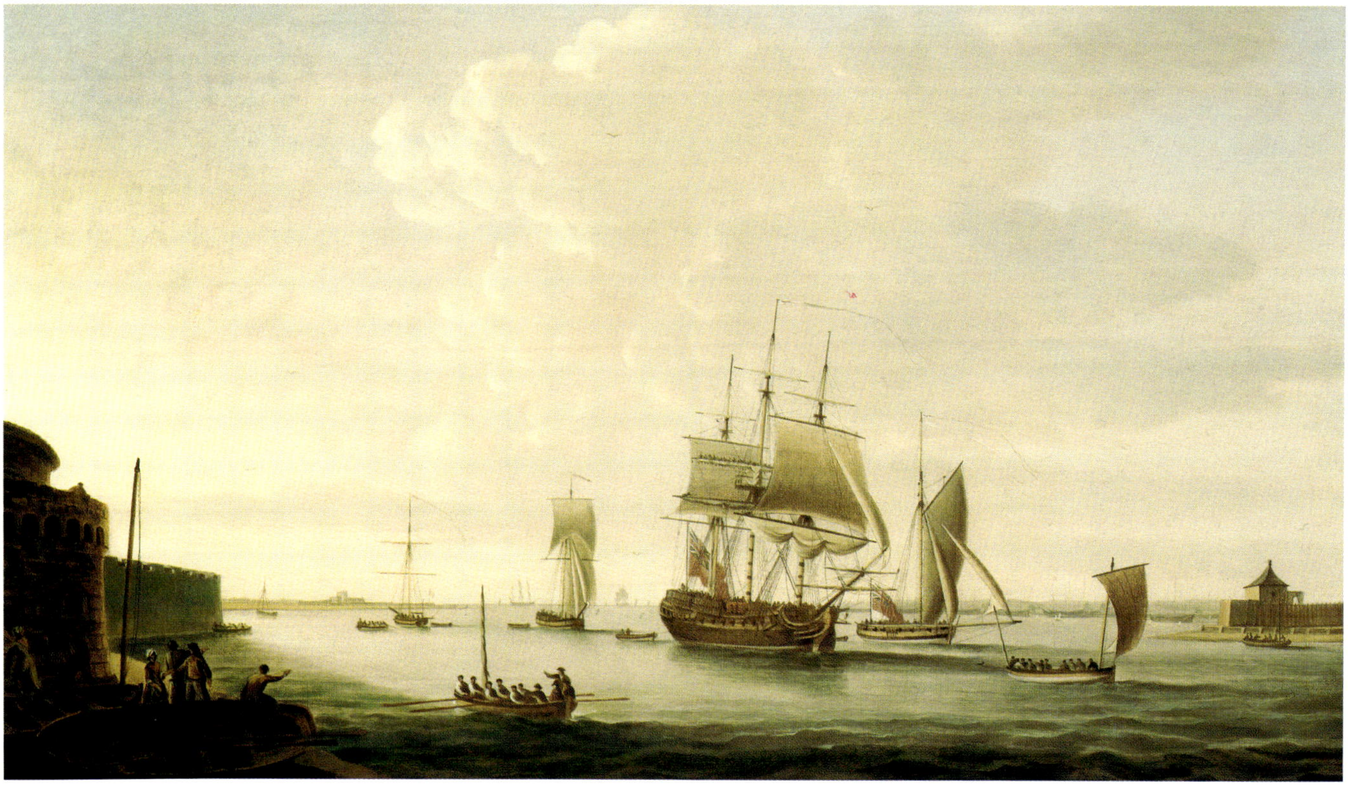

6/10
Thomas Mitchell (1735-1790). *Frigate off Portsmouth.* Signed and dated 1780. 17 x 28.
Richard Green Gallery

have set out to match the van de Velde reputation, but close copies of van de Velde by him are rare.

In about 1732 Monamy's career underwent a change, coinciding with the rise of his younger rival, Samuel Scott (c.1702-1772). Scott's work was not displayed at Vauxhall Gardens, which re-opened in 1736 and later exhibited major works by Monamy, as well as works by Hogarth (1697-1764), Hayman (1708-1776) and other English artists. With the advent of war against Spain and France in 1739 Monamy's style shed all continental influence, and he worked with renewed industry rather in the manner of his early years, dying at his house in Old Palace Yard in early February, 1749.

Hogarth painted a work in about 1729, *Monamy the Painter showing a sea-piece to a Patron*, see page 49. The sea-piece was painted by Monamy himself and is signed by him. There are two versions, one at Knowsley Hall, near Liverpool, England and the other in the Art Institute of Chicago. It is seldom mentioned in studies of Hogarth's oeuvre. This general lack of recognition by art historians has meant that a large quantity of inauthentic work has been ascribed to Monamy.

Peter Monamy was survived by his wife, still alive in 1761, and two daughters. The youngest, Ann, married a Thomas Cornwall in 1745. The other daughter, Mary, married the marine painter Francis Swaine in 1749. Their son, Monamy Swaine, was born in 1754 and he also became a sea painter.

See Chapter 1 pages 26, 27; Chapter 3 pages 49, 50; page 101.

MULIER, Pieter, the Elder 1615-1670

Born and died at Haarlem. Although he would have been only seventeen when Jan Porcellis died, the influence of Porcellis' work is so strong that he could have been his pupil. He adopted the grey tonal palette of the Dutch realist school and was mainly concerned with scenes of shipping in fresh breezes or storms.

OWEN, Samuel 1768/9–1857

Mainly a watercolourist of coastal and fishing scenes but having first exhibited *A Sea View* at the Royal Academy in 1794, his next exhibit was of the action off Cape St. Vincent in 1797. This was followed in 1799 by three paintings of the *Director*'s share of the Battle of Camperdown. His last exhibits, in 1802 and 1807, were general marine subjects. He died in Sunbury-on-Thames 8 December.

PATON, Richard 1717–1791

Born and died in London. Said to have been the youngest of an impoverished family, who sent him out as a child to beg in the streets. One day he accosted Commander (later Admiral) Sir Charles Knowles, on Tower Hill, and sufficiently impressed him to get an offer of a place in Knowles' ship, where he became assistant to the ship's painter.

From these unlikely beginnings, and presumably largely self-taught, he rose to be one of the principal painters of naval actions of the eighteenth century. In 1742, through some other patronage (not that of Knowles, who was in the West Indies), Paton was appointed Assistant Accountant in the Excise Office. Thus he was not dependent on his brush for a living and it does seem that he was a late starter as an artist. The first paintings to bring him to the public notice were of the Battle of Lagos 1759, and the capture of the *Foudroyant* in 1758, both of which were exhibited

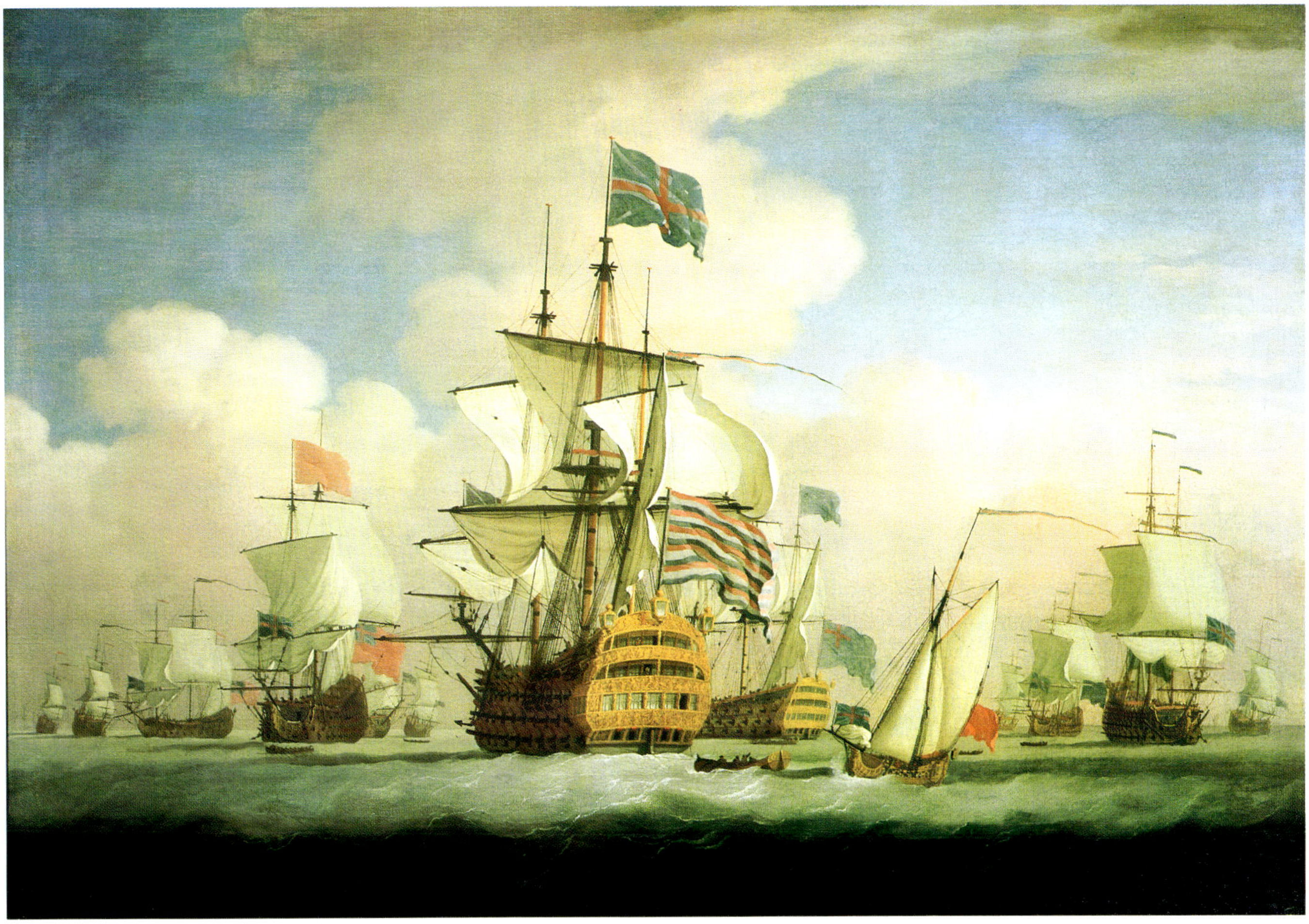

6/11
Peter Monamy (1681-1749). *An English fleet coming to anchor.* Oil on canvas, 34½ x 51, signed.
National Maritime Museum, London

at the Society of Artists in 1762 and subsequently engraved. He continued to exhibit views and actions until 1770, when he resigned from the Society after a dispute over the placing of his picture of the Battle of Finisterre, 1747. From 1776 to 1780 he exhibited at the Royal Academy.

Perhaps because he was self-taught and something of an experimenter, his work is uneven in quality and style; some of the best paintings show a strong influence of Samuel Scott, others that of Charles Brooking. He published engravings of his paintings, having them engraved by P. C. Canot. He undoubtedly knew Brooking, for after the latter's death Mary Brooking wrote to him at his address in Old Jewry, Cheapside in London, asking for advice.

See Chapter 5, page 80.

POCOCK, Nicholas **1740–1821**

Born in Bristol, he was the son of a well-connected Bristol merchant, who had married a cousin of the Duke of Roxburgh. He went to sea and in 1766 began a long period in command of the *Lloyd*, a merchantman belonging to Richard Champion, the maker of Bristol porcelain. He later commanded Champion's ships *Betsey* and *Minerva*, making twelve voyages in all, most to America. He was already an amateur painter and each day, when he wrote up his ship's log, he included a little wash drawing of her, showing the state of the weather or anything remarkable that had happened. Of the seven logbooks known to have survived, four are in the National Maritime Museum, Greenwich, one in the City of Bristol Record Office and one in the Mariners Museum, Newport News; the seventh is untraced.

Richard Champion's sister wrote in her journal that Pocock, 'having a fine taste for drawing, he sometimes talked of giving up the sea', and what is thought to be his earliest surviving watercolour is one showing two views of the *Ruby* of Bristol, dated 1759. It is fairly primitive.

In 1780 he married and this additional stimulus to leave the sea and settle down seems to have been artistically decisive. In that year he sent a picture to the Royal Academy and, though it arrived too late to be in the exhibition, he received an encouraging letter of advice from the President, Sir Joshua Reynolds. In 1782 he had two views around Bristol and two marines accepted, exhibiting thereafter every year until 1812, and finally in 1815.

In 1789 he moved to London where, like Dominic Serres before him, his immense practical knowledge of ships and the sea and a 'good address', immediately recommended him to naval clients to record their actions at sea. Indeed, Serres had only four years to live and Pocock was his obvious successor,

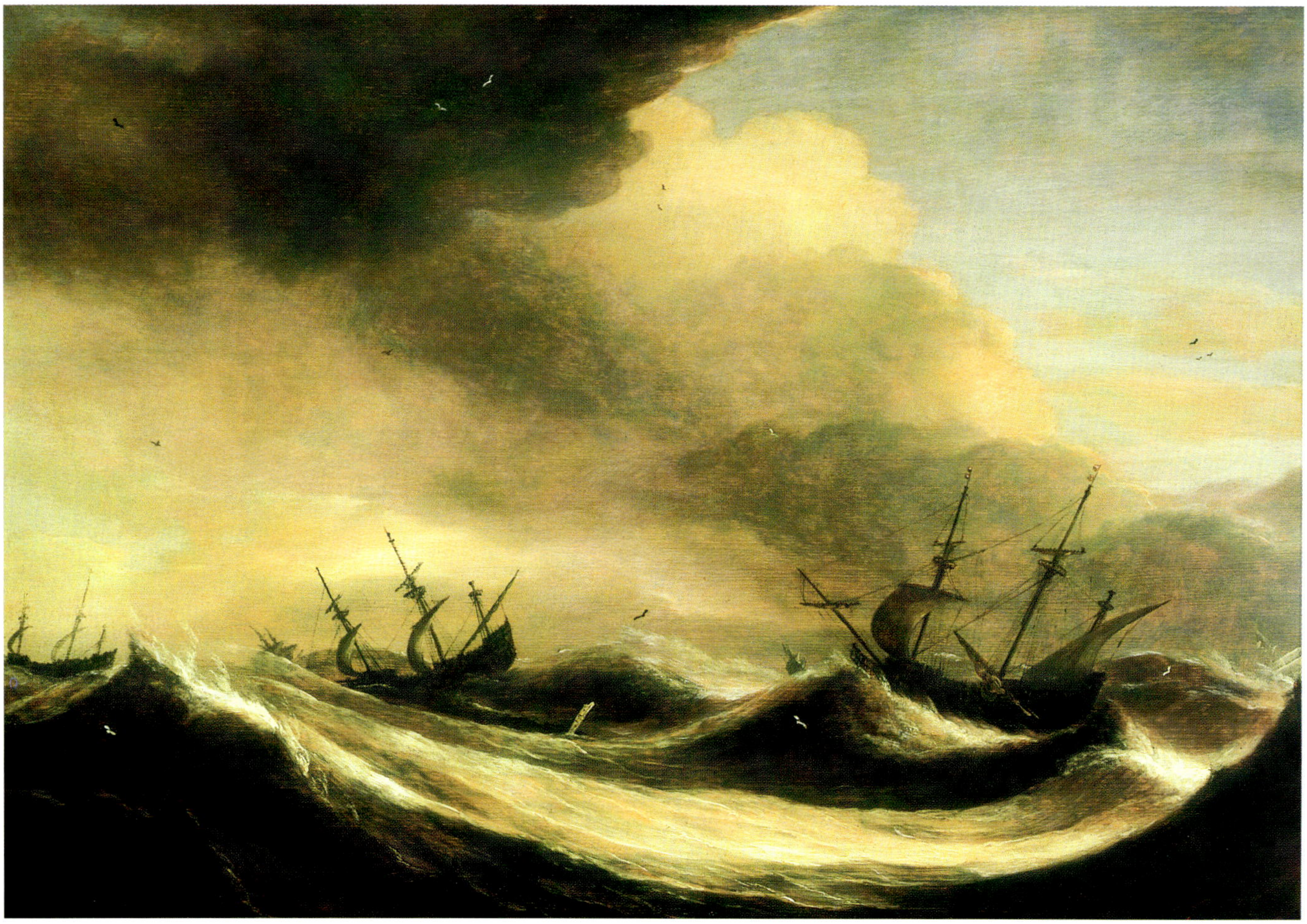

6/12
Pieter Mulier (1615-1670). *Ships in a heavy sea running before a storm.* Oil on canvas, 15½ x 23.
National Maritime Museum, London

though not without competition from such artists as Robert Dodd, Luny and Whitcombe.

Two of his sons, Isaac and William Innes Pocock, were also painters. The former, notable as a playwright, was a historical and portrait painter, the latter painted marines.

See Chapter 3, page 54.

POCOCK, William Innes, Lieut. R.N. 1783–1836
Son of Nicholas Pocock, he was born in Bristol in June. He followed his father's example and went to sea at the age of twelve. He seems to have been in merchantmen for some years, during which time he was involved in actions with the French. In 1805 he joined H.M. Frigate *Astrea* as a volunteer and fought the rest of the long Revolutionary Wars in the Royal Navy. In 1811 he became a lieutenant, but with the end of the wars in 1814 his employment at sea also ended.

His paintings are in his father's style and palette, so he may have been his pupil. During his service he kept sketchbooks of the places he visited, and in 1815, while Napoleon was on his way there, took advantage of the national interest in St. Helena to publish a set of five plates of the island with a lengthy description. The sketches for these were made when his ship, the *St. Albans*, put into St. Helena to repair storm damage about 1809. He did not like the place any more than Napoleon did.

PORCELLIS, Jan c.1584–1632
From the Spanish Netherlands, his family was of Spanish origins. He married H. C. Vroom's daughter in 1605 and is believed to have been his pupil at Rotterdam. He has strong claims to be the innovator of the new Dutch realist palette, moving away from the more colourful mannerist Flemish one and adopting a system of fairly low-key, closely-knit tonal values, based on the whole on the 'pearl grey skies of Holland'. This was to develop into an almost monochrome palette with some of the painters of the next generation, such as Simon de Vlieger and, in the extreme, with Jan van Goyen.

In his earlier works Porcellis' figures have a squat appearance reminiscent of Pieter Brueghel, though in later works they have a more 17th century look. He moved to Antwerp, where he became Master of the Guild in 1617, and then to Amsterdam and Haarlem, before finally settling at Soutermonde, near Leyden, where he died. His best known pupils were his son, Julius and, much more important, Simon de Vlieger.

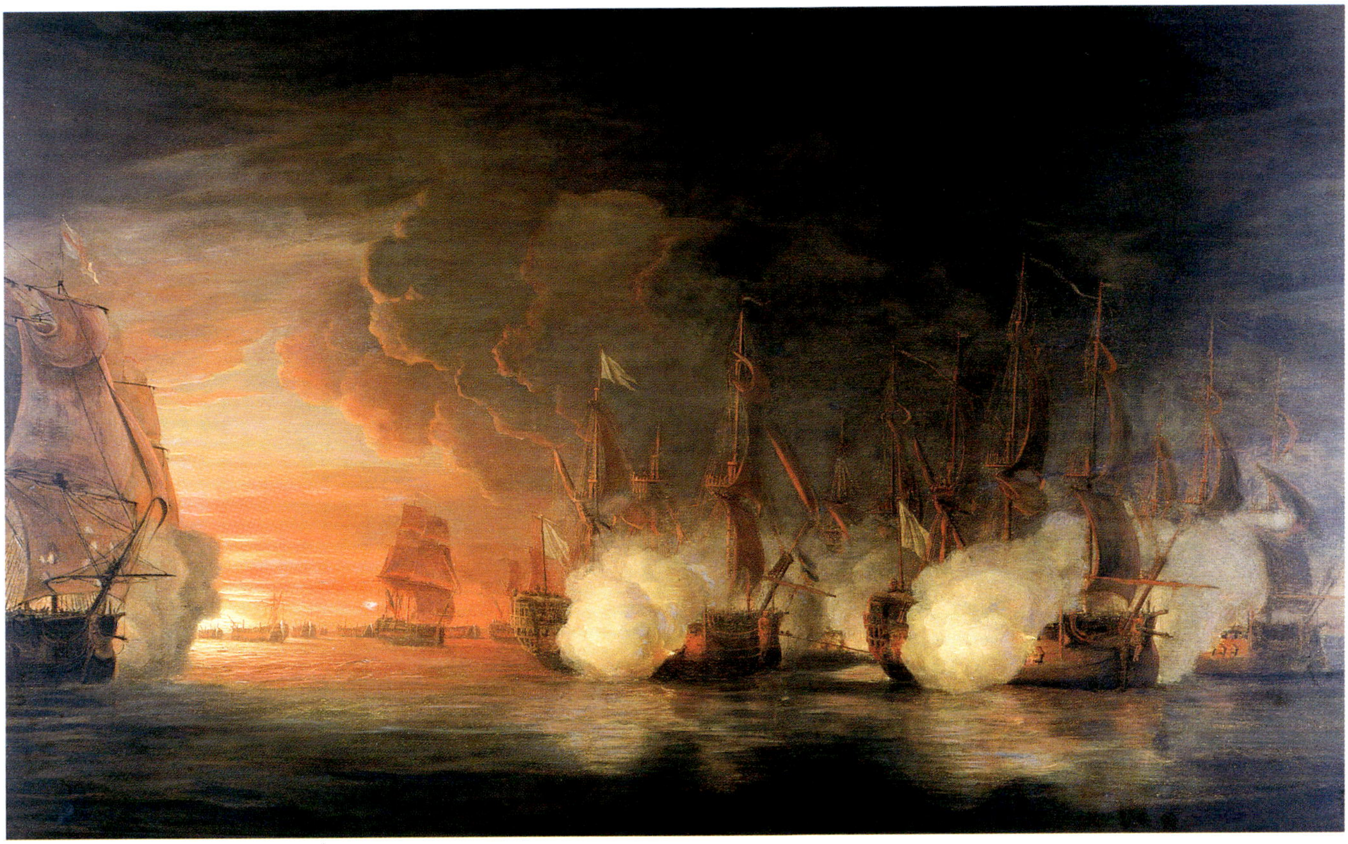

6/13
Dominic Serres (1722-1793). *The second Battle of Finisterre, 4 October 1747.* Oil on panel, 29½ x 48½, signed on reverse. Collection M. D. Joel

SAILMAKER, Isaac **1633/4–1721**

Born in Scheveningen, this painter was almost an exact contemporary of Willem van de Velde the Younger. Vertue says he came very young to London and was a pupil of George Geldorp; also that he did a painting for Oliver Cromwell of the fleet off Mardyke when that town was taken.

When the van de Veldes and some other Dutch artists of superior talent came to work in England in the early 1670s, Sailmaker was eclipsed, but he outlived them all to go on painting into his extreme old age. He died in London at the great age of 88 on 28 June at his house at King's Bench Walk, the Temple.

For a long time the lack of a signed painting by Sailmaker caused experts to doubt the traditional attribution of his works as not being good enough; a hand that has now been identified as that of Jacob Knyff was preferred. The identification of Knyff's work left a vacuum which was shortly afterwards filled when a well-documented Sailmaker painting of Rudyard's Eddystone lighthouse turned up and proved that the traditional identification had been correct. What is puzzling, bearing in mind how long he was active, is that existing identifiable works all appear to date from the last quarter of the seventeenth century and the first quarter of the eighteenth century. There are eleven engravings from his drawings.

SCOTT, Samuel **b.1701/2–1772**

Born in London. Though twenty years junior to Peter Monamy, Scott must rank with him as one of the two leaders in the first generation of English marine painters following on from the van de Veldes and the other Dutch immigrant painters who came to London in the 1670s.

We know nothing of his training as an artist but it is significant, in view of his subsequent city views, that in 1732 when the East India Company commissioned a set of paintings of some of their ports of call and factories abroad, the architectural subjects were painted by George Lambert, while Scott was commissioned to paint in the shipping parts. This suggests that Scott's admiration for the Thames views produced by Canaletto during his stay in London in the 1740s, prompted him to acquire similar skills; for it is on views of London that Scott's reputation chiefly rests.

He was very much a townsman – no pastoral scenes for him. He was a friend of Hogarth, another townsman, with whom he shared a fellow feeling and an eye for the workaday world. This is beautifully expressed in his painting of Custom House Quay in the Victoria and Albert Museum, a picture that could not have been painted during the preceding generation, whose painters would have felt that they had to romanticise it.

On the purely marine side, Scott accepted commissions for the actions of the War of Jenkins' Ear and the Seven Years War, as well as for general shipping pieces; all were painted in his studio in Covent Garden. Materially, he was more successful than Peter Monamy and much more successful than Charles Brooking, whose work he greatly admired, and justifiably. Since his work is comparable to that of Monamy and inferior to Brooking's, his success stemmed partly from his superior social talents and connections. He is said to have been a warm-tempered and kindly man. He was elected a Governor of the Foundling Hospital in 1746. Although any painting he may have given to the Foundling is now missing, it is suggested that it can be seen in part in an engraving entitled *Admission of Children to the Hospital by Ballot* by N. Parr after a drawing by S. Wale published 9 May 1749. See illustration 24, *Treasures of the Foundling Hospital*, by Nicholson, OUP 1972. It shows a large oil painting of a starboard stern view of a two-decker at anchor in a river with a cityscape immediately behind in Scott style.

His love of the sea and ships did not extend to a desire to sail in them, for apart from one trip to Helvoetsluys in one of the royal yachts of a squadron sent to collect George II, he never made another sea voyage. Indeed, one of the engravings commemorating a cruise down the Thames in a yacht with Hogarth and a party in 1732 shows him being pushed aboard.

Apart from his painting, which brought him a respectable income of £700 or £800 a year, he purchased the place of Deputy Clerk of Accounts to the Stamp Office; this brought in another £100 a year. Among his pupils were Sawrey Gilpin, who was with him from 1749 to 1758, and William Marlow from 1756 to 1761. About this time he retired to Bath to take the waters for gout and he died there 12 October. A bicentenary exhibition was held at the Guildhall Art Gallery, London, in 1972.

See Chapter 1, page 28 and Chapter 5, pages 74, 75.

SERRES, Dominic, the Elder **1722–1793**

Born near Auch, in Gascony, he came of a good family and was brought up in his father's country mansion at Beauperre. His uncle was an Archbishop of Rheims, and in Dominic's obituary in the *Gentleman's Magazine* he is called Comte Serres. He was sent to the famous English Benedictine school at Douai, which probably explains why he had no difficulties of communication when he came to England and accounts for his being a great anglophile.

His family intended him for the priesthood, but to avoid this he ran away, first to Spain and, once there, to sea. His education would have enabled him to grasp the intricacies of navigation and undoubtedly helped to bring him promotion and a command. He came to England after his ship had been captured, 'during the war of 1752', according to Redgrave. Since, however, there was no war in 1752, it has been generally assumed that he came to England near the outset of the Seven Years War in 1756. None the less, there exists a painting, surely done in England and dated 1754. It is thus possible that he was captured late in the War of the Austrian Succession (1741–48).

He knew Charles Brooking and was strongly influenced by him when he began to make a living by his brush. His early works strained after the commercial market and are luminous calms with ships in romantic settings. However, once success came to him he adopted a more immediate approach to his subjects, painting them far more realistically.

Like Samuel Scott and unlike Brooking, his success probably had much to do with his social gifts, for he was not only educated but also a most likeable and charming man. This must have commended him to his gentlemen patrons, as did the fact that he was a practical seaman to naval ones. Though a Frenchman, he became the most successful painter of the naval actions of the Seven Years War and the War of American Independence, from the British side. These paintings are most valuable historical documents and quite possibly more accurate than the written accounts. It must be admitted, however, that though well crafted they are often artistically dull.

Serres was a founder member of the Royal Academy in 1768 and in the last year of his life was its librarian; he was also made marine painter to George III. He exhibited at the Royal Academy from 1769 to the year of his death, when seven of his pictures were shown there. He also exhibited at the Free Society exhibitions and at the Incorporated Society of Artists, of which he became a member in 1765. He died in London 6 November 1793. At his four-day sale at Christie's in 1794 were 505 drawings and seven sketch books said to be by the van de Veldes, also three oil paintings by Brooking.

See page 103.

SERRES, Dominic, the Younger **c.1761/2–c.1804**

Born probably in London, he was the younger son of Dominic Serres, the Elder, and brother of John Thomas Serres. He first exhibited at the Royal Academy in 1778, when he was listed as Master Serres. If he began exhibiting at the same age as his brother, sixteen, then he must have been born in the second half of 1761 or the first half of 1762.

He continued to exhibit until 1787 and then there is a gap until 1804, when he exhibited a view of the Bay of Naples; he showed nothing more. It is said that he developed health problems of a cerebro-spinal nature and that he went to live with his brother, who looked after him. If this is so, he was not living at John Thomas' address in 1804 and one wonders whether his view of the Bay of Naples was done from firsthand knowledge of a visit there. From the evidence of his exhibited pictures, he did not follow his father and brother in choosing shipping subjects, though he painted some coastal views.

SERRES, John Thomas **1759–1825**

Born in London in December, he was the elder son and pupil of Dominic Serres, the Elder and was strongly influenced by the romanticism of Philippe de Loutherbourg and the Romantic movement, though he never approached the quality of that master. Indeed, had it not been for his father's position and prestige it is doubtful if he would have gained the honours and position that he did.

On his father's death he succeeded him in his appointment as marine painter to George III and the Duke of Clarence. Then in 1800 he was appointed Marine Draughtsman to the Admiralty. Ever since George Anson's first lieutenant, Piercy Brett, in the *Centurion* on the voyage round the world 1739–44, made drawings, subsequently engraved, of the coastlines they passed, the Admiralty had been conscious of the value of such views in identifying landfalls. Thus, Serres' task was to sail in naval ships round our coasts, down the western coasts of France and Spain and into the Mediterranean, making drawings in the form of elevations. A

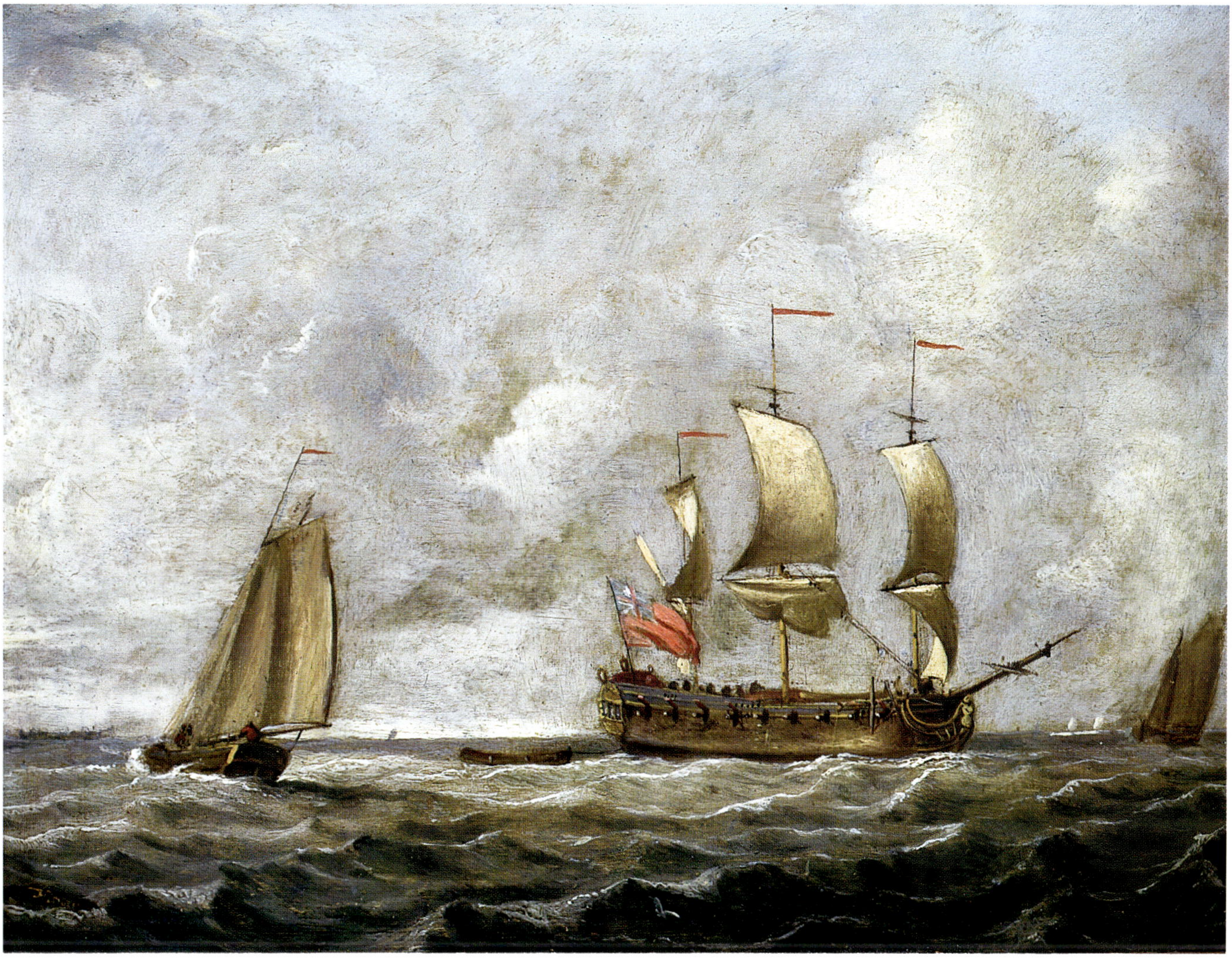

6/14
Francis Swaine (*c*.1720-1783). *A well armed merchant ship with other shipping in a fresh breeze.*
Oil on copper, 6⅛ x 8⅛. Mrs J.B. Joel

selection of these was subsequently published in a book entitled *The Little Sea Torch* (1801).

Serres also taught drawing for a time at the Chelsea Naval School and in 1805 published a work, *Liber Nauticus*; which aimed to help students draw ships and contained plates after his own work and that of his father, illustrating different types of vessels. He painted a few battle scenes, though none on the grand scale of de Loutherbourg, which is a little surprising considering his admiration for that artist. In about 1817 he became one of the proprietors of the new Coburg Theatre and subsequently its scenic director.

Sadly this considerable professional success was more than counterbalanced by his disastrous marriage to Olivia Wilmot, an extravagant and immoral woman with notorious delusions of grandeur. She claimed to be the illegitimate daughter of the Duke of Cumberland, calling herself 'Princess Olive of Cumberland' and passing on similar pretensions to her daughter. Her behaviour and debts ruined Serres, who lost all favour at court and died in a debtors' prison in London 28 December.

SWAINE, Francis ***c*.1720–1783**

In a list for 1735 of clerks and officers employed by the Treasurer and Commissioners of His Majesty's Navy, he is listed as a messenger; so the generally held estimate of his birth date, about 1740, cannot be right. We do not know how he came to be a marine painter but he was a close contemporary of Charles Brooking, whose work he sometimes copied. He was also strongly influenced by Peter Monamy, especially in his treatment of studio calms. This is why his work has been mistaken for both these artists' as well as John Cleveley's.

Swaine exhibited at the Free Society exhibitions from their inception in 1761 until the end of his life, and had put aside seven pictures for exhibition in 1783 which were included posthumously. The same thing was true for the Society of Artists exhibitions, where his work appeared from 1762 to 1783. It is curious that he never exhibited at the Royal Academy. He died in London. He had exhibited from an address near Avery farm in Chelsea.

On the whole Swaine liked to paint general shipping subjects and often on a small scale. He also took commissions for actions,

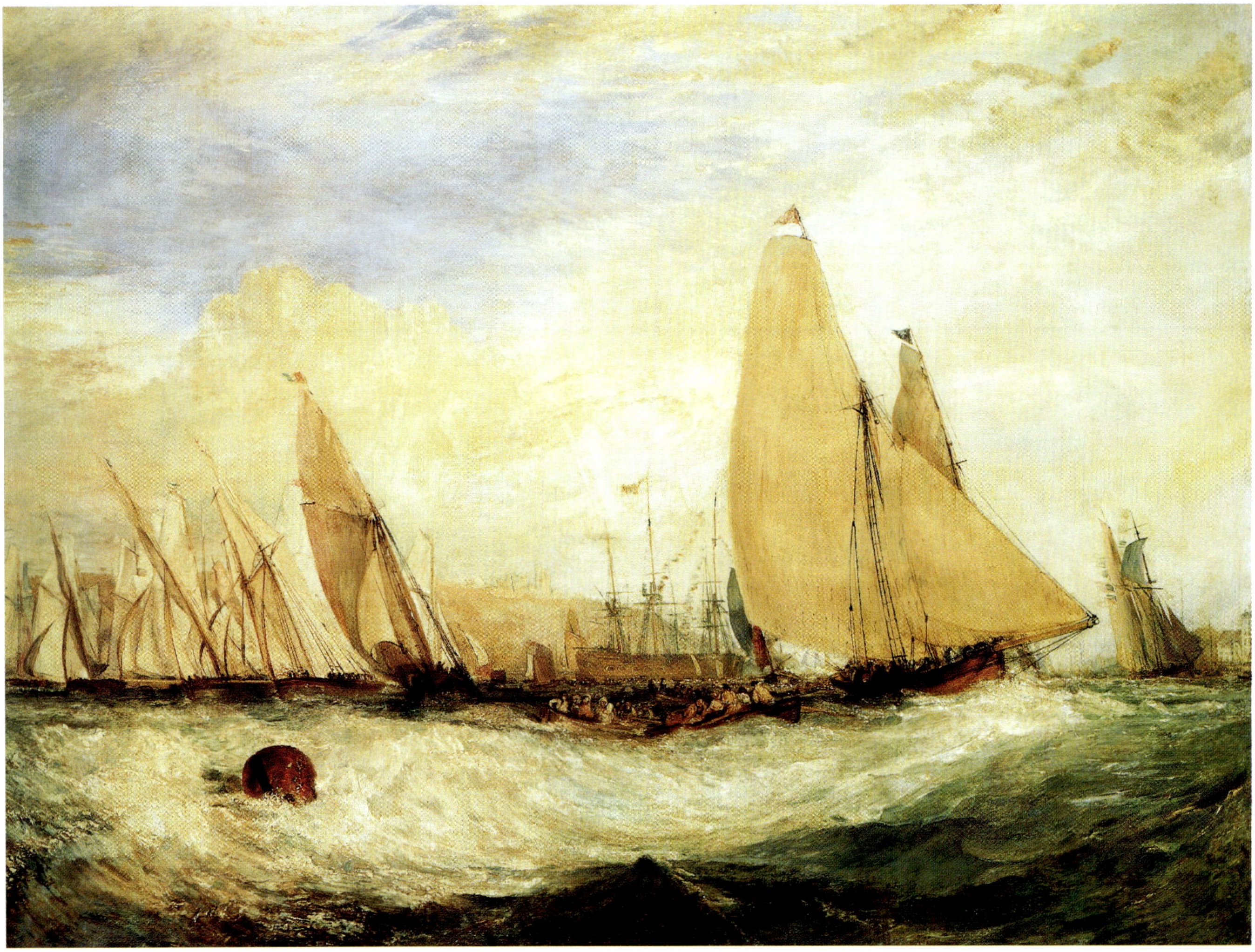

6/15
J. M. W. Turner (1775-1851). *East Cowes Castle. The regatta beating to windward.* Oil on canvas, 35½ x 47½.
Indianapolis Museum of Art, Gift of Mr and Mrs Nicholas Noyes

though in nothing like the numbers of Serres the Elder, and Paton.

Francis Swaine married Peter Monamy's daughter Mary at All Hallows, London Hill on 29 June 1749. They had two children, Anna Marie baptised 27 January 1750, and Monamy Swaine baptised 27 February 1754.

Researched by Harrison-Wallace. Pub. Societé Jensiaise Vol. 23 p.111 (1981) and Pallant House, Chichester, Catalogue Peter Monamy (1983).

See page 105.

SWAINE, Monamy **b.c.1754**
Probably born in 1754 since his first exhibited picture, not a marine, was at the Free Society in 1769, when he was described as 'Mr. Swaine Junior'. His first name honoured the memory of Peter Monamy, though his father, Francis Swaine seems to have had closer connections with Brooking since he copied some of his works. He continued to exhibit at the Free Society until 1774, only two of his pictures being marines. After this records on him and his work peter out, and it may be that he died about this time. His work, not always of high quality, shows the obvious influence of his father.

It is probable that Francis, his father, worked with Peter Monamy, for he was to marry Anne Monamy just after the old man's death. Thus Monamy Swaine is the grandson of Peter.

TURNER, Joseph Mallord William, R.A. **1775–1851**
Born in London 23 April, he was the son of a barber in Maiden Lane, Covent Garden. His interest in drawing was early and precocious and his father, who was later his business assistant, hung up some of his earliest drawings for sale in the barber's shop above which they lived. At fourteen he joined the Royal Academy Schools, and in 1790 the first of his paintings was accepted by the Academy for hanging in the annual exhibition.

His early marines were certainly encouraging, some being among the finest ever painted, such as *Calais Pier*, 1803, and the great picture of Dutch fishing boats, which the Duke of Bridgwater commissioned as a companion to his splendid van de Velde the Younger of a similar subject. His few attempts at naval historical subjects were not so happy. No doubt inspired by the blowing up of the French flagship there, he painted a Battle of

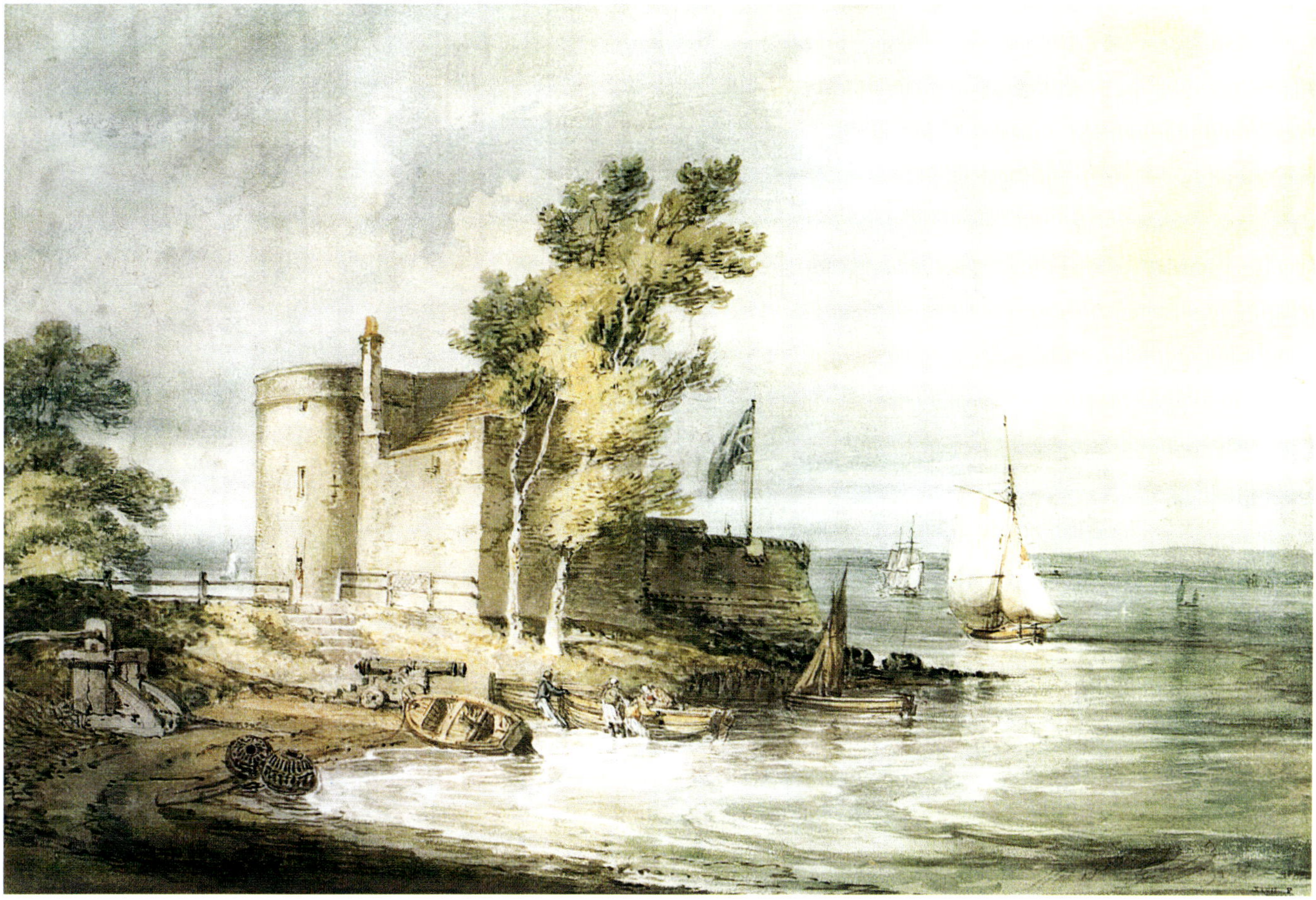

6/16
J. M. W. Turner (1775-1851). *Castle at West Cowes, Isle of Wight, 1795.* Sketchbook, watercolour.
RYS Collection

the Nile in 1798. In 1806 he began a painting of the Battle of Trafalgar, a deck scene rather than a marine, and unsuccessful. His next endeavour was a golden opportunity, which in the event proved a disaster. George IV wished to commission a Battle of Trafalgar to hang as a pair with the great de Loutherbourg of the Glorious First of June, in the ante-room of St. James' Palace. The Trafalgar was painted in 1824, and although containing fine passages with an impressive depiction of H.M.S. *Victory*, the picture as a whole fails. The King, who was as good a judge of art as any of his subjects, did not like it, the admirals hated it and the waiting ambassadors are said to have sneered at it. In the end the King got out of his predicament by giving both pictures to the naval gallery in Greenwich Hospital.

Only with *The Fighting* Temeraire *going to her last berth*, painted in 1839, did he really successfully combine art and a naval occasion.

Turner continued to exhibit at the Royal Academy until 1850, and at the British Institution between 1806 and 1846. He died in Chelsea on 19 December 1851.

On his death he bequeathed the very considerable contents of his studio to the nation. The Bequest material is now consolidated, at last and as Turner wished, in the new Clore Gallery for the Turner Bequest at the Tate, opened in 1987.

See page 106 and above.

VALE, H. **fl. c.1700–1730**

Paintings signed 'H. Vale' are by the earliest known English marine painter, on whom no information exists, except what can be deduced from his signed work. A large painting of the relief of Barcelona by Admiral Sir John Leake in 1706, and a portrait of the *Royal Katherine* of a somewhat earlier date are of good quality. A feature of both these paintings is a large decorative label in the top of the pictures, edged with shells and coral. According to Cockett there are now three more dated paintings signed H. Vale and dated 1713, 1714 and 1727 respectively.

VELDE, Cornelis van de **c.1675–1729**

His marriage entry in the Knightsbridge Chapel in 1699 anglicises his name to Cornelius, but he would undoubtedly have been Cornelis to his Dutch family. The marriage was to Bernarda, daughter of J. van der Hagen who was a friend and follower of Cornelis' father, W. van de Velde, the Younger.

Born in England after the family moved from Holland in 1672/3, he grew up to be an established marine painter, praised by J. C. Weyerman in his *De levens-beschrijvengen der Nederlandsche Kunst Schilders*, 1729, as being 'the best of all marine painters we could name'. In spite of this, his identity managed to sink into obscurity for many years.

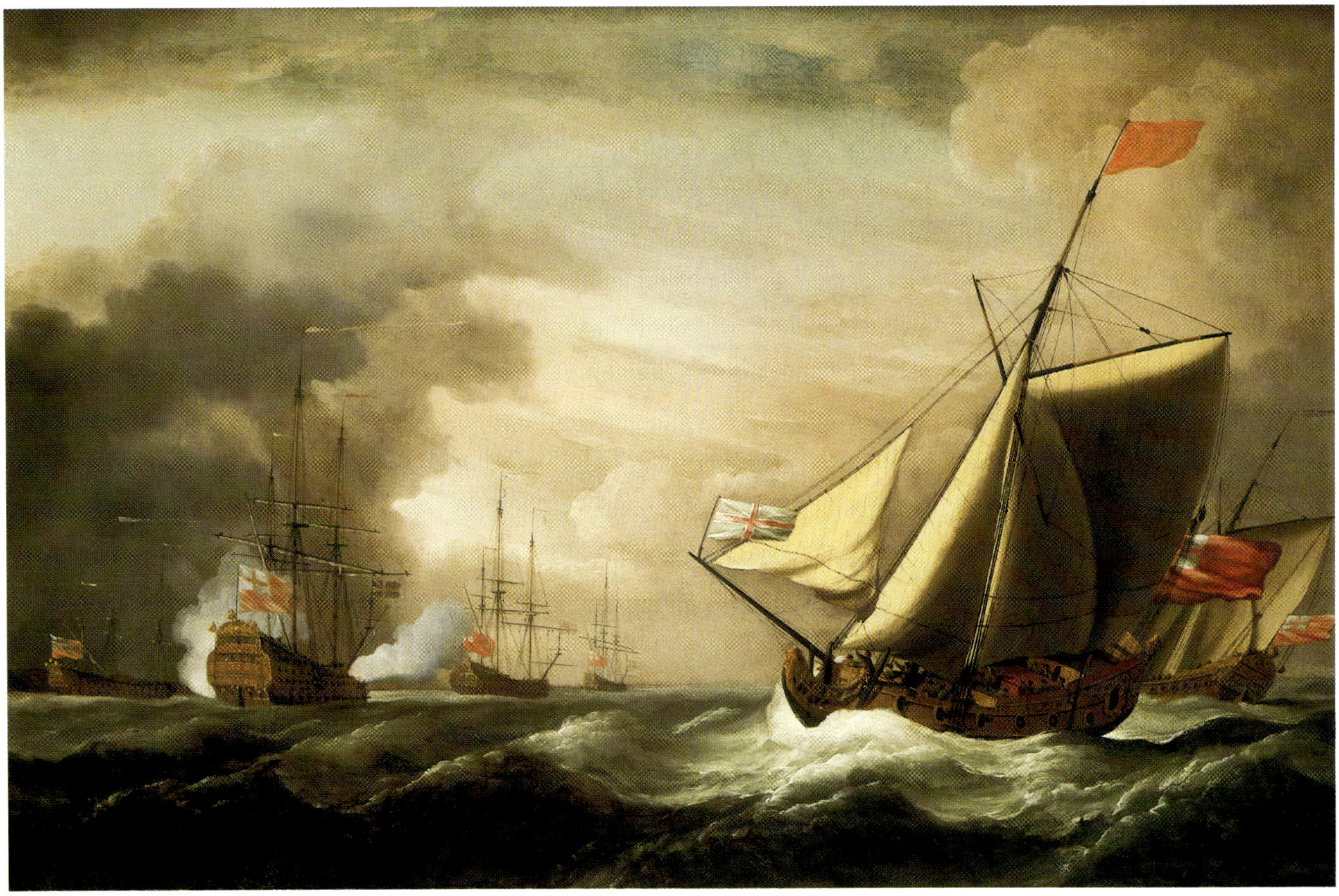

6/17
An Admiralty Yacht approaching an English Squadron of the Red, one of which fires a salute. This painting was recently sold as by 'follower of Peter Monamy'. On removal of an old relining canvas, this magnificent signature and date (right) were revealed. Lane Fine Art

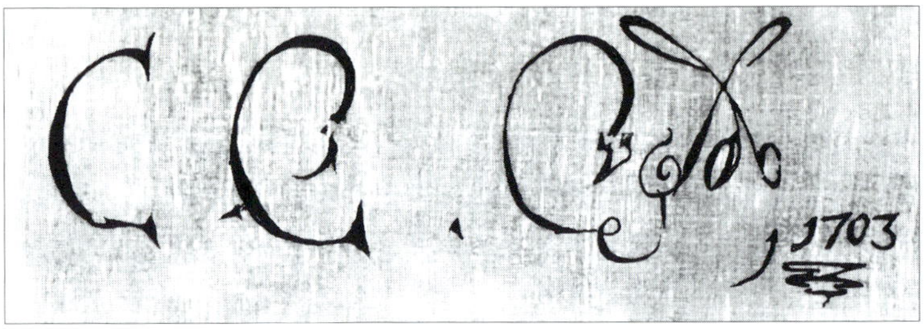

Speculation as to which hand was his ended when a signed storm piece appeared on the London market in 1965, and was bought by the National Maritime Museum, Greenwich. This picture enabled identification of a number of others. Later a couple of signed calms came to light, which completed the identification. These are in a highly finished and detailed style, more like the work of his grandfather, Willem van de Velde, the Elder than of his father. The calms have a characteristic pinkness in the sky.

One feature which may have contributed to Cornelis' long obscurity is his crabbed little signature, which is difficult to read. His standing as an artist in his lifetime, however, may be judged to some extent from his being asked to report on the progress of the work of Sir James Thornhill in the Painted Hall at Greenwich in 1717.

VELDE, Willem van de, the Elder 1611–1693
Born in Leiden, the son of a shipmaster, he went to sea as a boy. He married young and soon after the birth of his elder son, Willem, the Younger, in 1633, moved to Amsterdam; here his younger son, Adriaen, was born in 1636. Both boys were to grow up to be greater painters than their father, though only Willem inherited his father's love of the sea and ships. Adriaen, who was a pupil of his father, may have had too much of it as a child, for he turned his gaze firmly away from the sea and has left us rustic scenes of cows and people.

The elder van de Velde must be one of the earliest men, if not the earliest, to accompany a fleet into action as the official recording artist. Accompanying Marten Tromp's fleet in a galjoot in 1653, he was present at the Battle of Scheveningen and afterwards reported on it to the government. He was to repeat this, attending many Dutch Fleet actions. Up to this time van de Velde's finished works for sale had all been grisaille drawings – pen and ink drawings on prepared gesso panels, or sometimes canvases. It is not clear whether van de Velde developed this art form himself or whether he learnt it from Heerman Witmont,

6/18
Willem van de Velde the Younger (1633-1707). *The Morning Gun.* Oil on canvas, 26¼ x 20¾. Richard Green Gallery

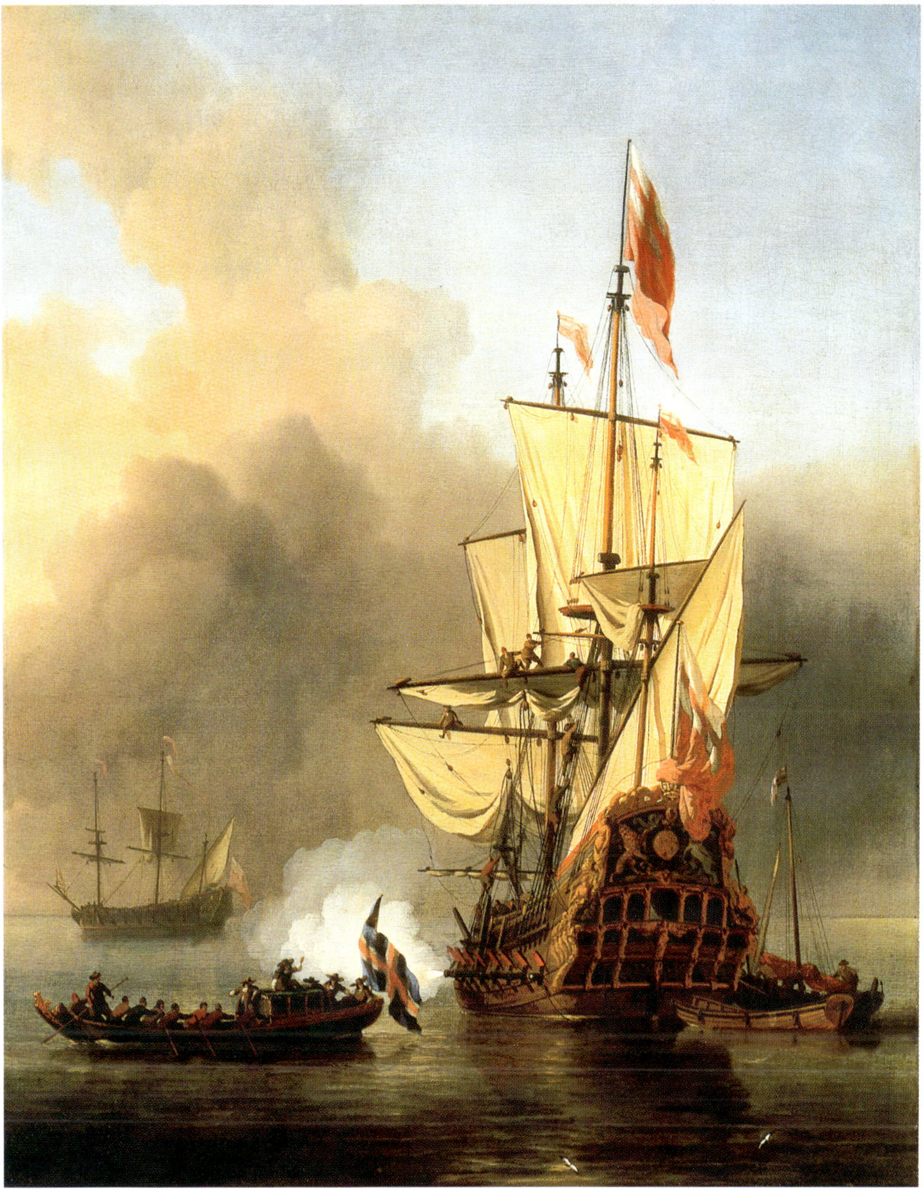

which seems the more likely. Unlike Witmont's work, which is generally done in sepia ink, van de Velde worked in black ink and he perfected his technique to a level never attained by anyone else; his grisailles, often four or five feet across, are one of the great glories of Dutch art.

It was a technique that enabled van de Velde to project in the finest detail his deep and expert knowledge of ships. The paintings did, however, take weeks or months to complete and must have been a strain on the eyes. This combination of reasons led him to turn to oils, an art he probably learnt from his son in the late 1660s when they were working in the same studio. His grisailles are signed on the front but oil paintings on canvas are usually signed on the back.

The van de Veldes came by invitation of Charles II in 1673 and immediately received royal patronage from the King and the Duke of York, to name but two, and the Elder van de Velde was soon in an English yacht accompanying the English fleet to record the two Battles of Schooneveld in June, this time from the English viewpoint. In August, Charles II would not let him accompany the fleet when it sailed to fight the Battle of Texel for fear he might be killed.

From this time and for the last twenty years of his long life (he died in Greenwich 13 December), the studio of van de Velde and his son Willem, dominated marine painting in England, and their style and approach to their subjects were the models and inspiration for the first generation of English marine painters.

Also working in van de Veldes' studio were other Dutch expatriates, J. van der Hagen, almost certainly Adriaen van Diest and probably Jacob Knyff, as well as the Elder van de Velde's grandson Cornelis. Van de Velde would have welcomed the company of his countrymen since he is not thought to have mastered English.

See Chapter 1, page 23.

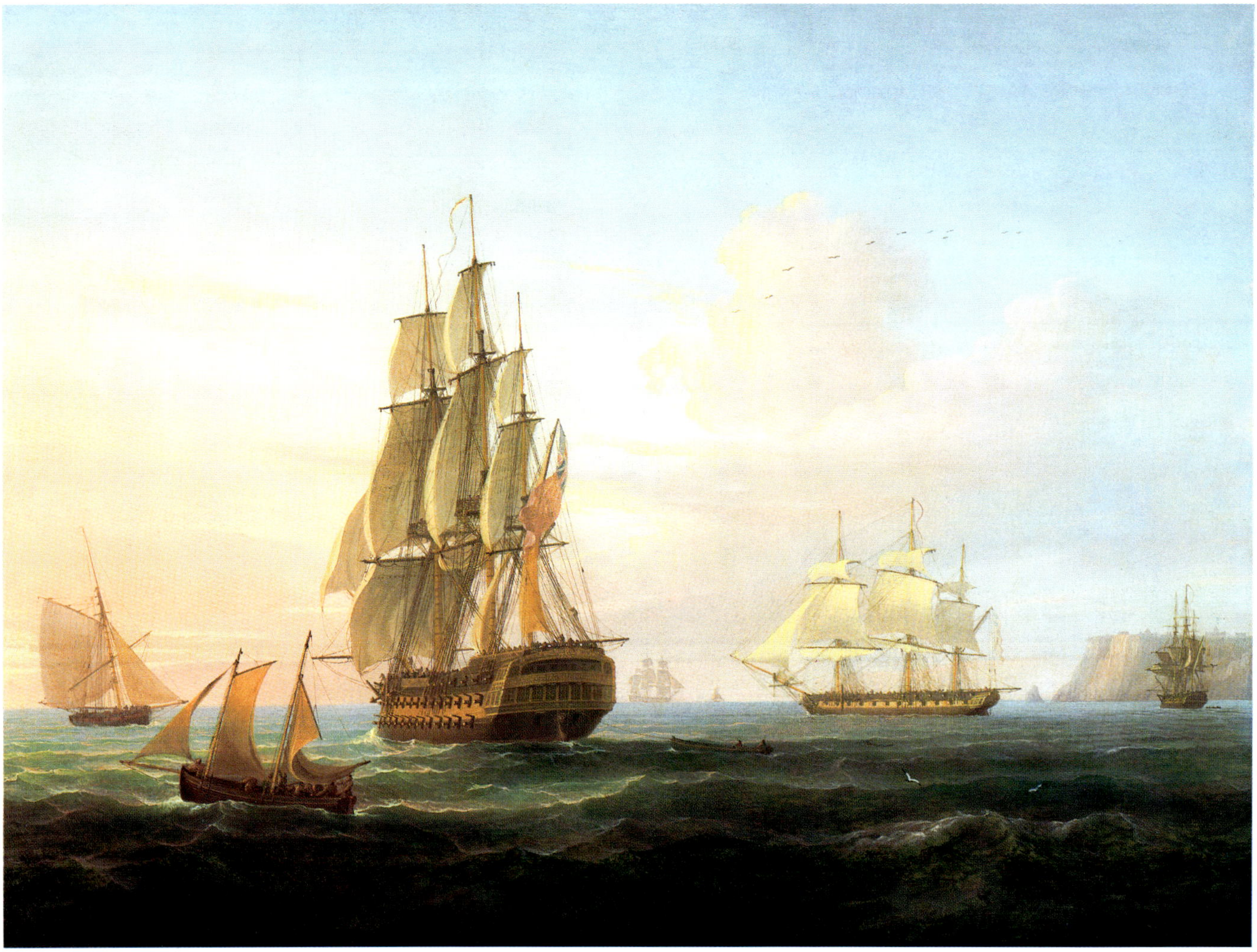

6/19
Thomas Whitcombe (*c.*1752-1824). Shipping off the Coast. Oil on canvas, 20 x 27. Signed and dated 1808.

VELDE, Willem van de, the Younger 1633–1707
Born in Leiden 18 December, he was the elder son of Willem van de Velde, the Elder. He inherited his father's love of ships and the sea. He was a pupil of his father, who taught him to draw; he then went to Simon de Vlieger who taught him to paint. His earliest known painting is at Greenwich and is dated 1651, when he was seventeen or eighteen. It is of ships driving on to rocks in a storm, and is very much like his master's style but not yet so good. His early works are highly finished and carefully crafted. As he got older and more confident his style broadened and he achieved his effects with more economy of brushstrokes. His palette changed too, from predominantly grey in his Dutch period to warmer browns in his English period.

Drawing was the basis of the van de Veldes' art, and both father and son poured out drawings all their lives. By these we know more about the appearance and decoration of Dutch, French and English ships of their time than we do about those of the 18th century.

Comparing father and son, the younger man excelled in painting; in drawing, though, he does not seem to have competed with his father in attempting grisailles. Even so, many of the ship portraits are very similar but under magnification the drawings of the carved figures on the ships do not read in the older man's work, as they do in the younger man's drawings.

Contemporary records in England relate that while the father made the live drawings of the actions at sea, his son translated them into oil paintings, though it is true to say that the Elder also made oils from his own drawings. Although the van de Veldes had received generous patronage both from Charles II and James II, they had no difficulty in welcoming Dutch William to the throne after the Glorious Revolution of 1688.

After his father's death in 1693, the mantle of marine painter to the King and Queen fell on Willem the Younger's shoulders, and in 1694 the commanders of the fleet were ordered to provide food and accommodation for him and his servant as long as he stayed aboard any of Their Majesties' ships. In the following year he accompanied the Straights Fleet to the Mediterranean.

Like his father, he is not thought to have acquired much knowledge of the English language, which could account for the lack of any known English pupil, although between them the van de Veldes worked for a period of thirty-five years in England. Van de Velde, the Younger died in Greenwich 6 April 1707.

He usually signed on the backs of canvases, but sometimes on the front; variously 'W. van Velde J', 'W.V. Velde der Jonge', 'W.V. Velde', 'W.V.V.', 'W.V.V.J.'

See Chapter 1, pages 24, 25; Chapter 5, pages 67, 71, 73.

WHITCOMBE, Thomas **c.1752–1824**

Information on the origins and death of this eminent artist still eludes us. Nobody contributed more to recording the naval side of the French Revolutionary Wars than Thomas Whitcombe and his output was vast. Apart from the paintings for the fifty plates in *The Naval Achievements of Great Britain,* published after the wars in 1819, he made paintings for at least one hundred more wartime engravings, as well as producing peaceful subjects.

He only exhibited one painting at the British Institution, in 1820, but at the Royal Academy he exhibited most years between 1783 and 1824, working from London addresses. His first exhibited painting, *The Destruction of the Floating Batteries before Gibraltar 1782* is very different in style from his mature work, which at its best is crisp and fresh. The rating for artistic quality of the four great recorders of the period, Nicholas Pocock, Thomas Luny, Thomas Whitcombe, and Robert Dodd, should place them in that order.

See Chapter 5, page 90; page 110.

WILKINS, Robert **c.1740–c.1799**

He painted a wide range of subjects, including portraits, landscapes and still lifes but also dockyard scenes and battles at sea. The Society of Arts awarded prizes between 1764 and 1768 for the 'best original sea piece on a canvas' and Wilkins won the first prize in 1765 and third prize the following year.

See Chapter 5, page 88.

WOODCOCK, Robert **1692–1728**

Clerk in the Admiralty with a keen interest in ships, he made drawings of them and at the age of thirty took up painting in oils. His admiration for the works of the van de Veldes led him to make many copies of their works. At Greenwich there is a remarkable version of the younger van de Velde's great painting of the *Gouden Leeuw* going into action at the Battle of Texel 1673, in which the latter is made into an English flagship and Spragge's *Royal Prince* into a Dutch flagship. When Woodcock died in London at the age of thirty-six, his style had not escaped from the influence of the van de Veldes but the versions of a third-rate getting under way show a confidence and originality which distinguishes his later works. One of these, dated 1726, is in the National Maritime Museum, Greenwich, which also owns a small painting based on the younger van de Velde's painting of the *Royal Sovereign* but depicting the *Royal William* instead.

He signed his work 'R.V.' or 'R. Woodcock'.

WRIGHT, Richard **1735–1775**

Born in Liverpool, he was called 'Wright of Liverpool', or 'Wright of the Isle of Man', the reason for the latter appellation is a mystery, though he did do a pair of paintings of Captain Elliot's action off the Isle of Man in 1760.

Wright was apparently self-taught and first exhibited at the

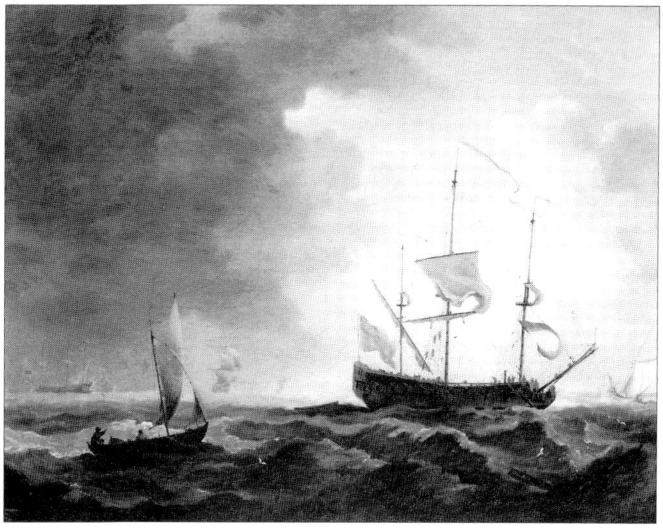

6/20
Robert Woodcock (1692-1728). *A third-rate getting under way.* Oil on canvas, 15½ x 20. National Maritime Museum, London

Society of Artists in 1762, and thereafter every year until 1773. In 1764 he exhibited one picture at the Free Society, *A Seapiece with a Squall of Rain*, a curious picture, also known as *The Fishery*. The picture won the highest prize of 30 guineas at the Society of Art's maritime painting competition in 1764. The cart in the foreground is explained by the fact that the picture was commissioned by a syndicate who planned an unlikely scheme to transport live fish in tanks full of sea water to inland customers. The weight factor in having enough water to support enough fish over rough roads and up and down hills must surely have been prohibitive.

Wright was aboard the royal yacht *Fubbs* in the squadron that went to Kiel in 1761 to collect Princess Charlotte of Mecklenburg-Strelitz to marry George III. On the voyage to Harwich three severe storms blew them towards Norway and the crossing took ten days. Wright did several paintings of the ordeal and one of these was his first exhibited picture at the Society of Arts.

See Chapter 5, page 87.

YATES, Lieutenant Thomas, R.N. **c.1760–1796**

Passed for a lieutenant in the Royal Navy in 1782. At what date he gave up the sea to be a painter is not clear but he first exhibited at the Royal Academy in 1788 and continued to do so until 1794, specialising in actions and views of good quality. When the French Revolutionary Wars began he started to publish pictures of actions from his own drawings.

His paintings are rare because of his short working life. He shared a London house that had belonged to his great-uncle (Richard Yates, the comedian) with a Miss Jones and in August 1796 they were in dispute about who owned it, though it had clearly been left to Miss Jones. After dinner on the afternoon of 29 August, his wife being out, Thomas took a stroll in the garden and Miss Jones locked him out. As he attempted to climb in through the kitchen window a Mr. Sellers, who had called in to protect Miss Jones, shot him. At the trial the jury returned a verdict of manslaughter; Sellers was fined one shilling (5p) and imprisoned for six months.

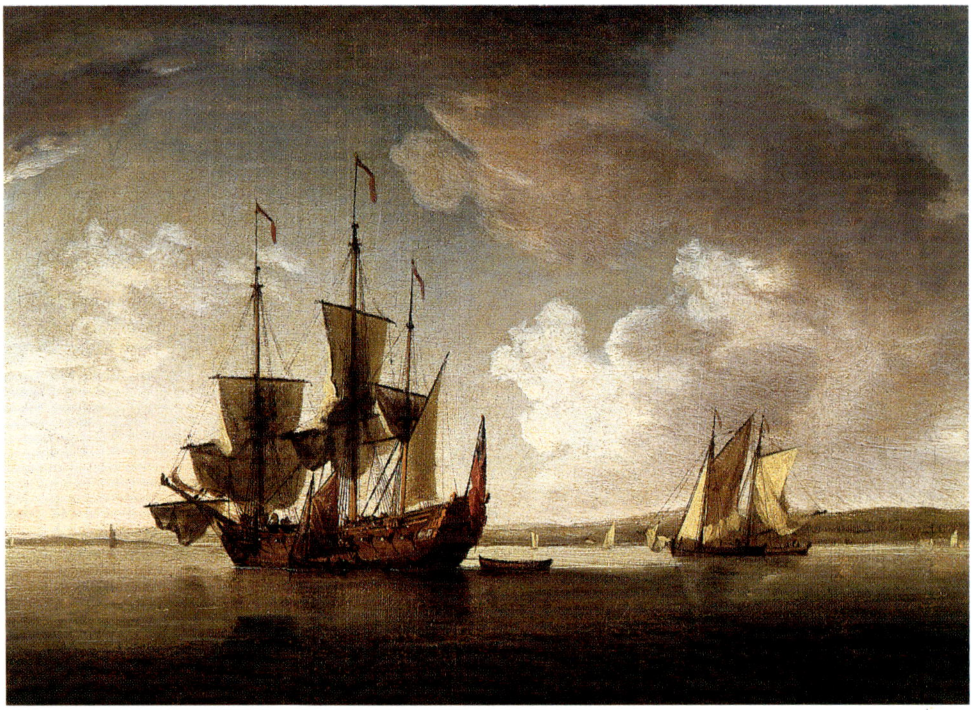

6A
A ship with two becalmed cutters off the land

Chapter 7

Catalogue

Introduction

The problem of indexing Charles Brooking's paintings is that only six of them are both signed and dated, whilst only just over half are initialled or signed. By 1966 about 90 of his paintings were extant and so it was decided to begin to catalogue the artist's work by the various grades of sea state from *calms* through *fresh breezes* to *gales* with a few extras like *shore scenes, ships on fire, battles, wrecks,* and *royal visits*. All known engravings and drawings are also illustrated and discussed.

The thematic breakdown of Brooking's work is as follows:

1-99	Calms
101-149	Shore Scenes
151-	Ships on Fire
201-230	Gales
231-	Fresh Breezes
351-	Battles
401-	Wrecks
450-	Royal Visits
700-	Drawings
600-	Engravings

Where Brooking has produced several versions of his compositions, these are grouped under alphabetical suffixes. Existing titles of paintings are used.

At the time of writing, the number of paintings discovered has risen to around 228 and we are fortunate if more than one or two are discovered in a year. These are supplemented by 29 drawings and 28 engravings. All measurements are given in inches.

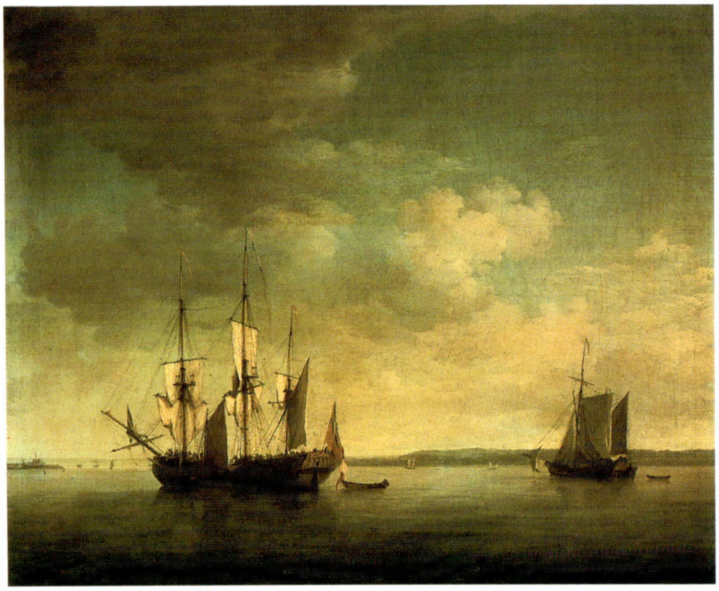

6B
An English frigate and two yachts at anchor in an estuary

CALMS

1A A ROYAL YACHT FIRING A SALUTE
Oil on canvas 14½ x 21¾. Signed C Brooking on the floating log in the left foreground. One of a pair. See 11B
Prov: John Smith 22 December 1857. A pair £60*
Christie's, 30 June 1894 170gns
Adrian Hope, 12 Langham Place, London
Sotheby's 15 July 1953 Lot 9. The pair £400
Partridge, Bond Street, London
Basil Mavrolean Esq.
Christie's 2 April 1965, Lot 44. 10,000gns.
Leggatt Bros
Private Collection
**John Smith's Day Book* Vol 4 p.492 (Victoria & Albert Museum) see 11B
An evening sky at sunset, with strato-cumulus clouds above cumulus and some blue patches. The sun is behind cloud and probably at the horizon signifying sunset, a very light air comes from the left of the picture.

To the right is a ship-rigged Royal Yacht post 1745, port quarter view firing to port from her aft midship gun. She is wearing the Royal Standard at the main, the Admiralty flag at the fore, the Union Flag at the mizzen, with the Red Ensign aft. This combination shows that the sovereign, King George II, is aboard. Her forecourse is loosed and main course clewed up, her mizzen is loose, fore and main topsails are mastheaded. A ship's boat is secured at her stern. In the left foreground is a two-masted fishing pink, port bow view, with five men aboard about to hoist sail; a skiff at her stern with mast down and one man in her, rowing. In the background to the left and in the gunsmoke is a small ship with a pennant with a Red Ensign and all courses set.

At the left of the picture is a hoy with topsail set. To the right of the picture is a pink with sails set but becalmed and beyond her a second Royal Yacht with jib and topsail set, main brailed up with flying jib bent on. There are three seagulls flying in the foreground.

The composition is of a more panaromic vista than van de Velde the Younger's composition which inspired it (see engraving 607). Van de Velde the Younger's oil painting is now in Schilderijenzaal, Prince Willem V, The Hague. Brooking's colouring is more carefully balanced giving a remarkable feeling of atmosphere. He has updated all the ships by fifty years or so from those in the van de Velde composition.

1B THE EVENING GUN (see title page)
Oil on canvas 14½ x 22½. Signed C Brooking on the log lower left
Prov: Property of a gentleman
Christie's 25 March 1899. Lot 66 135 gns
Bought Agnew's
Collection of J. Ackroyd of Manchester
Christie's 10 October 1958, Lot 1 850 gns
Bought Agnew's. Private Collection
A Royal Yacht wearing a Royal Standard. It is difficult to distinguish this painting from 1A except that the signature on the floating log in the lower left corner of the painting is further to the right. The right hand end of the log is in line with the middle of the bowsprit of the hoy above it.

1C THE EVENING GUN
Oil on canvas 14¾ x 22¼
Prov: Lady de la Rue
Christie's 15 November 1968, Lot 66 to L. Koetser
Exhibited L. Koetser May 1969
Private Collection
Christie's 15 April 1988 Lot 82 £35,000
Springfield Fine Art
Private Collection
This is very similar to 1A and 1B and depicts a Royal Yacht wearing a Royal Standard. However, the harp in the lower fly of the Standard is not visible. Also the spar for the mainsail of the pink at the right hand is yet to be hoisted. Some of the upper rigging has been repainted.

1D A CALM WITH AN ENGLISH YACHT SALUTING
Oil on canvas 15¼ x 23¼. Signed C. Brooking on plank lower left
Prov: Sir Bruce Ingram
Sotheby's 11 March 1964. Lot 5
(size incorrectly stated 15 x 22½ins) to Leggatt Bros for £15,500
Private Collection
In this painting there are several changes. The principal ship-rigged Royal Yacht is now a private ship with no Royal Standard flying. There is no man aloft in the port mizzen shrouds – he is in the fore shrouds instead. There are only three men in the single-masted fishing pink in the left foreground. The plank which bears the signature is at an angle to the horizontal and is further to the left. This is considered to be the best preserved of this series because the glazing and therefore the colouring is intact.
Exhib: Ferens Art Gallery, Hull. Early marine paintings 1951 No. 252
Mellon Foundation: Aldeburgh/Bristol June/July 1966, No. 31

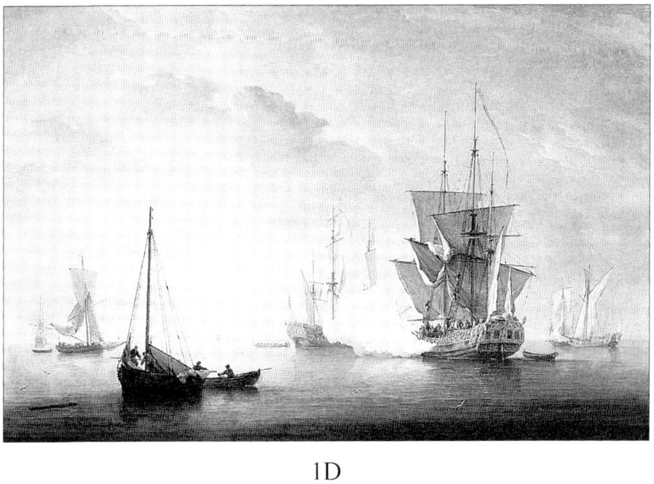

1D

1E THE EVENING GUN
Oil on canvas 15 by 22½
Prov: Sir Humphrey Browne CBE.
Christie's 16 July 1965. Lot 42 – 750 gns
Sir Raymond Smith
This painting has a different sky to the others in the series but must be attributed to a follower of Brooking because the drawing lacks the delicacy of touch and subtlety of effect of the others in the series. It does not exhibit the nautical accuracy commonly associated with Brooking. The principal ship-rigged Royal Yacht is wearing no standard. There are three men in the single-masted pink on the left with two seagulls on the left of the painting.

1F THE EVENING GUN or SUN SETTING
Oil on canvas 14½ x 22½
Prov: Christie's 16 July 1965. Lot 101
Private Collection
This painting is the reverse of an engraving by Boydell, 1753, of the painting by Willem van de Velde the Younger but the engraving has been modernised and this was very likely to have been done by Brooking, who was working with Boydell on a series of engravings at this time. The painting is likely to be by a follower of Brooking, perhaps from the engraving. Hopefully the original may yet be traced.

1G SHIP-RIGGED ROYAL YACHT FIRING AN EVENING GUN
Oil on canvas said to be 14 x 22 approx.
Prov: With Sir Patrick Donner in 1974
Stated by E. H. H. Archibald to be a likely looking picture in 1974.

2A SUNSET
Oil on canvas 12 x 15 (approx. sight size)
Prov: Given by Baron Winster in memory of his brother Herbert Fletcher, Master of Mathematics at Royal Naval College, Greenwich. Ex-Royal Naval College, Greenwich (was hung in the Stuart Room, King Charles building). In 1988 was in the Admiral President's house.

Sunset with cool blue sky with a line of cumulus clouds running diagonally across the painting with strato-cumulus above and puffy white cumulus around the horizon. A calm sea with two porpoises swimming in the left centre of the composition – the sun is below the horizon leaving an orange afterglow.

A Royal Yacht, starboard beam to quarter view on the right of the picture towing her boat; fore course, mizzen, fore main and mizzen topsails and spritsail set, jib bent on. Jack and ensign hoisted, commissioning pennant flying at the main mast. She is making way to the right where there is a two-masted sailing pink.

To the left of the picture a brigantine yacht under full sail with the main course half clewed up. To her left a hoy under full sail towing her skiff.

At the horizon, centre, are three other sailing vessels. In the foreground two porpoises are swimming to the right with dorsal fins showing.

This charming and elegantly coloured sketch was bequeathed to the Royal Naval College together with a fine collection of marine pictures, including oil paintings, watercolours, drawings and caricatures (42 in number). It is one of the few surviving sketches in oil by Brooking.

2B SUNSET. A SHIP-RIGGED ROYAL YACHT IN A LIGHT AIR WITH ANOTHER YACHT AND A CUTTER
Oil on canvas 10¼ x 15¼. Signed C Brooking
Prov: Private Collection
Exhib: Mellon Foundation: Aldeburgh June 1966, No. 34
The rigging has been rubbed away in places in this painting. It has been suggested that the yacht is either the *Carolina* or *Royal Charles*, the last named built in 1749.

2C SUNSET
Oil on canvas 10½ x 15½. Now signed C Brooking on a barrel centre foreground
Prov: Christie's 25 March 1966. Lot 22 – 2,300 gns
Richard Green
G. E. J. Robertson Esq.
Private Collection
When the painting was at Christie's it was badly damaged with two holes in the canvas and bore no signature.

2D SUNSET. A SHIP-RIGGED ROYAL YACHT IN A LIGHT AIR WITH ANOTHER YACHT AND A CUTTER (see Chapter 4, page 59)
Oil on canvas 9½ x 14¾. Signed C Brooking
Prov: Viscount Barrington
Vice Admiral B. C. B. Brooke
Sotheby's 17 June 1981. Lot 99 to Richard Green, for £7,000
Richard Green Marine Exhibition Catalogue 1981 No 6
Private Collection
In the left foreground can be seen a fishing basket which is not in any of the other three versions of this painting. A dead calm with not a breath of wind, with a tide of about one knot moving from the left to the right of the painting. The tide can be seen on the marker buoy in the right foreground as it lies to the tide with a pressure wave on its left side and a plume of disturbed water to the right. The sky is pale cerulean blue but through the centre of the painting rises a great mass of fair weather cumulus with a haze along the horizon suggesting the perfect English summer day. The sea is a ghostly calm in a deeper blue with long reflections of the shipping. To the left of the centre is a brigantine, starboard side to, with every possible sail set except the jib, the genoa, the fore topsail and the main course: she is wearing a Red Ensign at the ensign staff.

On her starboard side is a fishing hoy setting her sails and beyond her and to the left a hoy with sails set and two small fishing boats with mainsails set.

At the right of the painting is another fishing hoy with all sails being set by her crew of six men, one of whom is casting off a fishing boat on her starboard side – beyond and to the right is a ship at anchor, with sails furled.

At the left of this scene are two more small fishing boats, the larger with her jib furled around the forestay. The larger boat has a lobster post suspended over the stern.

Three seagulls are flying in the foreground, seven more fishing vessels are around the areas of the horizon. This is a late painting as shown by the disappearance of the fore part of the lateen mizzen yard in the brigantine.

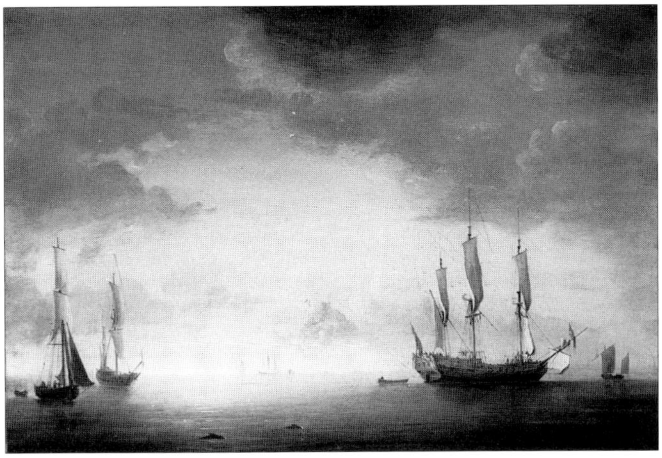

2E

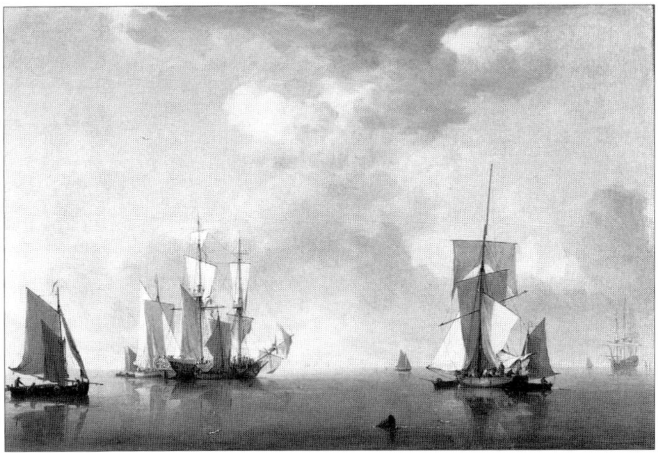

3A

2E SUNSET. A SHIP-RIGGED ROYAL YACHT AND OTHER SHIPPING IN CALM WATERS (see Chapter 3, page 51)
Oil on canvas 11⅛ x 16. No signature. Relined on to a new stretcher
Prov: Seen at Sotheby's July 1997. Lot No. H 239923-1 Label 14709
Private Collection (Midlands)

3A VESSELS IN A CALM (see page 5)
Oil on canvas 14¾ x 22½. Signed C Brooking on buoy in centre foreground
Prov: Sir Bruce Ingram
Sotheby's 11 March 1964 Lot 4
Sold to Leggatt Bros for £14,500
Private Collection
Exhib: Colnaghi Masterpieces of Maritime Art from the collection of Captain Bruce Ingram, 1938 No 5 (colour)
Ferens Art Gallery, Hull. Early Maritime Paintings 1951 No. 259
Royal Academy. European Masters of the 18th Century 1954-55 No 145
Walker Art Gallery 1958
Mellon Foundation: Aldeburgh/Bristol June/July 1966, No 27
Illustrated: *A Book of Ships*, E. Mitchell, Penguin 1941, Plate 12 (colour). *Sea Painters of Britain*, F. Gordon Roe, 1947, Plate 3 (colour).
A very delicate sepia and grey toned picture. A late painting, as shown by the disappearance of the fore part of the lateen and mizzen yard.

3B FISHING VESSELS IN A CALM
Oil on canvas 14 x 21½
Prov: William Wells 1890
Christie's 10 May 1890. 190gns
Agnew's
Mrs R. N. Bernard
Christie's 1 November 1963, Lot 34
To Leggatt Bros for 5,200 gns
Private Collection
Another fine example of this late painting. Very similar to 3A. Differences are to be found in the size of the lobster pot on the left hand fishing boat – it is larger, and the seagulls are in slightly different positions. Otherwise it is almost identical. This one is unsigned.

3C FISHING VESSELS IN A CALM
Oil on canvas 14 x 22 inches approx. Signed C Brooking
Prov: Sir Richard Boughey Bt in 1966
Mellon neg 4108
Judging from a photograph, this appears to be a similar composition to 3A and B with minor differences of ships on the horizon only.

3D FISHING VESSELS IN A CALM
Oil on canvas 14¼ x 22½. Signed C Brooking
Prov: Stafford Bourne Esq.
Christie's 3 July 1964
Private Collection
Sotheby's 21 March 1979, Lot 20 Sold for £17,725
Private Collection
This painting differs from the others in this series, and may predate them. The brigantine and fishing boats are in the same basic positions, but there is no ship at anchor with sails furled on the right. The sky is less dramatic with less cumulus. The buoy in the foreground is not there and there is no indication of tide. The ships on the horizon number seven, but they are in different positions to the other versions.

A calm day with a light breeze coming from the left of the painting. A summer blue sky, some altocumulus with towering cumulus rising at the horizon. Some dark cloud in the top left heralding perhaps a light squall with a shift of wind. The horizon is low, about one quarter of the way up the picture.

To the left an English 18 gun frigate starboard quarter to, with a cutter and two luggers beside her. The frigate has the fore course set, main course partly brailed, mizzen set. Fore and main topsails set, mizzen topsail being hoisted. She flies pennants at each masthead and a Red Ensign at the stern. A second frigate of 20 guns is at the horizon on the right with main and top course set, mizzen furled ghosting slowly to the right.

A fishing pink is in the right foreground with three crewmen and alongside her is a rowing boat with two men.

A marker stake is at the left foreground to the left of the

frigate and fishing boats. A similar stake is to the left of the right hand pink. There are four boats at the horizon.

4A EAST INDIAMAN BECALMED WITH CUTTERS AND LUGGERS (see Chapter 3, page 52)
Oil on canvas 22¾ x 32. Signed C Brooking
Prov: Hon Mrs Cecil Brownlow
Lt Col the Lord Lurgan OBE
Christie's 18 April 1986 Lot 73 £26,000
Fine Art Consultants
Private Collection
Exhib: Mellon Foundation: Bristol July 1966, No. 37
Sotheby's RNLI Exhibition Jan 1986 'Rule Britannia' Cat. No. 34
A majestic painting of a calm, which seems to be untouched by restorers. There are others in this series and also moonlight paintings of the same basic subjects. See 5A and 5B.

4B SHIPPING IN A CALM
Oil on canvas 21½ x 29½. No signature
Prov: Photographed at the National Maritime Museum in 1933
Christie's 7 Oct 1993 Lot 404 Sold for £9,400
Private Collection
The composition of the shipping is the same but there is low-lying land and islands at the horizon on the right. In the right foreground is a sand bank with a single stake only marking it. This stake has three supporting stakes arranged in a tripod at the base.

At the Christie's sale this painting was described as 'An East-Indiaman and fishing craft off Sheerness'. It is a very smooth, rather green sea painting and appeared to be in good condition.

4C A SHIP BECALMED WITH CUTTERS AND LUGGERS
Oil on canvas 15 x 23⅛. No signature
Prov: John Carr of Dunston Hall 1806 (see also 263)
Stafford Bourne Esq. (in 1960)
Private Collection
Exhib: Mellon Foundation: Bristol July 1966, No. 38
Both this painting and No. 263 belonged to John Carr and they both have similar carved frames. The cutter and two luggers beside the 18 gun frigate are in different positions in this painting to those in 4A and 4B.

4D A SHIP BECALMED WITH CUTTERS AND LUGGERS
Oil on canvas, size unknown
Prov: Major D. McCalmont, Eire 1969
Christie's Neg. 369184. Not yet seen
To date three paintings in this series have been traced. These paintings are related to series 4, which are broadly the daylight equivalent so far as the subject is concerned, with similarly disposed vessels off a muddy shore. In one of these Sheerness has been suggested, perhaps in relation to Brooking's trip to the Isle of Sheppey in August 1752 to make botanical studies with John Ellis, the Naturalist and Fellow of the Royal Society.

Moonlight Paintings (5A-C)

Brooking had experimented as early as the age of 17 in making a moonlight picture (see 152) and he also painted ships on fire at night (see 151 and 153) but later in life he painted three superlative moonlight paintings with the moon shining on the sea on an almost windless night. That the ships depicted in the paintings vary from men o'war to merchant brigs is noted, but in all three canvases there are a number of other vessels present, and all three show fishermen and fishing boats.

These paintings certainly show a degree of experimentation with the position of the moon which is central in 5C, but moved to the right in the other two, to give a varying balance to the scene. The clouds are also moved as well and reveal an ethereal night-sky, but no stars or planets.

All of them have a muddy foreground and also fishing stakes or marks, and one the remains of a jetty. One cannot help but feel that the painter was personally involved in this place, but we can only guess at its whereabouts. Wherever it is, all three paintings are beautifully controlled, atmospheric paintings of sea and sky.

5A A FRIGATE BECALMED BY MOONLIGHT WITH CUTTERS AND LUGGERS (see Chapter 1, page 31)
Oil on canvas 11 x 15. Signed C Brooking lower left
Prov: Lord Barrington
Commander David Joel RN
Mrs S. J. Herrtage
Exhib: Newtown Park Marine Exhibition 1983
This painting is the only one of the three in the series which is signed. Significantly, the man o'war has no commissioning pennants but has at least 16 guns on the main gun deck and probably more above. The mizzen sail is cut off and laced to the mizzen mast which M. S. Robinson and E. H. H. Archibald state occurred after 1760. However, this new research means that it must have happened at least 10 years earlier for this is a late painting by Brooking. There is a channel mark, a stake with a topmast in the right foreground.

5B AN ENGLISH MERCHANT BRIG AND COASTAL CRAFT BECALMED BY MOONLIGHT
Oil on canvas 15 x 23. Not signed
Prov: Christie's June 1975 catalogued as by Pether
E. H. H. Archibald Esq., MA
Christie's 12 April 1991 Lot 69 £11,000 to Cockett
Private Collection (USA)
Illus: *Dictionary of Sea Painters*, E. H. H. Archibald, Colour Plate XIV p.132.
This painting is also shown on the dust jacket of the 1st Edition (1980) of E. H. H. Archibald's *Dictionary of Sea Painters*. A magnificent moonlight painting showing in great detail the brig and other shipping. The lateen mizzen yard ends at the masts, so this rig must have been in use before Brooking died in 1759. Thus the rig must be earlier than either Robinson or Archibald suggest. It must have been in use by 1755 or even earlier.

The remains of a jetty are in the centre foreground, together with a fisherman who is making his dinghy fast to them.

5C AN ENGLISH FRIGATE AND COASTAL CRAFT BECALMED BY MOONLIGHT
Oil on canvas 14½ x 22. Not signed
Prov: From Sweden

Sotheby's 9 Nov 1994 Lot 3 £6,200
Private Collection
Basically the same as 5B but the cutters and luggers are in different positions, as are the clouds. The painter was experimenting.

The frigate is brig-rigged rather than ship-rigged. The mizzen yard is cut off at the mast to which the sail is laced. The sail is loose-footed, which reinforces the observation that this change in rig occurred in the early 1750s, and certainly before Brooking's death in 1759. Both Robinson and Archibald had reason to believe that this alteration was after 1760, but if it is shown in at least eight paintings by Brooking, some of which are signed by him, then it is fair now to assume that the change came about ten years earlier, in the 1750s.

The mud bank is in the centre foreground in this version with the remains of the jetty to the left. The channel mark, a stake without a topmast, is on the right of the picture.

6A A SHIP WITH TWO CUTTERS BECALMED OFF THE LAND (see page 112)
Oil on canvas 9½ x 13⅝. Not signed
Prov: Sir Bruce Ingram
Mr and Mrs Paul Mellon
Sotheby's 18 November 1981 Lot 81 £2,400
Private Collection
Exhib: Spink & Son 1966
Mellon Foundation: Aldeburgh/Bristol June/July 1966, No. 28
A calm day with little wind. Pale blue sky with dark cumulus high overhead, and towering cumulus at the horizon. Land across the horizon. An armed merchant ship (20 guns) moves port side on across the left of the painting towing her gig. On the right of the scene two cutters are becalmed alongside one another. Beside the ship, close alongside or perhaps secured beside her, are a small sailing cutter and another gig with several men in them. Perhaps the cutter is bringing a pilot on board as the ship heads for her anchorage to the left of the painting.

6B AN ENGLISH FRIGATE AND TWO YACHTS AT ANCHOR IN AN ESTUARY (see page 112)
Oil on canvas 24 x 29½. Bears another signature
Prov: Sotheby's 20 Nov 1985 Lot 5
Richard Green Gallery for £36,000
Private Collection
The same scene, but the ships have changed. If the ships are not anchored they are preparing to do so. The headland on the left appears to have a castle on the promontory. It could be the Solent with an ebb tide running off Fort Gilkicker or Calshot. This painting is much larger than 6A. The ship is a 26 gun frigate and the closer of the yachts appears to be a topsail cutter-rigged Royal Yacht.

7A TWO SMACKS AND OTHER SHIPPING BECALMED (see page 129)
Oil on canvas 15⅛ x 22. Not signed
Prov: Nicholas Argenti Esq.
Mrs Conran
Loan to National Museum of Wales, Cardiff
Exhib: Mellon Foundation: Bristol July 1966, No. 33
National Museum of Wales, Cardiff
Blue skies with large white puffy cumulus to quite a height across the whole horizon. Little wind, just a zephyr or two, sufficient to give the larger fishing boats steerage way. On the left, two cutter-rigged fishing boats overlapping one another. The nearer is towing a skiff with a man in it. To the right, three similar fishing vessels surround a small merchant brig, two to the left of her and one to the right. In the right foreground two men are rowing a boat towards the left of the painting. Five other vessels are on the horizon. Two of them could be men o'war.

7B FISHING BOATS, A BRIG, A ROWING BOAT WITH TWO MEN O'WAR AND OTHER CRAFT BEYOND IN A CALM SEA
Oil on canvas 14¼ x 22¼. Signed C Brooking lower left
Prov: Lieut Colonel D. M. Anderson (according to Witt Library)
Christie's 20 Nov. 1964 Lot 40 to Leggatt Bros (for £7,875)
David B. Goodstein, New York
This painting is almost the same size but much more detailed than 7A and it is signed on a floating log, lower left. There are more vessels on the horizon and it is evident that two are men o'war. All these ships are in slightly different positions to 7A. The skiff with a man in it has an oar poking out over the stern; the rowing boat, right foreground, has a spar sticking out from the bow. All five of these pictures show the brig with the mizzen laced to the mizzen masts and with the mizzen yard cut off at the mast. Thus they must be late paintings by Brooking. Other differences in this painting are five seagulls flying above the horizon and two porpoises swimming to the left in the centre foreground.

7C FISHING BOATS IN A CALM SEA
Oil on canvas 15 x 23⅞. Signed
Prov: Lady de la Rue Trust
Christie's 15 Nov. 1968 Lot 65 (£4,000)
Agnew's 1970
Private Collection
The same painting but the positions of the fishing boats vary a little. The big difference is that in place of the rowing boat there is a large round buoy in the centre of the picture and on it is written 'C Brooking'.

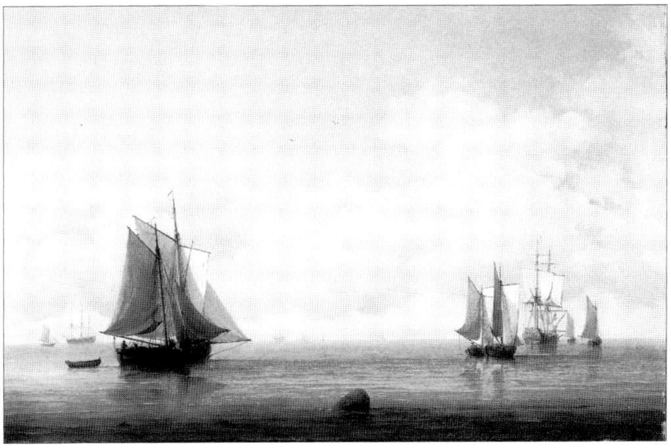

7C

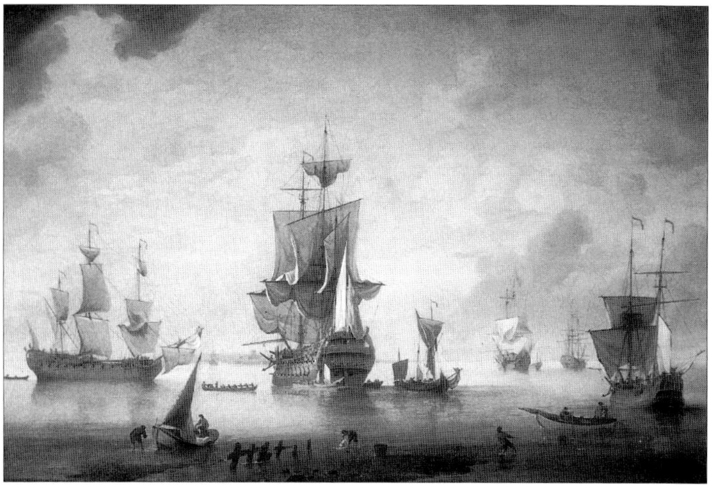

8A

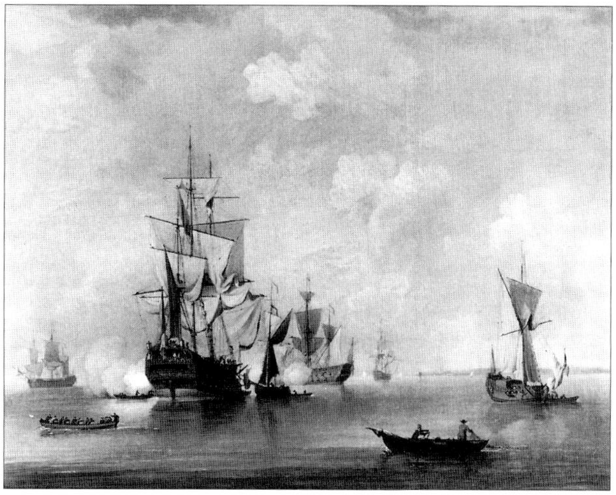

9A

7D VESSELS IN A CALM
Oil on canvas 15 x 22. Signed C Brooking lower left
Prov: John Mitchell Gallery (1958)
Sotheby's 8 July 1964 Lot 150 for £550
Private Collection
The last two in this series, D and E, depict the same shipping but are simplified. The two fishing boats have been moved almost to the centre of the painting and are nearer to the viewer. The brig which looks more like a snow is moved away and has only two fishing boats to the right of her. The men o'war have vanished and another fishing boat is to the left, but distant from the main group. The rowing boat and buoy are missing and the gaff of one boat is lowered. Only one gull is seen flying over the water in the foreground – none in the sky.

7E FISHING VESSELS IN A CALM
Oil on canvas 14½ x 20⅞. Signed C Brooking on log lower left
Prov: Countess of Craven. Coombe Abbey Sale No. 261
Sotheby's 27 Nov 1968 Lot 11 (sold for £1,700)
F. Sabin
Private Collection
Exhib: Ackerman & Johnson Dec 1996, No. 15
Very much the same as D above, but there are fewer men on deck in the snow and importantly the fishing boat in the mid-distance to the left of the main group is towing a dinghy. There are also three extra vessels on the horizon.

8A SHIPS BECALMED IN THE SOLENT (see page 8)
Oil on canvas 44 x 60. Signed Brooking lower left
Prov: National Maritime Museum (1943-63)
A series of three accomplished, but rather crowded, large paintings of a typical calm Solent day, the water green and with blue sky and a mass of high cumulus. The fort is almost certainly Southsea Castle and thus the painting is from the Isle of Wight shore. The main ships in all three pictures are a third rate of 64 guns, stern on with port side showing, in the centre of the scene and to the left, a sixth-rate of around 28 guns showing her full starboard side as she moves across the water. Additionally each painting has between six and eight other vessels, the remains of a jetty or breakwater in the mud of the centre foreground, with fishermen and two small boats.

8B
Oil on canvas 36½ x 52. Signed C Brooking lower left
Prov: Mrs Campbell-Watson
On loan to Walker Art Gallery Liverpool (1979)
In this version there are three ships of the line and a Royal Yacht on the right horizon (one extra ship of the line) and instead of the snow stern to in the right foreground, there is a fishing hoy moving out of the scene. It is the smallest of the series.

8C
Oil on canvas 37 x 55½. Not signed
Prov: Miss Allchin of Alverstoke
Sir William Henry Allchin
Private Collection
Again the main difference is on the right horizon, with only one ship of the line and the Royal Yacht shown. As in B above, there is a fishing hoy moving to the right.

9A BRITISH MEN O'WAR SALUTING AND FISHERMEN
Oil on canvas 27¼ x 33½. Signed C Brooking Pt lower left
Prov: Mrs P. A. Watson
Mrs Campbell-Watson
On loan to Walker Art Gallery, Liverpool 1979
Exhib: Walker Art Gallery 1958
Illus: *Illustrated London News* Nov. 1958
A calm, sunny day off a coast with towering cumulus sky. In the left foreground a two-decker seen from the stern and starboard quarter firing a salute, with another two-decker beyond, port side showing, also firing a salute. In the right mid-ground a small smack-rigged Royal Yacht of 8 guns. A third two-decker is on the left near the horizon. In the right foreground a man is rowing a small boat in which a fisherman is laying a net which stretches to the side of the picture. An eight-oared galley is being rowed in the left foreground to the left of the scene. A fourth two-decker is off the point of land.

9B
Oil on canvas 18¾ x 23½. Not signed
Prov: M. Bernard Gallery £1,500
Colonel Rupert Preston 1964
Illus: *Apollo* magazine July 1964

Private Collection
A smaller picture with one less two-decker. The galley with four men in it is made fast to the stern of the principal man o'war. There are two buoys in the left foreground together with three gulls flying just above the sea.

9C
Oil on canvas 24½ x 29½. Signed C Brooking on pile of jetty lower left
Prov: Duke of Sutherland, Donrobin Castle
Christie's 29 Nov. 1957 Lot 32
Agnew's
A similar composition to 9A and 9B, although there is a promontory in the left foreground and a mud bank across the painting on which are a grounded boat and two men. The right hand man is in the centre of the picture with a fish basket on its side. A galley with six oars is rowing from the left of the painting towards the main two-decker. In place of the Royal Yacht in B and C is a sailing fishing cutter.

10 A CALM WITH A MAN O'WAR SALUTING
Oil on canvas 14½ x 19¾. Signed on the log lower right
Prov: Christie's circa 1928
Sir Bruce Ingram
Lent to National Maritime Museum
Sotheby's 11 March 1964 Lot 6 for £3,000
Leggatt Bros
Private Collection
Exhib: Royal Academy of Arts, British Art, 1934 No 230
Illus: *Illustrated London News* 1 Aug 1931 and again 6 Jan 1934
Calm airs with six men o'war, the principal of which has just fired a gun. She is seen in the centre right of the design from her starboard quarter and has fired one of her port battery. An eight-oared gig has just left the ship with four officers wearing cocked hats – this boat is centre left proceeding to the left of the picture. A second two-decker is at centre ground left. The three remaining men o'war are near the horizon and appear to be sixth-rates. To starboard of the principal ship is another rowing boat with seven persons, the oars appear to be stowed. Further to the right is a sailing cutter under two jib sails. There are three buoys in the water and seven seabirds flying low over the sea. Full mizzens are set.

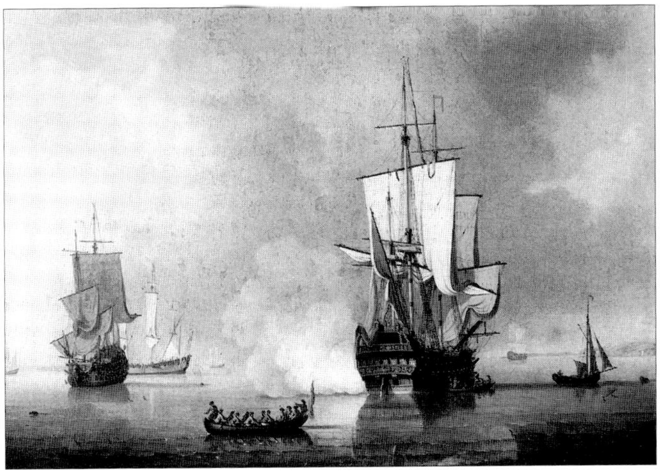
10

11A DUTCH FISHING BOATS MOORED IN A CALM ESTUARY (see page 129)
Oil on canvas 17½ x 24¼. Signed C Brooking by anchor lower left
Prov: Northwich Park Collection. Captain E. G. Spencer-Churchill
Christie's 25 June 1965 Lot 81 3,800 gns
Agnew's
Peter Green Esq.
Two Dutch fishing kaags to the left of the painting with a smaller boat beside them. The leading boat has an anchor out to the mud bank in the foreground. To the right two fishermen are moving another kaag off the mud – one is using a quant, the other is in the water and pushing. Between these boats, in the centre of the picture, are two figures wading out from the shore to the boats on the left. One has a fishing cran on his back and a staff in his left hand and on his right is a young boy. On the horizon are fourteen other vessels including the prow of a man o'war. The subject and composition of these two paintings is almost identical. The hard overworked nature of these paintings, and their lack of subtlety and delicacy of finish indicate that they were painted late in the artist's short life.

11B
Oil on canvas 14½ x 21¾. Signed C Brooking (below wading man)
Prov: John Smith 22 December 1857 A pair £60*
Adrian Hope Esq. 12 Langham Place, London
Good Sale. Sotheby's 15 July 1953 Lot 9. The pair £400
Partridge, Bond Street, London
Basil Mavrolean Esq.
Christie's 2 April 1965 Lot 45 unsold at 5,000 guineas
Leggatt Bros
Private Collection
**John Smith's Day Book* Vol 4 p.492 (Victoria & Albert Museum)
A pair – see 1A
The towering cumulus clouds in this version are not so dark as in A. There are only minute differences in the paintings. It is likely that they were produced at around the same time. Differences are in the positions of boats on the left horizon, the hoist to the mainsail is slack below the gaff on the nearest left hand yacht, the wading man's right foot is lower in the water, the luff line on the mainsail of the keel on the right is slacker. The ships on the right horizon are slightly larger.

12 DUTCH FISHING VESSELS BECALMED CLOSE TO A SHORE (see page 129)
Oil on canvas 14½ x 22. Signed lower left
Prov: Sotheby's 4 Oct 1944 Lot 15
Koetser
Spink & Son
Stafford Bourne Esq.
Christie's 3 July 1964 £577.10
B. Ingleby
Private Collection
Exhib: Mellon Foundation: Bristol July 1966, No. 36
Two Dutch kaags at anchor in the centre foreground port beam on with a rowing boat approaching from the right. To the right a Dutch two-decker man o'war firing a salute. Fishing boats

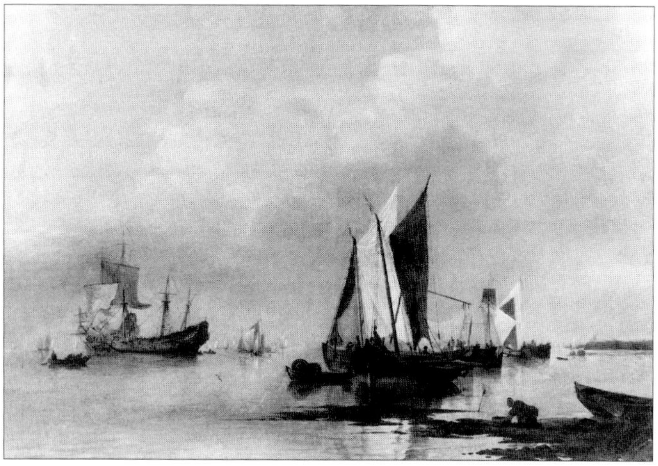

13

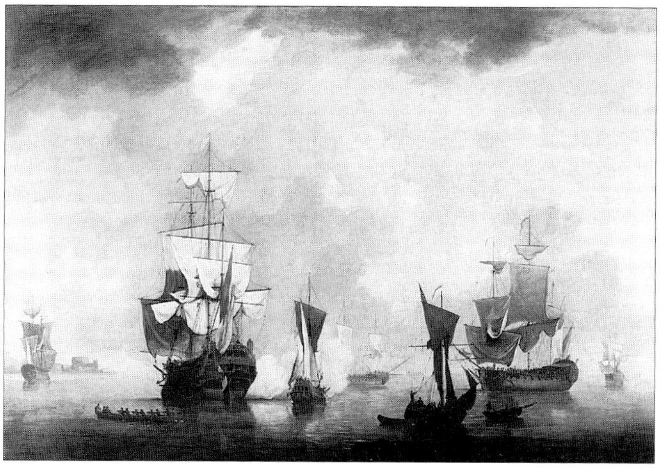

14

either side at the horizon, and also to the left, at the horizon going away, a second Dutch man o'war. Standing on the mud flat left foreground is a fisherman with a long stave on his shoulder carrying a fishing cran on his back. Blue skies with extensive cumulus.

13 DUTCH VESSELS AT ANCHOR IN A CALM
Oil on canvas 13½ x 19¾. No signature
Prov: Mrs Robert Somerset
Sotheby's 13 July 1966 Lot 89 £800
Speelman
Private Collection
Five Dutch fishing kaags in a line stretching into the right of the composition with land at the right horizon and a mud flat in the right foreground. Beyond and at the left are two Dutch men o'war of the 17th century and beyond them a large fleet of fishing boats. Kneeling on the mud flat between a stave mark and his dinghy is a cockle fisherman with a shallow cran basket. Though catalogued as a Brooking, this painting is more reminiscent of the work of Hendrik Dubbels. However, an almost identical painting measuring 15½ x 20 and signed 'Dominic Serres 1771' was with the Lowndes Lodge Gallery in 1967.

14 A BRITISH MAN O'WAR FIRING A SALUTE
Oil on canvas 40 x 58. Part signature lower right
Prov: Mrs K. M. E. Morris bequeathed in 1956
Tate Gallery London (T115)
In the centre of this painting is a small English smack-rigged Royal Yacht. To her left is an English two-decker, wearing a very large ensign, showing her stern and port quarter. She fires a gun to starboard just ahead of the yacht. Beyond the smoke is a partially obscured frigate, whilst to the right, port side to, is another English two-decker. At either side of the painting is another English man o'war. In the right foreground is a sailing smack with rowing boats on either side of her. Crossing the stern of the saluting ship is a four-oared gig carrying two officers. On the left horizon is land with a substantial castle. Calm seas with summer skies. The two-decker to the right has a mizzen sail laced to the mast and the forepart of the mizzen yard has been removed. It is a late Brooking therefore.

A superlative example by Brooking which the author has never seen exhibited!

15A A CUTTER AND OTHER VESSELS BECALMED
(see page 132)
Oil on canvas 19 x 31. Signed with initials on lower left buoy and C Brooking on its periphery
Prov: Mr Panton Betew, circa 1750
Christie's 13 April 1934 Lot 32C Estate of General Mackinnon £84
Spink & Son
Sir James Caird
National Maritime Museum 1934 (34-51)
Eng: R. B. Godfrey 14⅛ x 19¾ in reverse. See engraving No 611.
A calm sea with the tidal stream running to the right. There is a light wind, sufficient for all the vessels to maintain steerage way, and smaller craft are moving quite well. There is land with low cliffs across the right horizon. An 18 gun frigate starboard bow on is at left, another appears at anchor, port beam on, in the tideway on the right of the painting. Between them is a topsail cutter towing her dinghy moving to the right. There are six other boats and vessels, including two large men o'war off the point of land. In the left foreground is a wooden barrel marker buoy with cross pieces, on which are the initials CB.

15B SHIPS COMING TO ANCHOR AND A CUTTER BEFORE THE WIND
Oil on canvas 10½ x 14¾. Signed lower left C Brooking
The same scene with a breeze but only two men o'war, the cutter in the foreground without a topsail going well and another with the topsail as before in the left horizon. This is a small study for the bigger pictures, and one of a group of six paintings by Brooking which remained together until 1985. See 104, 203D, 210B, 257A and 402B.
Prov: Robert Taylor Esq. Solicitor Lincolns Inn (1840-1915)
Captain and Mrs Thomas 1915
David Messum Gallery 1984
Sotheby's 13 March 1985 Lot 19 £8,500
Private Collection
Exhib: Mellon Foundation: Aldeburgh/Bristol June/July 1966, No. 54

15C
Oil on canvas s.s. 19 x 30. Unsigned
This painting follows 15A very closely, and is very nearly the same size. Differences can be seen in the wakes of the craft and the heights of some masts. It lacks the boldness of the cloud formations in the right sky, etc, but it could still be by Brooking.
Prov: Speelman, about 1955 for £600
Private Collection, Sussex

15D
Oil on canvas 11⅛ x 16¼. Signed C Brooking bottom centre
A partly reversed copy of 15A. Engraved as *Noon* by Boydell in 1753.
See engraving 612.
Prov: Knoedler 1919 (see Witt Library)
Mr Carstairs (founder of Knoedlers)

15E
Oil on canvas 16½ x 20¼. Unsigned
Similar to 15A but much smaller. The same composition and ships but the spacings vary. There is no buoy in left foreground or seagulls over the water. The rigging has suffered from much inaccurate retouching.
Prov: Mrs J. E. Arnold
Sotheby's 9 December 1981 Lot 139 £1,800
Sidney Sabin
Private Collection

15F A MAN O'WAR WITH OTHER VESSELS IN THE THAMES ESTUARY
Oil on canvas 20¼ x 32¼. Signed with initials CB on buoy lower left
Like 15A but slightly larger. The man o'war right is not anchored but under way and there is less tide.
Prov: A dealer located in Reading, England 1945 to 1994
Sotheby's 13 July 94 Lot 2
Miles Joel

16 A SNOW LYING AT ANCHOR (see page 132)
Oil on canvas 25 x 30. Signed lower left
She is an English naval snow, as can be seen from the commissioning pennant, the jack and ensign. The snow is anchored in a strong tideway and port side to, in the centre of the painting with her galley moored astern. Across the horizon is land and behind her a massive low-lying fortress with a jetty, probably Southsea Castle. To the left a second snow is under way on the port tack heading for harbour. This is a splendid descriptive composition of snows, with their separate mizzen short mast.
Prov: Spink & Son 1936
Sir James Caird June 1936 £220
National Maritime Museum (1936-72)
Illus: *British Marine Painting*, Oliver Warner 1948, plate 12

17 FISHING SMACKS BECALMED NEAR A SHORE
Oil on canvas 10¾ x 33. Not signed (see page 7)
A remarkably fine painting taken from the shore showing over twenty fishing smacks in a calm with a merchant ship, probably a depot ship of some sort, to the right with smacks alongside her. There are five fishermen in two groups on the shore and two rowing boats. A tranquil scene with a greenish sea and blue skies.
Prov: Tate Gallery
Exhib: Mellon Foundation: Aldeburgh/Bristol June/July 1966, No. 32
Illus: *British Marine Painting*, A. L. Baldry, Studio 1919, p.35
Marine Painting, David Cordingly 1974, Plate 35

18 THREE ROYAL YACHTS, A SHIP OF THE LINE AND OTHER SHIPPING BY MOONLIGHT
Oil on canvas size unknown but large, signed C Brooking lower right
Two fishermen, one with a long staff, the other with a fish basket, stand on an old jetty in the left foreground on a calm moonlit night with a light breeze. Across the water from them on the left of the picture is a castle. Immediately before them

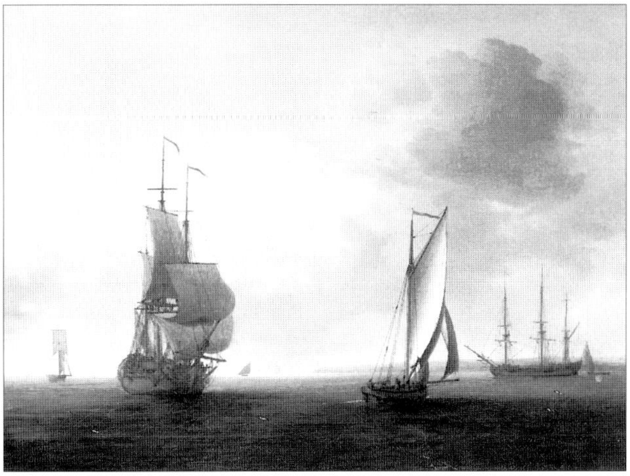
15B

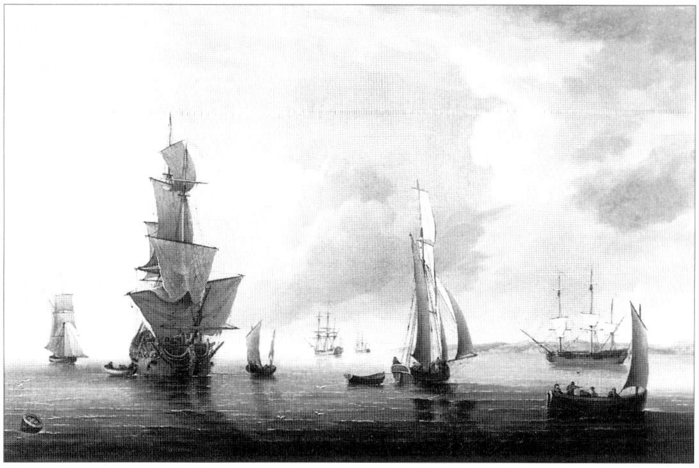
15F

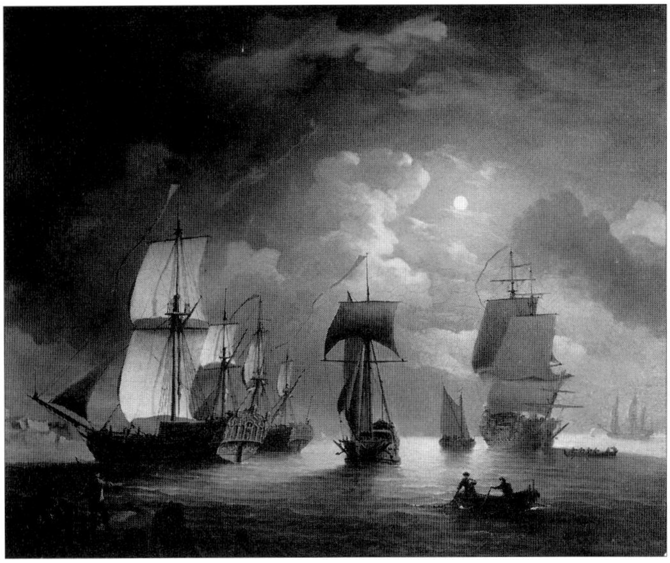

18

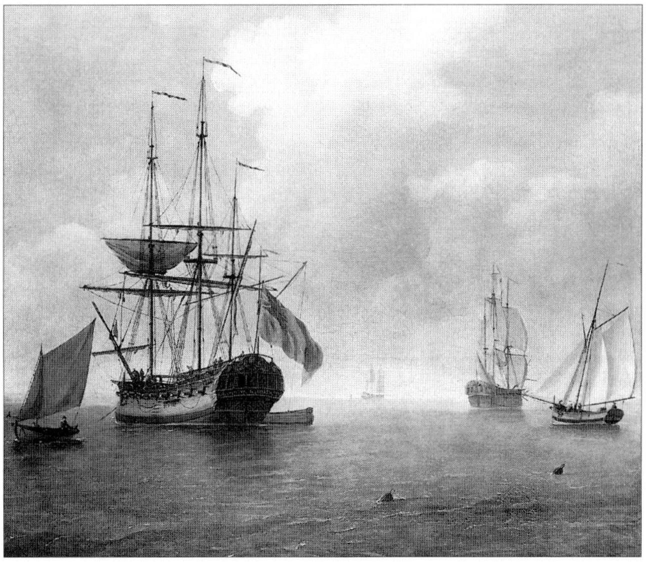

19

are two royal yachts port side on moving under full sail to the left whilst a third is moving bows on toward the viewer. To the right beyond, beneath the moon, is a fine two-decker moving bows on to the right where there is a four-oared gig with a passenger. Fishermen in a rowing boat are netting fish. There are other vessels to the right.
Prov: Not Known. Painting now missing. NMM Photo File PR/54/349 Cooper Neg 200145A

19 A SMALL SHIP AT ANCHOR WITH CUTTERS UNDER SAIL
Oil on canvas $23\frac{1}{8}$ x $26\frac{1}{8}$. No signature
Prov: Jolly's Saleroom Bath 1947 £25
R. R. Henshaw Esq.
Rupert Preston Gallery
Christie's 17 Nov. 1967 Lot 125
G. E. J. Robertson Esq.
Private Collection
Exhib: Mellon Foundation: Bristol July 1966, No. 56
A small but well-armed ship (20 guns) at anchor on the left of the painting with no sails set. A strange craft is on her starboard side. They are stemming the tide. To their left sailing out of the picture is a small sailing craft. To the right, middle distance, is an 18 gun single deck man o'war and to her right a sailing cutter. In the right foreground are two fishing buoys watching.

20 ENGLISH MAN O'WAR OFF A COAST
Oil on canvas $26\frac{1}{2}$ x $41\frac{1}{4}$. Signed on the buoy lower left
Prov: Martin B. Asscher 1951
J. H. N. Thompson Esq., Stanley Hall, Bridgnorth
Sotheby's 24 June 1964 Lot 35 £8,500
Leggatt Bros
To the left, broadside on, an English two-decker of 40 guns under almost full sail (except fore-topsail) broadside on towing her gig. Another man o'war, a second-rate, a three-decker of 90 guns, approaches from the right and is seen port bow on, under full sail except the fore topsail. Between the two main warships sailing to the right is an English Royal Yacht, ketch rigged. In the right foreground is an English lugger fishing boat dowsing her sails. Beyond her and to the right are land and rocks and a fine castle. A barrel buoy is in the left foreground.
Similar to engraving 603 *Morning*. See also painting 263.

21 A VIEW OF PORTSMOUTH HARBOUR WITH MEN O'WAR AND OTHER VESSELS WITH FIGURES ON THE SHORE (see page 132)
Oil on canvas $20\frac{1}{2}$ x $38\frac{1}{2}$. Not signed
Prov: Richard E. O. Cavendish Esq., Holker Hall, Cumbria.
Christie's 15 Nov 1968 Lot 77 (550 gns to Hughes) as by Charles Brooking
Christie's 9 May 1969 Lot 123 (350 gns to Wells) as by Charles Brooking
Private Collection
Bonham's 13 August 1998 Lot 255 (as a follower of Charles Brooking)
Private Collection
This panoramic painting is of Portsmouth harbour taken from the Gosport shore with ships' boats picking up their officers from the various sandy coves in the foreground, presumably in the morning. In the great harbour are two sixty-fours centre, three other men o'war and a merchantman, all at anchor on the ebb tide. A sixth-rate of 20 guns is under way to the right

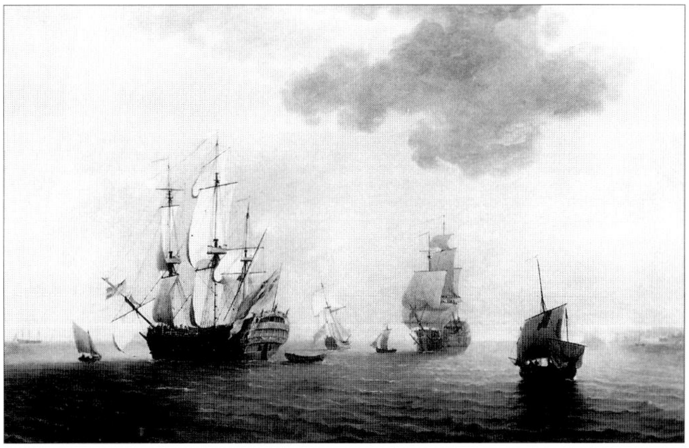

20

sailing down harbour moving out to Spithead, whilst to her right an incoming Royal Yacht sails by. In the right foreground, on the coveheads, are two groups of people and four boats seeing their passengers off to their respective ships.

The composition is based on the engraving by Samuel and Nathaniel Buck 'The West prospect of Portsmouth in Hampshire' published in 1749. It is known that the Bucks used Mr Scott and on one occasion Peter Monamy to draw in the ships in their harbour scenes.

The Bucks also used staffage for figures in their engravings. In some drawings they utilised sketches of people and animals by Gravelot or Chatelain, but in Plymouth and Portsmouth they used staffage drawings by Thomas Rosse (now in the British Museum). Since Monamy died in 1749 there is good reason to believe that Brooking may have been employed for the composition of ships and more importantly their boats for the work is considered superior to that of Scott.

The painting is believed to have come with the Chatsworth Bequest of Holker Hall via Admiral the Hon. Francis Egerton (1824-1895), second son of the first Earl of Ellesmere, who in 1865, as a Captain, married Lady Louisa Cavendish (1835-1907), daughter of the seventh Duke of Devonshire. Their first home after marriage was HMS *Victory*, afloat in Portsmouth harbour, of which he was the Captain from 1866 to 1867, 'A bit of a change from Chatsworth, Holker, etc., but how lovely' wrote Mrs Cavendish, who remembered this painting.

22A WHALERS IN THE ICE (see page 132)
Oil on canvas 11½ x 17. Signed C Brooking lower left
Prov: National Maritime Museum (1940-261)
Exhib: Mellon Foundation: Bristol July 1966, No. 59
Illus: *Country Life* 14 July 1966, E. H. H. Archibald p.116
Eng: Boydell in 1754, Engraving 605
Six whalers are in view and they have trapped three whales in this ice-floed area, of whom two are under attack from the ships' boats. The whale in the right foreground is spouting as the leading boat's harpooner thrusts a harpoon, by hand, into it. Beyond this action, the second whale has been cornered by three boats and is putting up a fight after being harpooned. To the left of the painting a third whale is spouting, whilst on the ice in the left foreground a polar bear is standing watching the scene. Further to the right on the same ice floe is a brown bear sitting on the ice!

22B WHALERS IN THE ICE
Oil on canvas 11 1/4 x 16. Signed C Brooking
A copy of 22A. It is unlikely that it is by Brooking.
Prov: Kendall Whaling Museum, Sharon, Massachusetts, USA, 02064

23A SUNSET – A CUTTER BEFORE A LIGHT BREEZE WITH A LUGGER LOWERING HER SAILS (see page 133)
Oil on copper 7 x 10. Signed CB
Prov: Sir Iver Proctor Beauchamp
Spink & Son 1961
Mr and Mrs Paul Mellon
Exhib: Royal Academy, Painting in England 1964/65 No 140
Yale University 1965 No 17
Mellon Foundation: Aldeburgh/Bristol June/July 1966, No. 30
Illus: *Connoisseur Yearbook* 1962 by Spink
This is a near calm but with a dramatic light coming from a well-observed sky, where some of the clouds obscuring the sun are painted with a heavy impasto unusual for Brooking. Dark cumulus overhead with lighter cumulus obscuring the sun and fleecy clouds to the horizon. This makes a wonderfully lit backdrop to the two fishing vessels. The cutter running to the right of the painting is towing her dinghy astern whilst the lugger is at anchor. On the log in the left foreground are the initials CB, whilst three gulls fly low over the water.

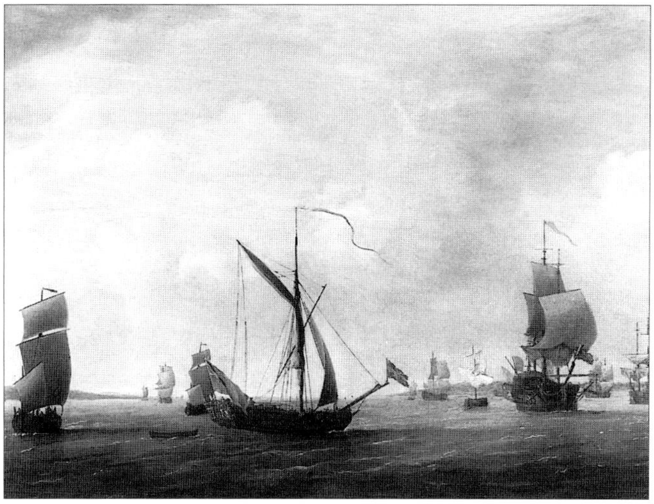

24

23B SUNSET – A CUTTER IN A SEAWAY
Oil on copper 7¾ x 11¼. Signed C.B. on post in foreground
Prov: Barbara Isherwood Kay
Sir David Piper
Private Collection
Very similar to 23A but it lacks three seagulls flying in right foreground and the two vessels on the horizon.

24 A ROYAL YACHT, A TWO-DECKER AND OTHER SHIPPING IN THE SOLENT
Oil on canvas 25½ x 35½. Traces of signature lower left
Cooper Neg 359132
Prov: Colonel A. T. Maxwell TD
Private Collection
A Royal Yacht (eight guns) is broadside-on in the centre of the painting sailing to the right under her jib towing her gig astern. To her left two merchant ships are coming towards. To her right is a large sea mark, a fishing hulk, with a mast and two yards on which square sails are set. Beyond this and to the right are six men o'war in formation led by the two-decker. This sea mark has not been seen in any other Brooking painting and may signify a meeting point for the yacht and the men o'war.

25 A FLAGSHIP, A THREE-DECKER AND A SHIP-RIGGED ROYAL YACHT OFF A CASTLE
Oil on canvas 30 x 39½
Prov: E. Bower Esq.
The flagship, a three-decker of at least 80 guns, is port quarter to the viewer and just right of the centre of the scene. She has six sails set, including the mizzen, and has just fired one of her starboard guns, behind the smoke of which is seen on the after port side of the ship-rigged Royal Yacht. A very substantial castellated castle is built on the rocks on the right side of the picture. Sailing away to the left is a smack-rigged Royal Yacht in the mid-distance, and to her left a two-decker, also firing a salute. There is a fishing boat high and dry on the left foreshore

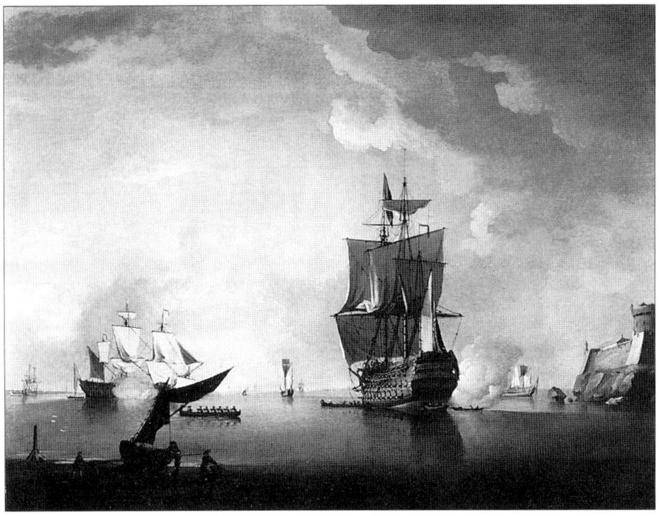

25

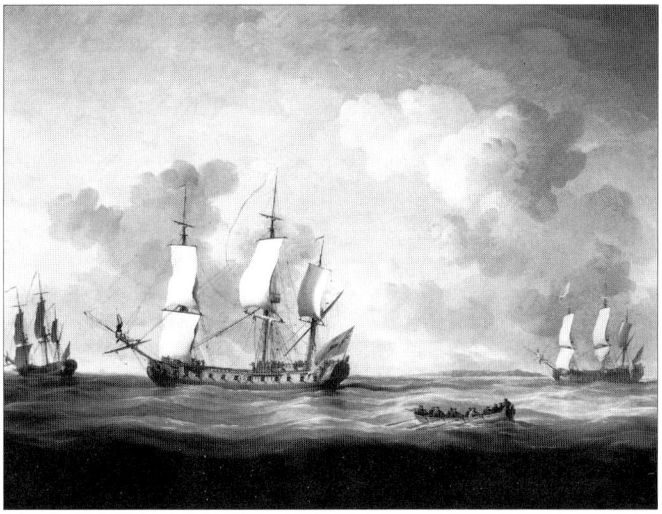

26A

and behind her a six-oared gig is being rowed toward the flagship, with two officer passengers. There is land in the distance on either side of the horizon with a lighthouse on each point. Ships are of the Blue Squadron.

26A A FRIGATE IN A SWELL BEFORE A LIGHT BREEZE WITH A BOAT PULLING TOWARDS HER (see page 8)
Oil on canvas 34 x 48. Signed C Brooking on a spar lower left
Prov: Abraham or Richard Wells, Deptford
By descent to Commander R. F. Wells OBE DSC RN
Phillip's 20 June 1995 Lot 22 to Richard Green
Private Collection
Exhib: Mellon Foundation: Aldeburgh/Bristol June/July 1966, No. 64
Illus: *Connoisseur* April 1966 p.240
Blue skies above with a wind from the right of the scene and towering cumulus inclined with the wind moving across the painting from right to left. The light is coming from the left. In this painting a 36-gun frigate, a single decked sixth-rate man o'war, is in the left centre and rowing out towards her is an eight-oared gig in a swell, carrying two officers. The frigate, under way, is rising gently on the swell with foresails set. On the horizon to the right is land, to the right of which in mid-ground is a flagship of the Red Squadron, a two-decker of at least 56 guns, making her a fourth-rate. To the left of this majestic scene is another frigate, but a Captain's command. The sea is calm but with a fair swell after some bad weather.

A late painting, probably of the frigate *Pallas* built in the Wells yard at Deptford in 1757. Her captain was Archibald Cleveland and master Samuel Brooking.

26B
Oil on canvas 12½ x 17. Not signed
Prov: Sharp Collection at Hill of Tarvit
Culzean Castle, Maybole, Ayrshire (National Trust for Scotland)
The same scene, with a little more wind. The high cloud is moved more to the left, where the second frigate heels more to the wind.

26C
Oil on canvas 12¼ x 17¼. Not signed
Prov: Parker Gallery
Private Collection
The same composition but in lighter tones than A or B. The ships to left and right of the painting are both unarmed merchant vessels, and the frigate appears to be of 30 guns, also a sixth-rate. Her crew and the boats stowed on deck between the main and fore are minor differences. The boat is rowing down a bigger swell as she approaches her mother ship which is inclined further off the wind than in A.

27 A FLAGSHIP FIRING A GUN AND ANOTHER TWO-DECKER GETTING UNDER WAY AT DAWN. THE ARTIST COMES ASHORE (see detail page 6)
Oil on canvas 20¾ x 27¾. Signed C Brooking on jetty lower right
Prov: Rupert Preston Gallery 1965
Commander M. D. Joel RN
Miss S. C. Joel
Exhib: Mellon Foundation: Aldeburgh/Bristol June/July 1966, No. 88
A pale blue sky at dawn with cirrus and cumulus clouds and a near calm. Two 64s, two-deckers and third-rates, are weighing anchor. To the right in the middle distance the flagship (Admiral of the Blue) port side on firing a gun. Astern of her is

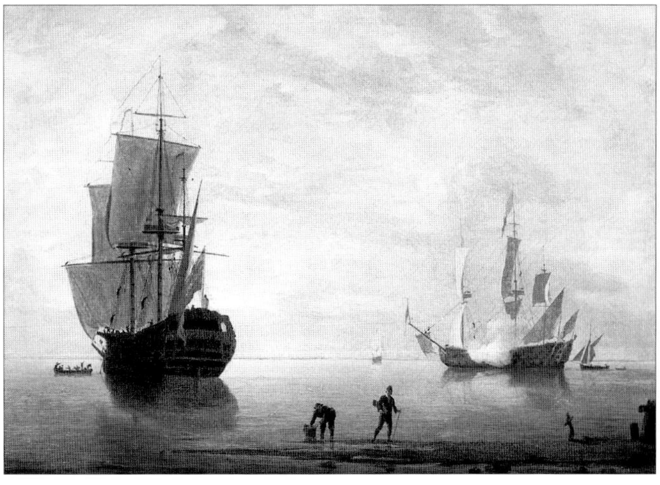

27

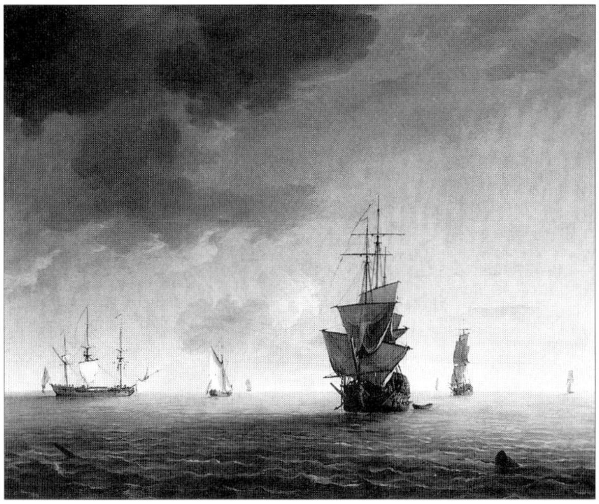

28

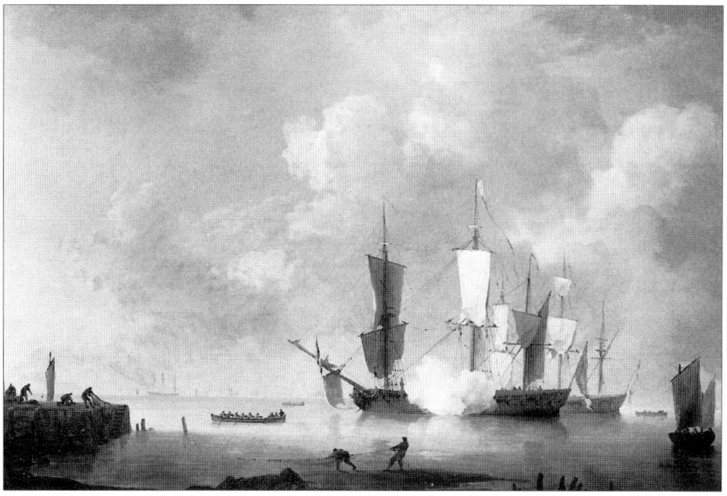

29

a cutter with mainsail brailed and two jibs set towing a dinghy. In the left foreground the other 64 port quarter towards about to hoist her gig. A jetty is at right with two men on the sand bars to the left. One a cockle fisherman with cran, the other an artist with a stave in his left hand and his sketch book in his right. Two other warships are in the centre horizon.

It is likely that Brooking has painted himself coming ashore here.

28 A TWO-DECKER, TWO FRIGATES AND A ROYAL YACHT ON A CALM DAY
Oil on canvas 24½ x 29½. Signed on spar lower left
Prov: J. Reveley Esq.
Sotheby's 24 February 1949 £320
Speelman Gallery
Rothschild
In the right foreground coming towards and towing her gig is the two-decker. In the left mid-ground is a frigate under mainsail and spritsail only. Between these two ships is a smack-rigged Royal Yacht and in the right mid-ground is the second frigate coming towards with four sails set. There is a circular buoy in the right foreground and a spar in the left.

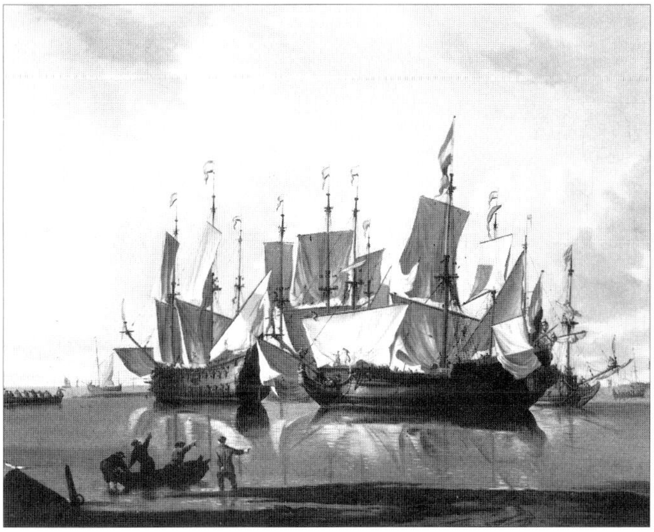

31

29 FRIGATES BECALMED NEAR THE SHORE, FIRING A SALUTE
Oil on canvas 23⅝ x 34¼. Not signed
Prov: Reverend H. B. George, Oxford
Dr & Mrs A. G. Peto
Exhib: Mellon Foundation: Bristol July 1966, No. 35
Below a blue sky with rising cumulus, two frigates broadside on in quarterline. To the left, a large jetty with fishermen tending nets on it. In the foreground are two fishermen working a net from the mud bank. To the right is a small two-masted lugger. Between the nearest frigate and the jetty a six-oared gig with passengers is moving to the left.

30 A SMACK UNDER SAIL IN A LIGHT BREEZE GOING DOWN RIVER (see Chapter 4, page 57)
Oil on canvas 14½ x 24½. Signed C Brooking
Prov: J. H. Anderson by 1865
Christie's 30 May 1879 Lot 100. Brought in by his descendant
Berwick sale 21 Oct 1949 Lot 18 (290 gns)
Agnew's
Mr and Mrs Paul Mellon 1968
Exhib: British Institution 1865 No. 170
Royal Academy 1872 No. 203
Agnew's 1968 No. 37
Yale Center for British Art 1977/78 No. 17
An unusual atmospheric painting of a smack under sail in the centre of the picture going down river with land on either side. To the left and well astern of her a covered barge is anchored and stems the current running to the right. There are many ships in the distant right shore area. The figure at the helm of the smack, which has jib and mainsail filled, is standing and sketching into a large sketch-book. Is this Brooking at work in his boat going down the Medway?

31 DUTCH MEN O'WAR DRYING SAILS BY A SHORE
Oil on canvas 21½ x 26. Signed C Brooking 1749 in red
Prov: Mrs Wakefield Saunders, Barbados
Major H. N. Du Boulay
Christie's 23 Nov 1973 Lot 110 withdrawn at 8,000 guineas
Christie's 11 April 1980 Lot 17
Tryon & Swann Gallery

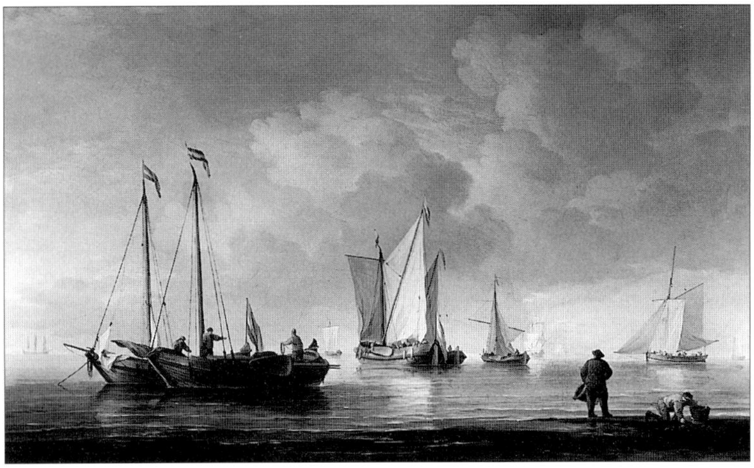

32

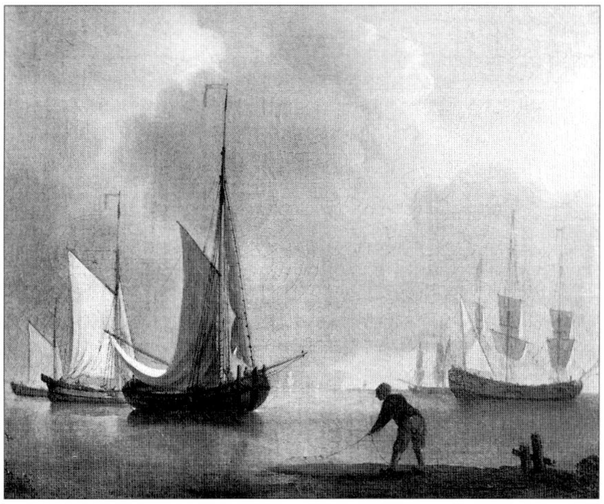

33

A. E. Edwards Esq.
Four large Dutch men o'war are lying port broadside on, whilst a fifth, just showing her foremast and beak bulkhead going to the right, is behind them. Other shipping is seen beyond and on either side of this close group. To the left and beyond them is a sandbank. Two boats are seen being rowed on either side. In the foreground another sand bank with a boat and four fishermen. To their left a circular buoy and an anchor. It is believed to be a copy of a Lieve Verschuier by Brooking in 1749. Brooking was no doubt specially commissioned to make the copy.

32 DUTCH FISHING BOATS OFF A SHORE IN A CALM
Oil on canvas 14½ x 22¼. Signed C Brooking
Prov: Captain F. Buddle Atkinson. Godalming Sale 30 September 1955
Agnew's
Sir James Elphinstone Bt
Lady Ursula Vernon
Sotheby's 26 June 1968 Lot 31
Agnew's
Private Collection
This is a fine example of a Brooking improvement on a van de Velde theme. See Michael Robinson, *The Paintings of the Willem van de Veldes* Vol. 1 p.444 No. 65 *Two weyschuits alongside each other near the shore*, circa 1671. The Brooking is a more striking version, and more authentic and with more incident than the van de Velde. But Brooking must have seen the van de Velde in order to turn the prosaic composition of the Dutch artist into this lyrical painting.

To the left, two small kaags at anchor. A kaag with sail half lowered is on her right (the spar is positioned at a more aesthetically pleasing angle than in the van de Velde). To the right of her an 18th century cutter has been convincingly added. The two figures, fishermen with crans on the foreshore, look very real in the Brooking.

33 VESSELS IN A CALM
Oil on canvas 11⅜ x 13⅝. No signature but on stretcher an old scratching Brooking
Prov: Ralph Edwards Esq.
On the left, three English gaff-rigged fishing boats. To the right two ships in the foreground; on the shore, a fisherman facing to the left hauling the nets. In the right foreground are two bits of a breakwater.

34 A CALM. A GALLIOT NEAR THE SHORE WITH BOATS UNLOADING
Oil on canvas 14 x 15¼. Unsigned
Prov: Sir Patrick Donner 1965
Exhib: Mellon Foundation: Aldeburgh/Bristol June/July 1966, No. 46
A group of boats and fishermen surround the galliot which has her mainsail set in the right side of this almost square painting. On the left horizon are four other vessels, including a Dutch ship. In the left foreground a fisherman wades to the right. He has a fishing net held horizontally in his left hand and a bucket in the right. Sitting in the nearest boat is an artist with a sketch-book. The artist is almost certainly Charles Brooking.

35A DUTCH FISHING KAAGS BY A SHORE AND A MAN O'WAR SALUTING
Oil on canvas 9¾ x 13¾. Signed Brooking centre bottom
Prov: The Earl of Warwick
A fisherman with hands clasped behind his back is on shore at left watching two small kaags with sails down and broadside on in shallow water facing left. Another kaag is under way port quarter on, on the right. Between them and at a distance a man o'war starboard broadside towards has just fired a gun. A calm day with mountainous cumulus. Remains of jetty at right.

35B
Oil on canvas 18½ x 20½
Prov: The Hon. James Bruce
Design as above but much larger. The fisherman at left is turned more to the left.
Paintings 35A and 35B are both in reverse of a composition by Willem van de Velde the Younger at Petworth House, Sussex. Van de Velde's painting dates from around 1672 and was later engraved by Thomas Major. Brooking has updated the man o'war in the background to 18th century hulls.

36 AN ENGLISH FLAGSHIP AND HER FLEET IN A CALM
Oil on canvas 36¾ x 43. Not signed
Prov: St Johns, College, Oxford

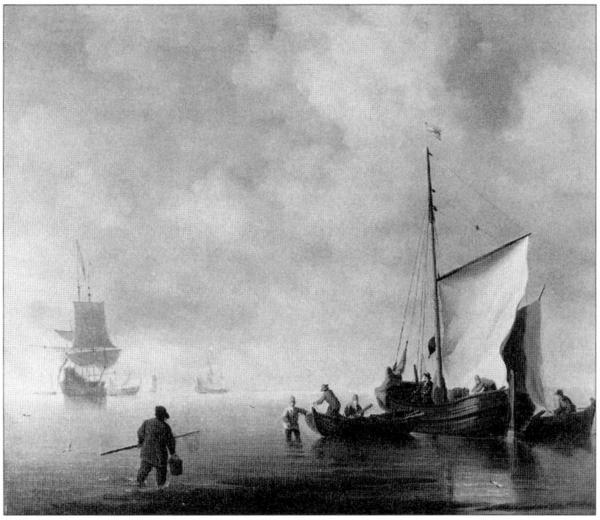

34

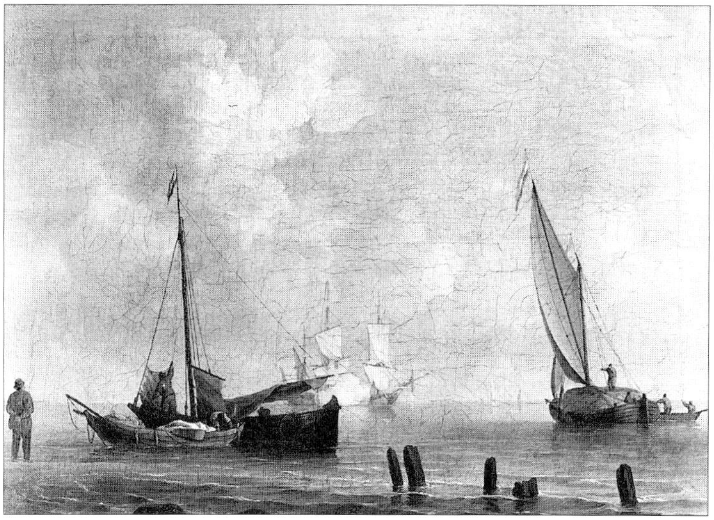

35A

A flagship, a three-decker at least a third-rate, flying an Admiral's flag at the fore, and possibly a Royal Standard at the main, becalmed starboard quarter to, with sails and flags limp, firing a port gun. She is on the right of the picture with three men o'war beyond. On the left of the picture six other men o'war in line ahead or turning and other vessels. Approaching the flagship are six captains' boats, all of eight oars, presumably for a conference. In the centre foreground a small rowing boat with two fishermen with their nets out to the right of the foreground.

37 THREE FRIGATES AND A CASTLE WITH A MAN O'WAR BEYOND
Oil on canvas 19¾ x 24
Prov. Spink & Son 1936
Mrs W. W. Bourne (until 1941)
Stafford Bourne Esq.
Private Collection
Illus: *Apollo* 1936 Vol.24 p.142
One frigate coming towards in the centre of the painting with a ship's boat at either side. To the left and beyond, a frigate is under way port side to and at her stern another more distant frigate is coming towards. Substantial coastline at the right of the painting with a large castle on the promontory. To the right of the castle a man o'war moving to the right under full sail. To the right of her and much closer is a fishing smack with mainsail brailed. In the left centre foreground a captain's gig broadside on under oars.

38 SHIPPING IN A CALM SEA WITH ELEVEN SHIPS
(see page 133)
Oil on canvas 15 x 23. Signed C Brooking
Prov: Williams & Son 1937
Spink & Son 1938
HM The Queen of Yugoslavia 1938 (ex Queen Alexandra) see 251C
John Mitchell & Son 1967
Mr and Mrs Paul Mellon 1967
This is a variant of Admiral of the Red (231), in that in the centre middle ground, starboard bow to under medium sail, is the same flagship of the Red with eight of her squadron in a group formation around her in a calm sea with a light wind

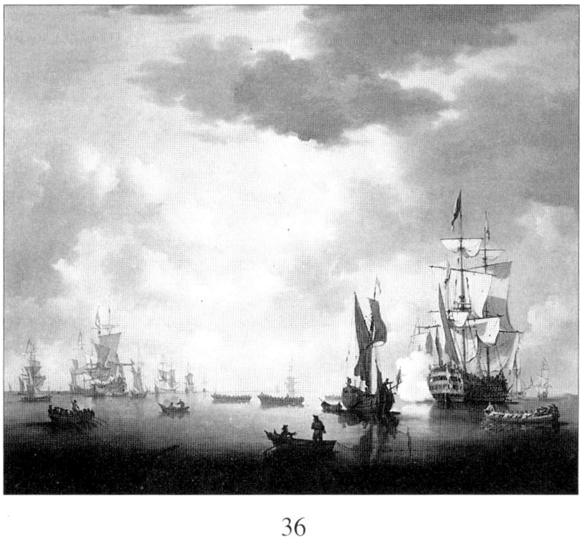

36

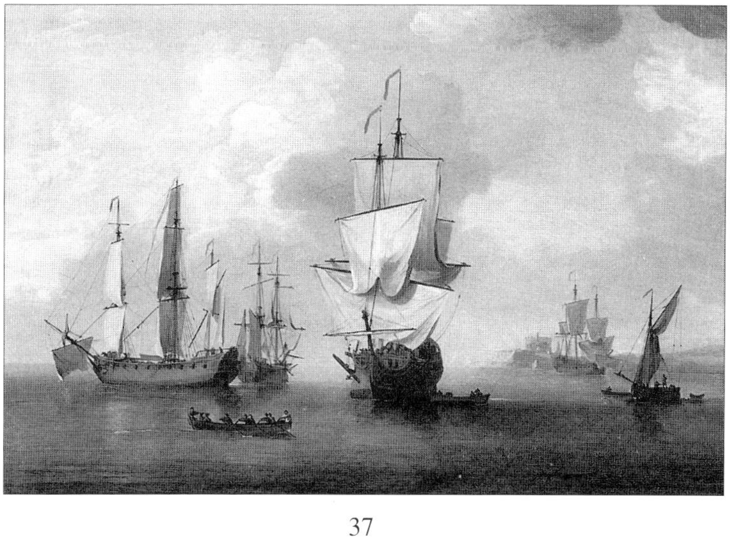

37

coming from the left. The sky is blue with cumulus and strato-cumulus top right. Two fishing smacks at the left of scene.

39A AN ENGLISH TWO-DECKER OF FORTY GUNS RIDING AT ANCHOR OFF A COAST WITH A GALLIOT CLOSE BY AND SIX MEN O'WAR BEYOND
Oil on canvas 22½ x 31½. Signed on stretcher C Brooking
Prov: Sir Alvarez and Lady Gascoigne, Lotherton Hall, Leeds
Leeds Art Gallery, Temple Newsham House (presented by the above)
Ref: M. S. Robinson, *The Paintings of the Willem van de Veldes* p.613 (2). Illustrated *Connoisseur* June 1956
This two-decker is left of centre port quarter on. From her stern shape she is a ship of about 1680 and may well have been inspired, or copied, from a van de Velde composition, although the frigate to the left which is broadside on is of a later date. The ensign is pre-1707. There is a second frigate behind that on the left and four further men o'war in the distant right. The galliot to the immediate right has her sails brailed and a small fishing boat approaches her. In the left foreground are two gigs approaching the two-decker, where there are already two boats at her port-side. There are two porpoises in the right foreground.

39B
Oil on panel 20½ x 31⅛. Unsigned
Prov: Sir Bruce Ingram (as a van de Velde)
Lieut General Sir Bertie Fisher KCB
Francis Fisher 1981
Private Collection
Ref: M. S. Robinson, *The Paintings of the Willem van de Veldes* p.613 (4)
Similar to 39A, with the exception that there is one less ship on the horizon far right. This painting has a wonderful blue sky with cirrus and cumulus clouds and sunshine. Two porpoises in the right foreground.

39C
Oil on canvas 21¼ x 27. Unsigned
Prov: Major A. D. Houston (1980)
Christie's 21 Nov 1980 Lot 123 not signed to Hahn for £6,500
Paul Hahn Fine Art Dealers, 47 Albermarle Street, London W1
Sotheby's 13 July 1994 bears signature lower left, P. Monamy £19,000
Private Collection
Ref: M. S. Robinson, *The Paintings of the Willem van de Veldes* p.613 (3)
A smaller, squarer version.

39D (see page 133)
Oil on canvas 21½ x 25. Unsigned
Prov: Sotheby's 12 March 1986 Lot 7 £17,000
J. Watman Esq.
Ref: M. S. Robinson, *The paintings of the Willem van de Veldes* p.614 (5)
This time the frigate to the left is replaced by a Dutch kaag and there is one less boat rowing toward the two-decker. Also, as in 39B above, one less man o'war at the right horizon. Two porpoises are in the right foreground.

40 BRITISH MEN O'WAR BECALMED WITH OTHER SHIPPING OFF A COAST (see page 136)
Oil on canvas 21½ x 29. Signed on the barrel
Prov: Lieut Colonel J. A. H. Moore-Brabazon
Lord Brabazon of Tara
Property of a Lady
Christie's 23 March 1979 Lot 54 £12,000
Richard Green
Private Collection
Sotheby's 15 July 1998 Lot 8. Private Collection.
Exhib: London 1905 – Naval, Shipping and Fisheries Exhibition
Ref: M. S. Robinson, *The paintings of the Willem van de Veldes* p.613 final para. Now numbered (7)
Very similar to the 39 series, but the two-decker is now modernised to around 1740 and the flags are post 1707. This also applies to the other five men o'war – the sixth is also missing from the right horizon. The other major change is the introduction of a substantial broken jetty at right which runs as far as the centre of the painting. There is a barrel in the lower left foreground.

41 AN EAST INDIAMAN BECALMED WITH FISHING BOATS (see pages 14 and 15)
Oil on canvas 20 x 30. Signed C Brooking on plank lower left
Prov: Sir John Molesworth Kt 2nd Bt. Vice Admiral of North Cornwall by descent to Lt Col Sir Arscott Molesworth-St Aubyn MBE 15th Bt.
One of a pair with 272
Another atmospheric calm based on the same sketches as the 39 series and No. 40. However there is a total of four men o'war of about 1740 and at either side of the painting are two fishing smacks in place of the rowing gigs.

42 DUTCH MEN O'WAR AT ANCHOR
Oil on canvas 39 x 52¼. Not signed
Prov: Neville Brown Esq.
Sotheby's 23 March 1960 Lot 135 as a Brooking
Agnew's
Private Collection
Eight Dutch men o'war from one to three deckers. In the left foreground a galliot starboard quarter to, towing a dinghy.
Note: Now believed to be by Samuel Scott.

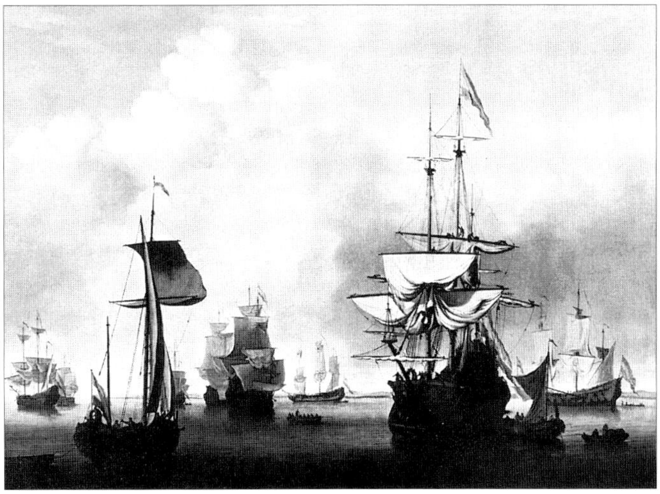

42

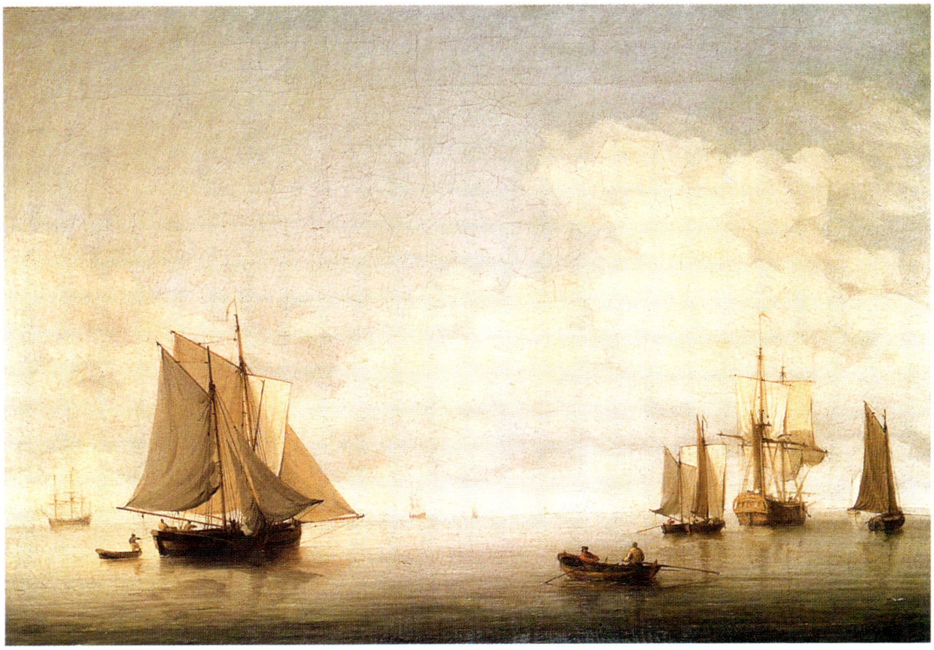

7A
Two smacks and other shipping becalmed

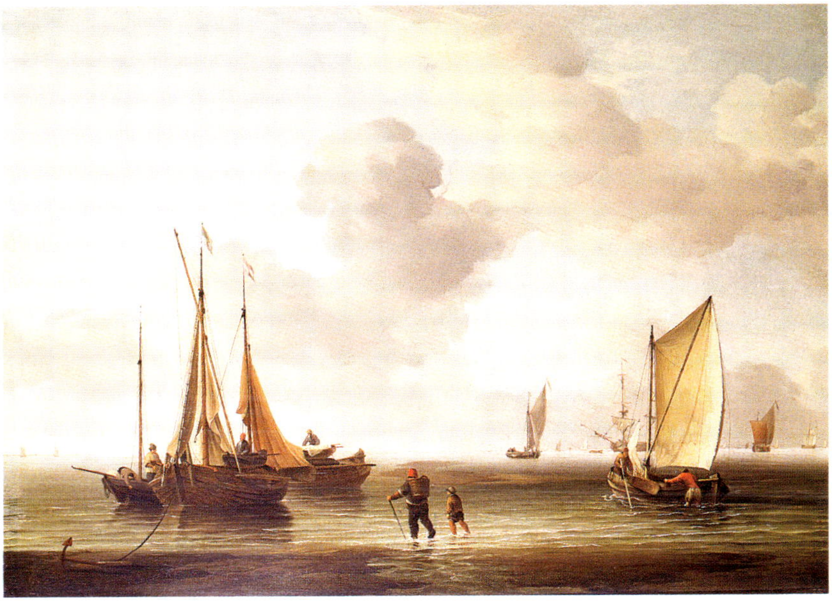

11A
Dutch fishing boats moored in a calm estuary

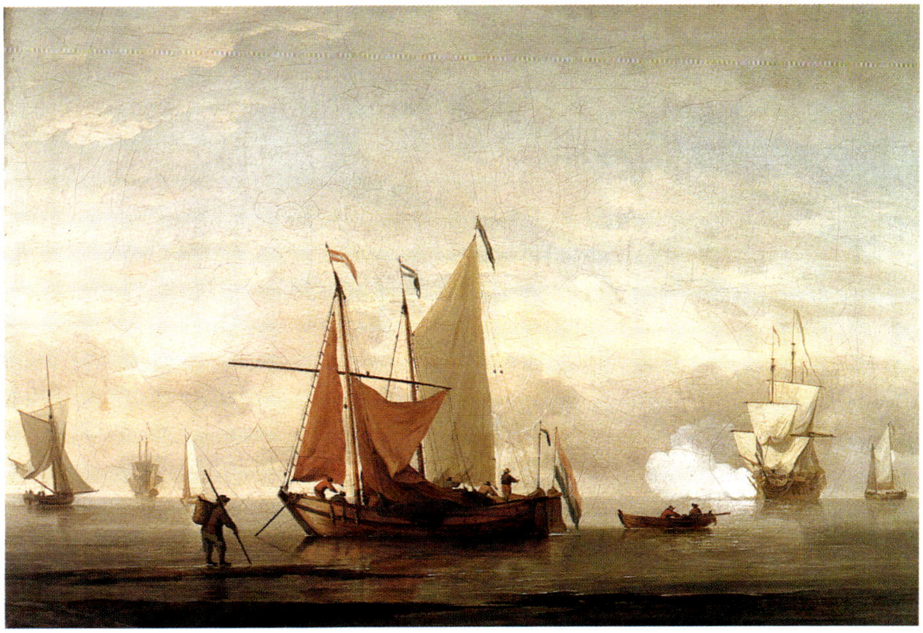

12
Dutch fishing vessels becalmed close to a shore

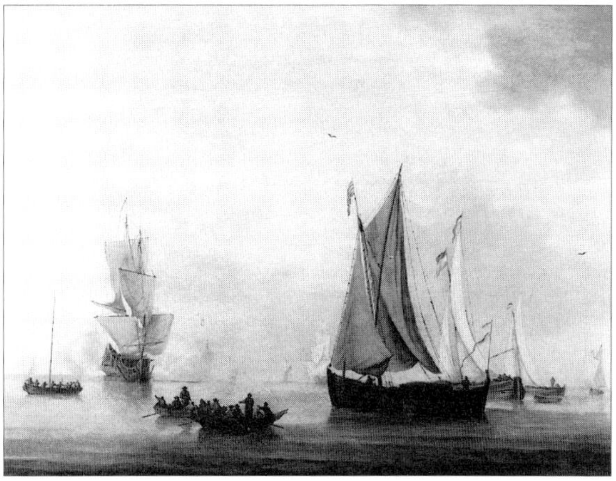

43

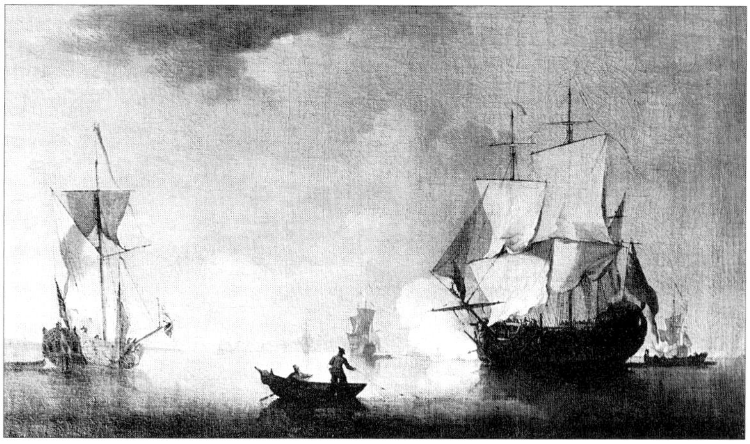

44

43 A DUTCH MAN O'WAR FIRING A SALUTE AND DUTCH KAAGS
Oil on canvas 17½ x 23. Not signed
Prov: Warwick Castle Sale 24 May 1968 No. 75. Bore a monogram
Georgian House, 300gns.
Koetser 1974
M. L. Lawrence Esq.
Lit Ref: *Old Sea Paintings*, Keeble Chatterton, 1928
Illus: Brian Koetser Autumn Catalogue 1973 No. 35 £5750
Three Dutch kaags and a smack on the right. To the left a Dutch two-decker firing a gun from each side as she approaches. In the left foreground three craft under oars in a calm.

44 AN ENGLISH MAN O'WAR FIRING A GUN AND A ROYAL YACHT
Oil on canvas 27 x 43½
Prov: Marquis of Ailsa, Cassillis Castle, Ayrshire
Ref: Witt Library No 3234
Left foreground a smack-rigged Royal Yacht, starboard quarter to sailing down an estuary. In the right foreground, under way, a two-decker, port bow on, firing a gun from her starboard battery and towing her captain's gig. Three other warships in the background.

45A FIVE DUTCH KAAGS IN A RIVER
Oil on canvas 13½ x 18. One of a pair with 45B
Prov: Spink & Son 1961
Illus: *Country Life* 11 May 1961
Spread right across the painting are five vessels. The first at anchor on the left has a dinghy moored astern. To her left is another small boat with fishermen netting. Current running to the right with a fine sky.

45B A DUTCH RIVER SCENE
Oil on canvas 13½ x 18. One of a pair with 45A
Prov: Spink & Son
Illus: *Country Life* 11 May 1961
On the left a great marker pole with a top mark. In the creek beside it a kaag unloading. In the river beyond three other kaags and beyond to seaward ten more sailing craft. In the foreground to the left three figures. To the right a rowing boat with two oarsmen and three passengers.

46 MEN O'WAR AT ANCHOR OFF THE COAST
Oil on canvas 29 x 52¾. Not signed
Prov: Sotheby's 26 Nov 1975 Lot 114 to David Messum Gallery £2,000

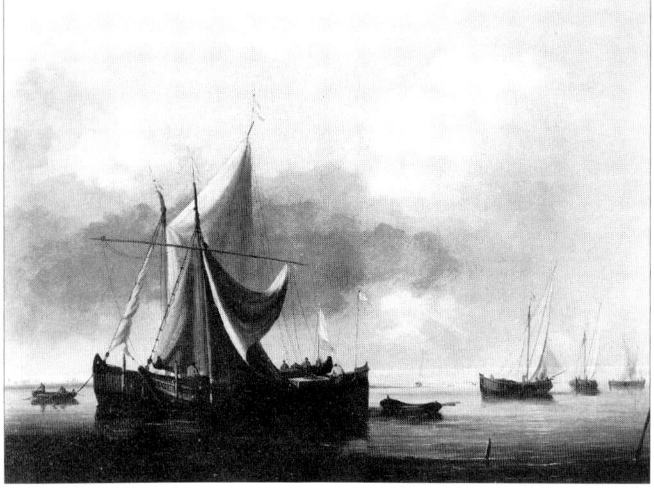

45A

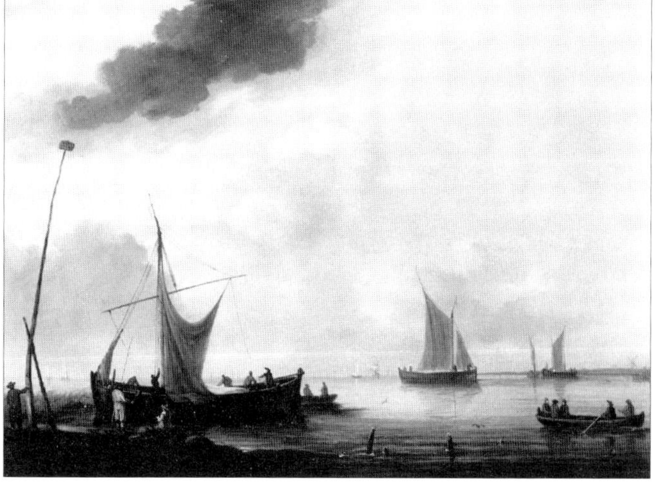

45B

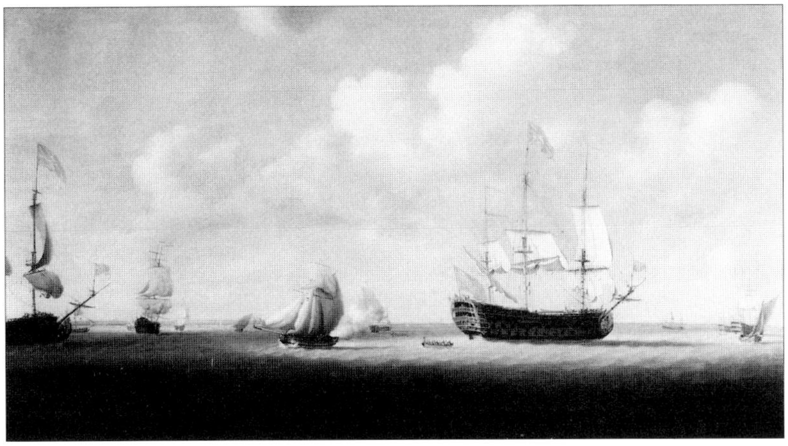

46

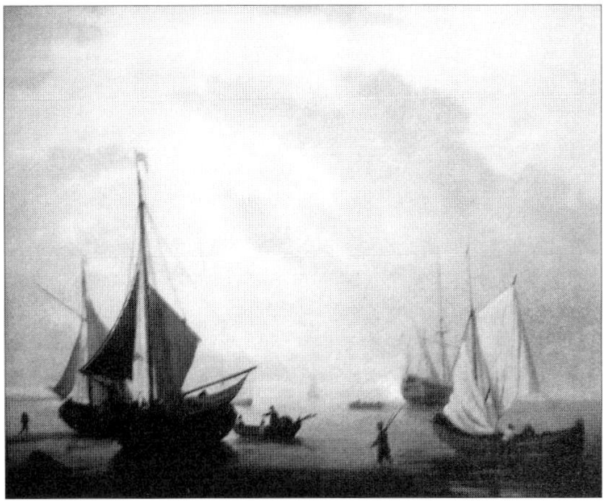

47

Private Collection
Sotheby's 15 July 1998 Lot 15 as by Richard Paton entitled *The Royal William and other shipping in the Thames estuary.*
Private Collection
An old photograph (A. C. Cooper Neg. No. 232163) exists of this painting which was sold at Christie's 30 June 1924 Lot 70. It would appear that the flagship at the left has been cut off just abaft the foremast. There is a Royal Yacht to its right firing a salute and then another large man o'war and a fishing craft.

47 THREE DUTCH KAAGS BECALMED ON A BEACH WITH A MAN O'WAR BEYOND
Oil on canvas 19½ x 23½
Prov: Koetser 1973
H. Hackman Esq.
Private Collection
Illus: Brian Koetser Autumn Catalogue 1973

48 MEN O'WAR AND OTHER SHIPPING BECALMED OFF THE COAST
Oil on canvas 36 x 48. Carved frame
Prov: N. R. Omell 11 October – 4 Nov 1977 No. 68
Sotheby's 12 March 1986 Lot 70
Edwinsford Collection, Tulley, Dyfed

Two galliots to the right and a Royal Yacht to the left with a man o'war of 1680 beyond various rowing craft. See Robinson's *The Paintings of the Willem van de Veldes* page 701. It is more likely to be an 18th century copy, painter unknown, of the van de Velde picture. See Robinson pages 699 to 700.

49 DUTCH BARGES IN A CALM
Oil on canvas 21 x 30¾. Not signed
Prov: Christie's 3 March 1916 Lot 165 to Smith 15 gns (as Cleveley)
L. Brietmeyer, Rushton Hall, Northampton
Christie's 27 June 1930 Lot 26
Sotheby's 6 April 1993 Lot 1 £7,000
Private Collection
Groups of Dutch fishing boats are at either side of this wide painting which surely must be in Holland with the outline of a village on the left shore. Looking down the centre of the picture is open water and on the land in the centre foreground are the fishermen. One has a long stave, whilst wading in the water a man stands holding a small fish basket. A rowing boat is aground on the right. The painting clearly shows the influence of Hendrik Dubbels and the van de Velde studio.

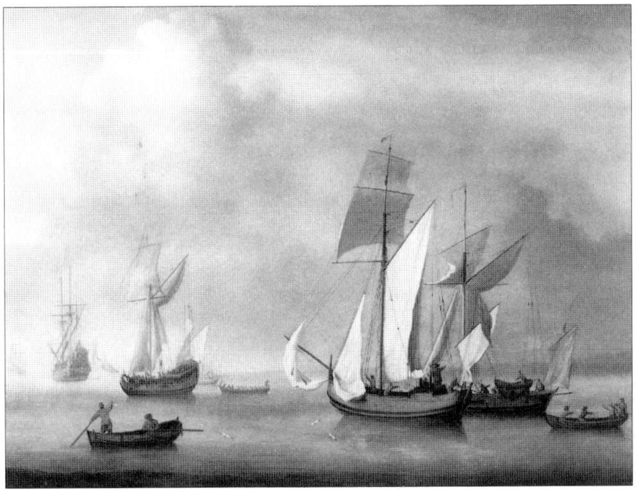

48

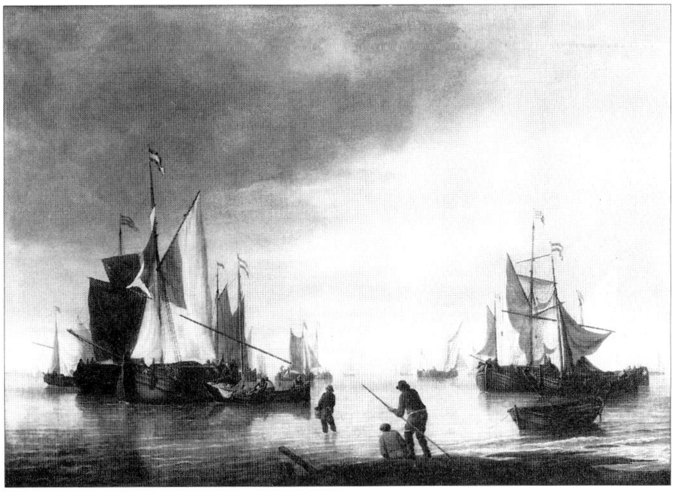

49

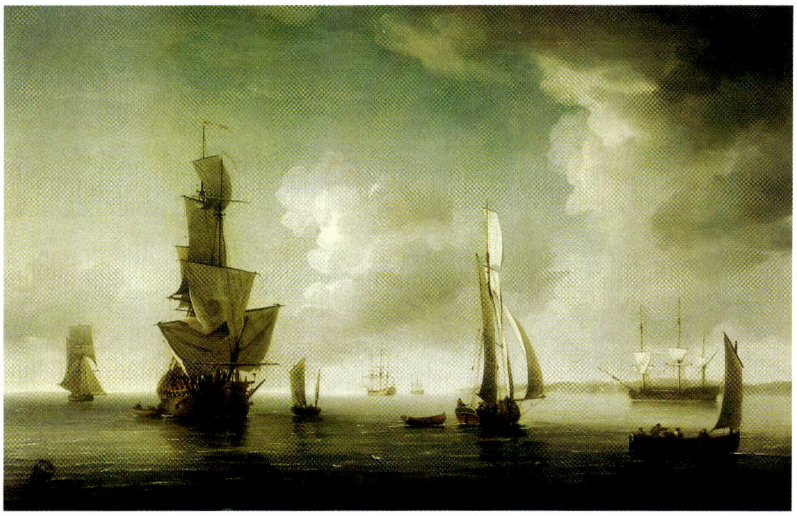

15A
A cutter and other vessels becalmed

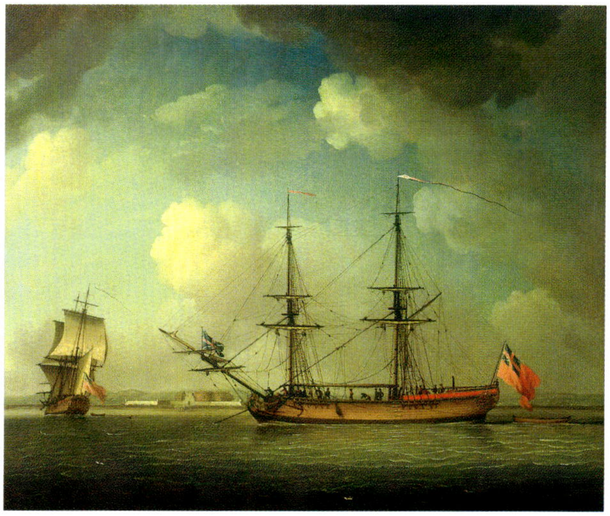

16
A snow lying at anchor

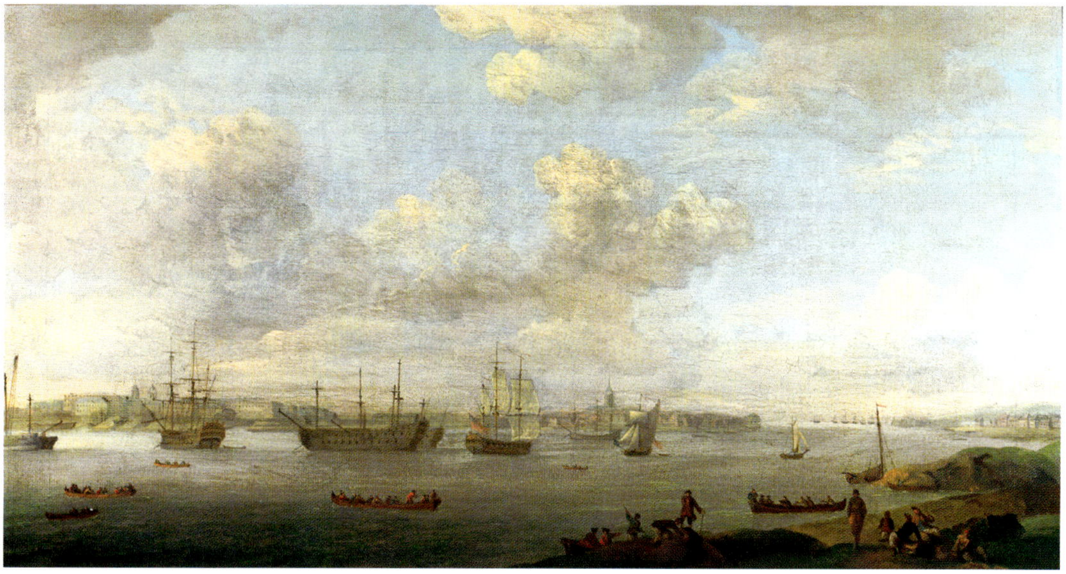

21
A view of Portsmouth harbour with men o' war and other vessels with figures on the shore

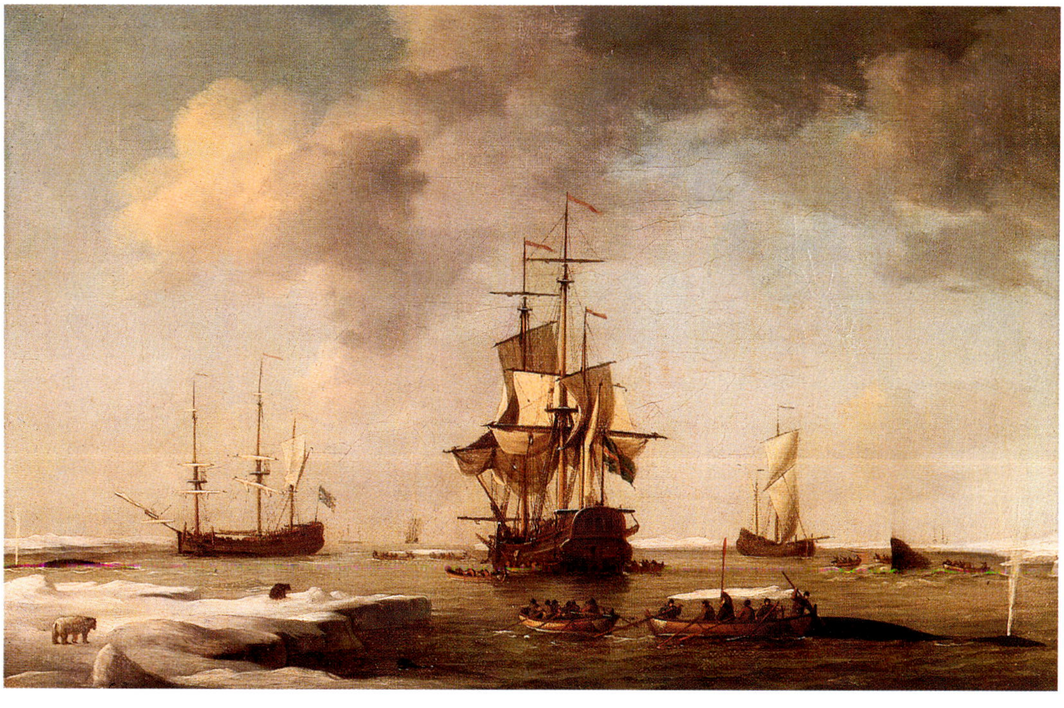

22A
Whalers in the ice

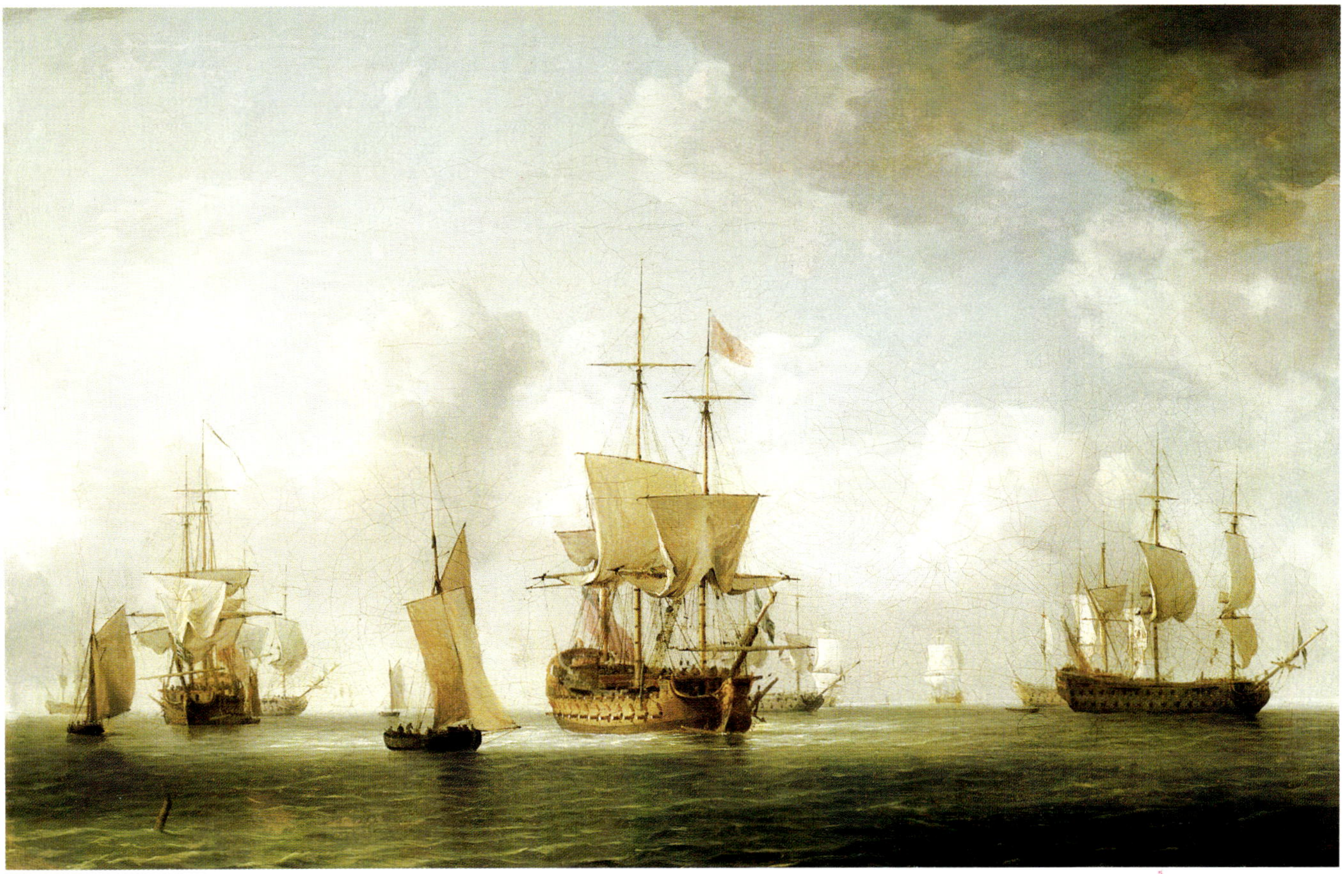

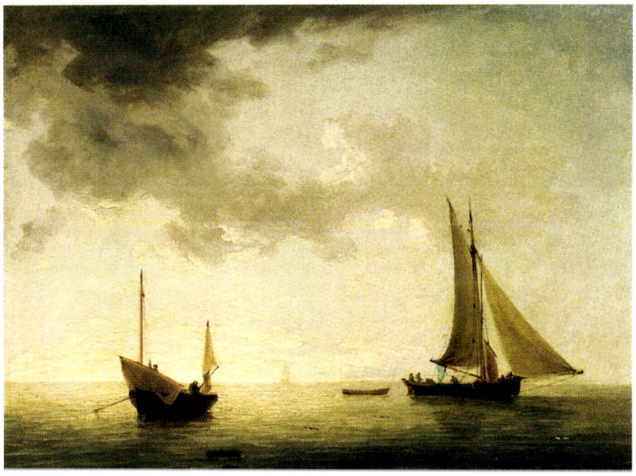

23A (Right)
Sunset – A cutter before a light breeze with a lugger lowering her sails

31 (Below left)
Dutch men o'war drying sails by a shore

38 (Above)
Shipping in a calm sea with eleven ships

39D (Below right)

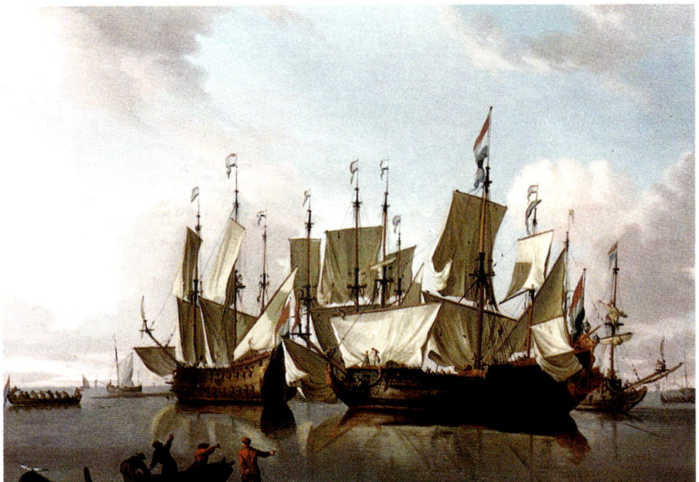

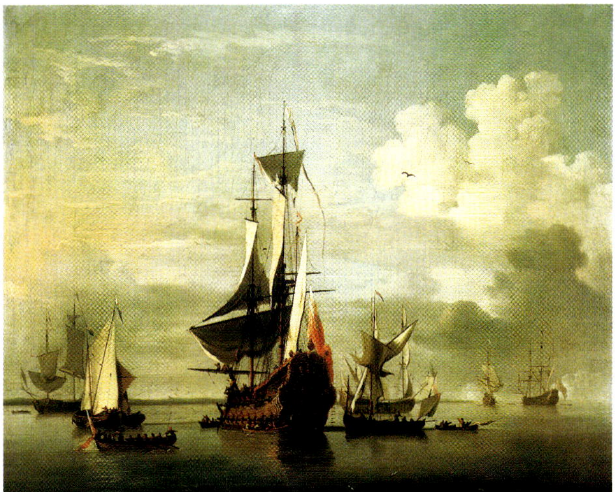

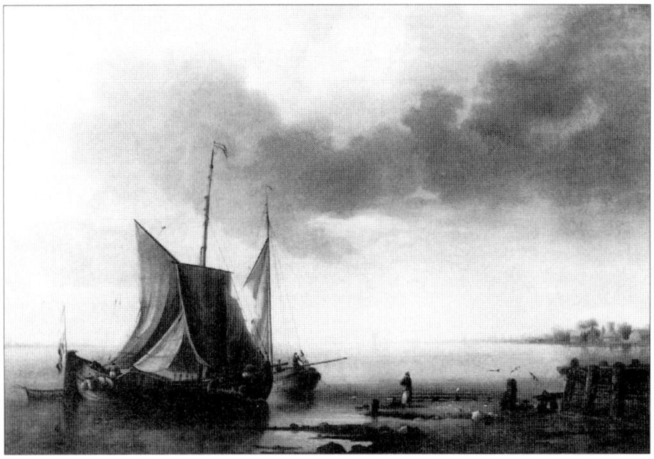

51

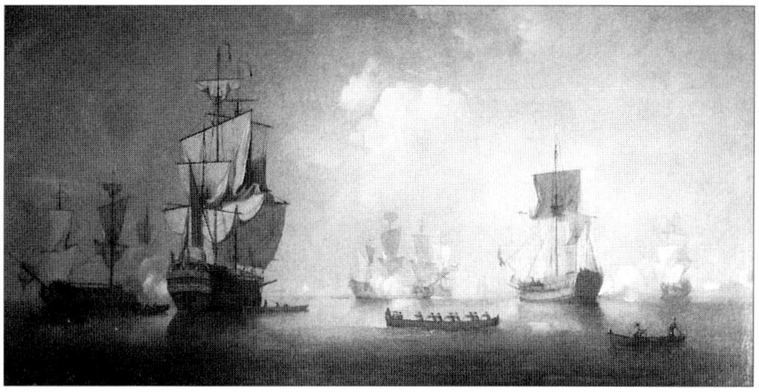

52

50 AN ADMIRAL OF THE RED AND OTHER SHIPPING IN A CALM (see page 136)
Oil on canvas 12½ x 20. Indistinctly inscribed lower right
Prov: Sotheby's 9 July 1986 Lot 5 £44,000
Private Collection
A fine 17th century English fifth-rate, with the royal cypher on her taffrail, fills the right hand side of the painting. She is port side to, towing two of her boats, with all sails set in a calm. At her mizzen topmast she wears the flag of a Rear Admiral of the Red. She has just fired a gun from the port battery. At the left horizon another English man o'war flying the flag of a full Admiral of the Red. In the left foreground a ship's six-oared galley is alongside a small fishing lugger to which an important passenger is being transferred. He wears white gloves and a cavalier hat. The land to the right could be the Isle of Wight seen from Keyhaven on the mainland. (The dirty varnish on this painting gives it a yellow appearance.)

51 DUTCH BARGES IN AN ESTUARY OFFSHORE WITH A FIGURE IN THE FOREGROUND
Oil on canvas 20¼ x 29¼. Unsigned
Prov: Sotheby's 18 December 1974 Lot 163 £600
Private Collection
Dutch fishing boats on the left of the painting, land on the right. A figure stands on the shore in the right foreground beside the remains of a jetty.

52 FIVE MEN O'WAR OF THE RED SQUADRON AND A ROYAL YACHT FIRING A SALUTE OFF A FORTRESS.
Oil on canvas 25 x 50. Signed C. Brooking pinxt lower right.
A pinnace rows important people to the distant shore to the right. Framed above a mirror of similar width, as an over mantel.
Prov: Miss Lawrence of Sandywell Park
Private Collection

SHORE SCENES

There are very few shore scenes by Brooking and those that do exist are based mainly on Willem van de Velde the Younger, and Simon de Vleiger.

101A THE COAST NEAR SCHEVENINGEN WITH FISHING PINKS ON THE SHORE (see page 136)
Oil on canvas 20 x 31¼. Signed C. Brooking lower right
In a fine carved frame
Prov: John Carr of Dunston Hill 1806
A. H. MacGeorge Esq., Kilmacolm, Ayrshire
Morrison McCleary, Glasgow sale March 1960 Lot 77
W. R. Drown Esq.
Spink & Son March 1960
Mr and Mrs Paul Mellon (Oct 1961)
Exhib: Mellon Foundation: Aldeburgh/Bristol June/July 1966, No. 39
Seascapes at Yale 77/78 No. 11
Illus: William Gaunt *Marine Painting* Plate 61
Apart from the omission of two figures in the foreground, this picture is almost an exact copy of a painting on a panel by Simon de Vleiger, now in the collection of the Wallraf-Richartz Museum, Cologne.

101B A BEACH SCENE NEAR SCHEVENINGEN
Oil on canvas 14¾ x 22½. Signed Brooking on boat right foreground
Prov: Spink & Son
Captain Bruce S. Ingram November 1936 bequeathed to The National Maritime Museum (1963-29)
A smaller version of 101A with minor differences.

102A A BEACH SCENE WITH MEN O'WAR IN THE DISTANCE (see page 136)
Oil on canvas 14¾ x 22¾. Signed C Brooking on spar left foreground
Prov: Sir Bruce Ingram
National Maritime Museum (1963-26)
Exhib: Art of the Van de Veldes NMM No. 148
Ref: M. S. Robinson, *The Paintings of the Willem van de Veldes* p.879
This is an updated version of the van de Velde the Younger, in the Lugt collection, Institut Nederlandais, Paris. A similar shore scene (*Breakwater at Den Helder*) by van de Velde was in a private collection in Los Angeles in 1974.

102B
Oil on canvas 15 x 23 approx. Signed C Brooking on spar left foreground
Prov: Colnaghi 1946

Private Collection
Ref: M. S. Robinson, *The Paintings of the Willem van de Veldes* No. 160 p.879
The spars left foreground and two of the ships at sea are in slightly different positions to 102A.

103A A BEACH SCENE ON A WINDY DAY, WITH A FISHING BOAT ASHORE
Oil on canvas 10¼ x 15¼. Signed C Brooking
Prov: Sir Edmund Bacon
Derived from a van de Velde the Younger composition, and now in the possession of Mr de Jonge. Another version by van de Velde was at the Schloss Museum, Weimar. It was stolen in 1945.

103B (see page 137)
Oil on canvas 9½ x 13½. Signed C Brooking lower left
Prov: Colnaghi 1958
Miss Donner
Exhib: Mellon Foundation: Aldeburgh/Bristol June/July 1966, No. 47
Illus: Grant *English Landscape*, 1925
Burlington Magazine, February 1958
Ref: M. S. Robinson, *The Paintings of the Willem van de Veldes* p.848

104 BLANKENBURG CASTLE OFF THE COAST OF FLANDERS (see page 137)
Oil on canvas 10½ x 14¾. Part signature C Brooking on horizontal log lower left
Prov: Robert Taylor, Esq.
E.M. Thomas, Esq. (1915)
David Messum Gallery 1984
Sotheby's 13 March 1985 Lot 20. Unsold
Sotheby's 20 November 1985 Lot 14 Sold £6,000
Private Collection
Exhib: Mellon Foundation: Aldeburgh/Bristol June/July 1966, No. 53
From a set of six Brooking paintings (see 15B)
This is a copy with some alterations of the original composition by Jan van Goyen. Brooking either saw the original oil painting or the engraving after it entitled *A View of Blankenburg Castle off the Coast of Flanders*. It was engraved by T. Major, and published 13 April 1754 at the Golden Head, Chandois St, near St. Martins Lane, London. The original painting was in the possession of William Herring Esq.

105 SHIPS NEAR A COAST OF SAND DUNES
(see page 137)
Oil on canvas 12 x 15. Signed C Brooking P
Prov: John Mitchell & Son 1962
Mr and Mrs Paul Mellon
Yale Center for British Art
Sotheby's 18 November 1981 Lot 111 for £2,000
Christie's 20 April 1990 Lot 84 for £8,500 Parker Gallery
Private Collection
Exhib: Virginia Museum of Fine Art 1963 No. 26
Royal Academy, Winter Exhib, 1964/65 No. 141
This is a close copy of a Willem van de Velde the Younger in the Manchester City Art Gallery (Assheton Bennett Collection No. 72).

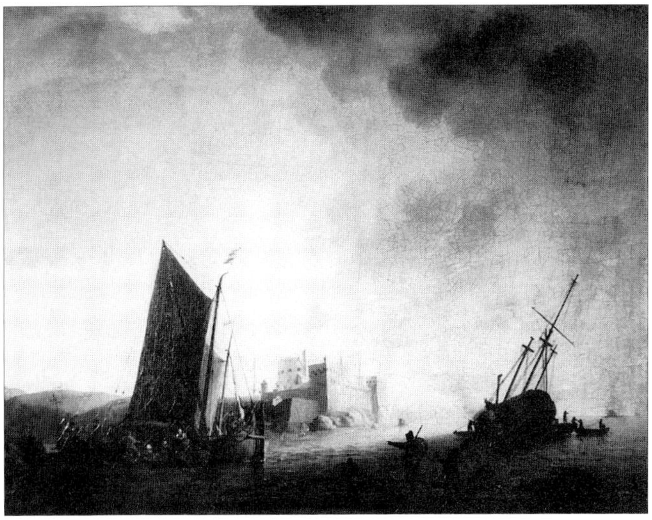

106

106 A SMALL SHIP BEING CAREENED OFF A CASTLE WITH DUTCH FISHING BOATS AT LEFT
Oil on canvas 21 x 28. Signed Charles Brooking
This unusual painting has been seen by David Moore-Gwyn, Sotheby's in the USA in 1990. The view is at the entrance to a creek to the left with land and a large fortress to the centre of the scene. On the right is a small ship with fore and mizzen masts struck being careened and attended by boats. On the left are two Dutch fishing boats with mainsails set, on the foreshore are four fishermen, one pointing to the left.

SHIPS ON FIRE

151 A TWO-DECKER ON FIRE AT NIGHT OFF A FORT (see Chapter 3, page 41)
Oil on canvas 10 x 12½. Signed C Brooking pinxit aged 17 years
Prov: F. M. Brotherhood Esq., Maryland, USA
Sporting Gallery, Middleburg, VA, USA
Mr and Mrs Paul Mellon November 1968
Yale Center for British Art 1976
Exhib: Mellon Foundation: Bristol July 1966, No. 8
This is his earliest known painting and if the signature is correct would have been painted in 1740. The fort has been tentatively identified as Elizabeth Castle, Jersey.

152 A BOMB KETCH BECALMED BY MOONLIGHT NEAR A FORT (see Chapter 3, page 42)
Oil on canvas 10 x 12. Signed C Brooking
Prov: F. M. Brotherhood Esq., Maryland, USA
Sporting Gallery, Middleburg, VA, USA
Mr and Mrs Paul Mellon November 1968
Yale University 1976
Sotheby's 18 November 1981 Lot 195
Private Collection
Exhib: Mellon Foundation: Bristol July 1966, No. 9
151 and 152 were a pair and there is no reason to suppose that the latter is not an early painting completed also around 1740.

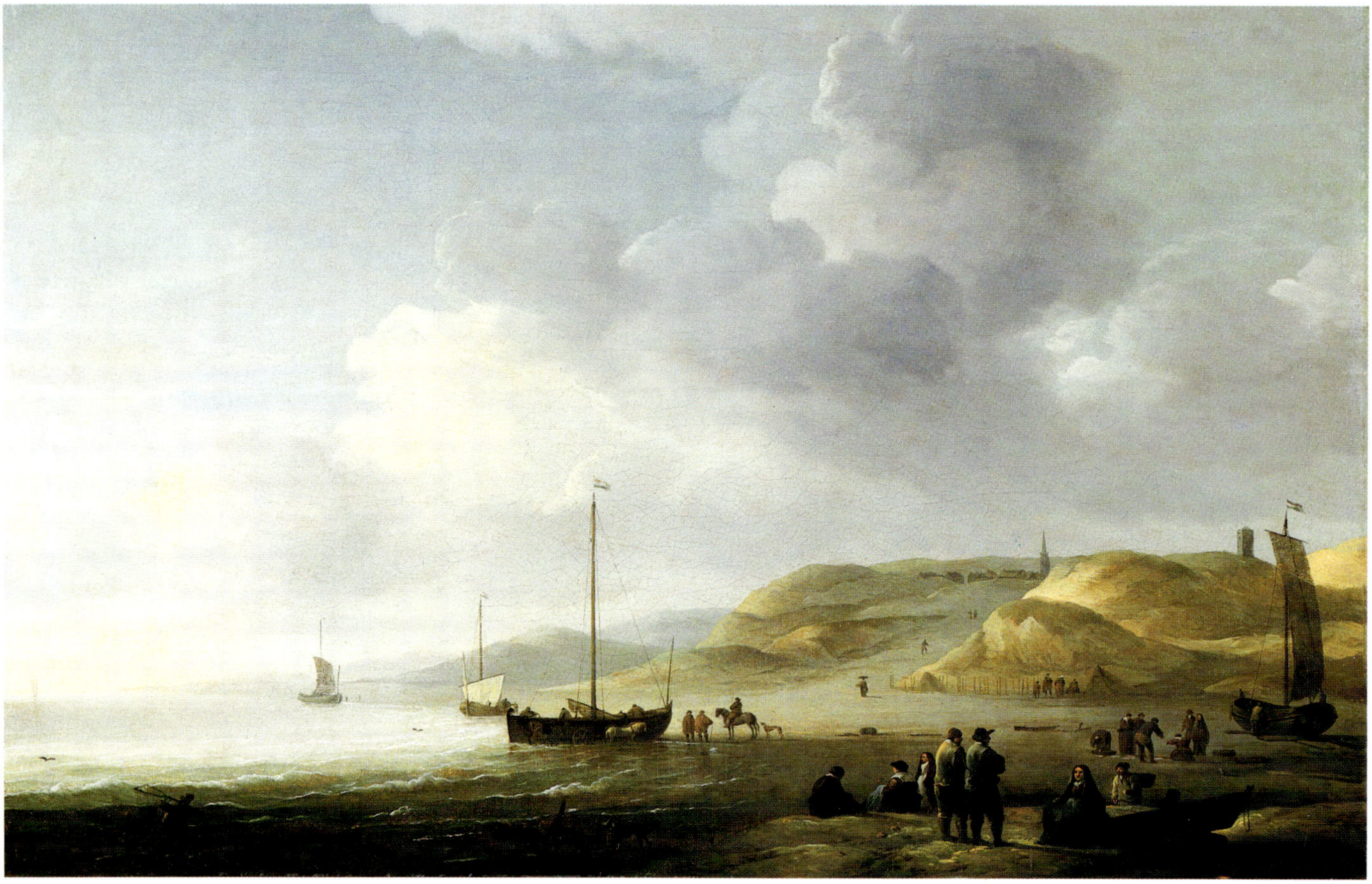

40 (Below left)
British men o'war becalmed with other shipping off a coast

50 (Below right)
An Admiral of the Red and other shipping in a calm

101A (Above)
The coast near Scheveningen with fishing pinks on the shore

102A (Right)
A beach scene with men o'war in the distance

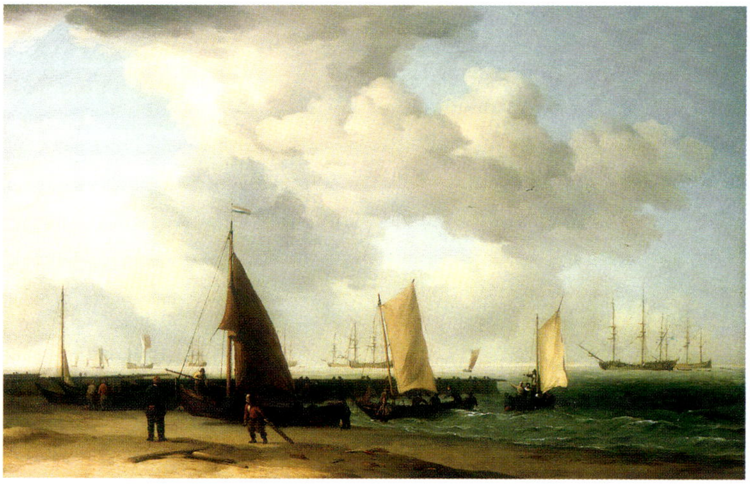

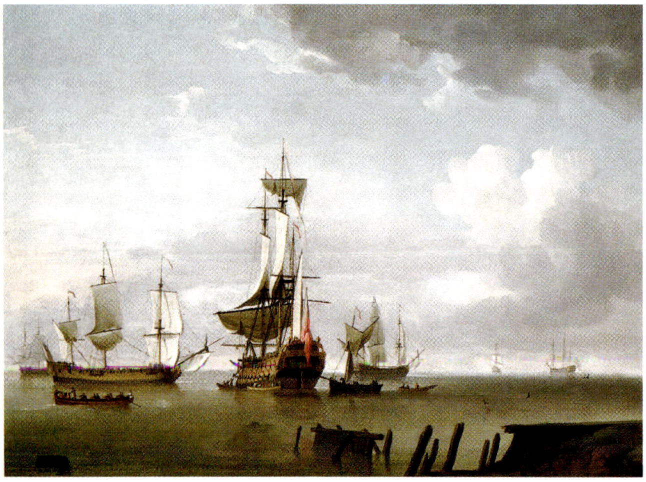

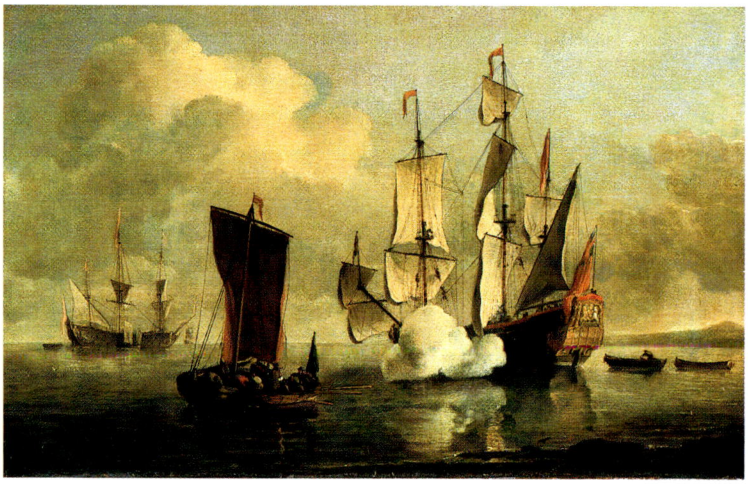

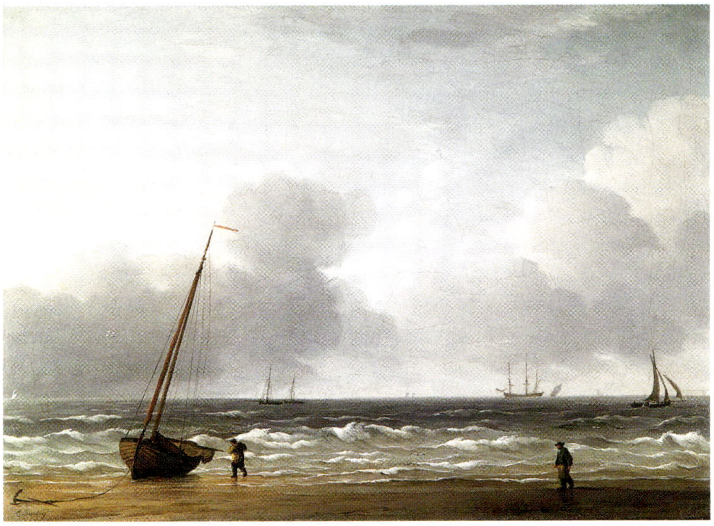

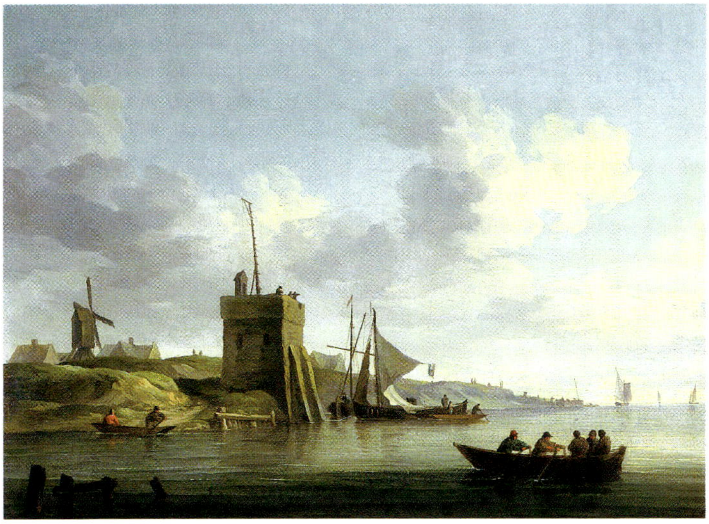

103B (Above left)

104 (Above right)
Blankenburg Castle off the coast of Flanders

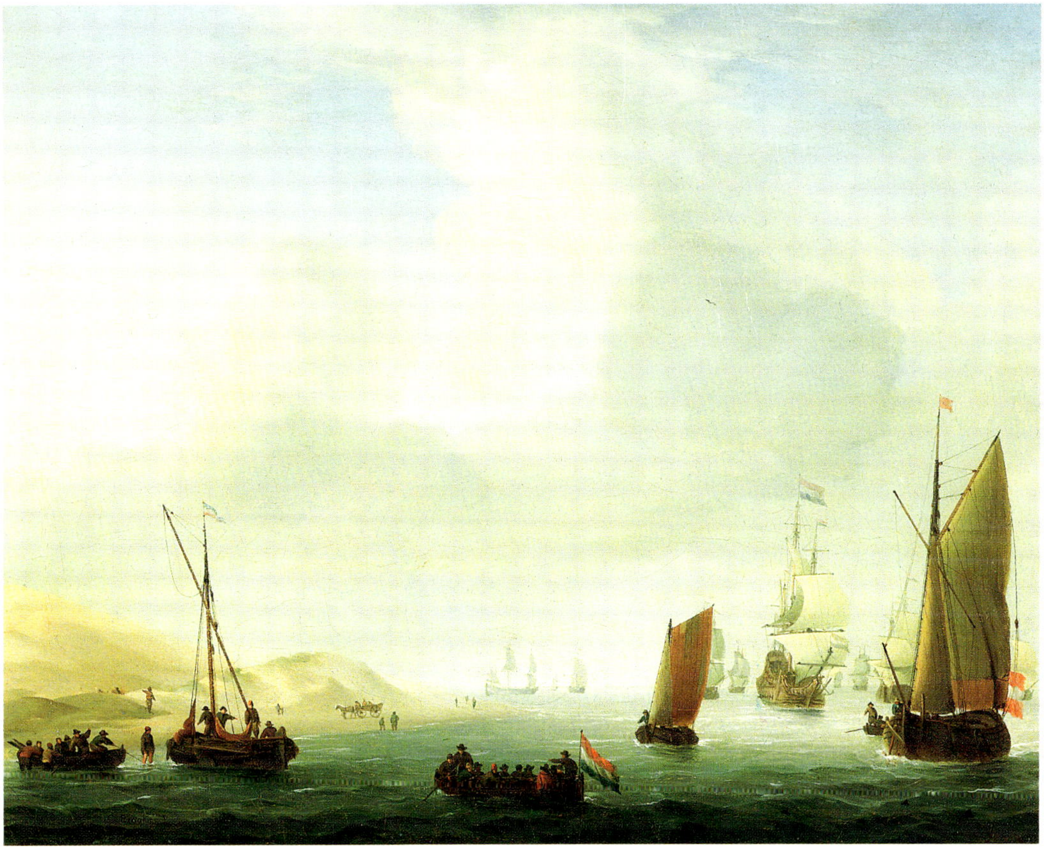

105 (Right)
Ships near a coast of sand dunes

154 (Below)
A ship on fire in a moonlit estuary by a castle

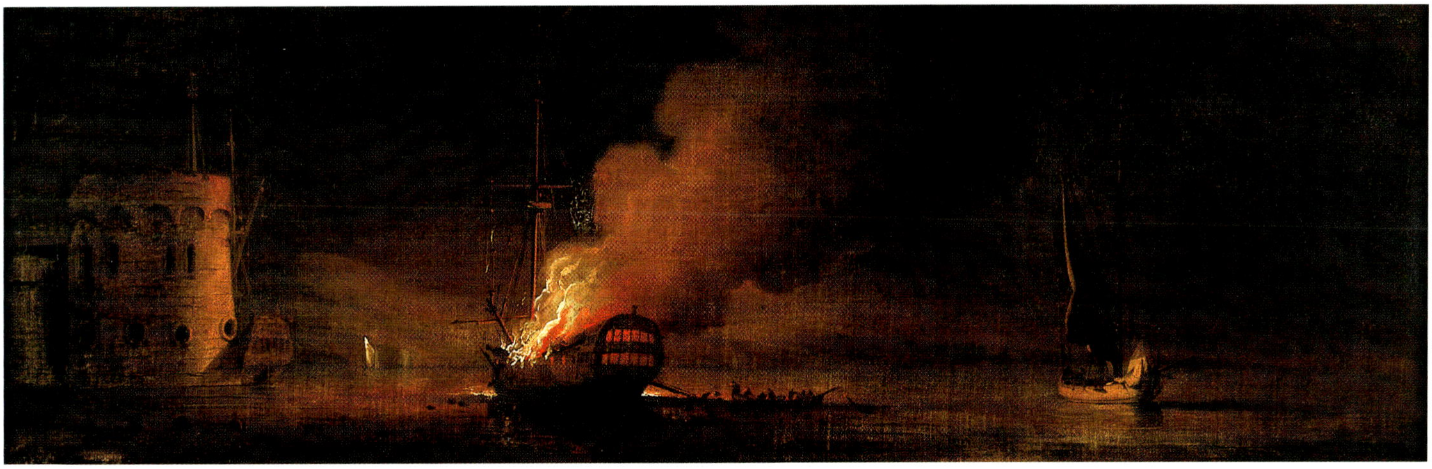

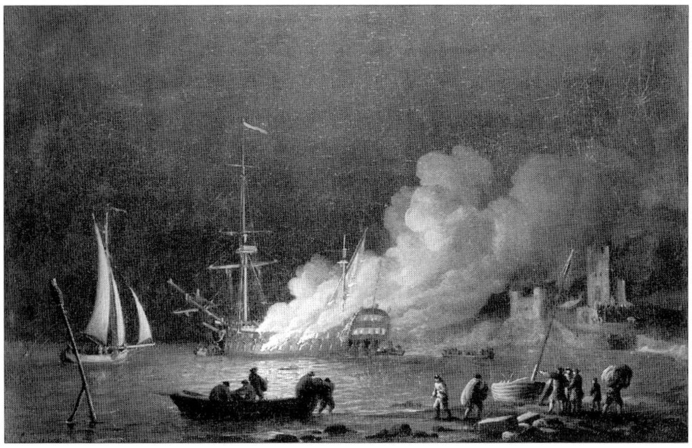

153A

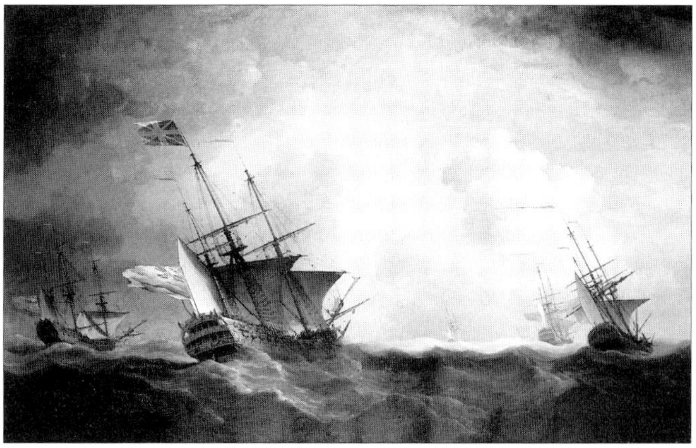

201C

153A A TWO-DECKED SHIP ON FIRE AT NIGHT CLOSE TO SHORE (see page 10)
Oil on canvas 12½ x 17½. Signed C Brooking lower left
Prov: Christie's 10 December, 1965 Lot 7 £420
Colnaghi
Mr and Mrs Paul Mellon 1965
Yale Center for British Art 1976
Exhib: Mellon Foundation: Bristol July 1966, No. 7
Yale Seascapes 1977/78 No. 16
Engraved by Boydell in 1756 entitled *Night* (see engraving 604)
This superb late painting depicts all the horror of a wooden ship on fire at night with the survivors coming ashore or proceeding up to the castle on the right for shelter. This painting may derive from No. 151, Brooking's earliest recorded oil painting of a similar subject.

153B
Oil on canvas 15 x 23. Signed C Brooking lower left
Prov: Arthur Kay, Edinburgh, 1926
Christie's 22 March 1929 Lot 10
Ellis & Smith
Private Collection
Christie's 24 November 1978 Lot 134 £2,000
H. Fritz-Dennville
Herr Peter Tamm, Hamburg
See engraving 604.
This painting was missing for many years, though there was a photograph of it in the Witt Library. It is beautifully painted but because it is wider than 153A and the scale of the figures is smaller, it is not so dramatic. The owner in 1926 was Arthur Kay of Edinburgh who also owned Degas' *Absinthe drinkers*, now in the Jeu de Paume, Paris.

154 A SHIP ON FIRE IN A MOONLIT ESTUARY BY A CASTLE (see page 137)
Oil on canvas 9½ x 29¼. Signed Charles Brooking lower right
Prov: Christie's 22 April 1949 Lot 144 Unsold as P. Monamy
M. Weare Dorset 1957
Sotheby's 18 November 1992 Lot 160 (as a Monamy) £890
M. D. Joel Esq.
A substantial fortress on the left, alongside which is a man o'war stern to. Just left of centre a two-decker is seriously on fire with her main and mizzen overboard. A longboat with eight figures is rescuing men in the water near her stern. To the right a fishing craft watches the awful scene as the fire intensifies in the calm of the night.

GALES

This late series of paintings of ships in gales shows in No. 201B the change in sail plan, with mizzen laced to the mast and the forepart of the mizzen removed, happening before Brooking's death in 1759. Thus it must have occurred before 1755, around 1750.

201A A SQUADRON GOING TO WINDWARD IN A STIFF BREEZE
Oil on canvas 34 x 50. Signed in full, lower left
Prov: Christie's 18 November 1938 Lot 14 £99.15 Rufford Abbey Sale
Spink & Son
Ferens Art Gallery, Hull
Exhib: Mellon Foundation, Aldeburgh/Bristol June/July 1966, No. 16
Illus: *Burlington Magazine*, August 1966
David Cordingly *Painters of the Sea,* Plate 21
This series of pictures is based on van de Velde the Younger's painting in the National Maritime Museum which measures 34 x 48ins. Brooking has updated the ships and painted the sea and sky in his manner and to the advantage of the composition.

201B SHIPS GOING TO WINDWARD IN A GALE (see page 140)
Oil on canvas 16 x 21½. Signed C Brooking
Prov: National Maritime Museum (1946-138)
Exhib: Mellon Foundation: Bristol June 1966 No. 62
Ref: M. S. Robinson, *The Paintings of the Willem van de Veldes* No 269 p.p.1058-60
In this dramatic version, which is freely painted, the flagship wears a red flag at the main whereas 201A has a union flag there instead.

201C A SQUADRON OF BRITISH MEN O'WAR IN OPEN SEA IN A GALE
Oil on canvas 33 x 42½
Prov: Anthony Whitaker, Esq.
Christie's 12 May 1967 Lot 54
S. Sabin 2,400 gns
Private Collection, Belfast

An even more dramatic version. The flagship wears a union flag at the main.

201D A SNOW CLOSE-HAULED ON THE STARBOARD TACK IN A FRESH BREEZE, OTHER SHIPPING BEYOND
Oil on canvas 11⅛ x 15¼
Prov: Lord Barrington 1773
William Barrington 1961, gifted to his naval cousin
Vice Admiral B. C. B. Brooke CB CBE
Sotheby's 18 March 1981 Lot 5 unsold
Private Collection
Exhib: Mellon Foundation: Aldeburgh June 1966, No. 18

201E A SQUADRON GOING TO WINDWARD IN A GALE
Oil on canvas 15 x 22½. Unsigned
Prov: Christie's 22 June 1973 Lot 141 £735
F. B. Cockett Esq.
Private Collection
Note: Mizzen laced to mast and fore part of yard removed.

202 A ROYAL YACHT IN A GALE (see Chapter 2, page 32)
Oil on canvas 14½ x 23½. Signed C Brooking lower left on spar
Prov: Beuckeleers-Donche
National Maritime Museum (1939-852)
This picture, painted towards the end of the artist's life, shows four Royal Yachts and a ship. The sea is very rough. Three forks of lightning are clearly visible. The nearest yacht wears the Royal Standard and is ship-rigged. Another yacht is also ship-rigged. Two others are ketch-rigged. The feature of the mizzen sail laced to the mast with the fore end of the yard removed can be seen in this picture.

203A A FLAGSHIP IN A GALE SHORTENING SAIL
Oil on canvas 14½ x 22. Signed C Brooking on spar lower left
Prov: Sir Bruce Ingram
Sotheby's 11 March 1964 Lot 8 £420
R. C. Porter Esq.
Sotheby's 17 June 1981 Lot 108 for £2,000
Private Collection
Exhib: Hull, Ferens Art Gallery, Early Marine Paintings 1951 No. 264
Mellon Foundation: Aldeburgh/Bristol June/July 1966, No. 58
This series of five paintings depicts a Vice Admiral of the Red (Red Flag at fore masthead) in heavy gales. The ships have all been damaged in the gales. See 203A, B, C and E. In 203D the two ships are in different positions, the main subject is fully broadside on and has no Vice Admiral's flag whilst the second ship to the right is more visibly moving up on the swell. There is also a ship's boat in the right foreground.

203B
Oil on canvas 14 x 22½. Signed C Brooking on plank lower left
Prov: J. W. Valpy (South Africa)
Sotheby's 3 April 1968 Lot 99
Lloyd
Christie's 15 November 1968 Lot 59 £1,600
Gomshall Gallery 1971
Private Collection
King & Chasemore 1986
Private Collection

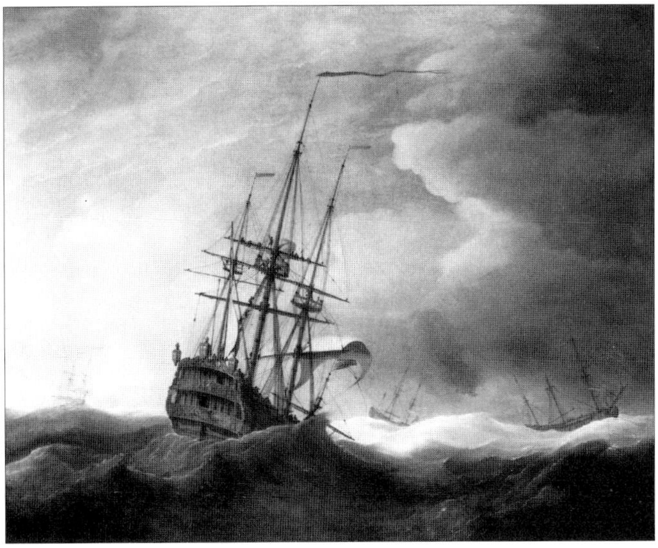

204

203C
Oil on canvas 19½ x 23¾. Signed C Brooking on spar left
Prov: Mrs L. E. Cookman 1949
Mr and Mrs G.M. Thomas
Exhib: Mellon Foundation: Bristol July 1966, No. 57

203D (see Chapter 4, page 61)
Oil on canvas 10½ x 14½. From a set of six Brooking paintings (see 15B). Signed lower right C Brooking
Prov: Robert Taylor Esq. (1840-1915)
E. M. Thomas Esq. 1915
David Messum Gallery 1984
Sotheby's 13 March 1985 Lot 23 £3,200
Private Collection
Exhib: Mellon Foundation: Aldeburgh/Bristol June/July 1966, No. 50

203E
Oil on canvas 10 x 14
Prov: S. G. Campion of Malvern
Rupert Preston Gallery October 1969
Private Collection

203F MERCHANT SHIPS IN ROUGH SEAS
Oil on canvas 17 x 26¼
Prov: Sotheby's 3 April 1966 Lot 4 £6,900
Private Collection.
This is the largest of the series. It shows three ships in very rough seas indeed. The predominant ship is just losing its main topmast which in turn is bringing down the mizzen as she ploughs into a huge wave. Surprisingly a ship's boat is rising violently on another wave in the right foreground. The two other ships are as yet undamaged.

204 BRITISH MEN O'WAR IN HEAVY SEAS
Oil on canvas 30¼ x 38
Prov: Col. Matchett
F. R. Lodge Esq.
Christie's 11 April 1980 Lot 16 (unsold) as van der Hagen
Sotheby's 9 July 1980 Lot 26

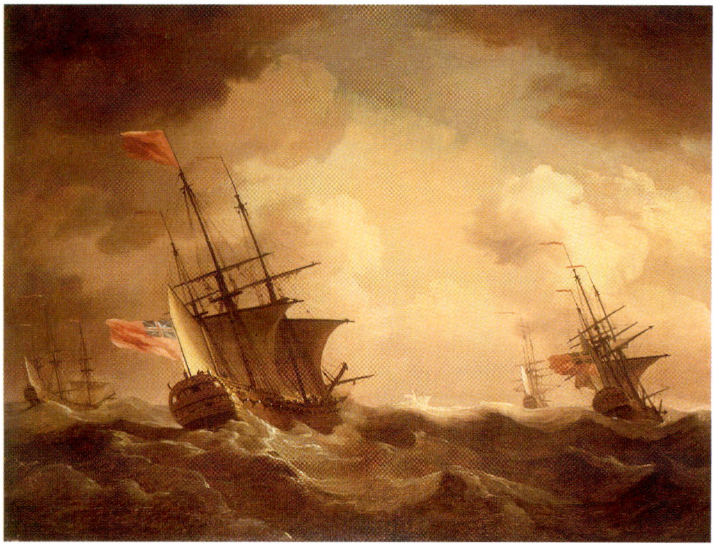

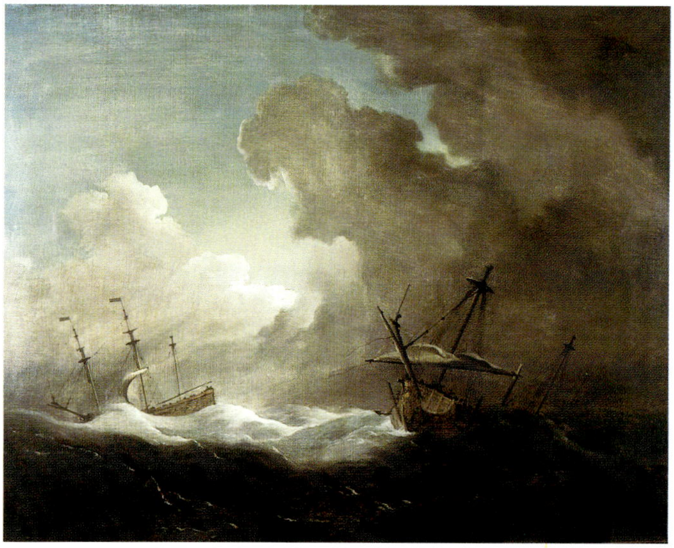

201B (Above left)
Ships going to windward in a gale

209 (Above right)
Storm at sea

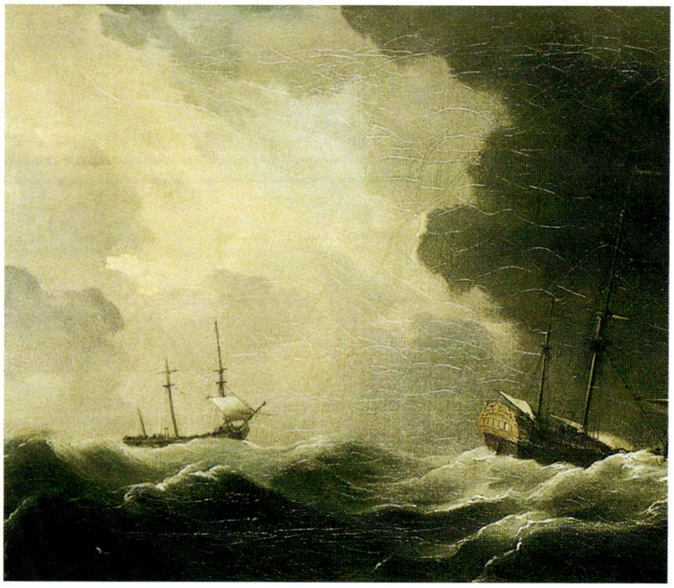

210A
Two ships scudding in a gale

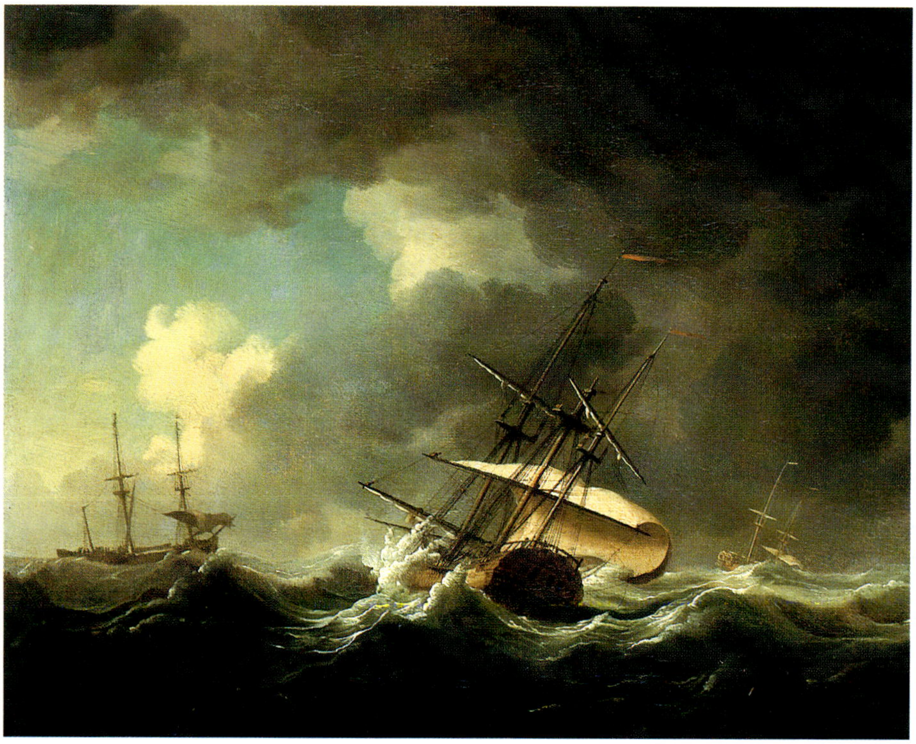

212B
A British man o' war in heavy seas

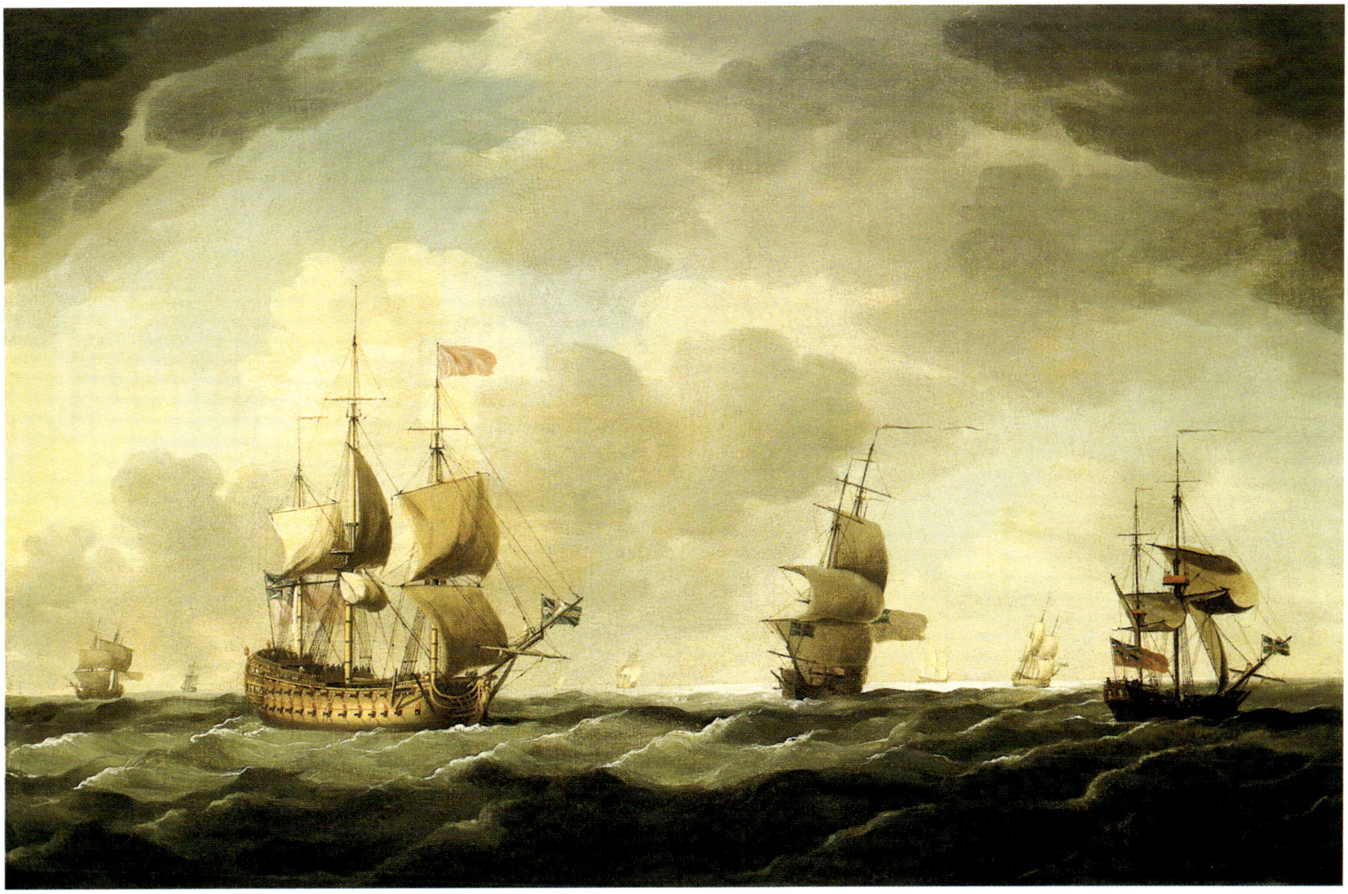

231D

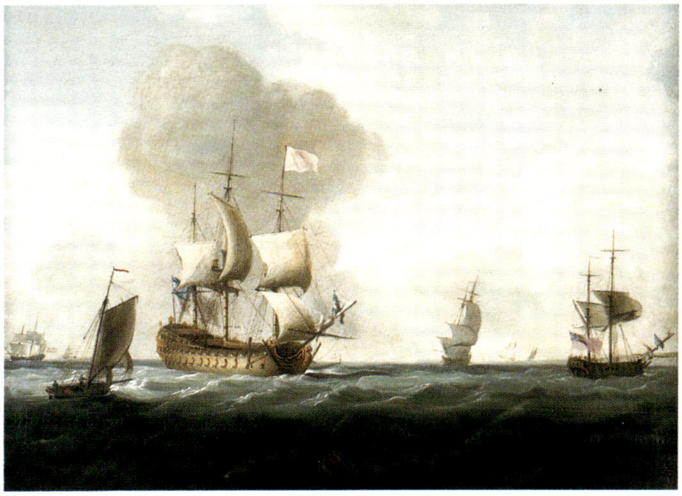

231C

231E

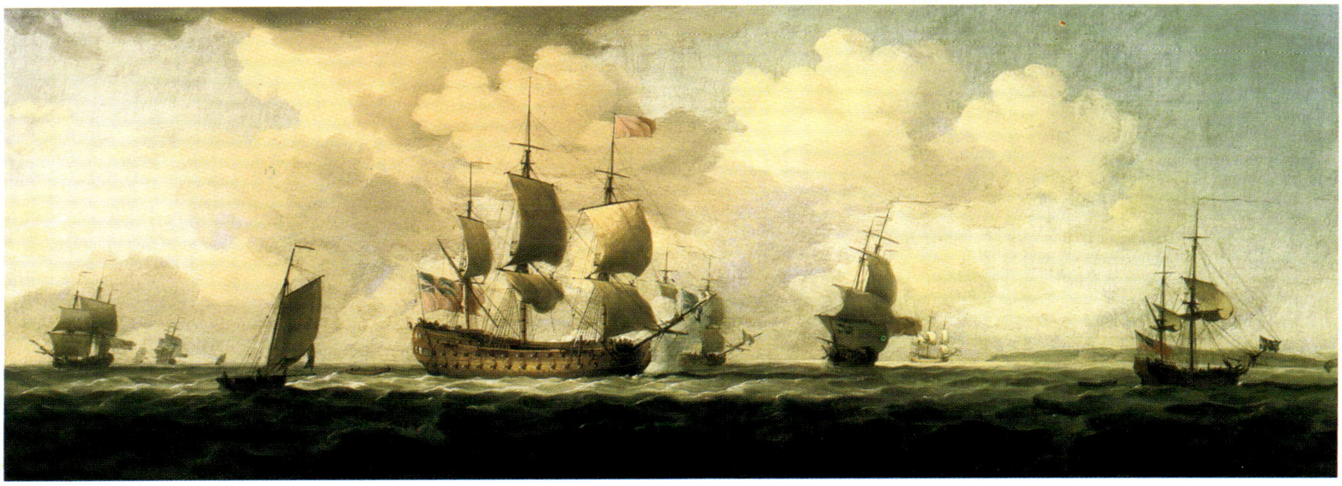

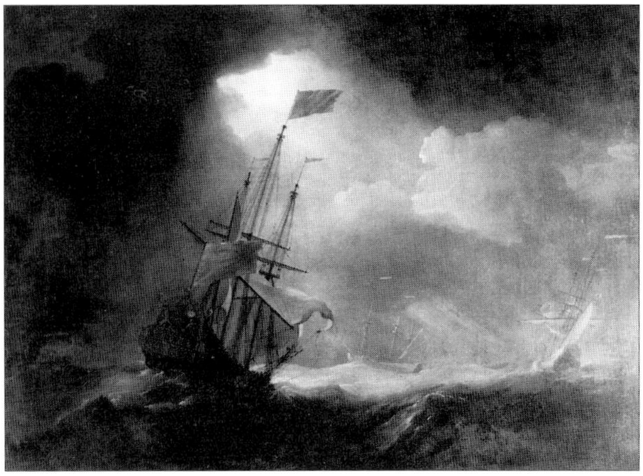

205

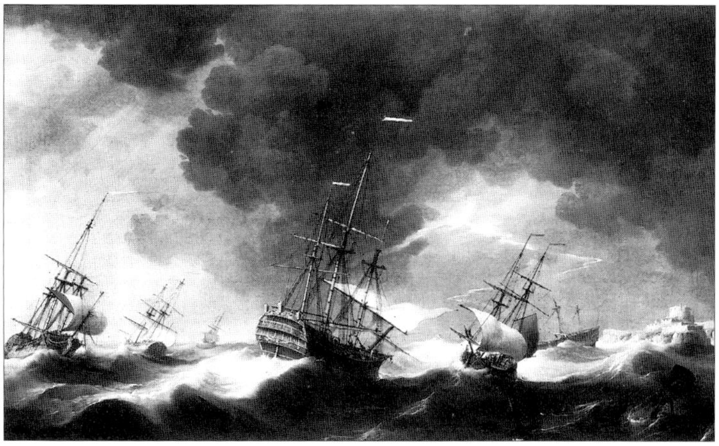

206

A. E. Edwards Esq.
Ref: M. S. Robinson, *The Paintings of the Willem van de Veldes* No. 503 p.1123
A fine two-decker going downwind and across seas under forecourse and reduced mizzen, with three other ships under reduced sail beyond in a storm.

205 A FLAGSHIP IN A STORM
Oil on canvas 26¼ x 35
Prov: C. E. Hill
Christie's 23 March 1979 Lot 50
Simon Carter Gallery, Woodbridge
Private Collection
A great storm with four ships of the line of an earlier period. Christie's attributed it to Johann van der Hagen. The painting style is closer to that of Brooking and he is a more likely candidate. If it is by van der Hagen it is an exceptional work.

206 INDIAMEN DRIVEN ASHORE IN A STORM
Oil on canvas 30½ x 50. Signed C Brooking Pinxit on spar lower left
Prov: National Maritime Museum (1947-85)
Seven Indiamen can be seen in this composition. A wild scene with lightning and a fortress at right that may be Elizabeth Castle in Jersey.

207 STORM SCENE ON A LEE SHORE (Three Men O'War in a storm)
Oil on canvas 17½ x 28
Prov: Christie's 21 December 1967 Lot 153 160gns sold to Lewis
(Cooper Neg: 353158)

208 SHIPS IN A GALE PASSING THROUGH A ROCKY PASSAGE WITH A SHIP-RIGGED ROYAL YACHT IN SUNSHINE BEYOND
Oil on canvas 25 x 33. Signed C Brooking lower left on spar
Prov: Christie's 1958. Not as a Brooking
Captain J. S. B. Holley New Zealand Shipping Company
Christie's 12 May 1995 Lot 549A £4,200
Private Collection
A fine early painting of a sea passage in a full gale. Daunting to any mariner. It shows the influence of Cornelis van de Velde and Johann van der Hagen.

209 STORM AT SEA (see page 140)
Oil on canvas 29 x 36½. Signed Brooking centre foreground
Prov: Southampton 27 October 1876
Archdeacon of Nottingham, The Ven M. R. W. Brown 1876
Neale & Son, Nottingham 5 July 1973 Lot 174
Commander David Joel RN
A dark and dramatic painting in the style of van de Velde the Younger showing two ships in a storm, one in the right foreground in shadow, the other in bright sunshine to the left, and beyond, both going down sea and wind.

210A TWO SHIPS SCUDDING IN A GALE
(see page 140)
Oil on canvas 15 x 23 approx
Prov: Brooke family
This is essentially a sepia-toned painting. In very rough seas two English merchant ships are running before a gale. The ship on the right is nearer with bows down and under a great wave. She has lost her fore topmast but prudently has struck the mizzen sail and mizzen topmast. The second ship to the left of the painting is riding on an even keel. She has lost her main topmast and most of the mizzen. Both ships have just their forecourse set.

210B
Oil on canvas 9 x 13½. From a set of six Brooking paintings
Prov: Robert Taylor Esq. (1840-1915)
E. M. Thomas Esq. 1915
David Messum Gallery 1984
Sotheby's 13 March 1985 Lot 21 £2,800
Private Collection
Exhib: Mellon Foundation: Aldeburgh/Bristol June/July 1966, No. 51
This is a beautifully toned greenish painting. See 15B

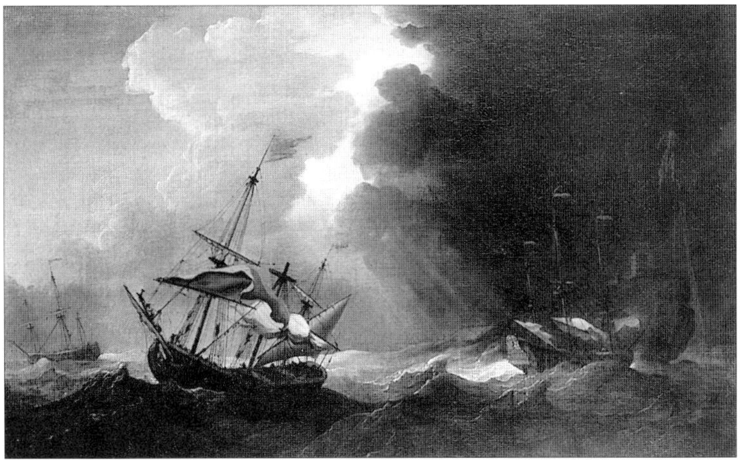

207

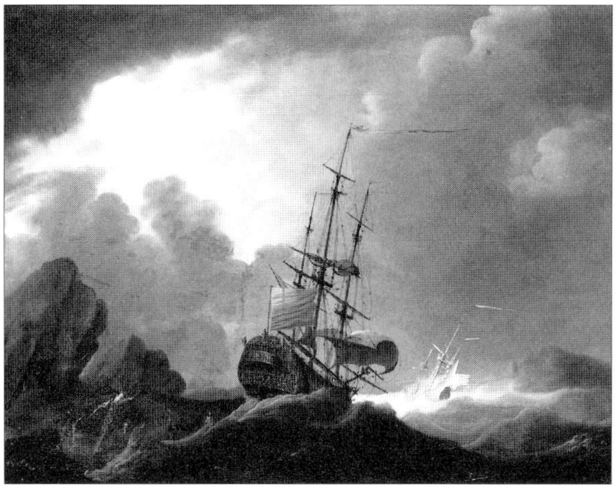

208

211 TWO SHIPS IN A GALE, ONE DISMASTED TO WINDWARD
Oil on canvas 23½ x 28½
Prov: B. Bullen Esq.
Bonhams 20 August 1995 Lot 306 £5,600
Royal Exchange Art Gallery Nov 1996 No. 2
Private Collection
Two two-deckers, men o'war in a very heavy gale. The ship to the left is further away with masts intact. The crew have lowered the forecourse to the deck and are having trouble in furling the sail. The ship to the right is much closer and in considerable difficulty, for the main mast has collapsed over the port side, whilst the mizzen has gone over the starboard. The foremast stands but the fore topsail has carried away as the crew attempt to bring home and furl the forecourse. Hopefully they are not on a lee shore.

212A THREE SHIPS IN A GALE
Oil on canvas 10⅛ x 14¼. Signed C Brooking P at lower left
Prov: S. G. Campion
Rupert Preston Gallery September 1969
Private Collection

212B A BRITISH MAN O'WAR IN HEAVY SEAS
(see page 140)
Oil on canvas 13½ x 17½. Signed C Brooking P lower left
Prov: Sotheby's 20 November 1985 Lot 8
Parker Gallery
Private Collection
Paintings 212A and 212B appear to be identical although the latter is considerably larger. They show three merchant ships (red pennants and no guns or gun ports) in a heavy gale with a large sea running. The principal ship is reaching into the picture under her main course only. She has lost her main topmast. Of the other vessels, on the left horizon, a ship is running down sea, broadside on under forecourse and she appears to have struck her mizzen top. On the right horizon a merchant brig is comfortably running out of the picture under her forecourse.

FRESH BREEZES

231A A FLAGSHIP, WEARING THE FLAG OF A VICE ADMIRAL OF THE RED, BEFORE THE WIND OFF THE ENGLISH COAST, WITH A CUTTER, A KETCH-RIGGED SLOOP AND OTHER SHIPPING (See Chapter 3, page 48)
Oil on canvas 68¾ x 121. Signed C Brooking Pinx lower left
Prov: The Foundling Hospital (presented by the artist in 1754)
Exhib: Burlington Fine Arts Club 1929 No. 1
Mellon Foundation: Bristol July 1966, No. 4
This is Brooking's largest oil painting and arguably his masterwork. Commissioned for the Foundling Hospital, Brownlow states that it was painted in 18 days. In return for the painting, Brooking was elected a Governor of the Hospital. The magnificent frame is reputedly to the design of William Hogarth, who is known to have supervised its manufacture.

So far as is known this is Brooking's largest painting. It is in a series of nine similar pictures, all of differing sizes. It was obviously a popular composition. The first in the series may be the small oil sketch, 231C, a cabinet painting, which would have been placed in his dealer's window, and from which others were ordered. In spite of the painting's popularity it is curious that no engravings of the subject have been traced, if indeed they were ever produced.

It was painted to hang beside a very large seapiece by Peter Monamy presented in 1737, *English Fleet in the Downs* 70 x 106½ ins, but Brooking made his picture 15ins wider. This great Monamy has been recently rediscovered in a private collection in London, having been missing for 90 years!

231B
Oil on canvas 14½ x 22½. Signed C Brooking lower left
Prov: National Maritime Museum (1962-13)
Bequeathed by Captain L. R. Hibbert in 1962 (see 250)
Exhib: Mellon Foundation: Bristol July 1966, No. 6
Illus: *Burlington Magazine* August 1966 p.441, article by W. Percival-Prescott
David Cordingly, *Marine Painting* 1974 Plate 34
David Cordingly, *Painters of the Sea* 1979 Plate 20

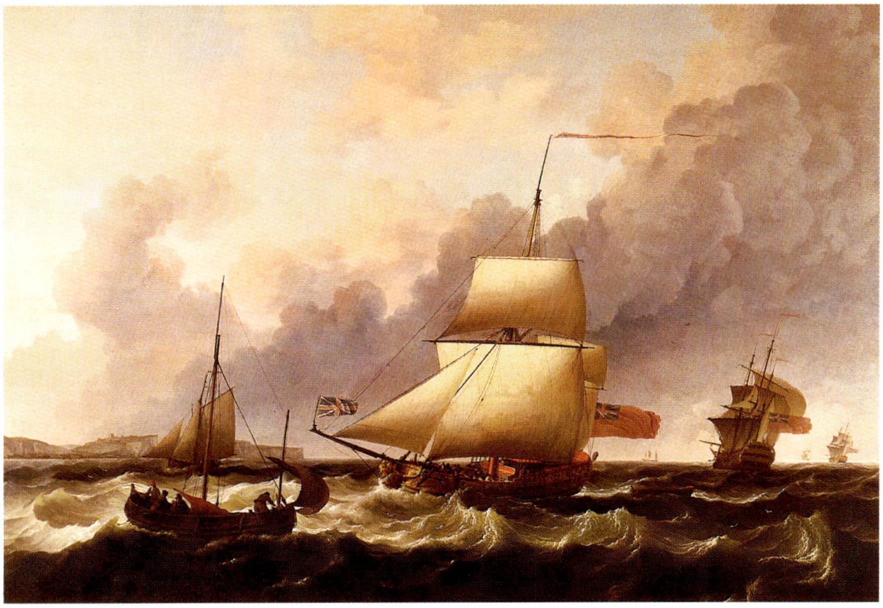

233A
A ketch-rigged Royal Yacht in a fresh breeze off Dover

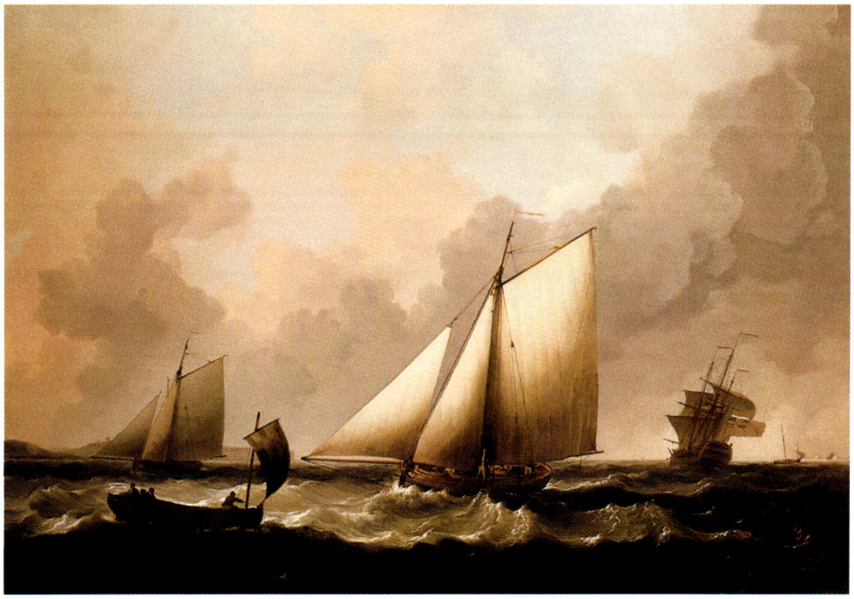

233D
Two cutters and a frigate in a fresh breeze off Dover

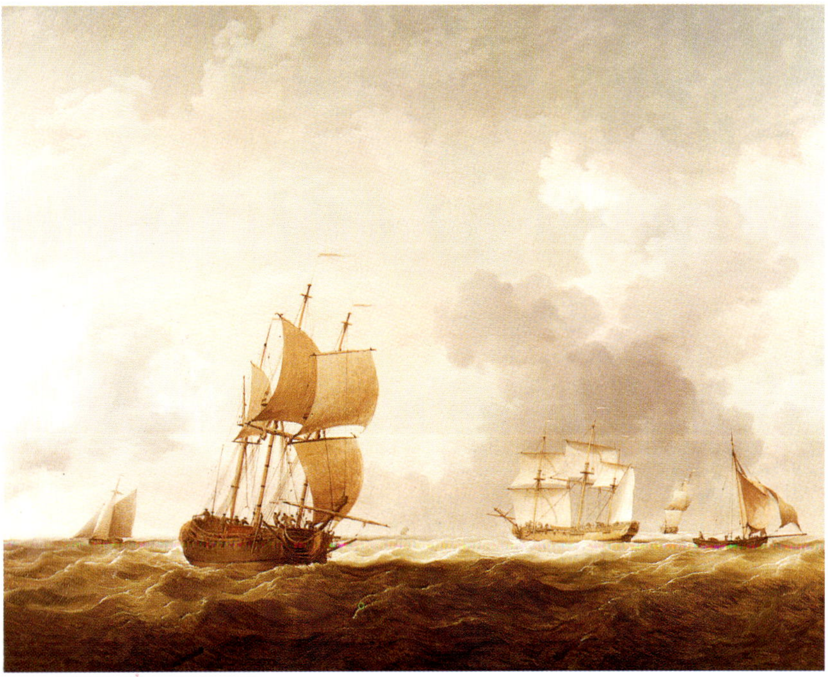

234A
A ship before a fresh breeze and another to leeward passing her

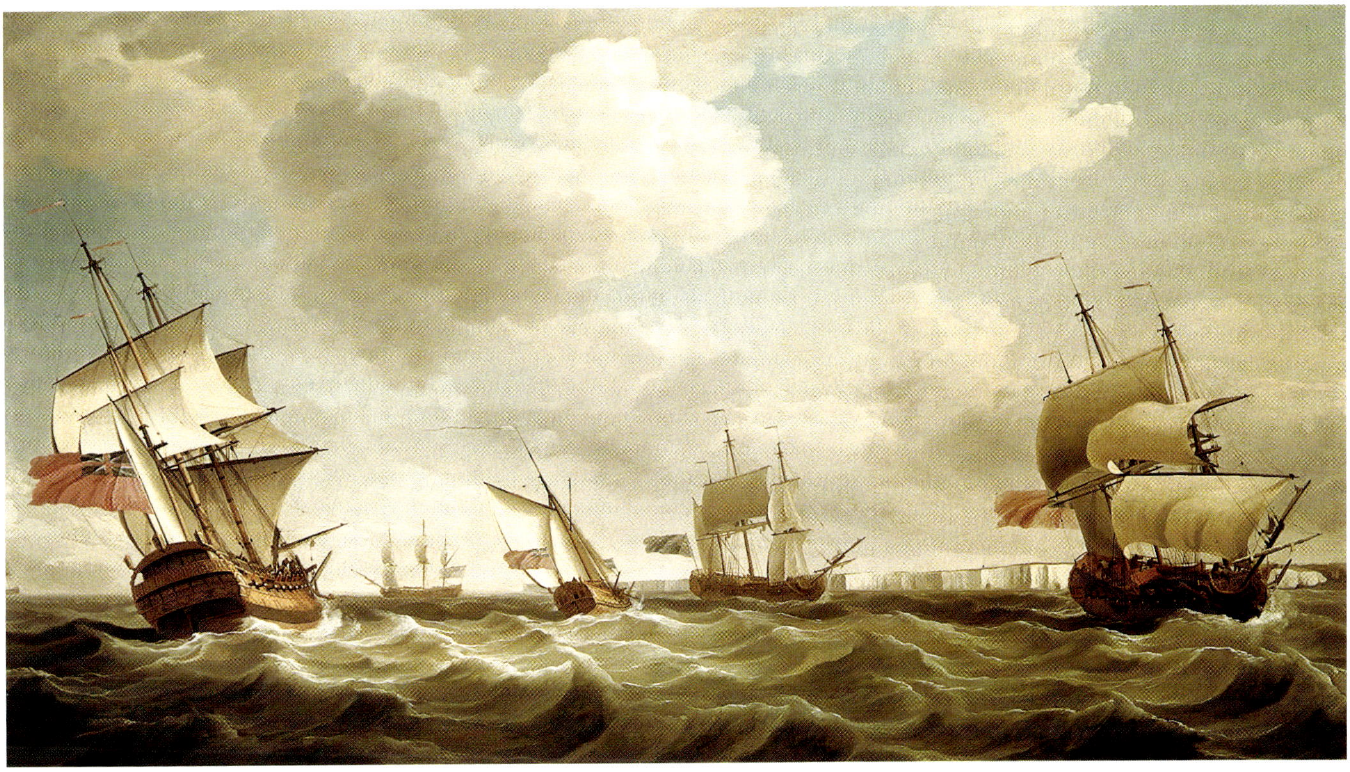

236
Shipping in a breeze in the downs

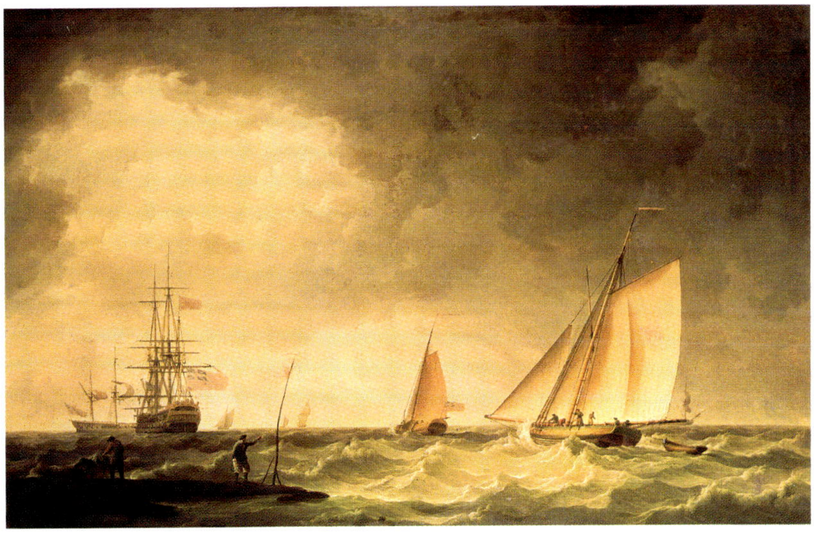

238A
Two cutters, English men o'war at anchor and other shipping in a breeze

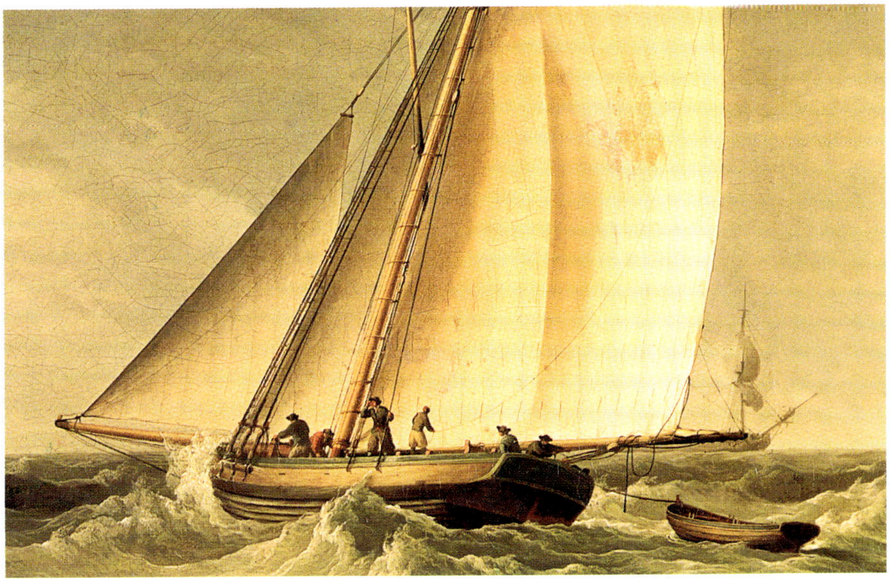

238A
Detail

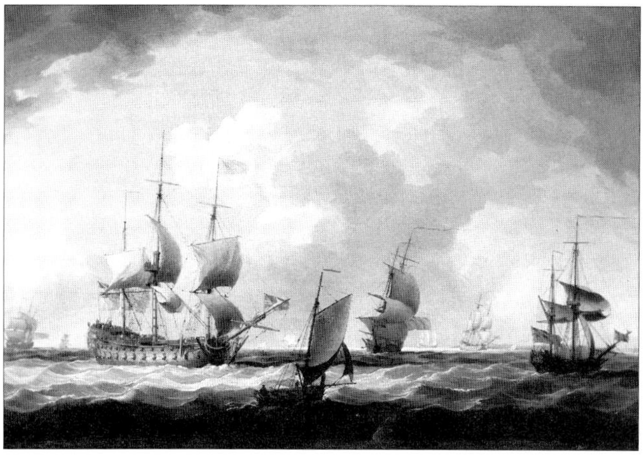

231H

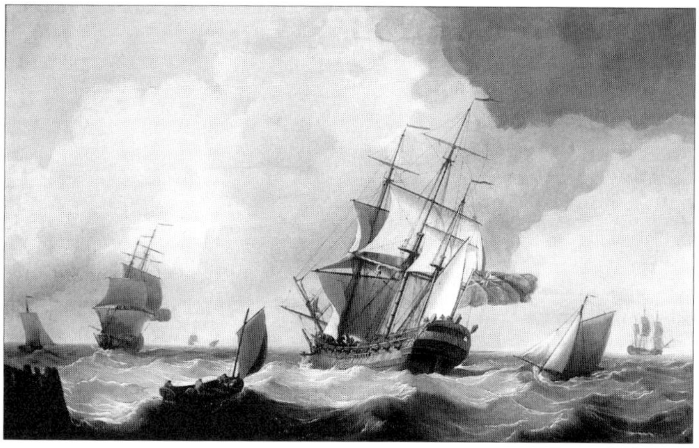

232E

231C (see page 141)
Oil on canvas 11 x 15⅞
Prov: The Lanes, Brighton
Commander David Joel, RN
Miss E.C. Joel
Exhib: Mellon Foundation: Bristol July 1966, No. 2
This small-scale work may well be the preparatory oil sketch from which the other versions derive. Other replicas, and versions, in various formats and sizes, were probably ordered from it in sizes to suit the customer

231D (see page 141)
Oil on canvas 14½ x 22½
Prov: Oscar and Peter Johnson 1964
Mr and Mrs Paul Mellon
Exhib: Yale 'Seascapes' 1977/78 No. 14
In this version the cutter has been omitted.

231E (see page 141)
Oil on canvas 14 ½ x 40
Prov: The Tate Gallery No 4003 Gift of Lt Gen Sir Gaspard Le Marchant Tupper, 1924
Exhib: The Mellon Foundation: Aldeburgh/Bristol June/July 1966, No. 3
Illus: The Tate Gallery 1969 p.30

231F
Oil on canvas 15½ x 23⅛
Prov: Brooke Family
In this version the cutter has been omitted.

231G
Oil on canvas 10⅝ x 16. Signed C Brooking
Prov: Lord Barrington 1773
William Barrington 1961 given to his naval cousin
Vice-Admiral B. C. B. Brooke, CBE
Sotheby's 12 November 1980 Lot 119 £13,500
Private Collection
Exhib: Mellon Foundation: Aldeburgh June 1966, No. 1

231H
Oil on canvas 11¼ x 16½. Signed C Brooking on spar lower left
Prov: McCorquodale Family
Agnew's
Richard Green
Spink & Son
Private Collection (USA)
Exhib: Agnew's Spring exhibition May 1975
Investigation has shown that no Vice Admiral of the Red flew his flag in a two-decker for the period 1744-54. Despite this fact, Brooking has faithfully portrayed his two-decker with 26 guns on the gun deck. There are 28 guns on the upper deck and this could only relate to one class of 70 gun ship, or one cut-down 90 gun three decker, named the *Torbay*. It seems that these nine paintings are based on this ship.

231J
Oil on canvas 9½ x 14½. Signed C Brooking
Prov: Christie's 2 April 1971 Lot 19 380 gns. Christie's Mark 428TD
R. Fulford
Parker Gallery
Private Collection

232A AN EAST INDIAMAN LYING TO IN A BREEZE
Oil on canvas 36 x 57. Not signed
Prov: W. T. Potts Esq. 1932
Sir James Caird
National Maritime Museum (1933-46)
Exhib: Royal Academy, British Exhibition 1934 No. 694
Weather quarter view of a 24 gun ship lying to on the port tack, fore course and topsail laid aback, reefed main with main and mizzen topsails and mizzen set. A red ensign at the stern. A fishing smack passing under her stern. In the left foreground a lugsail pilot boat running forward from the pier. There is another ship in the middle distance.

232B
Oil on canvas 21¼ x 29¾. Not signed
Prov: Sir Bruce Ingram

Sotheby's 24 June 1964 No. 37
Mrs Perpetua Ingram
Christie's 23 June 1972 Lot 49 6,000gns to Silva
Private Collection
Exhib: Mellon Foundation: Bristol July 1966, No. 13
Illus: Denys Brook-Hart, *Marine Painting* 1974 Plate 39
After restoration some of the rigging is now incorrect.

232C
Oil on canvas 36 x 56. Not signed
Prov: Frost and Reed 1970 £4,250 (attributed to Francis Swaine)
Private Collection (USA) 1971
This painting is the largest in the series and is set in a magnificent carved frame of the period.

232D
Oil on canvas 23½ x 43½. Signed C Brooking on diagonal pile at left
Prov: Leggatt Bros 16 Feb 1926
Private Collection (Hampshire)
Exhib: Mellon Foundation: Aldeburgh/Bristol June/July 1966, No. 12

232E
Oil on canvas 18¼ x 29½. Signed C Brooking lower left
Prov: The Midlands
Sotheby's 12 April 1995 Lot 5 £16,100
Royal Exchange Art Gallery 1995
Private Collection

233A A KETCH-RIGGED ROYAL YACHT IN A FRESH BREEZE OFF DOVER (see page 144)
Oil on canvas 48 x 72½. Signed C Brooking and dated 1756
Prov: Lord Shuttleworth
All five paintings in this series are on a large scale. All are signed and in addition three are dated. They were all painted towards the end of Brooking's life.

233B
Oil on canvas 48 x 72. Signed C Brooking on lugger foresail at left, dated 1754 on plank on right
Prov: D Stirling
Leggatt Bros 1957
National Westminster Bank, 41 Lothbury, London (January 1957)
Sotheby's 12 July 1995 Lot 2 £66,000
Richard Green
Private Collection
Exhib: Mellon Foundation: Aldeburgh/Bristol June/July 1966, No. 63
Illus: *Connoisseur*, August 1966 article by Dennis Thomas p.237

233C
Oil on canvas 32¾ x 41. Signed C Brooking P, on the planking of lugger at left
Prov: M. F. Hibbert
Christie's 11 April 1980 Lot 17 £9,000
Private Collection
Described as the Royal Yacht *Dorset* off Dover.

233D TWO CUTTERS AND A FRIGATE IN A FRESH BREEZE OFF DOVER (see page 144)
Oil on canvas 34 x 50. Signed and dated 1756
Prov: Exeter
David Messum Gallery 1974 £12,000
Private Collection USA
Illus: *Country Life* 20 December 1973
The most detailed painting of the series. The naval cutter in the foreground is about to either transfer a naval officer, or his despatch to a small boat.

233E A ROYAL YACHT CLOSE-HAULED ON THE STARBOARD TACK
Oil on canvas 35 x 58. Bears traces of a signature
Prov: National Maritime Museum (1947-272)
Inscribed: 'The Royal Yacht *Dorset* 164 tons. Built for the Lord Lieutenant of Ireland at Deptford Dockyard 1753'. Catalogued by the National Maritime Museum as by Dominic Serres.

234A A SHIP BEFORE A FRESH BREEZE AND ANOTHER TO LEEWARD PASSING HER (see page 144)
Oil on canvas 26½ x 34½. Signed Brooking on spar lower left
Prov: E. H. D. Thompson Esq.
Christie's 2 April 1965 Lot 47. Withdrawn
Mrs Christopher Dawnay
Exhib: Mellon Foundation: Aldeburgh June 1966, No. 55
A delicate greyish-green painting of a lovely breeze at sea.

234B
Oil on canvas 25 x 37 (approx)
Prov: Not known
Mellon Neg 4114

234C
Oil on canvas 15 x 22. Signed
Prov: Thomas Wise Esq. OBE
Earl of Hardwicke
Sir Bruce Ingram (1934) via Spink for £52.10.0
Sotheby's 11 March 1964 Lot 7 to Leggatt Bros £1,500
Private Collection
Exhib: Hull, Ferens Art Gallery, Early Marine Paintings, 1951 No. 254
This variation portrays the *Royal Caroline* yacht at the left hand side of the composition.

234D
Oil on oak panel 12⅞ x 25
Prov: Leggatt Bros 9 January 1948 for £155
F. F. Madan bequest to Ashmolean Oxford (1962)
Exhib: Colnaghi February 1962

234E
Oil on canvas 12½ x 17. Not signed
Prov: Sharp Collection at Hill of Tarvit
Culzean Castle (National Trust) Scotland

234F
Oil on canvas 15¼ x 23¼
Prov: A. E. Edwards Esq.

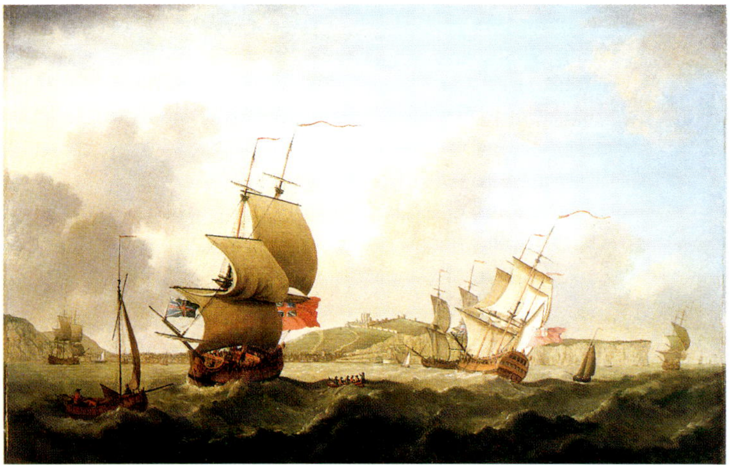

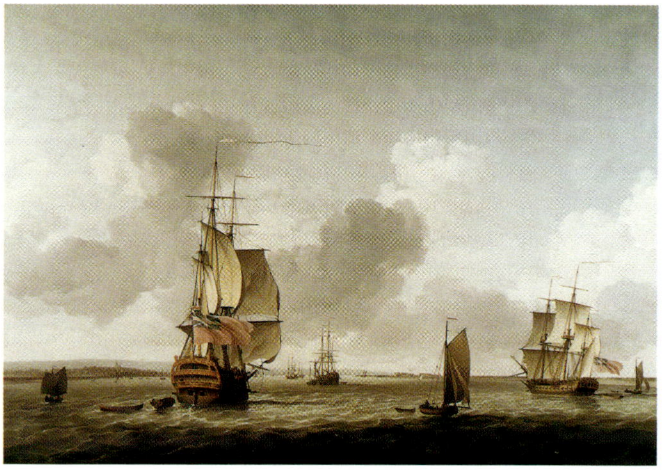

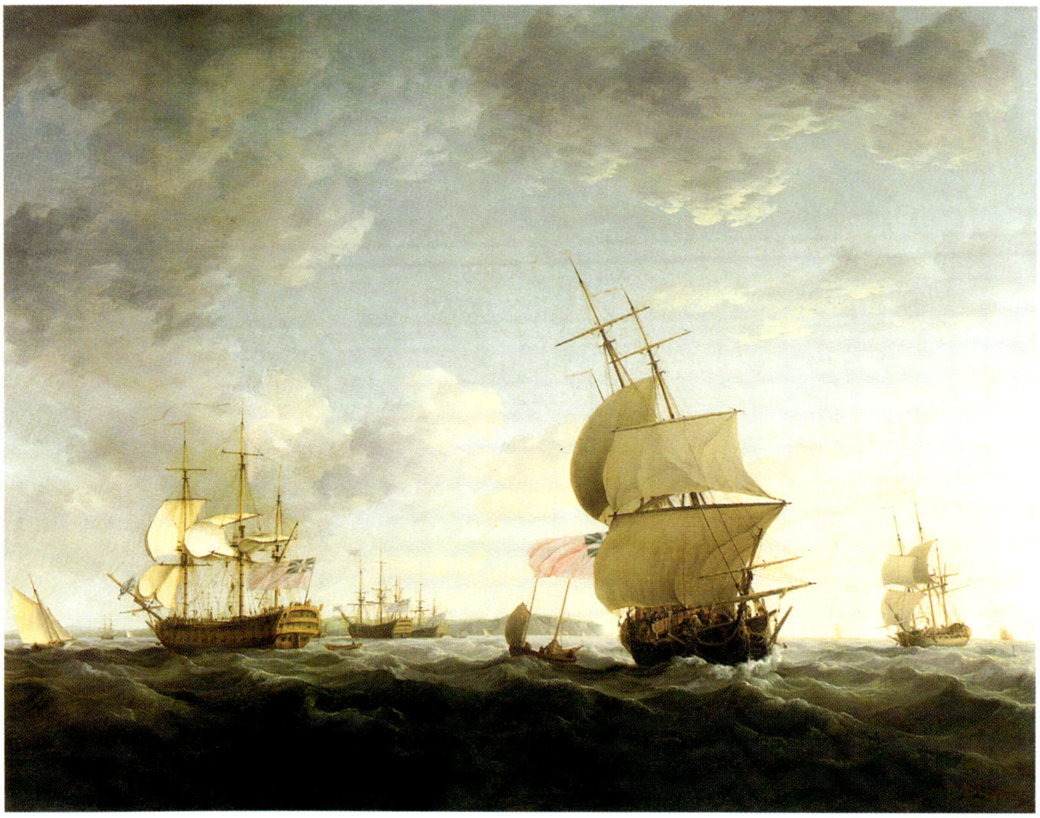

240 (Above left)
Shipping off Dover

243 (Above right)
A two-decker and a frigate running into Harwich

246A
A ship dropping a pilot in the downs, with a two-decker under easy sail

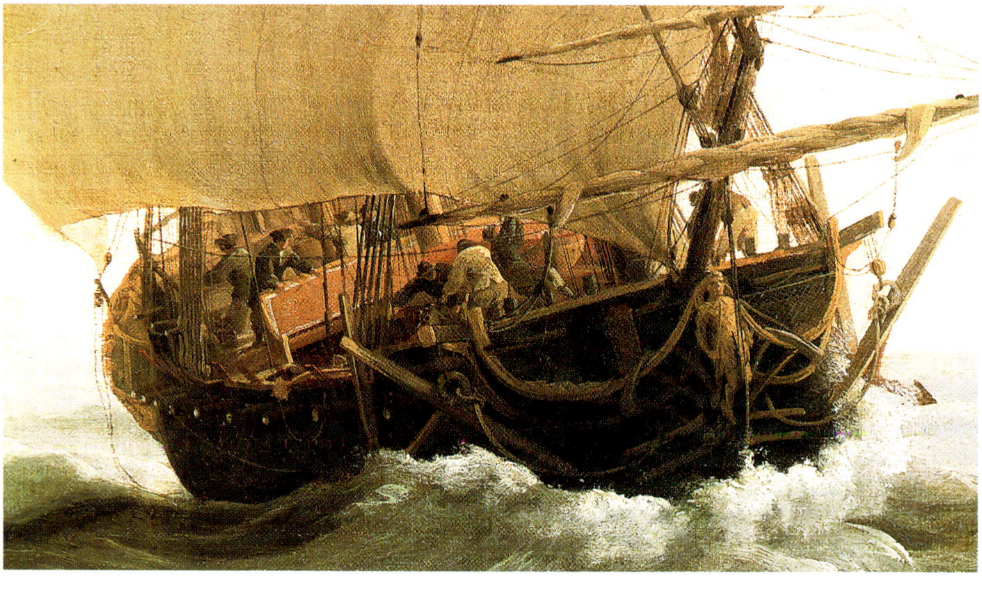

246A
Detail

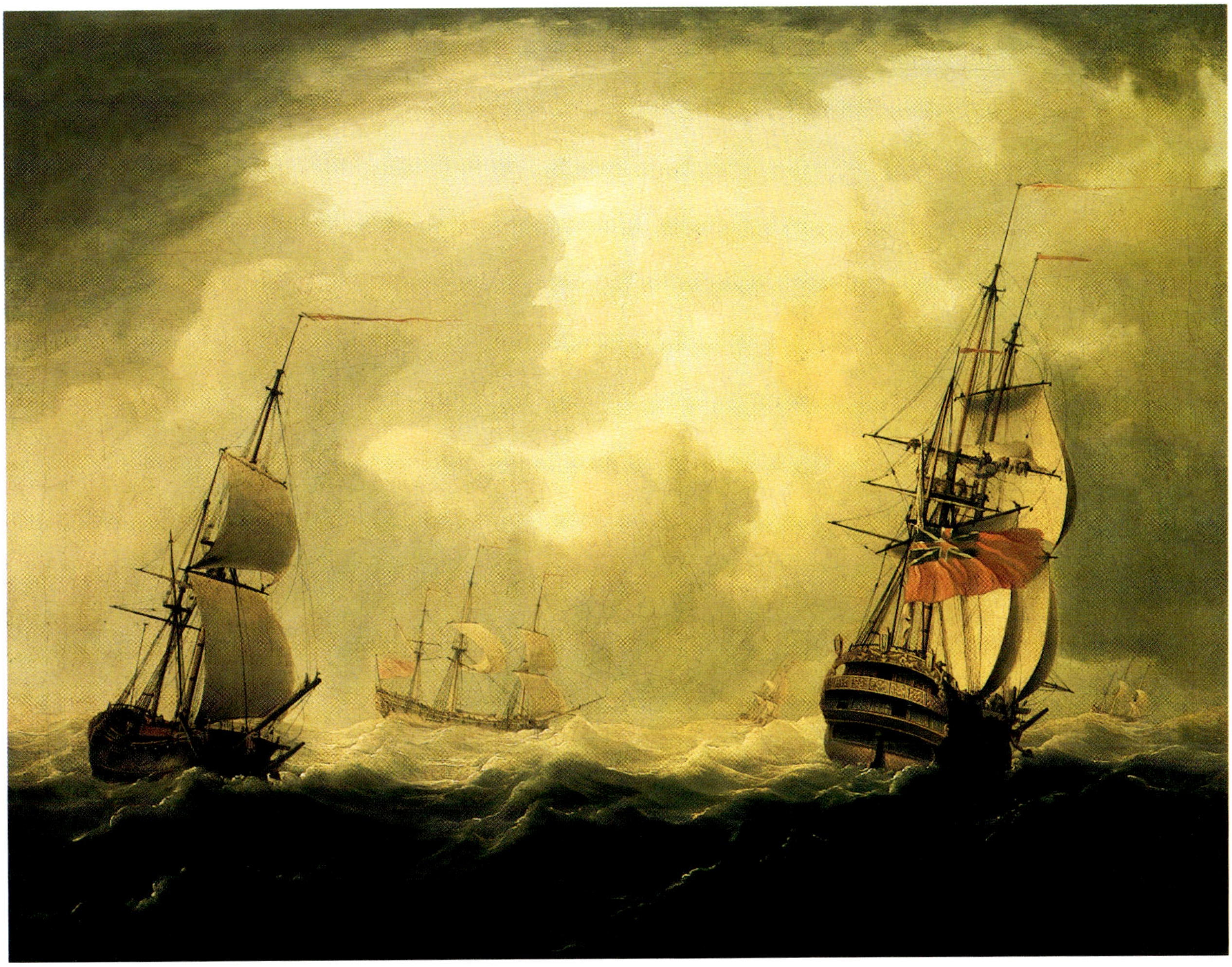

250
A bomb ketch, a two-decker and other shipping in a stormy sea

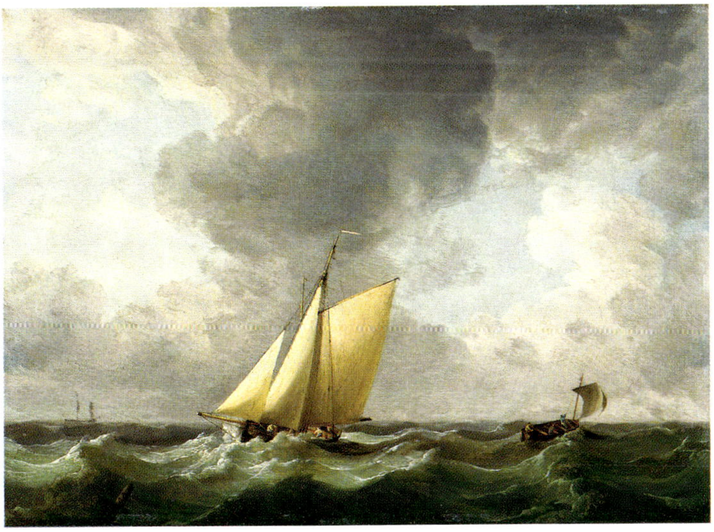

247A
A cutter hauled on the starboard tack in a fresh breeze

256
A snow close-hauled on the port tack off the English coast with a smack passing her

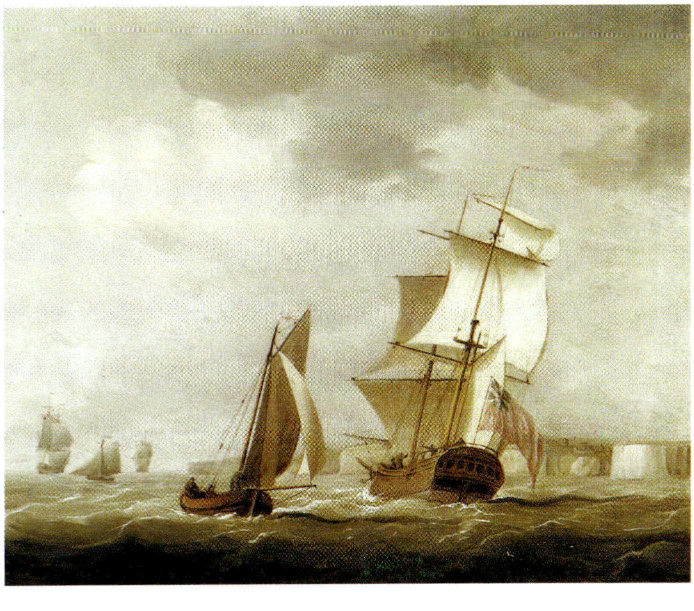

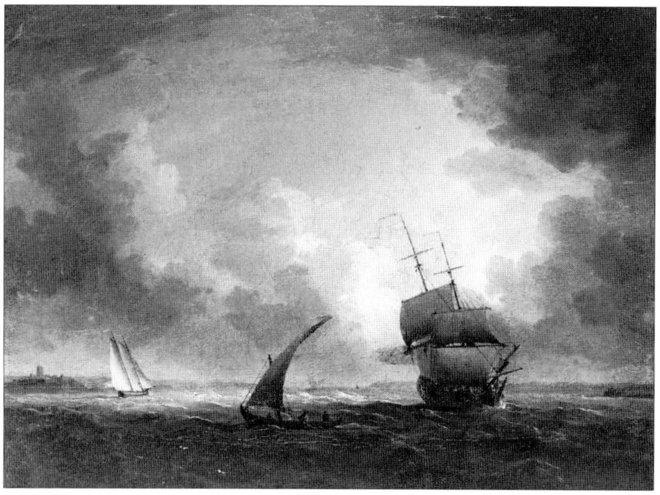

235

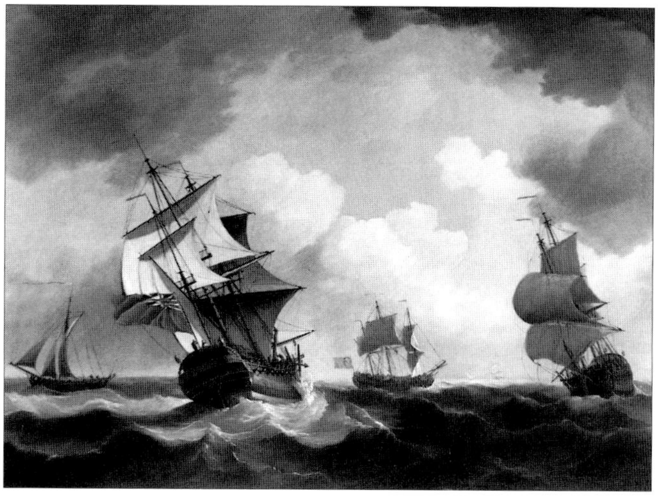

237

235 A SHIP CLOSE-HAULED ON THE PORT TACK WITH A LATEEN-RIGGED COASTAL VESSEL IN THE FOREGROUND
Oil on canvas 10½ x 14¼. Signed C Brooking right foreground with unusually large signature
Prov: Sotheby's 10 June 1964 Lot 222 £100
Appleby Bros £400
F. B. Cockett Esq.
Private Collection
Exhib: Mellon Foundation: Aldeburgh/Bristol June/July 1966, No. 21

236 SHIPPING IN A BREEZE IN THE DOWNS
(see page 145)
Oil on canvas 31¼ x 56½
Prov: Admiral Sir George Murray
Ship Hotel, Chichester (Allied Hotels) £7,000
Baskett and Day
Mr and Mrs Paul Mellon 1966
Yale University 1973
Christie's 17 November 1989 Lot 1 unsold at £26,000
Exhib: Mellon Foundation: Bristol June 1966, No. 11

237 THREE SHIPS AND A ROYAL YACHT IN A FRESH BREEZE
Oil on canvas 36 x 48
Prov: Biddle of Brighton
James Green Gallery Jermyn Street 1964, £4,000
Private Collection
Illus: *Apollo* June 1964 as Willem van de Velde the Younger

238A TWO CUTTERS, ENGLISH MEN O'WAR AT ANCHOR AND OTHER SHIPPING IN A BREEZE
(see page 145)
Oil on canvas 41¾ x 66¾. Signed C Brooking 1758
Prov: Leggatt Bros 1928
Lord Queenborough
Royal Society of St George
Christie's 7 July 1967 Lot 58 to S. Sabin £7,000
Private Collection, Belfast
Exhib: British Council: 18/19th Century British landscape to Japan 1970

If the date is correct, this must be one of the artist's last paintings. It is also one of his most accomplished works.

238B
Oil on canvas 42 x 65¾
Prov: J. Walter Thompson Ltd
Christie's 12 May 1967 Lot 58 9,000 gns
Gooden & Fox
Mr and Mrs Paul Mellon
A beautifully coloured late painting without the figures on the foreshore as depicted in painting 238A. Inscribed in paint on the reverse: 'Painted by Brooking, one of his best'.

239 A SHIP CLOSE-HAULED OFF DOVER
Oil on panel 40 x 50. Signed C Brooking lower left
Prov: Christie's 13 November 1936 Lot 108 £99.15
Spink & Son
Sir James Caird
National Maritime Museum (1937-1725)
A merchantman and a Royal Yacht off Dover. Originally catalogued at an Antique Dealers' Fair in London 1937 as HMS *Lion* off Dover.

240 SHIPPING OFF DOVER (see page 148)
Oil on canvas 28½ x 45. Not signed
Prov: Colonel Bernard Bevan

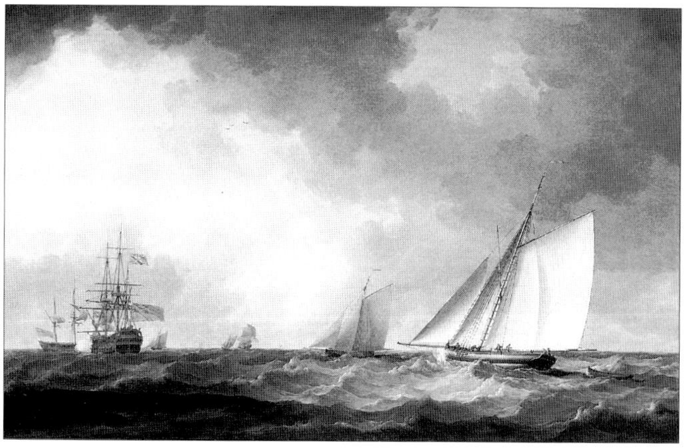

238B

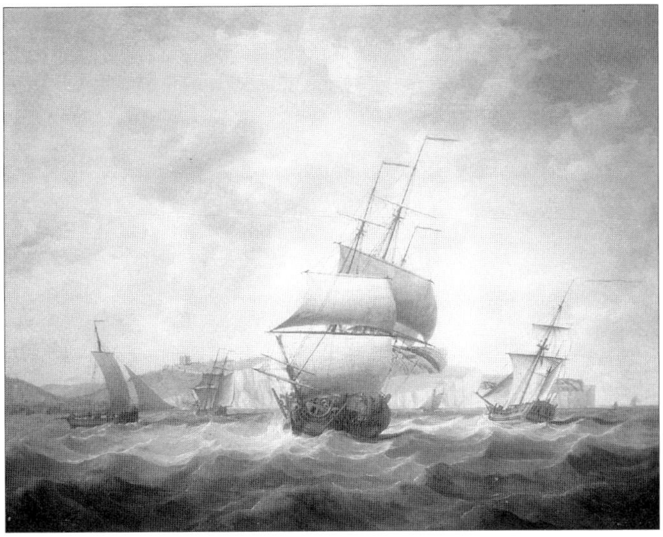

239

Phillip's Fine Art Auctioneers 12 December 95 Lot 26
Catalogued as Thomas Luny
Private Collection
A fine early painting with accurate topographical detail of Dover, its castle and the white cliffs.

241A A SMALL MERCHANT SHIP CLOSE-HAULED ON THE STARBOARD TACK IN A FRESH BREEZE (see frontispiece)
Oil on canvas 30 x 25⅛. Part of signature on spar bottom centre
Prov: G. D. Roper Esq.
Exhib: Mellon Foundation: Bristol July 1966, No. 25
Illus: *Connoisseur* August 1981 David Joel, 'Brooking's Marine Artistry', p.269
In this picture, note the change in the mizzen sail which is shortened to end at the mizzen mast and the sail laced to the mast. This was a major development in rigging technology. A remarkably brightly coloured painting for Brooking.

241B MERCHANT SHIPS PASSING IN THE CHANNEL (see Chapter 4, page 63)
Oil on canvas 13¾ x 17⅜. Traces of signature lower right
Reverse of 241A
Prov: Cooling Gallery London 1919
Howard Earl Hoover
Hoover Company (UK). Hung in their Boardroom
Bonhams 15 August 1996 Lot 246 (as John Cleveley)
Miles Joel

241C BRITISH FRIGATES IN A GOOD BREEZE
Oil on canvas 13 x 15 one of a pair
Prov: Sotheby's 13 Jan 71 Lot 76 to Baile £1,700 for the pair
Private Collection

242 A SMALL SHIP CLOSE-HAULED ON A PORT TACK OFF A FORT
Oil on canvas 20½ x 18½. Signed C Brooking P
Prov: William Ewing, bequest in 1874 to Glasgow Art Gallery & Museum
Exhib: Mellon Foundation: Bristol July 1966, No. 26

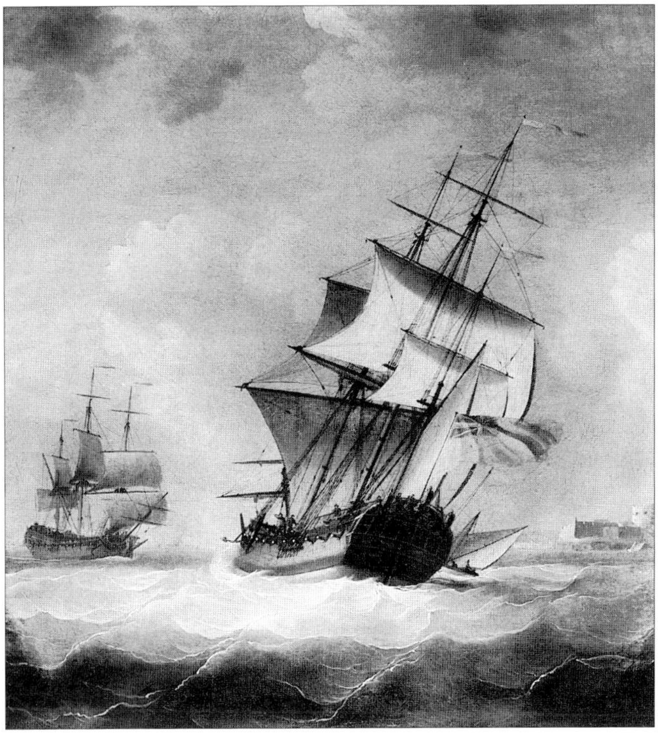

242

Note the forepart of the mizzen yard removed and the mizzen sail laced to the mast.

243 A TWO-DECKER AND A FRIGATE RUNNING INTO HARWICH (see page 148)
Oil on canvas 46 x 66. Signed C Brooking on spar lower left
Prov: Bernard Gallery 1956
Purchased by the Caird Fund for National Maritime Museum (1957-2)
Exhib: Mellon Foundation: Bristol July 1966, No. 60
Illus: *Connoisseur* November 1954 M. Bernard
F Gordon Roe *Sea Painters of Britain* Plate 21
It is a magnificent scene as these two large men o'war proceed up the narrow channel, which is filled with other shipping.

244 SHIPS IN A LIGHT BREEZE (see detail Chapter 3, page 43 and page 1)
Oil on canvas 27 x 27. Signed C Brooking on spar left foreground
Prov: Tooth & Son 25 March 1936
Spink & Son April 1936
Sir James Caird 1936
National Maritime Museum (1936-73)
Exhib: Mellon Foundation: Bristol July 1966, No. 61
Art of the Van de Veldes No. 150
Illus: *Illustrated London News* 17 April 1937
Oliver Warner *British Marine Painting* 1948 Plate 11
David Cordingly *Marine Painting* Plate 30, Plate 31 (detail), back cover illustration
W Percival-Prescott *Burlington Magazine* August 1966 Plate 75
One of the best known examples of the artist's work, and arguably his masterwork. This is a carefully balanced green

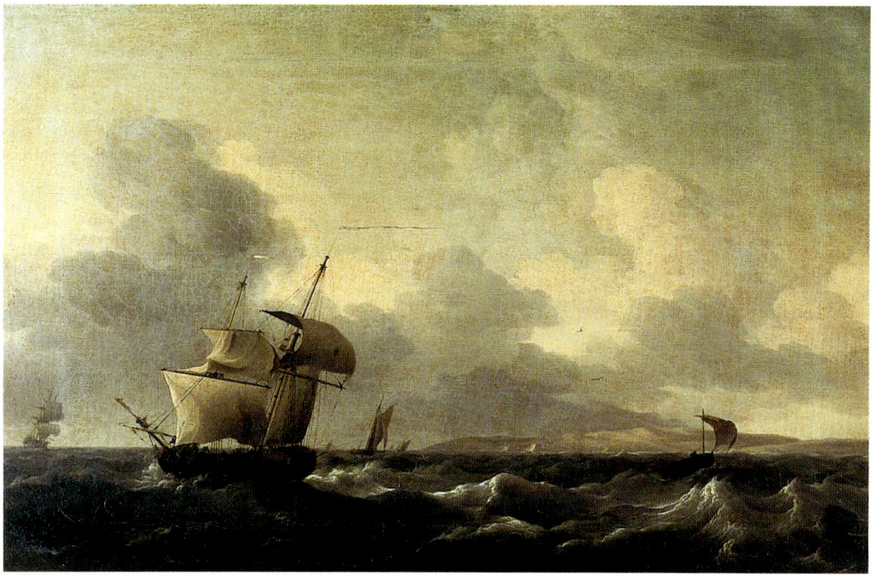

261
A brig and small boats offshore

265
Elizabeth Castle, Jersey with a frigate firing a gun at left and other shipping

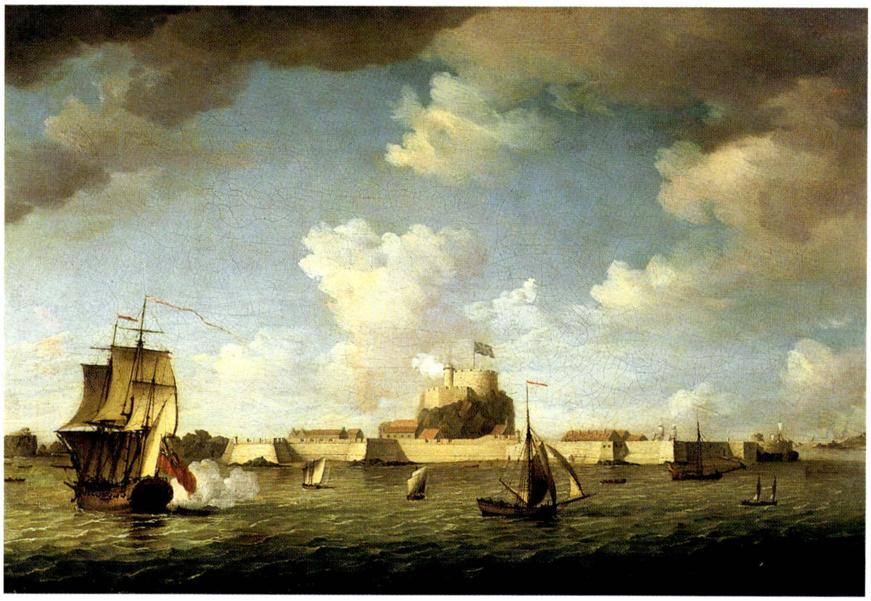

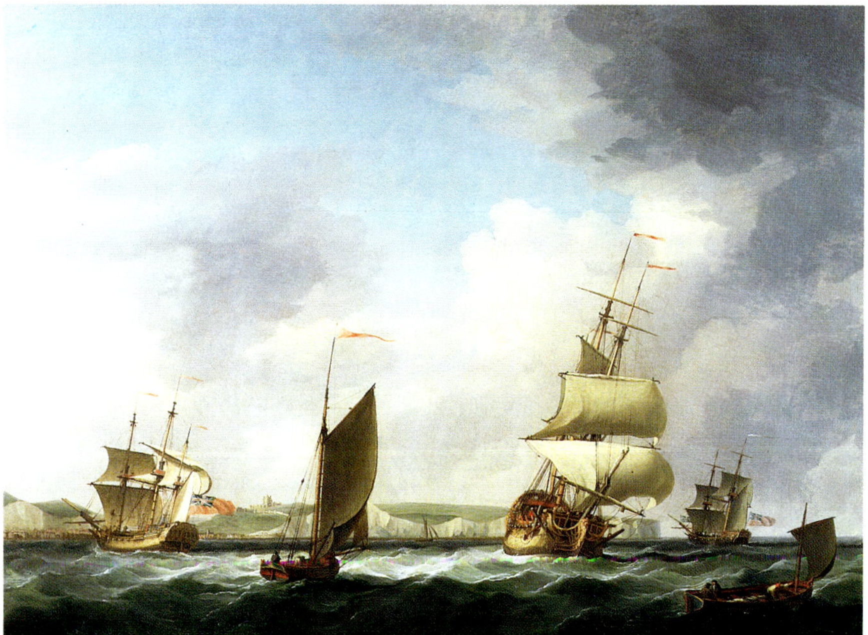

266B
A naval squadron off Dover

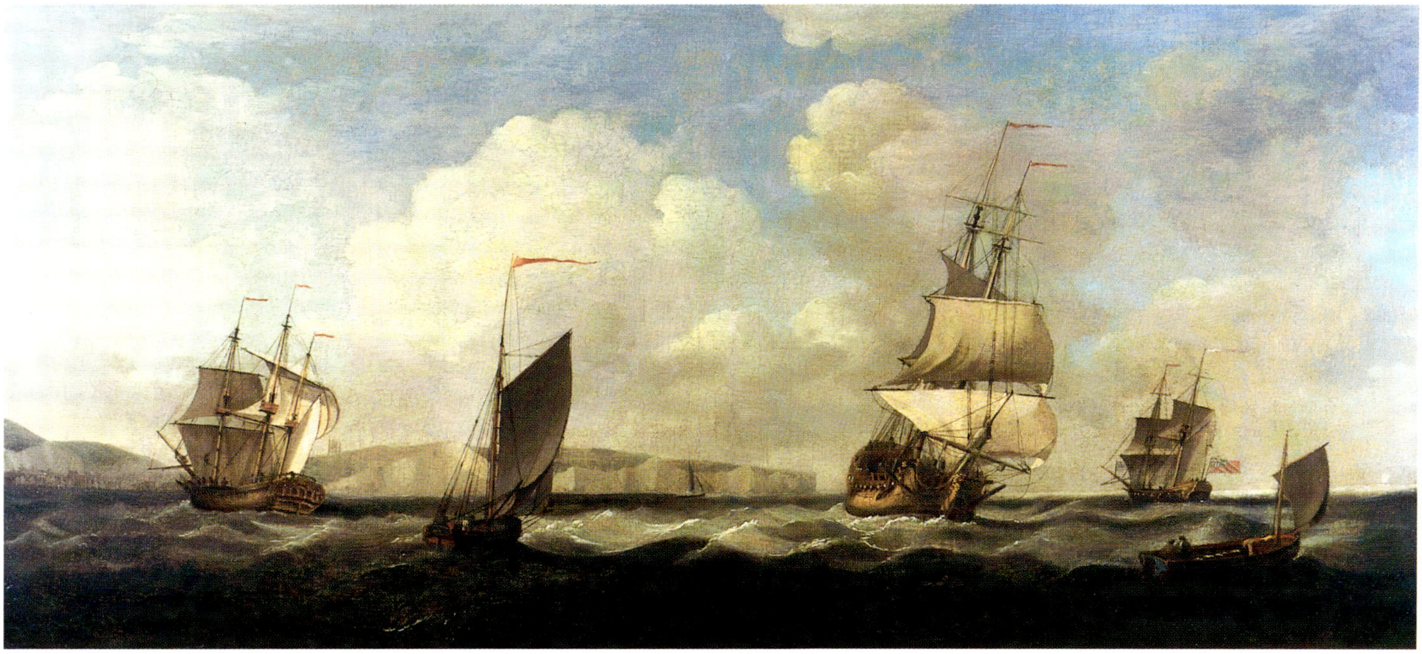

267
Two English frigates, a brig and other sailing vessels off Dover

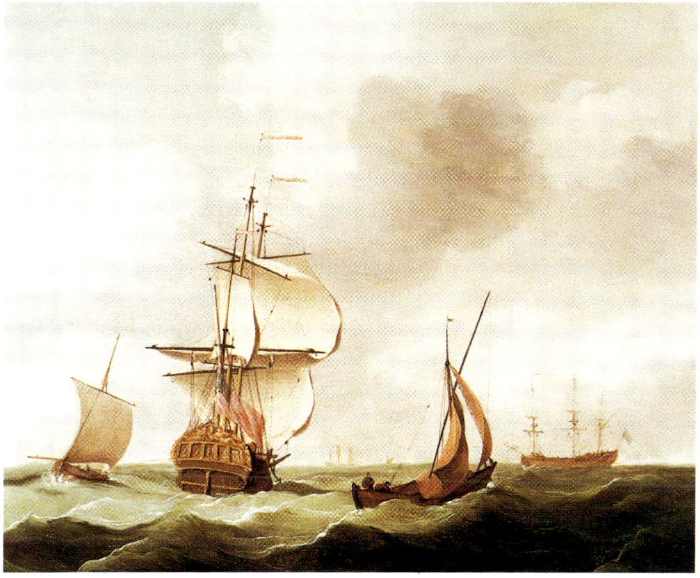

268
A small ship before the wind with a fishing vessel passing under her stern

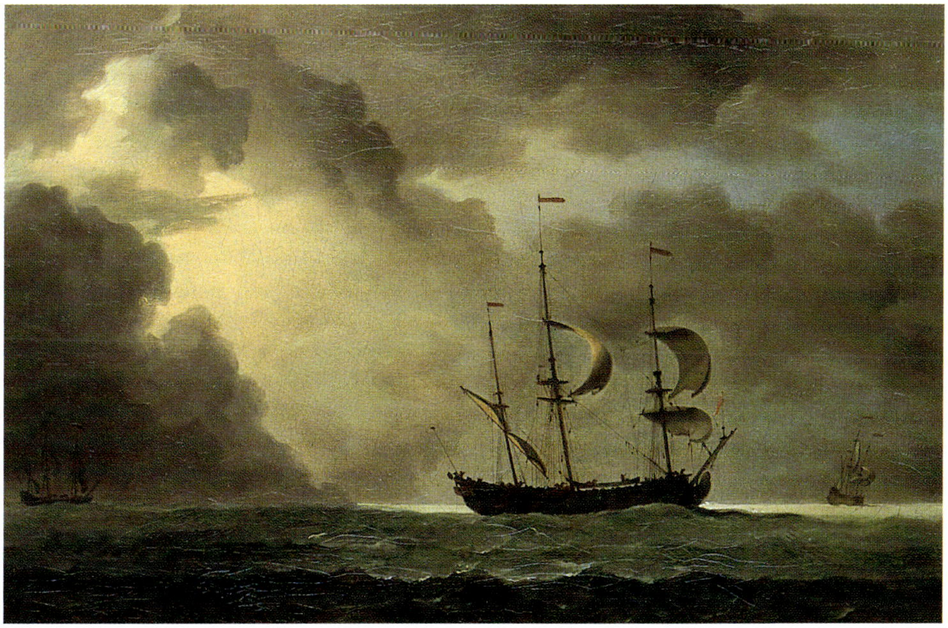

269
Men o'war approaching storm

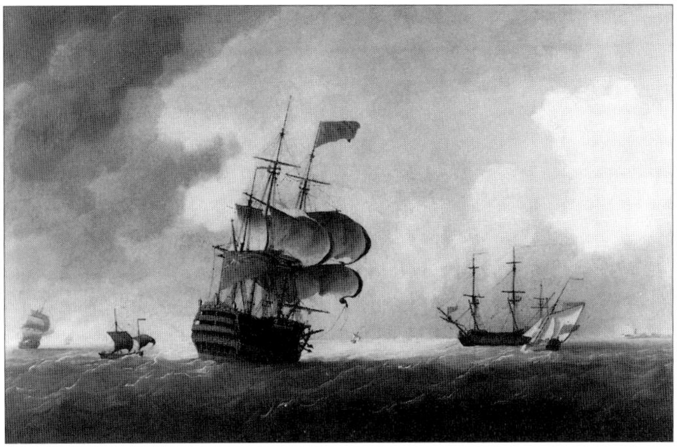

245

and sepia-toned painting, illustrating the effect of wind against tide. The two-decker is lee bowing the tide and thereby aiding her move to windward – a technique well-known to present-day racing sailors and also to Brooking and his contemporary seamen. The tide is pushing the ship physically to windward. This painting has also been entitled *An English third-rate running in a light breeze*. A gallery label attached to the reverse indicates the title *A 70 gun ship in a light breeze*.

245 A THREE-DECKER RUNNING IN TO HARBOUR WITH FORESAILS FLYING. PILOT BOAT COMING ALONGSIDE. A FRIGATE AT ANCHOR. A ROYAL YACHT AND OTHER SHIPPING
Oil on canvas 36 x 60 (approx). Not signed
Prov: Major General J A A Griffin (1969)
A fine painting of Brooking's middle period. It could be a scene at Spithead off Portsmouth.

246A A SHIP DROPPING A PILOT IN THE DOWNS, WITH A TWO-DECKER UNDER EASY SAIL (see page 148)
Oil on canvas 35½ x 48⅜. Signed C Brooking
Prov: J. G. Luard
Sotheby's 11 December 1929 Lot 151
Sir Bruce Ingram
Colnaghi 1962
Mr and Mrs Paul Mellon
Exhib: Ferens Art Gallery, Hull, Early Marine Painters 1951 No. 26
Virginia Museum of Fine Art 1963 No 25
Royal Academy 1964/65 No. 166
Mellon Foundation: Aldeburgh/Bristol June/July 1966, No. 14
Yale Seascapes 1977/78 No. 15
Illus: *Illustrated London News* 1 August 1931
F. Gordon Roe *Sea Painters of Britain* 1947, Plate 22 and cover painting
David Cordingly *Marine Painting* Plate 33
W. Percival-Prescott *Burlington Magazine,* August 1966 Plate 74 (detail)
Eng: Boydell in 1755 as *Evening*. See engraving 606

246B
Oil on canvas 11⅛ x 15 ¼
Prov: Lord Barrington
Vice-Admiral B. C. B. Brooke CBE

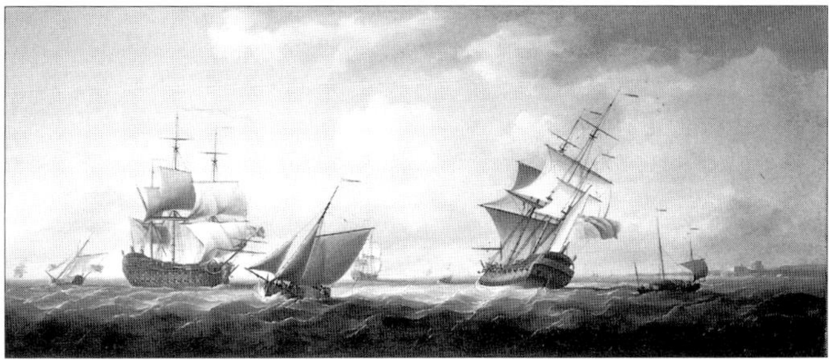

249

Sotheby's 18 March 1981 Lot 6 Unsold at £6,000
Private Collection
Exhib: Mellon Foundation: Aldeburgh June 1966, No. 15

246C TWO MEN O'WAR SAILING THROUGH THE DOWNS
Oil on canvas 25⅛ x 30⅛. Not signed
Prov: Marquess of Ormond gifted to the Royal Yacht Squadron in 1867
Sold to a member Royal Yacht Squadron in 1982
Private Collection
The main subject, a two-decker, is in the right mid-ground of the composition in a fresh breeze on the port tack. To the left and further towards the Downs is a frigate running to the left of the painting. Other shipping in the distance. There is considerable influence of Charles Brooking in this painting. Dominic Serres may have collaborated on this picture.

247A A CUTTER HAULED ON THE STARBOARD TACK IN A FRESH BREEZE (see page 149)
Oil on copper 7 x 10. Signed C B on spar lower left
Prov: Spink & Son 1961
Mr and Mrs Paul Mellon
Exhib: Royal Academy, Painting in England 1964/65, No 137
Yale Art Gallery 1965 No. 16
Mellon Foundation: Aldeburgh/Bristol June/July 1966, No. 29

247B
Oil on panel 7¾ x 10¾. Signed C B on plank lower left
Prov: Sotheby's 22 May 1991 Lot 110 as Koekkoek
F. B. Cockett Esq.
Private Collection
A dramatically lit painting to remarkable effect.

247C
Oil on canvas laid on board 8 x 10¾. Signed CB lower right
Prov: Sotheby's 8 November 1995 Lot 1 £8,800
Private Collection
In this version there is a second cutter to the right and in the left foreground a jetty with a long pole mark on it and two figures, one using a telescope.

248 INDIAMEN IN A FRESH BREEZE (see Chapter 4, page 55)
Oil on canvas 45½ x 48. Signed C Brooking on barrel left foreground
Prov: Taylor White Esq. (Treasurer of the Foundling Hospital)
By descent to R. J. M. Spranger Esq., Castle Keep, Reigate
Sotheby's 24 November 1954 Lot 131
Purchased by the Caird Fund for £65
National Maritime Museum (1955-3)
Exhib: Petit Palais Paris 1965 Marine Art No. 41

Arts Council 1965 Marine Paintings No. 18
Mellon Foundation: Bristol July 1966, No. 5
British Paintings Prague 1969 No. 6
Art of the Van de Veldes No. 149
A very fine late painting of four Indiamen in a force six wind with a good sea running. It belonged to Taylor White, Treasurer of the Foundling Hospital and was probably painted for him, remaining in his family until 1954.

249 SHIPPING IN A BREEZE WITH A CUTTER CLOSE-HAULED IN THE FOREGROUND WITH A CASTLE ON THE RIGHT
Oil on canvas 24½ x 59. Not signed
Prov: Dr Turner, Sussex Gardens 1868
The Misses Turner, Isle of Mull, 1965
Gifted to Ashmolean, Oxford by Miss Norah M. Turner in 1975
Exhib: Mellon Foundation: Bristol July 1966, No. 10
A splendid but rather stiff painting from the artist's middle period. The castle could be Elizabeth Castle, Jersey.

250 A BOMB KETCH, A TWO-DECKER AND OTHER SHIPPING IN A STORMY SEA (see page 149 and detail, Chapter 4 page 58)
Oil on canvas 26½ x 35
Prov: Captain L. R. Hibbert, bequeathed to National Maritime Museum (1962-14) (see 231B)
In this large painting there are eight seamen aloft furling the main topsail. Brooking has not just broadly suggested the seamen at work but actually takes the trouble to accurately render each man at his particular task.

251A A FLAGSHIP RUNNING IN A SEAWAY WITH A CUTTER AND OTHER VESSELS IN COMPANY
Oil on canvas 19½ x 29½. Signed C Brooking on barrel at left
Prov: Spink & Son 1947
Mrs G. B. MacKean
Exhib: Belfast 1961 No. 58
Mellon Foundation: Bristol June 1966, No. 24
A late painting, for the mizzen finishes at its mast, to which it is laced.

251B
Oil on canvas 20 x 29 (sight size)
Prov: Spink & Son
Mrs W. W. Bourne 1936
Stafford Bourne Esq.
Private Collection

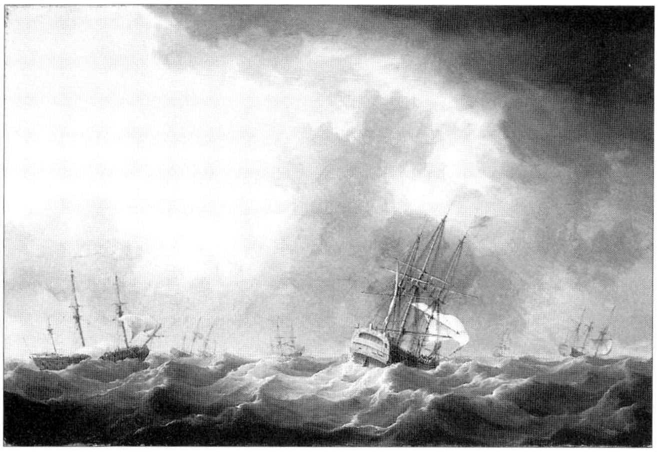

251C

251C
Oil on canvas 15 x 23. Signed C Brooking on spar at left
Prov: Williams & Son 1938
Spink & Son
HM The Queen of Yugoslavia (ex Queen Alexandra of Yugoslavia) see 38
John Mitchell and Son 1967
Mr and Mrs Paul Mellon

251D
Oil on canvas 14¾ x 23. Signed C Brooking on plank lower left
Prov: Molesworth St Aubyn family
One of a pair with 261

252 DUTCH MEN O'WAR AND FISHING CRAFT RUNNING IN A SEAWAY
Oil on canvas 30½ x 50½
Prov: Christie's 23 July 1965 Lot 82
Private Collection

253 BRITISH MEN O'WAR IN A CHOPPY SEA
Oil on canvas 17½ x 27½. Not signed
Prov: Oscar and Peter Johnson 1968
Christie's 9 May 1969 Lot 52 850 gns
Bartlett

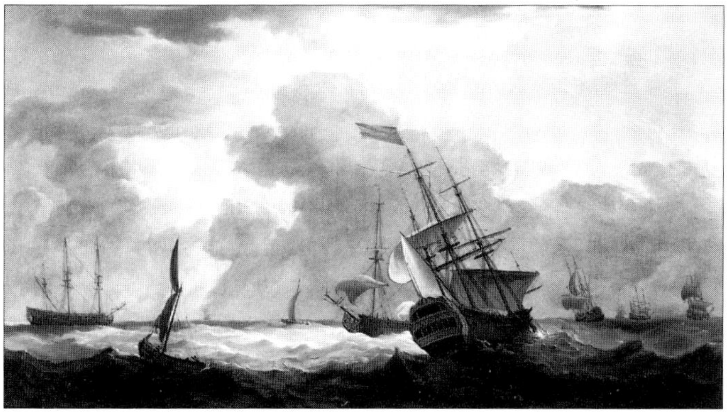

252

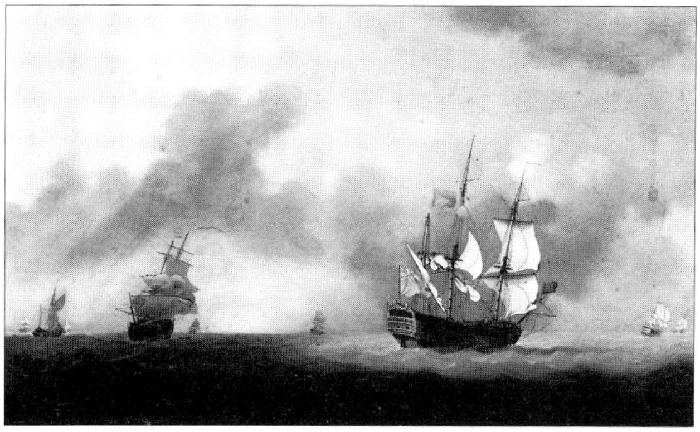

253

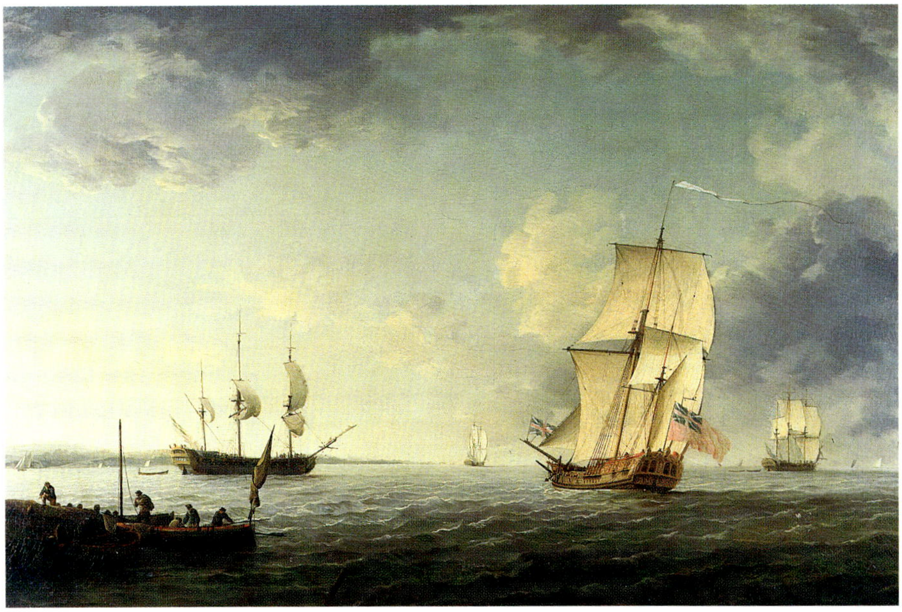

272
A brig-rigged yacht and two two-deckers in a breeze off a coast with a small fishing boat alongside the shore on the left

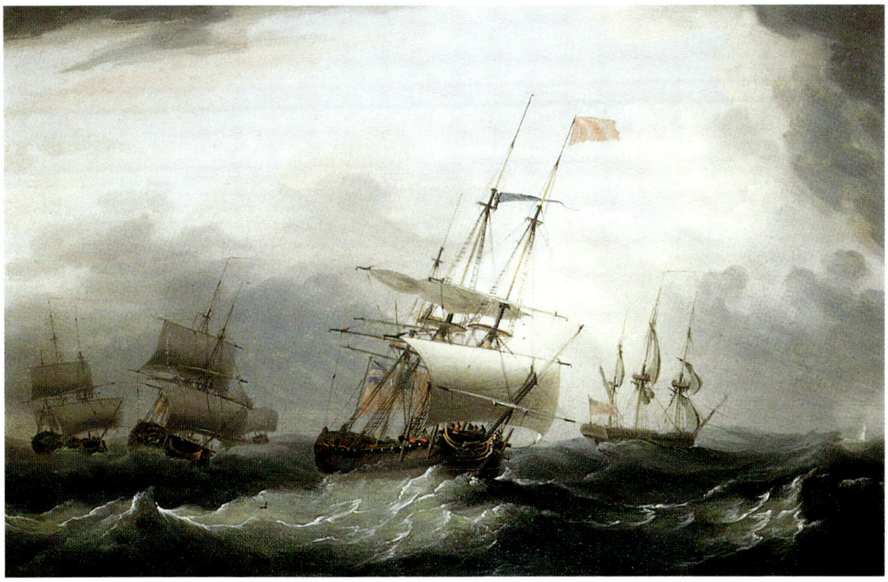

273
Five frigates manoeuvring in a choppy sea

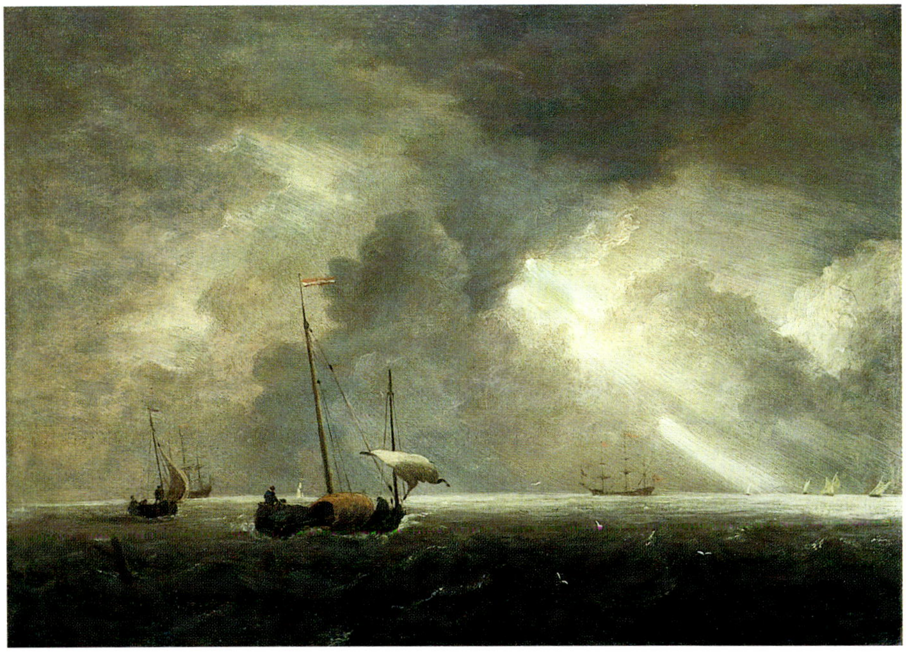

280
Dutch fishing vessels in coastal waters before a storm, a British man o' war beyond

352B

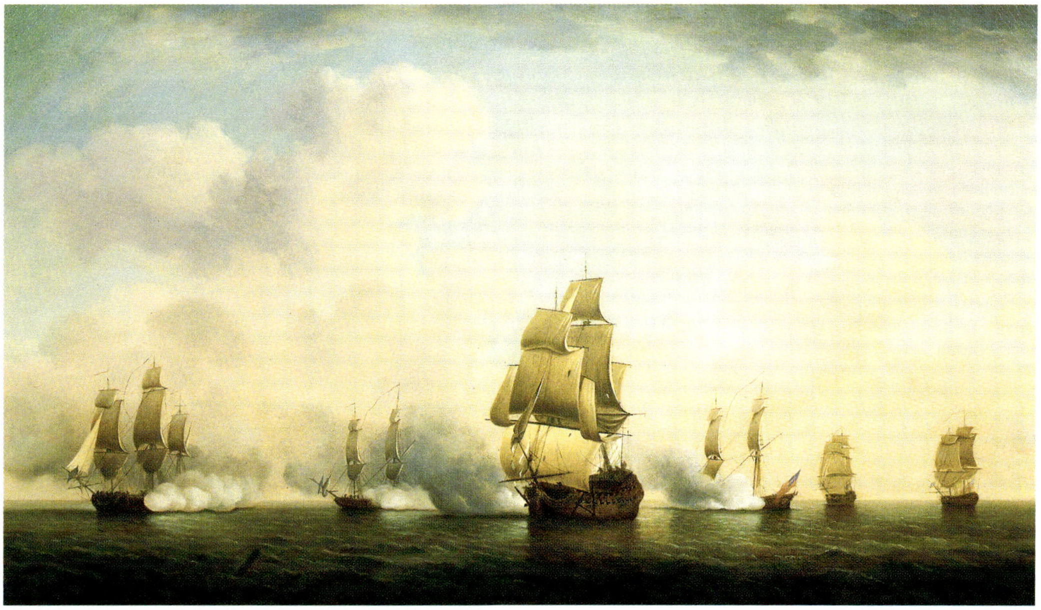

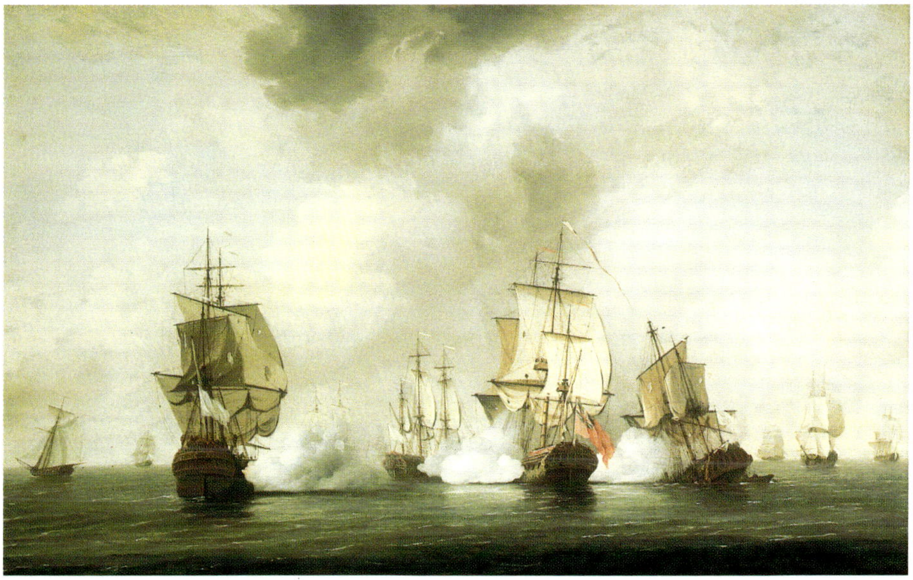

354
The Boscawen *engaging a fleet of French ships 23 May 1745*

355
Capture of the Marquese d'Antin *and the* Louis Erasme *10 July 1745*

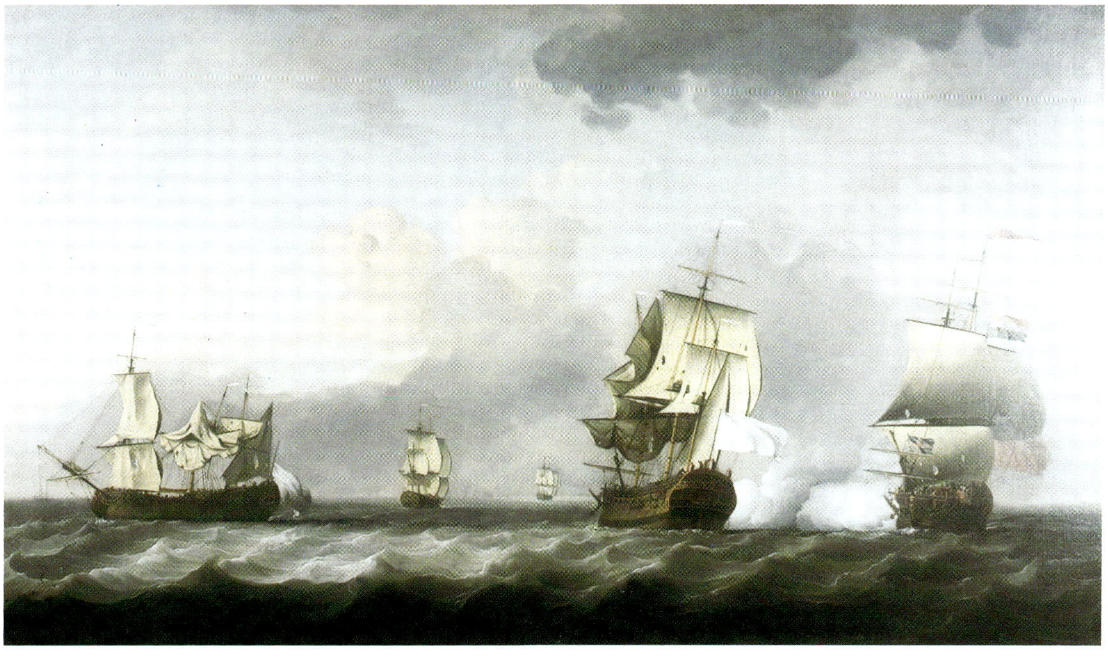

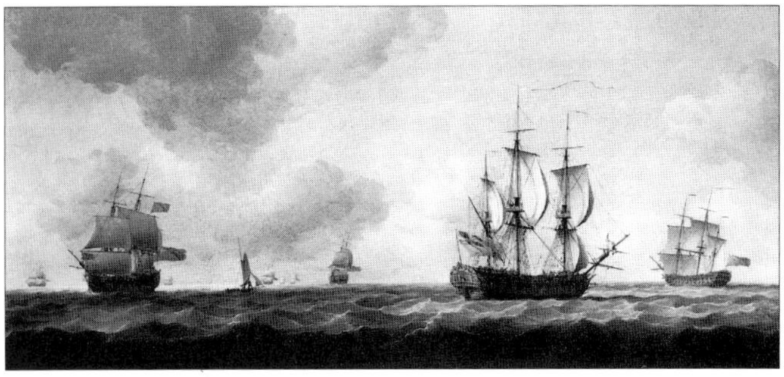

254

254 THE CHANNEL FLEET AT SEA
Oil on canvas 28 x 55
Prov: Captain George Cumming
Viscount Wimbourne
Private Collection
There are nine men o'war in this picture and one small cutter.

255 SHIPPING UNDER SAIL IN A FRESH BREEZE
Oil on canvas 19⅞ x 24
Prov: Spink & Son (1936)
Mrs W. W. Bourne
Stafford Bourne Esq.
Private Collection
Exhib: Mellon Foundation, Bristol July 1966, No. 22
Illus: *Apollo* magazine Vol 24 1936 p.142
In addition to the men o'war there is a frigate to the right wearing a blue ensign.

256 A SNOW CLOSE-HAULED ON THE PORT TACK OFF THE ENGLISH COAST WITH A SMACK PASSING HER
(see page 149)
Oil on canvas 13¾ x 17½
Prov: Lord Drogheda
H. F. T. Williamson
Christie's 19 November 1965 Lot 10
Mrs and Mrs Paul Mellon
Sotheby's 18 November 1981 Lot 99 £3,800
Private Collection
Exhib: Mellon Foundation Aldeburgh/Bristol June/July 1966, No. 48

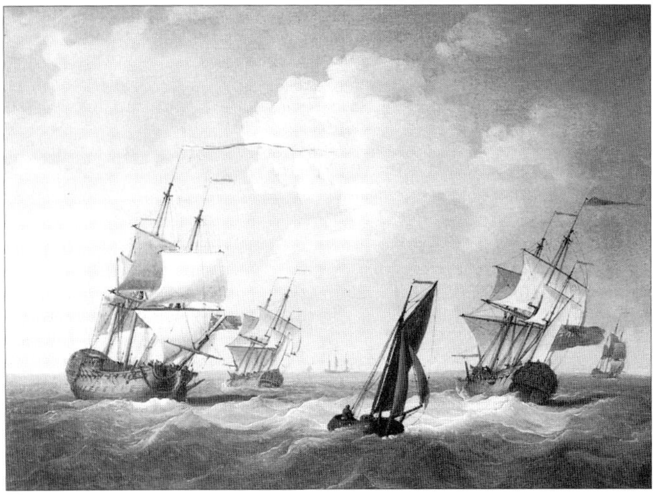

255

257A A BRIGANTINE IN A FRESH BREEZE OFF A FORT
Oil on canvas 10½ x 14¾. Part of signature Brooking right hand corner. From a set of six paintings (see 15B)
Prov: Robert Taylor Esq. (1840-1915)
E. M. Thomas Esq. 1915
David Messum Gallery, 1983
Stolen from this gallery 30 May 1983 and since recovered
Exhib: Mellon Foundation Aldeburgh/Bristol June/July 1966, No 52

257B
Oil on canvas 13¼ x 20. Unsigned
Prov: Captain W. R. Wells RN

257C
Oil on canvas 11⅝ x 15
Prov: Brooke family collection

257D
Oil on canvas 14 x 22¾. Unsigned
Laid down on board
Prov: P. Silo, Auctioneer 40 East 46 Street NY 1930
Ickes
By descent to Stephen Beecher Ickes NY
Sotheby's 14 Nov 90 Lot 3 £4,014
Commander David Joel RN

258 A TWO-DECKER BEFORE THE WIND
Oil on canvas 39 x 61
Prov: Leggatt Bros
Charles Hammond 1958
Sir Stanley Aubrey presented to Lloyd's of London Chairmans Office
Illus: *Apollo* magazine October 1957
An earlier work with a stylised sea.

259 A TWO-DECKER RUNNING UP THE THAMES
Oil on canvas 36 x 60
Prov: A. H. Brooking Esq. London N15
This painting was recorded in The National Maritime Museum in March 1952 as a possible early Brooking but no photograph is held.

260 FOUR TWO-DECKERS IN A RUNNING SEA WITH A SMACK IN THE FOREGROUND
Oil on canvas 20½ x 29. Bears traces of a signature

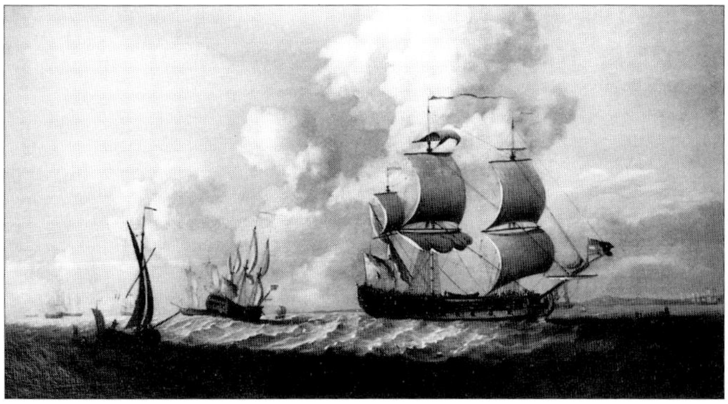

258

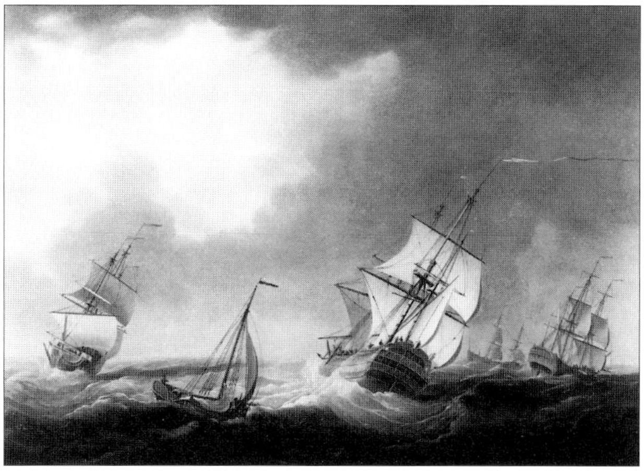

260

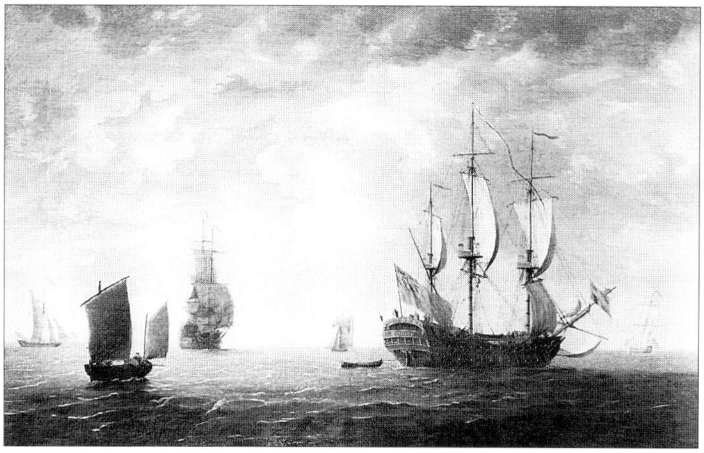

263

Prov: Rupert Preston Gallery 1966
G. E. J. Robertson Esq.
Private Collection

261 A BRIG AND SMALL BOATS OFFSHORE
(see page 152)
Oil on canvas 14¼ x 23. Signed C Brooking on barrel on right
Prov: Molesworth-St Aubyn family. One of a pair with 251D

262 TWO MERCHANT SHIPS WITH A SMACK ON THE RIGHT (see Chapter 4, page 56)
Oil on paper laid down on canvas 10⅛ x 15¼
Prov: Green and Hadfield 1958
W. K. Parkinson Esq.
Mr and Mrs B. Welch

263 A TWO-DECKER BEFORE A LIGHT BREEZE WITH A LUGGER UNDER SAIL
Oil on canvas 15 x 23
Prov: John Carr of Dunston Hall 1806
Stafford Bourne Esq.
Private Collection
Exhib: Mellon Foundation: Bristol July 1966, No. 23
Engraved and published as *Morning*, measuring 11½ x 16¼ by Boydell in 1753. See engraving 603 and painting 20.

264 THE PASSING SQUALL – MEN O'WAR AND MERCHANTMEN IN THE THAMES ESTUARY
Oil on canvas 29¾ x 38
Prov: Whereabouts unknown
Photograph in the NMM. The sea looks to be the work of Francis Swaine.
Mellon Copy Neg. No. 4126
Illus: *Walkers Monthly* January 1938

265 ELIZABETH CASTLE, JERSEY WITH A FRIGATE FIRING A GUN AT LEFT AND OTHER SHIPPING
(see page 152)
Oil on canvas 18¼ x 27¼. Not signed
Prov: The Misses Webb, Jersey
Peter Arnold Esq.
Sotheby's 10 November 1993 Lot 2 Withdrawn
Sotheby's 11 May 1994 Lot 55 £38,000
Private Collection
A very fine late painting which was engraved by Le Comte and published in 1818. See engravings 615A and 615B. The latter was engraved 28 years earlier drawn by James d'Auvergne, engraved by Boydell in 1790.

266A SHIPPING OFF DOVER
Oil on canvas 30¾ x 41¾. Signed C Brooking lower left
Prov: O. K. Whatley Esq. Cowden, Kent
Parke Bernet, New York 25 Sep 1968 Lot 10 Macy's Sale
Private Collection, USA
A very fine late painting with excellent topography of Dover, its castle and town and the white cliffs.

266B A NAVAL SQUADRON OFF DOVER (see page 152)
Oil on canvas 27⅞ x 35¾. Signed indistinctly
Prov: Leonard Koetser May 1973
Captain Prentice
Private Collection
Exhib: Ackerman & Johnson Dec. 1996 No. 13
Illus: Leonard Koetser Spring Exhibition 1973 (in colour)

267 TWO ENGLISH FRIGATES, A BRIG AND OTHER SAILING VESSELS OFF DOVER (see page 153)
Oil on canvas 21¾ x 48
Prov: Preston Gallery
Private Collection
Christie's 15 November 1968 Lot 83 £850
Christie's 22 March 1974 Lot 178 380 gns
Commander David Joel RN

268 A SMALL SHIP BEFORE THE WIND WITH A FISHING VESSEL PASSING UNDER HER STERN (see page 153)
Oil on canvas 15 x 17¾
Prov: Spink & Son 1946
Private Collection
Christie's 19 November 1965 Lot 9
Oscar and Peter Johnson
G. E. J. Robertson Esq.
Private Collection
Exhib: Mellon Foundation: Aldeburgh 1966, No. 49

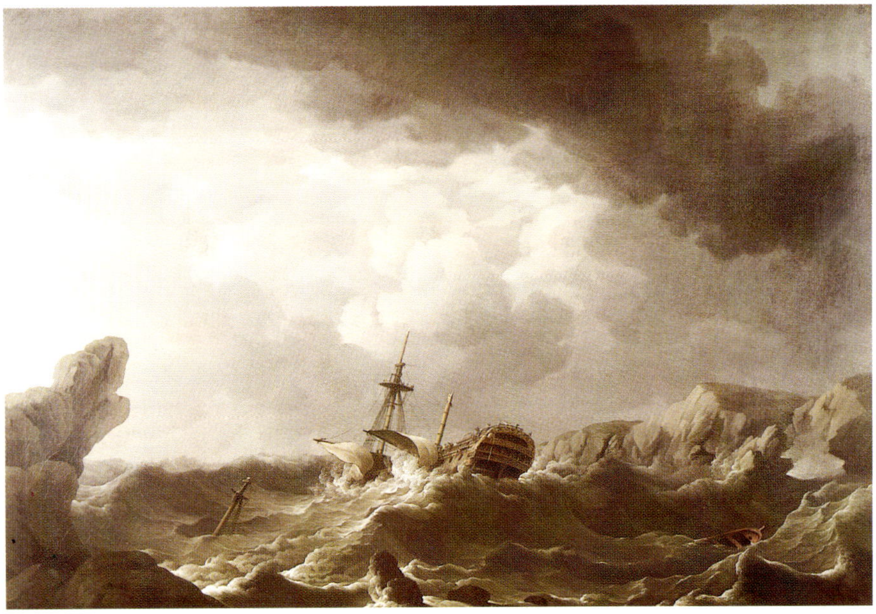

401C
A dismasted ship driving ashore in a gale

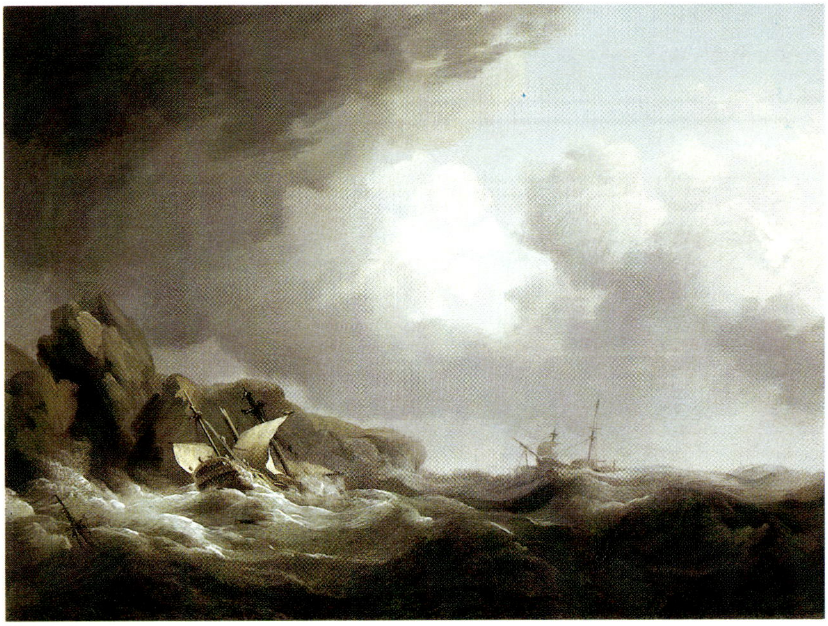

402B
The wreck of the Nuestra Senora *off Beachy Head November 1746*

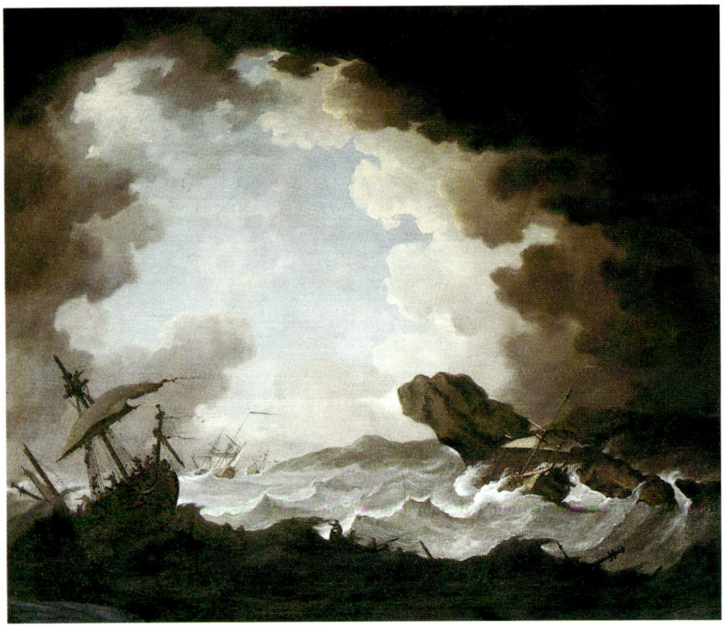

405
A tempest with four ships running on to a lee shore

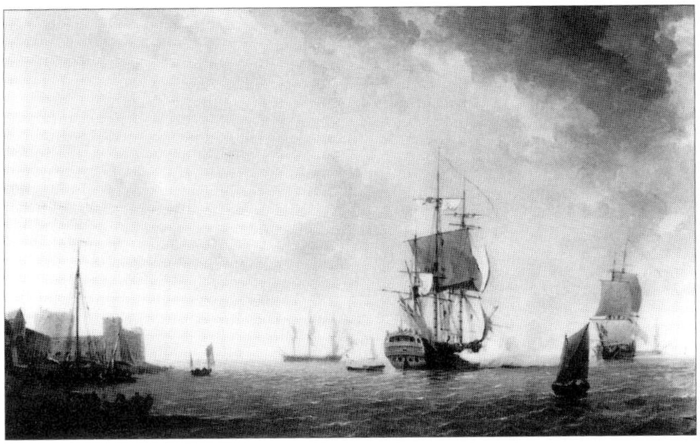

270

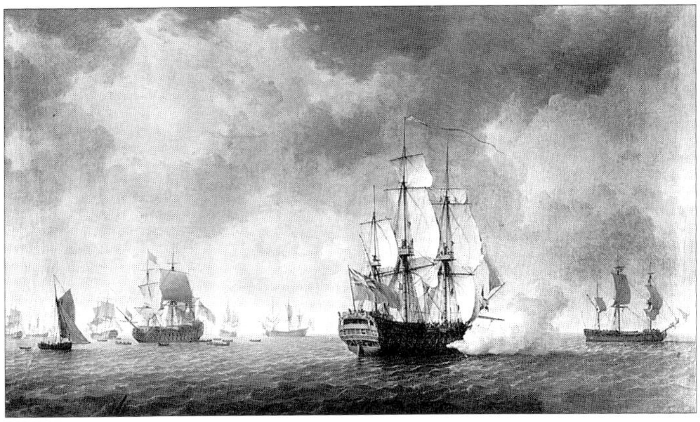

271

269 MEN O'WAR APPROACHING STORM (see page 153)
Oil on canvas 11½ x 17½. Signed C Brooking indistinctly on plank at left
Prov: Sandford Collection as P. Monamy
Sir Bruce Ingram until 1962 as P. Monamy
Colnaghi February 1963
Mr and Mrs Paul Mellon
Sotheby's 18th November 1981 Lot 82 £3,800
Private Collection
Exhib: Mellon Foundation: Aldeburgh/Bristol June/July 1966, No. 65
Previously exhibited as a Monamy in several major exhibitions, and inspired by a van de Velde.

270 MEN O'WAR OFF A CASTLE IN A LIGHT BREEZE
Oil on canvas 17½ x 27½. Signed
Prov: Robert W Symons 1927
Mrs M. McNab
Sotheby's 26 March 1975 Lot 103A – £4,800
Richard Green
Private Collection (USA)
This painting has also been entitled *Shipping near Calshot Castle, Southampton.*

271 BOATS OF THE FLEET REPAIRING TO A COUNCIL ON BOARD THE FLAGSHIP OF THE CHANNEL FLEET
Oil on canvas 22 x 32 (estimate only)
A fine late painting.

272 A BRIG-RIGGED YACHT AND TWO TWO-DECKERS IN A BREEZE OFF A COAST WITH A SMALL FISHING BOAT ALONGSIDE THE SHORE ON THE LEFT
(see page 156)
Oil on canvas 20 x 29¾. Signed C Brooking on spar left foreground
Prov: Molesworth-St Aubyn family
A lovely atmospheric painting. One of a pair with 41.

273 FIVE FRIGATES MANOEUVRING IN A CHOPPY SEA
(see page 156)
Oil on canvas 9¾ x 14½
Prov: Auction in Canterbury 1952
M. Lawrence Esq.
Sotheby's 9 July 1980 Lot 20 £9,000
Parker Gallery
Private Collection
A detailed late painting of ships in a seaway.

274 FOUR MEN O'WAR IN A FAIR BREEZE
Oil on canvas (oval) 25 x 34. Not known if it is signed
Prov: Daniel H. Farr, Philadelphia, USA
Exhib: Kirkham & Hall Gallery, New York 1922
In an oval frame and one of a pair. Whereabouts unknown.

275 SHIPPING IN A STIFF BREEZE
Oil on canvas 23 x 37½. Signed
Prov: Parker Gallery 1966
Private Collection
Illus. *Apollo* magazine November 1966

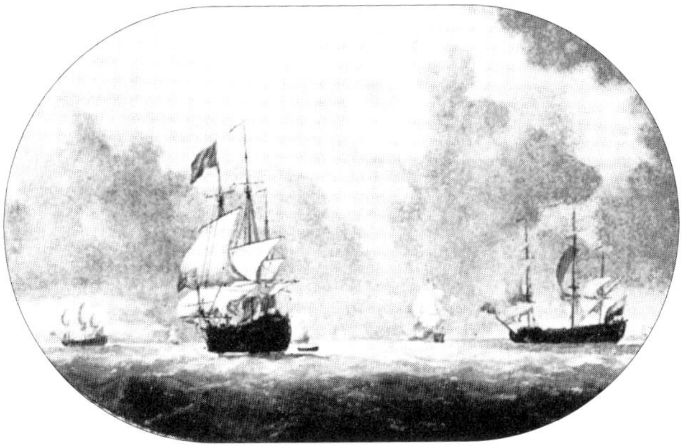

274

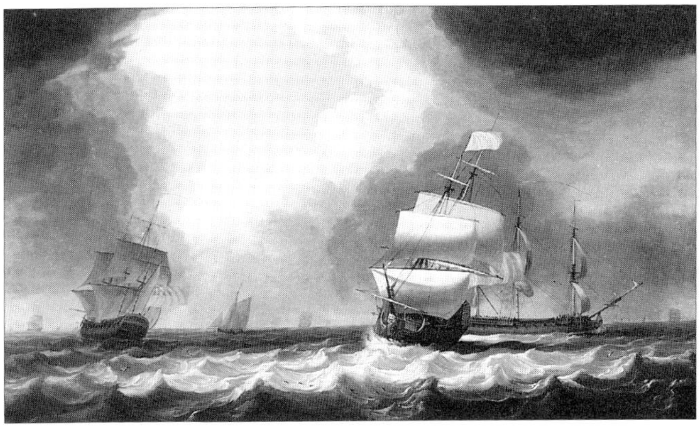

275

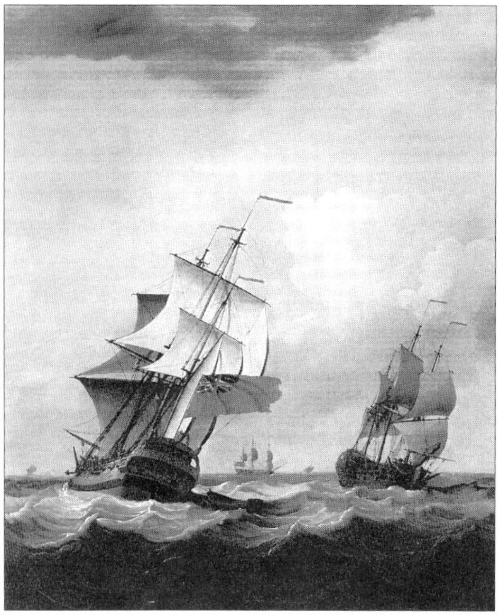

277

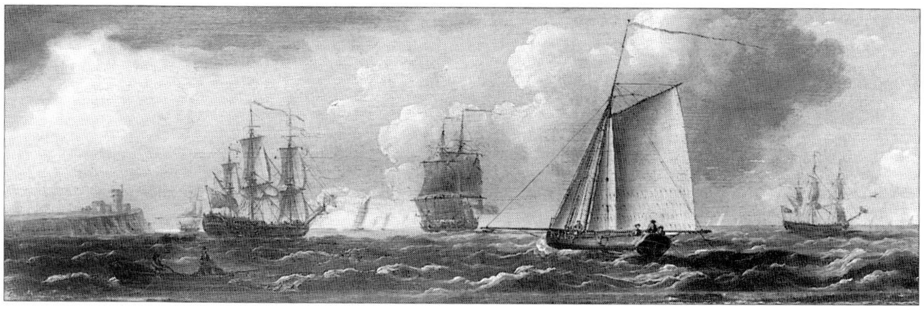

278

276 A FRIGATE, A CUTTER CLOSE-HAULED AND TWO SHIPS OF THE LINE, ONE AT ANCHOR, IN A BREEZE
(see Chapter 4, page 60)
Oil on canvas 17½ x 23½. Signed
Prov: Miss Honey
Christie's 8 March 1920 Lot 109 30 gns unsold
Christie's 23 June 1978 Lot 75 £4,800
David Messum 1978
Private Collection
A later painting.

277 EAST INDIAMEN IN A ROUGH SEA
Oil on canvas 50 x 40. Not signed
Prov: N. R. Omell 1979 asking £18,000
Private Collection
Illus: N. R. Omell 1979 Catalogue Plate 36
The Indiaman to the left is towing the captain's gig. The ship to the right has no mizzen yard which infers much restoration. Brooking had a preference for green-hued seas, evident in this picture.

278 A CUTTER CLOSE-HAULED ON THE PORT TACK
Oil on panel 8½ x 26. Unsigned
Prov: Macpherson Collection
National Maritime Museum (1927-326)
Illus: *Old Sea Paintings*, Keble Chatterton 1928

279 THE YACHT *ROYAL ESCAPE* IN A BREEZE ON THE PORT TACK OTHER MEN O'WAR IN THE DISTANCE
Oil on canvas 24¾ x 29¼. Not signed
Prov: R. R. Henshaw Esq. 1936
Rupert Preston Gallery 1966
C. D. Wilson Esq., Guernsey
John Millar Esq. FRICS FRSA 1972
Presented to Royal Yacht Squadron 1973
After the Battle of Worcester in 1651, the future King Charles II escaped to France in the coasting collier *Surprise*. On his return to the throne of England he bought her from Captain Tattersall in 1660, and she was moored for some years off Whitehall. She was in service as a smack-rigged Royal Yacht until 1673. Armed with two guns, she was 30ft 6ins in length, with a beam of 14ft 6ins, and a draft of 7ft. Brooking's painting is in fact a copy after van de Velde the Younger. See Robinson – *The Paintings of the Willem van de Veldes* Vol.2. No. 252 p.984. It is not an accurate copy of either sea or sky, nor is the vessel on the right horizon lifted too high. But it is based on the van de Velde composition.

280 DUTCH FISHING VESSELS IN COASTAL WATERS BEFORE A STORM, A BRITISH MAN O'WAR BEYOND
(see page 156)
Oil on canvas 11 x 15½. Not signed
Prov: Charrington Family
Sotheby's 9 July 1986 Lot 4 Unsold
Private Collection
This atmospheric painting with two shafts of silvery light on the right horizon with fishing boats in the left foreground, is based on William van de Velde the Younger's painting No. 380 circa 1700, entitled *A Dutch fishing pink at sea running before gale*, which was sold at the Sedelmeyer Gallery in Paris 25/28 May 1907 No. 196.

There is a record of a second version by Brooking of this composition in the National Maritime Museum's photographic archive by D. Cavat (negative No R26/6) in which there are two posts in the water at left. Current whereabouts unknown.

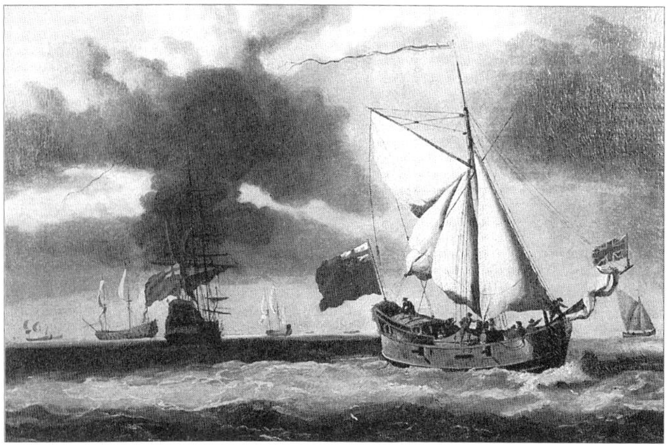

279

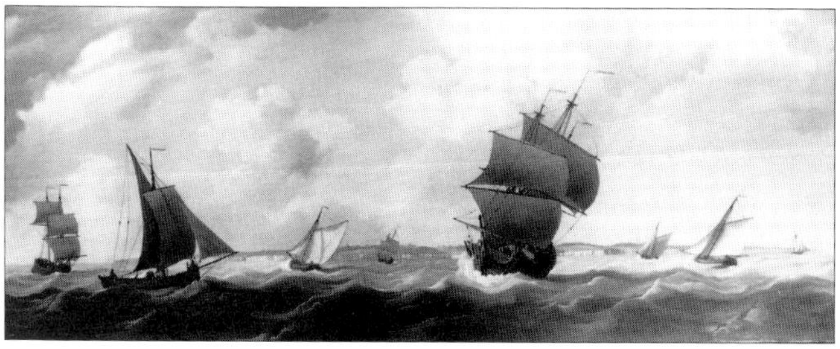

282

281 A MERCHANT SNOW AND TWO INDIAMEN, A LUGGER AND A CUTTER IN THE CHANNEL
Oil on canvas 19¼ x 30¾. Signed
Prov: Mr and Mrs Baussey
Richard Green (one of a pair, see 361) in 1987

282 SHIPPING IN THE ENGLISH CHANNEL
Oil on canvas 29 x 69. Not signed
Prov: Parker Gallery
Private Collection
A spectacular painting, related to the shipping off Dover series, 266A and B and 267. But in this example the scene is further up the English Channel with Dover in the centre background. The shipping is different too, with no less than five cutters.

BATTLES

351 THE TAKING OF THE *MARQUESE D'ANTIN* AND THE *LOUIS ERASME* BY THE *PRINCE FREDERICK* AND *DUKE* PRIVATEERS 10 JULY 1745 (see Chapter 3, page 44)
Oil on canvas 13 x 19⅛
Prov: Mr Panton Betew in 1766
Sotheby's 29 January 1964 Lot 46 for £650
Spink & Son
Mr and Mrs Paul Mellon
Exhib: Mellon Foundation: Aldeburgh/Bristol June/July 1966, No. 45
The Royal Family Privateers, so called because each vessel bore the name of a member of the Royal Family, were under the command of Commodore James Talbot. On 10 July 1745 the *Prince Frederick* and the *Duke* engaged and captured two Frenchmen, the *Marquese d'Antin* and the *Louis Erasme* which were found to be carrying over one million pounds in bullion. When the prizes reached Bristol, the treasure was loaded into 45 wagons and escorted to London by an armed guard, preceded by a band. The painting was engraved. See 621.

352A THE CAPTURE OF A FRENCH SHIP BY ENGLISH PRIVATEERS
Oil on canvas 22 x 33. Not signed
Prov: G. Scott 1894
R. C. Isaac
Lieut Col Sir Hutchinson Poe CB (by 1902)
Sir Bruce Ingram
Sotheby's 11 March 1964 Lot 3 £10,500
Leggat Bros
Private Collection
Exhib: Dublin Royal Hibernian Academy 1902-3 No. 104
Royal Academy British Art 1934 No. 351
Brussels Exposition Universelle. Cinq Siècles d'Art; 1935 No. 1102
Eastbourne, Towner Art Gallery 1946
Montreal Museum of Art, October 1957
Ottawa, National Gallery of Canada, November 1957
Toronto Art Gallery, January 1958
Toledo, Museum of Art, February 1958
Illus: F. Gordon Roe, *Sea Painters of Britain* Plate 23
This is supposed to be the same action as in 351, i.e. the capture of French ships.

352B (see page 157)
Oil on canvas 23½ x 41¼. Signed C Brooking on plank left centre
Prov: Property of a Lady (Lady Donner)
Christie's 22 June 1979 Lot 19 unsold
Sotheby's 16 November 1983 Lot 17 £15,500
Spink & Son, April 1987
Richard Green
Private Collection
Exhib: Mellon Foundation: Aldeburgh/Bristol June/July 1966, No. 44
In this painting the general composition is the same but the ships, a brig and ketch attacking seen in 352A, have been substituted with two ships and two brigs. This picture is meant to depict the capture of a Spanish Ship *Nuestra Senora de los Remedios* by the Royal Family Privateers 5 February 1746.

353 CAPTURE OF THE *GLORIOSO* 8 OCTOBER 1747 BY THE ROYAL FAMILY PRIVATEERS *PRINCE FREDERICK* AND *PRINCE GEORGE*
Oil on canvas 31 x 55. Signed C Brooking in the sea left of centre foreground
Prov: F. J. Goodlake
Christie's 28 November 1938 Lot 24 280 gns. A pair (with 355)
Spink & Son (1938)
Sir James Caird
National Maritime Museum (1939-400)
Exhib: Mellon Foundation: Bristol July 1966, No. 40
The *Glorioso* was a Spanish ship captured off Cape St Vincent and had a prize value of £700,000. Each seaman received £850 in prize money, a very large sum indeed in 1747.

354 THE *BOSCAWEN* ENGAGING A FLEET OF FRENCH SHIPS 23 MAY 1745 (see page 157)
Oil on canvas 20 x 31½. Signed C Brooking lower left
Prov: Sir Bruce Ingram
Spink & Son (1935)
Sir James Caird
National Maritime Museum (1935-40)
Commodore Walker's action with *Boscawen* and *Sheerness* engaging a fleet of French ships from Martinique, five of which were taken, one sunk and two escaping. See Engraving 609 and Drawing 714.
Illus: *Illustrated London News* 17 April 1937

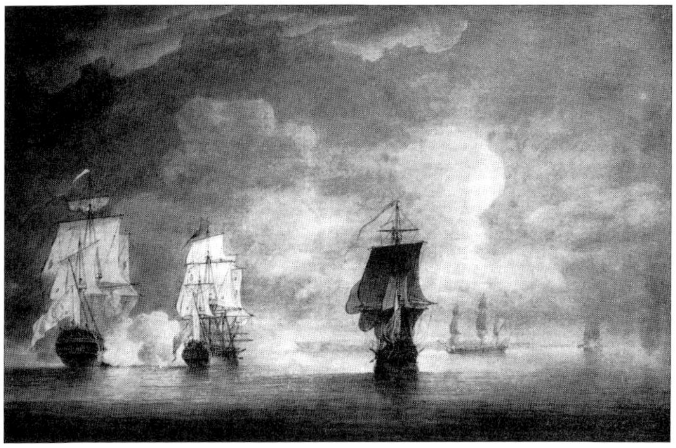

353

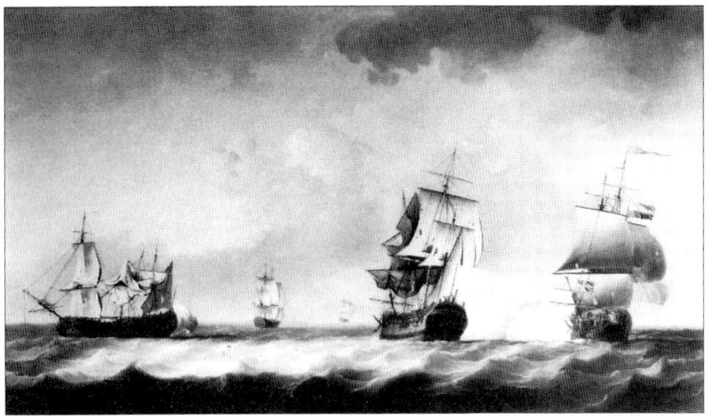

356

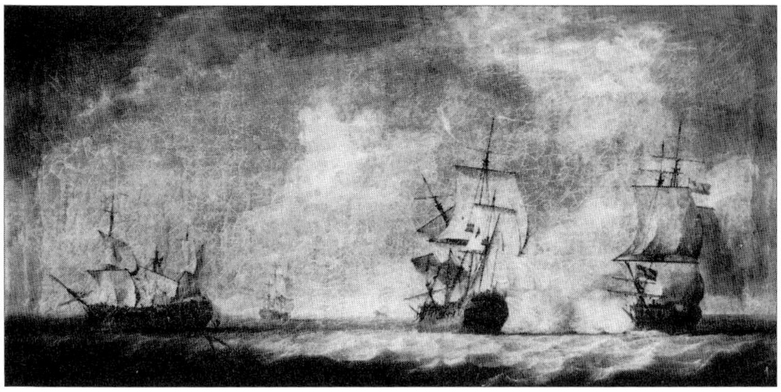

359

355 CAPTURE OF THE *MARQUESE D'ANTIN* AND THE *LOUIS ERASME* 10 JULY 1745 (see page 157)
Oil on canvas 31¼ x 54½. Signed C Brooking P
Prov: F. J. Goodlake
Christie's 28 Nov 1938 Lot 24 280 gns. A pair (with 353)
Spink & Son (1938)
Sir James Caird
National Maritime Museum (1939-399)
See 351 for further details of this engagement.

356 CAPTURE OF THE *MARQUESE D'ANTIN* AND THE *LOUIS ERASME* 10 JULY 1745
Oil on canvas 24 x 40
Prov: Spink & Son (1936) £65
Sir James Caird
National Maritime Museum (1936-45)
On loan to the Royal Naval College, Greenwich (Stuart Room), King Charles Building.
Note: Catalogued by the National Maritime Museum in the *Concise Catalogue of Oil Paintings* as 18th Century British School.

357 CAPTURE OF THE *MARQUESE D'ANTIN* AND THE *LOUIS ERASME* 10 JULY 1745 (see Chapter 3, page 45)
Oil on canvas 14½ x 24
Prov: R. Colin Smith Esq. (1946)
Exhib: Mellon Foundation: Bristol July 1966, No. 41
This subject was engraved by Ravenet and published by Boydell in 1753. It was published Whittle and Laurie in 1818. See Engravings 608A and 608B and Drawing 707A.

358 THE *ALEXANDER* IN ACTION WITH THE *SOLEBAY* OFF THE ISLAND OF RE – LA ROCHELLE – 10 APRIL 1746 (see Chapter 4, page 62)
Oil on canvas 44 x 95. Signed C Brooking centre foreground below the description of the action
Prov: 25/26 April 1777 (V & A Picture Catalogue 1755-1789) Lot 65
Rev Dr Friend and a gentleman of Weybridge
Rt Hon Earl Howe of Penn House, Bucks
Christie's 7 Dec 1933 Lot 3, 260 gns
Spink & Son (1933)
Private Collection
Exhib: Mellon Foundation: Aldeburgh/Bristol June/July 1966, No. 43
This large scale painting is unusual for Brooking in its adoption of a bird's-eye viewpoint. Brooking has represented the five phases of the engagement. No other recorded painting by him contains so much information of an engagement and its locale. It is as if he were present but there is no information which can either confirm or deny this supposition.

359 TAKING OF THE *MARQUESE D'ANTIN* AND THE *LOUIS ERASME* BY THE *PRINCE FREDERICK* AND THE *DUKE* 10 JULY 1745
Oil on canvas 23 x 46¾. Signed C Brooking left centre on wreckage
Prov: Sotheby's 11 July 1984 Lot 2 £16,500
Springfield Fine Arts, London, October 1985
Private Collection, Spain

360 AN ENGAGEMENT BETWEEN ENGLISH AND FRENCH SHIPS
Oil on canvas 11½ x 47½. Not signed
Prov: Sotheby's 11 March 1987 Lot 9 £7,500

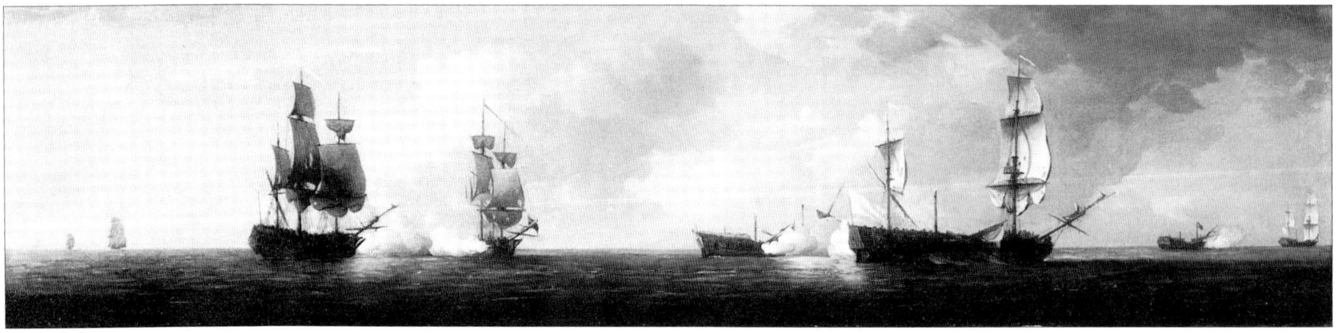

360

Private Collection
This painting was sold as by Charles Brooking by Sotheby's. It appears to be an action between an English frigate and a French two-decker with the action shown in four separate phases, going from left to right. Further research will undoubtedly identify the participants. But for the moment it would seem that the much smaller English ship, despite suffering enormous damage, including total dismasting, beats off the Frenchman who retires having lost her mainmast.

361 ACTION DURING THE FIRST CRUISE OF THE ROYAL FAMILY PRIVATEERS, THE *PRINCE FREDERICK*, THE *DUKE* AND THE *PRINCE GEORGE*
Oil on canvas 19¼ x 30¼. Signed
Prov: Mr and Mrs Baussey
Richard Green (one of a pair, see 281) in 1987
Private Collection, Spain

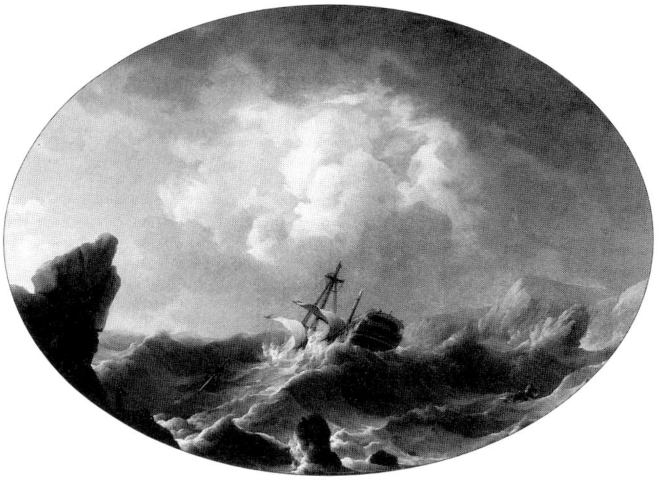
401F

WRECKS

401A A DISMASTED SHIP DRIVING ASHORE IN A GALE
(See Chapter 3, page 53)
Oil on canvas 12 x 13¾. Signed C Brooking on broken mast lower left foreground
Prov: Alan Rofe Esq. 1958
Agnew's 1970
Commander David Joel RN
Exhib: Agnew's September 1970
A remarkably detailed late atmospheric painting of an impending disaster, with men in the water and a swamped boat in the left foreground. In this version the mainmast is still standing.

401B
Oil on canvas 14½ x 22. Signed C Brooking on spar lower left
Prov: Mrs G. B. McKean
Leggatt Bros (May 1967)
Mr and Mrs Paul Mellon
Exhib: Mellon Foundation: Bristol July 1966, No. 17
Yale Seascapes 1977/78 No. 13
Illus: *Illustrated London News* 18 June 1966
In this version all three masts are damaged.

401C (see page 160)
Oil on canvas 34 x 50. Signed C Brooking lower left.
Prov: Christie's 1936 £50
Spink & Son (1938)
Private Collection
Bonhams (1960)
Private Collection
Exhib: Mellon Foundation: Aldeburgh/Bristol June/July 1966, No. 19
Ackerman & Johnson December 1996 No. 14
Illus: *Connoisseur* August 1966
This is the largest of this series. In this painting all three masts are damaged. There is in addition a very large outcrop of rock on the left of the painting. The owner suggests this may be HMS *Litchfield* wrecked on 29 November 1758.

401D
Oil on canvas 22½ x 32. Signed C Brooking lower left
Prov: Christie's 24 May 1968 Lot 74
Brandt
Private Collection
This painting, though smaller, is very similar to 401C.

401E
Oil on canvas 14½ x 22. Not signed
Prov: James Adams & Son Dublin 30 June 1965 – £24
Private Collection, Eire
This painting too is similar to 401C and 401D, with the same large outcrop of rocks on the left.

401F
Oil on canvas (oval) 22 x 31. Signed C Brooking left centre
Prov: Sotheby's 12 April 1995 Lot 7 £11,500
Private Collection
A highly detailed painting.

402A THE WRECK OF THE *NUESTRA SENORA* OFF BEACHY HEAD NOVEMBER 1746
Oil on canvas 20¼ x 31½. Signed C Brooking
Prov: Private Collection, Chelsea
Exhib: British Institution April 1817
A magnificent storm scene. See drawing 710 and engraving 601.

402B (see page 160)
Oil on canvas 10½ x 14½. Signed C Brooking on plank left foreground.
Prov: Robert Taylor Esq. (1840-1915)
E. M. Thomas, Esq.
David Messum Gallery
Sotheby's 13 March 1985 Lot 22 £3,000
Private Collection
Exhib: Mellon Foundation: Aldeburgh/Bristol June/July 1966, No. 20
See 15B. One of a series of six paintings under one ownership.

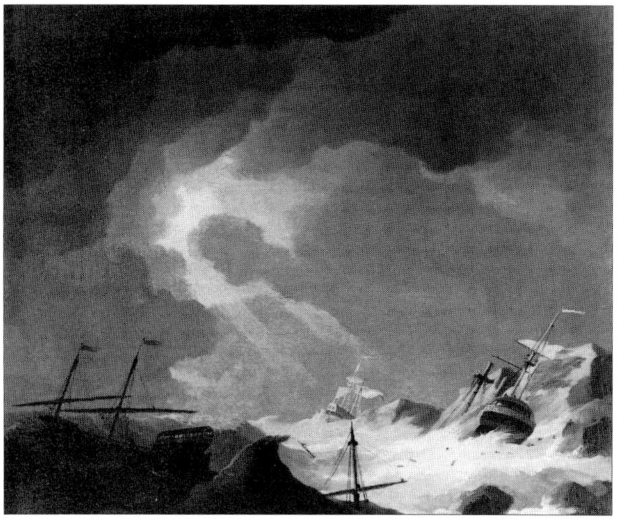

403

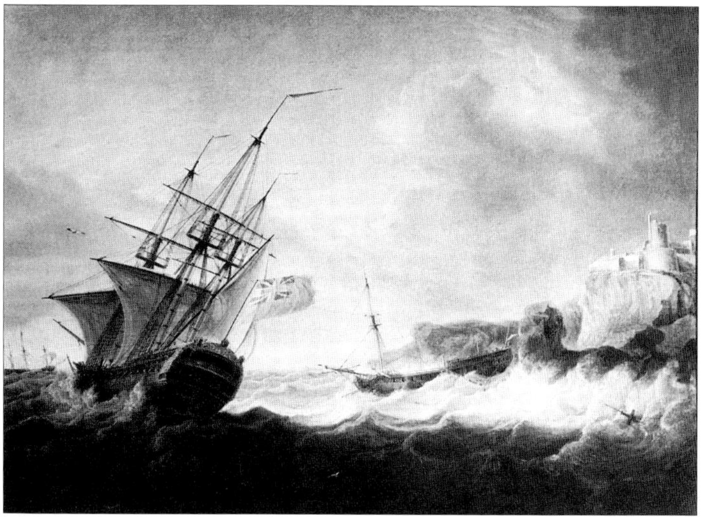

404

403 A GALLEY WITH OTHER VESSELS WRECKED ON A ROCKY COAST
Oil on canvas 12 x 14½
Prov: National Maritime Museum (1949-388/1)
This marine disaster of at least four ships nearing or on the rocks is here enacted with countless sailors struggling in an impossible foam, whilst in the galley they row in desperation to avoid the same fate, which seems inevitable.

404 A TWO-DECKER ABOUT TO BE WRECKED ON ROCKS ON A LEE SHORE WITH A CASTLE ABOVE, AS ANOTHER TWO-DECKER TRIES TO STAND OFF
A large painting (sight size approximately 20 x 30)
Prov: V Larby, Stockholm 1936
From a photograph in the Witt Library, the painting would appear to be by Brooking. Note below photograph states Sundbyberg Sweden.

405 A TEMPEST WITH FOUR SHIPS RUNNING ON TO A LEE SHORE (see page 160)
Oil on canvas 25 x 30. Signed C Brooking. In a fine carved frame
Prov: Christie's 25 November 1977 Lot 59. Sold as Peter Monamy but signed Brooking £800
David Messum Gallery
Sotheby's 20 July 1987 Lot 2 Martyn Gregory £2,600
Private Collection
There is a huge rock in the right centre of the picture. A very similar rock appears in several paintings by van de Velde the Younger and also in Monamy's work. Michael Robinson suggests this rock is called the Bec de L'Aigle on the Island of Aguila between Marseille and Toulon.

406 LARGE SAILING CRAFT IN A ROUGH SEA BELOW CLIFFS
Oil on canvas 14¼ x 19
Prov: Northwich Park. Captain E. G. Spencer-Churchill
Christie's 25 June 1965 Lot 80
Private Collection
Notes: Northwich Picture Catalogue 1864 No. 185
Northwich Picture Catalogue 1921 No. 243
Borenius No. 243

ROYAL VISITS TO THE FLEET

450A THE ROYAL VISIT TO THE FLEET IN THE THAMES ESTUARY, 10 SEPTEMBER 1673 (see Chapter 1, page 29)
Oil on canvas 25¾ x 38. Not signed
Prov: J. S. Beckett
Sir Hickman Bacon
Sir Edmund Bacon by descent
Sir Nicholas Bacon, Raveningham Hall, Norfolk
Exhib: Mellon Foundation: Aldeburgh/Bristol June/July 1966, No. 42
This painting, previously thought to depict the royal visit to the fleet on 6 June, 1672, is a copy, but not a direct one, after Willem van de Velde the Younger's painting now in the National Maritime Museum. The van de Velde the Younger measures 65 x 128ins. The painting is known to have been copied twelve times by various artists. It is believed by E. H. H. Archibald that Brooking's version was based on Elisha Kirkall's mezzotint engraving, after van de Velde's original composition.

The painting shows the scene with two Royal Yachts which have brought King Charles II and his noblemen down from London, on the left, and the *Royal Prince* at anchor on the right. The scene is fully described by Captain John Narborough (Pepysian Library, Cambridge MS 2555 p.61) and the history of the painting by Vertue (British Library Add M5 21111 f56).

Brooking has lowered the stern of the *Anne* yacht on the left and indeed has lowered the sterns of most of the ships in the painting, including that of the *Royal Prince*. He has lengthened the flags and ensigns of the ships and has also increased the sea state and by these means improved the picture.

Indications that Brooking has copied from a print rather than the painting are that the flags of the French boats are red and not white, as are the flag and ensign of the Admiral in the centre middle distance. There are other minor differences too. The *Prince* of 1670 had 90 guns.

450B
Oil on canvas 25½ x 47. Not signed
Prov: The Hon. Mrs Rhodes
Sotheby's 13 November 1968 Lot 87
Lord Elphinstone
Phillips 16 July 1973 Lot 67 £4,800
Private Collection
This painting is more extended than 450A, with greater distances between the ships *Royal Prince* and the *London*. The *Cleveland* yacht at anchor on the left shows the pendant being hoisted at the masthead as the Royal Standard is taken down, a feature not so far found in any version of a van de Velde or in 450A.

451 THE ADMIRAL OF THE FLEET IN HIS FLAGSHIP WITH FOUR SHIPS OF THE LINE
Oil on canvas 24 x 29. Not signed
Prov: Holburne Museum, Bath, Somerset No 111
A calm coast scene. A line-of-battle ship of the Red squadron flying the Union Flag at the main, at anchor broadside on, bow to left, close in shore, firing a starboard gun. To the right, another smaller one, stern on, flying a long pennant; a long-boat leaving her side; another, with a blue flag in the stern, rowing towards her. Three warships in the distance; a small cutter at anchor, and various small boats. In the immediate foreground to the left a boat with two men drawing a net to the shore, and right of centre, two men wading and some old timbers. Bright evening sky, blue to pale gold, with warm clouds.

DRAWINGS

701 TWO FRIGATES BEFORE THE WIND (see Chapter 4, page 57)
Pen, ink and grey wash 7⅞ x 10⅛. Signed C Brooking on the plank left foreground
Prov: Basil Taylor Esq. 1966
John Baskett 1970

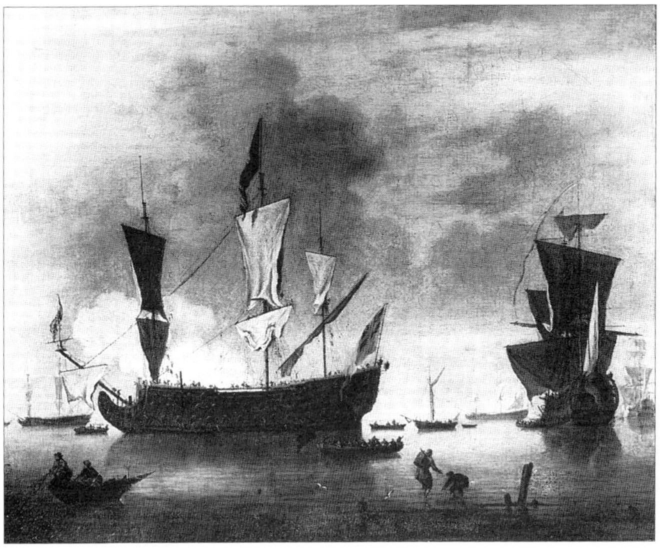

451

Mr and Mrs Paul Mellon
Exhib: Mellon Foundation: Aldeburgh/Bristol June/July 1966, No. 71

702 THE ROYAL YACHT *MARY* LYING OFF DOVER
Pen, pencil and wash 7¾ x 10⅛
Prov: Walter A. Brandt Esq.
Exhib: Mellon Foundation: Aldeburgh/Bristol June/July 1966, No. 66
The royal yacht *Mary* III was built at Dartford in 1727 and rigged as a ketch. Length 76ft, beam 22ft, 164 tons. The first *Mary* had been given to Charles II at his Restoration by the City of Amsterdam

703 A MAN OF WAR BRIGANTINE
Pen, ink and grey wash 13⅞ x 20. Signed C Brooking lower left
Prov: Mariners Museum, Newport News
Exhib: Mellon Foundation: Aldeburgh/Bristol June/July 1966, No. 67

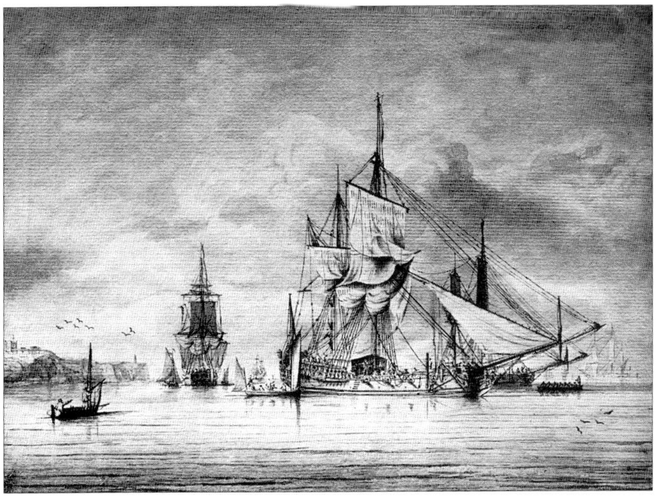

702

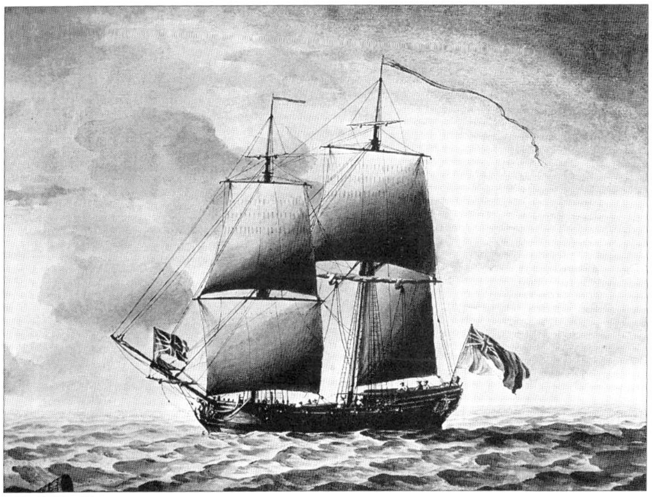

703

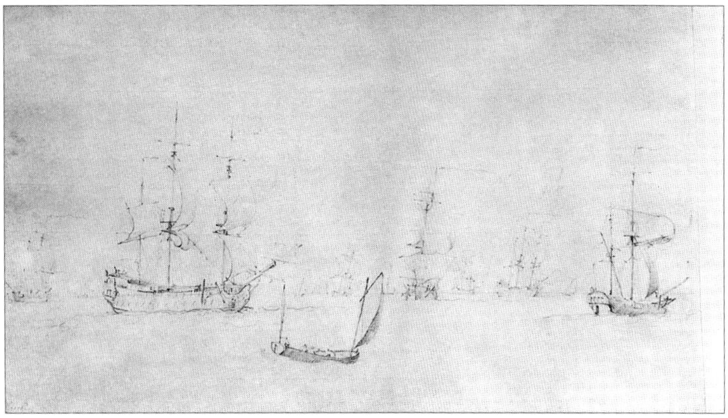

704

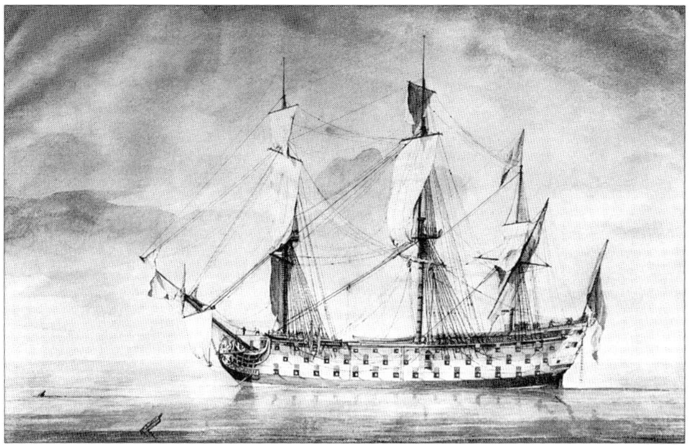

705

704 SHIPPING UNDER SAIL
Pencil 9⅛ x 16¼. Signed C Brooking lower left
Prov: Sir Bruce Ingram
Sotheby's 21 October 1964 Lot 8 £60
Private Collection
Sotheby's 16 July 1998 Lot 69
Exhib: Mellon Foundation: Aldeburgh/Bristol June/July 1966, No. 74

705 THE *ROYAL GEORGE* – 100 GUNS
Pen, ink and grey wash 12½ x 19⅛. Signed C Brooking on spar lower left
Prov: Royal Naval Club, Portsmouth
Exhib: Mellon Foundation: Aldeburgh/Bristol June/July 1966, No. 69
She was launched from Woolwich dockyard on 19 January 1756. For her time she was the world's most powerful man o'war and was to become Sir Edward Hawke's flagship at the battle of Quiberon Bay 20 November 1759. This is a beautifully finished late drawing.

706 A TWO-DECKER OF 74 GUNS IN A CALM
Pen, ink and grey wash 12 x 12½
Prov: British Museum (1875-8-4-949)

The John F. Kennedy Drawings

The following four drawings, 707A–D, were given to President Kennedy by James Graham & Sons New York in March 1961. The President accepted them in memory of his brother Lieutenant Joseph P. Kennedy Jnr USNR, providing that on his death they were given to the National Maritime Museum at Greenwich.

These drawings were in the Oval Room of the White House in Washington until the President's assassination on 22 November 1963. They were presented to the NMM in February 1965.
Prov: Parke Bernet New York, Heidseick Sale, 12 February 1943 Lot 109
James Graham & Sons 1014 Madison Avenue New York
President J. F. Kennedy
National Maritime Museum

707A TAKING OF THE *MARQUESE D'ANTIN* AND *LOUIS ERASME* BY THE *PRINCE FREDERICK* AND *DUKE* PRIVATEERS 10 JULY 1745 (see Chapter 3, page 45)
Wash drawing on cream laid paper. Stuck down on backing board 11½ x 17¾. Not signed
This drawing is closely related to 357 and engravings 608A and 608B.

707B TAKING OF THE *NUESTRA SENORA DE LOS REMEDIOS* 5 FEBRUARY 1746
Wash drawing on cream laid paper 11⅜ x 17⅞. Signed C Brooking Fecit 1746
This drawing is related to engraving 620.

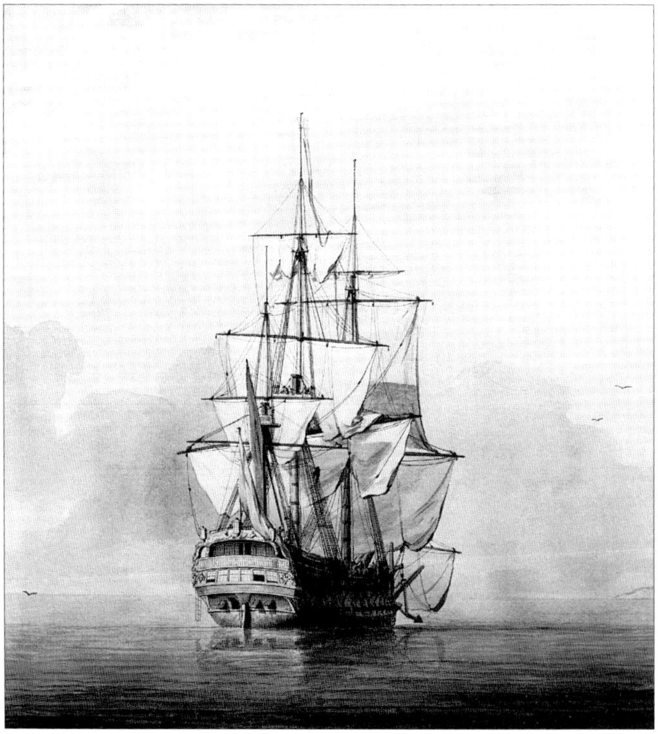

706

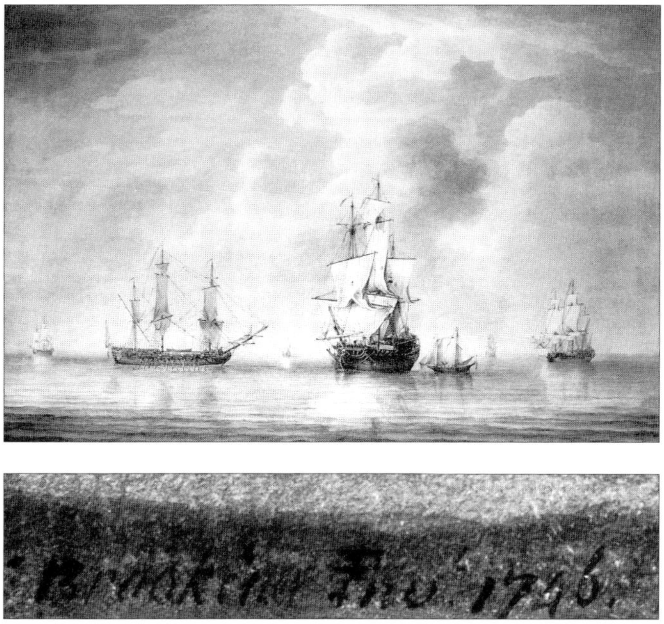

707B

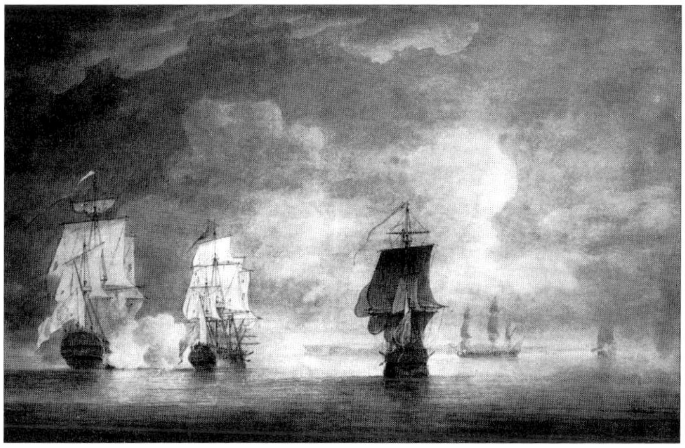

707C

707C THE *PRINCE FREDERICK* ENGAGING THE *GLORIOSO* 8 OCTOBER 1747
Wash drawing on cream laid paper 11½ x 17⅝. Signed Brooking The drawing is dark and stained. The signature slightly cut off. Related to engraving 613.

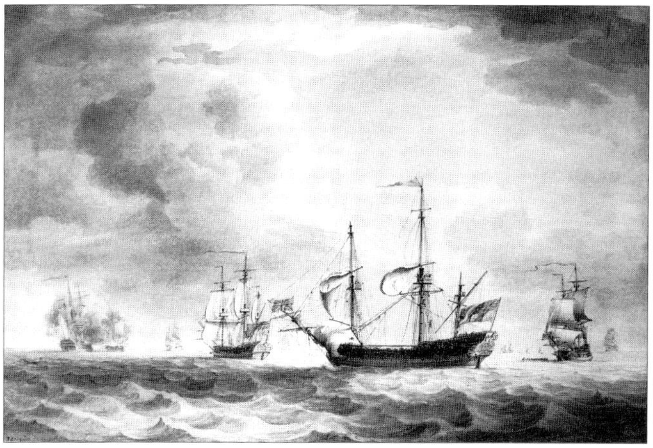

707D

707D THE *KING GEORGE* DISABLED DURING THE ENGAGEMENT WITH THE *GLORIOSA* 9 OCTOBER 1748
Wash drawing on cream laid paper 11½ x 17⅞. Signed Brooking. Related to engraving 616 and drawing 721. Drawing stolen from NMM (April 1995), recovered in 1998.

708 MEN OF WAR OFF THE ISLE OF WIGHT
Pencil 8 x 13. Signed C Brooking
Prov: Sir Bruce Ingram
Sotheby's 10 January 1965 No 412 £45
Captain J. S. B. Holley
Exhib: Mellon Foundation: Aldeburgh/Bristol June/July 1966, No. 75
This could have been a sketch for 246A (in reverse) or the engraving 606.

709 MEN OF WAR SALUTE ON PASSING AT SEA
Pen, ink and grey wash 5⅜ x 9⅞
Prov: Sir Bruce Ingram
Sotheby's 21 October 1964 Lot 8 £60
Private Collection
Exhib: Mellon Foundation: Aldeburgh/Bristol June/July 1966, No. 73
Previously described as men o'war about to engage. It now appears that the two-decker is a flagship under full sail plus two staysails and the one decker on the right is saluting her.

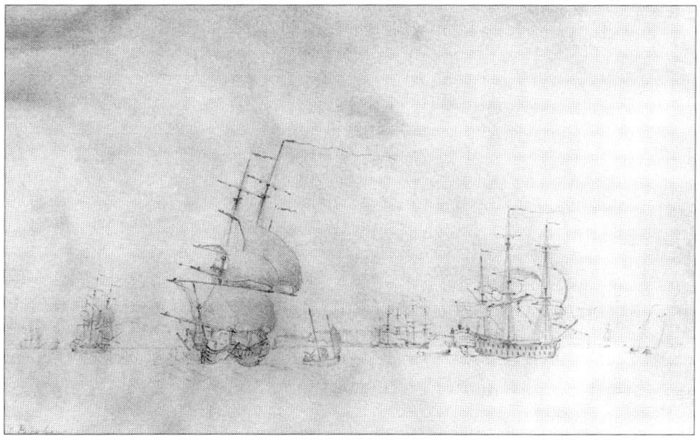

708

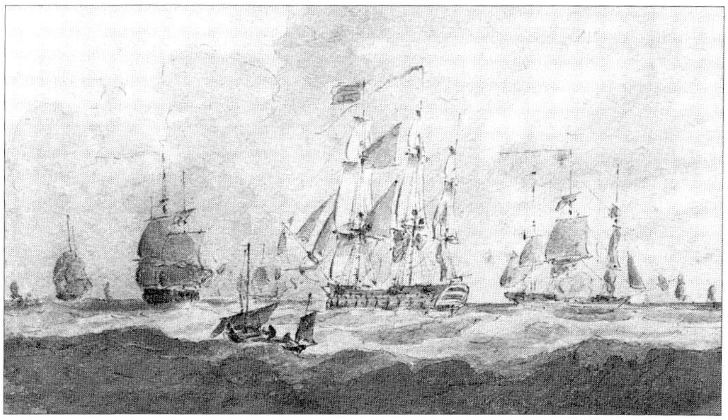

709

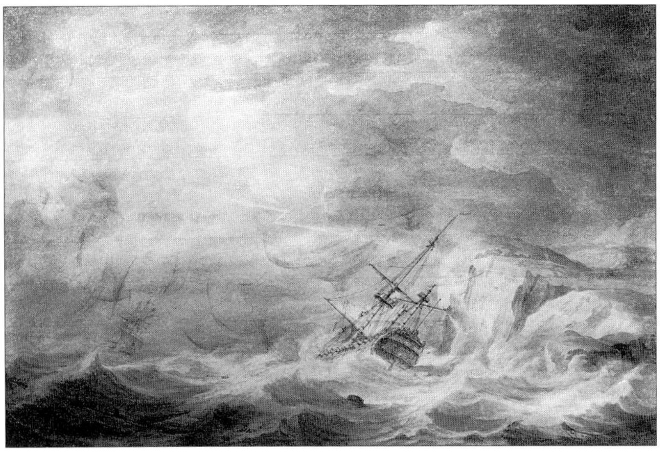

710

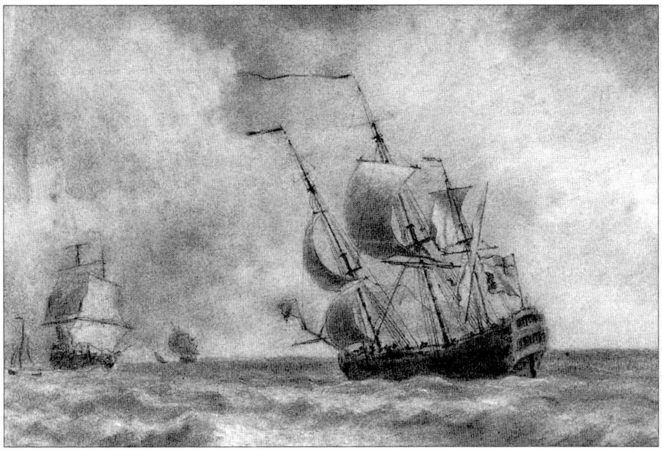

712

710 WRECK OF THE *NUESTRA SENORA DE LOS REMEDIOS* OFF BEACHY HEAD NOVEMBER 1746
Pen, ink and grey wash
Prov: V. N. Newman Sale 5 August 1923
Bought Philip Duval, New York Dealer 1923
This is the drawing for the engraving 601. See also 402 series, Frick Art Reference Library, Ref. 416.

711 MEN OF WAR IN A CALM
Pencil 9¼ x 5⅝. Signed
Prov: Sir Bruce Ingram
Sotheby's 21 October 1964 Lot 9 £45
Fine Art Society

712 SHIPPING STUDY
Pencil and white chalk on blue paper 10 x 14½. Not signed
Prov: Sir Bruce Ingram
Sotheby's 17 March 1965 Lot 784. One of 13 shipping drawings
F. B. Cockett Esq.
Note: Possibly by Samuel Scott.

713 MEN OF WAR BECALMED OFF SHEERNESS
Pen, ink and grey wash 5¾ x 7¼
Prov: Clouterbrook Trustees
Sotheby's 27 June 1968 Lot 135 £28
Agnew's

714 THE *BOSCAWEN* AND *SHEERNESS* PRIVATEERS ENGAGING A FLEET OF FRENCH SHIPS FROM MARTINICO (1745)
Pen, ink and grey wash. Size not known. Signed C Brooking Px.
Prov: W. H. McGraun (USA)
The drawing for engraving 609 in reverse. Frick Reference Library No 471. A superb drawing, now missing.

715 A SHIP COMING TO ANCHOR AND A CUTTER BEFORE THE WIND
Pen, ink and wash 10½ x16
Prov: Derek Clifford Esq.
This is the drawing for 15D and the engraving *Noon* 612. The paper has been oiled and is badly damaged.

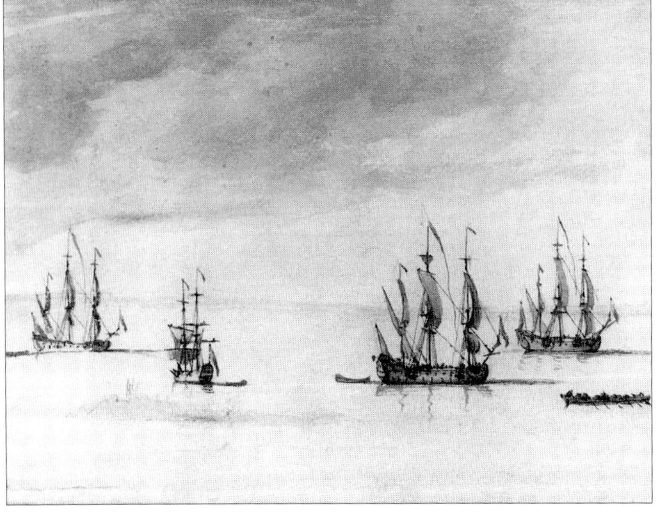

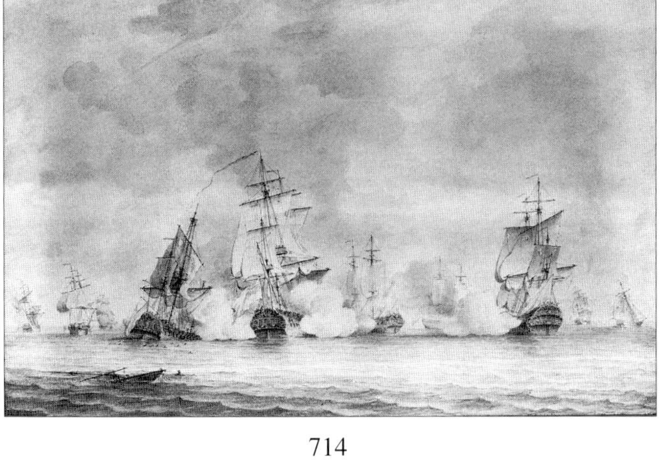

714

713

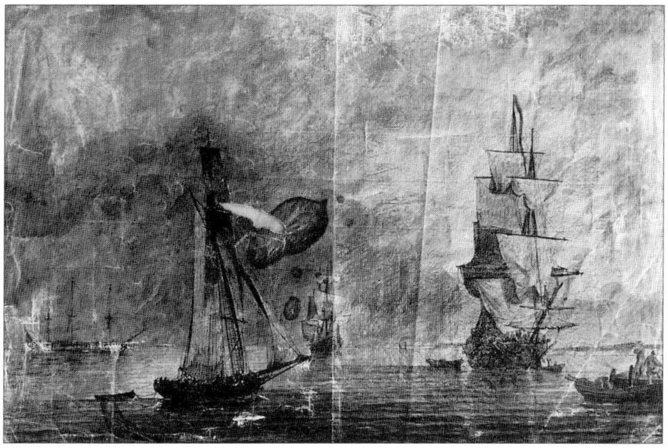

715

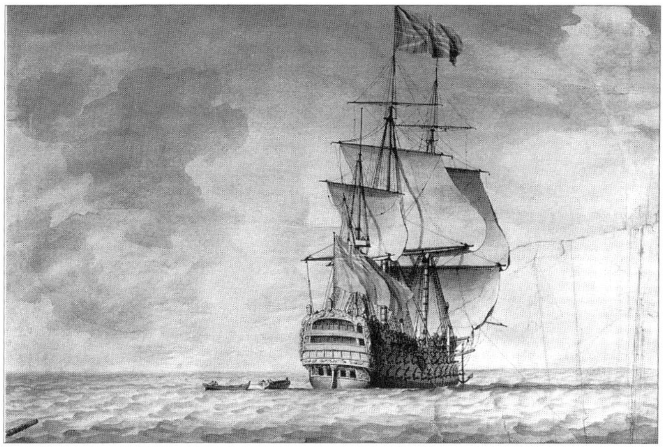

716

716 THE FLAGSHIP OF A COMMANDER IN CHIEF
Pen, ink and grey wash 11¾ x 18$\frac{3}{16}$. Signed C Brooking
Prov: Stanley Crowe Esq.
Mr and Mrs Paul Mellon 1965
Exhib: Mellon Foundation: Aldeburgh/Bristol June/July 1966, No. 70

717 TWO MEN OF WAR COMING TO ANCHOR IN A CALM
Pen, ink and grey wash 9¼ x 5¾. Signed C Brooking lower left
Prov: Walter Brandt Esq.

718 A 70 GUN THIRD-RATER LAYING AT ANCHOR
Pen, ink and wash 12¾ x 16⅞. Signed C Brooking lower left
Prov: Newman Sale, American Art Association, 7 February 1921 No. 15
Fairfax Murray Collection
A ship dated 1757 by its rigging. Superb, now missing.

719 A ROYAL VISIT TO THE FLEET
Pen, ink and grey wash 7¾ x 12 (s.s)
Prov: Dr R. C. Anderson
Mall Gallery, Bristol
Commander David Joel RN
A magnificent drawing. The King is in the first-rater, possibly the *Royal George*, which flies his Standard.

717 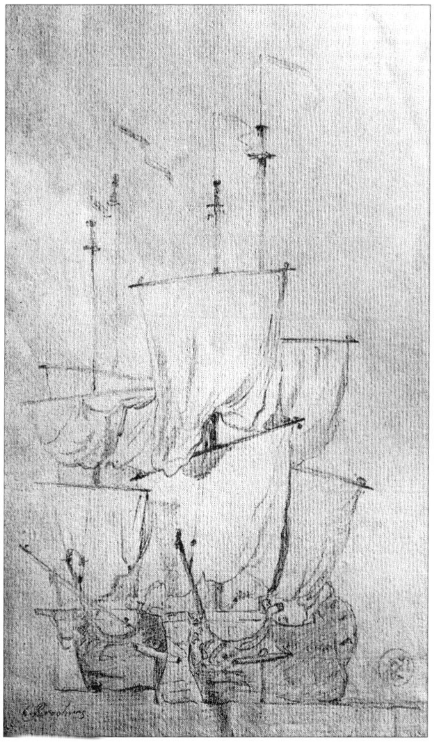

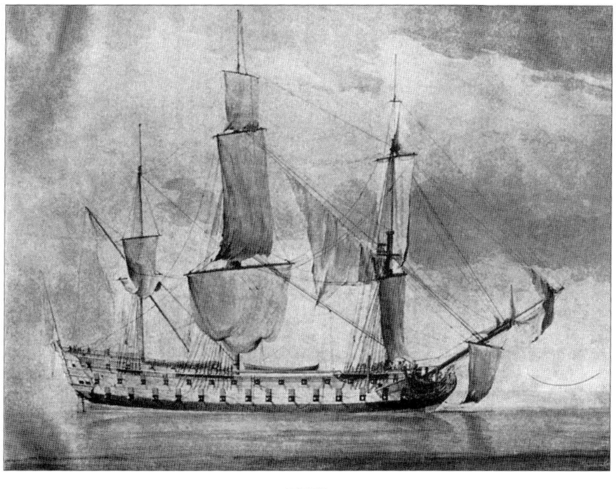

718

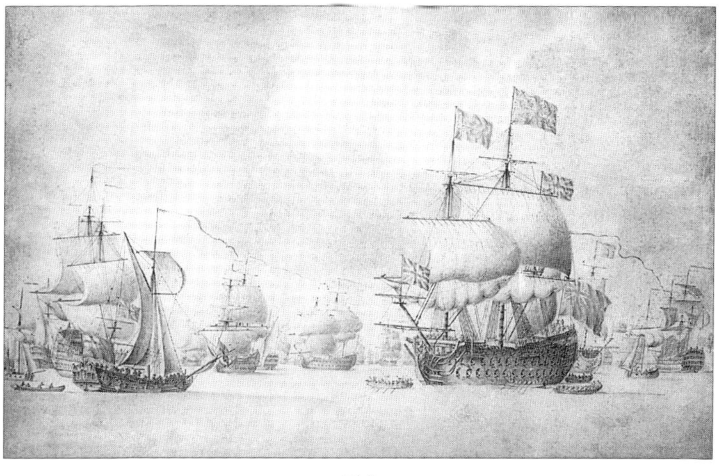

719

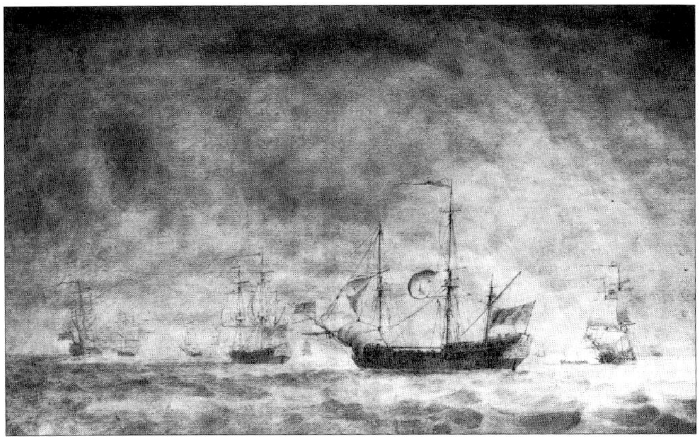

721

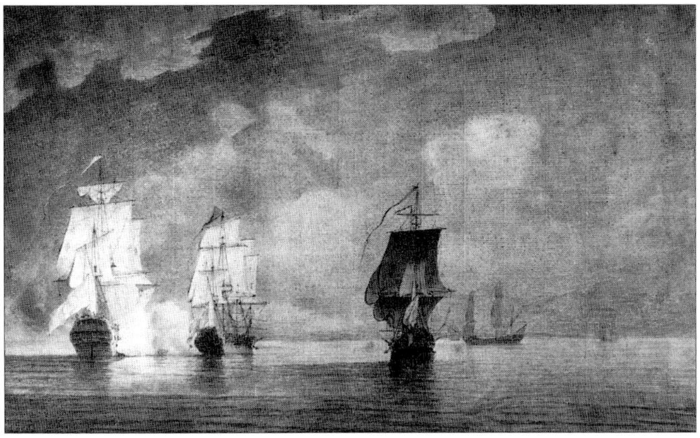

722

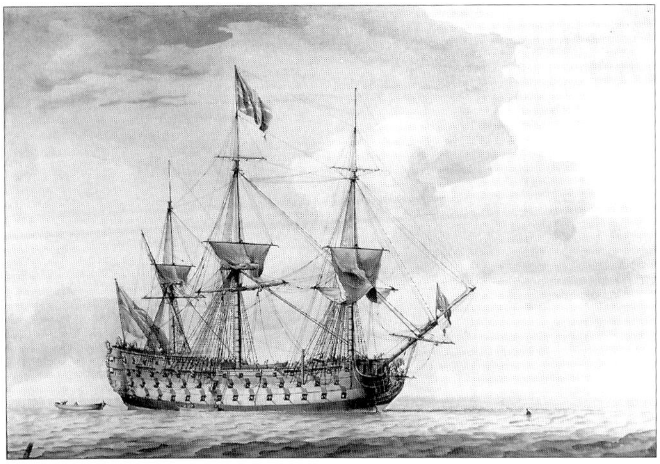

723

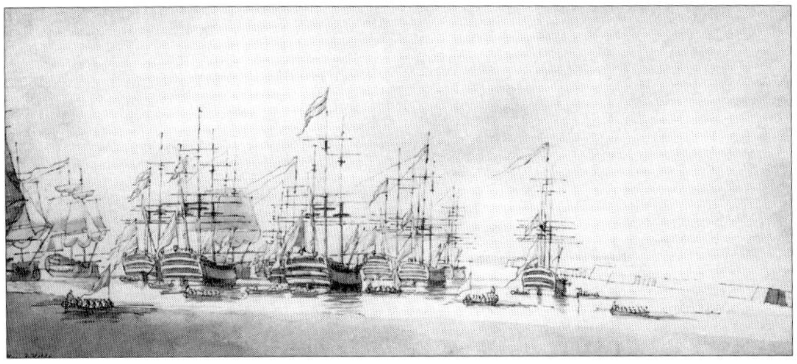

725

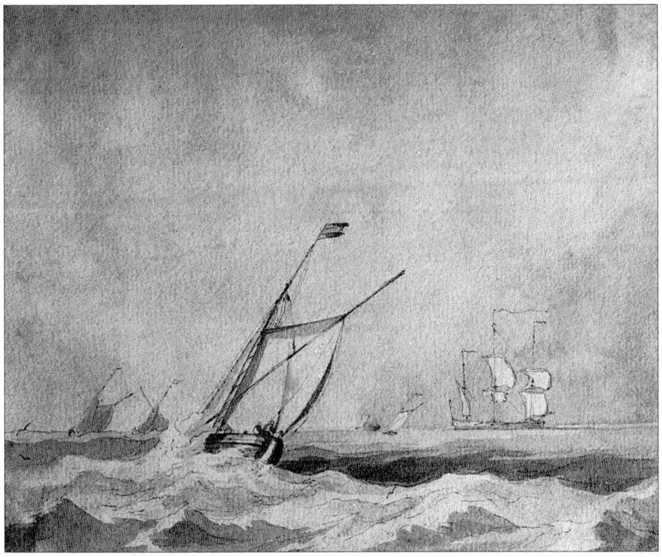

726

720 A THREE-DECKED MAN OF WAR FROM THE STARBOARD QUARTER (see Chapter 2, page 34)
Pen, ink and grey wash 12⅜ x 11½
Prov: Williams 1952 No 304
Victoria & Albert Museum
She wears a white ensign at the ensign staff and an Admiral's flag at the mizzen top.
Exhib: Mellon Foundation: Aldeburgh/Bristol June/July 1966, No. 68

721 THE *KING GEORGE* DISABLED DURING THE ENGAGEMENT WITH THE *GLORIOSA* 9 OCTOBER 1748
Pen, ink and grey wash 11½ x 18. Red chalk on reverse for tracing on to the engraver's plate. The wash has darkened, particularly in the sky. See engraving 616.
Prov: Private Collection
Exhib: Mellon Foundation: Aldeburgh/Bristol June/July 1966, No. 72

722 THE *PRINCE FREDERICK* WITH THE *KING GEORGE* ENGAGING THE *GLORIOSA* 8 OCTOBER 1748
Pencil and grey wash 11½ x 18. Red chalk on reverse. See engraving 613.
Prov: Sir Bruce Ingram
Leonard G. Duke Esq.
Christie's 5 March 1974 Lot 98 Unsold
Private Collection
Exhib: Mellon Foundation: Aldeburgh/ Bristol June/July 1966, No. 72.

723 THE *ROYAL GEORGE* AT ANCHOR
Pen, ink and grey wash 13¾ x 20¼. Signed C Brooking lower left
Prov: Christie's 4 March 1975 Lot 52 850 gns
Frank T. Sabin Ltd
Private Collection.

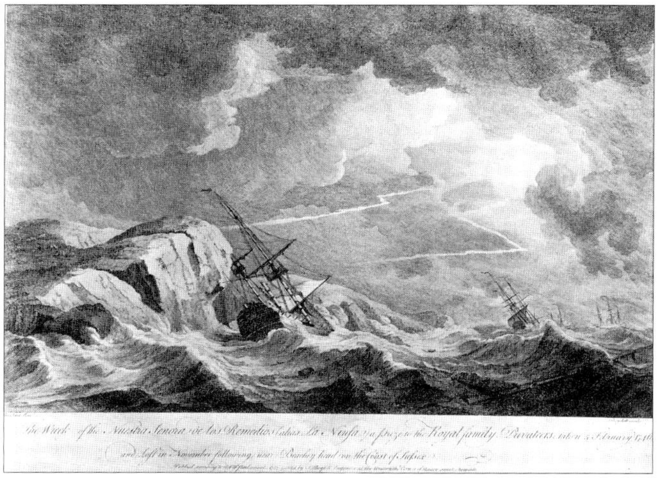
601

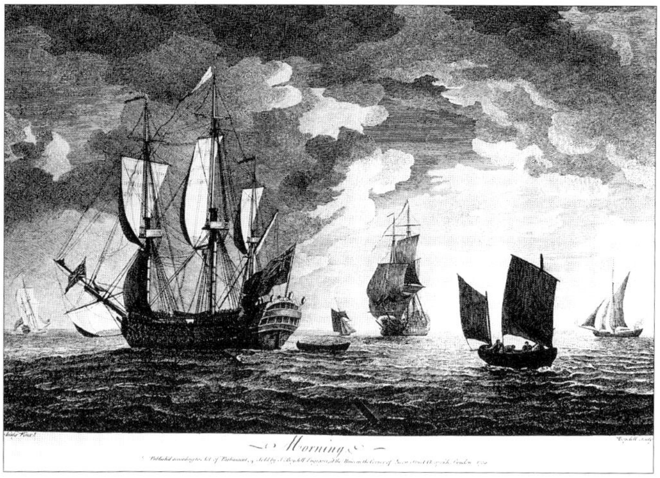

603

Exhib: Mellon Foundation: Aldeburgh/Bristol June/July 1966, No. 76
A very fine and detailed drawing.

724 THE THAMES – THE POOL
Pen and sepia wash 7¼ x 15½
Prov: Sir Robert Witt
Exhib: British Federation of Antique Collectors Exhibition 1932 No 134

725 A FLEET REVIEW
Pen, wash and faint trace of pencil 9 x 20½
Prov: Whitworth Art Gallery, Manchester
A note says Van de Velde, but the ships are of a later date.

There appear to be at least twelve ships of the line gathered in a calm around the flagship, with ships' boats converging on her. It is a most interesting and unusual drawing not repeated elsewhere. The men'o war are of Brooking's time. It is likely that this drawing is in fact by Dominic Serres, although the influence of Brooking is discernible.

726 A KAAG CLOSE-HAULED IN A STRONG BREEZE AND A HEAVY SEA
Pen, grey wash and traces of pencil approx 5½ x 6½. Traces of initials C.B. fecit
Prov: Sir Bruce Ingram (catalogued as Charles Brooking) Michael Ingram
Based on an oil painting No 707 by van de Velde the Younger. See p.802 M. S. Robinson, *The Paintings of the Willem van de Veldes* and illustrated Chapter 1, page 24 of this book.

ENGRAVINGS

Please note the titles are precisely those of the engravings. The prints are catalogued in the order in which they were discovered by David Cordingly, Colin Sorensen and James Taylor.

601 <u>The Wreck of the Nuestra Senora de Los Remedios (alias La Ninfa)</u> a prize to the Royal Family Privateers taken 5 February 1746, and lost in November following near Beachy Head on the coast of Sussex.
Engraved & Published by Boydell in 1753 at the Unicorn, Corner of Queen Street, Cheapside. 13⅜ x 18½. See painting 402 and drawing 710.

602 <u>A Cutter</u>
Engraved by Bickham 1768. Printed and sold by R. Marshall at No. 4 Aldermary Church Yard. 10 x 7 approx. See painting 238.
The engraver is almost certainly the London-based engraver, publisher and dealer George Bickham the younger (active 1730-71), perhaps best known for his satirical and political subjects. His father, George Bickham the elder, was also an engraver who died in Richmond in 1769. There are no records of the publisher and printseller R. Marshall.

603 <u>Morning</u>
Engraved and Published by Boydell in 1753 at the Unicorn, Corner of Queen Street, Cheapside. 11½ x 16⅛. See paintings 20 and 263.

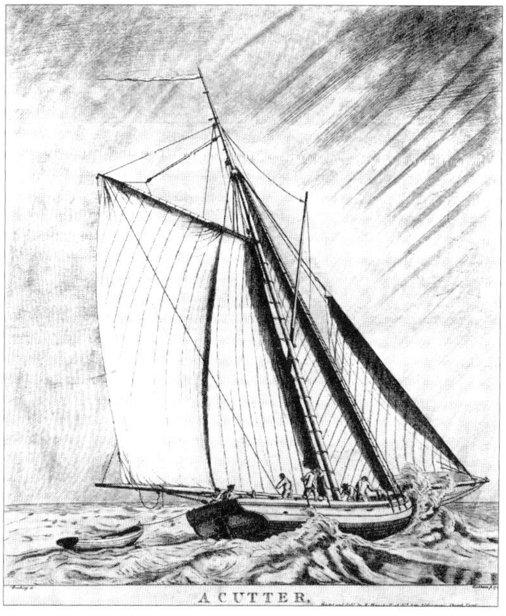

602

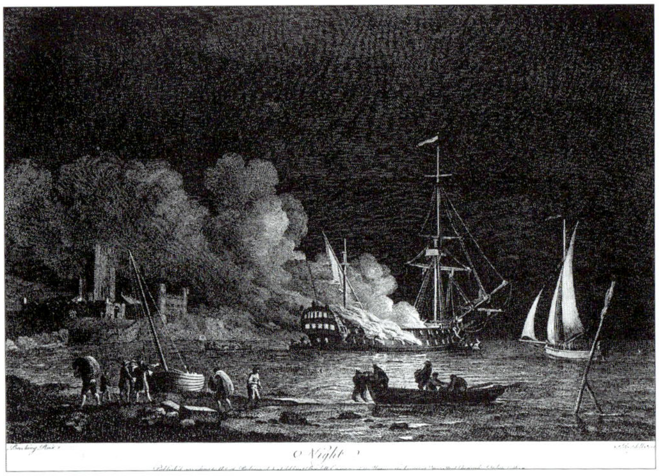

604

604 Night
Engraved and Published by Boydell in 1756 at the Unicorn, Corner of Queen Street, Cheapside. 11½ x 16⅝. See painting 153A.

605A Greenland Fishery (see Chapter 5, page 86)
Engraved and Published by Boydell in 1754 at the Unicorn. Corner of Queen Street, Cheapside. 11¾ x 16½. See painting 22A.

605B Greenland Whale Fishery – Peche de la Baleine a la Cote du Groenland
Engraved by Wilson. Printed for Robt. Sayer Map & Printseller at the Golden Buck in Fleet Street. Not dated. 7½ x 11.
The engraver Wilson may be James Wilson (active 1740s-80s).

605C Greenland Whale Fishery Plate 76
Coloured engraving 6 x 8.
Lit. & Ref.: *Whaling Prints in the Francis B. Lothrop Collection* by Elizabeth Ingalls, Peabody Museum of Salem, Massachusetts, 1987. See page **35**, no. 72.
A reverse copy of 605B. Of much cruder execution.

606 Evening
Engraved and Published by Boydell in 1755 at the Unicorn, Corner of Queen Street, Cheapside. 11 x 16½. See painting 246 and drawing 708.

607 Sun Setting
Engraved from a picture of Vandeveldes modernized and published by Boydell at the Unicorn, Corner of Queen Street, Cheapside, in 1753. See painting 1F.

608A The Taking of the Marquese de Antin & Louis Erasme two rich prizes from the South Seas by the Prince Frederick & Duke, Privateers with a view of the third ship which escaped. 10th July 1745. Lat: 43° 50'.
Engraved by Ravenet. No publisher given. 13¾ x 19. (Picture only 11$\frac{5}{16}$ x 17¾)
See painting 357.

608B Taking of the Marquese de Antin and Louis Erasme by the Prince Frederick and Duke, Privateers (see Chapter 5, page 77)
Engraved by Ravenet. Published 24 June 1818 by Jas Whittle and R. H. Laurie, No. 53 Fleet Street, London.
The plate seems to be the same as 608A but the inscription below is new. See painting 357. Size not yet known.

609 The Boscawen and Sheerness Privateers engaging a Fleet of French Ships from Martinico, five of which were taken, one sunk and two escaped 1745.
Engraved and Published by Boydell in 1753 at the Unicorn, Corner of Queen Street, Cheapside. 13¼ x 18¾. See painting 354 and drawing 714.

610A Hazy Weather (see Chapter 5, page 86)
After an Original Picture of Vanderveldt (Willem van de Velde the Younger). Engraved and published by Boydell at the Unicorn, Corner of Queen St, Cheapside. No date given. 11½ x 16¼. See painting 105.

610B Hazy Weather
Printed for Robert Sayer, Map & Printseller at the Golden Buck in Fleet Street.
No engraver, artist or date but it is the reverse of 610A. 7⅜ x 10⅞.
See painting 105.

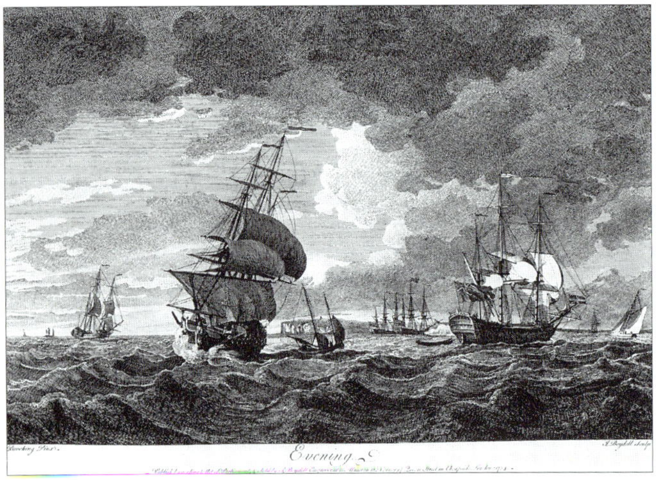

606

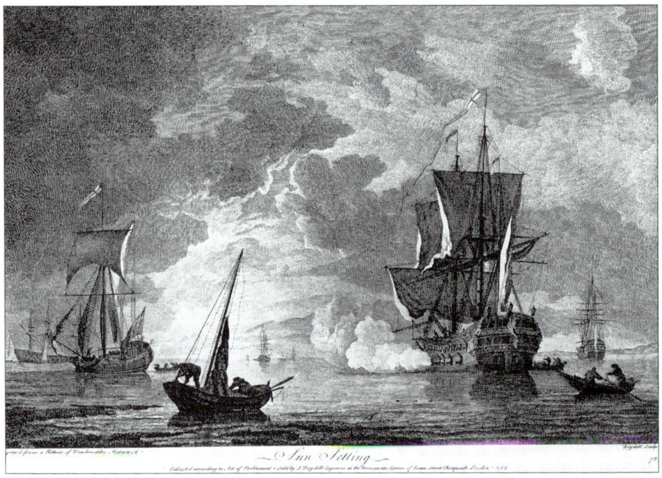

607

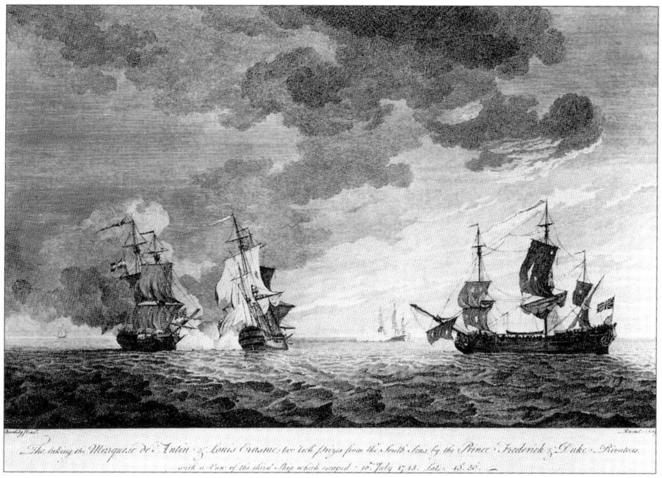

608A

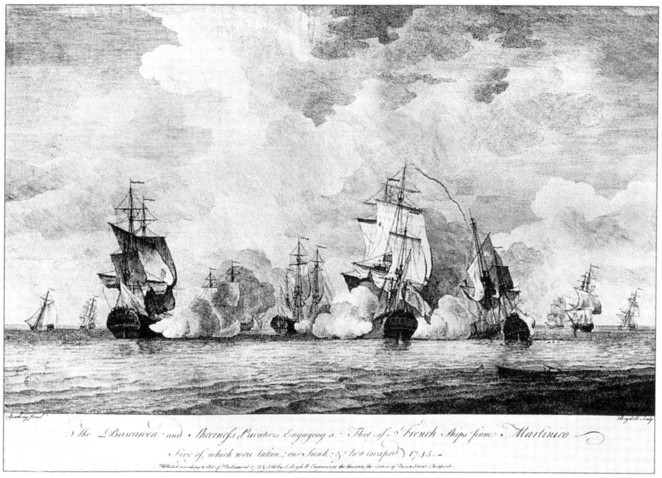

609

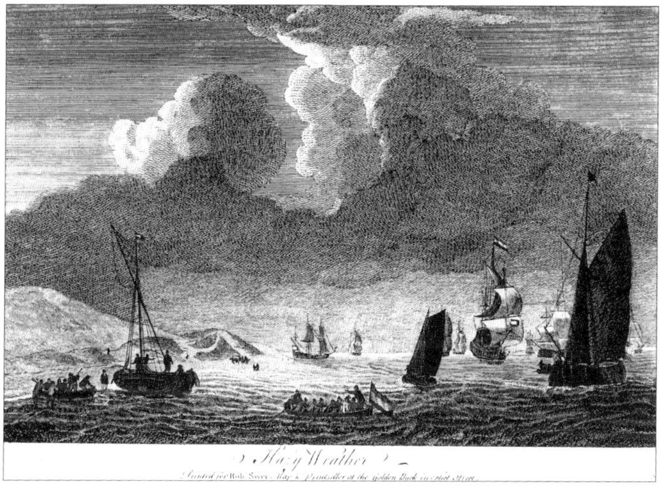

610B

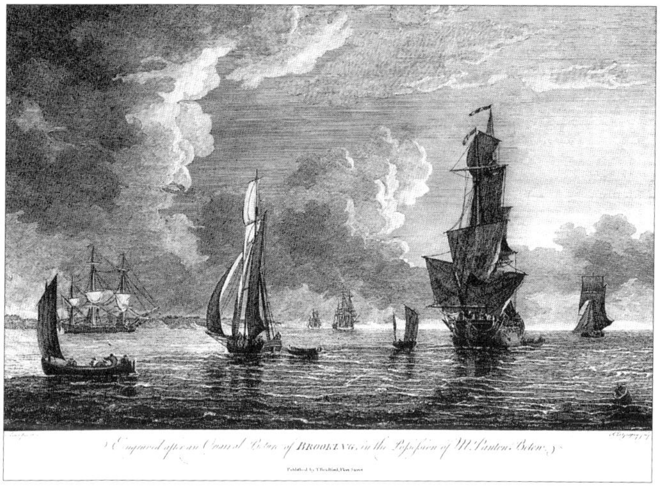

611

611 A Cutter and other vessels becalmed
Engraved after an Original Picture of Brooking in the Possession of Mr Panton-Betew.
Engraved by R. B. Godfrey and published by T. Bradford, Fleet Street. 14⅛ x 19¾.
There are few biographical details on the engraver Richard Bernard Godfrey. It is known that he was born in London in 1728. According to Timothy Clayton, author of *The English Print 1688-1802*, Thomas Bradford was the first Englishman to buy and then publish contemporary paintings.
Note: No date or title but it is taken from painting 15A which bears the title given above.

612 Noon
Engraved and published by Boydell in 1753 at the Unicorn, Corner of Queen Street, Cheapside, London. 11½ x 16$\frac{5}{16}$. See painting 15D and drawing 715.

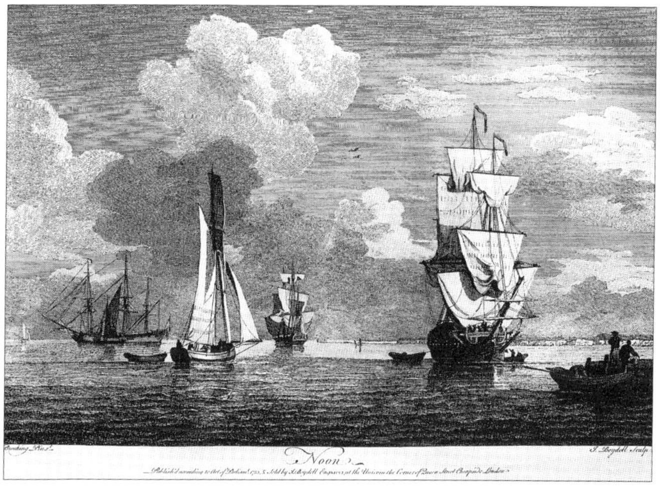

612

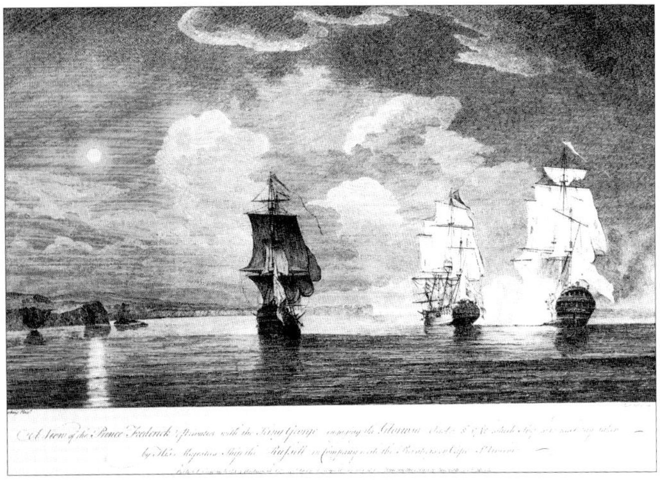

613

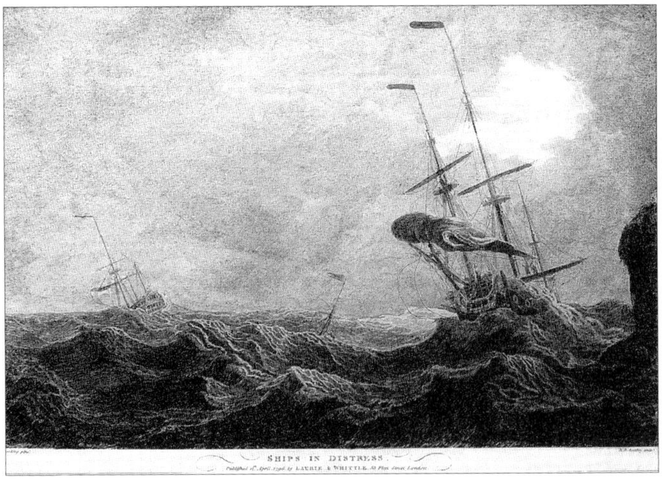

614

613 A View of the Prince Frederick privateer with the King George engaging the Gloriosa October 8th 1748 which Ship was next day taken by His Majesty's Ship Russell in Company with the Privateers off Cape St Vincent.
Engraved by Ravenet and published by Boydell in 1753 at the Unicorn, Corner of Queen Street, Cheapside. 13¾ x 18⅞. See drawing 707C.

613A The Prince Frederick Privateer, with the King George, engaging the Gloriosa, off Cape St. Vincent
Brooking Pinxt. Ravenet Sculpt.
Published 24th June 1818, by Jas. Whittle and R. H. Laurie, No. 53, Fleet Street, London.
Engraving. Hand coloured, 10 x 16½.
Lit. & Ref.: *Naval Prints from the Beverley R. Robinson Collection Volume I 1514-1791*, Beverley R. Robinson Colleciton. United States Naval Academy Museum, 1991.

614 Ships in Distress
Engraved by R.B. Godfrey and Published 12th April 1756 by Laurie & Whittle, 53 Fleet Street, London. 10½ x 15¾.
This engraving is taken from a plate by Peter Monamy engraved by R. B. Godfrey in the possession of Mr Bradford which is much earlier and which has been cut down by about an inch all around. Print-sellers lacked conscience 250 years ago!

615A A View of Elizabeth Castle in the Island of Jersey
Engraved by Le Comte and Published 24 June 1818 by Jas Whittle and R.H. Laurie. No 53 Fleet Street, London. 10¼ x 15¾. See painting 265.

615B East Prospect of Elizabeth Castle in Jersey (see Chapter 5, page 78)
Engraved and published by John Boydell. Plate size: 20⅞ x 28½ins
Pub: *A Collection of Views In England and Wales Drawn and Engraved by John Boydell To Which Are Added, Engraved By The Same Hand some miscellaneous Subjects After Various Masters*, sold by John and Josiah Boydell, No.90 Cheapside, and at the Shakespeare Gallery, Pall-Mall, London, 1790.
Title reads: 'To His Excellency John Huske Esq. Lieutent General of His Majesty's Forces, Colonel of His Majesty's own Royal Regimt of Welsh Fuzileers, Capt. Keeper and Governor in Chief of the Island of Jersey, and Commander in Chief of all the Castles, Forts, and Forces in the Same. This PROSPECT is most Humbly Presented by His Excellency's most Oblig'd and most Dutiful Servant Jas D'Auvergne.'
Based on engraving 620 but the plate has been reworked with a jetty and other vessels added.
This engraving incorporates a key indicating the names of buildings and hills, and their function. To the far left is St. Helier's Hermitage. The building to the right, with four chimneys, is identified as the 'Old Barracks'. The Union Flag flies from the 'Saluting Batterys'.

616 The King George disabled & the other Privateers in Chase with the Appearance of His Majestys Ship the Russell at the time the Dartmouth was blown up engaging the Gloriosa Oct 9th 1748.
Engraved and Published by Boydell in 1753, Corner of Queen Street, Cheapside. 13⅜ x 18½. See drawings 707D and 721.

617 An exact Representation of the taking of the Solebay Man of War by Captn Phillips of the Alexander Privateer of 20 Guns &140 Men belonging to Bristol. (see Chapter 5, page 76)
Published 25 Feb 1746 by T. Bakewell against Birchin Lane in Cornhill. 9¾ x 24⅝. See painting No.358 that was probably painted shortly after this action.
Thomas Bakewell (active 1729-48) moved his printselling business to Birchin Lane in 1745. He deserves to be better known, although his business has not enjoyed the same critical attention as Bowles, Sayer, or Boydell.

618 A Calm
Engraved and Published by Boydell in 1754 at the Unicorn, Corner of Queen Street, Cheapside, London. 11⅞ x 16½. Based on engraving 620 but the plate has been reworked with a jetty and other vessels added.

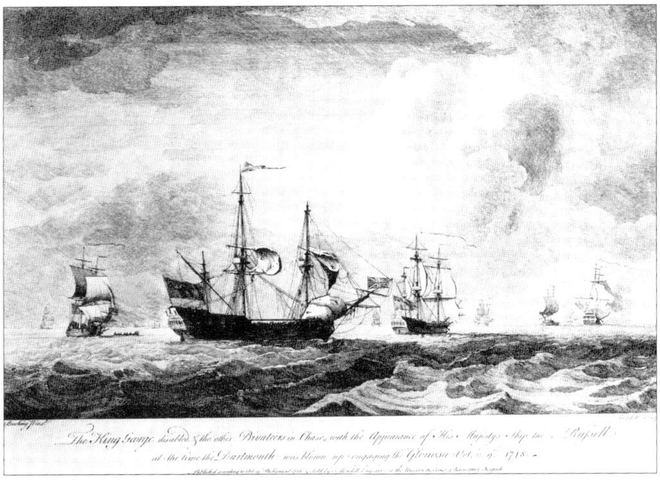

616

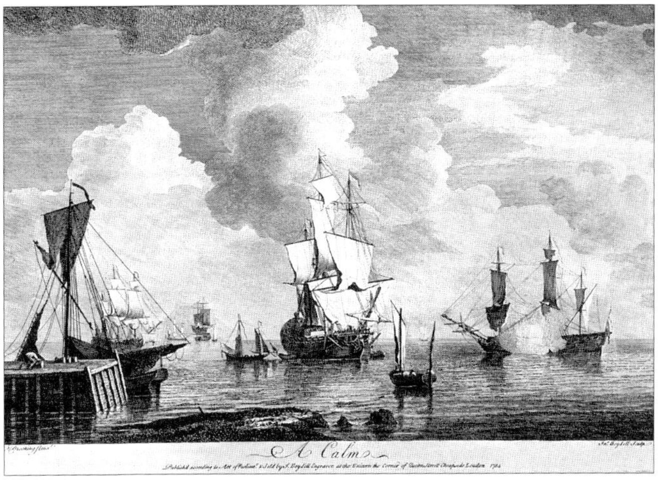

618

619 <u>A Small Breeze</u>
Engraved by Boydell, Hawarden 1753 and Published by Boydell at the Unicorn, Corner of Queen Street, Cheapside, London. 11½ x 16⁵⁄₁₆.

620 <u>The taking of the Nuestra Senora de los Remedios</u> a Spanish ship of 900 tons, 32 guns & 309 Men, very Richly Laden by the Royal Family Privateers 5 February 1746, off Cape St. Marys.
Engraved by Boydell. See drawing 707B which is dated 1746. 13¼ x 18½.

621 <u>Engraved from an Original Picture by Charles Brooking</u> in the collection of Mr Panton-Betew. Price 3 sh. 14¼ x 19¾
Engraved by P. Mazell and Published by Peter Mazell, Windmill Street, Tottenham Crt Road, London August 28th 1766. This is of the *Taking of the Marquese d'Antin and the Louis Erasme by the Prince Frederick & Duke 10 July 1745.* See painting 351 and engraving 611.
Peter Mazell is recorded in Benezit as an engraver who exhibited in London between 1761 and 1797. He is best known for his *Ruins and Romantic Prospects in North Britain* (1788).

622 <u>Corallines at low tide</u> taken from *Natural History of the Corallines* by John Ellis FRS. Illustrated by Charles Brooking and published in 1755.
The frontispiece, drawn in 1752, shows corallines in the Isle of Sheppey. But note the ships and their boats on the sea beyond. 9 x 6. (See Chapter 3, page 42)

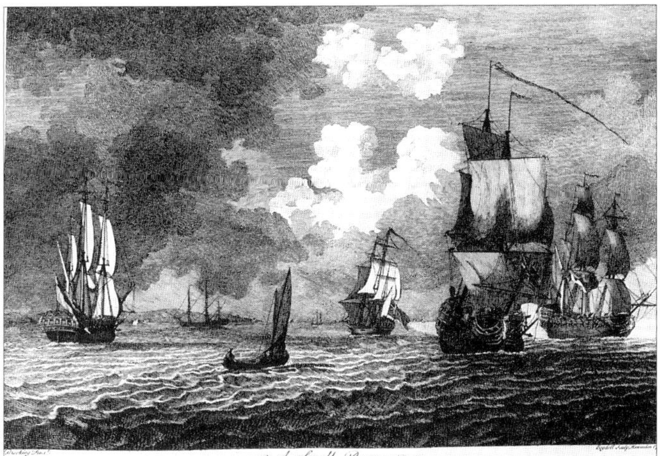

619

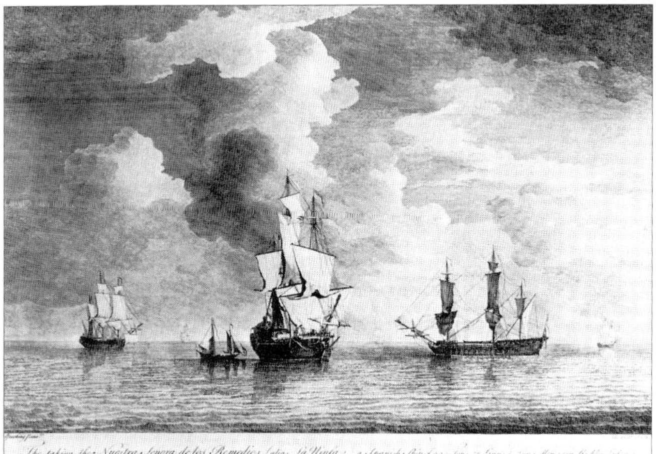

620

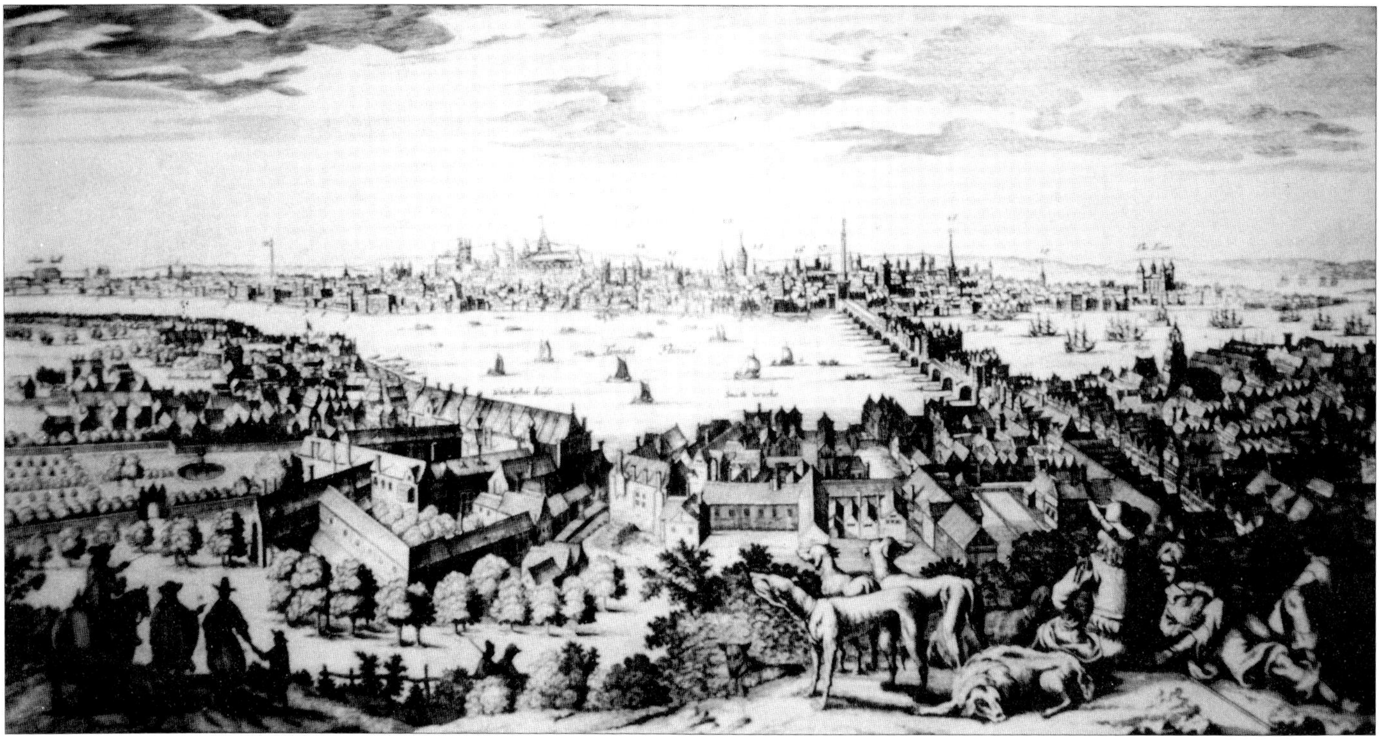

Appendix A

London during the 18th century

Guildhall Library map of London, view from the south of London Bridge.

The Great Plague broke out in England in 1665, five years into the reign of King Charles II. It was bubonic plague carried by the black rat and in London alone 68,000 people died. The next year witnessed the Great Fire of London, which lasted for four days and nights, destroying most of the wooden houses at the centre of the city and also St. Paul's Cathedral. These awesome events dictated a lengthy recovery time, as would be expected. St Paul's was rebuilt to Christopher Wren's design starting in 1673, to finish in 1711. Brooking was born just twelve years later, probably in Deptford, four miles down river from London Bridge, on the south bank of the Thames and about one mile from the Royal Palace at Greenwich.

By 1700 the population of England and Wales had stabilised at around 5.75 million persons, of whom only about 16 per cent, or 850,000, lived in towns and cities. The area around London, including all the surrounding villages, was said to have a population of no more than 700,000 but only 87,000 of these lived within the enclosing city walls in 1750. These numbers were all living within the area north of the Thames and between the Tower of London and Charing Cross. This was the area where Brooking was to live and work after moving from the dockyards at Deptford, Woolwich and Blackwall.

Samuel Pepys (1633-1703), the first Secretary to the Admiralty, records a great deal about London life including the events of the Plague and the Fire in his *Diary*, whilst William Hogarth (1697-1764) most ably records life in the early eighteenth century in his paintings. Hogarth is considered to be the first English-born picture maker of importance and the first of what is now a long line of national painters of distinction. Previous portrait and marine painters of any repute had all arrived from the mainland of Europe.

At the time of the Fire, London, like all medieval cities, had mainly timber and plaster houses fronting on to very narrow streets for the most part, the main reason for the rapid spread of the flames, coupled of course with the lack of water for fire-fighting. With so much of the old city destroyed, the opportunity was taken to improve the housing, by building in brick, stone and mortar, and to widen some of the narrow streets. Even so, the poorest section of the population, the majority, was crowded into most inadequate housing and diseases such

Map to show the lower Thames from Tilbury to Westminster

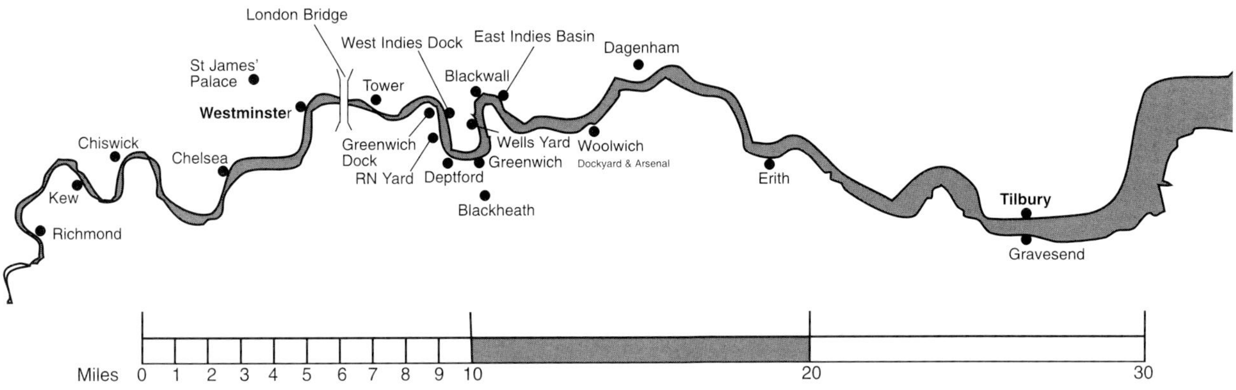

as typhoid, cholera and tuberculosis were endemic. Fresh water was hand-pumped from wells, whilst sewage and rubbish were poured into the street, eventually finding their way into the Thames, or taken out of the city and dumped on the countryside. The city was an evil-smelling place for the most part and, with the prevailing south-westerly winds, it was far more healthy to live in the west end of the city. To live in the east, at the Tower end, was most disagreeable. However, down river the separate hamlets of Deptford and Greenwich were in the country. Old London Bridge, where at one time Peter Monamy lived in one of the many large houses built upon it, must have been a comparatively healthy place to live. That bridge was so overloaded that the houses on it were removed in 1757. It was to be replaced by a new London Bridge in 1831, which was for traffic only with no houses on it at all.

The River Thames was much wider before the nineteenth century, which saw the infill of the banks to form roads on either side. However, in the time of the Old London Bridge, whose great breadth and width was supported on eighteen massive 'Starlings', the river tidal flow was much slower than today. This was because the river was so much wider and also because the 'Starlings' blocked both tide and current.

This hold-up of the water flow had the effect in heavily frosted weather of blocking the ice from passing under the arches and allowing the river to freeze over completely above the Bridge. So the great Thames Frost Fairs were made possible. There were six occasions when the frosts were sufficiently severe for this to happen: in 1608, 1683-84, 1715-16, 1739-40, 1788-89 and 1814. Strangely, neither Hogarth nor the marine painters recorded these events. William Hogarth would have seen the Fairs of 1715-16 and 1739-40. Indeed, we know that Hogarth attended the latter Fair, for he had one of those special tickets printed for his dog! Brooking must have been aware of the Fair too, but perhaps he was away at sea somewhere: we badly need to find out where he had been employed for, as Sawery Gilpin said, "he had been much at sea". So it was left to Dutch painters to record the scene. A quite brilliant painting by Jan Griffier the Younger recorded a 'View from the East near Whitehall' – the path across the ice from Whitehall stairs to Lambeth Palace for 1739-40, now in the Guildhall, London (see rear endpapers). Another important Fair painting by Abraham Hondius records 'The Frozen Thames in 1677' and shows the scene taken from the ice above Old London Bridge (now in the Museum of London).

Avercamp would have given much to depict these scenes, but as far as can be seen no English painter bothered with them. Perhaps there were no buyers who wished to remind themselves of those awesome cold spells or indeed the fatal accidents of those who, in the thaw, fell through the ice and were drowned.

It is tempting to think that with the small population of England and Wales it would have been an idyllic time to live there. Today, we have eight times that population and are relatively crowded, but this has to be put in perspective. This is where the insight given to us in Hogarth's pictures is important. London was a brutal place to live. Dirty, diseased, unhygenic, smelly, disorganised and downright foul to walk in. The only form of transport was a sedan chair or horse-drawn carriage for the well-to-do. For the remainder, travel was by foot and a lot of people could not afford shoes; or public horse-drawn car or coach, or horseback. With so many horses in London the streets were foul in any case. Rain to wash the streets clean would have been a blessing as long as you could stay dry. Transport by

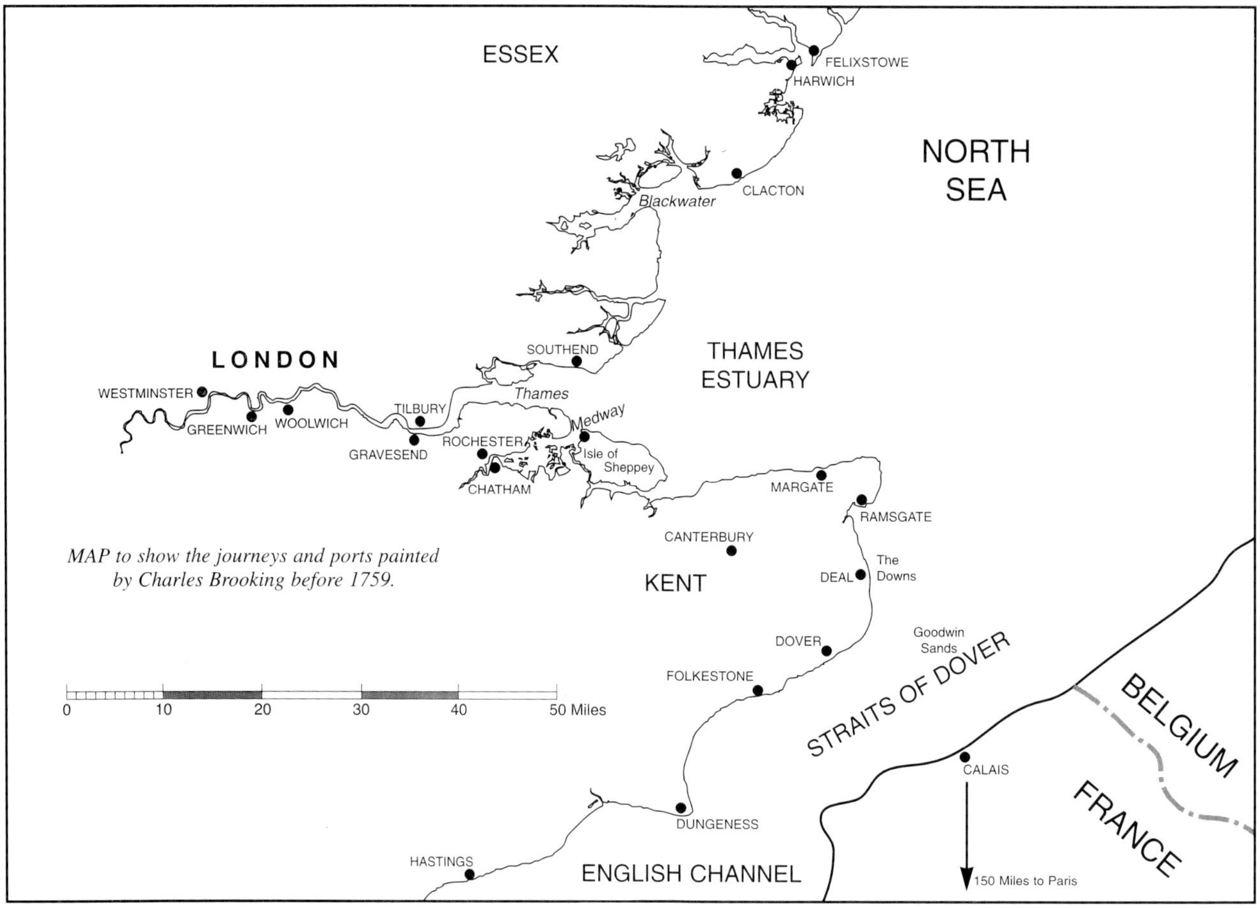

MAP to show the journeys and ports painted by Charles Brooking before 1759.

rowing-boat going down river would have been quite quick, but going up river against the tide could be time-consuming. But of course the pace of life was much slower. Equally, life was much shorter. To fall sick was a disaster, for the medical profession had barely got beyond using leeches to bleed people. Dentistry, as such, had not yet started.

For the poor there was little schooling available and few hospitals, none of which were free, no income support. Prison was the punishment for debtors and capital punishment for theft or anything worse than that. Housing conditions were quite deplorable, with large families occupying one room and even worse, one bed. There was a large number of unemployed. Thieving was endemic, filth everywhere; pity the poor woman in childbirth, many of whom did not survive, nor did their babies.

Until 1730 London had the unenviable reputation of being one of the worst lit cities in Europe, with candlelight only provided by householders in the winter months on dark nights. This was to change from 1736 onwards, when lights were hung out throughout the year in the city and really from then onwards there were improvements in every way. But most of this was too late for Brooking. For all of his life the water quality was awful and so indeed was the quality of bread, as records show.

It is strange to relate, but true, that "gin was the mother's ruin", a saying which is handed down to us. But this was a fact, particularly between the years 1720 and 1751, due to the very cheap and intoxicating liquor which was distilled and retailed indiscriminately in the city. This is all authoritatively researched and recorded in a remarkable book *London Life in the 18th Century* by Mrs Dorothy George, first published in 1925. In it she tells that, in 1725, there were over 6,000 houses and shops retailing spirits in the city, in one parish every fifth house. That in 1743 eight million gallons of spirits were sold. In Parliament it was stated that "gin was threatening to destroy the race". "The Chandlers shops provided the poorest classes with their staple food of bread, small beer and cheese – this staple fare became bread and gin, and it was even said gin only." A representation to the House of Commons in 1751 on the effects of spiritous

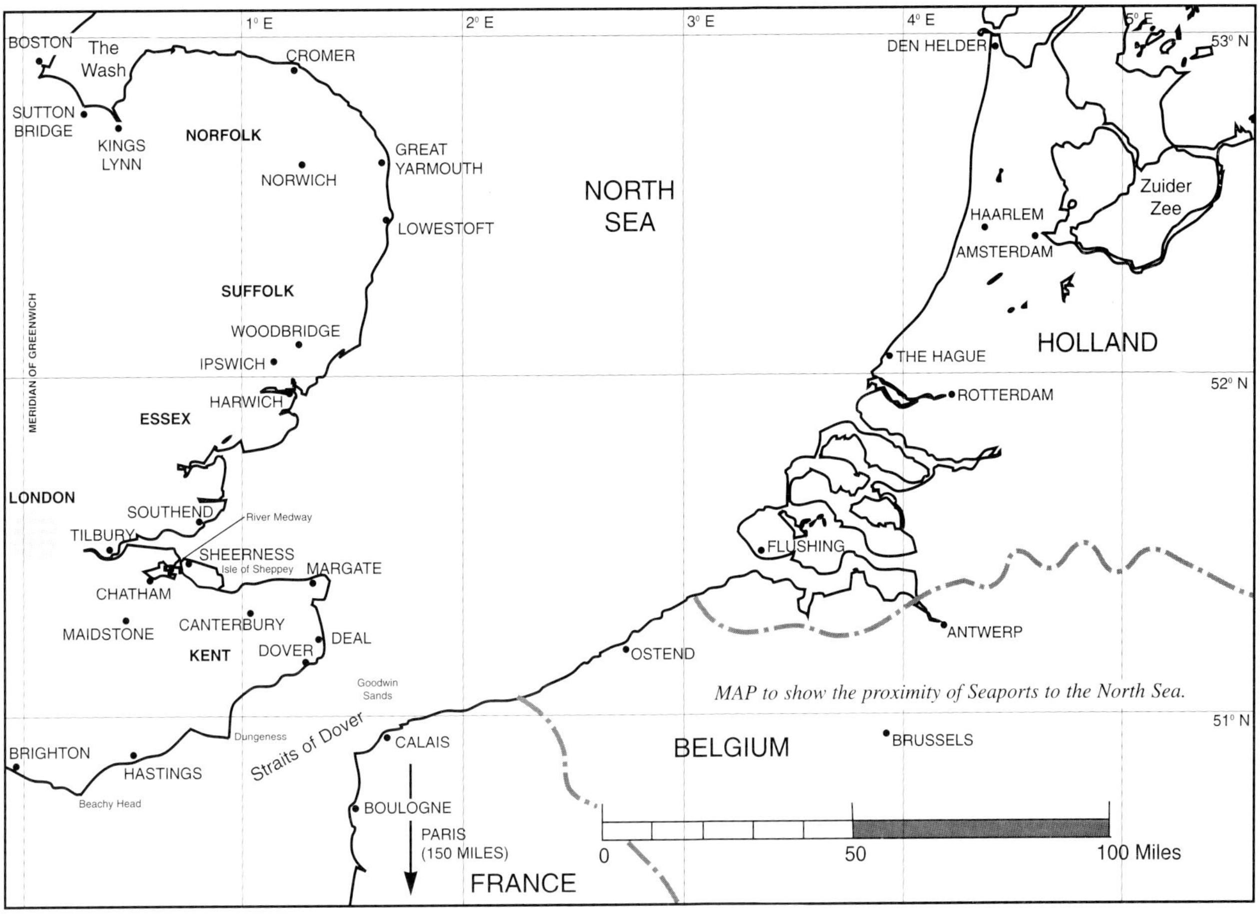

MAP to show the proximity of Seaports to the North Sea.

liquors estimated the annual loss in London since 1740 due to premature deaths of weak children under five and fewer births, as 9,323 – the population of the city, despite many new arrivals, actually fell in this period. In 1751 active measures were taken to reduce spirit consumption by making it too expensive, which after a period became fully effective, reducing the quantity drunk to one-eighth of the previous total.

This is recorded to show that Brooking's period of life in the City was one of the worst times ever to have lived there. It is not suggested that he was a spirit drinker, for he could not have made his pictures if he had have been. But all around him were drunkenness and unpleasant disorder, with frequent outbreaks of deadly diseases. The black rat, bad housing, bad water and food, coupled with desperately insanitary conditions, made life short and brutal for all the poor.

Brooking's places of abode

It is a reasonable assumption that the painter moved from the Deptford area to this great City of London around 1745, when he was twenty-two years old and when his first engraving was published by Ravenet. One can only generalise here, but we do know that he gave his address as Token House Yard, Lothbury on becoming a Governor of the Foundling Hospital in June 1754. Token House Yard is an important small yard off Lothbury, beside and on the northside of the Bank of England and adjacent to the little church of St. Margaret's Lothbury. One of its buildings housed an important branch of the National Westminster Bank, until recently the Directors' Boardroom. It was this branch which sold painting No. 233B in 1995, I suspect little realising that it may have been painted in a garret above their address at 41 Lothbury and that it was very valuable indeed.

The only other address we have is Castle Street, Leicester Square where Brooking is said to have died in March 1759. Leicester Square is only one mile from Token House Yard. Thus it would seem that with success he moved to the West and must have been familiar with the whole of the central area of London.

Appendix B

Collectors of Brooking's Paintings

The first known collector of Charles Brooking's paintings was the Barrister and Judge, Taylor White, who so far as we can discover was his first patron. It is known that he was the Treasurer of the Foundling Hospital. In 1754, after Brooking had presented his great painting of the 'Flagship before the Wind' as we call it to the Hospital, he was elected a Governor. A similar process had elected other outstanding painters of that period and this was very important to both the artist and the Hospital, for there was no National Gallery in those days. The Foundling Hospital became the prominent art centre in London, where the public could see collections of oil paintings, sculptures and decorative works, as well as visit the Foundling children. This became a fashionable thing to do.

So far as the painters were concerned, it was an excellent way of showing their pictures to the public and this continued until 1760, when the Society of Artists and later the Royal Academy were formed in central London.

When Taylor White died in 1774, there were three Brookings in his sale at Christie's, one of which, 'A Capital sea piece with a view of Dover', was sold for the remarkably large sum of £43.1s.0d (about £15,000 by today's wages).

One of the most colourful characters and collectors of Brooking's work during the artist's own lifetime was Panton Betew, or Panny to his friends. It is known that Betew's own collection included two recorded oil paintings by Brooking painted in the 1750s. They are: 'A cutter and other vessels becalmed' (No. 15A) now in the National Maritime Museum, Greenwich, and 'The Taking of the Marquese d'Antin and the Louis Erasme' (No. 351) now part of the Yale Center for British Art's collection, New Haven, USA. Both works were engraved. See Nos.611 and 621.

John Thomas Smith's *Nollekens And His Times* is the most comprehensive source on Betew. According to Smith, a former Keeper of Prints and Drawings at the British Museum, Joseph Nollekens (1737-1823), an acclaimed sculptor based in London, had engaged Betew in lively conversation during a sale at Greenwood's auction house. During the conversation Betew is credited with exclaiming "Ay I had many drawings and pictures by young artists, very clever fellows; but they are nearly all gone now. There was Brooking the Ship-painter; he died, poor fellow, just as he was getting into full song, as the saying is..."

Nollekens' biographer tells us that Betew had been "a silversmith of the old school, and also a dealer in pictures, drawings and other works of art. I recollect him well in my boyish days, at his house in Old Compton-street, Soho..." Betew was a friend of William Hogarth and sold pieces of armorial silver plate that Hogarth had engraved. Nollekens also reveals that Betew cut a dashing figure among dealers of the 18th century. Apparently his "...dress differed from the general mode: he wore a loose dark-brown great-coat with generally, a red cloth waistcoat...dark-grey worsted stockings, easy square-toed shoes, with small silver buckles and a large slouched hat with a round crown." Lamentably no such description of the garb of Brooking is known, although it is almost certain to assume he would have been attired in a more modest and sober manner. Although we know that Betew died in Chelsea, his exact birth and death dates have yet to be established.

William Wells, the shipbuilder, is also known to have owned Brooking's pictures. Farington records in his *Diary 1793-1821* in volume IV, with the entry of November 20th 1807, "William Wells of the East India Dock Office told Farington he would give me one of his paintings by Brooking". Whether he did or not, is not recorded.

The Wells family were well known shipbuilders at Deptford for several generations. The founder of the yard was Abraham Wells, who died in 1752. John Wells (1728-1794) was the next shipbuilder, to be followed by William, who made the offer to Farington. Until 1995 the descendants of this family had paintings by Brooking in their possession, Nos. 26A and 257B.

The first modern collection of Brooking's work was formed by the late Sir Bruce Ingram, the owner and editor of the *Illustrated London News*. Sir Bruce formed a magnificent collection of marine paintings in the 1920s and '30s and his munificent gifts to the National Maritime Museum formed no small part of the basis of the collection. He was a scholar and one of the first trustees of the Museum, which is deeply indebted to him. Sir Bruce died in 1963, having taken no small part in establishing the magnificent print room in the west wing, now wantonly destroyed.

His collection of paintings and drawings were sold at Sotheby's in eleven separate sales in 1964 and 1965. These sales included seven paintings by Willem van de Velde, four Monamys and no less than eleven Brookings. Their prices varied widely but the finest Brookings reached record prices, at that time the highest price being £15,500 for a version of the 'Evening Gun' (No. 1D).

In addition to the above, Sir Bruce gave a further three Brookings to the NMM, which owns the largest collection of the latter's paintings, all of which have been acquired since 1934.

Today, the NMM has no less than twenty-two oil paintings by Brooking, through the purchasing policy of its founders Sir James Caird and Professor Geoffrey Callender, and the gifts of Sir Bruce Ingram.

The National Collection in the Tate Gallery by comparison has only three Brooking oil paintings, and there are none in the National Gallery, which shows van de Velde, de Vleiger and Vernet instead. A Brooking in the National Gallery is long overdue. As the greatest maritime nation we need to put this right. We should honour our marine painters, more particularly when they are as good, if not better, than those from France or Holland.

The other great collection, formed since 1961, is that of the American the late Paul Mellon, KBE, whose Foundation for the Study of British Art sponsored the first ever Brooking exhibition at Aldeburgh and Bristol in 1966. Mellon, in the years 1961 to 1971, acquired no less than twenty oil paintings, two drawings and many engravings by Brooking via the London art market, many of which he has given to The Yale Centre for British Art at New Haven, Connecticut. Rather surprisingly they sold five of his paintings at Sotheby's in 1981, including his second earliest painting, the moonlight scene (No. 52).

There are two other large collections, both private, in the UK, one of which has ten oil paintings and the other six.

The story of the four Royal Family Privateer drawings is rather unusual. They had been sold in New York in 1943 and were given later to President John F. Kennedy, who hung them in the Oval Room in the White House in Washington. He accepted them in memory of his brother Lieutenant Joseph P Kennedy Jnr USNR, who died in the Second World War, on the condition that on the President's death they should be given to the National Maritime Museum in London. That dreadful assassination occurred in Dallas on 22 November 1963 and the drawings are now safely at Greenwich, London.

Other museums and art galleries which have paintings and drawings are listed as follows:

Ashmolean, Oxford	1 painting 234D
British Museum	2 drawings
Culzean Castle, Ayr	2 paintings 26A and 234E

Ferens Art Gallery, Hull	1 painting 201A
Glasgow Art Gallery	1 painting 242
Holburne Museum, Bath	1 painting 451
Kendal Whaling Museum	1 painting 22B
Leeds Art Gallery	1 painting 39A
Lloyds Committee Room	1 painting 258
Mariners Museum, Newport News	1 drawing 703
Royal Naval College, Greenwich	1 painting 2A
St John's College, Oxford	1 painting 36
Thomas Coram Foundation, London	1 painting 231A
Victoria & Albert Museum	1 drawing 706

Thus nearly one-third of all the Brooking paintings extant are now to be found in museums, in consequence his work comes only rarely to the auction rooms today.

Brooking paintings recorded in major 18/19th Century sales at Christie's

On 17-18 August 1772 Christie's sold the contents of Zoffany's house, garden and stables at his dwelling situated by the Six Mile Stone on the road leading to Brentford in the County of Essex. This included paintings attributed to Stubbs, Brooking, Rubens and Vernet etc.

In this sale, as in the others that follow, due to the lack of description, where the sizes are not given, it is impossible to identify paintings so briefly mentioned. But it does show which painters were considered important at the time. From Zoffany's sale we see that Brooking is aligned with other very well known painters.

The sale of Dominic Serres, Esq, RA, lasted for four days at Mr Christie's Great Room in Pall Mall from 13-15 March and again on 18 April 1794. On the first day of the sale no less than 505 drawings and seven sketch books said to be by van de Velde were sold for the sum of £6. 9s 0d and 14s. 0d respectively. Three oil paintings by Brooking were also sold. It is likely that among the enormous number of drawings assigned to the van de Veldes were sketches and drawings by Brooking.

At Richard Paton's sale, at Wardour Street, Soho by Christie's on 30 March 1792 lot no. 8 was a Brooking 'Sea Piece'. It was in good company with three Rembrandts, a Titian, three Brueghels, two Rubens, one Poussin and three Teniers, all belonging to Mr Paton, a fine collection indeed.

Mr. Christie's sale of 'A Valuable and Capital Collection of Pictures, Late the property of the Earl of Bute, deceased; Brought from his Seat at Highcliffe, in the County of Hants...' was held at his Great Room in Pall Mall, London on Saturday, March 19th 1796 and reveals a remarkable collection of English, Dutch and Flemish art from the seventeenth and eighteenth centuries. Mr. Christie proudly boasted on the front of the catalogue that the sale contained 'The very best Specimens of some of the most esteemed Masters, and the First Marine Collection ever offered to public.' It may not have been the first, but it was certainly the most significant maritime collection to be sold in the eighteenth century by a collector rather than an artist. In addition to paintings by van Goyen, Beerstraten, Cuyp, de Vlieger, the van de Veldes, Dubbels, Bakhuizen, Storck, Canaletto and Vernet, there were examples by Monamy, Scott, Serres, Wright, Paton and Luny. But by far the most popular artist in the late Earl of Bute's collection was Brooking.

Seven pictures were included in the sale and described as follows: 'A sea view with a brisk gale', 'A storm with a fleet in distress', A calm with shipping', 'A sea piece, a pleasing cabinet picture' [and two similar lots], 'A sea piece'.

The Earl of Bute's collection was appropriately housed at Highcliffe Castle in Hampshire, dramatically situated above the coast between Hurst Castle at the western approach to the Solent and the ancient town of Christchurch. Highcliffe Castle was destroyed after his death, although many of the pictures have survived. The sale total raised the relatively modest sum then of £1,084 19s 6d. Later on another castle was to be built on the same site at Highcliffe, but it bore little comparison to Bute's earlier magnificent fortified home.

In the following century at John Boydell's and his son Joshua Boydell's sale by their successor Mr Harrison at No. 90 Cheapside, in the spring of 1818, there is a quite remarkable catalogue of engravings and copper plates which were sold. An annotated catalogue is held at the Guildhall Library, London, which is revealing. No. A.1.5. No. 93 is the reference which shows that all of the engravings after Brooking by Ravenet, Boydell and Le Comte were sold with their copper plates and paper prints for mere shillings. Many were bought by Lawrie & Whittle and republished. Others were bought back by the successor Harrison, including that of Elizabeth Castle (Lot 35 and Lot 222).

To help my successors in this research, here are the addresses of the principal purchasers:

1819	LAWRIE	William. Printer and Engraver 146 Tooley Street, Borough (Southwark)
1820	LAWRIE	Richard H. Map, Chart & Print Seller 53 Fleet Street, London.
	LAWRIE	William. Printing Office 146 Tooley Street
1821	LAWRIE	Richard Holmes. Map & Print Seller 53 Fleet Street
1820	HARRISON	John, Copper Plate Printer 42, Little Sutton Street/Goswell Street
1820	HARRISON	T.R. Engraver & Printer 6 Lancaster Court, Strand
1821	HARRISON & THOME	Printers. 2 Red Lion Court, Fleet Street
	HARRISON	A.P. Engraver 4 Charlotte Street, Rathbone Place

Harrisons today are important printers. But could they or their predecessors have harboured the very important copper plates by Boydell and Brooking over the last 175 years? You never know. Research in some gloomy store might reveal them.

Appendix C

Brief notes on the history of Brooking's period of painting

Queen Anne was to outlive her children and when she died in 1714 her heir, a cousin, George, Elector of Hanover, became King George I of England. Charles Brooking was born in the ninth year of his reign which was to last until 1727, when he was succeeded by his son George II. So the remainder of the artist's short life was lived during this reign, and for the greater part of his life Sir Robert Walpole was Chief Minister in Whig administrations.

Surprisingly few wars or naval battles occurred in Brooking's lifetime. In the war of the Austrian Succession, 1740-48, Britain did take part with an army in support of Queen Maria Theresa of Austria. This army was actually led into battle by King George II, the last British Monarch to do this. He won a major victory over the French at Dettingen in Bavaria in 1742. This was ended with the Treaty of Aix-la-Chapelle in 1748. Thus Britain had helped to prevent the growth of French power in Europe at that time.

After this came the Seven Years War 1756-63 which could be divided really into two wars: The continuation of the fight between Britain and France for the control of India and North America and a war in Europe between Prussia and Austria. Britain was allied with Prussia, whilst this time France was allied with the Austrians.

At first Britain and Prussia suffered many defeats but in 1759 the tide turned, with a number of good victories. The British defeated the French at Minden in Germany and won control of Canada from the French, after Wolfe's Battle in Quebec. We also defeated the French at Quiberon Bay in 1759. Spain joined with France, in 1762, but by the end of the year Britain and Prussia had won the war and in 1763 the Treaty of Paris was signed, with Britain gaining Canada, most of the territory to the West of the Mississippi River and nearly all of the French West Indies. We also became the dominant power in India. It has to be said that the French always saw their Fleet as an adjunct to their Army, whilst the Royal Navy practised outright Sea Power.

Brooking died in the year of Hawke's great victory at Quiberon Bay, and it was left to Dominic Serres and Richard Paton to paint up that victory.

From all the above we see why the only battles in Brooking's time, which he was commissioned to paint, were small frigate actions, mainly by the Royal Privateers, and other minor but successful British actions, which in any case, involving few ships, were more to his compositional liking. In most of his paintings he showed a great sense of space between the ships, enabling a fine sense of sea, sky and often changing weather. He did not portray any crowded battle scenes.

NAVAL BATTLES AND EVENTS LEADING UP TO AND INCLUDING CHARLES BROOKING'S LIFETIME

1652-1654	FIRST DUTCH WAR
1655-1667	SECOND DUTCH WAR
1672-1673	THIRD DUTCH WAR
	The van de Veldes arrive in England and live at East Lane, Greenwich.
1691	The van de Veldes move to Sackville Street, Westminster.
1693	Willem van de Velde the Elder dies, aged 82, buried at St James' Church, Piccadilly.
1707	Willem van de Velde the Younger dies, aged 74, also buried at St. James' Church, Piccadilly.
1717	Cornelis van de Velde, brother of the Younger, actively painting in London. His father-in-law was Jan van der Hagen (marine painter).
1702-1713	WAR OF THE SPANISH SUCCESSION (against France and Spain)
1702	August 20-24. Four day action in the West Indies between Benbow and Ducasse. October 12. Rooke at Vigo Bay. Capture of the Treasure Ships.
1703	November 16. The Great Storm. London flooded. Eddystone lighthouse destroyed. Thirteen English men-of-war lost at sea.
1704	July 23. Rooke captures Gibraltar. August 13. BATTLE OF MALAGA
1707	October 10. H.M.S. *Cumberland* and consorts taken by De Forbin and Duguai Trouin. October 23. Sir Clowdisley Shovell wrecked off the Scilly Isles.
1708	May 28. Commodore Wager's Action with the Spanish Treasure Fleet off Carthagena, West Indies. October 30. Sir John Leake takes Minorca.
1713	Treaty of Utrecht. England keeps Gibraltar and Minorca (until 1782), Nova Scotia and New Foundland. England is acknowledged as the major sea power.
1715	First Jacobite rising.
1718-1720	WAR WITH SPAIN
1718	August 11. Sir George Byng defeats the Spanish Fleet off Cap Passaro.
1723	Charles Brooking born.
1739-48	THE WAR OF JENKIN'S EAR (with Spain)
1739	November 20. Admiral Vernon takes Porto Bello, Venezuela
1740-1744	Anson circumnavigates the World.
1741	March-May. Vernon fails to take Cartagena.
1743	June 20. Anson captures the Manila treasure ship *Nuestra Signora de Cavadonga* carrying an enormous treasure.
1744	February 11. Mathews and De Court off Toulon. October 4. Loss of Admiral Balchin in the *Victory* on the Casquets off Guernsey.
1745	The second and last Jacobite uprising. July 10. Commodore James Talbot and the Royal Family Privateers take the French ships *Marquese d'Antin* and *Louis Erasme* carrying over £1,000,000 in bullion landed in Bristol.
1746	February 5. The Royal Family Privateers capture the Spanish ship *Nuestra Senora de Los Remedios*. April 10. Captain Phillips in the *Alexander* cuts out the *Solebay* off the Isle of Ré. May 3. Two large French Privateers drive off *Greyhound*, 20 guns, and the brigantines *Baltimore* and *Terror*.
1747	May 3. Anson's victory in the First Battle of Finisterre. October 14. Hawke's victory in the Second Battle of Finisterre, painted by Dominic Serres.
1748	March 8. Capture of Port Louis – Cuba, painted by Dominic Serres. October 1. Knowles' action off Havana. October 8. The Royal Family Privateers capture the French ship *Gloriosa* off Cape St. Vincent.
1748	October. Peace with France and Spain, Aix la Chapelle.
1752	Dominic Serres taken prisoner off Havana, brought to England and lodged in the Marshalsea Gaol, Southwark, London.
1755	February 14. Admiral Charles Weston and Colonel Clive take the Private stronghold at Geriah.
1756-1763	WAR WITH FRANCE – THE SEVEN YEARS WAR.
1756	May-June. Byng's action off Minorca and the subsequent loss of the Island and the base of Port Mahon. February. Dominic Serres paints the Capture of Geriah.
1757	January 2. Admiral Watson takes Calcutta. March Capture of Chadnagore (painted by Dominic Serres). March 14. Execution of Admiral Byng at Spithead October 21. Captain Forest's action off Cape François, North America.
1758	February 28. H.M.S. *Monmouth* takes the *Foudroyant*. April 29. Admiral Pocock's action with Comte d'Ache's Squadron off Cuddalore. April. Hawke attacks Rochefort. January 5. The Hon. Richard Howe lands at St. Malo but fails to take it July 26. Admiral Boscawen takes Louisbourg. August. Howe destroys Cherbourg. December 20. Commodore Keppel captures the island of Goree off Dakar, painted by Dominic Serres.
1759	March. Charles Brooking dies.
1763	February 10. Treaty of Paris signed ending the Seven Years War.

Appendix D

Types of ships of the period and their boats

Some Profiles for the Rates of the Establishments of Men o'war of 1745

First, Second and Third-rates
All are three-deckers with 100, 90 and 80 guns respectively. Lengths on the gun-deck 178, 170 and 165 feet.

Figureheads
First and Second rates have individual figure heads. The Third rates and all the lower rates have a lion figure head.

Third-rates of 70 guns and 60 guns
A two decker of 160 feet and 150 on the gun-deck.

Fourth-rate
A two-decker of 50 guns, 144 feet on the gun-deck.

Fifth-rate
A two-decker of 40 guns, 133 feet on the gun-deck.

Sixth-rate
A two-decked ship of 24 guns, with most of her battery on the upper-deck, and oars on the gun-deck which measured 113 feet.

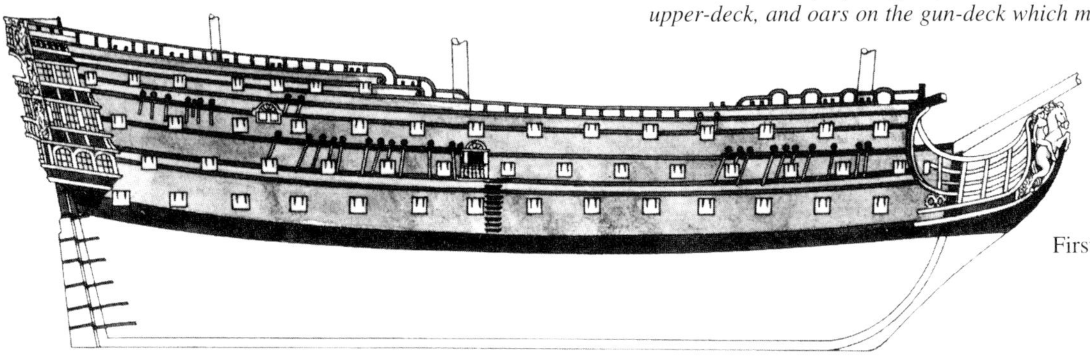

First-Rate (100 guns)

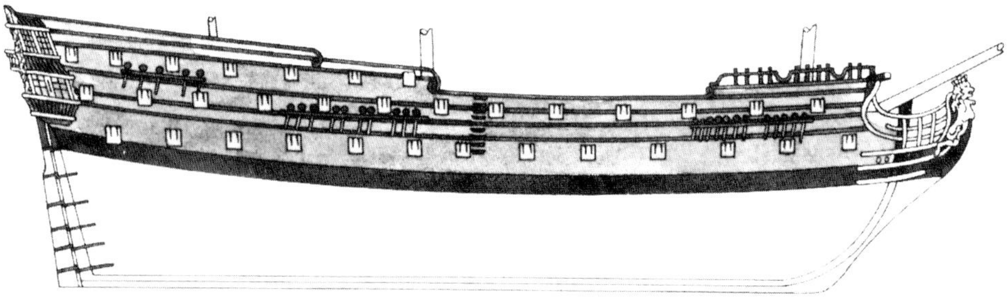

Third-Rate (70 guns)

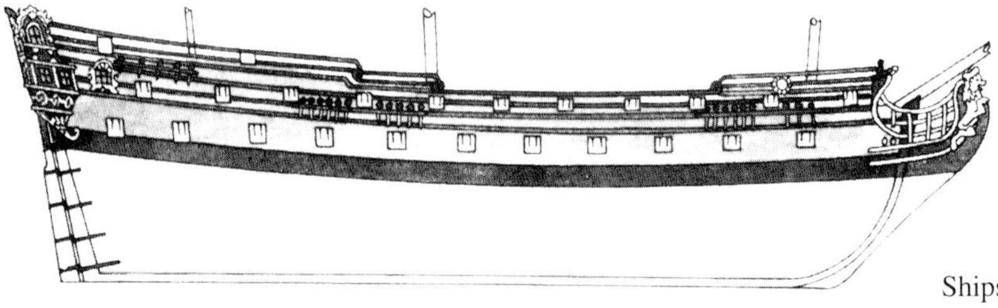

Fourth-Rate (50 guns)

Ships of the Battle Line (above)

Frigates (below)

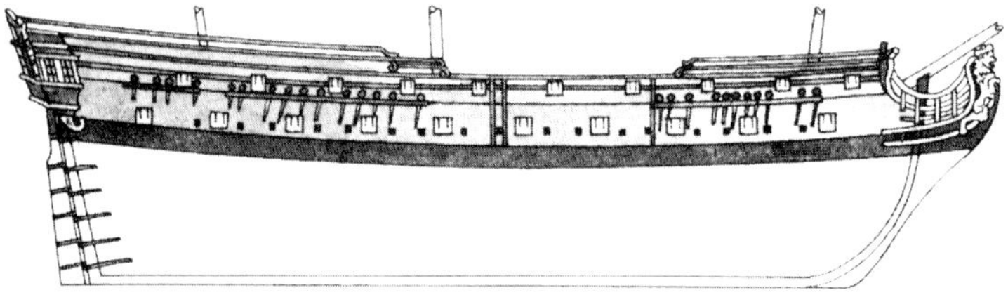

Fifth-Rate (40 guns)

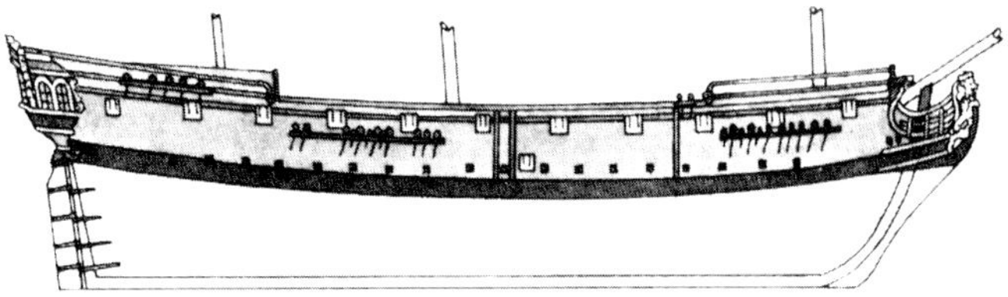

Sixth-Rate (24 guns)

Ships' boats in Brooking's paintings

The Royal Navy has always had a variety of boats best suited to each type of ship and the tasks they had to undertake. The designs of these boats, all of wooden construction, did not alter much with the passage of time. There were whalers, cutters, pinnaces, gigs, longboats, barges and others. It is useful to identify these eighteenth century boats in Brooking's paintings, particularly as he invariably illustrated the correct boat with its parent vessel, a detail which may have escaped the eye of the connoisseur but which would have been apparent to every sailor of the day. Indeed, to have shown the wrong boat pulling away from its parent ship would have been to show the artist's ignorance of naval matters.

There were, of course, circumstances in which the commander could insist on a more specially designed craft. For instance, in 1740 for Anson during his circumnavigation of the world, for Cook on his Antipodean and Pacific voyages and for HMS *Pandora* (Captain Edward Edwards) when she was sent specifically to Tahiti and associated Pacific islands to recapture Fletcher Christian and the *Bounty* mutineers.

Royal Yachts, and there were many of them, were stationed at strategic naval ports such as Yarmouth, Chatham, Dover, Portsmouth, London and Plymouth to act as despatch vessels for the Admiralty or Royalty and, like the Royal Yacht *Caroline*, carried more specialised boats and royal barges.

All men o'war and merchant ships had crews familiar with both rowing and sailing, thus most boats were dual purpose, with masts and sails to supplement the oars. Ships' boats within the fleet were regularly used for armed boardings, for landing marines and troops, for cutting ships out of enemy harbours and of course for attacking enemy forts and strongholds. They were also used for laying out anchors, transferring mail and provisions and for the thousand and one tasks required by a warship, ranging from ammunitioning, transfer of guns and for libertymen, moving to and from shore.

Six major types of ships' boats are illustrated from Brooking's era.

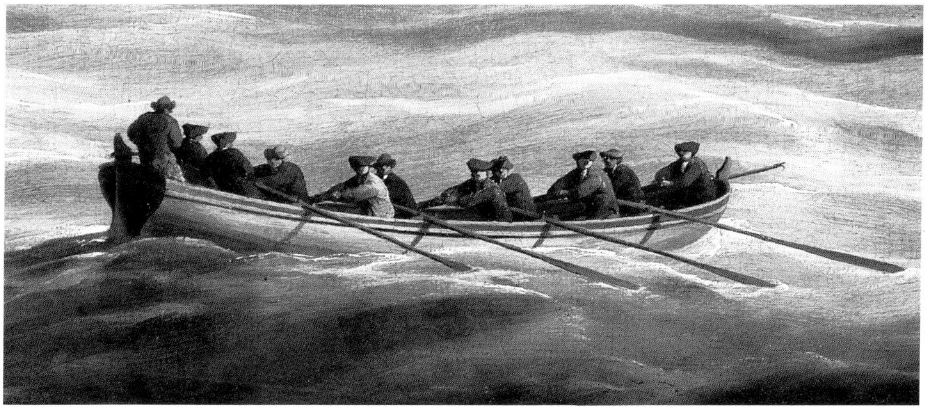

Detail of 26A. An eight-oared gig rows out towards the frigate *Pallas*. The captain was Archibald Brooking and the ship's master Samuel Brooking.

Ships' boats in Brooking's paintings

Royal Yacht *Caroline* - Barge 1749 - 8 oars - 27ft.

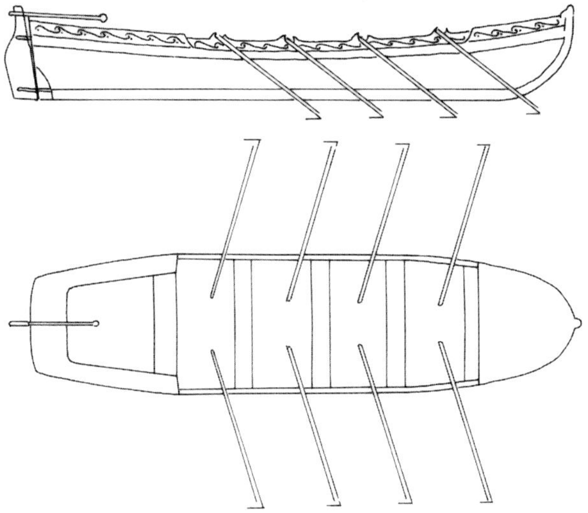

36ft. Longboat - 14 oars.

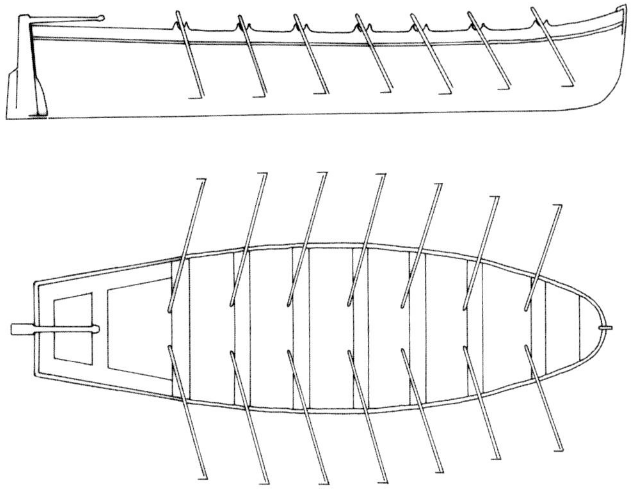

Pinnace - 32ft. (large) - 8 oars & 28ft. (small) - 6 oars.

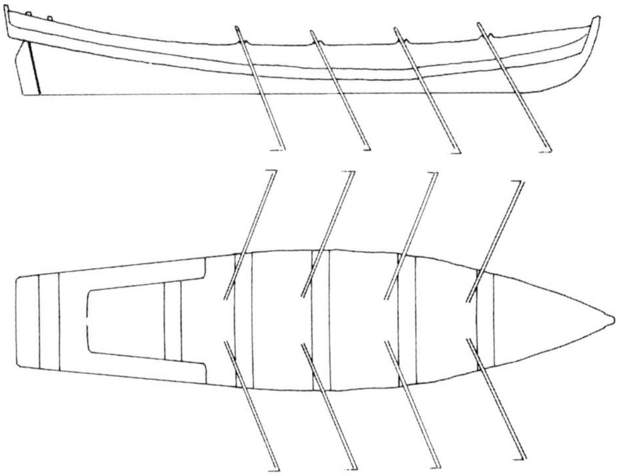

Gig - 27ft. Private boat - 6 oars.

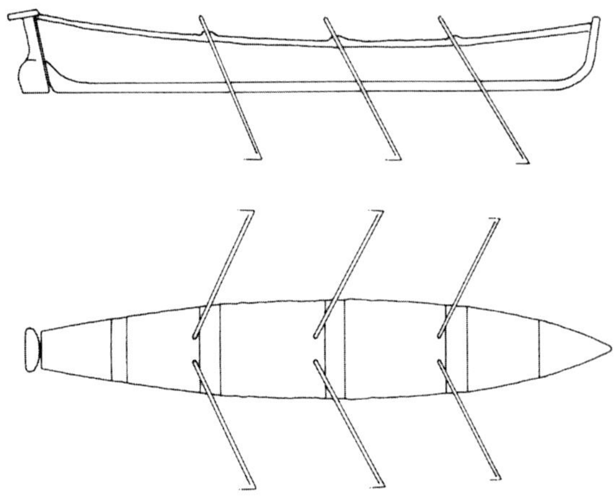

Cutter 25ft. (large) - 12 oars (max) & 18ft. (small).

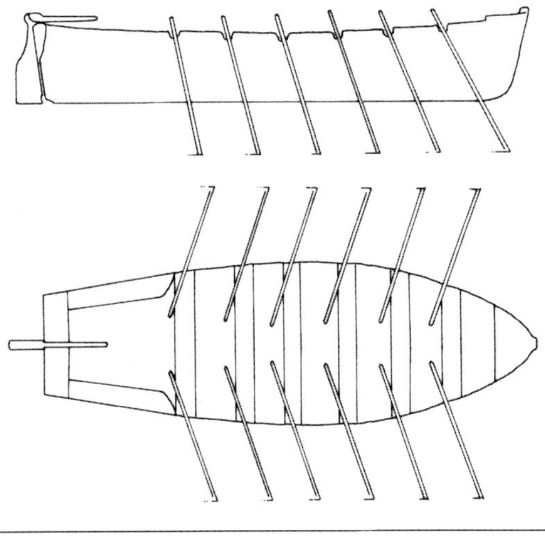

Yawl - 22ft. - 6 oars. Jollyboat 18ft. - 4 oars.

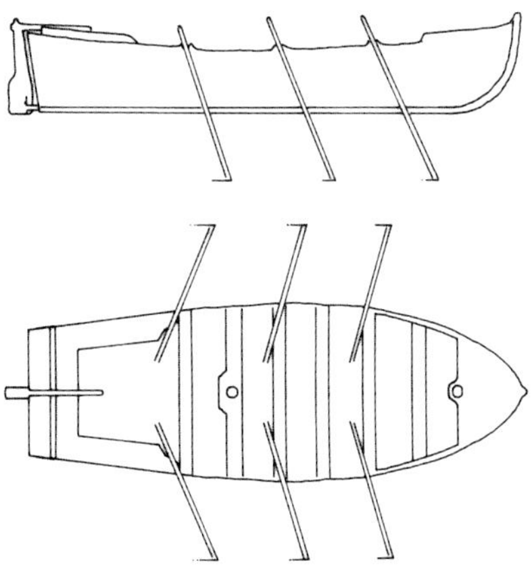

Types of 18th Century Merchant & Fishing Vessels

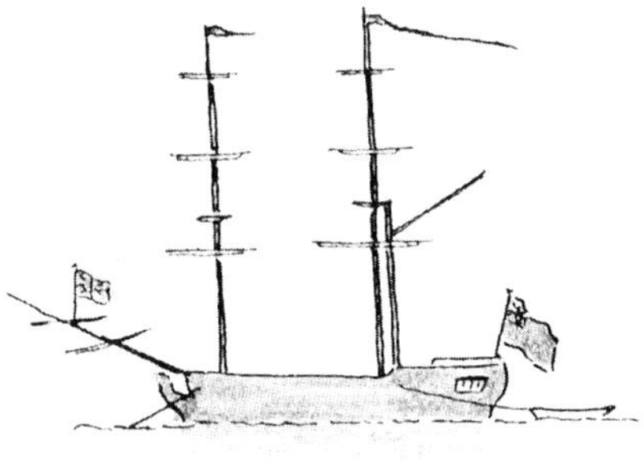

Snow

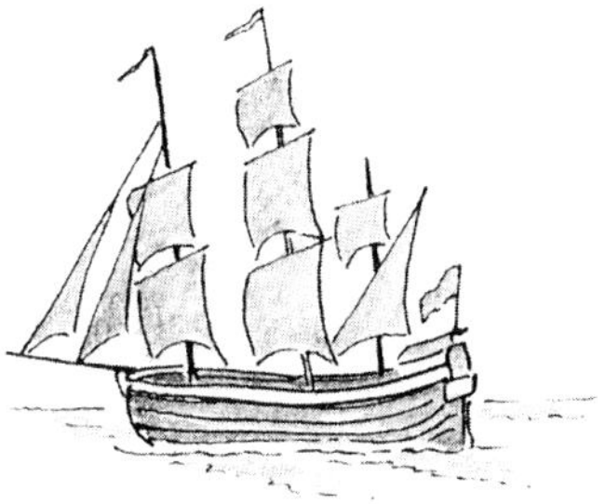

Flute or Flyboat

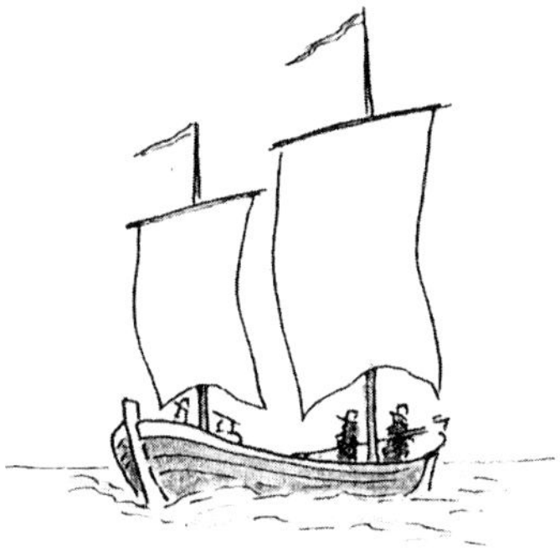

Pink

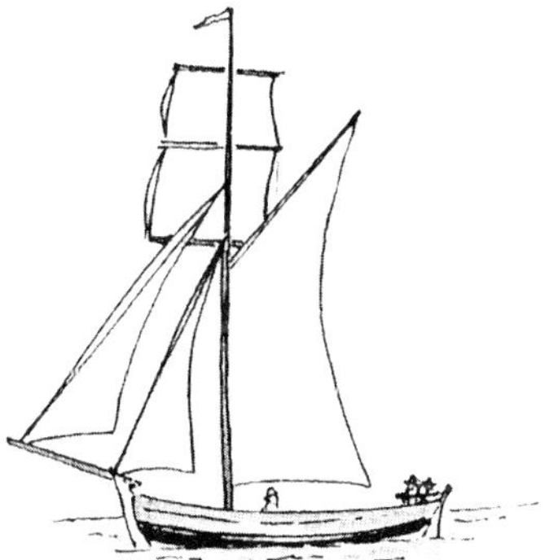

Hoy

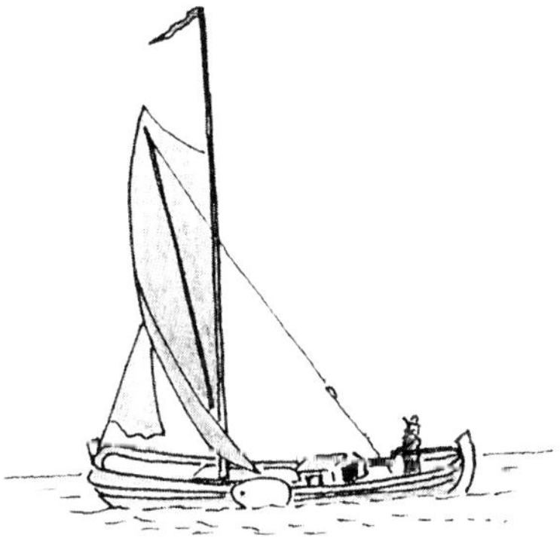

Kaag

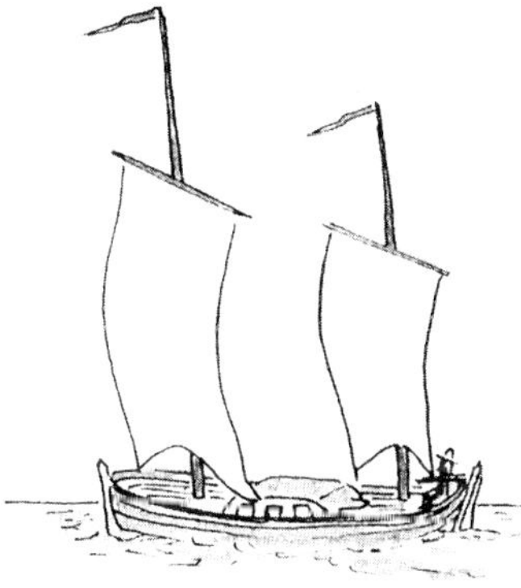

Hoeker

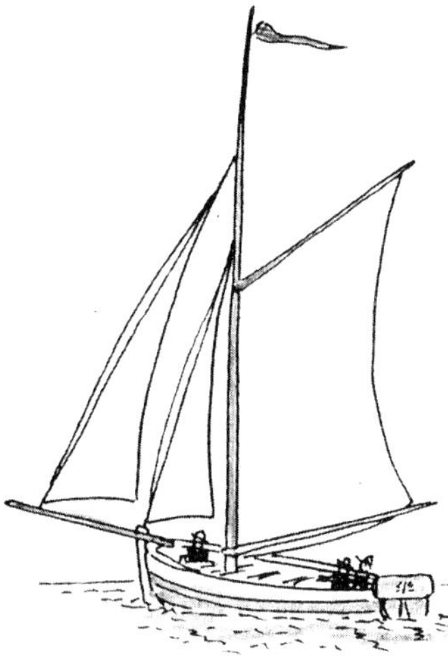

Smack

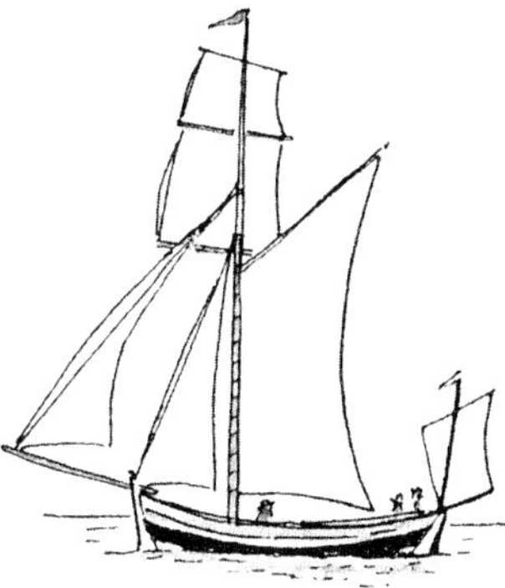

Galliot

Appendix E

Rigging of the period

STANDING RIGGING

based on drawings in C. Northcote Parkinson's book *Portsmouth Point*, Hodder & Staughton 1948.

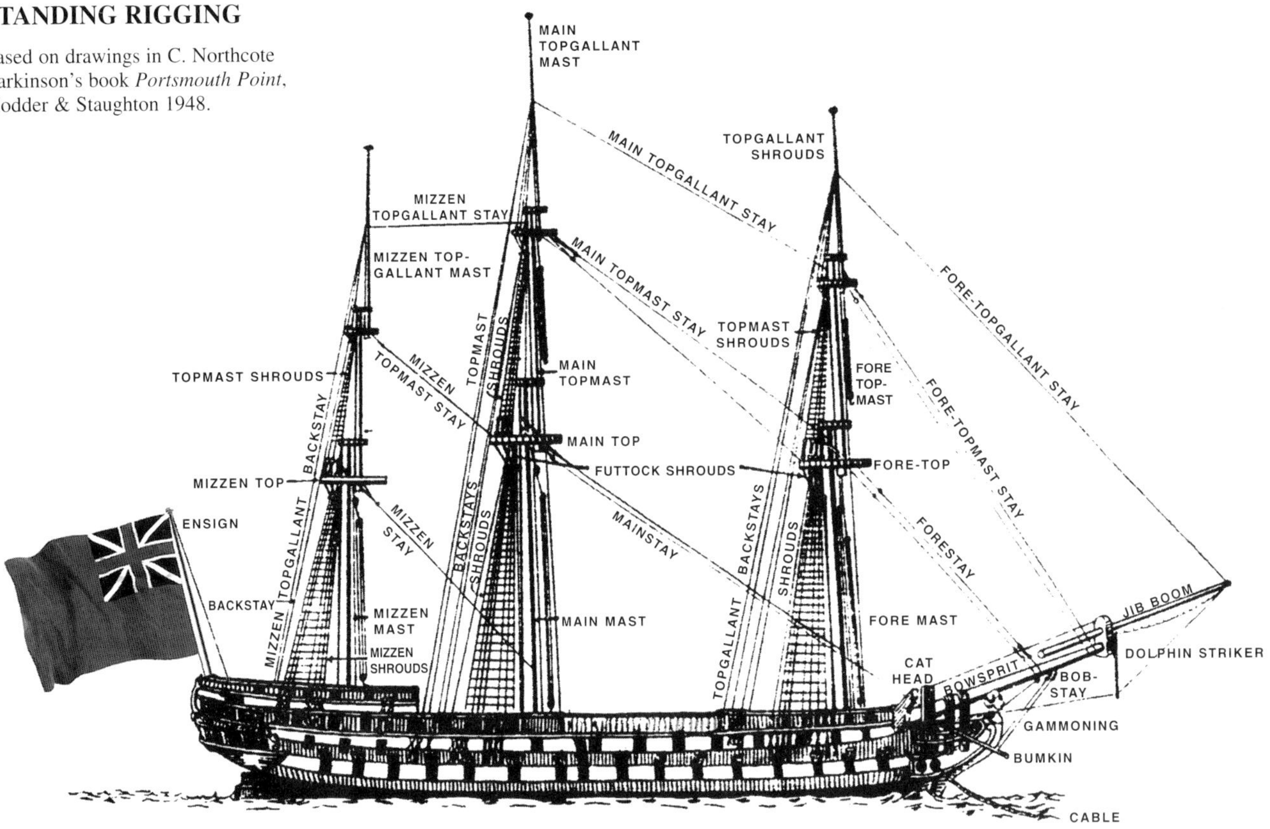

RUNNING RIGGING

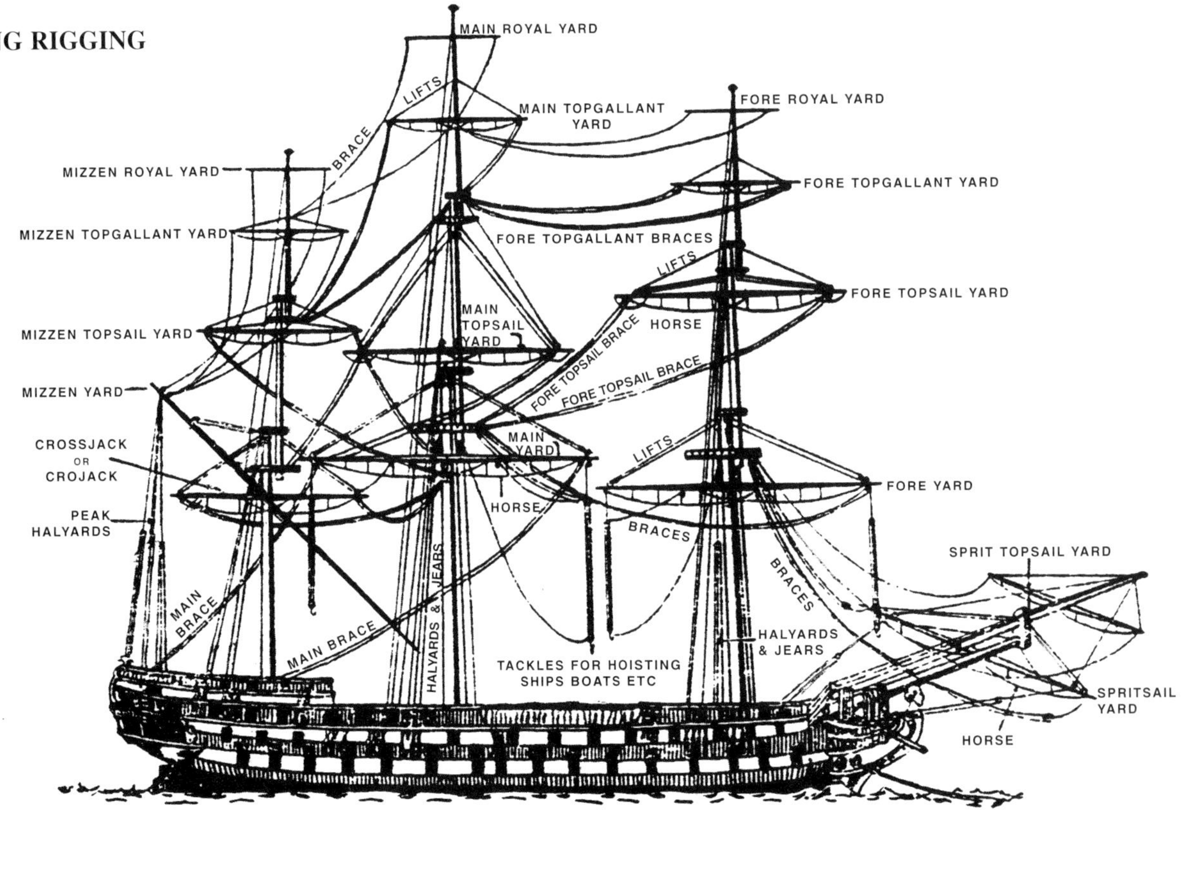

Appendix F

Flags of the period

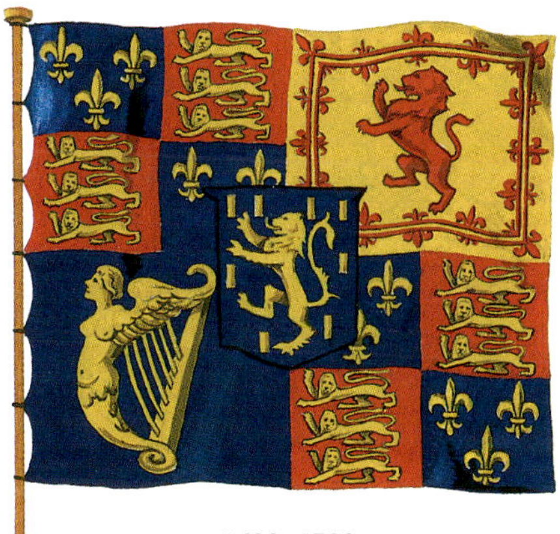

1689–1702

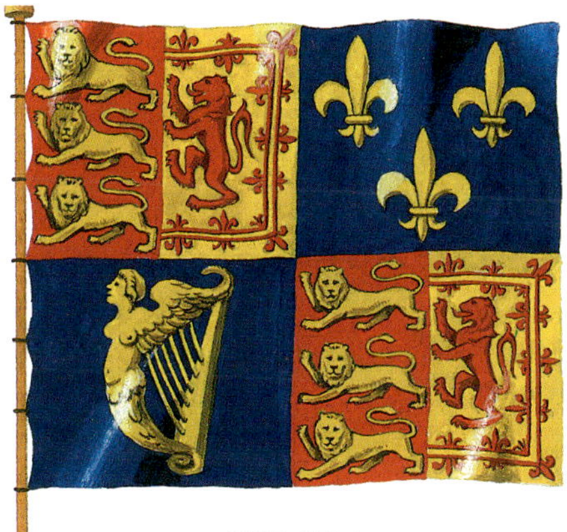

1707–1714

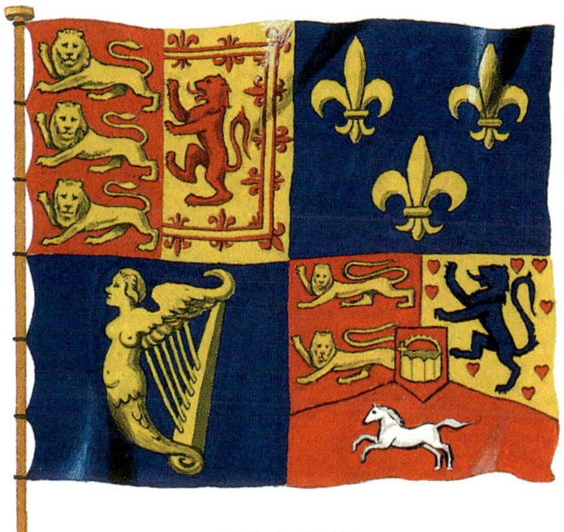

1714–1800

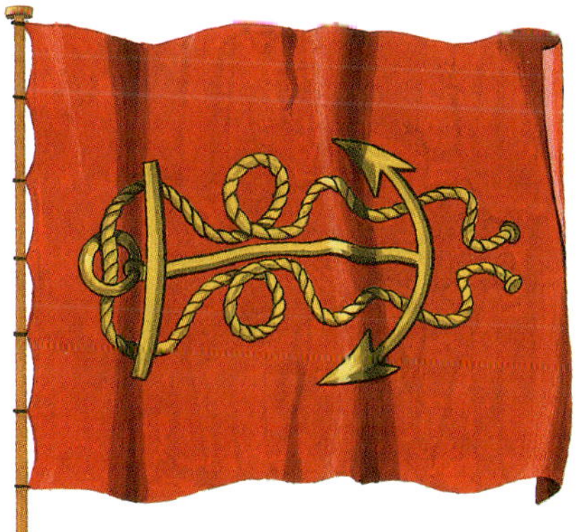

Lord High Admiral

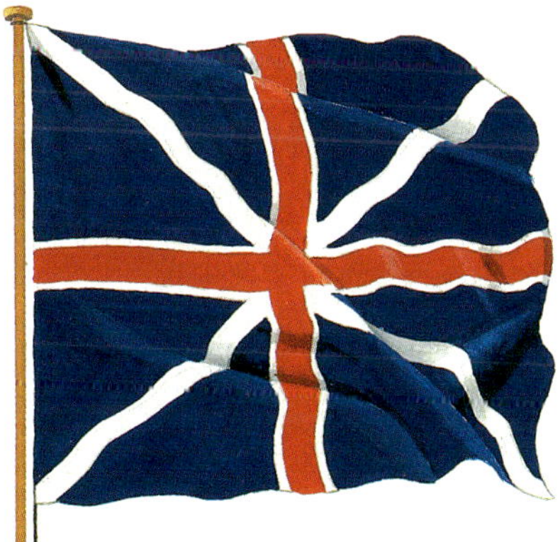

1606–1800

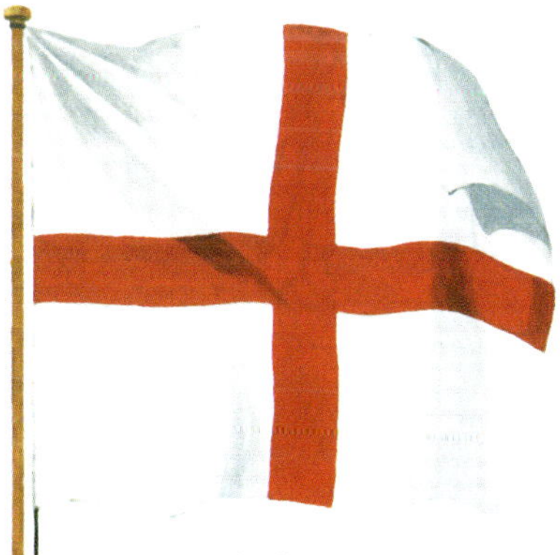

St George

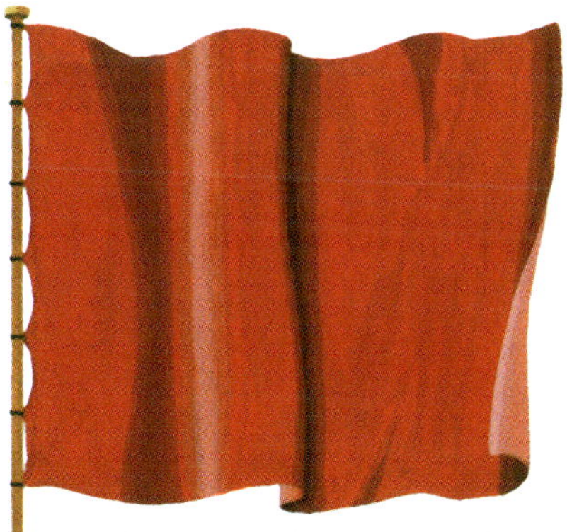

Red Squadron 17th Century–1864

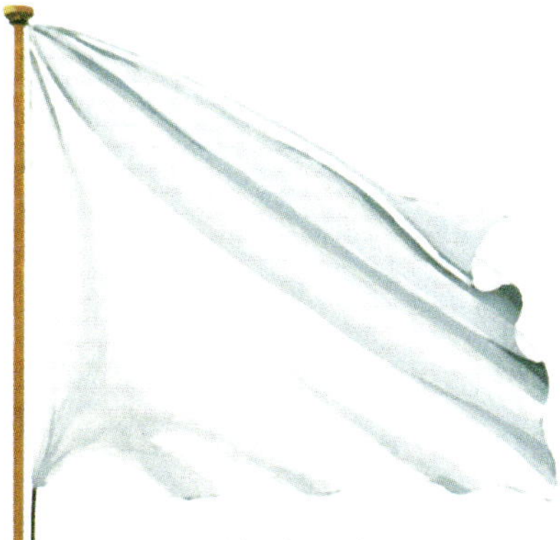

White Squadron

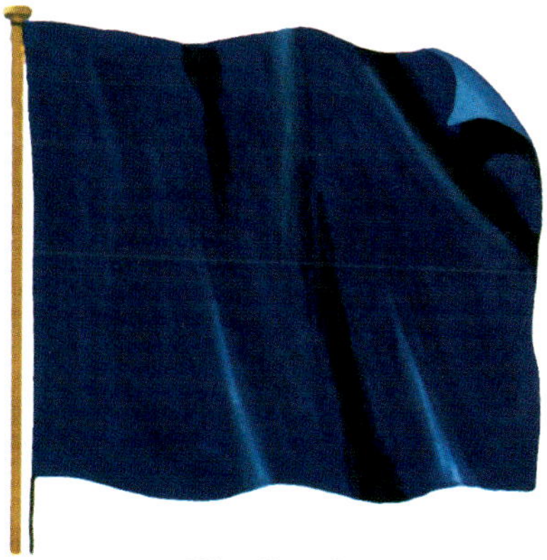

Blue Squadron

Pennants
Red, White and Blue Squadrons
and independent command

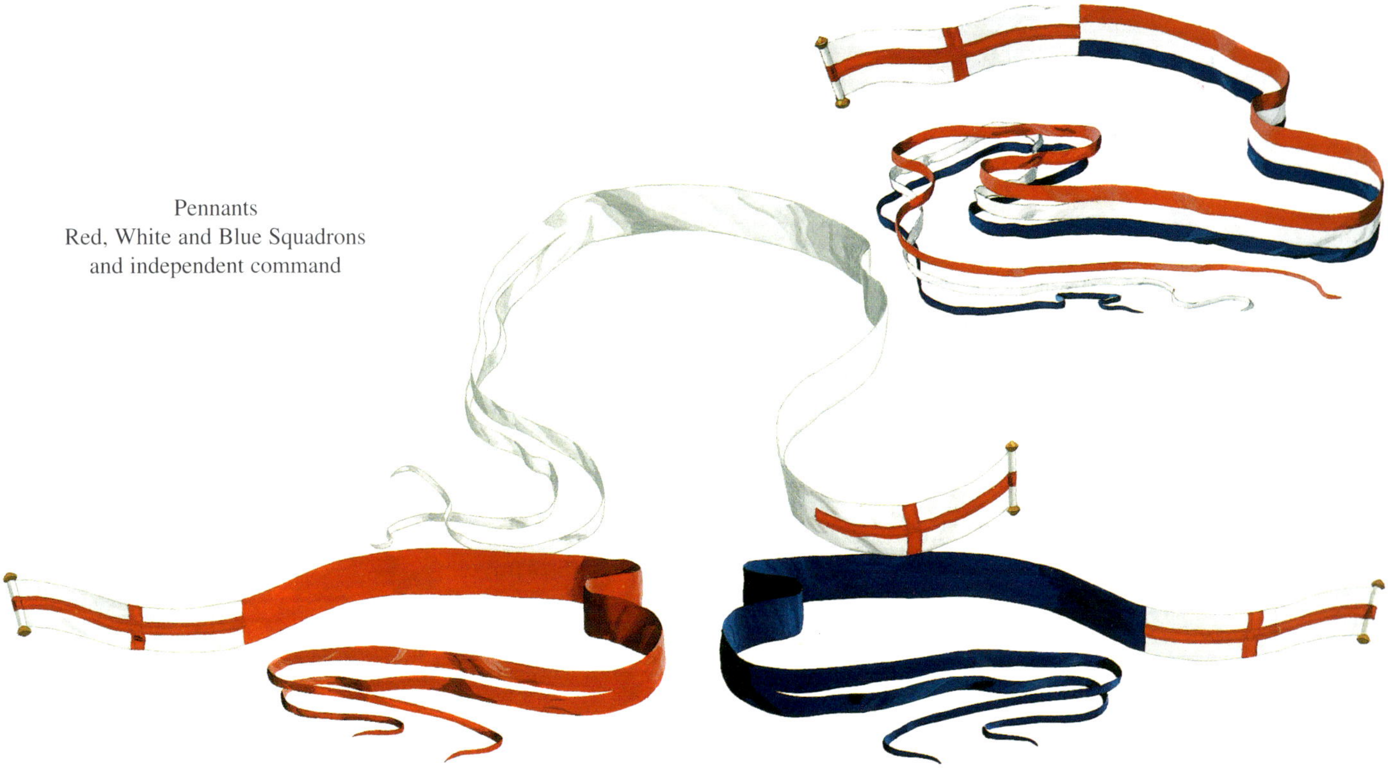

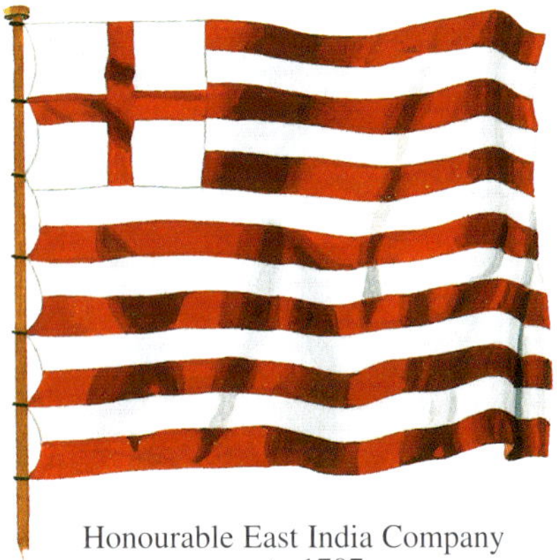

Honourable East India Company
up to 1707

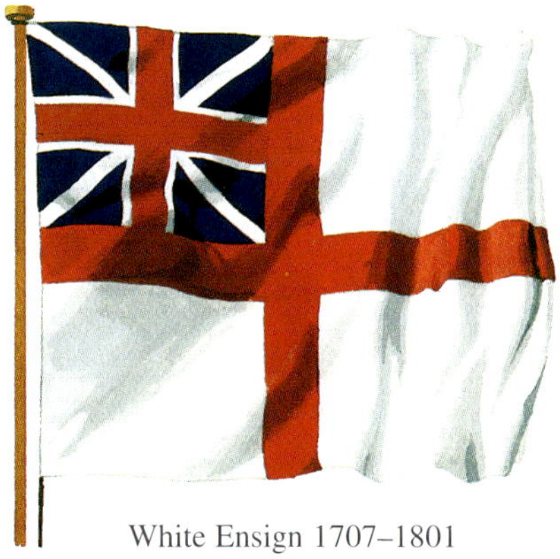

White Ensign 1707–1801

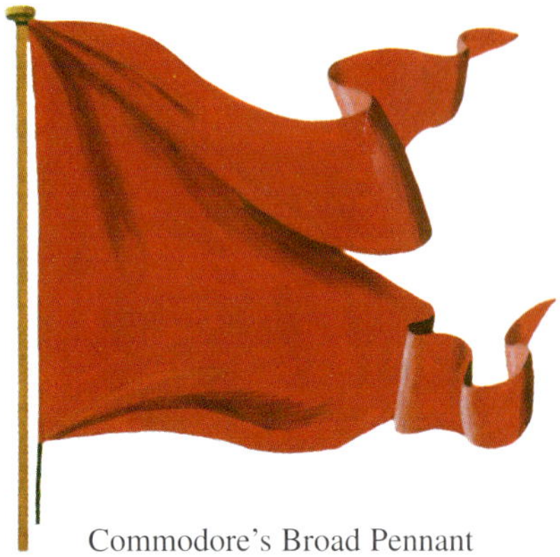

Commodore's Broad Pennant
early 18th Century to 1864

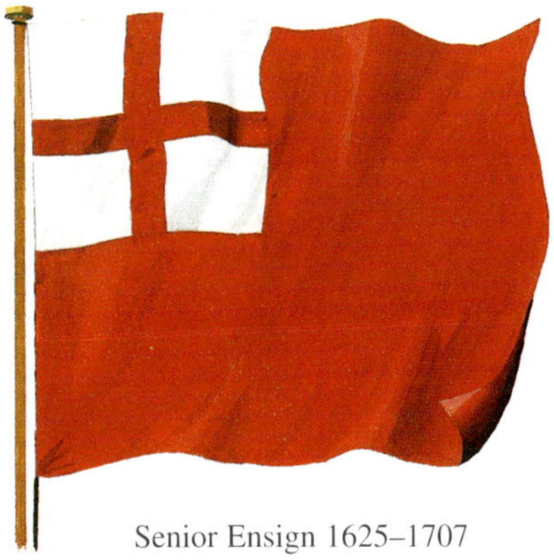

Senior Ensign 1625–1707

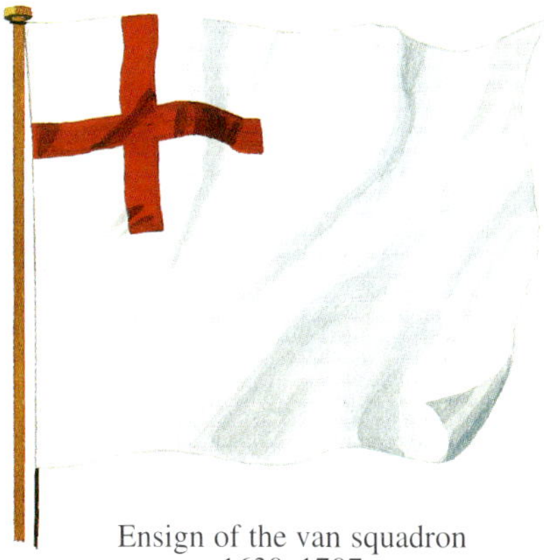

Ensign of the van squadron
1630–1707

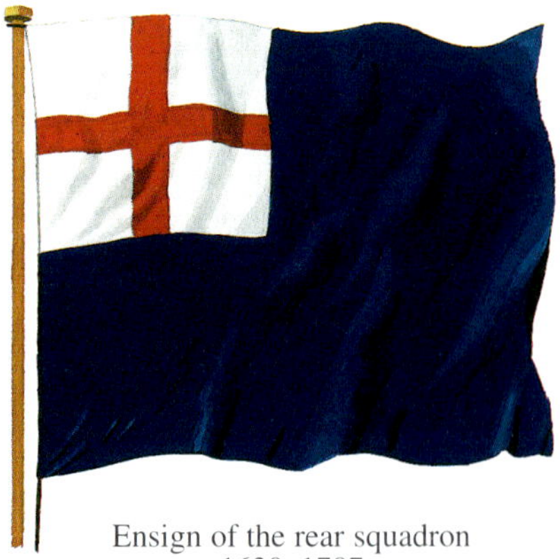

Ensign of the rear squadron
1630–1707

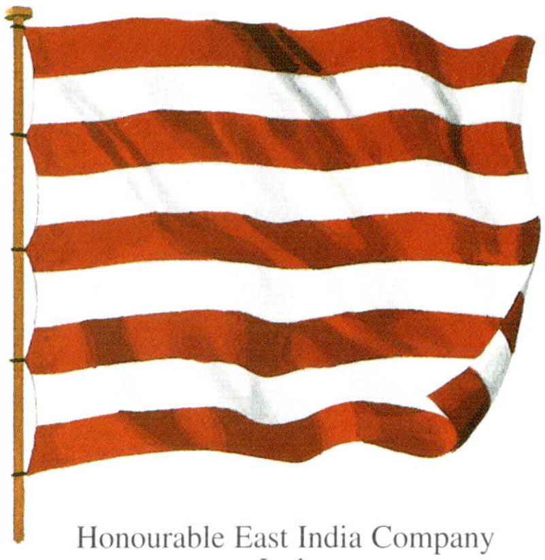
Honourable East India Company
Jack

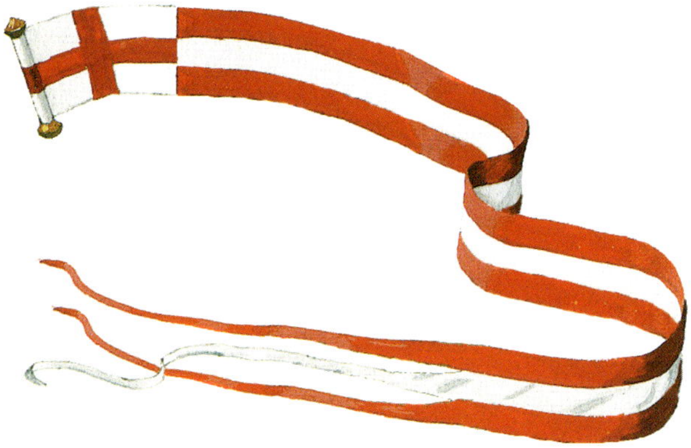
Honourable East India Company
Pennant

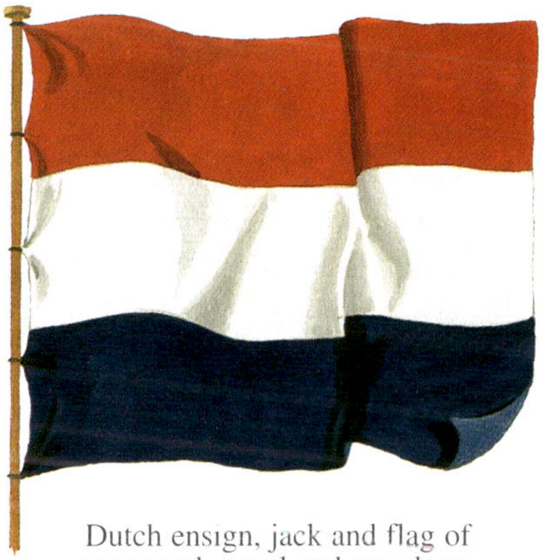
Dutch ensign, jack and flag of
command, naval and merchant,
from about 1625

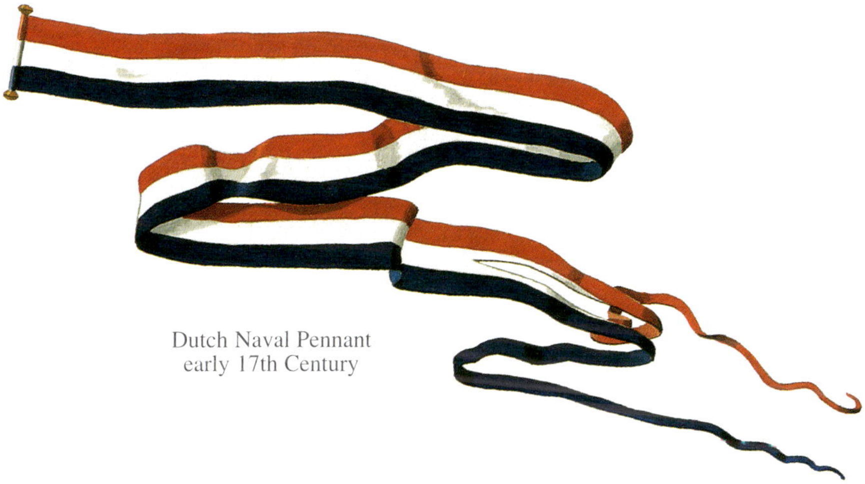
Dutch Naval Pennant
early 17th Century

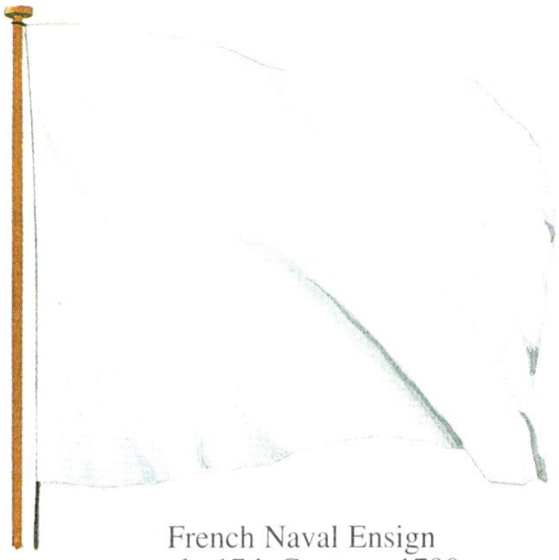
French Naval Ensign
early 17th Century–1790

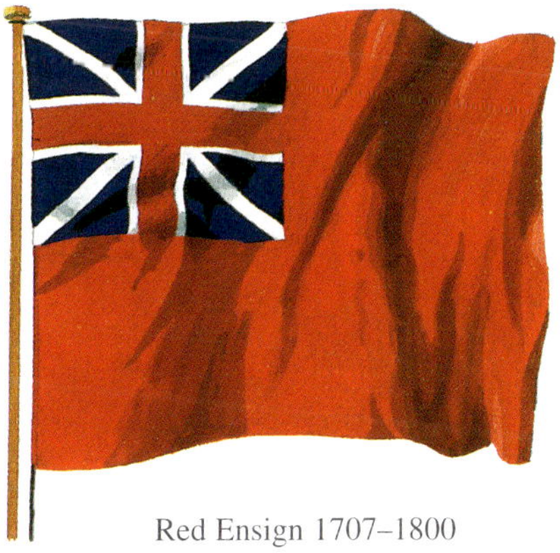
Red Ensign 1707–1800

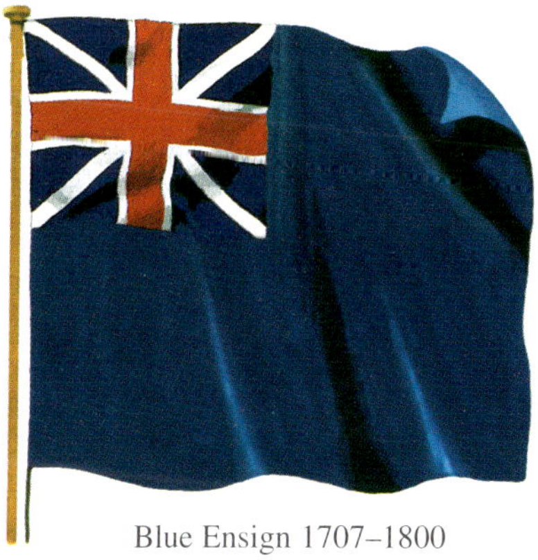
Blue Ensign 1707–1800

THE RED SQUAI

An English fleet, in three squadrons, of the reign of Charles II or James II.

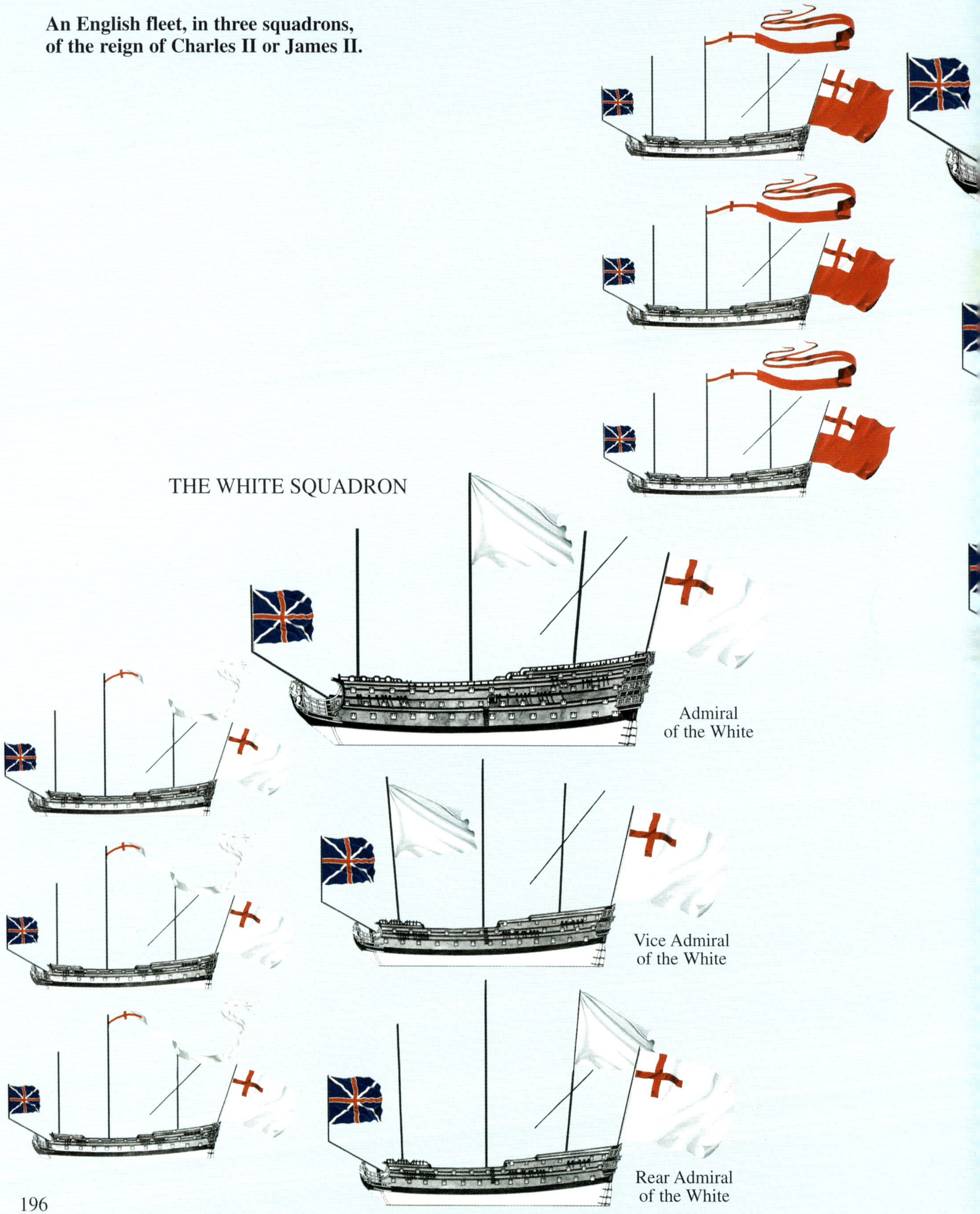

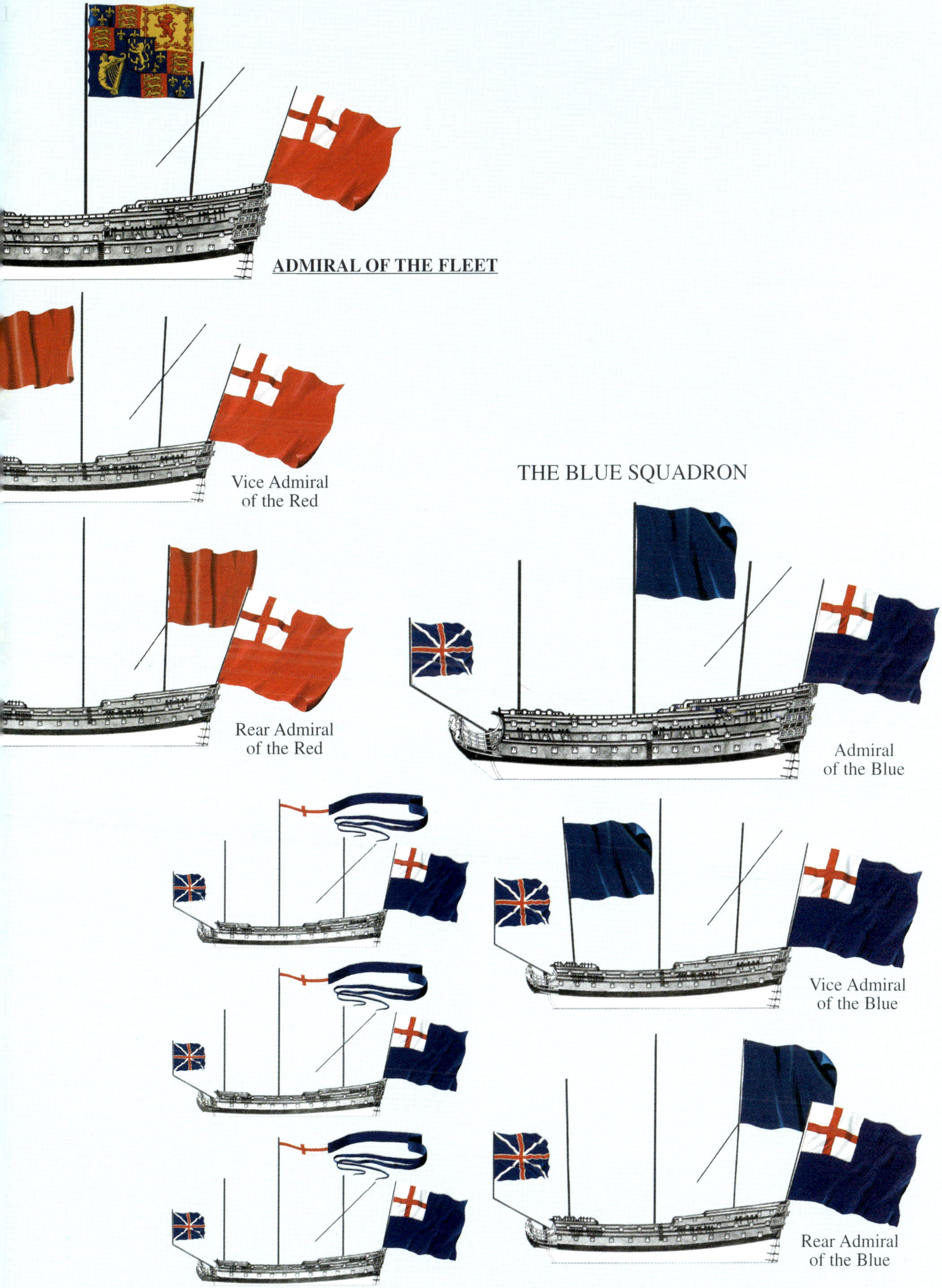
ADMIRAL OF THE FLEET
Vice Admiral
of the Red
Rear Admiral
of the Red
THE BLUE SQUADRON
Admiral
of the Blue
Vice Admiral
of the Blue
Rear Admiral
of the Blue

Appendix G

Dating of marine paintings of the 18th century

1677 Special red standard for the journey of Prince of Orange and Princess Mary to Holland.

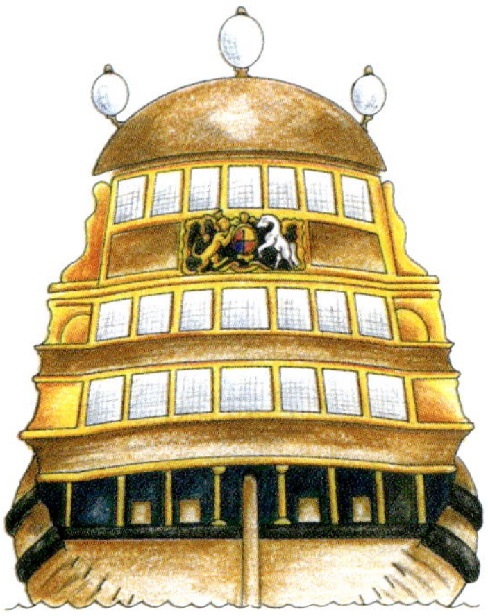

1678 First evidence of stern galleries with small coat-of-arms in English ships.

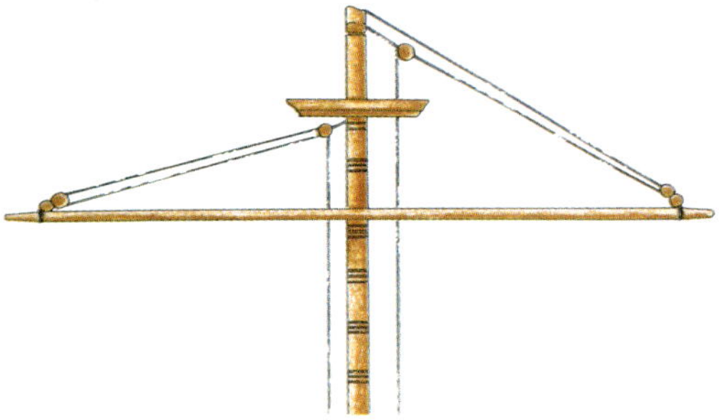

c.1680 Raising of lifts in English ships from below top to head of mast.

First mention of fore tack bumpkin; generally introduced in place of dead-block in head, *c.*1710 (foreign ships c.1740).

1682 Building of first Dutch three-deckers *Westfriesland* and *Zeelandia*.

Building of first ketch-rigged yacht *Fubbs*.

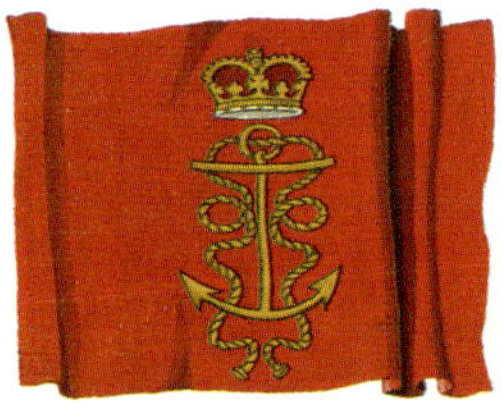

1685-88 Anchor and crown in Admiralty flag; anchor and crown in fly of red ensign in Royal Yacht having the King on board.

1688 Crown on Dutch lion figurehead.

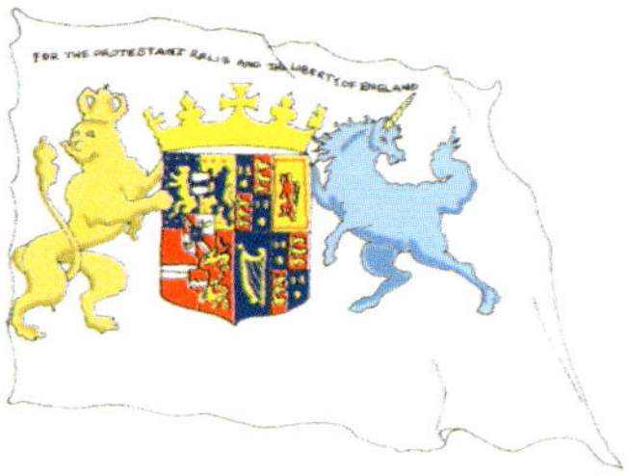

1688-89 Special white Standard for the journey of William and Mary to England.

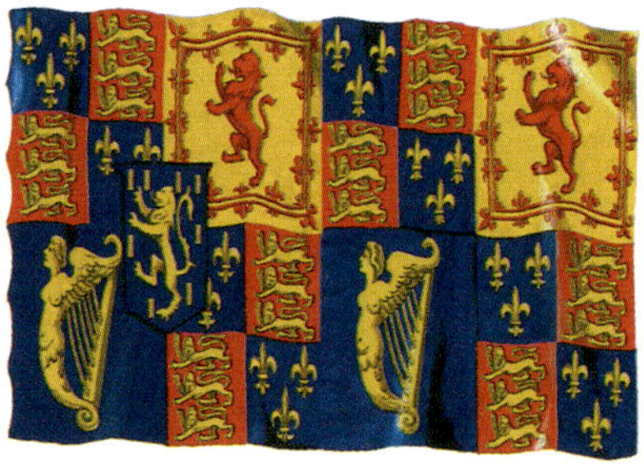

1689-94 Royal Standard with Mary's Stuart arms impaled with William's.

***c*.1690** Introduction of Budgee pendant with Union in chief for ships in Mediterranean.

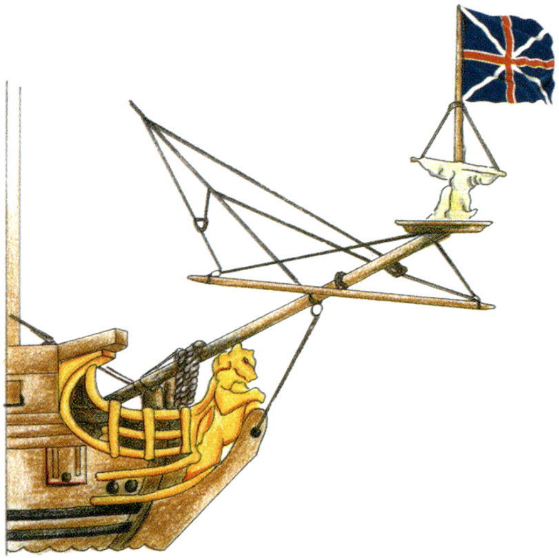

1691 First evidence of bobstay in large ships.

1695 Use of broad pendants in English Navy extended to senior captains of independent squadrons.

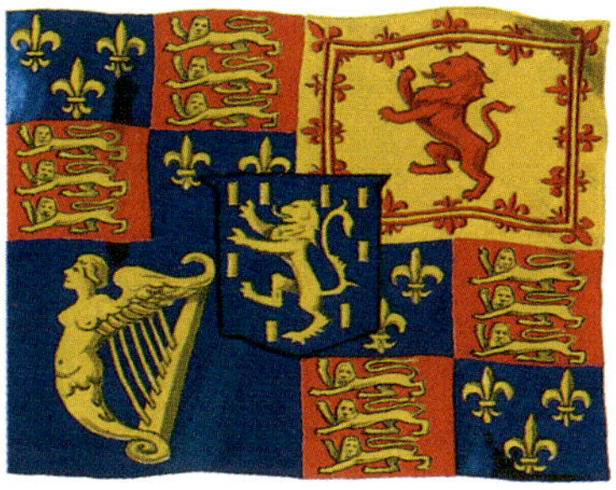

1695-1702 Stuart Royal Standard with inescutcheon the lion of Nassau.

***c*.1700** First evidence of one reef in mizzen topsail.

1702 Red cross placed in admiral's white flag and in white ensign.

1702-07 Stuart Royal Standard restored.

1703 Order to reduce decoration in English ships.

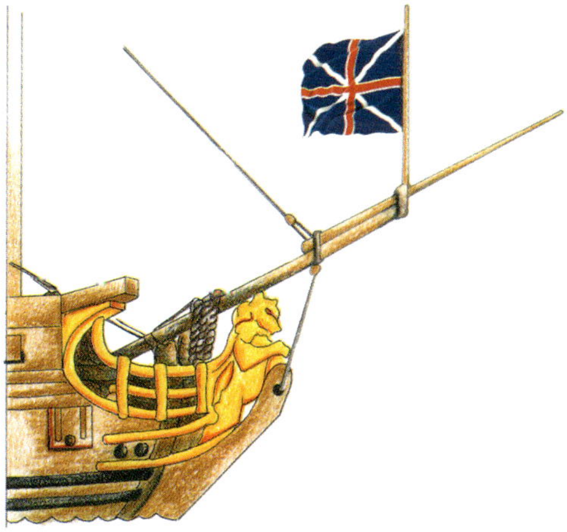

1705 First evidence of jibboom.

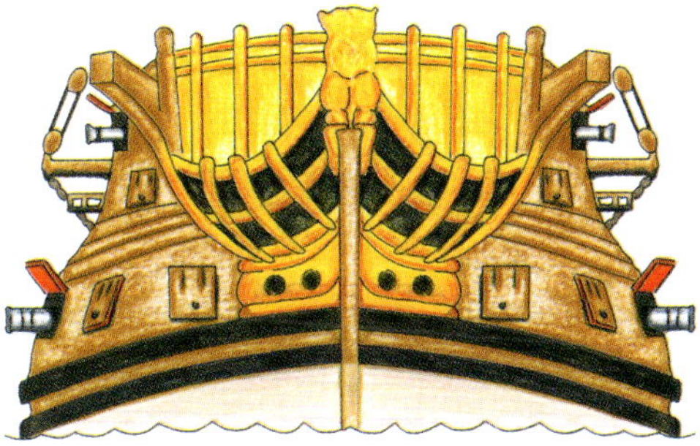

1706 Raising of channels to wale under upper deck guns in English three-deckers. (Raised experimentally in two ships in 1702.)

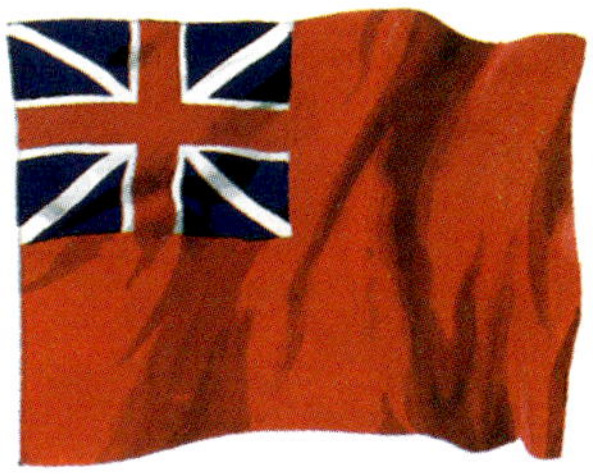

1707 Union placed in canton of ensign.

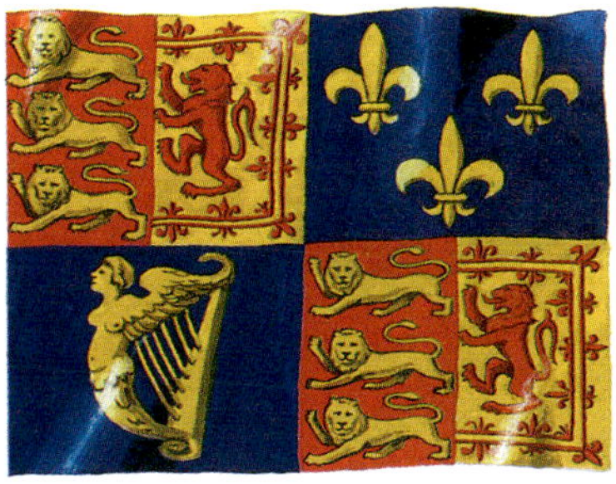

1707-14 Royal Standard with England impaled with Scotland.

***c*.1710** First evidence of third reef in fore and main topsails and of second reef in mizzen topsail.

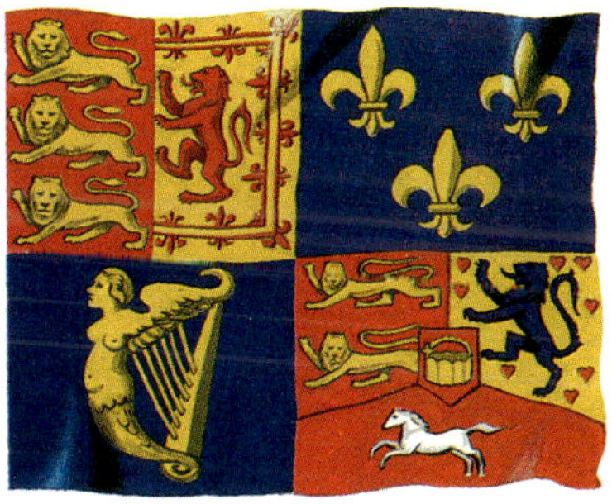

1714-1800 Royal Standard with Hanoverian arms in fourth quarter.

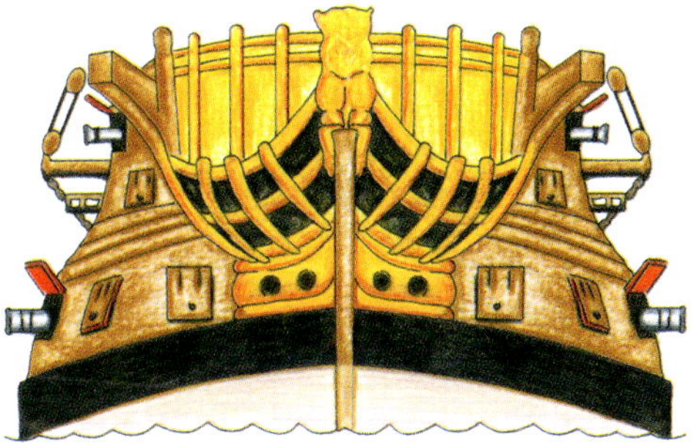

***c*.1720** First evidence of solid lower wale in English ships.

***c*.1730** Disappearance of spritsail topmast.

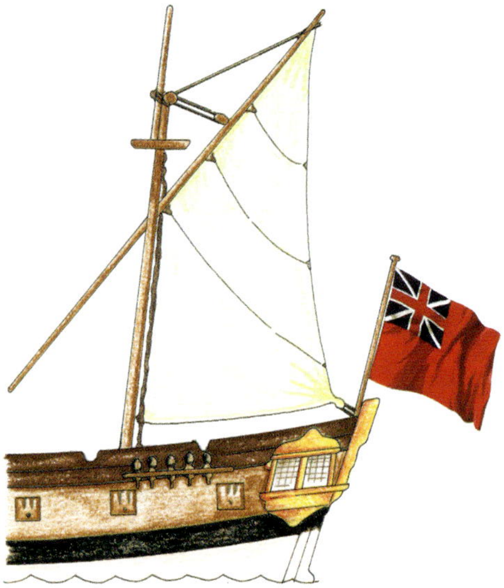

*c.*1745 Disappearance of fore part of lateen mizzen (but not of yard) in small ships.

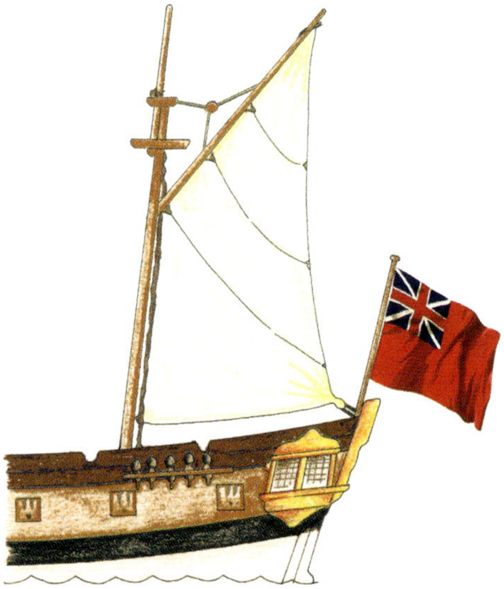

1749 Disappearance of fore part of mizzen yard in small ships.

1758 First evidence of round bow in place of beakhead bulkhead in English frigates.

1760 First evidence of luffs to staysails.

1771 Painting of name across counter of English ships introduced.

1773 Painting of ships in place of paying.

1775 First naval brigs.

1787 Channels in three-deckers raised above upper deck.

***c.*1790** General introduction of royals on all three masts. Four rows of reef points in topsails.

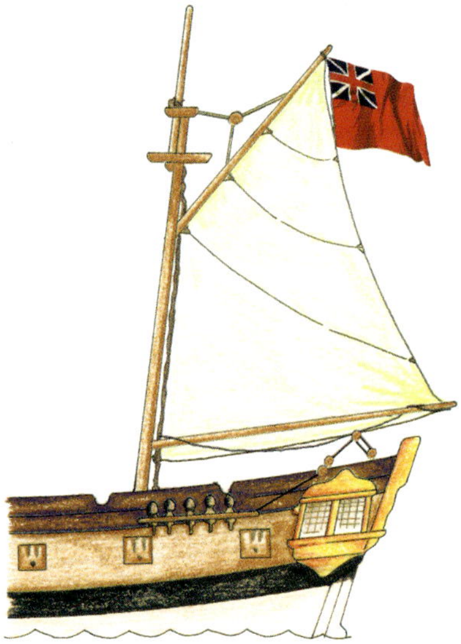

1793 First evidence in ships of boom to mizzen and ensign at peak when under way.

1794 First evidence of dolphin striker.

***c.*1795** Disappearance of fore part of mizzen yard in large ships.

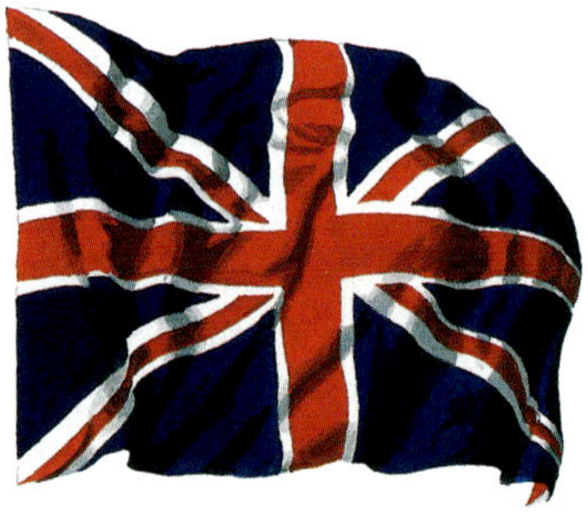

1801 Irish saltire placed in Union.

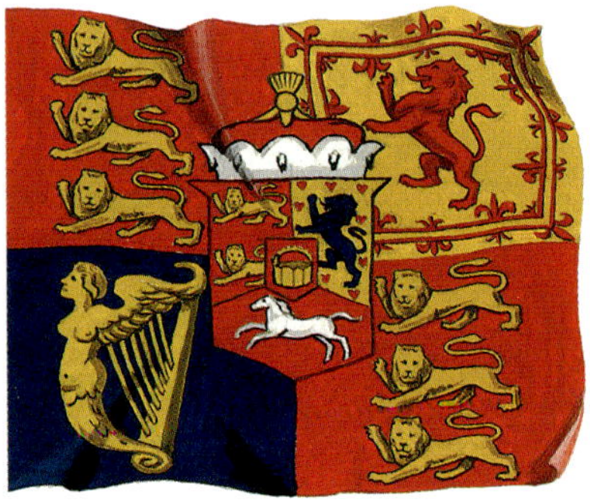

1801 Disappearance of fleur-de-lis from Royal Arms.

Appendix H

Letters supporting Chapter 3

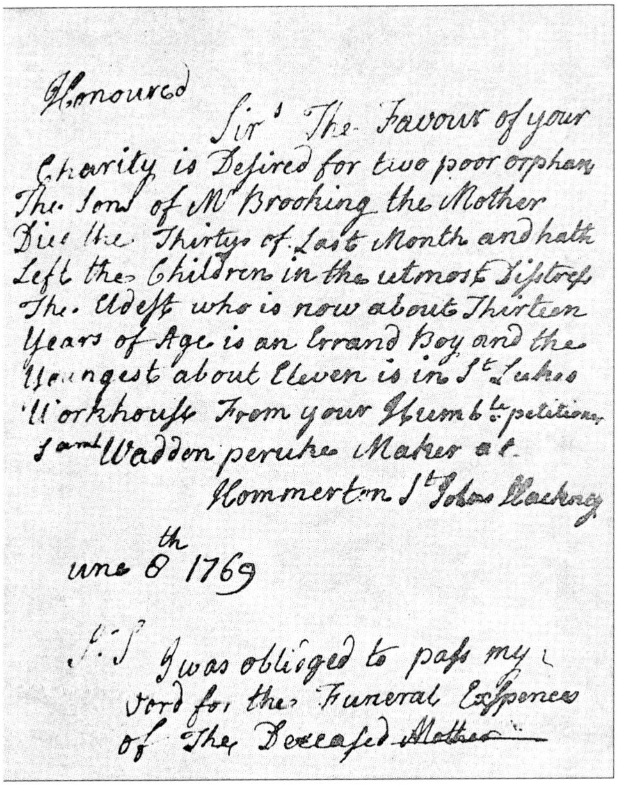

Honoured

Sir' The Favour of your Charity is Desired for two poor orphans The Sons of Mr Brooking the Mother Died the Thirty of Last Month and hath Left the Children in the utmost Distress The Eldest who is now about Thirteen Years of Age is an Errand Boy and the Youngest about Eleven is in St Lukes Workhouse From your Humble petitioner Sarah Waddon peruke Maker at Hommerton St Johns Hackney

June 8th 1769

P.S. I was obliged to pass my word for the Funeral Expences of The Deceased Mother

Sarah Waddon's letter, 8th June 1769. Mary Brooking (Charles Brooking's widow) re-married to become Mary Waddon and she died on 30 May 1769. Here, her sister-in-law writes on behalf of the Brooking children.

Society of Artists of Great Britain, held at the Royal Academy, London.

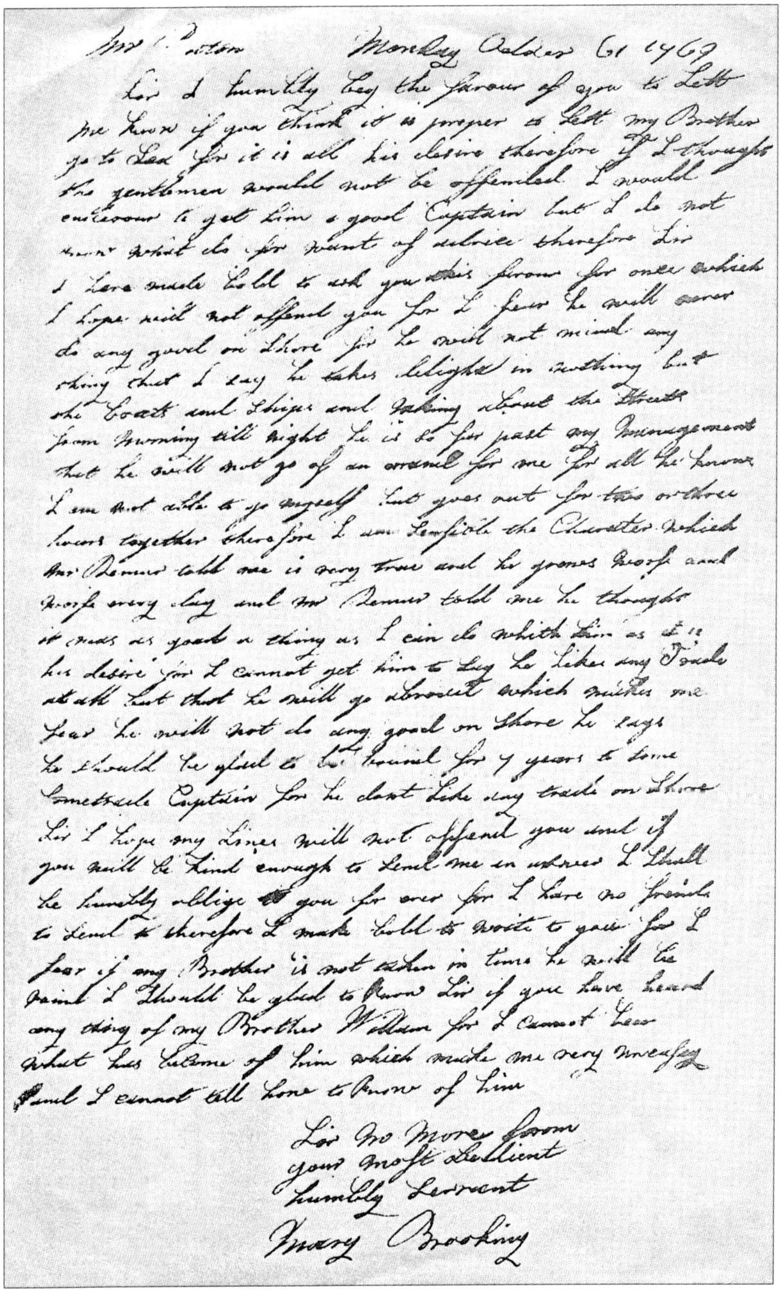

Mr Paton Monday October 16 1769

Sir I humbly beg the favour of you to Lett me know if you think it is proper to Lett my Brother go to Sea for it is all his desire therefore if I thought the gentlemen would not be offended I would endeavour to get him a good Captain but I do not know what do for want of advice therefore Sir I have made bold to ask you this favour for once which I hope will not offend you for I fear he will never do any good on Shore for he will not mind any thing that I say he takes delight in nothing but the boats and Ships and Walking about the Streets from morning till night he is so far past my management that he will not go of an errand for me for all he knows I am not able to go myself but goes out for two or three hours together therefore I am sensible the Character which Mr [illegible] told me is very true and he grows worse and worse every day and Mr [illegible] told me he thought it was as good a thing as I can do which him as it is his desire for I cannot get him to say he likes any Trade at all but that he will go abroad which makes me fear he will not do any good on Shore he says he should be glad to be bound for 7 years to some Sensible Captain for he dont like any trade on Shore Sir I hope my Lines will not offend you and if you will be kind enough to send me in answer I shall be humbly oblige to you for ever for I have no friends to send to therefore I make bold to write to you for I fear if my Brother is not taken in time he will be ruind I should be glad to know Sir if you have heard any thing of my Brother William for I cannot hear what his become of him which make me very uneasy and I cannot tell how to know of him

Sir no more from
your most Obedient
humbly Servant
Mary Brooking

Letter from Mary Brooking to Richard Paton, 16th October 1769 (see page 52).

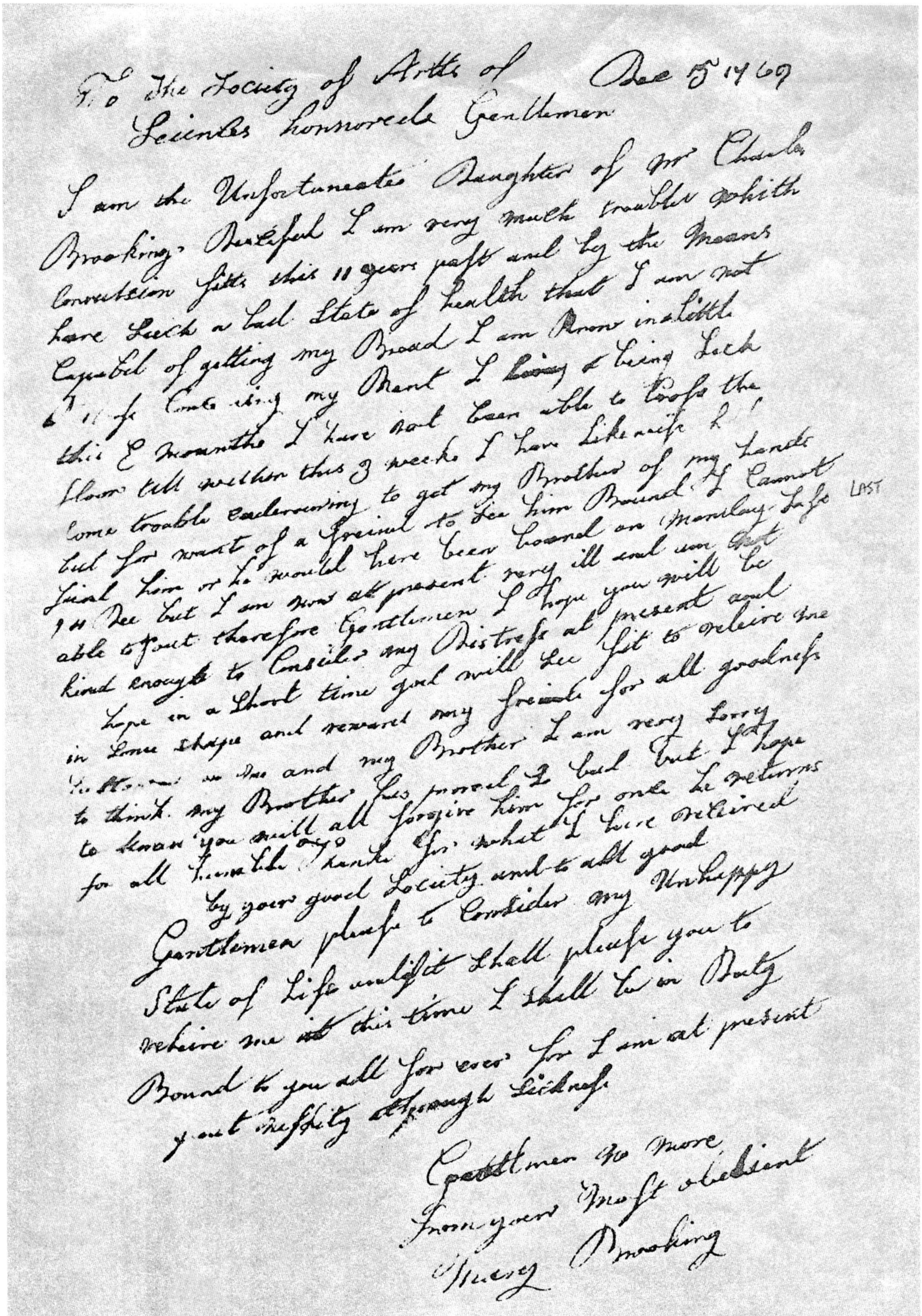

To The Society of Artts of Dec 15 1769
Sciences honnorable Gentlemen

I am the Unfortunate Daughter of Mr Charles Brooking Deceased I am very much troubled with Convultion fitts this 11 years past and by the Means have such a bad State of health that I am not Capable of getting my Bread I am Now in a little [illegible] of Continuing my Rent I [illegible] & being Such [illegible] this 8 monthe I have not been able to Cross the floor tell wether this 3 weeks I have Likewise had Some trouble endevouring to get my Brother of my hands but for want of a freind to See him Bound I Cannot find him or he would have been bound on Monday last 14 Dec but I am now at present very ill and am not able to put therefore Gentlemen I hope you will be kind enough to Consider my Distress at present and releive me hope in a Short time god will See fit to [illegible] in Some shape and reward my freinds for all goodness [illegible] me and my Brother I am very Sorry to think my Brother Has proved so bad but I hope to know you will all forgive him for once he returns for all [illegible] thanks for what I have received by your good Society and to all good Gentlemen please to Consider my Unhappy State of Life untill it shall please you to releive me at this time I shall be in Duty Bound to you all for ever for I am at present [illegible] through Sickness

Gentlmen No more
From yours Most obedient
Mary Brooking

LAST

Letter from Mary Brooking to James Payne, 15th December 1769. Society of Artists of Great Britain records held by Royal Academy, London.

Society of Artists of Great Britain, held at the Royal Academy, London.

Bibliography

Anderson, R. C., *Seventeenth Century Rigging*, 1977, Model and Allied Publications, Argus Books Ltd; *The Rigging of Ships in the Days of the Spritsail Topmast 1600-1720*, Marine Research Society, Salem, Massachusetts, 1927

Andrews, J. H., *Irish Georgian Society Quarterly Bulletin July – Dec 1980*, pp.33-43

Archibald, E. H. H., *The Wooden Fighting Ship*, Blandford Press, 1968; *Dictionary of Sea Painters*, Antique Collectors' Club, 1980, 2nd edn. 1989, 3rd edn. 1998; *The Willem van de Veldes*, Royal Society of Arts, 24 Feb 1982

Arts Council, *Marine Paintings Exhibition Catalogue*, 1965-1966

Baldry, A. L., *British Marine Painting*, Studio, 1919

Bellabarba & Osculati, *The Royal Yacht* Caroline *1749*, Conway Maritime Press, 1992

Brownlow, John, *Memoranda or Chronicles of the Foundling Hospital*, London, 1847

Brooking Society Records, *Geneology of the 18th Century Brookings*

Callender, Sir Geoffrey, *Sea Kings of Britain. Vol II 1660-1769 Abermarle to Hawke*, Longmans Green

Clayton, Timothy, *The English Print 1688-1802*, Yale University Press, 1997

Clowes, William Laird, *The Royal Navy, a History from the Earliest Times to the Present Day*, 7 Vols, London 1897-1903

Cockett, Frank B., *Early Sea Painters*, Antique Collectors' Club, 1995

Cordingly, David, *Marine Painting in England 1700-1900*, Studio Vista, 1974; *Painters of the Sea*, Brighton Art Galleries, 1979

Dayes, Edward, *Professional Sketches of Modern Artists*, T. Maiden, London, 1805

Edwards, Edward, *Edwards Anecdotes of English Painters*, Leigh & Sotheby, 1808

Farington Diary 1793-1821, edited by James Greig, Hutchinson & Co, 1922

Gaunt, William, *Marine Painting*, Secker and Warburg, 1975

Guildhall Art Gallery, *Samuel Scott Bicentary Exhibition*, 1972, catalogue

Harrison Wallace, Charles. *Peter Monamy 1681-1749 Marine Artist.* Pallant House Gallery, Chichester; *Heroes of the Surf. The Romance of Sailing*, David Coke, 1988

Ingalls, Elizabeth, *Whaling Prints in the Francis B. Lothrop Collection*, Peabody Museum of Salem, Salem, Massachusetts, 1987

Kemp, Peter, and Ormond, Richard, *The Great Age of Sail*, Phaidon, 1986

Kissane, Dr Noel, *Historic Dublin Maps*, National Library of Ireland, 1988

Lavery, Brian, *The 74 gun ship Bellona*, Conway Maritime Press, 1985

Macpherson, A. G. H., *Catalogue of Loan Exhibition of Paintings and Prints from the Macpherson Collection*, Whitechapel Art Gallery, 1929

May W.E., Commander R.N. *The Boats of Men of War*, N.M.M. 1974 & 1999 and Chatham Publishing

Mellon, Paul, KBE with Basketh, John, *Reflections in a Silver Spoon. A Memoir.* John Murray, 1992.

Miller, Oliver, *Zoffany and his Tribuna*, Paul Mellon Foundation for British Art, 1967

Mitchell, Charles A., *Book of Ships*, Penguin Books Ltd, 1941

N.M.M., *Concise Catalogue of the Paintings of the National Maritime Musuem*, HMSO, 1958; *The Art of the Van de Veldes*, 1982; *Concise Catalogue of Oil Paintings in the National Maritime Museum*, Antique Collectors' Club, 1988

Naval Prints from the Beverley R. Robinson Collection Vol. I, 1514-1791. Compiled and edited by Sigrid Trumpy, Curator, Beverley R. Robinson Collection, pub. Beverley R. Robinson Collection, United States Naval Academy Museum, Annapolis, Maryland, USA, 1991

Nichol, R. H. and Wray, F. A. *The History of the Foundling Hospital*, London, 1935
Nicholson, Benedict, *The Treasures of the Foundling Hospital*, Oxford University Press, 1972
Northcote Parkinson, C. *Portsmouth Point. Navy in Fiction 1793-1815*, Hodder and Staughton 1948
Perrin, W. G., *British Flags*, Cambridge Univeristy Press, 1922
Preston, Admiral Sir Lionel, *Sea and River Painters of the Netherlands in the 17th Century*, Oxford University Press, 1937
Preston, Colonel Rupert, *Seventeenth Century Marine Painters of the Netherlands*, F. Lewis Publishers, Leigh-on-Sea, 1974
Print Quarterly Volume 1 (1984), *A Checklist of Catalogues of British Print Publishers c.1650-1830*, Antony Griffiths
Purves, Alec A., *Flags for Ship Modellers and Marine Artists*, Conway Maritime Press, 1983
Quarm, Roger, and Wilcox, Scott, *Masters of the Sea, British Marine Watercolours*, Phaidon, 1987
Redgrave, Samuel, *Dictionary of Artists of the English School 1873*, Kingsmead Reprints, Bath, 1970
Robinson, Michael S. *Van der velde Drawings*, Cambridge U.P., Volume I 1958, Volume II 1974. *The Paintings of the William van de Veldes*, Volumes I & II, National Maritime Museum
Rodger, N. A. M., *Naval Records for Genealogists*, Public Record Office, 1984
Roe, Gordon F., *Sea Painters of Britain: Van de Velde to Turner*, F. Lewis Publishers, Leigh-on-Sea, 1947
Science Museum, *Sailing Ships, Their History and Development* by the late G. S. Laird Clowes, HMSO, Reprint, 1962
South Devon Family Historical Society 'Devon Extracts 1665-1850'
Sorensen, Colin, *Charles Brooking 1723-1759*, Catalogue of the Paul Mellon Foundation for British Art in association with the Aldeburgh Festival of Music, June 1966 and Bristol City Art Gallery July 1966. Foreword by Basil Taylor
Sutton, Jean, *Lords of the East, The East India Company and its Ships*, Conway Maritime Press, 1981
Taylor, James, *Marine Painting: Images of Sail, Sea and Shore*, Studio Editions, 1995; *Yachts on Canvas: Artists Images of Yachts from the Seventeenth Century to the Present Day*, Conway Maritime Press, 1998
Warner, Oliver, *An Introduction to British Marine Painting*, B. T. Batsford, Ltd, 1948
Whitley, William, *Artists and their Friends in England 1700-1799*, London, 1728 Vol I
Wilcox, Scott, *British Watercolour Drawings of the 18th and 19th Centuries from the Yale Center for British Art, Hudson Hills Press, New York in Association with the Yale Center for British Art*, 1985
Wilenski, R. H., *An Outline of English Painting*, Faber and Faber, 1933
Wilson, Timothy, *Flags at Sea*, HMSO, 1986

Index

Index of Dealers and Auction Houses involved with the sale of Charles Brooking's work

(Catalogue numbers follow the name of the dealer. Paintings sold by Sotheby's and Christie's are too numerous to list individually)

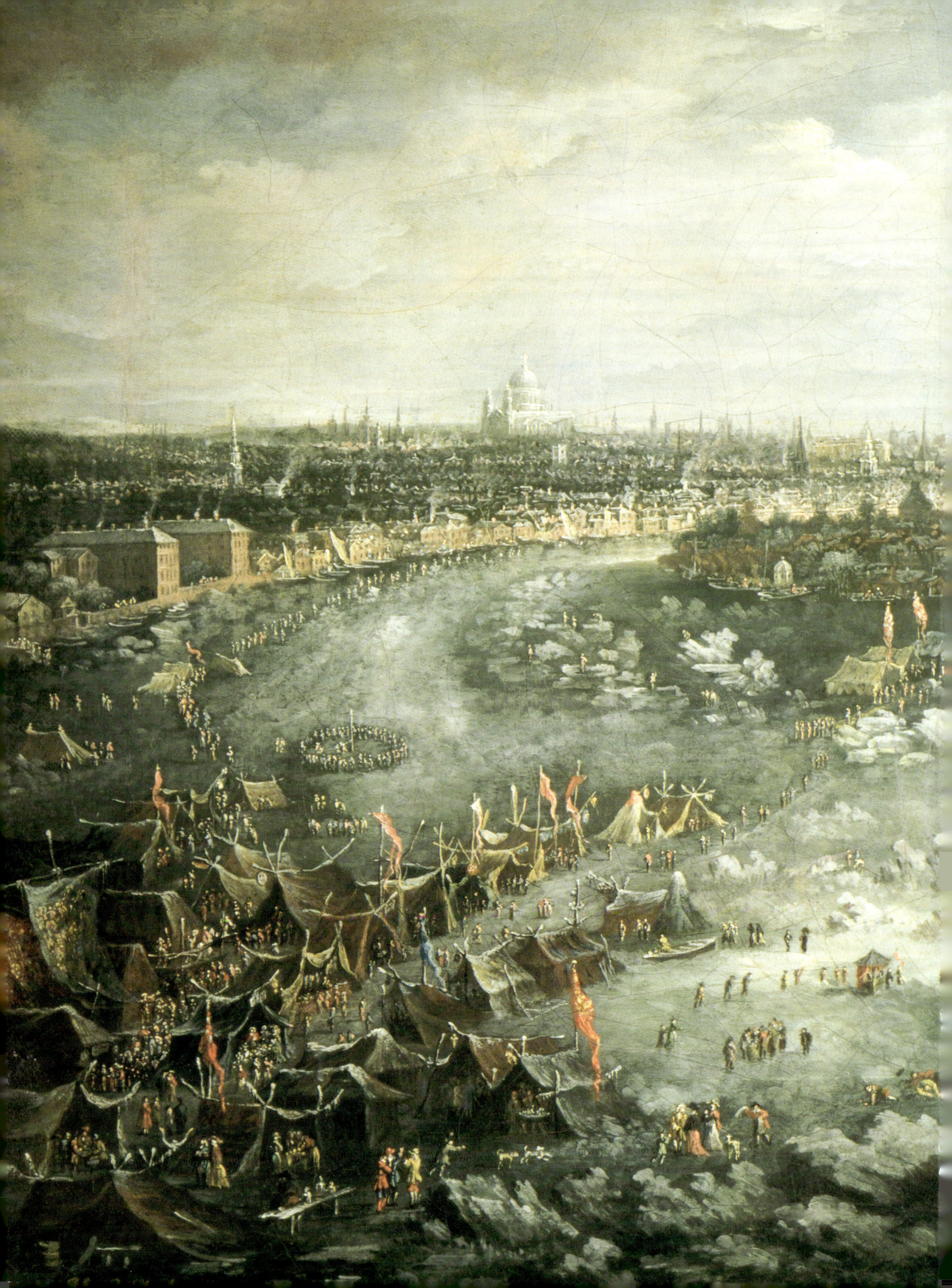